Operations Management

Production of Goods and Services

Operations Management

Production of Goods and Services

Second Edition

John O. McClain / L. Joseph Thomas
Cornell University

PRENTICE-HALL, INC.
Englewood Cliffs, New Jersey 07632

Library of Congress Cataloging in Publication Data

McClain, John O.
  Operations management.

    Includes bibliographies and index.
      1. Industrial management—Mathematical models.
  2. Production management—Mathematical models.
  3. Operations research. I. Thomas, L. Joseph,
  (date). II. Title.
  HD30.25.M38 1985   658.5   84-22325
  ISBN 0-13-637620-7

Editorial/production supervision and
  interior design: Maria McColligan
Cover design: Lundgren Graphics, Ltd.
Manufacturing buyer: Ed O'Dougherty

Printed in the United States of America

10 9 8 7 6 5

ISBN 0-13-637620-7   01

Prentice-Hall International, Inc., *London*
Prentice-Hall of Australia Pty. Limited, *Sydney*
Editora Prentice-Hall do Brasil, Ltda., *Rio de Janeiro*
Prentice-Hall Canada Inc., *Toronto*
Prentice-Hall Hispanoamericana, S.A., *Mexico*
Prentice-Hall of India Private Limited, *New Delhi*
Prentice-Hall of Japan, Inc., *Tokyo*
Prentice-Hall of Southeast Asia Pte. Ltd., *Singapore*
Whitehall Books Limited, *Wellington, New Zealand*

Contents

CHAPTER 9   Intermediate-Range Planning and Scheduling   *251*

**CHAPTER 10   Inventory Control: Ordering Systems for Independent
                      Demand   *282***

CHAPTER 11   Production Scheduling: Lot Sizing and Job Shop Control   *323*

CHAPTER 12   Multistage Manufacturing Systems   *360*

Preface

This text is designed to introduce upper-level undergraduate or first-year graduate students to the problems and techniques encountered in the production and delivery of goods and services—that is, operations management. Our purpose is to give future managers an understanding of the variety and importance of the management decisions faced in the operations area in different organizations, and to help them learn how to approach operations management problems. It is also our purpose to provide the foundation for further study in more specialized courses in production and operations management.

To accomplish our objectives, the book is oriented toward problem recognition and problem solving. Several chapters use large, integrative examples to illustrate the problems that can arise in actual situations. Analytical methods are used, but their limitations and potential misuse are also stressed. The extensive examples, caselets, and problem materials are designed to give the student not only an understanding of the details of many operational decisions, but also a broad view of operations. We also stress the similarities and differences of operations management in different settings.

In the second edition we have introduced new material on quality, productivity, technology, and production control systems. These reflect shifts of emphasis encountered in practice as managers seek better ways to respond to international competition. Although some of the new material is technical, most is focused on matters of judgment and strategy. This is particularly evident in the discussions of quality and productivity, two areas that are inextricably linked, and where choice of managerial philosophy and commitment to goals are vital.

In most organizations, production and delivery operations account for most of the expenditures and investments. The opportunities this creates makes operations management an interesting career, requiring an integrated view of the organization, a knowledge of marketing, finance and accounting, a knowledge of the application of mathematical and computer methods, and a high degree of interpersonal skills. We have found that an emphasis on the importance and complexity of operations management makes study in the area more enjoyable and challenging.

A WORD TO THE INSTRUCTOR

Several different types of courses can be based on this book. The extensive use of both manufacturing and service examples and problems has allowed us to use this book both as part of an MBA program and for a graduate course in the management of health care operations, in conjunction with some outside reading.

The operations research techniques of queuing, simulation, and linear programming are treated in technical appendixes. Each of these topics can be a significant part of the course, used only for reference, or deleted entirely. Sections in the text that require one of the appendixes are indicated by a footnote, and can be skipped. Thus the course can be designed to fit the backgrounds of the students as well as the desires of the instructors.

For the second edition, the LP appendix has been written to be compatible with the user-friendly LINDO package, available through Scientific Press. The section on managerial use of LP is presented as a dialogue between managers, a style that students enjoy. A directory to LP applications throughout the text is given in Section C-3.

At Cornell, operations management is a one-semester course and students have had a semester of statistics. Queuing and linear programming are taught in our course. We use several cases, spread throughout the semester, to supplement the text. The sequences of chapters we have used are as follows.

CHAPTERS OR APPENDIXES

Business students	1, 3–5, A, C, 6–13, 15–17
Health administration students	1,3–5, A, C, 6–10, 14–17

Because of the extensive examples and discussions and the inclusion of a few caselets, the text can be used either by itself, or supplemented by cases, or as background reading for a case-oriented course. The contents are extensive enough for a two-quarter course, or a two-semester course if cases and outside readings are used extensively.

A WORD TO THE STUDENT

Material, especially in examples and problems, should be examined using the techniques you have learned *and* common sense. You should develop a feeling for different problems that can occur while you are learning the technical material.

Each section in the book is followed by review problems designed to help you test your mastery of the material. You should complete them after reading each section, before moving on. After reading an entire chapter, try the problems assigned by the instructor. You should expect to need to re-read portions of the chapter as you are working the problems. The problems range from easy to difficult, and cover both analytical techniques and the managerial concepts of the chapter. Working on problems and cases is the best way to solidify your knowledge.

In this revision, we have added many new references, so that readers can do further study in a topic of special interest. Some of these references are technical in nature, but the majority are intended for a managerial audience. Since references can interrupt the flow, students are urged to read past references during a first reading of any topic. For term papers, subsequent courses, or research, the up-to-date references should prove useful.

ACKNOWLEDGMENTS

We are indebted to our past students for the improvements they have suggested. In addition, many of our colleagues have provided valuable comments. In particular, we would like to thank Professors Peter Billington of Northeastern University, Linda Sprague of the University of New Hampshire, Elliott Weiss of Cornell, Gabriel Bitran of MIT, Richard Steinberg of Columbia, Joel Knowles of California State University at Sacramento, and S. D. Deskmukh of Northwestern University. The Johnson Graduate School of Management of Cornell University provided us with clerical support, a good environment, and challenging students. Finally, we would like to thank our families for supporting our work and helping us to escape from it, too.

J.O.M.
L.J.T.

PART I

Perspectives on Operations Management

Part I is designed to give an overview of the important management problems found in the production and delivery of goods and services. This text is oriented toward recognizing and solving operations management problems, and Part I will describe different situations and the approaches to be used.

Chapter 1 defines and describes the area of operations management and gives a brief history of operations management. It gives a list of different problems and types of organizations, including a discussion of the similarities and differences between manufacturing and service organizations.

Chapter 2 contains a brief introduction to the methods of managerial economics, accounting, and finance that will be used throughout the book and discusses their application to operations management. It also contains a description of the systems approach, which is crucial to the study and practice of operations management. Even if you have prior background in these areas, it is worthwhile to read Chapter 2 quickly to see the application of the techniques to operations management and in particular to the integrative example used in Chapter 2, the Farm Supply Corporation.

Chapter 3 introduces the first special situation to be analyzed, the one-time project. One-time projects occur in manufacturing and in service industries, in profit and in nonprofit organizations. Such projects, and the methods of analysis used in Chapter 3, highlight the need for management control, in addition to management decision making. The techniques of PERT/CPM basically give operations managers good, timely information to use in exercising their judgment and management control.

CHAPTER 1

Managing Operations

There is no more important topic area for a manager than operations management. The operations area of an organization usually employs most of the people and uses most of the capital. In the last several years, U.S. managers have been castigated for allowing our competitive edge in productivity, quality, and technology to slip in comparison with many countries such as Japan and Germany (Hayes and Abernathy, 1980 and Deming, 1982). In some cases there has been a "growing pattern of mistrust and neglect between management and labor" (Abernathy and Corcoran, 1982).

The duties of an operations manager are broad. He or she must be able to motivate and organize the effort of many people, analyze capital investments, develop and use appropriate cost accounting numbers, and monitor and maintain quality. An understanding of the firm's marketing approach is also critical because the design of the operations area of an organization implies the level and type of service that can be delivered to the customers. In short, operations managers must be general managers with a broad-based perspective if they are to contribute to achieving the goals of the organization.

Much of the early effort in management of operations dealt largely with improving productivity. Improvements in productivity have had enormous benefits for labor, management, and consumers. However, in recent years the rate of productivity increase in the United States and many other Western countries has declined (Striner, 1982). In fact, the United States temporarily lost the lead in total productivity (*London Times*, November 3, 1983).

Over the past 100 years, the productivity of an average U.S. labor hour has increased about eightfold. Part of this productivity improvement has been

3

caused by inventions and ideas that allow workers to perform their jobs more easily. Many of the best ideas come from the workers themselves, as might be expected. Part of the gain has been caused by investment in capital equipment and part by better management, allowing more efficient utilization of the organization's resources. Operations managers must master all the ways of achieving productivity in order to best use the resources, both people and capital, of the organization.

Operations management is the process of obtaining and utilizing resources to produce useful goods and services so as to meet the goals of the organization. The organization can be a manufacturer, a hospital, a university, or a department store. The goals can be to maximize profit, provide the best possible service within a budget, or simply ensure existence. The resources used can be quite different, ranging from drill presses, classrooms, and cardiac care units to doctors, mechanics, professors, and unskilled laborers. The resources can always be categorized into "labor" or "capital."

Operations managers must manage the acquisition of resources, including a labor force, buildings, machinery, and inventories. In this process techniques of forecasting, capital budgeting, work-force planning, and many others support the basic element of sound business judgment. It is the goal of this book to introduce techniques that are useful in this regard and illustrate both their use and misuse. By including examples where quantitative approaches do and do not work, we hope to help lay a foundation for sound business judgment upon which your experience can build.

Operations managers must also schedule work assignments, plan inventory levels, and make many decisions and plans regarding what work will be done and when it will be done. Because of the immense amount of detail required in doing these tasks, managers find it difficult to keep in mind the overall goals of the organizations and take a "systems" view of the process. Yet this is extremely important. For example, it may look good for an inventory manager to have a low inventory, but it may also ruin the company if too many sales are lost due to stockouts. Chapter 2 introduces some fundamentals of systems analysis. Several other chapters describe problems of scheduling and planning the utilization of resources and indicate ways of attacking these problems, while keeping the overall goals of the organization in mind.

The history of improvements in production methods goes back to the wheel, lever, and inclined plane. The last two centuries have seen several major improvements, beginning with the development of interchangeable parts by Eli Whitney, between 1798 and 1800, while working on a government contract for muskets. In 1913, Henry Ford instituted the first assembly line, allowing specialization of tasks and faster rates of production. Throughout the time period preceding Ford's accomplishment (1895–1913), Frederick Taylor (the "father of scientific management") was investigating ways of improving workers' output by analyzing the methods and tools involved in a work assignment. Taylor's efforts were followed by many other industrial engineers, notably Henry Gantt and Frank and Lillian Gilbreth. (The Gilbreths are known to movie fans from the old movie "Cheaper by the Dozen.") All these efforts were oriented toward studying work in great detail and dividing it into smaller segments to allow specialization and greater efficiency. Recently, the trend to specialization has been questioned and, in some cases, reversed. Managers have found that employees are unhappy with tasks that are too specialized and that employees are often unable to exercise their intelligence for the good of the organization.

Better coordination of individual work efforts has improved productivity in many service and manufacturing organizations. Coordination, achieved using methods of operations management, can make each worker more productive by reducing idle time and by having people and materials available when and where they are needed. These methods not only improve overall efficiency, but often increase employee satisfaction as well.

Efficiency is important to organizations, and to our society, because efficiency in one area allows greater efforts in another. A business firm that reduces its inventories while maintaining its level of customer service has more funds available to invest in developing new products. This leads, in turn, to more jobs. A school board that reduces its transportation costs has more money to spend on special reading programs for elementary school children. A society that satisfies its housing and sustenance needs more efficiently has more resources (including time) to expend in improving the quality of life. Thus efficient utilization of resources is one major way for an operations manager to contribute to achieving the goals or objectives of the organization and of our society.

Peter Drucker has said that "efficiency is doing things right; effectiveness is doing the right things." Good operations managers must be both effective and efficient. The operating system must be designed to achieve correct goals. Managers must manage in a way that can utilize workers' intelligence and motivation as well as their hands, and the resulting system must be managed efficiently. Combining effectiveness and efficiency in operating systems is a challenging, rewarding, and important career.

1-1 OPERATIONS AND THE OPERATIONS MANAGER

Operations management is not just manufacturing management. Textbooks in the area, however, have historically spent more words on manufacturing organizations than on nonmanufacturing organizations, in spite of the fact that the service sector has grown to over half of total consumption expenditures. Service organizations such as banks, hospitals, and the Postal Service are increasingly finding that the techniques of operations management can be effectively used to reduce costs and improve service.

We define operations to include any process that accepts inputs and uses resources to usefully change those inputs. For example, an outpatient health clinic accepts patients and utilizes doctors, nurses, drugs, and capital (buildings and, indirectly, money) to treat the patient. A mail-order house accepts physical goods and customer orders and utilizes material handling, delivery capability, and capital to change an unsatisfied need for an item at the customer's home to a satisfied need. In the Postal Service the inputs and outputs are (supposed to be) identical, with only the time and place having been transformed. A bank accepts money, checks, and other forms of paper input and changes them to transactions on a computerized account record. A steel plant has inputs of iron ore and coal (plus several others depending on the precise product) and produces steel of several types.

In an ongoing operation, the operations manager must supervise the flow of inputs and outputs and manage the use of the resources involved. To be effective, the manager must be able to pinpoint the important problems and the resources that are most limited. The operations manager must plan the use of resources, predict the impact on goals, and coordinate the implementation of the plan. For example, a plant manager might plan to produce 5000 toasters, based on a sales forecast, during a month. The plan would predict a certain contribution to fixed costs and profit and would predict an end-of-month inventory level. Based on the plan, detailed decisions on batch size (for different styles), overtime and other work force variables, quality control procedures, material ordering, and many other procedures would be implemented. The plan may not be followed perfectly since quality problems may occur, the sales forecast may prove to be in error, or for any of several other reasons.

Before an operation is begun, an operations manager must design the physical facilities, including the location and capacity, as well as the staffing and work flow to be used. For example, a rural area with one hospital may choose to add satellite outpatient clinics in other locations in order to meet the health needs of the area. The number of examination rooms, the staff size (doctors, nurses, aides, secretaries), and the location must be planned, considering not only patient convenience, but also problems of coordination with and access to the parent facility.

Each of these problems is discussed in this book—facility and job design, capacity and location analysis, forecasting, planning work-force variables, inventory ordering procedures, material requirements planning, quality control—as well as many others. Each of the organizational settings mentioned above—consumer durables plant and satellite outpatient clinic—is also discussed. Tables 1-1 and 1-2 list several organizational settings that require operations management expertise, together with some of the problems that they face.

These lists of organizations and problems are by no means exhaustive. For example, forecasting is required in all the examples given, and maintaining quality of the product or service is important for all organizations. Other examples and problems will be discussed throughout the book.

Operations can be characterized in several different ways, but one of the most common is "service" versus "manufacturing." Service organizations provide personal services (e.g., teaching, healing, or postal service). Manufacturing or-

TABLE 1-1 SERVICE SECTOR ORGANIZATIONS AND SOME OF THEIR OPERATIONS
MANAGEMENT PROBLEMS

Organization	TYPICAL PROBLEM AREAS	
	Before Operation	During Operation
Outpatient clinic	Design facility and staffing plan	Schedule patients and employees
Hospital	Design facility and staffing plan	Schedule operating room; schedule elective patients; staff emergency room; schedule employees; maintain quality audit; maintain inventories of blood and supplies
School board	Design or modify facilities and geographic coverage	Design bus routes; schedule classes; operate lunch programs
Retail store	Design facilities and product-line strategy	Maintain inventories; schedule employees
Mail-order house	Design distribution system (capacity and location of warehouses and transportation links); design order-entry system	Maintain inventories; expedite late orders; develop transportation plans
Banks	Design information-flow system; locate and design branch banks	Maintain and audit quality of information; plan employee schedules

ganizations physically transform inputs to produce a more useful finished product
(house, car, or bread).

Another way to contrast operations is by the nature of the demand placed
by customers. At one extreme is the demand for a standard product, with that
demand being high in volume and arriving fairly continuously for some period
of time (e.g., the demand for refined oil products or preinduction physicals). At
the other extreme is a one-time project (building a house or developing a new
product). In between are "job shops," where each job may be different, but
they all use the basic capabilities of the organization, and jobs arrive continuously.
(A university health clinic and a specialty steel products manufacturer are examples.)

A final way to characterize operations is by the type of process. This is,
of course, strongly related to the type of demand. If there is a high-volume,
stable demand for a single product, a continuous operation (such as an assembly-
line or mail-sorting operation) is likely to be used. If the demand is for several
different products, a batch operation (such as a cosmetic firm with the same
equipment used at different times for several products) is likely. In the case of
"special but similar and frequent" demands, the operation will probably be
designed to allow most products to flow smoothly. That is, a "process" layout
will be used, and this type of operation is called a job shop. Examples include
branch banks and computer installations. The different types of demand and
process will be analyzed differently. These demand and process differences are

TABLE 1-2 MANUFACTURING ORGANIZATIONS AND SOME OF THEIR OPERATIONS MANAGEMENT PROBLEMS

	TYPICAL PROBLEMS	
Organization	Before Operation	During Operation
Air-conditioner manufacturer	Design building and assembly line, including task assignments	Plan material requirements; plan seasonal inventory accumulation and work-force patterns; maintain quality control system; maintain material-flow system
Cosmetic manufacturer	Design facility for "batch" operations	Obtain raw materials and packaging; make sequence and batch-size decisions for various items
Multilocation food product manufacturer	Design all facilities; choose location, capabilities, and capacity of plants, warehouses, and transportation links	Obtain raw materials (perhaps choosing long-term contracts with suppliers); determine which products are to be made at which plants; determine shipment patterns; plan "safety stocks" and seasonal inventories
Building contractor	Purchase capital equipment and obtain skilled work force	Sequence activities; obtain materials; perform quality checks; schedule work crews (perhaps at several locations)
Computer manufacturer	Design facility to be flexible for future products, to accept design changes easily, and to produce verifiably high-quality products	Plan production of each product line; schedule modifications requested by customers; manage quality control to guarantee good finished products
Manufacturer of specialty steel products, such as structural members for buildings	Design facility, with emphasis on production capabilities and material flow	Maintain materials inventory; sequence different jobs in the facility; manage "work-in-process" inventory; plan completion times

summarized in Table 1-3. The service-manufacturing difference is discussed further in the next section.

Review Problem[1]

What kind of operations problems does a book publishing firm that runs its own printing operation have, both before operations begin and during? What kind of demand and process would it probably have?

[1] Review problems should be completed before proceeding to the next section. Each review problem will be followed by a solution.

TABLE 1-3 TWO CATEGORIZATIONS FOR TYPES OF OPERATIONS

Demand types:	One-time	Special, but similar and frequent	High volume
Example:	Construction	University health clinic	Film production

	CONTINUOUS		BATCH	
Process type:	Distribution	Manufacturing	Producing standard products	Producing special products
Example:	Postal service	Oil refinery	Cosmetic production	Computer installation

Solution

Before operation they must choose the capacity, location, and quality of their printing operation. They must design their distribution system. During operation they must make run-size decisions, schedule personnel, arrange for book distribution, and maintain inventories. There are, of course, other things that can be said about the firm's operations problems. The firm's demand is of the high-volume type, in that many orders are for the same, standard product (such as an operations management text). The process would be "batch, producing standard products."

1-2 SIMILARITIES AND DIFFERENCES BETWEEN MANUFACTURING AND SERVICE OPERATIONS

In this section we will briefly explore some of the similarities and differences of manufacturing and service industries in order to understand which of the topics in this book should be of interest to managers in different organizational settings.

One basic difference is that services cannot be inventoried in the ordinary sense. Manufacturing organizations use inventories to smooth transitions between production phases and to meet peak seasonal demands. The physical unit is produced before it is needed for use. Services can often be partially performed before use. This book is one example. As we write and organize this book, we are providing you with a service in advance, instead of appearing in person in your home or classroom. Similarly, part of a physician's service can be inventoried by providing pamphlets concerning various health matters. Retail stores provide part of their service by carefully arranging items to facilitate search. A pharmacy purchases and inventories its service by purchasing premixed and presized drugs. Restaurants can inventory part of their service (save labor at the time of sale) by buying individual portions rather than a side of beef.

An inventoried service may not be identical to the service it replaces. It usually requires more active participation of the customer and may be referred to as *self-service*. Also, many services cannot be inventoried. For example, next week's garbage must be picked up next week. The use of the maternity suite of a hospital cannot be inventoried by using a waiting list, because of the urgent nature of the service.

The reason for concern over inventory possibilities is that a major problem for all producers of goods and services is the coordination of supply and demand. Inventory is the most common tool to use; a plant may produce at a constant rate while meeting demand fluctuations out of inventory. If that is uneconomical, they may alter the production rate during the year, or they may try off-season sales to alter the demand pattern. There are many other possible actions available to achieve coordination, and they are more or less desirable in different organizations. It is convenient to categorize possible actions according to whether they are manipulations of the production process or attempts to modify the demand pattern. A strong parallel emerges, as can be seen in the Table 1-4 list of potential actions.

Many manufacturing organizations use inventories, work scheduling, and subcontracting to avoid having to use items 1, 2, 3, and 5 under demand modification. However, many other industrial firms operate using a backlog, in which a demand is filled several weeks or months after an order is placed. These firms are using a waiting line, analogous to that of a grocery store, but with longer waiting times. Service organizations typically use demand modification, including customer waiting and scheduling, as their basic tool in coordinating supply and demand to avoid the requirement for excess capacity. Using inventory is frequently impossible for service organizations. However, items 2 through 5 under production manipulation can be used. For example, certain types of patients may be sent to another hospital (subcontracting), excess capacity (on average) is maintained in snow-removal equipment, and retail sales personnel often perform other duties when customer demand is low.

In summary, while demand modification is more common in the service sector, all the approaches to demand-supply coordination are found in both

TABLE 1-4 ACTIONS TO COORDINATE SUPPLY AND DEMAND FOR PHYSICAL GOODS AND FOR SERVICES

Production Manipulations	Demand Modifications
1. Inventory the good or service	1. Have the customers wait (in a queue)
2. Schedule workers according to demand (time of day, season, etc.)	2. Schedule customers by appointment
3. Subcontract to another organization	3. Provide substitute goods or services
4. Diversify work (e.g., do maintenance or preparation during a slack time)	4. Diversify demands by entering new markets to balance seasonal demand patterns
5. Provide excess capacity so that peak demand can be met	5. Turn some customers away during peak demand period

service and manufacturing. Therefore, it is more important to carefully consider the feasible options for a particular organization than to worry about the service-manufacturing distinction. There is very little material in this book that is not used in both sectors.

Review Problems

Refer to Table 1-4 and indicate which methods of demand–supply coordination would most likely be used in each of the following organizations:

1. A large public accounting firm.
2. A furniture manufacturing firm with nationwide distribution.
3. A doctor's office.

Solutions

In all three examples, the methods used will vary from one organization to another. Thus answers other than those given here are possible.

1. The accounting firm managers would certainly plan vacations at low demand times, and they might hire some extra clerical assistance for peak demand periods. They probably have some excess capacity on average, and they have attempted to enter other markets (management consulting) to partially balance the work load.
2. The furniture manufacturing managers would inventory their products, and they also frequently make customers wait for a particular color-fabric combination. They may use seasonal employees, and they will do maintenance and preparatory work during low demand periods. They may diversify demand by entering (say) the institutional furniture market, which is less seasonal than retail sales.
3. The doctor's office uses a queue and a customer schedule. They may turn some customers away, perhaps to another doctor's office. They will schedule support personnel to match demand patterns. They may choose not to have excess M.D. capacity, because of the high cost of such capacity.

1-3 GOALS, POLICIES, AND THE EXTERNAL ENVIRONMENT

An organization has many constituencies. Owners, managers, workers, governments, and communities all have an effect on the organization. The owners, managers, and workers often have (or should have) policies that can be expressed as "shared values." Peters and Waterman (1982) discuss how vital it is for all parties to agree that, for example, quality must be as near perfect as possible, regardless of the short-term cost. Firms often provide service that looks too expensive in the short run, but in the long run develops a commitment among employees and advertises it to the world.

The external environment affects an organization's operations in many ways. For example, a chemical firm must meet air and water pollution standards specified by law. A hospital must explain cost increases to health insurance firms and customers, and they must also meet quality standards required by governments and the physicians who practice at the hospital. A trucking firm must be aware of the myriad regulations that the federal (Interstate Commerce Commission) and state governments place on them. Laws, regulations, and other environmental factors place limits on the operations manager.

Internal policies that determine a firm's treatment of employees or customers dramatically affect operations. For example, a firm may establish a policy that workers are not to be fired except for gross negligence or theft. This might have the effect of improving employee morale and productivity as well as community relations. The firm might choose to do this because the policymakers feel it is beneficial economically, because they feel it is the proper way for a firm to act, or for a combination of these reasons. Whatever the reasons, this policy has a major impact on the manner in which the operations manager meets seasonal or economic fluctuations in demand.

Many other policies are indirectly connected to external influences. For example, a firm may choose to maintain a high-quality image for its products and to compete on that basis. Another firm may choose to develop a low-price (or value per dollar) image and to compete on a price basis. Such policy decisions must be made by top management, using subjective judgments. Once such a policy is set, the day-to-day operations are guided by the policies. In turn, the effect on operations must be considered when establishing policies. Otherwise, the overall goals of the organization will not be achieved.

Overall goals are, in effect, policy statements. Nearly all organizations have multiple goals, and the trade-offs among the different goals are usually unclear. A university has as its basic goal academic excellence (or some other such nebulous phrase). This translates into the more tangible goals of "have a well-known faculty" or "produce the best students possible." (People do not agree on how to achieve these goals.) Another significant goal for many schools is to try to guarantee their existence in the face of budget pressures and declining enrollments. Trade-offs among these three goals must be made in many instances. It is the president's job, in conjunction with the board of trustees and/or the state legislature, to see that the trade-offs are made in a consistent manner.

Goals, policies, and the external environment have a major impact on decisions. Operations management decisions must be made considering the environmental and policy context, as well as the detailed costs and benefits of the particular decision at hand. Policies, goals, and environmental considerations are aimed at guaranteeing the long-run health of the organization. Minimizing cost in the short run may not be the best approach in some cases, but then neither is ignoring the quantitative cost–benefit data. In this book we will stress the analytical cost–benefit analysis, but always in conjunction with the application of managerial judgment to the situation at hand. Table 1-5 gives a few examples of policy, goal, and environmental influences on operations decisions.

TABLE 1-5 EXAMPLES OF POLICY, GOAL, AND ENVIRONMENTAL INFLUENCES ON OPERATING DECISIONS

Setting	Policy, Goal, or Environmental Influence	Possible Effect on Decision
Film manufacturer	Maintain highest-quality image	Use stringent quality control standards, even if they are expensive in the short run
Hospital	Never turn away emergency patients	Do not fill hospital past (say) 95% capacity; that is, allow room for emergency arrivals
Mass transit agency	Increase number of riders, or decrease personal car use	Make runs at times and places that will lose money in the short run to generate long-term customers
Manufacturer	Provide stable jobs for employees	Carry inventory to meet seasonal peak demand; do not have seasonal layoffs
Mail-order house	Maintain very fast response time to customer orders	Maintain large inventories at several warehouses in different parts of the country, and/or use fast mode of shipment
Mail-order house	Use price competition to increase sales	Maintain low inventories at a centralized warehouse and use a cheap mode of shipment

Review Problem

Consider an established firm that is trying to enter the dining room chair market. Their assembly plant is in an area in the United States that has a strong demand for labor. List three possible goals of the firm and explain how they might be in conflict. Choose one of those goals and explain what effect it might have on the firm's operations decisions.

Solution

Possible goals are to make a profit, obtain a market share of over $X\%$ (so they can make money in the long run) and to have an employee turnover rate of less than 5% per year after startup. They also might want to establish themselves as a high-quality producer. The goals may conflict because two ways to establish a high market share are to advertise and sell the item at a fairly low price. One way to hold turnover rates down is to pay high wages. One way to obtain quality products (and, thus, a quality image) is to expend money on quality control and production. (This short-run expenditure may be paid back by less rework and material waste as well as in higher sales.) All of these may hurt the firm's chances of making a short-run profit.

The goal of a high market share would have several effects on decisions other than those listed in the foregoing paragraph. For example, they would want the product to be easily available, so they would need many outlets and high inventories. It would also help to have some design feature to make their chairs stand out as better or at least different.

1-4 Summary

Operations management has the responsibility for the production and delivery of physical goods and services. Consequently, it is an important topic of study for a potential manager, especially considering the broad definition of the field that we use. This book will discuss many significant operations problems and management tools which have been applied to them. Our examples will include challenges and opportunities that arise in service and manufacturing organizations, in profit-making and not-for-profit organizations.

The differences between manufacturing industries and service industries are not as strong as they would seem at first. Table 1-4 and the associated discussion indicate ways of coordinating supply and demand, and we found that each method can be used by either a manufacturing or a service organization. The subsequent chapters take advantage of this substantial overlap whenever possible. Only a few chapters are specifically limited to either service or man- ufacturing problems. In studying this material we must learn to consider the applicability or lack of applicability of each approach in the context of the particular situation.

Finally, all operations management decisions should be made considering goals and policies of the organization, and the influences that the external environment should have on decisions. A decision may look good based on short-run and narrow-scope criteria and still prove to be inappropriate from the larger and longer-run perspective. The other side of the coin is that policies and goals must be carefully defined using an understanding of operating problems so they can act as guidelines for detailed decisions. The operations manager must, therefore, help to define the policies and goals, and see that they are carried through.

PROBLEMS

***1.** Name some operations management problems that occur in a bank.

2. Name some operations management problems that occur in constructing a building.

***3.** Why is efficiency important to an agency that has a specified budget that cannot be exceeded and must be spent?

4. To describe the history of productivity improvement we identified three basic categories: (1) machines (wheel, lever, etc.), (2) task specialization and its ramifications (assembly line, better work methods, etc.), and (3) coordination of work efforts. How are each of these used in a construction project?

5. Refer to Problem 4. Which of the three improvements is probably of most importance in construction? Is there any one that *may* not be an improvement overall?

*6. Name one key difference between service and manufacturing operations management. How does this difference impinge on decisions?

7. What three demand types were discussed in this chapter? Name at least one example of each, other than the example given in Table 1-3.

*8. The Postal Service has an essentially continuous process. Yet some of their key decisions involve batch decisions: how often to make deliveries (of a batch of mail), how often to pick up mail from collection points, and how many collection points to have. What major considerations are involved in these batching decisions?

9. What capacity-related design considerations and demand modifications are most important to a city that is planning to build a sports arena?

*10. Name an operation in which the basic method of demand–supply coordination is to inventory the product during periods of relatively low demand.

*11. Name three goals that a hospital might have and state some ways in which they conflict with each other.

12. In your opinion, is the trend toward specialization in jobs being reversed? Should it be reversed?

13. In your opinion, what should the goals of a mass transit agency be? How should managers make decisions when these goals are in conflict?

14. In your opinion, how can a firm decide what pollution abatement, employee stability, and community relations policies to follow?

*15. Place yourself in the position of manager of production for a medium-size consumer goods manufacturer that introduces several new products each year. As manager, you are part of a new product committee. Marketing has suggested a new product for introduction next year called a flubscrub.
   (a) Why would you be asked to serve on a new product committee?
   (b) Other members of the committee include representatives from the marketing and finance areas. What information will you need from them concerning the flubscrub?
   (c) What information will you have to provide the committee to aid in the decision of whether to market the flubscrub or not?

16. For each of the following organizations, give a few examples of inputs, resources, and outputs. State whether the operation would be labor- or capital-intensive.
   (a) Telephone company.
   (b) Restaurant.
   (c) Book publisher.
   (d) Furniture reupholstery shop.
   (e) Steel mill.

17. For the organizations listed in Problem 16, describe some production ma-

nipulations and demand modifications that would be used to coordinate supply and demand. Refer to Table 1-4.

18. Laborsaving devices have provided an important source for productivity increases in manufacturing. Compare the growing service sector with the manufacturing sector in terms of methods and rate of productivity increases.

REFERENCES

ABERNATHY, W., AND J. CORCORAN, "Relearning from the Old Masters: Lessons of the American System of Manufacturing." *Journal of Operations Management,* Vol. 3, No. 4 (August 1983).

DEMING, W., "Improvement of Quality and Productivity through Action by Management." *National Productivity Review*, Vol. 1, No. 1 (1982).

Economic Report of the President, 1983.

HAYES, R., AND W. ABERNATHY, "Managing Our Way to Economic Decline." *Harvard Business Review*, July–August, 1980.

London Times, November 3, 1983.

PETERS, T. J., AND R. H. WATERMAN, JR., *In Search of Excellence.* New York: Harper & Row, 1982.

STRINER, H., "Regaining the Lead in Productivity Growth." *National Productivity Review*, Vol. 1, No. 1 (1982).

Survey of Current Business, recent issues.

CHAPTER 2

Analysis for Operations Management

Studying methods of analysis for operations management is of crucial importance because analysis can be done well or poorly in several different ways. Four basic mistakes have occasionally placed analytical methods in bad repute: solving the wrong problem;[1] using incorrect inputs into any mathematical or computer models; choosing a model or method that does not fit the situation; and using the results of the analysis incorrectly. It is possible to solve the wrong problem by, for example, examining the wrong organizational unit. If we examine a distribution system one warehouse at a time, it is possible to develop a solution that is good for the warehouse but bad for the overall system's effectiveness. If incorrect data inputs are used, the analysis will lead to solutions that are appropriate for those incorrect inputs but not appropriate for the world as it is. Of course, even good data cannot save an incorrect analytical approach. Finally, and most important, all analysis, from problem definition to data gathering to implementation of the solution, should be viewed as an aid to managerial judgment. Good analysis and good judgment are supportive of each other. Managers gain intuition about their operations from viewing the results of analysis, and the weaknesses and incompleteness of analytical methods can be filled in by an experienced manager.

---

[1] In statistic courses Type I and Type II errors play an important role. They are: believing an assertion is true when it is in fact false; and believing the assertion is false when it is in fact true. In the real world, the Type III error—solving the wrong problem—is more common and typically more costly. The Type IV error—solving the right problem but too late to be useful—is sometimes called paralysis by analysis, and we must be careful not to make this error by overanalyzing operational problems.

In this chapter we will examine four very important topics that will be used throughout the text. Section 2-1 discusses systems and their importance to operations management. As mentioned above, mistakes can be made by examining a subunit of an organization. On the other hand, one cannot examine the entire organization for every problem. Defining the system to be studied is an important first step to analysis.

Second, we will examine trade-off analysis. For example, other things being equal, the more inventory a retail store has, the more likely it is that the customers' needs will be satisfied. There is a trade-off between inventory and customer service. The trade-off is not simple because the speed of response to a shortage, selecting the correct inventory to hold, and several other factors also affect customer service. There are even cases where trade-offs can be viewed incorrectly. Many authors and managers now feel that a trade-off between cost of production and quality of the item does not exist; rather, they argue that building units correctly the first time may actually reduce total costs. In analysis for operations, it is necessary to be aware of the trade-offs that do exist and to make a proper choice for the value of each item.

Third, we will briefly introduce some mathematical models for operations. It is in this area that we must guard most carefully against solving the wrong problem. As an example, perhaps the most common model in operations is the economic order quantity formula which we will introduce in this chapter. It balances the cost of initiating a production batch against the cost of holding inventory until the next batch. Viewing this problem, Japanese companies, including Toyota, reduced the setup cost rather than managing around a large setup cost. The analysis used to derive a proper trade-off between initiating batches and holding inventory is not incorrect, but it is not the most useful way to approach the problem in some manufacturing settings.

Finally, we will examine methods of obtaining and using cost data for operations management. In many situations, standard accounting numbers cannot be used to make correct operational decisions. Operations managers must be aware of these problems and of appropriate financial analysis to be used in making managerial judgments. Since these topics are covered extensively in other courses, we will only scratch the surface in this chapter.

The references at the end of this chapter contain further discussion of many of these topics. We will use an extensive example throughout the chapter to illustrate the points we wish to make.

An Example: Farm Supply Corporation

Harry LaRoe is the manager of distribution services for the Farm Supply Corporation. Farm Supply sells a large number of items, but most of their business comes through sales of heavy machinery such as silo loaders, baling machines, and milking machines.

As part of the firm's marketing strategy, they provide a parts supply service designed to quickly respond to customers' needs. Many of their products are items that their users cannot do without for an extended period of time. For this reason, the firm had over $44 million of its $206 million inventory (as of January 1, 1985) in spare parts. The percentage of the total inventory allocated to spare parts has grown significantly in the last 15 years. In addition, they have received an increasing number of complaints from their customers about the lack of spare-parts support. These two symptoms caused LaRoe to commission a study, involving internal people as well as external consultants, of the spare-parts distribution system. In preparation for the study, he wrote a brief description of the system.

Farm Supply has one plant that produces the spare parts made by the company. The company also purchases some parts from outside vendors. However, the plant maintains a very small inventory of spare parts. Instead, parts are shipped to three distribution centers (DCs) when it fits the plant's production schedule. The DCs ship spare parts on demand to a total of 250 stores, each of which maintains a spare parts inventory. The current breakdown of the $44 million inventory is: $16 million at the stores, $24 million at the DCs, and $4 million at the plant. The current system is shown pictorially in Figure 2-1.

LaRoe asked the study group to describe areas for potential improvements in the service system. He was specifically interested in the following questions.

1. How could the inventory be reallocated to provide better service, or, alternatively, how could the same level of service be obtained with less total inventory?
2. Should the New York DC be expanded, since some shipments that should go through that DC have to be handled by the Ohio DC because of capacity constraints?
3. Until a possible expansion, how should stores be assigned to DCs, considering the capacity constraint?
4. What information on inventories and costs of distribution is currently available, and what information should be available? How can this information, including accounting numbers, be used to better manage distribution?

LaRoe has stated that the overall goal is to have the best distribution system possible, at the least cost. To do this, a definition of the system is required. Section 2-1 deals with systems in general so that we can proceed with Farm Supply's problem.

2-1 SYSTEMS

Figure 2-1 is a pictorial representation of Farm Supply's distribution system. The distribution system itself would consist of the units depicted in Figure 2-1, the trucks and trains used to link the system, and the people and facilities used to handle the flow of both physical goods and information. This system has the

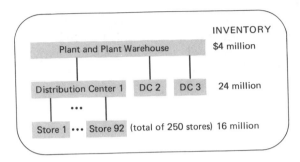

Figure 2-1 Spare-parts distribution at farm supply corporation.

dual goals of providing excellent service to customers while operating as inexpensively as possible. In considering how to provide service, several alternatives can be considered. If a large amount of inventory (of the proper items) is maintained at the retail level, a slow mode of transportation can be used. If frequent and fast shipments are made to the retail units, they can provide service using less total inventory. If money is invested in maintaining accurate up-to-date inventory information, the inventory level can be reduced by proper management techniques.

LaRoe is considering modifying the distribution system *design* by expanding the capacity at one of the DCs (question 2 in the introductory section). The system must be *operated* and *controlled,* and LaRoe is considering several questions related to these functions (questions 1, 3, and 4). Finally, provision must be made for *evaluating* the performance of the system so that modification in the design or operation and control procedures can be considered. Question 4 is partially related to such an evaluation procedure.

The preceding two paragraphs illustrate many of the important concepts in systems theory. These concepts are discussed further below.

The Nature of a System

The pioneering work of Frederick Taylor, briefly discussed in Chapter 1, made its contribution to operations management by dividing a task into many very small parts and studying each part separately. This process of dividing a unit into subunits is frequently an appropriate way to obtain important insights. However, the basic concept of systems theory is that the entire unit (the Farm Supply distribution system, for example) is more than just the sum of the parts. The entire system has goals, interrelationships, and ways of performing tasks that transcend the functions of the subunits. If the subunits are analyzed separately, an understanding of the overall system does not necessarily result. The system must be viewed as a whole, in addition to examining the subunits in detail.

A system is a collection of interrelated components that performs tasks and has goals pertaining to the entire system.

If a distribution center (DC) is viewed as a separate system rather than as part of a distribution system, it may be managed inappropriately. For example, if the retail units carry a large inventory of an item, the DC may wish to carry a small inventory of it. If the DC is managed separately, it may, instead, have more inventory than is needed in that item. The system should, at least initially, be viewed in its entirety, focusing on the overall goals and the relationships among the components. Otherwise, some opportunities for better management will be overlooked.

Defining the System

In the introduction we discussed what has been (jokingly) called the Type III error—solving the wrong problem. If we solve the wrong problem, it makes very little difference whether the answer obtained is right or wrong. *Defining the system under study is a way of deciding what problem to solve.* It is a crucial and frequently misunderstood step in operations management.

Everything is related to every other thing, in some way. But we cannot study the world every time a problem arises. The system must include only those interrelated components that *significantly* interact with each other in search of the common goal or goals. On the other hand, all such components must be included or the wrong problem may be solved. The distribution system is related to the rest of the Farm Supply Corporation and the firm's customers and competitors. However, the distribution system is large enough to contain most significant aspects of the spare-parts supply problem. An individual store or DC is not an appropriate unit of analysis, since it would not contain some important aspects of the problem.

As an example of system definition, consider question 2 posed by Harry LaRoe: Should the New York distribution center be expanded? The problem cannot be solved by considering only the New York DC. LaRoe must consider: (1) How many units should flow through each DC if the new capacity were available? (2) What effect would the reduced load have on the average cost per shipment at the other DCs? and (3) What effect would there be on the total-system transportation cost? The system to be studied must be the entire distribution system.

Operations Management and Systems

The system described above can be thought of as a *hierarchical system.*

A hierarchical system is composed of subsystems, and each subsystem is part of only one system. In turn, a subsystem may be composed of smaller subsystems.

Figure 2-1 illustrates a hierarchical system. The distribution system is composed of three DC systems as subsystems. The DC systems in turn have subsystems. No retail store is in more than one DC system. If pushed to the limit, such a system would imply that no store ever received goods from any other store or from any DC other than its own. In practice, emergencies arise and such shipments do occur, but a system of this type typically operates hierarchically. Most operations organizations are designed in this fashion. There are several managerial benefits involved, and these are discussed below.

A hierarchical system allows establishment of clear authority and responsibility. Harry LaRoe is in charge of Farm Supply's distribution system and responsible for its performance. A manager could be placed in charge of one DC system and not have to worry directly about retail stores in other DC systems. A hierarchical system allows top-level strategies and plans to be passed down to the operating levels in a rational manner. *Strategic* plans and decisions involve goal determination and large-scale resource allocation. These decisions constrain and guide the management of lower levels. Within the guidelines provided, *tactical* plans are made as to how to allocate the available resources to the projects the organization has chosen. These tactical plans, in turn, guide and constrain *detailed* planning such as: "What truck should be loaded next?"

This strategy–tactics–details view of the functions of a goal-seeking system is very old for military organizations. Research and experience have shown that hierarchical systems facilitate such planning, and that the organizations thus operated are more adept at achieving the overall organizational goals. Strategic planning can only be accomplished when considering the system as a whole. The tactical and detailed plans are devised to achieve the overall goals, and they can do that best with guidance from the strategic planning level of the organization. We will discuss this organization of the planning process on many occasions in this text, recognizing that every topic should be viewed in the context of how an organization would use it to achieve organizational goals and what guidelines would be appropriate to assist in that process.

Finally, a hierarchical organization can allow for orderly interaction among different systems within an organization. In Farm Supply, the distribution manager and the marketing manager share common goals and problems. They should interact to achieve those. This is done in two ways: by informal communication between the two subsystem managers and by formal direction from the manager to whom they both report.

The discussion of systems management thus far has focused on organizing the system and planning its operation to achieve system-wide goals. In addition, in order to achieve these goals, purposeful systems must be managed to *control* and *maintain* performance.

Control of a system is typically achieved through *feedback* mechanisms. The standard example of feedback control is a thermostat, which maintains a room temperature in a close range by sensing the temperature and adding heat to the room (or extracting heat from the room) if the temperature drops below (or rises above) a specified level. That is, information is received from the system on which corrective action or feedback is based. The basis for action is comprised of the data obtained from the system. This means that a manager must establish regular sources of information from the system. The output from the system and the interaction with the outside environment should be monitored and used to modify both the inputs and the system itself. For example, the number of times an item is demanded when it is out of stock may be used to adjust inventory policies, thus affecting the purchasing of materials and production scheduling.

Johnson et al. (1967, p. 107) describe this monitoring and corrective-action process as follows: "Summary and exception reports are generated by the control system and become a part of higher level control in terms of adaption or innovation of goals and objectives. Subsequent planning activity reflects such feedback and the entire process is repeated. Over time, an organization 'learns' through the process of planning, implementing, and feedback."

One purpose of control is to achieve stability. In the thermostat example, stability of room temperature is the objective of the control mechanism. In management situations the systems are more complex and stability is not so easy to define. Farm Supply may wish to satisfy 95% of all orders from the retail stores' shelves. To achieve this stability, inventories in the system must be free to vary dramatically from season to season. System-wide stability may be achieved by having widely fluctuating system components. Management must be careful to keep the overall stability in mind. If stability of the system components is used as a goal, the overall system may be unstable, because of external influences. A stable inventory for Farm Supply would lead to many stockouts during the busy season and to excessive inventory during the slack season.

The final part of managing a system is maintenance. Unless effort is applied to stop it, all systems will become disarrayed. (This, believe it or not, is a law of physics—the second law of thermodynamics. It also applies to systems in the management context.) In a distribution system, effort must be expended frequently to see that inventory records are accurate, or they will become useless. Through frequent (or constant) effort, a manager can keep records up to date and maintain good information flow.

A manager must also maintain a good informal information network among the members of the organization. Maintaining a commitment among all organization members to work for the good of the overall organization is a difficult but necessary task. This requires that members of the organization be given tasks and goals that will lead to achieving the organization's overall goals and that they understand why that is so. Each manager must keep the overall system goals in mind, so that his or her actions and those of subordinates can be guided appropriately.

Review Problems

Ann Sharp is the manager of the bus transportation system for a school district with six elementary schools, two junior high schools, and one high school. She is considering how to route the buses to pick up the children for the various schools. The schools use several different starting times.

1. Since there is only one high school, is it reasonable to work on the high school bus routing problem as if it were a separate system? If not, how might the different school subsystems be related?

2. If the different schools share buses, we cannot think of each school bus system as a subsystem in a hierarchical system. The clear benefit of sharing buses is cost savings. What is a potential disadvantage, and how does this indicate the value of a hierarchical system?

3. The stability that is desired in the system is arrival of nearly all children at their destination within a few minutes of the prescribed time. Give one example of a control mechanism that might be used in this situation to achieve that stability.

Solutions

1. No; since the different routes will share buses and drivers, it is inappropriate to work only on one of the routes.

2. The potential disadvantage of sharing buses is that a single bus can cause problems for several of the schools if it fails for some reason. The value of a hierarchical system is that this is not likely to happen. In Farm Supply's case, a truck problem in one DC system will not affect another DC system. Even so, in the school situation it is much cheaper overall to share buses.

3. A log of arrival times could be kept, with an eye toward changing starting times or realigning the routes. Perhaps different bus starting times would be used for different road conditions.

2-2 TRADE-OFF ANALYSIS

This section might well be titled "you don't get something for nothing." In almost every managerial situation, there is a trade-off between two or more quantities. Deciding how to make such trade-offs is the essence of management. The trade-offs can involve strictly quantitative measures, or they may involve qualitative factors.

For example, many common stocks are viewed as having a high potential gain, but the same stocks invariably have a high potential loss as well. To obtain a high potential gain the investor must be willing to undergo a high risk. In setting a price for a new product a manager knows that a higher price will cause more revenue per unit, but, probably, fewer units will be sold.

As discussed in Chapter 1, nearly all operations managers are faced with multiple goals, and they must find some way of dealing with them. The trade-offs are frequently difficult to make. Even in a profit-making organization, the link of service level performance to long-run profits is so unclear that a manager often must make a subjective trade-off between immediate cost and service level. (In addition, most firms today do not act as if simple profit maximization were their goal.) In a nonprofit organization, cost and level of service must still be traded, but the manager is frequently doing so for a diverse group such as the "public." As an example, a school superintendent must decide how large a library to have. The public can give policy guidance only through their votes on bond issues and for school board members, but the management must make numerous quality–cost trade-off decisions within the given guidelines.

In manufacturing, the trade-off between quality and cost has been debated in recent years. Many people feel that so much money is spent on rework when quality is low that quality and cost can be improved simultaneously. Deming (1982) describes Japanese companies that take "zero defects" as an achievable goal and reject the notion that there is a trade-off between finished product quality and cost. If we accept this idea, there still is a quality–cost trade-off. The number of points in the process to monitor quality must be selected, and each monitoring operation costs money. The trade-off then becomes the cost of monitoring quality versus the value added in the process that may be lost when a defect is discovered. This trade-off exists even if all finished items are inspected so as to obtain 100% quality.

Two Examples of Trade-Off Analysis

We will be discussing trade-offs throughout this text. The purpose of this section is simply to familiarize ourselves with the process. To do so, we will consider two examples, one involving strictly quantitative data and one involving qualitative factors.

The first example involves the economic order quantity (EOQ), which we will study in more detail in Chapter 10. The real-world complexities of such decisions will be discussed there (not here), but the trade-off discussed below is a commonly faced problem.

In Farm Supply's manufacturing plant a bulk cattle feed is produced in batches. The feed is demanded at a rate of 100 metric tons per week. It costs $90 to clean the processing equipment and begin a batch, no matter what size batch is to be produced. The product costs $250 per metric ton, and the firm thinks that dollars tied up in inventory cost 13% of the dollar value per year, or $\frac{1}{4}$% per week.

If they produce once per week, they will make a batch of 100 metric tons. The average inventory will be $100/2 = 50$ tons, since they start with 100, deplete to zero, begin with 100 again, and have 50 on the average. The inventory cost per week would be: average inventory times cost per unit times the $\frac{1}{4}$% per week cost of inventory dollars, or $(50)(250)(0.0025) = \$31.25$. The weekly cost of cleaning and beginning a batch would be $90, since one batch is begun per week. If they begin a batch every other week, the inventory cost will be twice as much, and the cleaning cost will be one-half as much. They will place one order every other week, so they will place $\frac{1}{2}$ of one order per week, on the average. The batch size will be 200 units, so the average inventory will be 200/2 units. Several calculations are given in Table 2-1.

Table 2-1 seems to indicate that producing 2 weeks' worth is optimal. In Chapter 10 we will use calculus to get a precise answer. Here we are interested only in seeing the trade-off between the inventory cost and the cost of beginning a batch. The trade-off can be entirely quantified, and a "best" solution can be found.

This trade-off becomes more complex if we enlarge the possibilities to

TABLE 2-1 TRADE-OFF OF INVENTORY COST AGAINST THE COST OF BEGINNING
A NEW BATCH

Order Size	Average Inventory	Orders Per Week	Weekly Inventory Cost	Weekly Cost of Beginning New Batches	Total Cost Per Week
100	50	1	$ 31.25	$90.00	$121.25
200	100	$\frac{1}{2}$	62.50	45.00	107.50
300	150	$\frac{1}{3}$	93.75	30.00	123.75
400	200	$\frac{1}{4}$	125.00	22.50	147.50

include spending money for machinery to reduce the cost of beginning a batch.
If that cost is reduced from $90 to $10, the optimum batch size becomes very
small. This approach has been used by Toyota in their "just-in-time" system
of production. (See Monden, 1981. He describes a reduction in setup time from
several hours to several minutes.) Changing the setup cost does not alter the
form of the trade-off between number of batches in inventory. However, managerial
effort is directed at a very different problem; how can we change the setup cost
so that the proper trade-off leads to a very small batch size and thus to a very
small work-in-process inventory? This approach and the method of managerial
control it implies are discussed further in Chapter 12.

The second example involves the qualitative factor of level of service. At
the retail stores, Farm Supply carries more units than they expect to sell so that
most customers will find what they want. They would like over 95% of the items
requested to be available "off the shelf." The benefit of having an item present
is twofold: (1) Farm Supply makes the sale and obtains the revenue from the
sale, and (2) they generate a reputation among their customers that causes customers
to return to the store. This second factor (and the opposite, ill will if the product
is not available) is hard to quantify. Farm Supply can avoid this ill-defined cost
by carrying large, excess inventories in every item, but they should not do so.
It would be too expensive. Instead, they should choose a trade-off point between
the two extremes of too much and too little inventory. We will give a simplified
example of this below. Trade-offs of service level versus inventory size are
discussed extensively in Chapters 10 and 13.

Farm Supply's top-quality electric drill is ordered by store 1 every week.
During a week, they sell between 5 and 20 drills of this type. The weekly sales
data for the past year are shown in Table 2-2. (We are ignoring advertising and
the seasonality of sales for now. These factors will be considered in later chapters.)

If they believe this pattern of sales will continue, Farm Supply can use it
to determine the trade-off between inventory and service level. For example,
if they had begun every week with 20 drills, they would have always had enough
drills. Assuming, as we will, that last year's data will persist, stocking 20 drills
at the beginning of every week will ensure a 100% service level. If they stock
19 drills, they expect to be out of stock for one customer during the year. If

TABLE 2-2 WEEKLY SALES DATA FOR ONE YEAR FOR FARM SUPPLY'S BEST ELECTRIC DRILL

Sales	Frequency (weeks)	Sales	Frequency (weeks)	Sales	Frequency (weeks)
6	1	11	6	16	3
7	3	12	7	17	2
8	1	13	6	18	2
9	4	14	5	19	1
10	6	15	4	20	1

Total for 52 weeks: 646 units sold.

the stock level is 18, during one week 19 will be demanded and during one week 20 will be demanded, so there will be a total of 3 (one week times 20 minus 18 plus one week times 19 minus 18) units requested for which no drill is in stock. Table 2-3 gives the results of several such calculations, and Figure 2-2 displays the results pictorially.

Figure 2-2 is a *trade-off curve,* displaying the trade-off between inventory level and unfilled demands. It can be used as information for a manager who is having difficulty setting a service goal. If 13 is used as the inventory level, 53 unfilled demands are expected to occur out of a total of 646 expected demands. If the store manager is willing to carry 7 more units at all times, out-of-stocks can be eliminated (unless the demand pattern changes). Seven units seems a small price to pay until we remember that a store such as this one might carry close to 5000 items, and 7 more of everything might not fit within the budget or the physical space. Since the total inventory is really the quantity of interest, a trade-off curve giving total inventory versus the total number of unfilled demands would be more helpful than Figure 2-2. Trade-off curves are usually given in this total form; this is discussed further in Chapter 13.

TABLE 2-3 NUMBER OF UNFILLED DEMANDS VERSUS INVENTORY LEVEL AT THE BEGINNING OF THE WEEK

Beginning Inventory Level	Unfilled Demands During the Year	
20	0	= 0
19	1	= 1
18	$1(20 - 18) + 1(19 - 18)$	= 3
17	$1(20 - 17) + 1(19 - 17) + 2(18 - 17)$	= 7
16	$1(20 - 16) + 1(19 - 16) + 2(18 - 16) + 2(17 - 16)$	= 13
15	$1(20 - 15) + 1(19 - 15) + 2(18 - 15) + 2(17 - 15) + 3(16 - 15)$	= 22
14	$1(6) + 1(5) + 2(4) + 2(3) + 3(2) + 4(1)$	= 35
13	$1(7) + 1(6) + 2(5) + 2(4) + 3(3) + 4(2) + 5(1)$	= 53

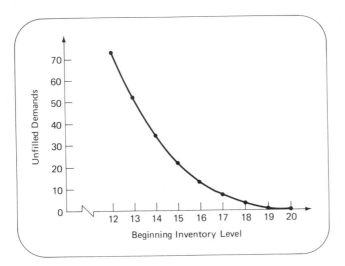

Figure 2-2 Pictorial representation of inventory versus out-of-stock trade-off.

The foregoing examples illustrate the importance and, occasionally, difficulty of making proper trade-offs among multiple quantities and/or goals. Once again, the key is to ask the right question (properly structure the trade-off to be considered) and obtain good data on which to base managerial judgment.

Review Problems

1. Make the trade-off calculation for the feed-order-quantity example of Table 2-1 for producing 160 units every 1.6 weeks. This would be analogous to making a batch every eighth working day if the plant is on a 5-day week.
2. Make the trade-off calculation for the electric drill example for an inventory level of 12. Comment on the value of carrying the thirteenth unit.
3. In considering how many checkout counters to run in a supermarket during a busy period, what trade-off should a store manager consider? Explain briefly how this peak-load problem is solved.

Solutions

1. The new row in Table 2-1 would be

$$160 \quad 80 \quad 100/160 \quad 50.00 \quad 56.25 \quad 106.25$$

2. The expected unfilled demands during the year would be

$$1(8) + 1(7) + 2(6) + 2(5) + 3(4) + 4(3) + 5(2) + 6(1) = 77$$

The thirteenth unit would reduce the expected annual backorders from 77 to 53, a larger decrease than any unit above 13 will give.

3. The basic trade-off is between the cost of staffing additional checkout counters (and/or adding "baggers" to speed up the lines) and the waiting time of customers. Stores solve the peak-load problem by having personnel

who are doing other jobs (stocking shelves, changing prices, or managing) fill in at extra checkout counters when they are needed.

2-3 MODELS IN OPERATIONS MANAGEMENT

A model is an abstract representation of reality. Automobile designers build clay models of their car designs to see how the finished car will look. This type of model is a *physical* model. Economists build computer models of the economy to predict future economic trends or the effect of a tax reduction. This type of model is referred to as a *conceptual* model. Operations managers use both types of models to help them choose inventory levels, design a facility layout, choose warehouse locations, and to make many other decisions.

Models are used for several reasons:

1. To eliminate the myriad of details surrounding a problem and allow concentration on the key factors.
2. To perform "experiments" (see what would happen if . . .) without altering the real system (thus lowering the cost of experimentation).
3. To allow a computer to choose an "optimal" solution from among the large number of alternatives.

A manager's job in using any model of a real system is threefold:

1. To see that the model and its assumptions accurately represent the key factors in the real system.
2. To see that the model is being used to ask the right question(s).
3. To use the information obtained from the model, along with managerial judgment and other inputs, in reaching the decision.

Some models allow us to find an "optimal" solution to the question posed. Of course, the solution may be optimal only for the abstract version of the question as captured in the model. The manager's role in assessing the validity of a model cannot be overemphasized. Judgment regarding factors not included in the model must be incorporated into the actual decision. In actuality, managers "satisfice" rather than "optimize;" that is, a sufficiently good solution is sought rather than an optimal one. Herbert A. Simon, who won the 1978 Nobel Prize in economics, did the pioneering work in dealing with managerial decisions in this more realistic way. Managers can use models as an information source in seeking a satisfactory solution. In simple situations, a model can be programmed to make the decisions, with the possibility of managerial intervention if necessary. In complex situations, such as strategy formulation, a model can only be one of several sources of information.

In fact, we have used some models already. For example, in the order-quantity decision for cattle feed, the total cost per week is composed of:

total cost/week = inventory cost per week + weekly cost of beginning the batches

$\quad$ = (weekly cost of money tied up in inventory) · (value per ton) · (order size in tons, divided by 2) + (number of batches per week) · (cost of beginning a batch)

$\quad$ = (0.0025)(250)(order size in tons, divided by 2)

$\quad\quad + \left(\dfrac{\text{weekly demand in tons}}{\text{order size in tons}} \right) (90)$

$\quad = (0.0025)(250) \dfrac{Q}{2} + \dfrac{100}{Q} (90)$

where Q is the order size, in tons.

For any order size we might consider, we can plug in the value for Q and compute the total cost.

$$\text{TC} = (0.0025)(250) \frac{Q}{2} + \frac{100}{Q} (90)$$

is a model of the inventory-related costs for one example. For more generality, we could use symbols for the cost of money, value per ton, weekly demand, and the model would be as follows:

$$\text{TC}(Q) = F_I C_u \frac{Q}{2} + \frac{D}{Q} C_T \tag{1}$$

where $\quad$ $\text{TC}(Q)$ = total cost, as a function of order size

$\quad\quad$ F_I = cost of money tied up for one period in inventory (an interest charge)

$\quad\quad$ C_u = variable cost of 1 unit of the item

$\quad\quad$ D = demand rate per period; this period and the period referred to in F_I must be the same period (week, year, month, etc.)

$\quad\quad$ C_T = transaction cost; cost of beginning a batch (setup cost)

Formula (1) is a model of relevant costs involved in the order-size decision. It does not represent all the factors related to producing cattle feed. A manager uses a model if he or she believes that it represents the important factors involved in a particular decision. Formula (1) has been successfully applied, and it has also been misused on many occasions. The misuse will be discussed more extensively later, but several examples are given here. If demand does not arrive at a smooth rate but in chunks (say for the firm's assembly operation or for large customers), the average inventory is not likely to be $Q/2$. Then the model does not represent reality and other methods (requirements planning, Chapter 12) are appropriate. If the product is cheaper to produce in large batches, perhaps due to a quantity discount for raw materials, the model has omitted a relevant cost, production cost, and the model is inappropriate. (If production cost is constant, it need not be included, since the batch-size decision would not have any effect on production cost.)

Formula (1) is an *abstract or mathematical model* in that the costs are modeled using only mathematical symbols. It is a model that can be optimized; that is, we can find the best decision from among the infinite number of possible Q values. We will study several models of this type, using calculus and mathematical programming techniques to perform the optimization. Using the computer, it is possible to include more realism in models, to make the model act like the real system in several important ways. Such models can be called *analog* models or *simulation* models. The distinction between a mathematical model and a simulation model is frequently unclear. Typically, large simulation models are not optimized due to their complexity, but they are used to evaluate alternatives specified by management. An example would be evaluating the effect of a tax reduction using a large computer model of the U.S. economy.

Examples of Models

Harry LaRoe's third question related to the Farm Supply Corporation distribution system was: Until a possible expansion, how should stores be assigned to distribution centers, considering the capacity constraints of the DCs? With 250 stores, several thousand products, and three DCs, the number of possible shipping patterns is huge—too large for even a large computer to examine all possibilities. Problems of this type (minimize cost or maximize profit, subject to several constraints) can frequently be modeled using a *mathematical program*. The mathematical program will then find the optimal solution to the problem as modeled. This type of model is discussed extensively in Appendix C. Here we will give an example of the approach, without many details.

The objective is to minimize costs. The constraints are of two kinds: (1) the amount of throughput in any DC is limited, and (2) the demands of each store must be met. Any model involves simplifying reality. Here we are going to assume that the demands at each store, measured in truckloads, are known and are constant throughout the year. Since we are only seeking an assignment of stores to DCs rather than a detailed trucking schedule, this assumption may be reasonable, but the manager must always consider the assumptions very carefully. Given our assumptions, a model of the following form would result. Let

X_{ij} = truckloads shipped from DC i to retail store j, where $i = 1, 2,$ or 3 and $j = 1, \ldots, 250$

CAP_i = throughput capacity per week, in truckloads, at DC i, where $i = 1, 2,$ or 3

DEM_j = demand per week, in truckloads, at store j, where $j = 1, \ldots, 250$

C_{ij} = cost of shipping one truckload from DC i to store j, where $i = 1, 2,$ or 3 and $j = 1, \ldots, 250$

Then the mathematical programming formulation is

$$\text{minimize} \sum_{i=1}^{3} \sum_{j=1}^{250} C_{ij} X_{ij} \qquad \text{(minimize the sum of} \qquad (2)$$
all shipment costs)

subject to

$$\sum_{i=1}^{3} X_{ij} = \text{DEM}_j \qquad \text{for each store, } j = 1, \ldots, 250 \qquad (3)$$

$$\sum_{j=1}^{250} X_{ij} \leq \text{CAP}_i \qquad \text{for each DC, } i = 1, 2, \text{ or } 3 \qquad (4)$$

$$X_{ij} \geq 0 \qquad \text{for all DCs, } i = 1, 2, \text{ or } 3 \text{ and} \qquad (5)$$
stores, $j = 1, \ldots, 250$

The first constraint, equation (3), says that in total, enough truckloads must be shipped to each store to satisfy the demand. The second constraint, equation (4), says that in total, each DC must ship no more than its capacity. The third constraint, equation (5), reminds the computer that negative shipment is not allowed in this model. There are $3 \times 250 = 750$ variables. There are 250 constraints of the first kind, 3 constraints of the second kind, and 750 nonnegativity constraints. This model can be solved to give the minimum possible value of the objective function (2). How this is done is discussed in Appendix C. The output of the program would be the number of truckloads to be shipped from each DC to each store. A manager would use the solution as a significant input into the actual decisions to be made.

Harry LaRoe also wants to decide whether or not to expand the New York distribution center. In considering that decision, it may be that he wants to consider the seasonality of demand, several different scenarios for future demand, and the fact that demands are not known but are random variables.

Mathematical programming cannot deal with all these complexities, so a *simulation* model might be used. LaRoe would decide on a possible expansion plan, and the model would indicate how it might be expected to perform. Figure 2-3 gives a rough sketch of how this could be done.

Figure 2-3 leaves many unanswered questions, such as, "How can we obtain good forecasts and randomly generate weekly sales data that are consistent with those forecasts?" These questions are dealt with later in the book. Simulation is discussed at length in Appendix B.

Simulation models typically are not designed to obtain optimal solutions, as mentioned above, but rather to test pre-specified alternatives. However, a program can be written to generate alternatives to be tested. Such a program is called a *heuristic program*. If the simulation is written for interactive operation, a manager can test alternatives, observe the results, and use that information to generate the next alternative to be tested. While the simulation model cannot be used to generate an optimal solution, it has more flexibility in modeling than does a mathematical program. Simulation models can be very realistic. Since

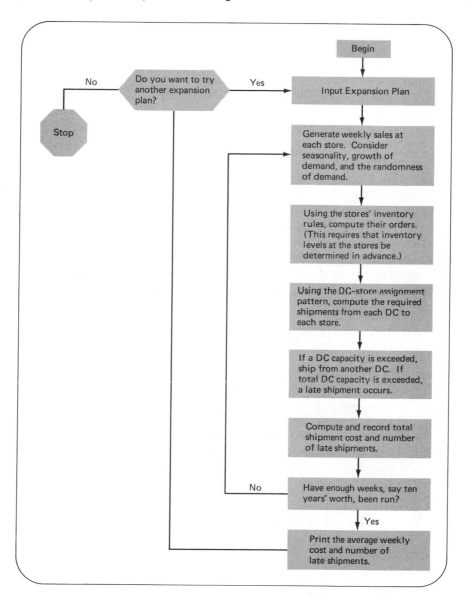

Figure 2-3 Pictorial representation of simulation procedure for farm supply.

optimization is not considered, they can give the manager output values on more than one criterion, such as cost and number of late shipments.

We will use many other models in this text. All of them, through the use of mathematical symbols, computer statements, or physical representation, try to represent the important components of a real system. The models will be imperfect in several ways, but good models will accurately reflect the factors that are important in the decision context at hand.

To help deal with imperfections in the model or the input data, we need *sensitivity analysis*. Sensitivity analysis is a process of seeing if a model's decisions are sensitive to possible errors in the model or its inputs. To perform a sensitivity analysis, a model is run with several different input values or model configurations. The results are examined to see if the changes might lead to bad decisions, not just different decisions. Sensitivity analysis is very important, and we will use it in many different settings in this text.

For example, if Farm Supply is considering an expansion of a distribution center, they should see if forecast errors will change their decision and lead to greatly increased cost. If even a large forecast error will not change the decision, they can feel comfortable. If a large forecast error will change the decision but either decision (no expansion or expansion) will perform well under the new scenario, they still can relax. Only if a large forecast error will cause the proposed decision to perform much worse than an alternative choice should Farm Supply expend time and money to try to improve forecast accuracy. Alternatively, they may try to find a decision (such as a smaller expansion) that will perform acceptably well under any of the possible future scenarios.

Review Problem

In the inventory cost model, where

$$TC(Q) = F_I C_u \frac{Q}{2} + \frac{D}{Q} C_T$$

the cost of producing the items was omitted. This is incorrect if the variable production cost changes as a function of the number produced. Suppose that the item costs $250 per ton to produce any amount less than 100 tons, but it costs $230 per ton to produce any number greater than or equal to 100 tons. Show how the cost model would change. (There is more than one way to answer.)

Solutions

$$TC(Q) = \begin{cases} F_I(250) \dfrac{Q}{2} + \dfrac{D}{Q} C_T + D(250) & \text{if } Q < 100 \\[3mm] F_I(230) \dfrac{Q}{2} + \dfrac{D}{Q} C_T + D(230) & \text{if } Q \geq 100 \end{cases}$$

The production-cost term (annual production cost = annual demand times unit price) must be added, and there are two parts to the cost model.

2-4 OBTAINING AND USING COST DATA FOR OPERATIONS MANAGEMENT

Managers deal with cost data every day. It is crucial for organizations to collect good cost information and to use it in an appropriate manner. Much of the material in this section would be covered much more fully in a text or course on managerial or cost accounting and/or in a text or course in financial analysis.

(Some references are given at the end of the chapter.) This section, while sufficient for reading this text, is not sufficient background in these areas for an operations manager.

We will continue to use the Farm Supply Corporation to illustrate basic concepts. Farm Supply Corporation had some problems with cost data at the store level. Harry LaRoe had, in fact, commissioned a study of the distribution system problems to include a discussion of data problems. The lengthy report included many technical details, some new ways of optimizing the inventory, and the following brief excerpts.

Farm Supply owns most of its stores, but it allows almost total autonomy in their operation. Thus there is no consistent method of inventory control. Farm Supply supports their managers by allowing them to "pay" for merchandise when it is sold, not when it is shipped to the store. The stores are profit centers, and they are not charged any inventory carrying cost as part of their profit computation. (A profit center is a unit of a business organization that buys and sells products within and from outside the firm. A profit computation for the subunit is made, and the manager of the profit center is evaluated using that profit.)

Many of the storage managers stock only one to two hundred of the spare parts. (There are about 9200 stock-keeping units, SKUs, in Farm Supply. An SKU is simply a product for which an inventory record is maintained.) In our opinion this is because of the complexity of managing more items than this and because spare parts is not the store's main business. However, of the items carried, many items are carried to excess. We found up to 50 times last year's sales of some items at some locations. (While 50 was an unusually large value, 5 years' worth of many items was carried at some locations.) This is because there is no perceived cost to the store manager of having inventory, but there is a cost to being out of an item when it is needed, in that one of the customers is upset.

In an emergency situation, a part from the DC is shipped by bus or airfreight. For regular shipments, company-owned trucks make weekly shipments to each store. In either case, the cost of the part to the store is the same. The store is never supposed to receive spare parts from a source other than their own DC, but they frequently call around to other stores in their vicinity to find spare parts (or other items) that they do not have in stock.

Based on our examination of the system we have several suggestions for your consideration.

1. The profit centers should be assessed an inventory charge based on a percentage of the value of the inventory, valued at store cost. The percentage should include a cost of the money tied up and a charge for the risk of obsolescence.

2. Technical assistance in establishing inventory levels should be given by the corporate office. A central responsibility for corporate inventory control, under Harry LaRoe, should be established. The individual assigned should set DC inventory policy, both overall and detailed, and recommend inventory policies to store managers. The latter responsibility would be the only change over the present system.

3. Many items, including many spare parts, are strongly seasonal and have only a short selling period per year. We recommend that such items be identified, and that the inventory charge until the next selling season be assessed within 1 month after the current season. The implication would be that managers would closely watch inventories of seasonal items and have an incentive to reduce prices at the end of the season. We feel these changes would reduce the overall inventory in an appropriate manner.

4. Emergency ordering costs should be charged to the individual stores.

Data for Management—Incentives and Transfer Prices

To make proper decisions, managers must have good information and the proper goal. Farm Supply's store managers have not properly managed the inventories, partially because of poor information and improper incentives. One of the most important tasks for LaRoe is to establish incentive systems for the store managers. The store managers are measured on the profit they make, but they are, in essence, given interest-free loans to purchase inventory. Also, they are not charged the emergency ordering cost. The first of these two facts gives a store an incentive to carry excessive inventory. The second gives them a reason to ignore many low-demand items and to count on expensive emergency shipments.

Interdepartmental charges in an organization should be designed to make managers properly consider the organization's goals. The report given to LaRoe explains one way to improve the incentive system. (There are several other ways, and there would not be general agreement in Farm Supply about which methods should be used.) Notice that the changes will not all cause reduced inventory. Suggestions 1 and 3 are incentives to reduce inventory, while suggestion 4 is an incentive for managers to increase inventory. The point is that the managers will be making more appropriate trade-offs.

The most common charge used in operations management is a *transfer price*. That is, a physical unit flows from one unit in an organization to another, and the receiving organization is charged a transfer price for the unit. There has been much written on transfer pricing, but the basic notion is, again, that transfer prices should cause managers to act in accordance with overall goals. (See Bierman et al., 1986, for a discussion of transfer pricing methods.)

Review Problem

Another control that might be employed in Farm Supply regarding seasonal products would be to give stores a rebate on items sold after the season, to encourage end-of-season sales. What problems might there be with this procedure?

Solution

There are several possible answers here. One answer is that the store owners would have an incentive to carry excess inventory if they feel they have any chance of selling it at a sale price. The store might benefit while the company does not. (Customers might come to expect end-of-season sales and postpone purchases.)

Contribution and Break-Even Analysis

One of the key ideas contained in a management education is the notion that fixed costs are irrelevant to decisions. Any cost that is not going to be affected by the decision at hand should be ignored in making that decision.

For example, in considering how many units to produce at a time, the variable costs of production (which may be different for different order sizes) and the costs of initiating a batch are relevant. The heat for the building, the president's salary, and the cost of the water treatment facility are not relevant, since they will not change based on the order size used.

In deciding, say, whether or not a product is helping a firm, the *contribution* is an appropriate measure. Revenue per unit minus variable cost per unit is the *contribution margin* per unit. A product that brings in a total of $5 *contribution margin* times 100 units sold can be said to have produced a *contribution to fixed costs and profits* of $500. That is, there is $500 available to pay the heat, president's salary, stockholders' dividends, and so on. If fixed costs are used in computing the cost per unit, incorrect decisions can be made. The following story will help to verify this fact.

A firm with three divisions shared one productive facility. There were no costs other than the fixed cost of running the facility, which was $30 million per year. The three divisions had revenues of $20 million, $12 million, and $8 million, respectively, a total of $40 million. The $10 million profit made everyone happy.

Then someone decided that fixed costs should be allocated to the divisions, so each division was charged $10 million. The divisions then had profits of $20 - 10 = +10$, and $12 - 10 = +2$, and $8 - 10 = -2$. The third division had to go. After the third division was axed, each of the two divisions "owed" $15 million. They had profits of $20   15 = +5$ and $12 - 15 - -3$. The second division had to go. And then . . . .

Often fixed costs are more difficult to spot than in the example above. For example, in some manufacturing settings there is a setup crew that does not produce items but prepares production equipment for running the next batch. Sometimes this is done overnight on the third shift or on the weekend. If the setup crew is busy only half of the time (as is sometimes the case), the marginal cost of one additional setup is zero as far as labor cost is concerned. The accounting cost for a setup may include a labor cost that contains several hours of time at perhaps a fully allocated rate. Similarly, what is the cost of using an additional hour of time of a machine that is only utilized 20% of the time? On the other hand, consider the cost of using 1 hour of time of the machine that is the bottleneck in a production process. This machine may keep us from producing, say, a $5 million computer. The marginal cost of time for this machine is very high indeed. The marginal cost of time for an underutilized machine may be zero.

The accounting system cannot maintain true marginal cost in every situation. The situation changes from time to time. An underutilized machine may become fully utilized, for example. Operations managers must be aware of the idea of marginal costs (the irrelevance of fixed costs), and they must make decisions accordingly. When we study mathematical programming in Appendix C and in several chapters that use it we will see that the notion of *shadow prices* helps us see the true marginal cost of a constrained resource. In most cases, however, the operations manager must use his or her judgment rather than mathematical programming.

Having just demonstrated the irrelevance of fixed costs in some circumstances, we should discuss their relevance in others. If a manager is considering whether to enter a particular venture, the potential fixed costs are not yet fixed. For example, suppose that a small hospital is considering a radiology unit. The unit would cost $40,000 per year for equipment rental and maintenance, $80,000 per year for a radiologist, and $20,000 per year in other salaries. The total, $140,000 per year, is all fixed cost. The average charge for each service the radiology unit performs is $20, and the average variable cost, for materials such as film, is $2. Symbolically:

$$FC = \text{fixed cost} = \$140,000 \text{ per year}$$
$$VC = \text{variable cost per unit} = \$2$$
$$REV = \text{revenue per unit} = \$20$$
$$N = \text{units (number of radiology visits) per year}$$

The total revenue per year is

$$(REV)(N) = \$20N$$

The total cost per year is

$$140,000 + (VC)N = 140,000 + 2N$$

These two relationships are graphed in Figure 2-4.

The fixed costs of $140,000 are the key to the economic side of the decision to begin a radiology unit or not. (Medical considerations must be included, of course.) The point where the two lines cross in Figure 2-4 is the *break-even point*, the minimum N (number of radiology visits) necessary to cover the fixed costs. Symbolically,

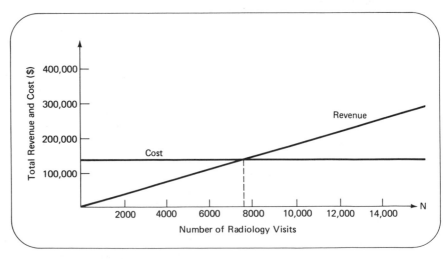

Figure 2-4 Graph of total revenue and total cost, radiology problem.

$$FC + (VC)(N) = (REV)(N) \qquad \text{at the break-even point.}$$
Solving yields

$$N = \frac{FC}{REV - VC} = \frac{140,000}{20 - 2} = 7778$$

If more than 7778 visits to radiology are made per year, the radiology unit will make money for the hospital.

It may be that the amount of fixed costs depends on the number of visits, or on output of the product in a manufacturing setting. For example, at 10,000 visits, another radiologist may be necessary. The rest of the unit is still sufficient. The extra $80,000 expense is referred to as a *semifixed cost*. The new cost relationships are shown in Figure 2-5.

The second break-even point occurs at $N = 12,222$. Between 10,000 visits and 12,222 visits, the hospital would again lose money on the radiology unit. Whether or not to start the unit and whether or not to hire a second radiologist will depend on their estimate of N, the demand for the service.

A final point about break-even analysis is that cost curves often are not really linear as shown. In a production situation people learn how to produce an item as they make it, so the cost per unit may decrease. However, since unit costs are an output of engineering estimates or a cost accounting system, linear cost functions (constant unit costs) are typically used. It is a manager's job to be alert to any glaring errors in the cost assumptions of a break-even analysis.

Review Problem

Show how the second break-even point in Figure 2-5, at $N = 12,222$, can be computed.

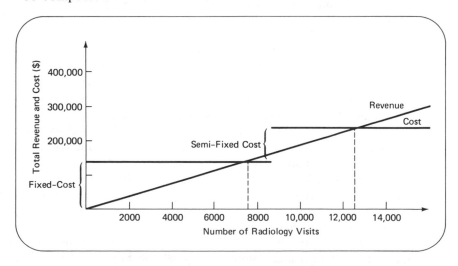

Figure 2-5 Costs and revenues of radiology unit, including semifixed costs.

Solution

The fixed and semifixed costs must both be recovered past $N = 10,000$. Thus fixed FC = 220,000, REV = 20, and VC = 2, and the second break-even point is $220,000/(20 - 2) = 12,222$.

Investment Analysis

A break-even analysis as described above does not consider the fact that a dollar today is worth more than a dollar next year. That is, future revenues should be *discounted*; they are worth less than a current revenue. Analyzing capital investment projects is a well-developed science (see Bierman and Smidt, 1984). In this text we will give only a brief introduction to the topic, using an example.

Harry LaRoe's second question, stated at the beginning of the chapter, was: Should the New York distribution center be expanded? There are two plans, A and B, under consideration. A report from the consulting team, using a simulation model, indicates that shipment costs would decrease in the entire distribution system by $475,000 per year, for each of the next 10 years, if the facility is expanded using plan A. The 10-year period represents the expected time until major refurbishing is needed for the distribution center at which time the net value of the investment will be zero. The investment required for the expansion using plan A is $1,400,000. Plan B would save $550,000 per year and cost $2,100,000. Which, if either, of these investments should be made?

The simplest method of investment analysis is to determine a *payback period*. This has serious flaws and should be used only for a quick calculation to indicate obvious acceptability or unacceptability. The payback period is the time by which the investment is recovered.

For example, plan A pays back $475,000 per year. The investment cost is $1,400,000. By the end of year 3, plan A will have returned $1,425,000; thus plan A's payback is 3 years (or slightly less). Plan B takes slightly less than 4 years to pay back the $2,100,000 investment.

An organization such as Farm Supply might use a maximum payback period of anywhere between 2 and 5 years, depending on their capital situation and the perceived riskiness of a venture. Suppose that the criterion level is 4 years. That means that any investment with a payback period less than or equal to 4 years is acceptable. Thus both plans are acceptable, and we do not know how to choose between them. If we were using payback with a 4-year criterion level, we would know that some expansion is appropriate.

A preferable method for investment analysis involves *net present value* (NPV). In an NPV analysis, cash flows are *discounted* back to the present in a manner analogous to the compounding done by the bank to figure the future value of a current bank account.

The total savings of $475,000 times 10 or $4,750,000 must be discounted back to time zero and compared against the $1,400,000 investment. (We will treat the savings as if they occurred entirely at the end of the year rather than spread evenly throughout the year. Using integral calculus it can be done assuming a constant rate throughout the year, but the result is essentially the same.) The rate of discount to use is discussed extensively in finance texts such as Brealy and Myers (1981). For business organizations with access to capital markets, the cost of debt and the cost of equity capital must be considered. For nonprofit organizations, the cost of debt, if debt is available, must be considered. If any type of organization is under capital constraints, a discount rate must be set high enough that only available funds are invested.

Discounting of future cash flows is accomplished by multiplying them by

$$\left(\frac{1}{1+i}\right)^t$$

where i is the discount rate and t the number of years in the future. (If monthly periods are used for t, a monthly discount rate must be used.)

A proper analysis of an investment problem should consider the tax benefits (investment tax credits and tax effects of depreciation). Before illustrating those complexities, we will show a before-tax analysis. This is used by many profit-making organizations and by nonprofit organizations. A firm such as Farm Supply might use $i = 0.18$ on a before-tax basis. Then the present value of the cost savings would be

$$(475,000)\left(\frac{1}{1+0.18}\right)^1 + (475,000)\left(\frac{1}{1+0.18}\right)^2 + \cdots + (475,000)\left(\frac{1}{1+0.18}\right)^{10}$$

$$= (475,000)\left[\sum_{t=1}^{10}\left(\frac{1}{1.18}\right)^t\right]$$

$$= (475,000)(0.84746 + 0.71819 + \cdots + 0.19107)$$

$$= \$2,134,700$$

The net present value of plan A is the present value of the cost savings minus the investment cost. Thus, for plan A, using a discount rate of 18%,

$$\text{NPV} = 2,134,700 - 1,400,000 = \$734,700$$

A positive NPV implies that an investment is worthwhile, since it earns more than the required rate of return, which was 18% in the example.

Two comments are in order here. First, there is an easy formula to use in evaluating an *annuity,* which is a stream of equal payments for T periods, as above. When A is the annual amount, i the discount rate, and T the number of years for which the payments will occur, the present value of an annuity is

$$PV = A\left[\frac{1 - (1 + i)^{-T}}{i}\right] \tag{6}$$

For plan A we obtain

$$PV = (475,000)\left[\frac{1 - (1.18)^{-10}}{0.18}\right] = (475,000)(4.494) = \$2,134,700$$

We will use formula (6) several times below. There are, in fact, formulas for many such situations, and these can be looked up in books on the mathematics of finance or engineering economics. Also, inexpensive calculators can compute present values.

Second, we can find, by trial and error or search procedures using calculators or computers, the discount rate that causes NPV to be zero. That rate is the *internal rate of return* of the investment. For plan A, that value is approximately 31.8%. An investment that returns 31.8% is an attractive investment for most organizations. Having seen the foregoing calculations, LaRoe made the same calculations for plan B, using formula (6). First, using $i = 0.18$, he obtained

$$\text{NPV} = 550,000\left[\frac{1 - (1.18)^{-10}}{0.18}\right] - 2,100,000 = \$371,700$$

The discount rate that gives NPV $= 0$ is 22.8%, or 0.228. Based on this analysis, Farm Supply should select plan A. They should select the plan with the larger net present value. The internal rate of return is useful management information, but it should not be used to select between different plans in a situation such as the present one. The reasons for this are discussed extensively in finance texts.

After-Tax Analysis

After-tax analysis depends on the investment tax credit in effect at the time, the depreciation method used, the firm's tax rate, and the firm's after-tax cost of capital. All these topics are discussed in Bierman and Smidt (1984), as well as in courses and texts on finance and accounting. This method is preferable in profit-making organizations because it properly measures the actual monetary effect on the firm. There are four steps.

1. Deduct the investment tax credit from the investment.
2. Deduct taxes that must be paid on all returns.
3. Include the tax saving due to depreciation as a new stream of cash flows.
4. Find the net present value of the investment using the amounts given above and the after-tax discount rate. (The after-tax discount rate is lower than the before-tax rate, but it will not in general be the before-tax rate times 1 minus the tax rate. Ways of computing before- and after-tax discount rates are discussed in finance texts.)

For example, suppose that $i = 0.11$ is the after-tax discount rate for Farm Supply, and the tax rate is 0.48. An investment tax credit of 8% applies to the entire investment in either plan A or plan B. Finally, we will use straight-line depreciation over the 10-year life of the investment, still assuming zero value 10 years from now. This implies that $\frac{1}{10}$ of the investment is deducted from income in each of the 10 years. For plan A, this means that $(\frac{1}{10})(1,400,000) =$

$140,000 depreciation expense is incurred every year, and the tax rate times that amount, $(0.48)(140,000) = \$67,200$, is saved each year in taxes. There are other methods of depreciation that allow a firm to obtain the tax benefits faster, thus favoring the capital investment. These methods will not be discussed here. The after-tax analysis for plan A is shown below.

$$\text{net investment after deducting tax credit} = (1,400,000)(1 - 0.08)$$
$$= \$1,288,000$$
$$\text{after-tax yearly saving} = (475,000)(1 - 0.48)$$
$$= \$247,000$$
$$\text{yearly tax saving due to depreciation} = (\tfrac{1}{10})(1,400,000)(0.48)$$
$$= \$67,200$$
$$\text{total saving per year} = 247,000 + 67,200$$
$$= \$314,200$$

Using formula (6), with $A = 314,200$, $T - 10$, and $i = 0.11$, the net present value of the saving is

$$(314,200)\left[\frac{1 - (1.11)^{-10}}{0.11}\right] = (314,200)(5.89) = \$1,851,000$$

The net present value, after taxes, of plan A, is

$$1,851,000 - 1,288,000 = \$563,000$$

Properly accounting for the time value of money is crucial for an operations manager. In business firms, obtaining a high rate of return is a primary objective. In public organizations, which nearly always have limited capital, the dollars that are available must be used in the most advantageous way.

Financial analysis is only part of the decision process, as is illustrated by considering investments in new technologies in manufacturing. Projects involving group technology, flexible manufacturing systems, and/or automation often involve large capital outlays. In spite of this, many consultants believe that the advantages of these new technologies are difficult to assess using financial analysis, and thus they recommend that financial analysis not be used. Rather, they suggest that these investments should be made based on faith.

We strongly disagree that financial analysis is inappropriate. The advantages of some of these technologies include inventory reduction (Boucher and Muckstadt, 1983), quality improvement, a reduction in time required to manufacture a product with a concomitant improvement in perceived service to the customer (Thomas, 1983), a reduction in factory floor space needs, and reduced labor cost. Such projects are often viewed only as laborsaving devices. Such a narrow view would make any analysis inappropriate. Financial models are very useful when the decision is viewed properly. These topics will be discussed further in Chapter 5.

Review Problem

Find the net present value, after taxes, of plan B. The annual savings are $550,000 and the investment required is $2,100,000. Use $i = 0.11$, a tax rate of 0.48, an investment tax credit of 0.08, and straight-line depreciation over a 10-year life.

Solution

$$\text{net investment after deducting tax credit} = (2{,}100{,}000)(1 - 0.08)$$
$$= \$1{,}932{,}000$$

$$\text{after-tax yearly saving} = (550{,}000)(1 - 0.48)$$
$$= \$286{,}000$$

$$\text{yearly tax saving due to depreciation} = (\tfrac{1}{10})(2{,}100{,}000)(0.48)$$
$$= \$100{,}800$$

$$\text{total saving per year} = 286{,}000 + 100{,}800$$
$$= \$386{,}800$$

Using formula (6), the net present value of the saving is

$$(386{,}800)\left[\frac{1 - (1.11)^{-10}}{0.11}\right] = (386{,}800)(5.89) = \$2{,}278{,}000$$

The net present value, after taxes, of plan B, is

$$2{,}278{,}000 - 1{,}932{,}000 = \$346{,}000$$

The company should select the larger net present value—plan A. In this case, both a before-tax and an after-tax analysis suggested the same decision; this will not always be so.

2-5 Summary

The material in this chapter is essential to studying operations management and being an operations manager. Section 2-1 is perhaps the most important but is surely the least specific. The basic message is to study the right system and ask the right question. Asking the right question occurs when a manager knows what is important in a given situation. System definition is part art, part science. There will be many occasions in this book to practice that skill.

Once the system is defined, such as the distribution system for Farm Supply, the manager must decide what goals the organization wishes to achieve. (Frequently, these will have been previously stated.) In almost every situation, there will be a trade-off to be made: between inventory level and service level, between money spent now and money received later, or between inspection cost and wasted production time. Recognizing the trade-offs and obtaining good information as to what the quantitative trade-offs are provide a manager with a sound basis for making decisions using the quantitative data and management judgment.

In performing an analysis leading to a management judgment, data are necessary. For example, Harry LaRoe needs to know inventory levels, cost figures and demand rates if the system inventory is to be properly managed. A management information system must be designed to provide the data necessary for management planning and control. However, too much data can be as bad as too little. Proper summaries of information must be made if information is to be of value to management.

Models are often used to analyze management information. These models are always based on simplifying assumptions. If the assumptions of the model are not reasonable, the model may lead to errors that are as serious as those caused by using incorrect or inappropriate data. This means that a manager must decide if it is appropriate to use a specific model and how much to rely on the information provided by the model as compared to other information. A model will never consider all the factors present in a problem, but it can be a very useful input into the decision-making process.

An important aspect to the use of any model is sensitivity analysis. Sensitivity analysis consists of seeing whether errors in input data or model formulation will lead to bad decisions (not just a change in a decision).

Finally, there are situations where a model fits well enough, considering the importance of the decisions at hand, that the model's recommendation can be directly implemented. In these cases the manager's role is reduced to occasional monitoring and modification of the model, freeing the manager for other tasks. An example would be setting the weekly order quantities for Farm Supply's 9200 items at one of the DCs. An automatic procedure, with the possibility of overrides, can perform very well. Even in such situations the responsibility rests with the manager, not the model.

Section 2-4 deals with the use and analysis of cost data. Providing proper incentive systems is often more important than choosing a good model. Thus managerial accounting systems are very important in operations management, particularly in allocating costs and determining transfer prices. In deciding whether to proceed with a project or not, investment analysis is used to ensure that high-enough returns are obtained from invested capital. Since the returns can (and do) include nonmonetary benefits, investment analysis is only part of the decision process.

PROBLEMS

*1. The Farm Supply Corporation has 250 stores, three distribution centers, and one plant. In analyzing the layout for one store, what system definition is appropriate? Why?

2. In determining the proper long-term staffing level for a station in a metropolitan fire department, what system definition is appropriate? Why? Assume that an overall budget is known.

3. What are the advantages and disadvantages of hierarchical systems in the operations management context?

*4. Are the following decisions strategic, tactical, or detailed decisions? Why?

 (a) Selecting a yearly budget for nursing personnel and assigning portions of the budget to the separate units.

 (b) Determining the total size of a major addition to a hospital.

 (c) Establishing the shift schedule for nursing personnel for the next week.

 (d) Establishing the method of monitoring patients in the intensive care ward.

5. Explain the meaning of stability in systems. Why are some components of a stable system unstable?

*6. Farm Supply Corporation currently maintains its own trucking operation and ships from the DC to each store twice per week. They are considering making daily shipments to each store. What trade-offs are involved in this decision?

7. A regional blood bank makes daily shipments of fresh blood to each hospital in the region. They are considering shipping every other day. What trade-offs are involved in this decision?

8. A publisher is considering how many copies of a new book to print. What trade-offs are involved in this decision?

9. Given a trade-off curve such as Figure 2-2, how can a manager select an optimal point for inventory? Why is it better to have a trade-off curve giving total inventory (all items) and the total number of unfilled demands, rather than a curve related to only one item at a time?

*10. In Section 2-3 the following equation was introduced:

$$TC(Q) = F_I C_u \frac{Q}{2} + \frac{D}{Q} C_T$$

A firm is considering order quantities for a \$5 item. They use $F_I = 0.15$ per year and $C_T = \$2.50$. The annual demand is 4000 units. They are considering order quantities of 200, 500, or 1000. Which should the firm choose?

11. This problem uses the data introduced in Problem 10. If the unit cost is \$5 in batches of 200, \$4.96 in batches of 500, and \$4.91 in batches of 1000, what order quantity should the firm use?

*12. Consider the mathematical program of equations (2) to (5). Suppose that we change equation (3) to

$$\sum_{i=1}^{3} X_{ij} \leqslant \text{DEM}_j \qquad \text{for each store,} \qquad j = 1, \ldots, 250$$

What solution would the computer think is optimal?

13. Consider the mathematical program of equations (2) to (5). Suppose that we change equation (4) to

$$\sum_{j=1}^{250} X_{ij} = CAP_i \qquad \text{for each DC,} \qquad i = 1, 2, \text{ or } 3$$

What problems may the computer encounter?

*14. What are the main advantages of simulation models?

15. What is sensitivity analysis and why is it important? Give an example in which sensitivity analysis would be necessary.

16. In Section 2-4, four suggestions were given for improving the management of Farm Supply's inventory system. Do you agree with the suggestions? How would you modify them? Would your answer change if Farm Supply were a *cooperative,* whose stated goal was to provide the best service possible, subject to a constraint of breaking even each year?

*17. An accounting firm is considering opening an office in a new city. The annual fixed cost of operating a new office is $115,000. The average revenue from a client is $18,000 per year, and the average marginal cost of a client is $9000. How many clients do they need in order to break even? How might an analysis of this type be improved?

18. In Section 2-4, two break-even points were computed for a radiology unit: one to cover the $140,000 fixed cost and one to cover the $80,000 semifixed cost. The semifixed cost must be paid if N (the number of visits) exceeds 10,000. Suppose that if N exceeds 20,000 visits, another $80,000 must be expended. The revenue from one visit is $20 and the marginal cost is $2. What value of N would be required to break even and cover the 140,000 + 80,000 + 80,000 = $300,000 fixed and semifixed costs? What does the answer mean?

*19. Compute the net present value of a $1,000,000 investment that will return $400,000 at the end of 1 year, $500,000 at the end of 2 years, $600,000 at the end of 3 years, and no other returns. Use a discount rate of $i = 0.15$.

*20. The manager of traffic and distribution for a large firm is considering renting trucks rather than purchasing them. The rental agreement would cost $2,000,000 per year for the next 5 years. The purchase cost would be $5,000,000. Maintenance would be the same under either plan, and the trucks would be worthless after the 5 years of intensive use. Ignoring the tax effects and using a discount rate of $i = 0.16$, should the manager buy the trucks?

21. This problem uses the data from Problem 20. The investment tax credit is 10% of the investment. The tax rate is 0.48. The firm is using straight-line depreciation. Using an after-tax analysis with a discount rate of $i = 0.09$, should the manager buy the trucks?

*22. This problem refers to Problems 20 and 21. Would the following changes tend to make buying the trucks look more or less attractive than shown in the Problem 21 analysis? Why?

(a) A salvage value at the end of the 5 years.

(b) A faster depreciation method, such as the sum of years' digits or double declining balance.

23. A machine shop manager has two machines that can do the same milling operation. Machine *B*, which is designed for high volume, has a larger initial setup cost but lower per unit variable costs.

Machine	Setup Costs	Variable Cost per Unit
A	$ 8	$0.24
B	80	0.09

The manager wants to determine which machine to schedule to minimize total cost when an order requires milling.

(a) Determine the total cost equation for each machine.

(b) Plot these two equations on one graph.

(c) At what volume do machines *A* and *B* have the same total cost?

(d) What decision rule should the manager use when determining which machine to use for a particular order requiring milling?

24. An entrepreneur is considering introduction of a new morning newspaper in New York City. Her direct competitors charge $0.20 at retail, with $0.05 going to the retailer. For the level of reporting she desires, she determines the fixed cost of editors, reporters, rent, pressroom expenses, and wire service charges to be $250,000 per month. The variable cost of ink and paper is $0.10 per copy, but advertising revenues of $0.05 per paper will be generated. Assume 25 weekdays in a month.

(a) How many copies per day must be sold to break even at a selling price of $0.20 per paper at retail?

(b) What would be the break-even volume per day if she undercut her competitors by $0.05 at retail?

(c) What would be the break-even volume at $0.25 per copy retail?

(d) How do the answers found in parts (a), (b), and (c) help the entrepreneur make a decision whether to publish or not?

REFERENCES

BIERMAN, H., AND S. SMIDT, *The Capital Budgeting Decision,* 6th ed. New York: Macmillan, 1984.

BIERMAN, H., T. DYCKMAN, AND R. SWIERINGA, *Managerial Cost Accounting,* 3rd ed. New York: Macmillan, 1986.

BOUCHER, T., AND J. MUCKSTADT, "The Inventory Cost Effectiveness of Group Technology Production Systems." *Annales de Sciences Économiques Appliquées* (Belgium), Vol. 39, No. 1 (1983).

BREALY, R., AND S. MYERS, *Principles of Corporate Finance.* New York: McGraw-Hill, 1981.

CURTIS, D., "Manufacturing's Most Strategic Resource: Workforce Commitment." *Operations Management Review,* Fall 1983.

DEMING, W. E., "Improvement of Quality and Productivity through Action by Management." *National Productivity Review,* Vol. 1, No. 1 (Winter 1982).

JOHNSON, R., F. KAST, AND J. ROSENZWEIG, *The Theory and Management of Systems,* 2nd ed. New York: McGraw-Hill, 1967.

KAPLAN, R., *Advanced Management Accounting.* Englewood Cliffs, N.J.: Prentice-Hall, 1982.

KAPLAN, R., "Measuring Manufacturing Performance: A New Challenge for Managerial Accounting Research." *The Accounting Review,* October 1983.

MONDEN, Y., "What Makes the Toyota Production System Really Tick?" *Industrial Engineering,* January 1981.

MUCKSTADT, J., AND J. THOMAS, "Improving Inventory Productivity in Multi-level Distribution Systems," in *Productivity and Efficiency in Distribution Systems,* D. Gautschi, ed. New York: North-Holland, 1982.

THOMAS, J., "Incorporating Marketing Considerations into Capacity Planning and Detailed Scheduling." *Annales de Sciences Économiques Appliquées* (Belgium), Vol. 39, No. 1 (1983). Also available as a Cornell Graduate School of Management working paper.

CHAPTER 3

Project Coordination with PERT/CPM

The life of a manager is a series of projects. As one's career progresses, the scope of the projects expands, and with it the potential losses and gains to the organization. Since the effectiveness of a manager is often judged by the quality of performance on projects, it is important to have effective methods of coordinating and controlling people and resources. The best methods help to anticipate potential future difficulties in a project so that contingency plans can be made. Surprises are usually not welcome in management.

Projects have four interrelated elements—goals, timing, resources, and environment. The *goal* of a construction project might be to meet an established deadline at minimum cost. The goal of a project to implement a new, computer-controlled inventory system might be to minimize processing errors during implementation, to minimize the likelihood that the new system will be rejected. Cost minimization is often a goal, but the previous examples show that it is not always paramount.

The *time* element of a project includes not only deadlines, but also the lead times that are needed to procure resources, and the schedules of personnel and equipment. Idle time is to be avoided, and it is also desirable to anticipate when very busy periods will occur.

Resources are used to attain the goals of the project and to change the time required to perform various parts of the project. Resources include personnel, equipment, and materials. Identifying the needed resources is an important part of project planning, but coordinating these resources through time is far more difficult.

The *environment* of a project, including factors such as weather, material shortages, and so on, causes uncertainty regarding the cost and timing of a project. The goal may be made unattainable, the timing may be radically altered, and the availability of resources may be changed due to environmental factors external to the project itself. Thus uncertainty is a key element of the environment. The purpose of this chapter is to introduce PERT/CPM, a method for project planning and control.

Network Planning Methods

The United States Navy was faced with an immense coordination problem in the development of Polaris, the first weapons system that could launch a long-range ballistic missile from a submerged submarine. In order to coordinate the activities of 11,000 contractors, a new method was invented to manage this project; they called it PERT—Program Evaluation and Review Technique. This method was used to evaluate proposed changes in schedule to prevent delays in the ultimate completion date. The application, described by Malcolm et al. (1959), was considered very successful, and led to widespread use of the technique.

At about the same time, the Critical Path Method (CPM) was developed at DuPont, in consultation with Remington-Rand. It was soon recognized that PERT and CPM were the same idea. Since that time, both have evolved substantially, but the essential concept remains the same.

PERT/CPM planning is based on a *network diagram*. In the diagram method we will use, arrows are used to show *precedence relationships* among activities. A precedence relationship states that (for example) activity X must be completed before activity Y can begin. The resulting diagram has several uses, as we will see. It can be used to identify potential scheduling difficulties, to estimate the time until completion of the entire project and to improve the project's coordination. Computer programs are available to estimate completion times and draw the diagrams. The diagrams are large and detailed, sometimes covering whole walls with information such as when each activity is scheduled to begin and notes such as "continued in corridor G, second floor."

Disenchantment with PERT/CPM

An unfortunate consequence of the increasing sophistication of PERT/CPM programs was an increasing reliance on the tool, at the expense of good, commonsense management (Vazsonyi, 1970). For example, the computer would produce an estimate of the project completion time, perhaps with an associated statistical confidence interval, accurate to five decimal places. But then the project would "run over" far beyond the planned completion date, and everyone would point fickle fingers at PERT/CPM. "Obviously inadequate!" "Machines can't think!" "Worthless!" And so on.

Closer inspection often discloses a different story. A typical example involves the incentives sometimes faced by the mid- and lower-level managers. Because the activities for which they are responsible have been "scheduled" within a designated time slot, there is a tendency to try to meet the schedule at all costs. This may lead to inadequate testing and/or redesign at several key project phases. The results are not felt until near the scheduled project completion time when the project does not function as specified. This may lead to costly delays for design modifications. This is not a criticism of PERT/CPM but rather of the way it was used.

The strength of PERT and CPM is that they are easy to understand and use. Elaborate, computerized versions are sometimes appropriate for large-scale programs, but manual calculation is quite suitable for the moderate projects of everyday management. The trade literature abounds with applications, ranging from "new product introduction" to "opening a new hospital."

In this chapter, project planning will be described in three phases—analysis, scheduling, and control. *Analysis* consists of preliminary data gathering, constructing the diagram described above, and identifying critical elements of the project. *Scheduling* makes use of this information to coordinate the project, considering where changes in personnel or other resources will have the most beneficial effect. Once the project is under way, PERT/CPM can be used to *monitor and control* the project's progress.

3-1 PHASE ONE: PROJECT ANALYSIS

"I'm glad we're doing this. I've never been this systematic in planning a project. Now I feel we're getting a good overall view at the outset. Even if your fancy technique fails, this session is worthwhile." This is a typical comment of a manager engaged in *activity analysis,* in which a project is broken down into its major steps (*activities*). At the same time, the parties who will be responsible for each step are identified and the duration of each activity is estimated. The definition of each activity is then refined, in consultation with the person responsible, who can also provide more detailed time estimates based on previous experience.

The time estimation should be approached carefully. One method is to ask for "worst-case" and "best-case" estimates before requesting the "most likely activity duration." This allows a person to express concerns and uncertainty about the future before making a "best-guess" forecast. In addition, the difference between the worst and best cases can be a useful measure of uncertainty, as we shall see later.

In addition to defining activities and estimating the required time, *precedence relationships* are also recorded: for each activity, a list of "immediate predecessors" is constructed. For example, the list for "activity X" would contain the activities that must be completely finished before X can begin. The list is kept as short as possible by excluding all but the "immediate predecessors." Otherwise, activities near the end of the project would have gigantic predecessor lists. (Thus, if A precedes B and B precedes C, A is not an "immediate predecessor" for C.)

TABLE 3-1 ACTIVITY DATA FOR INSTALLING A NEW OFFICE PROCEDURE, USING NEW EQUIPMENT WHICH HAS ALREADY BEEN DELIVERED

Activity	Activity Code	Activity Time (days)	Predecessors
Preliminary training	A	5	—
Procure full supply of forms	B	8	D
Train personnel to use new forms	C	6	A, D
Modify forms for new system	D	11	—
Train personnel on new equipment	E	7	A, C

Other details of the activity are also recorded, such as number and type of personnel required, equipment, procurement lead times for materials, and special requirements such as "dust-free environment" or "clear weather." Each activity has a substantial file at this point, and it is therefore convenient to assign a code to each activity, using either numbers or letters. For our example, we will use a letter code. The result of an activity analysis of a project to implement a new office procedure is presented in Table 3-1.

The Network Diagram

This information is used to construct an arrow diagram or *network diagram.* There are two ways to accomplish this. By far the easiest, for hand computation, is to represent each activity by a circle or box (a node) and use arrows to show precedence.[1] The procedure for producing a network diagram is given below, using the data in Table 3-1 as an illustration.

How to Draw a Network Diagram

1. First, draw a node (circle) called START, at the left-hand side of the page.
2. Draw a node for each activity that has no predecessors, and draw an arrow from START to each node. (In Table 3-1, activities A and D would be chosen first. See Figure 3-1a.)
3. Choose any activity on the diagram that has not yet been crossed off the list of activities. Call it "the candidate." (Activity A could be the first candidate in the example. It will eventually be "crossed off" from Table 3-1 once steps 4 and 5 are finished.)
4. Search over the predecessor lists of other activities, looking for the candidate's code. Each time you find it, draw an arrow to the corresponding activity from the candidate node. If the activity does not have a node on the diagram, draw one, and then draw the arrow. After the arrow has been drawn, cross off the candidate from the precedence list. (Activity C is the

[1] Another version will be described later, in which arrows represent both activity and precedence.

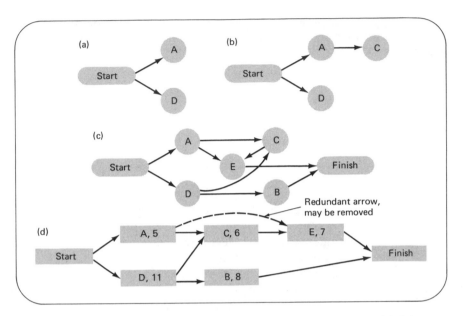

Figure 3-1   Constructing an arrow diagram to match the data in Table 3-1.

first with *A* as a predecessor. See Figure 3-1b. "Cross off" the *A* in *C*'s predecessor list in Table 3-1.)

5. Repeat step 4 with the same candidate, until it no longer appears in any precedence list. Then cross off the candidate from the list of activities. Return to steps 3 and 4 until all activities and predecessors have been crossed off. (After nodes *C* and *E* are drawn, "cross off" *A* from the activity code column of Table 3-1.)

6. Draw a FINISH node. Look for "dead-end" nodes (those with no outward-pointing arrows) and connect them to the FINISH node. (See Figure 3-1c. Activities *B* and *E* are dead ends.)

7. Now, go back and clean up the mess you have made. This time, use rectangular nodes, and reduce the number of arrows that cross each other to a minimum. Eliminate any redundant arrows, such as from *A* to *E* in Figure 3-1d. (Can you explain why this arrow is not needed?)

8. On each node, write in the "most likely" activity time.[2]

Activity-on-Arrow Diagrams. As mentioned earlier, another common network diagramming method is to force the arrows to do double-duty, representing both activity and precedence. Such a diagram results when the boxes in Figure 3-1d

---

[2] As we shall see later, one may wish to use the "expected activity time" = [worst + 4(most likely) + best]/6.

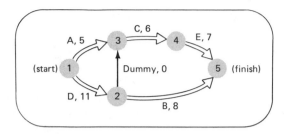

Figure 3-2 Activity-on-arrow diagram, equivalent to Figure 3-1d.

are flattened into arrows and stretched until they meet. This requires two kinds of arrows, however, as illustrated by the "dummy activity" running from D to C in Figure 3-2. The dummy is needed to show that C has both A and D as predecessors, but B has only D.

The "nodes" (circles) in this diagram are numbered only for reference. Each node signifies an event. For example, node 3 is "activities A and D are both finished." Focusing on events has certain advantages, and this technique is widely used.[3] In the next section, we will develop charts in which the length of the arrow on the chart is an indication of the activity's duration. In such a time-scale chart, the distinction between the two methods of drawing the diagram disappears.

Precedence Diagramming. Based on the activity-on-node approach, precedence diagramming allows arrows to be drawn from the end of one activity to the end of another (note that all arrows in Figure 3-1 are end-to-start) as well as start-to-start and start-to-end. The computations and interpretation are very similar to the usual PERT/CPM method. Wiest (1981) describes this method and some unusual characteristics that it has.

Calculations Using the Network Diagram

Earliest Start and Finish Times. Time zero is defined to be the earliest start time of the project. Each activity also has an earliest start (ES) time, which supposes that all activities start as early as possible, given the precedence relationships. The earliest finish (EF) time of an activity is simply the earliest start (ES) time plus the activity time (AT):

$$EF_i = ES_i + AT_i \qquad \text{for each activity } i \tag{1}$$

However, the earliest start time depends on the predecessors. Since an activity cannot start until all its predecessors are completed, then

$$ES_i = \max \left\{ \begin{array}{l} \text{EF of the predecessors} \\ \text{of activity } i \end{array} \right\} \tag{2}$$

---

[3] Activity-on-arrow diagrams are usually associated with PERT, whereas CPM commonly uses nodes as activities and arrows for precedence. All the arrows in a CPM diagram are dummies.

in which "max" means maximum, or in this case, the *latest* completion time among the predecessors of activity i.

To use these formulas, one must work from left to right in the diagram. For example, in Figure 3-1d, activity A has ES = 0, EF = ES + AT = 0 + 5 = 5 days. Similarly, activity D has ES = 0 and EF = 11. But activity C has a tougher situation. Look at Figure 3-1d to see why C cannot begin at time 5 (when A is completed) but must wait, instead, until time 11 to begin (after both A and D are completed). All predecessors have to be done, or else the activity cannot begin. (For example, in a building project, you cannot pour the foundation until digging is finished and forms are in place for the concrete.)

Using formula (2) for activity C yields

$$ES(C) = \max \{5, 11\} = 11$$

Now, we apply formula (1) to find its EF:

$$EF(C) = ES + AT = 11 + 6 = 17$$

The ES and EF times for each activity are computed as soon as all predecessors have EF times. These are written on the node, as shown in Figure 3-3. The ES time for the "finish" node can then be computed, which indicates that the project can be finished by time 24, at the earliest, in our example.

After following the calculations, you can now see why the arrow from A to E was unnecessary—there is a path from A to E through C. Satisfying that sequence guarantees that A will precede E.

Latest Start and Finish Times. In this small diagram (Figure 3-3) it is easy to see that the path D–C–E is *longer than any other,* and is therefore the one that determines when the project can be completed. This *critical path* may be harder to find in a larger diagram, but another set of calculations will identify it. This time, the calculations are designed to find out how *late* each activity could start

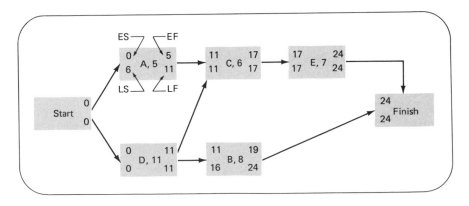

Figure 3-3   Calculating Early Start (ES) and Early Finish (EF) times.

without delaying project completion. The latest start (LS) and latest finish (LF) times are calculated by working backward (right to left) through the diagram, with the following formulas:

$$LF_i = \min \{LS \text{ of the successors of activity } i\} \tag{3}$$

$$LS_i = LF_i - AT_i \tag{4}$$

Arbitrarily assigning time 24 as the latest start for the FINISH node (since 24 was the earliest finish time), we can immediately write 24 as the LF for E and B, since they have no successors other than FINISH. The calculations proceed smoothly until we get to D, which has two successors—C and B.

Applying formula (3), $LF(D) = \min \{11, 16\} = 11$. The reason that LF for D is 11 rather than 16 is that, if we finish D later than 11, activity C will be pushed beyond its LS, pushing back E and thence the project completion. Thus there is no *slack* on the path D–C–E. However, activity B has some slack. It could start as early as 11 or as late as 16 without changing the project completion. Figure 3-4 shows all LS and LF times for our example.

Slack and Critical Path. The difference between LS and ES is the *total slack* (TS). For activity B, this is $16 - 11 = 5$ days. That is,

$$\text{total slack of an activity} = TS_i = LS_i - ES_i \tag{5}$$

The critical path is easy to identify now, by calculating TS for each activity. Let Tmin be the smallest TS in the diagram. Activities with TS = Tmin define the critical path. *The critical path is the longest path in the network, the one that determines project completion time.* There can be more than one critical path.

The importance of these numbers and concepts will be demonstrated by example in the Review Problems.

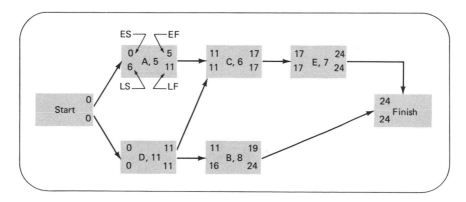

Figure 3-4   Arrow diagram with Early Start (ES), Early Finish (EF), Late Start (LS), and Late Finish (LF) times.

Review Problems

1. Activity A is the preliminary training session, in the example of Figure 3-4, and D is the modification of existing forms. The instructor wishes to have at least a preliminary draft of the new forms to use in the introductory sessions. How long can A be delayed, to procure these drafts, without affecting the project completion time?

2. The supplier of the forms considers 8 days a rush order and is charging a premium price. An additional week of lead time (5 working days) would eliminate the premium. Should we continue the rush-order status?

3. Additional resources are available to speed up activity D. What would be the result of cutting its duration to 6 days? 5 days? 4 days?

4. Path A–C–E is the shortest path through the network. Why not take that path rather than D–C–E?

Solutions

1. The LS of activity A is 6. Therefore, if preliminary forms are available within the first 6 days, the delay in waiting for them will not delay the project completion date.

2. Activity B has 5 days of slack, or 1 working week, so we could cancel the rush order. However, there would no longer be any slack for activity B, and any unanticipated delay in delivery would delay project completion. Depending on the costs, one might wish to continue the rush-order status, just for protection. Notice that if B takes 13 days, there would be *two critical paths, D–C–E* and *D–B*.

3. Activity D is on the critical path, and will remain critical unless it becomes shorter than activity A (look at Figure 3-4). Therefore, reducing D's activity time from 11 days to 6 or 5 days will shorten the entire project by a like amount (to 19 or 18), but if D takes less than 5 days, *the critical path shifts to A–C–E* and project completion is no longer influenced by D. (The project completion time would be 18 days.)

4. We do not "take a path" through this type of network. We must perform all the tasks in order to complete the project.

3-2 SCHEDULING WITH PERT/CPM

It is sometimes convenient to use a time scale in conjunction with a network diagram. Figure 3-5 shows one way to do this with the example from the preceding section. Notice that each rectangular box has been expanded to a length proportional to the activity time; START and FINISH have been reduced to vertical lines, since they have zero activity time. In Figure 3-5, each activity begins at its earliest start time. The horizontal arrows are remnants from the previous diagram, showing the precedence relationships. For example, after A,

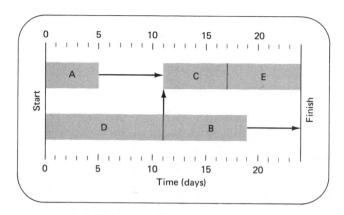

Figure 3-5 Time-Scale PERT/CPM chart for the new office procedure example of Table 3-1.

the arrow is 6 time units long, exactly the amount of slack in this portion of the network. The vertical arrow is a dummy activity, showing that *D* must precede *C* as well as *B*. Most of the arrows from Figure 3-4 have been eliminated—they were squashed between the expanding blocks.

The time-scale diagram presents an improved picture of the project. Slack is visible (in the form of horizontal arrows), and the critical paths are therefore easy to identify, by the absence of "slack" arrows. (In Figure 3-5, path *D–C–E* is critical.) The effects of changes, like those discussed in the preceding Review Problems, are also easier to interpret. (It would be worth your while to redo Review Problem 3 in Section 3-1 using Figure 3-5.)

Coordination of resources is also facilitated with the time-scale chart. Figure 3-6 shows a chart of a construction project; each activity has a list of the required number of carpenters (*c*), plumbers (*p*), and unskilled laborers (*u*). At the bottom of the chart is a summary of the total number of each kind of worker through time. This schedule can be improved by moving some activities within their slack times. For example, delaying the start of activity *C* until day 5 would reduce the peak number of carpenters from 3 to 2 during the first 11 project days, and peak laborers from 7 to 6. (Activity *C* can begin at 5 and end at 9 so that *F* is not held up by the shift.) Further analysis will be left for a review problem.

The preceding is an example of *resource leveling*. The philosophy is that a nearly constant usage of resources is easier to manage and less costly than an uneven schedule with widely varying peaks of activity. Computer routines have been developed for resource leveling. They are based on heuristics, which are rules, designed intuitively, to develop good plans. (They cannot guarantee an optimal solution.) The Project Management Institute (1980) published a survey of CPM computer software and other project control programs.

Time–cost trade-offs are also common in the use of PERT/CPM. Two examples were given as Review Problems 2 and 3 in the preceding section—a rush order at extra cost, and assignment of more personnel to speed up an

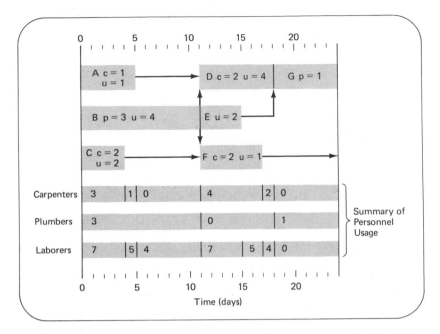

Figure 3-6 Construction project, with usage of carpenters (c), plumbers (p), and unskilled laborers (u).

activity. There are usually limited resources that can be utilized in these trade-offs, so one often can speed up an activity only at the expense of slowing down another. However, since some activities are "more critical" than others, such trade-offs may improve the overall project performance.

The simplest situation is when there is a single resource, which can be used to change some of the activity times. Whether the resource is personnel, equipment, or something else, it can often be expressed in dollar terms, and the typical cost curve looks like Figure 3-7—shortening the activity increases the cost, but there are upper and lower limits on activity time.

As an example, suppose that an activity could be speeded up from 12 days to 7 days by doubling the number of personnel working on it. This would double the hourly cost but would not cut the time in half, and therefore the activity would cost more in its shortened version. Of course, some activities cannot be shortened at all (concrete takes a certain time to harden), so that no amount of money can reduce the activity time. A few activities may speed up in direct proportion to resources expended, so that no additional cost is incurred in reducing the activity time if the resources are available. Mathematically, these may be viewed as special cases of Figure 3-7. That is, if $L_i = G_i$, the activity cannot vary, whereas if $b_i = 0$, there is no cost for varying the activity. We can now formulate a linear program (LP) to suggest an allocation of resources to change activity times to our best advantage. (LP is discussed in Appendix C.)

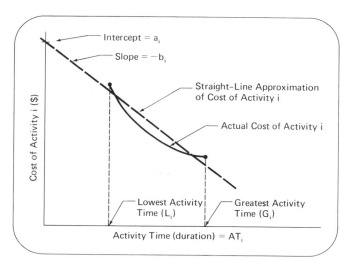

Figure 3-7 Typical time–cost trade-off for an activity.

The formulation in Table 3-2 makes use of the linear approximation of actual costs, described in Figure 3-7. There are three alternative objectives—either minimize the project completion time (PD) within a fixed budget (B) for project costs, or minimize costs while meeting a prespecified project deadline, or minimize total project costs, including penalties for late completion.

A typical penalty function for late project completion is shown in Figure 3-8. It is a simple matter to include a "piecewise-linear" function such as Figure 3-8 in an LP. In fact, if desired, a piecewise-linear approximation could be used in Figure 3-7 as well.

Constraints (9) and (10) in Table 3-2 assure that the start time of each activity satisfies the precedence relationships, since $ST_j + AT_j$ is the finish time of activity j, which is a predecessor to i. Constraint (11) keeps the project within its overall limit, PD, which is variable if objective function (6) or (8) is used. Constraint (12) keeps activity times between the limits shown in Figure 3-7, and (13) keeps the entire project within a budget limit B, which is variable under objective function (7) or (8).

For a large project, there may be hundreds or thousands of activities, and many thousands of precedence relationships. The LP formulation would, therefore, be extremely large. However, LPs that are derived from networks (such as the PERT/CPM diagram) are much easier to solve than the ordinary LP, and efficient algorithms exist that can solve this problem for most projects.

This LP suggests a schedule based on costs and project deadline. However, resource leveling is not considered in this formulation, so the suggested solution may have to be modified to better reflect the reality of limited resources.

Time–cost trade-offs can be generated by hand in small problems. Begin by solving for the critical path using normal times, then reduce the critical path

TABLE 3-2 LP FORMULATION[a] OF TIME–COST TRADE-OFFS IN A PERT/CPM NETWORK

Definitions

$$ST_i = \text{start time of activity } i$$
$$AT_i = \text{duration (activity time) for } i$$
$$PD = \text{project deadline or project duration}$$
$$B = \text{amount of funds budgeted for the project}$$
$$f(PD) = \text{penalty cost function based on project duration (see Figure 3-8)}$$
$$L_i = \text{lowest activity time for } i \text{ (see Figure 3-7)}$$
$$G_i = \text{greatest activity time for } i \text{ (see Figure 3-7)}$$
$$a_i \text{ and } b_i = \text{intercept and negative slope shown in Figure 3-7}$$

Objectives (three are given—take your pick)

(6) Minimize PD within fixed B
(7) Minimize B within fixed PD
(8) Minimize $B + f(PD)$

Constraints (all constraints apply, regardless of which objective function is used)

(9) $ST_i \geq 0$ for all activities that have no predecessors
(10) $ST_i \geq ST_j + AT_j$ for all pairs of activities i and j in which j is a predecessor of i
(11) $ST_i + AT_i \leq PD$ for all activities that have no successors
(12) $L_i \leq AT_i \leq G_i$ for all activities
(13) $\sum_i (a_i - b_i AT_i) \leq B$ (summation is over all the activities)

---

[a] Fulkerson (1961) published the first version of this LP.

sequentially by finding the activity (or set of activities) that is cheapest (per unit time) to speed up. When there are multiple critical paths, as there will be as reductions are made, they must all be reduced simultaneously. The cost of each schedule is computed and plotted as in Figure 3-9. When a critical path is composed of activities at their crash times, no further reduction is possible.

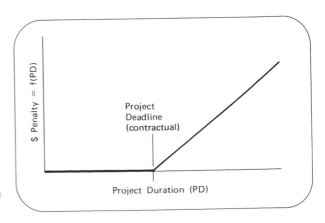

Figure 3-8 Typical penalty for late project completion.

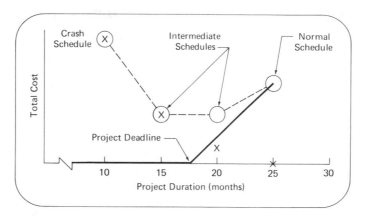

Figure 3-9   Time–cost trade-offs for a project.

In the figure, X denotes project costs, derived from functions such as Figure 3-7, and the solid line is the late completion penalty from Figure 3-8. The circles denote total cost (direct costs plus penalty costs).

Review Problems

1. Rearranging Figure 3-6, smooth the utilization of personnel as much as possible within the 24-day limit. Once a carpenter or plumber is on the job, it is best to keep that worker there as long as possible.

2. In time-cost trade-offs, why is it not necessarily true that doubling the personnel on an activity will cut the activity time in half?

3. In Figure 3-6, suppose that activity D can be crashed, cutting its duration from 7 days to 3 days. By how much will this shorten the critical path?

Solutions

1. The following start times really smooth things out for carpenters: $B = 0$, $A = 2$, $C = 7$, $D = 11$, $E = 11$, $F = 18$, $G = 18$. One carpenter begins at time 2, a second at time 7, and both remain until F is completed at time 24. Three plumbers are needed for B and 1 for G, but there is no way to move B and G together.

2. There may be other factors, such as limited equipment or "waiting for the paint to dry," which limit the effectiveness of additional personnel.

3. Activity E is 4 days long and must precede G. Therefore, crashing D from 7 to 3 days will shift the critical path to B–E–G, which requires 21 days, a saving of only 3 days, compared to the 4-day reduction in D. The extra day becomes slack for D.

3-3 *UNCERTAIN ACTIVITY TIMES: SIMULATION METHODS*

All the analysis has relied on the time estimates obtained in the early phase of planning. But these are not always reliable, particularly if an activity involves new product development or depends on uncertain elements such as the weather. Some authors distinguish between PERT and CPM by noting that variability in activity times is an integral part of the PERT methodology, but not included in CPM as described by its developers. However, as the methods have evolved, the emphasis on formal use of probabilities has diminished among PERT users, and elements of randomness have been adopted in many CPM-based approaches.

Today, the formal use of probabilistic methods in PERT/CPM is not common. However, there are two alternative approaches that are used. The first is to represent uncertainty on a time-scale graph. The second is to use more highly developed, computer-supported techniques. Both of these are discussed in this section.

One method of eliciting a forecast of activity time is to ask first for an optimistic time (call it a) and a pessimistic time b, and then ask for the most likely time m. The range, $b - a$, is one indicator of the expected precision of the forecast. PERT's developers went one step further and converted these three time estimates into an expected time (ET) and a standard deviation (σ) for each activity. The formulas[4] are

$$ET = \frac{a + 4m + b}{6} \tag{14}$$

$$\sigma = \frac{b - a}{6} \tag{15}$$

The expected time ET may be used wherever AT (activity time) occurs in the critical-path calculations. However, the standard deviations enter the picture in a more complicated fashion.

For example, in Figure 3-10, the uncertainty in activities has been represented by attaching triangles to the activity blocks. The base of the triangle is 2 standard deviations long, indicating (very roughly) that there is about a 2.3% probability of the actual task completion time extending beyond the end of the triangle. We shall discuss how the numbers were derived later, after interpreting the significance of the triangles.

First, consider activity A. We now see that the slack time following A is substantial enough that we may fully expect A to remain noncritical. However, the triangle following B extends well beyond what was the end of the diagram. Therefore, it is possible that the project will be delayed beyond 24 days because of a delay in B, *which was not on the original critical path.* Thus we may

---

[4] These formulas are based on the assumption that activity time has a Beta probability distribution. However, the mathematical development is unimportant for our purposes. See Malcolm et al. (1959) and MacCrimmon and Ryavec (1964).

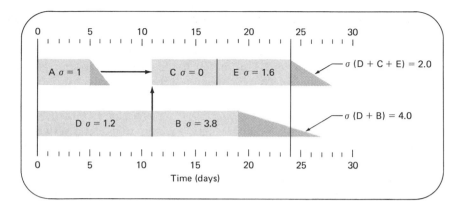

Figure 3-10 Time-scale diagram with 2σ confidence intervals (the triangles). Activity-on-arrow diagram, not drawn to a time scale.

conclude that some "noncritical" activities are more critical than others, depending on how large σ is compared to slack time.

The critical path, D–C–E, also extends beyond 24 days and, in fact, extends beyond the D–B triangle. This indicates that D–C–E is more likely to be the longest path than D–B, but there is no guarantee that this will actually occur.

Based on the discussion so far, one should be cautious about treating 24 days as a program target, particularly if the firm's reputation were hanging in the balance. Attempting to convert the triangles into numbers (probabilities) requires assumptions that are often unrealistic. This analysis has gone about as far as it should.[5] Many attempts have been made to refine this approach, but most have fallen into disfavor because of added expense or poor performance.

Now to explain the triangles. First, σ was estimated for each activity using equation (15). For example, if the optimistic estimate for activity A is 2.0 and the pessimistic estimate is 8.0, then $\sigma_A = (8.0 - 2.0)/6 = 1.0$. The other values, $\sigma_B = 3.8$, $\sigma_C = 0$, $\sigma_D = 1.2$, and $\sigma_E = 1.6$, are not calculated here.

Second, these were combined along each path using a statistical formula:

$$\sigma^2(\text{path}) = \sum_i \sigma_i^2 \qquad \text{with the summation for } i = \text{all} \qquad (16)$$
$$\text{activities along the path}$$

That is,

$$\sigma^2(D + B) = \sigma^2(D) + \sigma^2(B) = 1.2^2 + 3.8^2 = 15.9$$

so $\sigma(D + B) = \sqrt{15.9} \approx 4.0$. This formula is valid only if the duration of activities B and D are statistically independent. There are many situations that

---

[5] MacCrimmon and Ryavec (1964) carefully analyzed the PERT assumptions and the calculations. They concluded that the overall project completion time, as estimated by PERT (or CPM), is always biased optimistically (actual time is likely to be longer than PERT estimate). In their example, the bias ranged from 10 to 30%.

violate this assumption, so the length of the triangle must be taken only as a rough indicator of variability.

Many projects are more complex than a PERT/CPM diagram indicates. For example, Taylor and Moore (1980) describe a research and development project in which some activities may need to be repeated, or may fail altogether. They applied Q-GERT to model the complex and random character of the R & D project. Q-GERT is a type of simulation program (simulation is described in Appendix B) designed to make it relatively easy to model a network with random elements and arrows that form loops indicating an activity that may have to be repeated. Simulation is the only reliable method available for managers of such projects who want a good estimate of project duration and the probabilities of delay. Unfortunately, this requires the use of a computer and the collection of extensive data beyond that usually required for PERT/CPM. Nevertheless, computer simulation is finding wider application in project planning as well as other areas of management.

Review Problems

1. In Figure 3-10, compute σ for the critical path D–C–E. Using the σ value, ET = 24, and the normal probability law (Table 2, Appendix D), what is the probability that D–C–E will be completed within 25 days? 28 days?

2. Explain why activity B in Figure 3-10 could turn out to be on a critical path, even though it is shown as ending before E, and its "triangle" (2σ confidence interval) also terminates first.

3. What complication is introduced if the triangle following activity A extends beyond day 11, the early start of activity C, in Figure 3-10?

Solutions

1. (a) $\sigma^2(D + C + E) = 1.2^2 + 0^2 + 1.6^2 = 4$, so $\sigma(DCE) = \sqrt{4} = 2$ days.
   (b) With a mean of 24 days and $\sigma = 2$ days, we compute $z = (25 - 24)/2 = 0.5$.

   Using Table 2, Appendix D, for normal probabilities, the result is a probability of 0.692 or 69.2% of 25 days or less. For 28 days, $z = (28 - 24)/2 = 2.0$, and the probability is 97.7%. Please remember that these probabilities are based on guesses about activity times and some questionable assumptions. They are only ballpark estimates.

2. There are several reasons. Everything may go "normally" for activity E and everything may fall apart in B. Or, E might come in ahead of schedule. The point is that the triangles in the figure indicate uncertainty, and the uncertainty in the outcomes of B and E may differ.

3. This would indicate the possibility that A would use up all its slack and delay activity C. Unfortunately, the triangle following C is now understated, since it was calculated from path D–C–E, assuming that A did not intervene.

This is another way that the probabilistic approach to PERT/CPM gets complicated.

3-4 PROJECT CONTROL

Once the project begins, the nature of the game changes. Effective project control requires quick and reliable feedback of the progress to date. Experience has shown that the simplest reporting methods are usually the best, since more complex reports are generally more expensive to complete and more likely to either arrive too late to be useful or be ignored because of their length and complexity.

One method of control is to require weekly revisions of estimated activity completion time. These estimates are used to update the network diagram in an attempt to anticipate upcoming "bottlenecks." An activity qualifies as a bottleneck if it has important successor activities and appears to be falling behind schedule. Such an activity would be a prime candidate for management attention, perhaps requiring a *contingency plan* for diverting resources to alleviate the bottleneck, if necessary.

PERT-COST was developed as a management control tool, to report on cost and time performance of the responsibility centers as the project progresses. (See Bierman et al., 1986.) In addition to bottlenecks, PERT COST forecasts budget overruns (or underruns) by keeping an ongoing comparison of actual to planned spending.

The calculations are relatively simple. However, implementing PERT-COST imposes significant requirements on the cost accounting system as well as the organizational structure used in project management. Consequently, it is much more expensive to use, although the potential payoff is also higher, compared to a conventional PERT/CPM system.

The network diagram itself is a useful tool in project control, particularly when it is scaled with reference to time. The diagram should be constructed in a way that is easy to modify. For example, if the activities are represented by strips of plastic or heavy paper, changes in the schedule may be represented by physically moving the appropriate strips. Or, if the computer is being used, new diagrams can be printed with each revision. Whichever method is chosen, the value of the visual representation is the rapidity with which one can get an overall view of the project and focus attention on potential trouble spots.

Review Problems

1. In Figure 3-10, which activity qualifies as a potential bottleneck? Why?
2. Suppose that, after 6 days had elapsed, we found that activity D could not be finished until day 14 rather than day 11, as scheduled.
   (a) What does this do to the critical path?

(b) Where would you expend resources to try to meet a deadline of day 26 for total project completion?

Solutions

1. Activity *D* is on the critical path and has two immediate successors. Its delay would have the most significant project-wide effects.

2. (a) The same path remains critical (*D–C–E*) since the expected completion times of both *D–C–E* and *D–B* are lengthened by this 3-day delay. However, the length of the critical path is increased by 3 days.

   (b) This depends on costs and feasibility. It is tempting to concentrate on *D*, because it is the bottleneck. However, day 6 may be too late to implement effective changes for *D*. The next most likely candidate is path *C–E*, since there is no slack. However, Figure 3-10 indicates that simultaneous plans should be made for speeding up *B*, since it has a high degree of uncertainty.

3-5 Summary

Our discussion of project management has been far-ranging, even though the topic has focused on PERT/CPM as a tool. It is unusual when a single method addresses both the overall picture and the details of an operation, but network analysis does. The diagram provides both a broad overview of project phases and a detailed schedule of individual activities. Indeed, it is common to have at least two levels of charts, with the highest-level chart having "activities" that are actually subprojects, and the second level consisting of detailed diagrams for each subproject.

As part of an information system, PERT/CPM transforms data on individual activities into information about the project as a whole. The most fundamental information is identification of the critical path or paths and pinpointing where slack time and potential trouble spots exist in the system. These serve to focus management's attention on key problems and opportunities—suggesting activities that are primary candidates for contingency planning and crash programs (critical or near-critical activities), and pointing out activities that can be easily rescheduled to improve resource utilization. At the same time, the system provides a forecast of overall project completion time, and it can be used to summarize the projected utilization of key resources through time.

Because of these features, there has been a tendency to rely too heavily on the numbers that come tumbling out in legion. It is important that these numbers play their proper support role and not be allowed to supplant management judgment and control.

PERT/CPM is a valuable tool for planning and control, but not a substitute for good judgment, with attention to organizational and behavioral implications. It is common practice, for example, to build in a certain amount of slack at various stages of a project, to allow for unpredictable delays. The network diagram can be used to decide where to locate the slack.

Judgment is central to every phase of project management with PERT/CPM: deciding what version of network planning to use; assigning responsibilities; estimating requirements; scheduling; contingency planning; and so on. PERT/CPM helps the manager to keep on top of the situation, to focus attention on the most significant decisions, and to sort out the implications of a decision.

PROBLEMS

1. (a) How does one recognize the critical path in a PERT or CPM diagram?
   (b) Define "total slack."
   (c) Explain, in one sentence, the advantage of knowing the critical path.
   (d) Explain how knowledge of the total slack can be useful in managing a project.
   (e) For what type of network would the PERT estimate of "expected project duration" be biased? In what direction might it be biased?

2. (a) Draw a PERT diagram for the following project.
   (b) Calculate ES, EF, LS, LF, and slack for each activity.
   (c) Indicate the critical path.
   (d) Lay out a time scale, being careful to make equal time intervals from zero to the EF for the project. Then make a time-scale PERT diagram, with activities starting at their ES times.

Activity	Time Required (Weeks)	Predecessors
A	2	C, B
B	2	C
C	3	None
D	3	C, F
E	3	C, D, F, G
F	4	None
G	4	F

*3. Examine the following time-scale PERT chart.

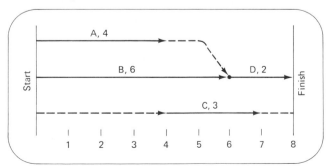

(a) What is unusual about the placement of activity *C* on the chart? How much slack is there for delaying this activity as shown? Why is that different from the total slack for *C*?

(b) As a manager, which of the activities would you monitor most closely for possible delays of the project? Which is least worrisome? Why?

*4. (Refer to the diagram below)

(a) Calculate ES, EF, LS, LF, and total slack for each activity, *using a deadline of 20 days for project completion.*

(b) Indicate the critical path and its completion time.

(c) Management is worried that activity *D* might be delayed beyond day 12 (start time). Discuss briefly how we could decide which activities would be most likely to cause such a delay.

(d) What is the earliest finish time for the project? Discuss briefly the accuracy of this number for planning purposes, and the sources of possible errors.

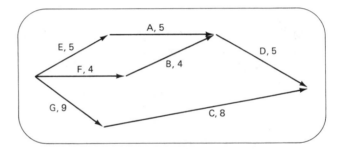

5. The BPA Distribution Co. has obtained exclusive rights, nationwide, for sale of a new product. They want to plan its introduction and set up a plan for inventory control. The new product introduction requires the following steps:

Activity	Predecessors	Time Required (Weeks)
A. Laboratory tests	None	3
B. Home tests	*A*	6
C. Design advertising campaign	*A*, *B*	5
D. Implement advertising campaign	*C*	4
E. Test market in a small region	*B*	6
F. Make decision as to whether to continue or not	*E*	1
G. Ship supplies to all regional warehouses	*F*	3
H. Deliver supplies to retail outlets	*D*, *G*	3

(a) How long, at a minimum, will the project take, and what items are on the critical path? (Show the diagram.)

(b) How much total slack does task *C* have?

(c) The project manager argues that all items which have some slack and which also have early start times before task *F*'s completion should be postponed to begin as late as possible. What items would be affected and what would the new start times be? Finally, what are the basic arguments for and against the project manager's policy?

*6. The curriculum committee of a well-known MBA program has decided that MBA programs are too long. They have decided to try a modular approach to curriculum planning, where each person proceeds at his or her own pace through the modules, but there is a system of prerequisites. Some of the activities, average times, and prerequisites are as follows:

Number	Activity	Average Time[a] (Modules)	Immediate Predecessor
1	Accounting	3	None
2	Quantitative methods	4	None
3	Economics	4	None
4	Finance	3	1, 3
5	Operations management	2	2
6	Business policy	2	4, 5

[a] Average times are in terms of 5-week modules.

(a) Draw the network diagram, and find the critical path and expected time of that path. Show the earliest and latest finish times on the diagram.

(b) Is the "critical-path time" a good estimate of the average time a student would take to complete the program? Explain.

7.

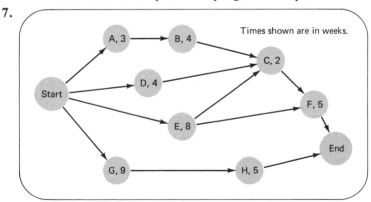

Times shown are in weeks.

(a) In the accompanying PERT diagram, what is the critical path? (Show or tell how you know!) How long does it take?

(b) What is the *least critical activity*?

    (c) Of the activities on the critical path, which one is most likely to be delayed because of its *immediate* precedence relationships?

    (d) What happens if *E* takes 7 weeks instead of 8 weeks?

*8. The accompanying diagram shows the network representation of a planned rearrangement of the machine shop in a manufacturing firm. The foreman is almost satisfied with the diagram, but he has a couple of problems.

    (a) He understands that activities on the critical path are the ones most likely to cause a delay. Which *other* activities should he be watching carefully because of their potential for delaying project completion?

    (b) How much does the activity time of *D* have to increase in order to change

        (i) The early start time of *H*?

        (ii) The early start time of *I*?

        (iii) The early completion time of the project?

    (c) He feels that activity *C* should be a predecessor to activity *F*.

        (i) Which activities will have their *earliest start* times changed and by how much?

        (ii) Which will have their *latest start* times changed and by how much?

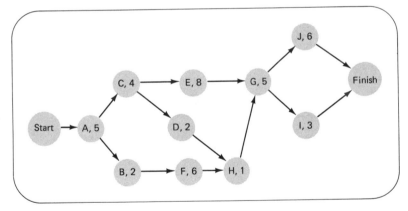

9. The PERT methodology can be adapted to handle deadlines for portions of the network (project). Consider the following project:

Activity	Time Required (Days)	Predecessors	Deadline for Completion
A	1	None	None
B	3	*A*	None
C	7	*A*	None
D	2	*B*	7
E	2	*C, D*	None

    (a) What is the EF time for *D* without considering the deadline? Can the deadline be met?

(b) How would you modify the formula for LF to accommodate deadlines?

*10. *NOTE:* Read the whole problem before beginning—a piecemeal approach will waste time.

(a) In the accompanying table, activity *D* depends on the arrival of a particular piece of equipment that won't become available until day 12. Does this affect the project completion time? Show in detail how you arrive at your answer.

(b) Which is the "least critical" activity (in timing, that is) in the project? How do you know? (Ignore part (a) for the rest of the problem.)

(c) Activity *G* can be speeded up by adding more personnel. How many days would its activity time have to be reduced before another critical path appears? How do you know?

Activity	Time Required (Days)	Predecessors
A	14	*D*
B	9	None
C	7	None
D	7	*C, B,* and arrival of equipment
F	12	*D*
G	14	*C*
H	14	*G*

*11. American Bottle Company (ABC) produces several types of glass containers. They have recently reduced capacity at several of their plants. Glass manufacturing involves large, expensive machines (including ovens), several of which were turned off in the capacity reduction. The machines were hard to shut down and to start up. In the event of a surge in demand, they wanted to know how quickly they could start one. How quickly can they start a new oven using normal times? What is the fastest time in which a new oven can be started, and how much additional cost is involved?

Cost per Unit Time Reduction	Activity	Normal Time (Hours)	"Crash" Time (Hours)	Predecessors
—	*A.* Preheat glass	8	8	*C*
—	*B.* Preheat oven	12	12	*D*
$40/hr	*C.* Obtain materials	4	2	None
$20/hr	*D.* Check valves	4	2	None
$20/hr	*E.* Check pressure seals	2	1	*B*
—	*F.* Add glass to oven	2	2	*A, E*
$50/hr	*G.* Prepare bottlemaker	6	3	*E*
—	*H.* Run test production	4	4	*F, G*
$50/hr	*I.* Examine test quantity and make adjustments	4	2	*H*
—	*J.* Refill oven with glass	2	2	*H*

12. The accompanying table contains a list of activities and sequencing requirements that comprise necessary activities for alterations on a medical school science building.

Activity	Predecessors	Expected Time (Weeks)
A. Preparation of preliminary application to NIH for funding alteration to medical science building	None considered here	4
B. Approval of preliminary application by NIH and subsequent request for detailed application	A	8
C. Preparation of narrative for application	B, E	4
D. Review and submission of application by medical center board of trustees; request for site visit	C	3
E. Development of cost estimates for grant application	I	4
F. Revision of application following site visit by NIH	G	3
G. Site visit by NIH team	L	1
H. Approval of grant application	F, G	16
I. Programming and schematic design by architects	B	8
J. Design development by architects	I	12
K. Final drawings by architects	J	12
L. "Rehearsal" of medical school faculty by planning committee for NIH site visit	D	2
M. Application for and approval of alterations in building and sidewalk to City Building Department and Traffic Department	J	16
N. Out to bid to contractors	K, M, H	2

(a) Draw a time-scale network diagram and find the critical path, using expected activity times.

(b) The site-visit team will be able to give a virtually certain statement of the eventual approval or disapproval of the application, at the end of their visit. Activities I, J, and K cost $100,000 each, so they would like to delay them until after the site visit. How much would the project completion date be delayed if activity K is so delayed? Activities J and K?

(c) Total construction costs of $10 million are escalating at the rate of 10.4% per year. Any cost above the $10 million would not be covered by the grant. There is a 90% probability (in the opinion of the managers) that the application will be accepted (by the site-visit team). Of the three activities I, J, and K, which should be delayed?

*13. Metropolis General Hospital is installing a linear accelerator in their radiology department, replacing a cobalt unit. The accompanying table represents the main phases of the project (excluding training of personnel, which has already been completed). Today is June 1. Delivery of the accelerator is scheduled for June 12. Once the cobalt unit is removed, every day that the unit is out of operation means a net loss of revenue of $500. However, of the activities shown, only the wiring may be speeded up, and this may be accomplished by working the electricians overtime, up to 3 hours per day (a normal day is 8 hours), at an additional cost of $50 per hour of overtime for the crew.

(a) Draw a critical path diagram and calculate ES, EF, LS, LF, and slack for each activity. Identify the critical path.

(b) Should the electricians work overtime? If so, how much overtime, and what savings accrue? If not, explain why not. If you feel that you must make some assumptions to answer, state the assumptions briefly.

Activity	Predecessors	Activity Time (Days)
B. Install new floor mounts for accelerator	D	8
C. Install new wiring	None	14
D. Remove cobalt unit	None	2
E. Install accelerator	B, C, D	7
F. Test accelerator	E	14

14. A division of Generous Motors has decided to install a computer to record and collate test results. It has been projected that the plant will save $300 per day with the new system. All activities can be speeded up (except *E*) by using overtime labor. The electricians are employed by the company at a rate of $5 per hour for a normal 8-hour day. They may work 4 hours overtime at an additional cost of $40 per hour for the crew. The carpentry work is done by contract. This crew may work overtime at a cost of $20 per hour for the crew for a maximum of 4 hours. The computer is expected to arrive on day 14. Using the accompanying table:

(a) Draw a PERT diagram and calculate ES, EF, LS, LF, and total slack for each activity. Identify the critical path.

(b) Should overtime labor be used? If not, why not? If so, how many hours overtime for what activity? What savings result?

(c) Construct a time-scale PERT chart [this can be done as part of part (a)].

Activity	Predecessors	Activity Time (Days)	Crew
A. Build a raised floor	None	4	Carpenter
B. Wire auto analyzers to feed results into computer	C	5	Electrician
C. Wire computer room	None	6	Electrician
D. Install air conditioning	G, B	2	Electrician
E. Wait to take delivery of computer	None	(see above)	Administrator
F. Install computer	A, C, D, E	10	Electrician
G. Build vents	A	3	Carpenter
H. Hook up to auto analyzer wiring	C, B, F	4	Electrician

15. The Eljay Samoht Construction Company builds houses. They want you to do a network analysis of their construction process. The data are given in the accompanying table.

Activity	Normal Time (Days)	Fastest Time (Days)	Total Additional Cost to Reduce Entire Amount of Time	Predecessors	Standard Use of Bulldozers	Standard Use of Workers
A. Rough in driveway	2	1	$200	none	1	2
B. Dig foundation	4	2	500	A	1	2
C. Finish driveway	2	1	100	A	1	3
D. Pour foundation	6	6	—	B	0	4
E. Construct framing	10	6	200	D	0	4
F. Construct roof	10	6	400	E	0	2
G. Siding	8	4	200	E	0	2
H. Plumbing	8	6	200	F, G	0	2
I. Wiring	6	5	100	F, G	0	2
J. Interior walls	10	6	300	H, I	0	3
K. Interior carpentry	14	8	800	J	0	3
L. Flooring	8	6	200	J	0	3
M. Finish lawn grading	2	1	200	G	1	2
N. Exterior painting	12	8	160	G	0	2
O. Interior painting and finishing	18	14	240	K	0	3
P. Landscaping	6	4	300	M	0	4

(a) Using all normal times, find the critical path, earliest start times, latest start times, length (in days) of the critical path, and planned usage of workers and bulldozers, starting all activities at early start times.

(b) Develop time–cost trade-offs for reductions of at least 24 days. State the basic assumption you are making.

(c) In part (b) an assumption was necessary. Comment on the validity of the assumption in this case. Would a reexamination make any changes in your answer to part (b)? Be brief.

(d) Assuming that skills are transferrable, it makes sense to lower peak usage of workers and bulldozers since the different skills can be used at different job sites at different times. State a *simple* heuristic to lower peak usage and use it. After applying the heuristic, do you see any better solution? If so, state it.

*16. A project manager has done a PERT analysis and found that the critical path contains the following tasks:

Task	Time Estimates		
	Optimistic	Mode	Pessimistic
A	3	4	5
D	7	7	7
G	5	10	21
H	2	5	8

(a) What is the estimated time for completion of the critical path, and what is the standard deviation?

(b) What is the probability of completion by a time of 30?

(c) Is the answer to part (b) biased? If yes, in which direction and why?

17. A project manager has the following PERT diagram of his project:

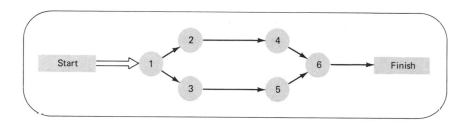

The time estimates are as follows:

Activity	Optimistic	Mode	Pessimistic
1	3	3	3
2	4	6	8
3	2	3	10
4	5	7	15
5	1	3	11
6	4	4	4

(a) Find the critical path and its mean and variance using the PERT assumptions. (You may use inspection to find the critical path if you prefer.)

(b) Using the PERT method, what is the probability of completion of 25 time units? Which way is this *probability* biased?

(c) As an estimate of total project duration, what can you say about the mean value calculated in part (a), making reference to the slack available to the noncritical activities?

18.

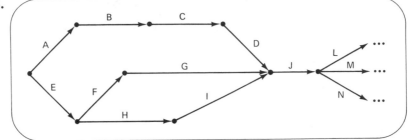

The preceding PERT chart is not drawn with a time scale. Activity *J* has been identified as a potential bottleneck because it has many successor activities. Management desires an estimate of the start time of *J*. There is substantial uncertainty in several of the preceding activities, so that a likely range for the ES time is desired. The analysis has led to an apparent contradiction: The critical path was assumed to be the longest one, or *A–B–C–D*. However, when the question ''what is the probability of being finished by time 20?'' is asked, another path appears to be ''more critical.''

(a) Calculate the ES time of *J*.

(b) Explain, with words and numbers, using the data below, the contradiction.

Activity	Expected Activity Time (Weeks)	Variance
A	4	1
B	4	1
C	4	1
D	4	1
E	5	3
F	1	0.5
G	1	0.5
H	5	3
I	5	10

(c) What is the probability that all activities (*A* through *I*) will be finished by time 16?

(d) Given your answer to part (b), is the expected start time of *J* above or below its ES time from part (a)? Explain.

REFERENCES

BIERMAN, H., T. DYCKMAN, AND R. SWIERINGA, *Managerial Cost Accounting,* 3rd ed. New York: Macmillan, 1986.

FULKERSON, D. R., ''A Network Flow Computation for Project Cost Curves.'' *Management Science,* Vol. 7, No. 2 (1961).

MacCrimmon, K. R., and C. A. Ryavec, "An Analytical Study of the PERT Assumptions." *Operations Research,* Vol. 12, No. 1 (1964).

Malcolm, D. G., J. H. Rosenbloom, C. E. Clark, and W. Fazar, "Application of a Technique for Research and Development Program Evaluation." *Operations Research,* Vol. 7, No. 5 (1959).

Moder, J. J., C. R. Phillips, and E. W. Davis, *Project Management with CPM and PERT,* 3rd ed. New York: Van Nostrand Reinhold, 1983.

Project Management Institute, *Survey of CPM Scheduling Software Packages and Related Project Control Programs.* Drexel Hill, Pa.: PMI, 1980.

Scott, D., C. Alsop, and R. L. Chandler, "Planning the Opening of a New Hospital." *The Hospital and Health Services Review,* March 1974, pp. 86–90.

Taylor, B. W., and L. J. Moore, "R&D Project Planning with Q-GERT Network Modeling and Simulation." *Management Science,* Vol. 26, No. 1 (1980).

Vazsonyi, A., "The History of the Rise and Fall of the PERT Method." *Management Science,* Vol. 16, No. 8 (1970). (Title in French, text in English.)

Wiest, J. D., "Precedence Diagramming Method: Some Unusual Characteristics and Their Implications for Managers." *Journal of Operations Management,* Vol. 1., No. 3 (February 1981).

PART II

Systems Planning and Design

Part II discusses operations management decisions that affect the organization for a long period of time. These are often called "design" decisions, in that the physical facilities, the organizational structure, or the tasks to be performed by management or labor are designed by the choices. Design decisions typically have long-lasting effects and impose constraints on the shorter-term problems to be discussed in Part III.

Chapter 4 introduces design problems in operations management and describes their interaction with marketing, finance, and personnel policies. Chapter 4 also describes several ways of developing the necessary long-range forecasts of sales, technology, or consumer tastes.

Chapter 5 describes methods for designing physical facilities, including different types of layouts and their relative advantages in different situations. The chapter includes an extensive analysis of the advantages and disadvantages of new technologies, including automation, in factories. Financial, marketing and behavioral aspects are analyzed, together with the societal impact of automation.

Chapter 6 introduces the problem of improving productivity. Methods are described for motivating employees and designing organizations so that an employee's range of abilities can be utilized. The difficulty involved in measuring productivity is discussed, together with some ways to improve productivity in both manufacturing and service operations.

Chapter 7 presents the related problems of capacity and location—where should the organization locate facilities, and what size should they be? These decisions typically involve facilities that will last for many years and involve large amounts of capital. The strategic aspects of capacity planning are discussed, including the organizational value of small capacity units and the competitive value of having large capacity. The chapter describes the differences among decisions in retail, warehouse, and plant settings as well as the use and limitations of several quantitative techniques.

CHAPTER 4

Introduction to Long-Range Planning and Design for Operations

Problems of long-range planning and system design are characterized by the facts that (1) a long look ahead (planning horizon) is used when considering them, and (2) the decisions made have an impact over a long period of time. This chapter gives an overview of this important area, discussing the many factors to be considered and the data needs involved in long-range planning and system design. A detailed example, the Somerton Health Maintenance Organization, will be used for illustration throughout this chapter.

The Somerton Health Maintenance Organization, SHMO, is faced with the problem of planning for health care for the Somerton metropolitan area. Somerton is a midwestern city with a metropolitan area population of 160,000 individuals. A health maintenance organization (HMO) is an organization providing prepaid care, where an individual pays a set amount each month and receives whatever medical care, including checkups, is required. The patient may pay a small fraction of the cost of a service in addition to the monthly charge.

SHMO owns and operates the only hospital in town. They are in the process of establishing satellite clinics around the city to provide primary care. Needless to say, they do not have sufficient funds to do everything they would like. (This problem, shortness of funds, is also faced by profit-making organizations, operations managers, and even professors.) SHMO needs assistance in designing their health care delivery system and in planning operations for the future. So that we can better assist them, their executive vice-president, Clare Voyant, has gathered some information.

Figure 4-1 is a representation of the metropolitan area, showing borough boundaries, population information, and the present hospital site.

Category	Population Density (Persons/km²)	Regions	
I	0–500	11, 13, 14, 16	(av. density = 380 persons/km²)
II	501–1500	4, 7, 12, 15	(av. density = 1210 persons/km²)
III	1501–3000	3, 6, 9, 10	(av. density = 2650 persons/km²)
IV	>3000	1, 2, 5, 8	(av. density = 3940 persons/km²)

The cost of a satellite clinic depends on the location. A new clinic to accommodate 3000 individuals for primary care costs $900,000 to build and equip in boroughs 1, 2, 5, and 8; $750,000 in boroughs 3, 6, 9, and 10; and $600,000 in all other regions. The operating cost per year is $750,000 when fully staffed, including costs of maintaining and updating the building and equipment. Each individual member of the HMO will pay $57 per month on the average.

The 400-bed hospital costs $45,000,000 a year to operate, including the cost of repaying a bond issue that was used to expand and refurbish the hospital 4 years ago. The $45,000,000 also includes the cost of necessary maintenance and improvements. An average bed is occupied 81% of the time.

The hospital accepts both SHMO members and patients who are not members. Nonmembers are charged $345 per day of hospitalization on the average. Members pay no additional fee over the monthly charge. The hospital has an outpatient clinic that is used both for nonmembers and for members. That clinic can serve a population of up to 10,000 members in addition to the expected load from all nonmembers. The hospital also has an emergency room. The outpatient clinic and the emergency room generate an average of $90 per visit from nonmember patients.

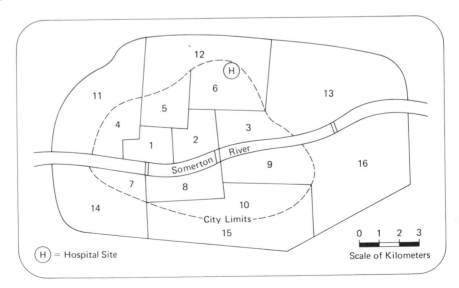

Figure 4-1 Somerton metropolitan area.

SHMO currently has 10,000 members, all of whom are treated using the hospital's outpatient clinic as their "doctor's office." Based on data from other HMOs, Voyant estimates that each member generates 0.84 hospital day per year, while nonmembers in the Somerton population generate 0.75 hospital day per year. Members generate 3.1 outpatient or emergency visits, while each nonmember generates 0.4 outpatient or emergency visit per year.

It is difficult to estimate how many members will be generated by a new satellite clinic. Many factors affect the rate of growth in members. We will study this prediction problem in more detail later in the chapter, but for now Voyant has given us an educated guess to work with. She estimates that a new satellite will attract 10% of the population within a 1-kilometer radius of the site in its first year of operation. A satellite will draw 1% of the population beyond 1 kilometer but within a 5-kilometer radius in the first year. Some of these will be drawn from members who previously belonged to another SHMO facility. The membership will double in the second year and again in the third year if capacity allows.

SHMO has a grant of $1,500,000 to use in establishing satellite clinics. The organization has no other funds at the present, but they plan to use some of their revenues in the future for satellites.

SHMO and Voyant would like some assistance in designing the future health care delivery system. They want to plan expansion over the next several years. The plans will be reviewed first by SHMO's board of trustees, then by a health planning agency representing the county. The health planning agency must approve the plan, since the HMO operates on a charter granted by the county government. Voyant says that the health planning agency is concerned with delivery of health care to outlying areas.

To assist SHMO, we will begin by discussing planning and design for operational systems.

4-1 LONG-RANGE PLANNING AND SYSTEM DESIGN VERSUS OPERATIONAL PLANNING AND CONTROL

The operations area of an organization should be designed using a long planning horizon (planning for a long period of time). In many design problems resources are being committed that will be used for a long period of time; thus their usefulness over that period must be considered. For this reason long-range planning and system design are frequently considered simultaneously by operations managers.

Operational planning and control, on the other hand, is the process of deciding what to do with the personnel and facilities that are available, and controlling the execution of the plans for the next day, week, month, or longer time period. These functions are usually constrained by the design decisions that have been made previously, and they usually involve a shorter time horizon.

SHMO is facing a long-range planning and system design problem, in that they are deciding what their organization will look like in the future. Each day they will face the operational planning and control problems of scheduling doctors and nurses, purchasing supplies, and all the other problems associated with utilizing the system within their control, but the main concern at the moment is with designing that system.

For simplicity, we will, in the following sections, often use "design" to mean long-range planning and system design and "control" to mean operational planning and control. These shortened phrases are used in many texts. The distinction between design and control is often unclear. This is true for several reasons. First, operating problems are constrained by design decisions, so the two areas are interrelated. An example is a manufacturing plant that must produce for inventory well in advance of its peak sales season, since it does not have capacity to meet the peak sales in season. This pattern is frequently optimal for a firm; the point is that design implies the mode of operation. Thus the mode of operation and the costs thereof must be considered in the design. Second, some design problems are faced frequently and are easy to change, so they essentially become a portion of the control mechanism. An example is the design of work assignments. Tasks can be redesigned easily in some situations, and the operations manager may do so to obtain more efficiency, happier personnel, or better material flow. In this case, redesign is one tool in the ongoing management of the operation. Finally, there are some topics that belong to both design and control. One example is product design, where "product" can mean a service as well as a physical good. Modifying and updating a product line is a continuing process, used to maintain a market position. Products are also designed and redesigned to make their production easier.

The design phase deals with some of the most important problems faced by the organization. SHMO, for example, wants to expand its size, a major goal of the organization. To achieve this goal, the organization is considering facility location decisions. It has apparently made a capacity decision, since figures are given only for outpatient facilities that can serve 3000 persons. SHMO will also face a facility layout problem in that each facility must have waiting rooms, examination rooms, magazine racks, drinking fountains, and so on. They must develop job assignments as well, determining the tasks to be performed by nurses, nurses' aides, paramedics, doctors, and clerical staff. Of these many design problems, the location problems are the most important. Location decisions through time are the key component of SHMO's long-range planning.

We will discuss many design decisions in this book, including production processes such as an assembly line and service systems such as a grocery store checkout area. Basic design differences between some Japanese, American, and European manufacturing systems are highlighted. We will find that the design approach critically depends on the goals of the organization and that there are both differences and similarities between profit-making and nonprofit organizations.

The remaining sections of this chapter will discuss marketing considerations; the interface of systems planning and design with the personnel, finance, and engineering functions; and forecasting for long-range planning. We will also try to assist SHMO in designing an expansion plan.

Review Problem

In Chapter 2 we dealt with Farm Supply Corporation's distribution system. They had one plant, supplying three distribution centers (DCs), which in turn supported a total of 250 stores. In several years, the distribution centers will be old enough to need significant repair. At that time the firm may totally redesign the system. The stores and plant will remain fixed, but the number and location of the distribution centers may change. Briefly what are the major objectives involved in the design of the distribution system? What trade-offs are there between these goals? How does the design affect the management of the system? (You need not refer to Chapter 2 to answer these questions.)

Solution

The main objectives in the design are to minimize the cost of transportation, to provide quick response to requests from stores, and to reduce total system inventory. Having many DCs provides quick response, but that would cause increased inventory investment (due to more locations for each item) and transportation cost (due to smaller average shipment size). The design affects the trade-off between service level and total system inventory; thus it affects the ordering decisions throughout the system. The design will also affect the mode of transportation and frequency of shipment used.

4-2 MARKETING CONSIDERATIONS IN THE DESIGN OF OPERATIONS

Marketing includes the delivery of a product or service to a customer, the process of finding out what the customer wants or needs, and convincing the customer that he or she wants the product or service. Marketing decisions constitute a major portion of the strategy for both nonprofit and profit-making organizations. As an example, SHMO wants to grow using satellites so that it can eventually provide health care for most of the Somerton metropolitan area. The location decisions are not only a system design problem but also a marketing problem, since locations will attract customers.

The customers do not view the analysis that goes into a systems design decision. They do not view each of the management decisions that are made, such as personnel scheduling, inventory ordering, transportation decisions, and so on. The customers see only the results of the management process, and the firm's image is projected to the public through the characteristics of the product or service. The three main characteristics of a product or service are price, quality (or perceived quality), and availability, where availability includes several subcategories to be discussed below.

Price is typically not determined by operations managers, although they have an input into the decision. Price affects the operations manager in that a low price implies higher demand to be met and the need for tight cost control.

Policy statements on quality often come from top management, but operations managers are usually responsible for the control of quality. Product quality has a major impact on the organization both in the short run and long run. The organization's image and reputation depend largely on product quality over a long period of time. In the short run, repeat customers depend on each product's quality.

Examples of the impact of the quality image abound. Consider IBM's entry into the personal computer market. The IBM image for quality of product and service, attained over many years, has helped them to be the largest force in the personal computer market in the mid-1980s, even though they started in the early 1980s, later than their major competitors. Japanese automobile manufacturers were able to make a large impact on the automobile market in the 1970s and 1980s for several reasons, but one important reason was that their product was perceived to be of higher quality. Quality is an operational as well as a marketing factor. Garvin (1983) says that "improving product quality is a profitable activity." Andrews (1983) says that "product quality is . . . the hallmark of long term success in competition and the keystone of vitality." This is one very important area where marketing and operational considerations overlap.

Availability involves many operating decisions, such as location and amount of inventories, the selection of modes of transport, and the choice of hours of operation. In some industries availability is not measured by whether an item is immediately available or not but by how long it takes to get it. In either case, the customers' viewpoint and the associated marketing considerations must be taken into account by operations managers who are designing and controlling the organization's operations.

An example of the effect of operational decisions on product availability (and thus on customer service) is given by Thomas (1983). In this article, a situation is described in which a company is able to provide dramatically better service to customers by expanding production and changing their method of production control. The financial justification for the product depended on the marketing benefits. Marketing benefits are often very difficult to quantify, but they are of great importance and cannot be ignored.

The customers' viewpoint, then, most directly affects the following operations design areas: (1) product or service design, including the range of products (the product line) or services to be offered; (2) location of the facilities that interact with the customers; and (3) the capability of the system to respond to customers' needs that are not fulfilled by the unit that first contacts them. Each of the three areas is discussed further below.

A product line that contains many items will make a firm known as a "full-line supplier." The products help to sell each other. However, a line composed of many products implies that the organization must have either many productive facilities or flexible productive facilities. A line composed of many products also implies high inventories per dollar sold, for reasons that we will discuss in later chapters. The same idea is true in service facilities. The fewer services an organization offers, the better the facility can be designed for those services. For example, SHMO must consider whether to have an X-ray unit and/or an EKG unit at each satellite clinic. The more services they offer, the more patients they may attract. However, the specialized facilities may not be fully utilized if they are placed at many locations.

In the case of individual product design, products can be designed to minimize cost, maximize appeal, or make a trade-off between the two. The packaging can also be designed to maximize appeal, minimize shipping costs, or make a trade-off between the two.

Item 2, location, requires marketing–operations interaction, because of the different needs of the two areas. Having many locations for customer contact may increase sales, but the cost of building and operating the locations may be excessive. In the case of production facilities, many facilities may allow quicker customer service, but economies of scale are forgone. SHMO's location decisions are to be used to obtain customer service. There is no significant economy of scale in such facilities past a minimum efficient size. Thus the sites are to be chosen based on the demand they can create. Location decisions are discussed extensively in Chapter 7.

Item 3, the ability to respond to customers, raises questions such as: who should respond to an unfilled request; what transportation links should be maintained between a customer contact point and other units; and what goods or services should be centralized at one or a few locations? For example, in a distribution system that supplies many items, should the slow-moving items be stored at one central location and sent by airfreight to the customer? (Maintaining access to airfreight is, at least partially, a system design decision.) Should a plant be designed to allow ease of changeover to another product so that small batch quantities can be produced and emergencies can be handled quickly, even though the cost of such a design may be high? In SHMO's case, the design question of this type is: What facilities should be centralized at the hospital to allow fuller utilization? Examples of such a "facility" would be a neurologist, an anaesthesiologist, or a pathologist.

To illustrate the effect marketing has on operations area decisions, we will consider SHMO's location decision. We will consider only the demand-creation aspect of the location decision here. This might be a first step in gathering evidence for use in making a final decision. Further analysis of the problem will be given in later sections.

Question Using only demand-creation considerations, where should the first SHMO satellite be placed? How many new members can SHMO expect to have in the first, second, and third years?

Analysis We will use the data presented in Figure 4-1. We will also have to make several assumptions, and, as in most real location problems, we will be satisfied with a good solution rather than an "optimal" one.

The location should be in a heavily populated area, but far enough away from the hospital to minimize taking the hospital's outpatients. On the line between regions 1 and 2, about 1 kilometer from the river, would be a good choice. The average population density is 3940 persons per square kilometer for regions 1, 2, 5, and 8. A 2-kilometer radius around the location lies almost entirely in those regions. A 5-kilometer radius includes regions of types I, II, III, and IV. We will assume a 2-kilometer density of 4000 and a density from 2 to 5 kilometers of 1500.

Ms. Voyant estimated that SHMO would gain 10% of the population within 1 kilometer of the satellite and 1% of the population from 1 to 5 kilometers during the first year. She predicted that enrollments would double in the second and again in the third year. However, she feels that all hospital members will stay at the hospital. Using these figures and the assumed population densities, we can compute an initial estimate of new enrollments. (Remember that the area of a circle is πr^2.) First:

$$\text{area within 1 kilometer}\quad = \pi r^2\ =(3.14)(1^2)=(3.14)(1)=3.14$$

$$\text{area from 1 to 2 kilometers} = \pi(2)^2-\pi(1)^2=(3.14)(3)=9.42$$

$$\text{area from 2 to 5 kilometers} = \pi(5)^2-\pi(2)^2=(3.14)(21)=65.94$$

Then the initial predictions of new enrollments are:

First year: $(0.10)(3.14)(4000)+(0.01)[(9.42)(4000)$

$+(65.94)(1500)]=2622$

Second year: 2622 will double to 5244

Third year: 5244 will double to 10,488

Next we need some assumption about the fraction of these members who already belong to SHMO, since they probably will not be attracted to the new clinic. Since the two locations are a little more than 5 kilometers apart, about 30% of the satellite's 5-kilometer area is in the hospital's 5-kilometer area. (If they were 5 kilometers apart, 39.1% would be included. How's your plane geometry?) A conservative assumption would be that all this area is lost to the satellite, and that the area of overlap contains 30% of the potential customers. Thus we will assume that 30% of the potential members already belong to the HMO and cannot be attracted to the satellite. Reducing the numbers above by 30% gives 1836 (70% of 2622), 3671, and 7342. The last two must be reduced to the 3000-member capacity. Since no net increase or decrease in hospital members can be attributed to the satellite, the total new members predicted in SHMO are 1836, 3000, and 3000 in years 1, 2, and 3.

All these assumptions should make you uneasy. Two comments are in order. First, such assumptions are frequently necessary and are based on informed judgment. Second, we will study long-range forecasting problems, such as forecasting the number of members here, in Section 4-4.

The interaction of operations management and marketing will be discussed again as we discuss both design and management control topics. The main point is that operations-area decisions must be made realizing the effect on marketing, and vice versa. As an example, Henry Ford, in discussing customers' preference for automobile colors, once said they could "have any color they want as long as it's black." The paint department can operate very efficiently in that mode, but the customer may not like it. In fact, General Motors, under the leadership of A. P. Sloan, used marketing effort, including colors, to overtake Ford in sales in the automotive industry. Henry Ford would have done better to have incurred the additional paint department cost.

However, lest you think that a broad product line is an eternal verity, Japanese automobile manufacturers have successfully used a limited product line in recent years to guarantee lower cost and higher quality. One firm advertised that choosing red or black is the only decision you will have to make.

Review Problem

A firm is considering replacing three machines that are used to produce their main product with one new machine that will be able to produce more units on the average at less cost than before. What marketing and operations factors should be considered? Why might they not buy the new machine?

Solution

The key operations factors here are the lower cost and higher capacity. The key marketing factor may include the cost (allowing lower prices) and the ability to fill larger orders quickly (this may be very important), but the possibility that one machine can break down and close off the entire supply is of prime importance. They might not buy the machine because they do not want to increase the risk of losing all their productive capacity for a time. Also, they might not have the money to buy the machine, even though it can pay for itself.

4-3 INTERFACES WITH PERSONNEL, FINANCE, AND ENGINEERING

The design of a production facility determines the environment in which many people spend over one-third of their waking hours. Personnel and labor relations policies must be considered in the design of a work area, and vice versa. As an example, in the U.S. automotive industry much of the labor is performed using assembly lines. The work is boring, but the rate of pay is high compared to jobs of similar skill levels in many industries. Alternative methods have been tried in some Japanese and European companies, where more group-oriented work assignments are tried. The physical facility can be designed with the purpose of allowing more meaningful work for the individual and encouraging worker commitment. Curtis (1983) says that "turnover is the ultimate in lost productivity to an organization." The U.S. automobile companies have had high turnover until recently. Design decisions and management styles that reduce turnover and gain worker commitment will pay for any short-term cost with long-run benefit.

Companies that provide services instead of physical goods must also consider the work environment when designing facilities. For example, in the SHMO clinics, each physician may want his or her own office for consultation, even though little time is spent there and shared offices would be "sufficient." In designing a school building, classrooms should not be large if the contract with (or policy related to) the teachers' organization specifies a maximum number of pupils per class.

In both manufacturing and service organizations, personnel policies, such as the commitment to quality circles, quality-of-work-life programs, and open communication systems imply methods of designing and managing operations. The type of training required and a firm's commitment to long-term employment affect the attitude toward automation. (See Vedder, 1982, for a discussion of the effect of automation on employment.) If employees are asked to suggest productivity improvements, they must feel that they will benefit rather than suffer. In general, the kind of work situation we want employees to have should be a major factor in designing facilities (discussed in Chapter 5) and in designing jobs (discussed in Chapter 6).

Another interface that is difficult to manage is the interface of production with engineering. A product may or may not be designed so that it is easy to build. Frequent redesign of a product may keep it up to date in the marketplace but add dramatically to production cost. Commonality of parts and design may add somewhat to the immediate production cost but reduce the cost of supporting the product in the field. Commonality of parts is not always the correct solution. Limiting the number of times a product can be redesigned is not always appropriate. However, it is appropriate to predict the costs of these changes and to make the correct trade-off. One difficulty in doing this is that the data base has typically not been common between engineering and production. Proper information management can assist both engineering and production to work toward the good of the overall organization. (See Gallagher and Gullo, 1980, for example.)

In nearly all design problems in operations management, an investment of money is needed to implement the design. Thus financial considerations are of paramount importance. Investments in plant and equipment can reduce costs, increase revenues, or allow reduced inventories due to improved ability to respond to customer demands. Operations managers should interact with the finance area in describing potential design investments, computing the expected financial returns, and selecting the most promising investments.

Business firms will usually demand higher returns from risky ventures. Thus a plant to produce a new product line may be viewed as more risky than an investment in cost–savings methods in an existing plant. A firm may use a different *discount rate* (see Chapter 2) for the different situations. They may also decide that a new product line is crucial to maintaining their market position in the future; then, by policy judgment, they might undertake an investment in that product line, even though the dollar return is relatively low. When this happens, it implies that the firm believes that there are benefits other than the ones used in computing the rate of return. In this situation the firm's strategy, financial considerations, and long-range planning and system design are all intertwined. Examples of this interconnection are seen in automation projects. The benefits in this case are many and varied as discussed in Chapter 2. Not only a financial analysis based on short-run cost, but also the firm's commitment to decrease marginal cost and receive the benefit of learning how to use automation should be included in these decisions.

Finance and operations design are related in nonprofit organizations as well. A school board is constrained in designing new facilities by the size of the bond issue the voters will approve and by the interest rate they can obtain when they issue the bonds. SHMO is constrained in their expansion plans by the funds they can generate either through borrowing or revenues. The extent to which they would be willing to use borrowing depends on the rate of return a new satellite would have.

The financial analysis of a new satellite clinic for SHMO is illustrated below. Other considerations are discussed in the Review Problems for this section.

Question   What cash flows will an investment in a new satellite have? Is it a good investment?

Analysis   As before, only rough estimates are possible. Based on the location selected in Section 4-2, we estimated new membership due to the satellite would be 1836, 3000, and 3000 in years 1, 2, and 3, respectively. Other data used below were introduced at the beginning of the chapter.

Each new member pays $57 per month, which is $684 per year. However, as a nonmember (i.e., if the satellite is not built) they each would have had an expected 0.75 hospital day at $345 per day and 0.4 emergency room visit at $90 per visit. Therefore SHMO's added revenue per new member is an expected value[1] of $684 − 345(0.75) − 90(0.4) = $389.25 per member per year. (Notice that we assume that people who join are not more or less sick than average.)

---

[1] The concept of expected value is discussed in statistics books such as Neter et al. (1982).

Assuming that the satellite is fully staffed immediately, the cash flows in dollars are as follows:

	TIME			
	0	**1**	**2**	**3 and After**
Building cost	− $900,000			
Operating cost		− $750,000	− $750,000	− $750,000
Additional revenue		(1836)(389.25) = 714,660	(3000)(389.25) = 1,167,750	1,167,750
Total	− $900,000	− $35,340	$417,750	$417,750

The cash flows will continue for a long time. We assume that the costs and revenues will inflate equally, so that a net revenue of at least $417,750 will continue into the future. It takes over 3 years to get the initial investment back. If SHMO discounts at 10%, the satellite has a positive net present value (NPV) after the fourth year. That is,

$$-900,000 - (35,340)\left(\frac{1}{1.0 + 0.1}\right) + (417,750)\left(\frac{1}{1.0 + 0.1}\right)^2$$

$$+ (417,750)\left(\frac{1}{1.0 + 0.1}\right)^3 + (417,750)\left(\frac{1}{1.0 + 0.1}\right)^4 = \$12,310$$

There are no tax effects, since SHMO is a nonprofit organization. Also, they believe they can borrow money at the assumed 10% rate. If SHMO thinks the satellite will last, it is a good investment. They have $500,000 to use in starting clinics, and they may be able to borrow more.

Several points should be made:

1. The lost revenue in hospital days and emergency visits cannot be ignored, since new members used the hospital as nonmembers.
2. The presumption of the satellite's existence past 3 years is necessary to make it a viable investment.
3. The assumptions about demand are crucial.

Review Problems

The analysis above and in Section 4-2 centers on current marketing and financial considerations in the system design.

1. Personnel and political considerations may militate against the chosen location. Why?
2. What future decisions might affect the profitability of the satellite?

Solutions

1. The political authorities seem to have some preference for serving outlying areas. Also, medical employees may be hard to find to staff a downtown location.

2. As the organization adds more satellites, they will have a harder time attracting new members, and they may reduce the membership of existing satellites. Even if all of Somerton is enrolled, the hospital, which now has 81% utilization, will be sufficiently large. (0.84 day per member times 160,000 members would give 134,000 hospital days. This is only 91.3% utilization for a hospital with 400 beds and 365 days per year.) However, the emergency room may not be sufficient as the number of members increases; expansion may be required in this area. Many other answers are also possible. For example, changes in the membership fee may make previously marginal satellites good investments, and obtaining subsidies for providing care to inner-city or rural patients may do the same.

4-4 FORECASTING FOR LONG-RANGE PLANNING

Any long-range plan or facility design requires some forecast (or forecasts) for an extended period of time. We will say that a long-range forecast is for at least 1 year, and more often for 2 to 10 years, or even more. SHMO wants to predict new members as a function of location decisions. As another example, in deciding whether or not to build a coal gasification plant, a manager would want to forecast the demand for the product (gaseous heating fuel) during the life of the plant. As part of that forecast, the expected technological breakthroughs in solar, wind, or nuclear energy would have to be reviewed.

SHMO's board of trustees would like to have half of Somerton's 160,000 individuals enrolled within 10 years. That is their goal. It is not the forecast. Goals should be based on forecasts, not the reverse. However, many managers set a goal and "make it happen." Thus the goal becomes a self-fulfilling prophecy and a forecast. Nothing we will say in this section about forecasting is meant to reduce the importance of proper goal-setting and motivation to reach those goals. Rather, it is suggested that a forecast should be made based on the best available information and that goals should be based on the forecast. If the forecast is insufficient to meet a strategic plan for penetration, management can try to change something to make a higher forecast appropriate. Ways to make a higher forecast appropriate might include a larger building budget in SHMO's case, or a larger sales force or advertising budget for a business firm.

Good forecasts are made using several sources of information. These include:

1. Grass-roots information (including guesses and a "feel" for the market) from sales personnel and first-line management. Management must provide for timely feedback of this information.

2. Judgments made by managers and technical experts as to new sources of competition, technological advances, and other factors that affect sales (or some other variable of interest).

3. Past sales records that can be analyzed to find trends and seasonal patterns in sales. Techniques to do this are more useful for short-term forecasts, discussed in Chapter 8, than for long-term forecasts.

4. Other quantitative information that can help in predicting sales and other variables. For example, past values and predictions of average disposable income are available from the government. (The Department of Commerce publishes a plethora of information in the *Survey of Current Business*.) Another key source of useful data and forecasts is an industry association. Such associations, composed of firms from a specific industry, collect and distribute data concerning industry-wide sales, costs, and so on. They also publish forecasts of industry sales for the next several years. These data sources are useful because they measure trends that affect the sales of most firms. Explanatory models, using regression and other techniques, are often used for this sort of long-range forecasting.

In developing long-range forecasts and plans it is crucial for the manager to organize data gathering to include any of the four categories listed above that are relevant. Keep in mind that the biggest errors in long-range forecasting and planning have not been in misestimating a number for sales of a particular item, but in not knowing that the item would be obsolete or that a new product would totally redefine the market. That is, in long-range forecasting, it is important to try to predict what the shape of the market will be in the future.

We will discuss categories 1 and 2 under the heading "Group and Individual Judgments." Category 3 is postponed to Chapter 8, where it will receive extensive attention. Category 4 will be discussed here. Chambers et al. (1971) discuss each of the four categories.

Group and Individual Judgments

In processing information, people have certain common weaknesses. These are extensively discussed by Hogarth and Makridakis (1981) in a very interesting article. Summarizing many research studies, they state that in acquiring data people have selective perception in several ways. First, we all tend to weigh our own experience much more heavily than statistical information. (If I buy a particular make of car and it is a "lemon," I probably will not be convinced by a good quality report in *Consumer Reports*.) People also tend to downplay conflicting data when they arrive and to collect data that are consistent with previous opinions. (As one example of this, the group that pays more attention to automobile advertisements than any other is the group of people who have just purchased automobiles.)

Two other limitations are of particular importance in long-range forecasting. First, research shows that logical displays blind people. That is, a long list of the good and bad things that might happen to our corporation, artfully presented, makes people less able to come up with innovative ideas about the future than before they read the logical display. This means that some thinking about the long-range future should be done without reference to other information.

The second limitation is that in processing information, most people sift through the possibilities until they get to the one they consider most likely. Thereafter, people frequently ignore the wide range of things that might happen even if they had thought of them during the data gathering process. For long-range forecasting this can be particularly dangerous, since a long-range plan must be able to deal with many possible futures that the company might face.

Individual judgments are used for long-range forecasting in many ways, but perhaps the most common is to obtain a feel for the market. Salespeople know whether or not the customer is satisfied and what changes the customer would like in the product. This information must be routinely collected, collated, and used in planning. However, in addition to the limitations mentioned in the preceding paragraphs, salespeople are likely to consistently over- or underestimate sales. This misestimation should be computed and used in one of two ways: (1) as feedback to the salesforce to improve their accuracy, or (2) as an adjustment of the individual forecasts to eliminate the bias. The authors have a strong preference for method 1, since method 2 can eventually lead to managerial difficulties. Of course, a long-range forecast should not be based on grass-roots information alone.

In developing long-range forecasts and long-range plans an organization must make predictions of major changes in the technology or the markets. For example, will a new product eliminate half of our current business in the next 10 years, or will a currently small competitor dramatically increase their market share? Forecasts of important changes such as these are often best made by individuals applying their informed judgment. Major changes occur infrequently, and they are often ignored in short-range forecasting. However, ignoring such developments in long-range forecasting invites disaster. Mechanical calculators, flash cubes, and medium- to high-priced watches were all basically removed from the marketplace due to a new product innovation. In the calculator industry, the entrance of many companies into the field reduced prices and sales to a point where many companies were forced to leave the business.

Group judgments can be used to predict such market and technological changes. Since time is expensive, group judgments are used more frequently for major long-range plans than for day-to-day management. In using group judgment to address technological or market forecasts, it is important to select the right group. The group should not be composed of people who all think alike, because coming up with an unusual idea is a basic purpose of the exercise. The individuals interact either face to face or through intermediaries as they move toward a consensus forecast. When intermediaries are used this method is called the *Delphi technique* (for an example of Delphi, see Basu and Schroeder, 1977). In the Delphi technique, all information is passed in written form (or using computer terminals), and some information is lost due to the form of message. However, Delphi has the advantage that one person will not dominate the decision due to force of personality, debating skill, or management position. We do not feel that Delphi is always preferable to a group consensus approach where people openly debate the issue. We do feel it is important for an organization regularly to address potential major changes in a formal way, so that long-range planning can be more effective. The manner in which potential market and technological changes are addressed is less important than making sure that they are not ignored.

Group consensus approaches have several very useful functions. Consider the following sample question. "In what year (if ever) do you expect electric cars to capture 10% of the market?" Beginning with that question, a group would first try to define the market. Does the market include golf carts, for example? After the question is refined, a group would try, by passing messages back and forth or by discussing the topic, to determine what technological and market changes would have an impact on this question. For example, the future price of oil is clearly relevant. The group should contain someone with knowledge in that area. Technologically, future breakthroughs in battery storage of energy would be needed. For example, what discoveries are expected to make light batteries that can propel a car for over 100 miles, while being rechargable in a matter of a few minutes? Consumer response to the style of car that would be built around an electric propulsion system would be important. Different people adding different information would be needed.

One final point relates to the effect of an organization's competitors. To predict the future of an industry, it is necessary to have competitor and industry forecasts. These are discussed extensively by Porter (1980). It is common, for example, for three or four firms in an industry to have long-range plans that predict a total of 150% of the market share between them. Clearly that cannot happen, so in developing plans the effect of competitors' probable moves must be included. Are different strategies likely to clash?

In predicting the industry structure it is useful to construct *scenarios* for the future of the industry. A scenario is an internally consistent view of the future. That is, if we make the move we are considering, what might our major competitor and other competitors do? Based on their possible responses, how might we counter? This line of reasoning can be followed, including estimates of how successful different moves will be, to project a future for the industry. However, it is not usually safe to use one scenario; we suggest developing several. The main benefit for this effort is the learning process that goes on, whereby we seriously consider our place in the market. Long-range plans can then include contingency plans. If a plan is beginning to fail in a particular way, what will we do about it? A plan that can be repaired is better than one that cannot handle contingencies. Decision analysis, including *decision trees* (see Neter et al., 1982, for example), can be used to help managers examine alternative futures and their effect on current plans.

Survey Methods and Conjoint Measurement

When a new product or service is being considered, as in SHMO's case, potential demand is often measured by consumer surveys. Recent developments in statistical analysis have brought survey methods into the realm of "complex, causal methods." By careful design of the survey instruments, the researcher can find out not only what the consumer prefers, but also which *attributes* are the most significant in the consumer's decision. For example, in a survey concerning health care, McClain and Rao (1974) identified three groups of consumers who could be distinguished not only by their choice of a health plan, but also because they disagreed as to what aspect of a health plan was most important. The attributes were "method of payment," "hours of operation," and "use of physician's assistants"; by asking the consumers to choose among health plans, the researchers were able to discover, indirectly, how each attribute was valued, without asking the respondents.

   The name *conjoint measurement* is applied to this kind of approach because two things are jointly estimated from the same data—overall preferences for different alternatives (e.g., different health plans) and the underlying values (or utilities) of the attributes that describe the alternatives. Green and Wind (1973) describe a number of ways to perform the analysis and provide extensive discussion of the kinds of assumptions and judgments which are required, on the part of the forecaster, in choosing a method.

   The two major advantages of this approach are (1) that it does not require historical data (data are collected by a survey), and (2) that the detailed understanding of the consumer's preferences may lead to new ideas, such as a new product or service that combines some of the most preferred attributes. However, it is also among the most expensive methods, primarily because of the cost of the survey.

Using Quantitative Data and Regression Models

The basic idea in forecasting using regression models is that the manager tries to find numerically valued variables that can explain the quantity to be forecasted. For example, a U.S. automobile company's annual sales can partially be explained by average disposable income in the U.S. population. This statistic is available for the past, and forecasts are made of the future. *Linear regression* is a statistical technique that will give a linear equation to relate the variable to be forecast to values for the other variables. This might be

   car sales per million registered drivers

$$= 550 + 0.6(\text{per capita U.S. disposable income})$$

or

$$y = 550 + 0.6x$$

Then if disposable income is \$16,000 per capita, the car sales are expected to be

$$y = 550 + 0.6(16,000) = 10,150 \text{ per million registered drivers}$$

The manager's job in this analysis is to be certain that the explanatory (independent) variable or variables used are logically related to the variable to be forecast (the dependent variable). In addition, the manager must examine the forecast equation and the particular forecast to see that they make sense. It is easy to obtain a nonsensical result, and it is the manager's responsibility to check results for reasonability.

There are several common errors to look for in applying regression.

1. Both y and x (or several x variables) may be increasing or decreasing due to another variable that is not included in the analysis. In this case, the independent variables must be changed to include variables that more directly cause changes in y.

2. The relationship between y and x may be incomplete. There may be another x variable that should be included.

3. The relationship between y and x may be nonlinear, and forcing a linear relationship to hold between them gives a bad result.

4. The forecast may require extrapolation beyond the x values included in the regression calculations. Thus, if advertising varied between \$1000 and \$4000 heretofore, it is very risky to use the relationship found using that data to predict sales if the advertising budget is increased to \$7000. Nevertheless, forecasting by some kind of trend-line extrapolation beyond past experience is common.

5. The relationship found in the regression study may be useless in forecasting. For example, a relationship between annual sales and average temperature in the same year is not useful unless accurate forecasts for next year's average temperature are available. A useful independent variable must be known in advance of the time when the forecast is needed.

Points 1 and 2 are best avoided by careful choice of the independent variables and careful scrutiny of the resulting equation and forecast. Point 3 is best avoided by plotting the data and seeing if a linear relationship is reasonable. Point 4 is best avoided by not extrapolating beyond the data used in the calculations (unless we have to, in which case we worry about it). Point 5 is best avoided by always keeping the purpose of the analysis (such as forecasting) in mind, so that a useless relationship is not obtained. These topics are discussed at length in books such as Neter et al. (1983).

Turning our attention to SHMO's forecasting problem, you will recall that Clare Voyant made a rough estimate that a satellite would attract 10% of the population within 1 kilometer and 1% of the population within 5 kilometers in the first year. The membership was expected to double in the second year of operation and again in the third year. Recognizing that these estimates are critical to the planning problem, she has analyzed data from several other HMOs, concentrating on those that were the only HMO in their metropolitan area.

After extensive analysis, the equation that fit the best *and* made sense was as follows.

new (additional) members at a satellite in a 1-year period

$= a + b_1$ (unsubscribed individuals within 2 kilometers)

$+ b_2$ (unsubscribed individuals beyond 2 kilometers but within 6 kilometers)

$+ b_3$ (monthly membership fee, adjusted to the current price level using an inflation factor)

$+ b_4$ (total membership of the entire HMO)

This equation was used to predict new members until the capacity of the satellite was reached. The values of the constants were

$$a = -40.0 \qquad b_1 = 0.09 \qquad b_2 = 0.01 \qquad b_3 = -6.0 \qquad b_4 = -0.001$$

The negative values for b_3 and b_4 imply that high prices reduced an HMO's attractiveness and that as an HMO increased in total size, the remaining people were harder to attract. As one final piece of information, Census Bureau figures indicated that Somerton was not currently increasing or decreasing in population, so 160,000 could be assumed for the next several years. Voyant felt that the equation was reasonable and could be used in planning.

Question 1   For long-range planning, assume that SHMO has added the satellite referred to in Section 4-3, on the line between areas 1 and 2 in Figure 4-1. Further, it has reached its capacity for members at 3000, and the hospital still has 10,000 members. The price per member is expected to be $57, and other costs are also the same as before. A satellite at the intersection of areas 9, 10, 15, and 16 in Figure 4-1 would please the planning agency since it wants the rural areas to be served. Use the forecast equation above to predict the membership pattern of the new site.

Analysis   As in Section 4-3, many assumptions will be needed. The population within 2 kilometers of the site is roughly $\frac{1}{4}$ in region 9, $\frac{1}{2}$ in region 16, $\frac{1}{8}$ in region 10, and $\frac{1}{8}$ in region 15. Using the population figures below Figure 4-1 and the fact that a 2-kilometer-radius circle contains $\pi(2)^2$ square kilometers, we obtain

$$\pi(2)^2[\tfrac{1}{4}(2650) + \tfrac{1}{2}(380) + \tfrac{1}{8}(2650) + \tfrac{1}{8}(1210)] = 16,800$$

individuals within 2 kilometers. Of these individuals, only a few percent will belong to the HMO before the new satellite is in place, since the other satellite is over 6 kilometers away. We will use 16,000 as the number of unsubscribed individuals within 2 kilometers, initially. Similarly, there are (very roughly) 95,000 individuals beyond a 2-kilometer range but within a 6-kilometer radius of the new satellite, and close to 10,000 of these may already belong to SHMO. Thus 85,000 is the initial value of the second variable in the equation. The current monthly membership fee is $57, and the total existing membership at HMO units is 13,000. The forecasts are given below.

Year 1—Additional members:

$$y = -40.0 + (0.09)(16,000) + (0.01)(85,000)$$

$$-(6.0)(57.0) - (0.001)(13,000)$$

$$= 1895$$

total members at this satellite $= 1895$

Year 2—Additional members:

$$y = -40.0 + (0.09)(14,560) + (0.01)(84,150)$$

$$-(6.0)(57.0) - (0.001)(14,895)$$

$$= 1755$$

where numbers have been changed in year 2 because of the additional members in year 1.

However, capacity will not allow 1895 + 1755 new members. The total members at this satellite will therefore be 3000; capacity is reached, and replacements can be found to fill vacancies that occur in the future. The satellite will have roughly 2000 members by the end of year 1 and will reach capacity during year 2, according to the forecast equation.

Question 2   Is this new proposed location an economically viable site? What does the answer imply about SHMO's long-range expansion plans?

Analysis   As you may recall from the beginning of the chapter, the building cost is lower at this site than for the site analyzed at the end of Section 4-3. The revenues will be higher, since the forecast equation now predicts more members in year one, and capacity is reached sooner. The operating cost here will be the same as in Section 4-3. Since the site analyzed previously was a good investment, so is this one. This analysis seems to imply that SHMO can profitably build several satellites on the edge of the city limits, to satisfy outlying areas. The sites should be chosen so that they are not within 2 kilometers of one another. If at some future time a large fraction of the population are members (say one-third or more), SHMO may have to slow down their expansion as a result of competition among the satellites. (This competition appears in the forecast equation, since the unsubscribed population is used to compute the forecast for new members.)

Review Problems

1. Which of the variables used in SHMO's regression equation might have a different effect in different metropolitan areas? Why?
2. What else might affect the attraction of new members?

Solutions

1. Potentially all of them. In certain cities, people are used to driving long distances to get to things. Thus b_1 and b_2 might vary with driving habits. The value of b_3 will depend partially on the average income in the area. The value of a and b_4 will depend on attitudes toward HMOs, which will vary with location.

2. Many other factors might affect the attraction of new members, but no study can include every possible factor. Examples of other factors would be the number of non-HMO physicians per 1000 people in the population and the average age of the population.

4-5 Summary

Long-range planning and design of operations is a process of deciding what facilities an organization will have, where they will be, and what they will be able to do. It includes the strategic consideration of what products and/or services the organization will offer. The plan involves committing large amounts of resources over a long period of time (from 1 year up to perhaps 20 or more).

The design of the operations facilities must be reviewed periodicially to see that the facilities will be able to deal with future contingencies that may occur. The facilities must be able to deliver goods and services that are in demand by the public. The design should facilitate the strategic plan of the organization with regard to entering new markets and in maintaining a high-quality and/or low-cost position. In the design phase, the various concerns of operations, marketing, personnel, engineering, finance, and other areas must be balanced by the top-level management of the organization.

In SHMO's situation, the design problem centers on increasing size through planned facility expansion. The problem is similar to that of a fast-food company that is expanding the number of outlets. Differences include the limited competition for SHMO and the fact that new fast-food outlets often use the franchisee's cash rather than the company's. The problem is also similar to the refurbishing plan of a business firm that is not expanding, but is stable or even contracting.

A key to many, if not most, operations design problems is a long-range forecast of the overall sales of the organization. How long will a particular product line exist and at what sales level? What new technology will arise in the next several years and how can the organization react to it? Questions such as these are difficult to deal with, but they must be addressed in any long-range plan. A plan can be selected because of its ability to deal with several possible futures, as well as for its ability to deal with the most likely future. The long-range forecast must be revised from time to time to allow periodic revision of the long-range plan and to aid in the ongoing design of the operations area of the organization.

The remaining chapters of Part II will deal with designing the work situation, considering the needs of people and products, and planning the capacity and location of facilities. However, since the distinction between long-range planning and design and operations planning and control is frequently unclear, we will return to design questions throughout the remainder of the book.

CASELET: SOMERTON HEALTH MAINTENANCE ORGANIZATION

This caselet is a continuation of the SHMO case. As in the chapter, several assumptions and guesses are necessary. The questions have more than one answer, and the goal is to achieve a good long-range plan, not an optimal plan. To refresh your memory, some of the significant data are stated below.

Population densities—shown below Figure 4-1

Member charge per month—$57

Nonmember charge per: hospital day—$345
                      emergency visit—$90

Expected hospital usage per: member—0.84 day per year
                             nonmember—0.75 day per year

Expected outpatient and emergency use per member—3.1 visits
                                          nonmember—0.4 visit

Operating cost per satellite—$750,000 per year

Construction cost per satellite—$900,000 in regions 1, 2, 5, and 8
                                $750,000 in regions 3, 6, 9, and 10
                                $600,000 in all other regions

Forecast equation: given at the end of Section 4-4, with $a = -40.0$, $b_1 = 0.09$, $b_2 = 0.01$, $b_3 = -6.0$, and $b_4 = -0.001$

In the following problems, assume that only the satellite between regions 1 and 2 has been added, that it is fully subscribed at the 3000-member capacity level, and that the hospital clinic has 8000 members.

Required

1. Predict the membership pattern for a site in the middle of region 16.
2. Is the site described in Part (1) economically viable? Assume that SHMO can borrow money at 10% interest, that the full $750,000 operating cost is required in each year, and that the facility will last for at least 10 years with no refurbishing.
3. How many satellite clinics would be necessary to meet SHMO's goal of having 80,000 members (half of Somerton's population)? Somerton has an area of approximately 150 square kilometers. How much coverage can an average satellite have? Would a downtown site have more or less than this average?
4. If 23 satellites have been added and are fully subscribed, is a twenty-

fourth site economically viable? Assume that it is placed downtown. Some guesses will be necessary.

5. Roughly, how fast can satellites be added if SHMO cannot obtain extra funds except through their operations? They have money to build the first two units, and the hospital can be assumed to produce $4,500,000 per year above its operating cost.

6. Using the answers to parts 1 to 5, devise an expansion plan for SHMO that makes sense and is economically viable. Assume that satellite clinics can be prepared for operation in a few months.

PROBLEMS

1. Define "long-range planning and system design" and "operational planning and control."

*2. Are the following problems "design" problems or "control" problems?
   (a) Deciding whether to run a plant for two shifts or three shifts for the foreseeable future.
   (b) Deciding whether to establish a policy of using two police officers or one in each patrol car.
   (c) Deciding whether to have a policy of using airfreight or truck to transport all products.

3. Are the following problems "design" problems or "control" problems?
   (a) Deciding what products to make during the next shift in a job shop.
   (b) Deciding what officers to assign to which patrol cars for the upcoming month.
   (c) Deciding which items from today's output to ship via airfreight.

*4. When the capacity of a plant is determined, what operational planning and control problems should be considered?

5. How does the design of a fire protection system (number of stations, equipment, and personnel at each station) constrain the day-to-day operations? Give an example.

6. Why would a health maintenance organization such as SHMO want to centralize the X-ray facilities at the hospital? Why would they want to have one at each satellite clinic?

*7. What important interactions are there between the design of a new plant for a furniture manufacturer and the marketing plans for the organization?

8. In designing an assembly line and its method of operation, a company wants to use the following guidelines: (1) use several groups of workers, with each completing a recognizable portion of the finished product, rather than in-

dividual, seemingly unimportant tasks along the line; (2) place a work-in-process inventory between each group; (3) allow each group to set its own hours of operation, subject to meeting a specified level and quality of output.

(a) Why would the firm want to use guideline 1?

(b) What is the trade-off between guidelines 2 and 3?

9. An operations manager in an electronics company is considering a $2 million investment in equipment which will currently save money at a rate of $1.2 million per year. She says that the investment should not be made. Explain how she could be correct to turn down such an investment.

*10. An operations manager in a nonprofit health care organization is considering a $2 million investment in equipment which will save $0.5 million per year for the next 10 years. He wants to make the investment. What rate of return will the investment earn? Why might the manager not make the investment?

11. In making a long-range plan for a metropolitan mass-transit agency, what major changes in the agency's operating environment should be considered?

*12. A forecasting expert told a newspaper editor to "keep an eye on cable television." What impact might cable TV have on newspapers in the future? How might this affect their systems design in the long run?

13. Select an industry and discuss possible major changes in the competitive environment 20 years from now. The automotive industry, sports industry, or television industry are some of the possibilities. Also discuss how the operations of the industry must change in response to that environment.

*14. What independent variables might be appropriate in using a regression analysis to predict the sale of refrigerators for one large manufacturer? Justify the choices and state whether each coefficient would be expected to be positive or negative.

15. What independent variables might be appropriate in using regression analysis to predict the number of applications to a graduate school of business?

REFERENCES

ANDREWS, K., "Letter from the Editor." *Harvard Business Review,* September–October 1983.

BASU, S., AND R. G. SCHROEDER, "Incorporating Judgments in Sales Forecast: Application of the DELPHI Method at American Hoist & Derrick." *Interfaces,* Vol. 7, No. 3 (1977).

BREALY, R., AND S. MYERS, *Principles of Corporate Finance.* New York: McGraw-Hill, 1981.

CHAMBERS, J. C., S. K. MULLICK, AND D. C. SMITH, "How to Choose the Right Forecasting Technique." *Harvard Business Review,* July–August 1971.

CURTIS, D., "Manufacturing's Most Strategic Resource: Workforce Commitment," *Operations Management Review,* Fall, 1983.

GALLAGHER, G., AND J. GULLO, "Developing a Closed Loop MRP System—What's in It for the Design Engineer?" *Production and Inventory Management,* 4th Quarter, 1980.

GARVIN, D., "Quality on the Line." *Harvard Business Review,* September–October, 1983.

GREEN, P., AND Y. WIND, *Multi-attribute Decisions in Marketing.* Hinsdale, Ill.: Dryden Press, 1973.

HOGARTH, R., AND S. MAKRIDAKAS, "Forecasting and Planning: An Evaluation." *Management Science,* February 1981.

KOTLER, P., *Marketing Management,* 5th ed. Englewood Cliffs, N.J.: Prentice-Hall, 1984.

LAWLER, E., AND G. LEDFORD, "Productivity and the Quality of Work Life." *National Productivity Review,* Vol. 1, No. 1 (1982).

LEVIN, D., *The Executive's Illustrated Primer of Long-Range Planning.* Englewood Cliffs, N.J.: Prentice-Hall, 1981.

MCCLAIN, J., AND V. RAO, "Tradeoffs and Conflicts in Evaluation of Health System Alternatives." *Health Services Research,* Spring 1974.

NETER, J., W. WASSERMAN, AND G. WHITMORE, *Applied Statistics,* 2nd ed. Boston: Allyn and Bacon, 1982.

NETER, J., W. WASSERMAN, AND M. KUTNER, *Applied Linear Regression Models.* Homewood, Ill.: Richard D. Irwin, 1983.

PORTER, M., *Competitive Strategy.* New York: Free Press, 1980.

RAO, V., AND J. COX, *Sales Forecasting Methods: A Survey of Recent Developments.* Cambridge, Mass.: Marketing Science Institute, 1979.

THOMAS, J., "Incorporating Marketing Considerations into Capacity Planning and Detailing Scheduling." *Annales de Sciences Économiques Appliquées* (Belgium), Vol. 39, No. 1 (1983). Also available as a Cornell Graduate School of Management working paper.

URBAN, G., AND J. HAUSER, *Design and Marketing of New Products.* Englewood Cliffs, N.J.: Prentice-Hall, 1980.

VEDDER, R., "Robotics and the Economy," prepared for the Joint Economic Committee, U.S. Congress, March 26, 1982.

WIND, Y., *Product Policy: Concepts, Methods, and Strategy.* Reading, Mass.: Addison-Wesley, 1982.

CHAPTER 5

Facility Design

Facility design often determines how smoothly work can flow, how people feel about their jobs, and how easily the organization can respond to changes in their product line or product mix. Well-designed facilities allow an organization to respond to customers and hold down inventory and production cost. This chapter will discuss facility design for both manufacturing and service operations and the many objectives it must address.

Facility design affects and is affected by *job design,* one of the subjects of the next chapter. In both chapters, separation of the topics is impossible to maintain. The facility determines how people will work and similarly, the organization of work determines the appropriate facility design. Thus Chapters 5 and 6 form an important pair, leading to the design of facilities and jobs in such a way that the organization can be productive.

In manufacturing systems, new methods of production are causing (or allowing) major changes. Automation and computer control has allowed new methods of organizing plants called *flexible manufacturing systems* (FMS) or *computer-integrated manufacturing* (CIM). Computer graphics and other breakthroughs have allowed *computer-aided design* (CAD) and *computer-aided manufacturing* (CAM). Flexible manufacturing systems work best if products and facilities are grouped together to facilitate short processing times, using *group technology.* These, and other concepts, are changing the way factories are designed and operated in many situations. In this chapter we will describe the foregoing concepts, the new problems and opportunities that arise because of the concepts, and the effect on the work force.

We will address such questions as: How can one tell if automation is appropriate for a particular operation? Should we stop automating plants because of the unemployment effect? (The number of people employed in manufacturing is expected to decline in the future, as agricultural employment did before.) What effect does automation have on a company's strategy? How can a labor force be managed to avoid or reduce obsolete skills? And how can automation be introduced with minimal negative feeling among the work force? The recent automating of certain manufacturing processes has been called the Second Industrial Revolution. Will its effects be similar to those of the first Industrial Revolution?

Section 5-1 describes some basic types of facility layout, without reference to automation. These layout types have been around for many years, and they apply to both manufacturing and service industries. Section 5-2 defines and discusses the topics mentioned in the preceding paragraph—new manufacturing methods. Section 5-3 discusses managerial aspects of automation and some ways of designing plants for different control methods. One of our examples will be the *just-in-time* (*JIT*) system, which is typically implemented without computer control mechanisms. Section 5-3 will also discuss the societal impact of automation, and Section 5-4 presents a summary.

5-1 FACILITY LAYOUTS AND PROCESSES

In this section we will discuss layout designs for facilities; that is, how will the different pieces of equipment and work areas be arranged? There is much more to the design of facilities, including equipment selection, architectural design for function and aesthetics, limitations placed by the building or site, and so on. Most of these topics are specific to a situation, and they are the province of the manufacturing engineer or architect. Thus we limit our discussion to layouts. The facility layouts are categorized as *process layout*, *product layout*, and *fixed-position layout*, depending on the function of the facility.

Designing a Process Layout

Patients come to the NIH Clinic[1] for various diagnostic and treatment procedures. Accordingly, the clinic is arranged in a *process layout*, with separate functional areas. The layout focuses on the process; for a particular job, similar tasks (or tasks requiring the same equipment) are grouped together, and the job (a person in the clinic in our example) moves to the facility. Each functional area has a particular purpose and is staffed by one or more people trained specifically to perform that function. Figure 5-1 is a *flow diagram*, showing the functional areas and the typical routes taken by patients in the clinic. The *flow process chart* of

[1] This example is an abstraction of a report on the Acute Leukemia Clinic of the National Institutes of Health. See Perrault (1973).

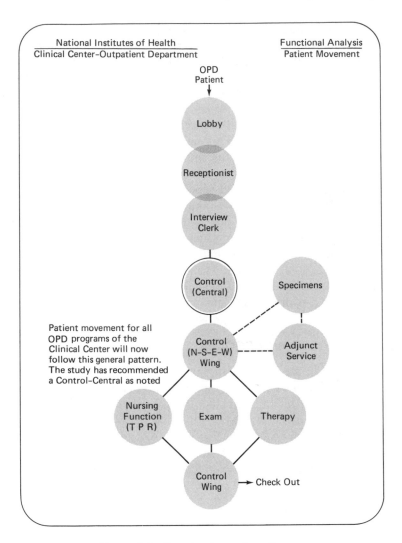

Figure 5-1 Functional area flow diagram.

Figure 5-2 describes, for a particular kind of patient, the expected sequence of visits and delays.

Flow of people or materials between functional areas is often referred to, in the industrial context, as a *load*. Typically, facility layout is evaluated by the amount of traffic between locations, so that two locations joined by an especially high flow rate should be located near one another. However, the location analysis must allow for special circumstances, such as:

1. An area may be required to be at an exterior door (e.g., a receiving department).

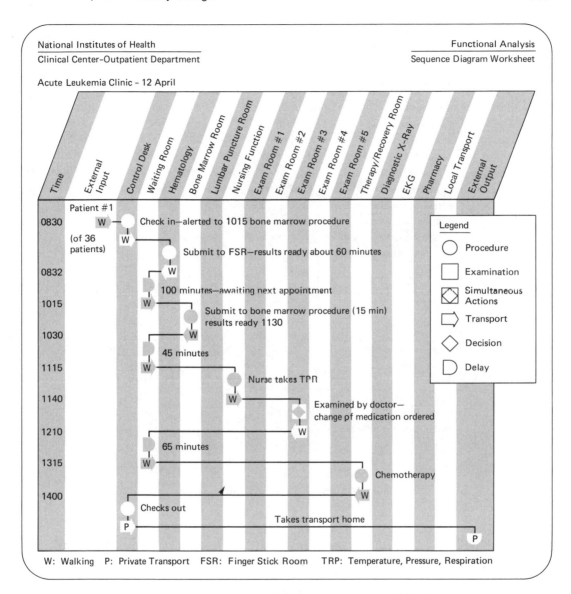

Figure 5-2 Flow process chart.

2. A location may be permanently fixed (e.g., a heating and cooling system).
3. There may be absolute requirements concerning proximity (e.g., control desk must be adjacent to the waiting room).

A *proximity matrix* is used to display these special requirements and their rationale in Figure 5-3a and 5-3b. For example, 5-3a shows that it is important

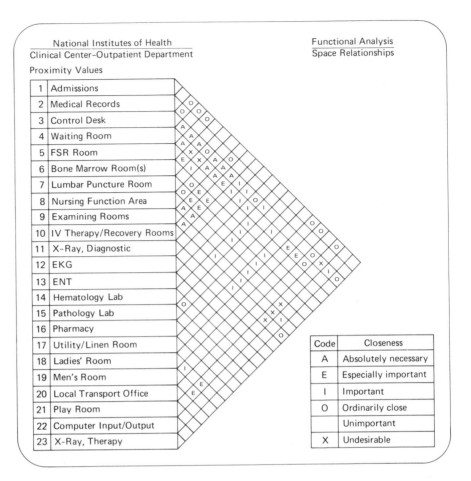

Figure 5-3a   Proximity matrix with proximity requirements.

(but not necessary) for the hematology lab to be near the control desk, and Figure 5-3b indicates that this would promote rapid transfer of test and exam findings.

A first cut at an ideal facility layout may be derived from the proximity matrix by a trial-and-error method. Figure 5-4 shows the result of such a procedure. Notice that there is a central core of functional areas which are highly interrelated by the proximity matrix. This is not unusual, and locating these areas first simplifies the trial-and-error method significantly.

It then remains to fit the functional areas into the actual floor plan in a manner that resembles the schematic diagram but allows proper floor space, hallways, and so on. This is sometimes done with templates, cut from cardboard or plastic, to represent the floor space needed for the work areas. More efficiently,

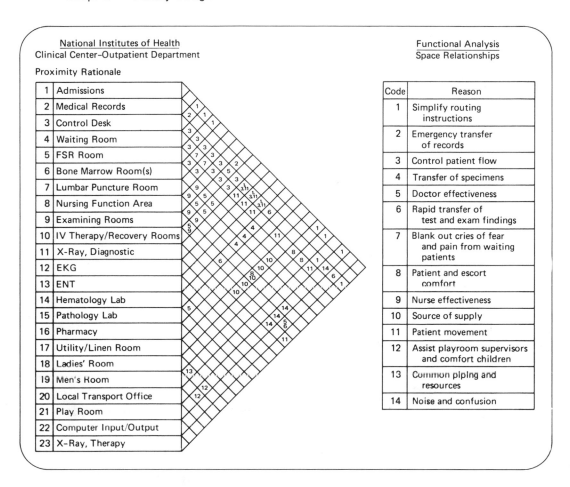

National Institutes of Health
Clinical Center–Outpatient Department

Functional Analysis
Space Relationships

Proximity Rationale

1	Admissions
2	Medical Records
3	Control Desk
4	Waiting Room
5	FSR Room
6	Bone Marrow Room(s)
7	Lumbar Puncture Room
8	Nursing Function Area
9	Examining Rooms
10	IV Therapy/Recovery Rooms
11	X-Ray, Diagnostic
12	EKG
13	ENT
14	Hematology Lab
15	Pathology Lab
16	Pharmacy
17	Utility/Linen Room
18	Ladies' Room
19	Men's Room
20	Local Transport Office
21	Play Room
22	Computer Input/Output
23	X-Ray, Therapy

Code	Reason
1	Simplify routing instructions
2	Emergency transfer of records
3	Control patient flow
4	Transfer of specimens
5	Doctor effectiveness
6	Rapid transfer of test and exam findings
7	Blank out cries of fear and pain from waiting patients
8	Patient and escort comfort
9	Nurse effectiveness
10	Source of supply
11	Patient movement
12	Assist playroom supervisors and comfort children
13	Common piping and resources
14	Noise and confusion

Figure 5-3b   Proximity matrix with rationale.

one can use computer graphics that allow interactively changing the design, while the computer keeps track of total distance traveled or other statistics of interest. Using either method, several alternative floor plans can be tried. If an area's size and shape is not completely specified by its function, different building blocks must also be tried. (A room that is 2 meters by 4 meters might be as good as one that is 3 meters by 3 meters.) The value of a visual representation, using templates or computer graphics, is that a person obtains a better understanding of the important relationships of the functions and areas. Visual methods are particularly effective when planning minor modifications, such as moving a few departments but leaving most areas as they are.

The NIH Clinic, for example, discovered that they could increase the number of examination rooms in the available floor space by reducing the size of the rooms to a generally accepted standard. Several alternative layouts were

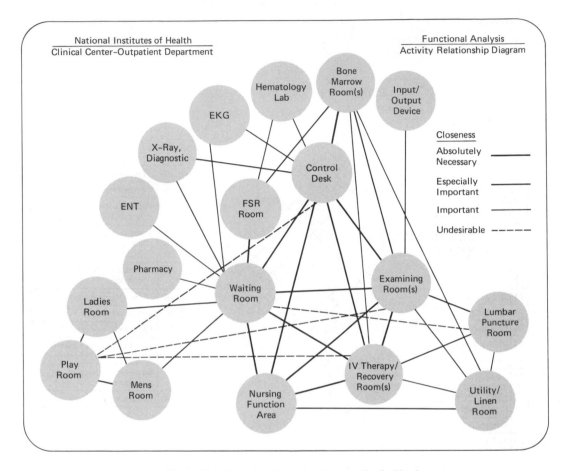

Figure 5-4 Rough schematic diagram of a facility layout.

tried on the NIH floor plan. The final design reduced groups of three large exam rooms to four standard rooms plus a small waiting area. This plan was consistent with the proximity matrix and served to reduce corridor congestion.

The proximity matrix contains the information necessary to evaluate alternative layouts. A commonly used method is to assign numerical values to the proximity requirements. (Referring to the code in Figure 5-3a, A = absolutely necessary = 4 points, E = 3 points and so on, with X = undesirable = -1 point.) Then an index of the quality of the layout would be obtained by multiplying the distance between each pair of centers times the proximity value, and adding up the results. The objective of the analysis would be to minimize this index:

$$\text{minimize} \sum (\text{prox. index})_{ij} \times (\text{distance})_{ij}$$

(Here i and j refer to functional areas: for example, $(\text{distance})_{37}$ = distance between areas 3 and 7.) If the objective is to reduce the length of the average trip between areas, the daily number of trips would be used as the proximity index. One disadvantage of using proximity indexes is that it is impossible to determine, typically, whether a 4 is really four times as important as a 1. It might be more or less, but we cannot be sure. Still, a manager can see the effect of trying different values. Computer programs are commercially available for aiding in physical layout design. The best of these allow for most of the special requirements (such as fixed location for certain areas) and result in a diagram of a proposed layout, printed by the computer. The programs are based on heuristic methods for generating good solutions and therefore do not claim to always find the best layout. However, the speed of the computer allows it to try out many more patterns than is possible by hand. Several computer algorithms are described, with references, in Foulds (1983). An algorithm for multiple-floor layout planning is given by Johnson (1982).

Congestion, Inventory, and Idle Time in a Process Layout

A *job shop* is a work area that is designed to handle many different types of jobs. A job shop that uses many different machines (sometimes called a machine shop) may be designed to handle a wide variety of jobs by grouping machines into functional areas (grinders, millers, etc.). This is a process layout. Each job follows a more-or-less unique path through the maze of machines, with each stop representing one step toward its completion. An alternative design approach is to put machines into groups that can handle all the production needs for a set of products. *Cellular manufacturing* or the automated equivalent, *flexible manufacturing systems,* can dramatically reduce movement of parts. They are discussed in the next section.

To prevent chaos in a job shop, a good information system is required which keeps track of the location of each job, the workload at each machine center, and the progress of each job toward its deadline. This facilitates planning of work force, acquisition and distribution of raw materials and tools, and the schedule of release of new jobs to the system. Some of the methods for job-shop scheduling are described in Chapter 11. However, some basic design principles can be illustrated without reference to the more intricate details of scheduling.

One of the most basic principles of job-shop management is to make sure that all operators have at least one job awaiting their attention to avoid unnecessary idle time. This waiting line (queue) of jobs represents the major portion of work-in-process inventory, and the capital invested in that inventory represents an opportunity cost. Inventory also requires floor space, often resulting in clutter and congestion. Therefore, work-in-process inventory should be minimized. However, management cannot minimize both work-in-process inventory and operator idle time; there is a trade-off between them. Unfortunately, the trade-off is often difficult to understand.

Methods commonly used to study this problem include queuing theory and computer simulation (see Appendixes A and B.) Queuing theory pictures each machine center as a set of servers, with each machine a server and each job a customer. The wide variety of jobs and the complex routing of jobs is represented by assuming that processing times and arrival of jobs at a center are governed by probability distributions. We shall use a simple queuing model to demonstrate the following principles.

Principle 1. It is more efficient for all identical machines in a work center to share a queue than for each machine to have its own supply of waiting jobs.

Principle 2. In a heavily loaded center, small increases in productivity can yield substantial reduction of work-in-process inventory.

Principle 3. In a lightly loaded center, substantial reductions in idle time can be achieved with only small increases in inventory.

Example   Ten identical machines are each capable of an average output of 5 jobs per hour. The average arrival rate of jobs is 45 per hour.

Discussion   Table 5-1 shows the predicted behavior of two different organizations of the machine center. The first row shows that, at the current load of 45 jobs per hour, there are 81 jobs waiting to be processed in the parallel queue configuration, compared to only 6 when there is a single, shared queue. This organizational change has reduced the in-process inventory by 92.6% with no increase in average machine utilization, other than a short period of high activity while the queues are being reduced.

Thus the sharing of queues can obtain substantial benefits, provided that sharing is not ruled out by other factors, such as layout of the work area or bulk of the jobs. This is Principle 1. This principle applies to flexible manufacturing systems also, as discussed by Buzacott and Shanthikumar (1980).

Principles 2 and 3 are two sides of the same coin. Referring again to Table 5-1, if the load is high (say 49 jobs per hour), either a small increase in productivity (increase speed to 5.16 per hour) or a small decrease in the load (down to 47.5 jobs per hour) will decrease a shared queue from 45.5 to 15.7 jobs, on the average. However, at a very light load (say 30 jobs per hour) the average queue is already so small that increased productivity has almost no impact on the in-process inventory.

Queuing-theory models of the type used for Table 5-1 can sometimes help to quantify the trade-off between idle time and work-in-process inventory, but the usual situation is too complex for available queuing models. Computer simulation may be used in such situations if quantification is necessary. Although the three principles illustrated above are general, the magnitude of the trade-off depends very much on the details of shop scheduling, to be discussed in Chapter 11.

Assembly Lines—Product Layout

When goods or services are to be produced in large quantities, efficiency gains are attainable using a *product layout*. The term "product layout" is used because

TABLE 5-1 TRADE-OFF OF MACHINE IDLE TIME AGAINST IN-PROCESS INVENTORY FOR TWO DIFFERENT MACHINE CENTER ORGANIZATIONS

			ORGANIZATION			
			10 PARALLEL QUEUES, 10 SERVERS		10 SERVERS SHARING ONE QUEUE	
Total Load (Jobs Arriving per Hour)	Speed (Service Rate, Jobs per Hour per Machine)	Machine Utilization (Load per Machine Divided by Speed)	Idle[a]	Queues[b]	Idle[a]	Queue[b]
Current load 45	5	0.90	1.0	81	1.0	6.0
Heavy load 49	5	0.98	0.2	480	0.2	45.5
49	5.16	0.95	0.5	181	0.5	15.7
47.5	5	0.95	0.5	181	0.5	15.7
Light load 30	5	0.60	4.0	9.0	4.0	0.152
25	5	0.50	5.0	5.0	5.0	0.036
30	6	0.50	5.0	5.0	5.0	0.036

[a] Average number of idle machines.

[b] Average number of jobs in queue, from queuing-theory tables.

the organization of the work is dictated by the sequence of production or service steps, common to most or all jobs. An assembly line is the most common type of product layout. Examples include machine shops dedicated to a single product, vaccination clinics, car washes, fast-food assembly areas, and customs areas in airports. Another example is automobile assembly. This product layout may or may not be automated, depending on economic variables. The conditions for automation are discussed in the next section; the general characteristics of product layouts and assembly lines are discussed here.

Assembly lines typically operate with a "forced" work pace, dictated by the speed of a conveyer on which the jobs are transported between work stations. Careful balancing of tasks is required so that operators are able to finish their tasks in the prescribed amount of time. Some flexibility in job design can be obtained by utilizing conveyers that have provision for storage of jobs (a queue) waiting to be processed. In this design, the important criterion is that the *average* output rate of each work area be equal, since the between-station queues can absorb short-term deviations from the average.

Another example of product layout is a factory designed for *continuous* product flow (often called *continuous processes*) such as oil refineries. The product moves continuously through the system. Industries that use continuous processes are called *process industries,* as opposed to batch production industries or discrete-parts production. Most of the design considerations for process industries are technical in nature, and we will not discuss them here.

Assembly-line Balancing

An assembly line is said to be perfectly balanced when all workstations (workers and machines) are 100% occupied, working at standard speed (with allowances for errors, personal time, etc.). However, it is neither possible (as we shall see), nor necessarily desirable, to have perfect balance. With an unbalanced line, one has the opportunity to either assign the better workers to more demanding stations, with higher pay, or to rotate people through the easy stations so that everyone has a chance at an easy day now and then.

Kitchen Products Corporation has several major products, one of which is the KPC jingflopper.[2] During assembly, each jingflopper is carried on a belt moving past the workers at a steady pace. The desired production rate is 3 per hour. Table 5-2 contains data on the elementary operations needed for assembly of a jingflopper. The operations are designated A to N. Components of the product are designated B-1 to B-11, and subassemblies are designated SA-1 to SA-3. If it were possible for one person to learn all these tasks to 100% proficiency, and to organize all the subassembly supplies, tools, jigs, and so on, around a single work station, one person could assemble 1 item in 100 minutes, or 0.6 per hour. However, since the desired output rate is 3 per hour, or 1 unit every

----

[2] An automatic pancake turner, with an optional attachment for turning fried eggs.

TABLE 5-2 ASSEMBLY OPERATIONS FOR A JINGFLOPPER

Operation Label	Time (Minutes)	Description	Predecessors
A	2	Inspect frame and place on conveyor	None
B	7	Attach B-4 to frame	A
C	5	Attach B-2 to B-1	None
D	2	Attach B-3 to B-1	None
E	15	Test SA-1	C, D
F	7	Attach SA-1 to frame	A, E
G	6	Attach B-6 to B-5	None
H	4	Attach SA-2 to frame	B, G
I	9	Attach B-7 to frame	A
J	10	Attach B-9 to B-8	None
K	4	Attach B-10 to B-8	None
L	8	Attach B-11 to B-8	J, K
M	6	Attach SA-3 to frame	A, L
N	15	Test item	All others

Total = 100 minutes

20 minutes, five operators would be necessary, each with a complete set of tools and supplies. Most of these tools would be idle most of the time. In contrast, if the assembly were subdivided into five stages, much of the duplication of equipment could be avoided. The jobs would be easier to learn, and, because of their repetitive nature, the workers may perform them relatively more quickly. However, as we shall discuss in Chapter 6, there is a trade-off because the subdivided jobs are probably more boring and lead to lower self-esteem.

The "Gozinto" chart (assembly chart) of Figure 5-5 shows one possible sequence for the assembly process. Item SA-3 is a subassembly, and item B-8 "goes into" SA-3, as do B-9 and B-10. Then B-11 is attached and SA-3 goes into the partially completed jingflopper near the end of the assembly sequence.

There are many sequences in which a jingflopper can be assembled, and each sequence can be represented by a Gozinto chart. However, a different diagram is more useful in assigning tasks to people in an attempt to balance the production line. Figure 5-6 is a *precedence diagram* for the assembly, showing which sequences are allowed. Each operation is represented by its label (from Table 5-2) and its time. The arrows indicate which operations must come first. To divide the operations among five workers, the simplest method is to draw five loops on the chart, each loop enclosing tasks to be assigned to a workstation, making sure not to violate any of the sequence requirements. The target is five stations with 20 minutes of work per station, to achieve a production rate of 3 per hour.

One possible assignment is shown in Figure 5-7, in which the longest assembly time is 22 minutes at stations 2 and 4. Therefore, the items must be spaced at

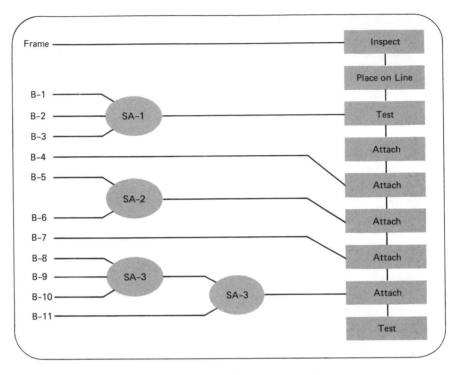

Figure 5-5 Gozinto (assembly) chart for a jingflopper.

least 22 minutes apart on the moving belt, and each station has that amount of
time. The spacing actually used is called the *cycle time* of the line.

It should now be evident why it may not be possible to achieve a perfect
balance. There is a limited number of combinations that satisfy the sequence
requirements, and, for a given sequence, it may not be possible to obtain exactly
20 minutes per station, since the elementary operations are not divisible.

The quality of a solution is measured by the *balance delay,* which is the
idle time induced by the imperfect solution. With five workers and a cycle time
of 22 minutes at each station, there are (5)(22) = 110 worker-minutes expended
per item assembled (including idle time), compared to the required productive
time of 100 minutes from Table 5-2. Therefore, the balance delay is 10 minutes
of idle time per item, which is 9.1% of the worker's time. Expressed as a formula,
we have

$$\text{balance delay} = \frac{nc - T}{nc} \tag{1}$$

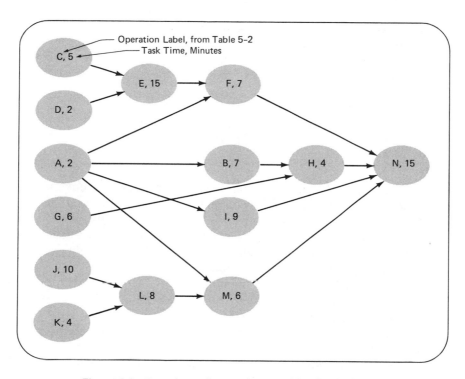

Figure 5-6 Precedence diagram for assembly of a jingflopper.

where n = number of workstations

c = cycle time = inverse of production rate of the line (c cannot be less than the assembly time required at the slowest station)

T = total amount of work time required per item

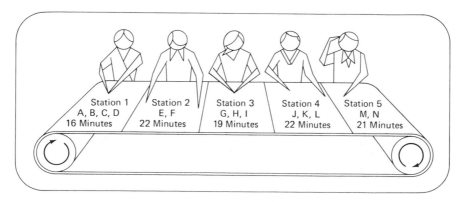

Figure 5-7 Schematic of an assembly line.

Note that the proposed solution does not meet the desired production rate of 3 per hour. (Cycle time = 22 minutes means production rate = 60/22 = 2.73 per hour.) Actually, 3 per hour (1 every 20 minutes) would require perfect balance, which we now know is unrealistic to expect. There are four alternatives.

1. Be satisfied with the lower rate.
2. Work overtime.
3. Add another worker (and another workstation).
4. Find some way to increase the line speed.

The line speed could be increased if faster workers were placed at the most difficult work stations. The premium wage necessary to attract and keep such workers must be compared against the costs of the other alternatives.

If we add another worker and station and then rebalance the line, the slowest station has an assembly time of 18 minutes. The desired cycle time of 20 minutes can therefore be attained. The balance delay of this solution is $[(6)(20) - 100]/(6)(20) = 20/120 = 0.167$ or 16.7%. Part of this balance delay occurs because we have an externally imposed cycle time of 20 minutes, slower than the 18 minutes of the slowest station.

If we are free to choose the production rate, we can reduce the balance delay. Equation (1) can be minimized by setting c *equal to* the assembly time of the slowest station. The result is called the *internal balance delay*. In this example the internal balance delay is $[(6)(18) - 100]/(6)(18) = 8/108$ or 7.4%. This part of the balance delay is due to the indivisibility of the assembly tasks.

Finding the best solution to a large line-balancing problem is an immense task because of the many combinations and sequence requirements. It is helpful to have a good solution as a starting point from which one may make improvements and changes to fit the unique requirements of the company. The following set of rules is a simple heuristic that often obtains a good solution (Hegelson and Birnie, 1961):

1. For each task, compute the sum of its time and the times of all tasks that must be done later because of the precedence relationships. (This is made easier by the precedence diagram, Figure 5-6.)
2. Rank the tasks, largest first, using the total times from step 1.
3. Form stations by considering tasks from the list in step 2. Add a task to a station if
   a. The total station time will still be less than the required cycle time, c.
   b. The predecessors of the task are done.
4. Start new stations when necessary. Stop when all tasks are assigned.

Use of this heuristic is illustrated in the problems at the end of the chapter.

The assembly line and the job shop are at opposite ends of a scale. The assembly line is organized for a high-volume product and paced by a conveyor system, resulting in very rigid, repetitive jobs. In contrast, the job shop is organized into functional areas, and each operator uses his or her talents on many kinds of jobs each month. Between these extremes are a variety of organizations with the layouts dictated by the products but which typically have more product variety than an assembly line and more repetition than a job shop.

Computers have been used to balance assembly lines, with programs much more sophisticated than the heuristic above. Furthermore, the typical problem size is 100 tasks and 15 workstations, which makes manual solution extremely time consuming. The computer programs tested by Mastor (1970) and Dar-El (1973) are based on heuristic methods designed to solve large problems in reasonable time. Pinto et al. (1983) present a mathematical programming approach that allows for processing alternatives, thereby considering more of the design problem.

Fixed-position Layouts (Where the Workers Move)

Among many examples where the worker must travel between operations is the warehouse, or *storage layout*. Most service and manufacturing facilities have an area dedicated to storage of goods. In retail stores, it is common to have most of the inventory displayed in customer self-service areas, designed for maximum marketing appeal. However, in hospitals, mail-order houses, factories, distribution centers, and military supply depots, the storage areas are designed for minimum cost, with important considerations being rapid access, easy and accurate control, possibility for future expansion, and so on.

Two-stage systems are used when items are removed from storage in smaller quantities than the containers in which they are received. Open containers are kept in the "pick" area (or central supply), where an individual order is filled by a person who moves through the area. Large-volume distributors use vehicles with personnel lifts to quickly access the appropriate bins. This requires that aisles be one-way and wide enough to maneuver the machines. Where distance is a factor, high-volume items will be kept nearest the control area. When vehicle congestion is a problem, high-volume items may be kept in more than one location, and aisle lengths are shortened by inserting either perpendicular or diagonal cross-aisles.

The second stage involves the bulk storage area, which has less activity and hence can have fewer aisles. There are two ways to organize such an area: by stock lines or by individual locations. With a stock-line storage layout, each type of item has part of the warehouse allocated to it, so the storage area is equivalent to many small warehouses. The main advantage of this layout is ease of control. The operator always knows where to find a given item, and visual inventory inspection is facilitated. However, stock-line layout typically leaves large areas unused as the inventory of each stock-line decreases between replenishments.

In contrast, individual-locations storage layout uses flexible storage assignment. Typically, each location has a label indicating the aisle, a distance down the aisle, and a height (shelf number). One system of control has a card for each location, kept at the controller's desk. When the location is empty, the card is kept in a slot corresponding to the location. When an item is placed in the location, the card is placed in a file corresponding to the item. Thus, the inventory of an item may be ascertained by counting the cards in that item's file, and available storage locations may be spotted by scanning the occupied card slots.

Hausman et al. (1976) have considered rules for assigning locations to items in an automated storage and retrieval system. Computerized systems of inventory control are often designed to interface with the warehouse in a manner similar to the card system described above. Such systems are capable of generating shopping lists for stock picking, as well as making location and retrieval assignments for bulk storage. The computer may also have direct control over a stacker crane in the bulk storage area, dispatching these robots-on-rails to store and retrieve items in an efficient manner. The Farm Supply caselet, at the end of this chapter, asks the reader to consider the design of a warehouse, including a large stacker crane.

A hospital provides another example where workers move to the work. The majority of the service is provided by nurses, who move among a variety of work areas, including patients' bedsides and nursing stations. The criteria for effective work area design in such instances include fast response time (the patient should not wait long for service) and high utilization of the server. A circular floor plan, with rooms on the periphery and a central nursing station, is one effective means of obtaining both these goals. However, other designs are more suitable on other dimensions.

In this section we have described three layout types: process, product, and fixed location. Product layout takes maximum advantage of high volume by subdividing tasks to a level that allows a worker to learn quickly and to be very proficient. This specialization restricts flexibility in job design, as we shall discuss in the next section. Therefore, there is an increasing interest in modification of assembly-line and similar operations to allow more room for consideration of the worker's needs and desires.

In process layout, similar operations are grouped together and jobs may take long and individualized paths through the facility. This is acceptable only if there are low quantities of many job types to be produced. In fixed-position layout, the "jobs" hold still and the workers visit the jobs.

A few design methods have been introduced in the context of specific facility layouts. However, in reviewing these tools, one should reflect on their more general applicability. For example, how could a proximity matrix be useful in designing a storage layout? Many more detailed and elaborate methods are described in the industrial engineering literature. (See, for example, Francis and White, 1974.)

Review Problems

1. Apply the three principles discussed in the section "Congestion, Inventory, and Idle Time in a Process Layout" to the problem of assigning nurses to

patients, treating the patients as customers who signify their "arrival" by pressing a call button.

2. In Figures 5-3a and 5-3b, interpret the proximity values between the waiting area and
   (a) The FSR (finger stick room).
   (b) The bone marrow rooms.
   (c) The lumbar puncture room.
   (d) Are these all well represented in Figure 5-4?

3. What is the meaning of the balance delay function? Why is it usually impossible to achieve perfect assembly-line balance?

Solutions

1. (a) Assigning patients to nurses will result in longer waiting times than having nurses available for calls from any patient.
   (b) Postponing part of the nurses' duties is advisable during periods of heavy patient activity.
   (c) Broadening the role of the nurse will decrease idle time.

2. (a) The FSR should be close to the waiting area (code A = absolutely necessary in Figure 5-3a) for purposes of patient control (code 3 in Figure 5-3b).
   (b) and (c) Both of these areas should be located away from the waiting area to prevent unpleasant sounds from disturbing waiting patients.
   (d) The layout satisfies these requirements, but the interconnecting lines are not all there. For example, in Figure 5-4 there should be a dashed line from the bone marrow room(s) to the waiting rooms.

3. It is an estimate of the percent idle time attributable to the organization of the assembly line. Sequence requirements and indivisible tasks prevent perfect balance.

5-2 NEW MANUFACTURING METHODS

This section has the ambitious goal of explaining automated techniques in manufacturing and discussing their costs and benefits. We will define terms, discuss economic analysis, and introduce methods of control. Table 5-3 lists some of the most common terms used in connection with modern automation of manufacturing. It also gives references for many of the terms. Definitions will be given below. We are purposefully vague about the word "new" here, since some of the ideas are not new but simply repackaged or once again fashionable. Still, their common usage in manufacturing is relatively new.

The terms listed in Table 5-3 are not all-inclusive. Worse, the ideas are not distinct, but overlap. For example, a robot is part of an automated system and group technology is typically part of a flexible manufacturing system. Finally, not everyone uses the terms in exactly the same way. For these reasons, we

TABLE 5-3 SOME NEW MANUFACTURING METHODS: TERMS AND ACRONYMS

Term	Acronym (if any)	Partial List of References
Automation		Groover and Hughes (1981) Roth (1983)
Computerized, numerically controlled	CNC or NC	Ayres and Miller (1982)
Robot		Kamali et al. (1982) Ottinger (1981) Potter (1983)
Artificial Intelligence	AI	
Cellular manufacturing		Black (1983)
Group technology	GT	Desai (1981) Dunlap and Hirlinger (1983)
Computer-integrated manufacturing	CIM	Meredith (1981)
Flexible manufacturing systems	FMS	Klahorst (1981)
Automated storage and retrieval systems	AS/RS	Zisk (1983)
Automated guided vehicle systems	AGVS	Glenney (1981)
Asynchronous material handling		Lofgren (1981)
Computer-assisted process planning	CAPP	Houtzeel (1981)
Computer-aided design	CAD	Bishop and Miller (1981)
Computer-aided manufacturing	CAM	Groover (1980)
CAD integrated with CAM	CAD/CAM or CADICAM	Wang (1983) Wang (1981) Zimmers and Plebani (1981)

will provide a structure for discussing the terms and define them in turn. The structure given below is from COMEPP (1982).[3]

Flexible, Automated, Responsive, and Versatile Systems

There are several motivations behind the new manufacturing thrusts. These are summarized in the following ideas. A manufacturing facility can be:

FLEXIBLE: designed to allow quick changeovers, small lots, and ease of material handling.

AUTOMATED: designed so that machines perform the labor rather than people.

RESPONSIVE: designed to allow easy engineering changes, new products, and other responses to the marketplace.

VERSATILE: designed to produce many different items.

[3] COMEPP is the Cornell Manufacturing Engineering and Productivity Program, of which the authors are members. The structure we will use was developed for COMEPP by Professors Maxwell and Muckstadt.

The desired characteristics for a manufacturing facility depend on the nature of the demands placed on it. For example, a volatile product line, with many engineering changes, requires a *responsive* system. A large number of products, each produced in small batches, requires a system that is *flexible* and *versatile* whether or not it is *automated*. Using these ideas we can define the terms in Table 5-3. The references in Table 5-3 can be used for follow-up reading.

Automation. Automated systems supply machine functions to replace human functions. They reduce labor, accept obnoxious tasks, and provide consistent quality. Versatility and thinking are not necessarily implied.

Industrial robots are automated, but they also include some decision making. They can do different things to different items. They can remember a set of actions and decide which to use, perhaps based on sensory input. Robots consist of a *manipulator* (a mechanical "arm"), a *power supply* (hydraulic, electric, or pneumatic), and a *controller* (a "brain"). Some robots have variable speeds based on feedback (servo robots), whereas others do not. In the future, robots will use *artificial intelligence*, meaning that their range of possible actions and discretion will improve. They will "think" in many ways similar to people, learning by experience.

Robots currently are used for many tasks, including welding, painting, loading, and so on. Kamali et al. (1982) discuss the advantages and disadvantages in different tasks of robots vis-à-vis human labor.

Numerically controlled (NC) machines have programmable automation. The instructions are stored on a device such as magnetic tape, and interpreted by a controller unit which directs the machine. Early forms of NC were incorporated in looms more than a century ago.

Direct numerical control (DNC) is the use of a computer to input the instructions to a number of NC machines.

Computerized numerical control (CNC) is a result of the development of microprocessors, so that each NC machine has its own computer.

Flexible Systems. Cellular manufacturing is a type of layout that is used in situations where *process layout* was used heretofore. Instead of having lathes together and grinders together, one or more manufacturing *cells* are established that have the variety of machines needed to do most or all of the work for a set of items. These can be *manned* or *unmanned* (operated by a robot). With a cellular layout the items do less traveling, so inventory control can be tighter. Workers (or robots) are multifunctional. Since they can perform several tasks, they are less likely to waste time, and productivity is increased. Other benefits will be discussed later for cellular manufacturing and flexible manufacturing systems. Figures 5-8 and 5-9 illustrate manned and unmanned cellular manufacturing units.

Group Technology (GT) refers to methods of analysis for grouping products with similar manufacturing requirements. This allows manufacturing economies. For example, properly designed manufacturing cells can complete the work for

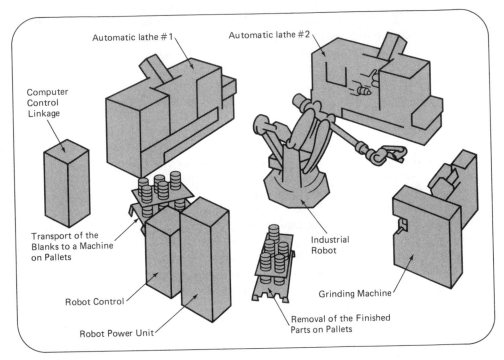

Computer
Control
Linkage

Automatic lathe #1

Automatic lathe #2

Transport of the
Blanks to a Machine
on Pallets

Industrial
Robot

Robot Control

Grinding Machine

Robot Power Unit

Removal of the Finished
Parts on Pallets

Figure 5-8 Example of unmanned cellular manufacturing system in which NC machine tools and robot work together to produce turned and cylindrically ground parts. Reprinted from J. T. Black, "An Overview of Cellular Manufacturing Systems and Comparisons to Conventional Systems," *Industrial Engineering,* Vol. 15, No. 11 (1983), published by the Institute of Industrial Engineers, Atlanta, Georgia, by permission of the Institute.

a group of items with minimal time lost for changeovers. Groups are formed using a manufacturing plan for the facility and a coding system for the items. There are two basic ways of coding, termed hierarchical and nonhierarchical. The code for a new part must determine which manufacturing cell will be used. Even if a small amount of work must be done outside the cell, the reduction in total production time can be significant.

Flexible manufacturing systems (FMSs) are the highly automated version of cellular manufacturing. Both material handling and production are automated, and these two functions are integrated by computer control. [Some people use the terms *computer-integrated manufacturing* (CIM) and *flexible manufacturing* synonymously.] These systems are expensive, but they allow some of the benefits of fixed-position automation to be gained in a firm with a broad product line and small batch sizes.

Automated storage and retrieval systems (AS/RSs) are computer-controlled, high-density storage facilities, such as stacker cranes. AS/RS can feed production and withdraw and store finished products.

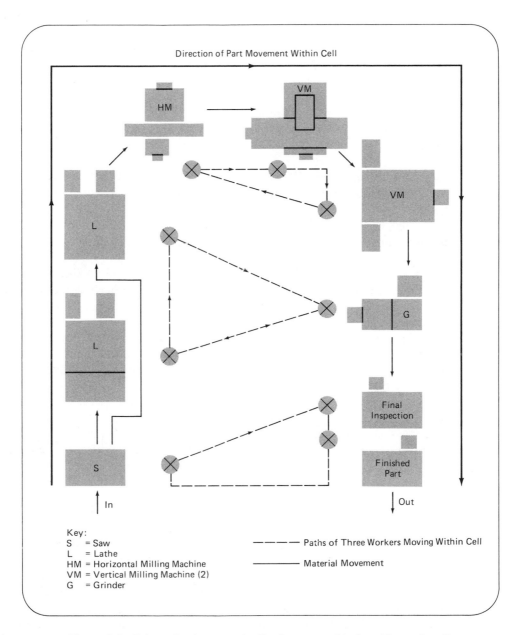

Figure 5-9 Schematic of a manned cell using conventional machine tools—all laid out in U-shape and staffed by three multifunctional workers. Reprinted from J. T. Black, "An Overview of Conventional Manufacturing Systems and Comparisons of Conventional Systems," *Industrial Engineering,* Vol. 15, No. 11 (1983), published by the Institute of Industrial Engineers, Atlanta Georgia, by permission of the Institute.

Automated guided vehicle systems (AGVSs) are what the name implies—automated vehicles moving work to and from storage and production.

Asynchronous material handling systems allow different parts of a conveyor to move at different rates. This is important in flexible systems since different facilities may process items at different rates, and each facility should be supplied with work. A single-speed conveyor can be used for an assembly line, but FMSs process different parts in different cells. The slowest machine at one time may be the fast one for the next part. If we always wait for the slowest part, production time will be lost.

Responsiveness to Change. The key to faster response is reducing the time required to convert an idea into a product. Three computer-assisted methods fall in this category.

Computer-aided process planning (CAPP) is a computerized method of using group technology product codes and selecting the process to be used in production.

Computer-aided design (CAD) is a tool for the design engineer. Extensive data bases are developed that allow an engineer to try different designs and test their performance. This substantially reduces the time required to bring an idea into production.

Computer-aided manufacturing (CAM) is a broad term that encompasses direct use of computers in process control, such as CNC, and indirect means such as cost estimation, work standards, and developing NC input media (see Groover, 1980).

CAD/CAM or CADICAM, the integration of CAD and CAM, is largely an unrealized dream at the moment. The ultimate goal is a system that will take the engineer's (computer-assisted) design directly to the (computer-assisted) manufacturing stage. In effect, by pushing a button, the picture would become a real object. Less ambitious goals are currently being achieved by integrating data on manufacturing difficulties into the engineering design system. The future of CAD/CAM is very promising.

Versatile Systems. A versatile system is one that can be used for many different products. Many of the concepts discussed above, such as cellular manufacturing, asynchronous material handling, NC machines, CAD, and CAM can contribute to versatility. However, a system can be automated, flexible, and responsive but not versatile. This occurs in the case of a highly automated facility designed specifically to produce a narrow line of high-technology items. It is flexible if production changeovers among the items are easily accomplished. It is responsive if changes in the market for this line of items can be readily accommodated. However, major redesign of the facility might be required to produce a variety of items, so the facility is very limited in versatility.

Although versatility is desirable, it often comes at a cost of reduced productivity. A system that is versatile may be "jack of all trades, master of none."

Narrow focus often allows production technology that is highly efficient but single-purpose. Thus, a company with versatile facilities will have a competitive advantage in moving between markets, but it may face higher marginal production costs as a result.

You may believe you have seen all the acronyms in the world in the discussion above. Alas, that is not so. We have not discussed methods of managerial control. These methods of control, such as MRP-II and JIT (manufacturing resource planning and just-in-time production) also overlap. They fit well with some forms of automation and not with others. We will discuss these two at more length in Chapter 12, but we will briefly discuss the relation of JIT with automation in Section 5-3, together with financial accounting and marketing topics related to managerial control of automated production.

Layout Implications

The manufacturing methods and concepts of this section are closely associated with facility layout. *Process layout and product layout* represent two ends of a continuum from small batches to large batches to continuous production. The larger the batch and the smaller the product variety, the closer to a continuous process a plant can be designed. When quantity is sufficient, this type of plant can have very low unit production costs.

Cellular manufacturing, group technology, and flexible manufacturing systems attempt to obtain the benefits of product or continuous layout for firms with smaller batches and larger variety. The ability to keep manufacturing cells busy with small batches holds down inventory and production cost. Different layouts and different organizational structures are needed. Figures 5-10 and 5-11 show two layouts for a mythical two-product firm. The "new" organization uses a cellular manufacturing approach. The review problems for this section ask you to consider a cellular approach to a service system.

Whether a flexible, automated, responsive, or versatile system is appropriate depends on many factors, but two key ones are breadth of product line (variety) and quantity to be produced. The more items, the more flexibility is needed. The larger the volume, the more automation can be justified. Several authors give numerical guidelines for automation decisions (Roth, 1983, Ayres and Miller, 1982, Jenkins and Raedels, 1983, and Groover and Hughes, 1981, for example). We prefer to use a detailed financial analysis rather than guidelines. However, the ideas have been captured in Figure 5-12. Figure 5-12 suggests that high volume reduces the need for flexibility. High-volume items can have dedicated production facilities. However, at low volumes, there will often be a wide variety of items that share facilities, increasing the need for flexible systems.

Computer Control

The automated equipment described above exists and is being improved. Several thousand robots are in place in the United States, and the number is projected

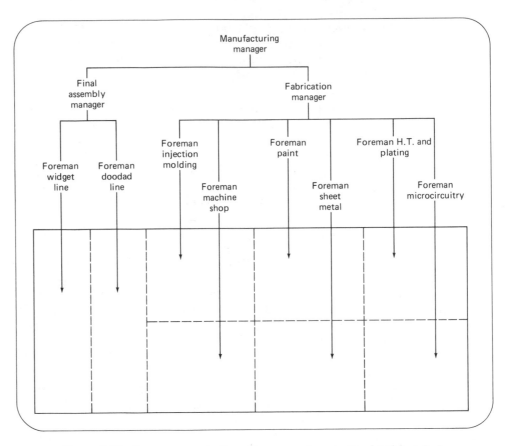

Figure 5-10 Common organization with common layout. Reprinted from R. J. Schonberger, "Integration of Cellular Manufacturing and Just-in-Time Production," *Industrial Engineering*, Vol. 15, No. 11 (1983), published by the Institute of Industrial Engineers, Atlanta, Georgia, by permission of the Institute.

to grow dramatically by 1990. Although the United States is behind some countries, notably Japan, in introducing automation, Americans appear to be the leaders in developing the next generation—thinking robots. A partial list of robot manufacturers is given by Ottinger (1981) and Foulkes and Hirsch (1984).

In our opinion the difficult, unsolved problem is that of overall system control. That is, how do we control the entire facility so that it meets the overall objectives? Klahorst (1981) speaks of three levels of control. Level 1 is simply control of NC machines, to drill a hole of the correct diameter, for example. Level 2 is localized control of parts flow and interface with level 1. Level 3 is a true management information system with decision-making power. Where should parts be sent? When can an order be completed? Systems at levels 1 and 2 are in place and operating. Level 3 remains unsolved, but the methods

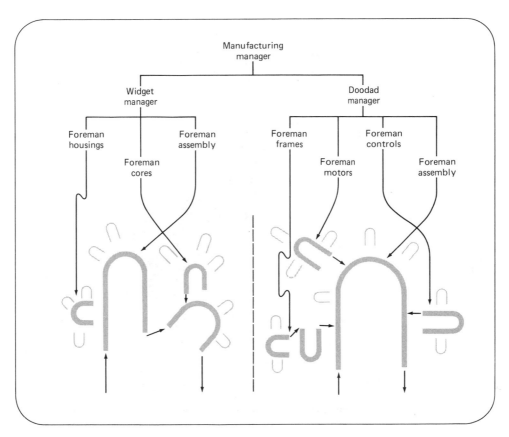

Figure 5-11 New manufacturing plant and organizational realignment. Reprinted from R. J. Schonberger, "Integration of Cellular Manufacturing and Just-in-Time Production," *Industrial Engineering,* Vol. 15, No. 11 (1983), published by the Institute of Industrial Engineers, Atlanta, Georgia, by permission of the Institute.

we will describe in Chapters 11, 12, and 15 can be part of an integrated system of control. Many manufacturing and consulting firms are trying to be the first to control an entire automated plant well. Putting the pieces together will require a knowledge of the hardware, excellent computer skills, and, most important in our opinion, a good "feel" for overall systems of production.

Review Problems

1. Review Table 5-3 to be sure that you understand the terms.
2. Why is cellular manufacturing replacing process layout in some situations?
3. An engineering design department has 10 electrical engineers, 10 mechanical engineers, 10 draftspersons, and 10 programmers. They receive requests for major design projects from other units in the organization. Typically,

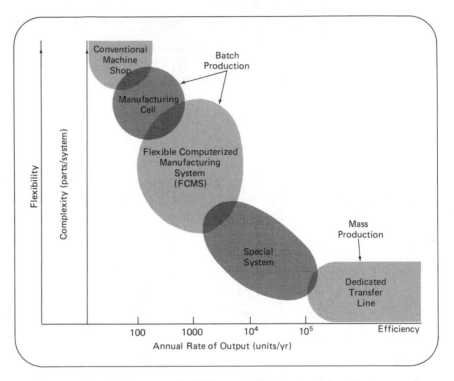

Figure 5-12 Efficiency vs. flexibility tradeoffs. Reprinted from R. Ayers and S. Miller, "Robotics, CAM, and Industrial Productivity," *National Productivity Review,* published by Executive Enterprises Publication Co., Inc., New York, by permission of the publisher.

persons from each subgroup are assigned to each project. Their current layout is shown below.

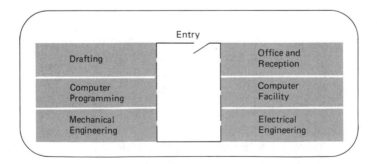

There are no requirements regarding adjacent groups. (All groups use terminals to interact with the computer, for example, so that they do not need to be next to the computer.) Suggest a cellular manufacturing approach to layout. What is this department's product? How might the product's characteristics affect layout?

Solutions

2. Because cellular manufacturing seems to give the benefits of product layout without losing all the advantages of process layout.

3. Each of five "cells" might contain two draftspersons, electrical engineers, mechanical engineers, and computer programmers. Each design job would be given to a cell. This may work, since each member of the team would know how the job was progressing.

   The product, a design, can be divided into parts. For example, the electrical engineers can do part of their work independent of other groups. A project manager can oversee the entire project. Because of this possibility of dividing the work, the advantage of a cellular layout may be less than for a manufacturing situation that requires physical closeness.

5-3 MANAGING AUTOMATED SYSTEMS

Financial Justification

Roger Smith, Chairman of the Board of General Motors, has said: "Every time the cost of labor goes up $1 an hour, 1,000 more robots become economical" (*The New York Times*, October 14, 1981). The main reason given by many managers for automating operations is labor saving. Examining automation only as a laborsaving device is myopic in two very different ways. First, workers will not be committed to a firm if they perceive that the firm is not committed to them. Second, the potential savings extend far beyond labor saving. We will address the second problem first.

Estimates vary dramatically, but most industrial equipment is in productive use only a small fraction of the time. Zisk (1983) mentions 10 to 15%, with a possible increase to 80 to 90% due to a FMS. If such increases are possible, total investment in equipment can decline in the long run. Also, FMSs often require less factory space than do other configurations.

A second advantage is that the total time spent in manufacture of an item can decline dramatically. Bradt (1983) estimates that items are being transformed only 5% of the time. The rest of the time is spent waiting. Thus huge reductions in total time are possible if the correct parts arrive at the correct machine at the right time. This has two effects. First, work-in-process (WIP) inventory can be reduced dramatically and almost eliminated. Also, response time to customers can be reduced so that it may be possible to reduce finished goods inventory. If customer service improves, market share may increase.

Quality often improves with automation due to a machine's precision. Material usage improves; there is less waste. This reduces scrap and rework cost.

If labor cost is reduced, some overhead costs will decline at the same time.

Often, the labor that is saved is in operations involving hazardous conditions, so safety improves.

These savings often outweigh labor savings. Unfortunately, they may be hard to quantify. It is important to attempt to estimate them, because, as Potter (1983) says: "If [indirect savings] are not used in the justification of a project and the savings truly do exist, the analysis is more incorrect than it would have been if educated estimates had been used." Financial analysis can be used to evaluate automation projects; financial analysis can be misused by not including all benefits.

Two final points should be made. One point is that the first project helps an organization learn how to use automation and to see how operations can be integrated to give greater total benefits. Thus a firm may not meet short-term financial goals on an automation project, but the eventual payoff may be sufficient. The second point is that automation drives down the marginal cost of a unit of production. A company with a lower marginal cost of production is more able to survive either a price war or simply increased competition. It may be that automation is necessary as a strategic weapon in order to survive. These intangible benefits must be included using managerial judgment.

Cost Accounting and Marketing

Manufacturing organizations often use direct labor as a basis for generating management accounting numbers. This basis makes no sense if there are few workers. In a highly automated environment, the average direct labor hour could easily generate $1000 worth of cost. Decisions should not be made using such numbers. Machine hours is a better basis if the capital cost is large, but no simple basis can be as good as a sound economic analysis of the managerial question at hand.

Marketing strategy is affected by automation because different layouts fit different product lines. Figure 5-12 shows layout styles that are appropriate for different numbers of products and annual demand. However, as a matter of strategy, the product line and the factory design (and subsequent modification) should be determined together. More automation (and therefore lower cost) is possible if a firm limits its number of finished products, uses common parts wherever possible, and limits engineering changes. A simple product line may improve quality and reduce cost. Customers may buy more of these products, and profits may increase. This is not to say that a small product line is always appropriate. Rather, automation plans and factory design in general should go hand in hand with product line management.

An Example of Production Control with Automation: The Just-In-Time System

The Japanese *just-in-time (JIT) system* is a very simple, but effective, method of production control in the right situation. We will describe JIT more fully in

Chapter 12 and discuss the prerequisites for its use. Here we discuss only its use as part of automated systems and its layout implications.

The basic idea of JIT is that parts move to the next stage of manufacture *just in time* to be used. An order for a finished product causes cards (called "kanbans") to be issued that instruct workers to finish the product. The finishing department selects components and assembles the product. They then pass a kanban back to predecessor stations to replenish the components. Almost no work in process is stored. Lot sizes are as small as possible, preferably 1. The kanbans are placed where they can be seen by the appropriate employees, so they know what to produce next. The process goes back all the way to material suppliers.

Such systems are often highly automated, but there is no system-wide computer control. Individual machines may still be controlled by computers, but managerial control of production along the process occurs only using the kanbans. Schonberger (1983) argues that cellular manufacturing and JIT fit together well. The cells would be departments that produce one stage of components, to pass on to another cell. Automated material handling can be used. Only the need for detailed level 3 computer control of production is eliminated, and that is due to the simple guiding principle of the JIT system.

A vital key to success of JIT is the reduction of machine setup times to near zero. This allows each work unit to respond quickly to a kanban and makes small lot sizes economically feasible. To achieve this performance the product line must not be highly varied, and substantial investment must be made in research and equipment. Automation is often an important element. If JIT fits, it is a magnificent system. As discussed in Chapter 12, it does not fit everywhere.

Finally, special layouts are appropriate for JIT systems. The different work groups should be close together physically. Within each work group, individuals should be able to view the kanban. Since setup time must be low, it may be necessary to allow space to do preliminary setup work while the automated equipment is doing another job.

Automation: Behavioral and Societal Issues

Robots can accept boring, tiresome jobs. They can handle heavy loads and hazardous environments such as spray painting in an enclosed room. Comparisons of robots and people, with a discussion of the types of jobs best suited for each, is given by Kamali et al. (1982). Robots can improve safety, reduce boredom, and work odd hours. Yet they are thought of by many workers as a bad thing because they can also reduce the number of jobs.

Introducing any change to an organization is difficult, but a change that can eliminate jobs often causes very negative reactions on the part of the work force. For example, in the *Wall Street Journal*, Saga (1983) writes of the Japanese experience: "Automation is particularly bad news for older workers. Their traditional skills suddenly obsolete, many find themselves working under the supervision of younger employees.'' Silk (1983), in *The New York Times*, even reports on robots being allowed to join the union, with the Fujitsu Fanuc Company paying their dues, because the union was losing membership and its funds were diminishing.

Minimizing the difficulties of automation requires planning. Some companies announce that no employees will be laid off due to automation. If this can be done, that eliminates one major concern. Even if layoffs are deemed essential, employees should not be kept guessing. Foulkes and Hirsch (1984) say that ''in the interest of maintaining cooperative bargaining relations, the conscientious employer should not wait for the union to request advance notice of new technology but should voluntarily extend this courtesy.''

Once the employment situation is clear, the problem of education must be addressed. The operators must be trained, of course, but skills of engineering, supervisory, and other support staff may also need to be improved. Learning how to design products, determine production schedules, and monitor quality with automated equipment takes time and commitment. Everyone's help should be solicited, and attention must be paid to all concerned. The implementation process requires extensive technical work, but also extensive education, communication, and management.

The benefits of automation can be large, but individuals can lose jobs. Thus we conclude this section with a discussion of the societal impact of new manufacturing technologies. First, a history lesson. The Industrial Revolution began in the late eighteenth century and had its greatest and earliest effect in Great Britain. The technology that received the most attention replaced 200 workers with one worker and one set of machines in the textile industry. Several groups, including the *Luddites*, believed that machines were bad because of their effect on jobs. They even went so far as to smash textile machines. However, the increased productivity was so great and the cost so low that demand for textiles grew, sufficiently to allow total employment to increase (see Vedder, 1982).

This amazing story of increased productivity, increased wealth, and increased demand leads many people to believe that the current automation and computerization trends are a Second Industrial Revolution and will have a good effect on employment (see Vedder, 1982 and Cichowitz, 1984). They say that negative effects are often overstated and that the negative effect should be short term. Ayres and Miller (1982) give a detailed estimate of jobs that could be lost in the metalworking industry (the industry most susceptible to automation); they then extend that estimate to all of the 20 million manufacturing operating jobs in the United States. They estimate that a 20% reduction could occur over a 20-year period; 4 million jobs would be lost. Even so, the *annual* effect would be less than 1% per year of manufacturing jobs, and $\frac{1}{4}$% of all U.S. jobs, per year.

We agree that in the long run, productivity improvements will be good for society. In fact, automation will be needed in the early twenty-first century to compensate for a potential shortage of labor. The population bulge known as the ''baby boom'' will retire, leaving fewer people working. Service jobs will substitute for manufacturing jobs and standards of living can improve. However, there will be significant pockets of unemployment that will be present for extended periods. Older workers in industrial towns will find work hard to obtain. Many of the jobs created by change will not be filled by the workers who lost their jobs. Companies and government will be forced to ameliorate the unemployment by training programs. Striner (1982) shows that the United States is behind many other countries in training expenditures. If a 20-year employee can be trained for new assignments, presumably a more dedicated employee will be the result.

Finally, automation is coming, for better or worse. In free economies, companies that do not automate to reduce cost will lose sales to lower-cost producers. Although companies cannot avoid using new technologies, they may be able to use training and other approaches to preserve their work force's job security.

Review Problems

1. Do highly automated factories always require extensive computer controls?
2. A company expected that new automated equipment would reduce the total manufacturing time from 10 weeks to 2 weeks. In addition to labor savings, what benefits might the company observe from this change?
3. Is automation good or bad for society?

Solutions

1. No. The just-in-time system substitutes physically observable cards for computer control, for example.
2. Work-in-process inventory will be reduced and customer service will improve. We cannot be certain what other benefits would accrue, but quality may improve, waste and finished goods inventory may be reduced, and the firm may be in a better competitive cost position.
3. It is both good (productivity will increase, thereby adding to total wealth) and bad (some workers will lose jobs and have difficulty being trained for new ones). There are many other points that can be made here. For example, since work helps define people in our society, reducing work may not be good. Also, automation is inevitable, whether it is good or bad.

5-4 Summary

The basic types of layout for operations are process, product, and fixed-position layouts. All of these are still important in our economy. However, many operations that formerly used process layout are changing to cellular manufacturing, a form of product layout. Managers must carefully analyze their special situation to see which kind of layout is best for them. Then they can consider techniques for optimizing that kind of layout—techniques using proximity matrices for process layout or assembly-line balancing methods, for example.

Since operations management is important to all organizations, including services and all types of manufacturing, it is impossible to survey in detail the new equipment that is and will be available in each situation. Still, we have attempted to introduce terms for new manufacturing technologies. Our purpose is to indicate the areas that a manager must understand. The details for a specific type of operation are best learned on the job, but the issues can be understood in advance.

Agriculture is a sector of Western economies that has benefited greatly from improved technology. The fraction of labor involved in agriculture has declined to where a few percent of the work force feeds us better and more cheaply than ever. This does not mean that agriculture is unimportant. The labor force will decline in manufacturing as new technologies are introduced. Agriculture and manufacturing will remain a key source of wealth creation even as their part of the work force declines.

The effects of automation are as profound in the service industries as in manufacturing. Consider the new diagnostic equipment in medical care, the capabilities of office automation systems, and the effect of computer operations on stock markets, for example.

As we change technology, we change the nature of work and even who can obtain work. Different skills are in demand and thus are paid well and respected. Technology changes the fabric of our society. Operations managers must understand not only the technical issues and methods of strategic, financial, and operational analysis, but also the human issues in organizations and in society. In the long run, taking care of the work force and the community is good for the entire organization.

CASELET: FARM SUPPLY CORPORATION'S AUTOMATED WAREHOUSE

Farm Supply Corporation (also discussed in Chapter 2) has three partially automated warehouses, called distribution centers (DCs). They distribute several thousand stock-keeping units (SKUs) through the DCs, including products such as paint, pet food, hardware, small power tools, and gardening items. Each warehouse receives shipments from a few Farm Supply plants and outside vendors. Shipments into the DCs are in full rail car or truckload quantities, and nearly all items are palletized, meaning they are delivered on 40- by 48-inch wooden pallets for ease of handling.

Each DC ships to about 100 stores. These shipments are in small quantities (less than full pallets) which are loaded into trucks that visit several stores. Each store receives two shipments per week. The truck routes are not always the same, since the demands for truck space vary and a truck that can satisfy four stores on Monday may be able to satisfy only three stores on Thursday.

Layout. Currently, each DC is composed of three main parts: (1) the office area, including the computer system; (2) the high-density, computer-controlled stacker crane for storing full pallet lots; and (3) a low-rise area with one or two pallets of each item in racks. A schematic diagram is shown in Figure 5-13.

Control and Operation of the DC. All inbound and outbound orders are tracked by computer so that a *perpetual inventory* system is maintained. Orders by the stores are fed into a program that generates *picking lists*. Items are withdrawn (picked) from low-density storage in the order that they will be loaded into the delivery truck. The tow-line truck is sent around with a list; operators with specialized trucks read the lists, then ride the aisles retrieving items.

High-demand items have two pallets in the low-density storage area. Items that are demanded less than once per week (70% of the items) have one pallet. When the last of a pallet is used, another is ordered from the high-density storage. The stacker crane is computer controlled and retrieves only full pallets, automatically. The stacker crane is moving less than 20% of the time, but it is cost-effective due to the good physical control of the inventory it allows.

Costs. Farm Supply has an annual labor cost of operating each DC of approximately $2,000,000, including all personnel. Equipment maintenance costs roughly $200,000 annually. Finally, each DC has $50,000,000 in inventory. Before automation, these figures were $2,000,000, $50,000, and $80,000,000, respectively.

Required

1. Farm Supply is considering automating more of the process. What might you consider automating, and why? On balance, do you think that your suggestion is a good one?
2. How important is it for Farm Supply to efficiently plan "stores" and "retrieves" for the stacker crane? Why? At the plant, where shipments are in full pallets and the crane is busy most of the time, is the answer different? Why?
3. Briefly describe an easy heuristic that you might use to determine which stores will be serviced by which trucks.
4. Which category of cost is most important? Why?
5. Which kind of layout is represented by this DC? Are there any layout changes that you would suggest?

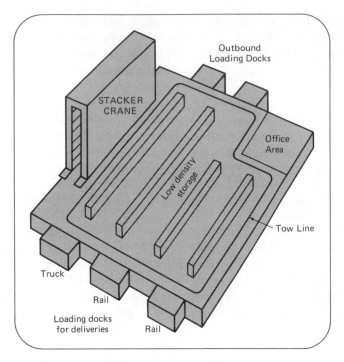

Figure 5-13 Farm supply distribution center.

PROBLEMS

1. For each of the following, would the layout be a product, process, or fixed-position layout?
   (a) The location of departments and/or academic fields within the buildings in a large university.
   (b) A blood donation center.
   (c) A self-service cafeteria.
   (d) A building construction site.
   (e) An airline terminal's customer areas.

2. An ethical drug manufacturer must expand plant capacity to meet increasing demand. The company has two alternatives to consider: (a) build a specialized plant with a product layout for its largest-selling product, or (b) build additional capacity using process layout similar to its current facilities. Discuss the possible impact on long-term profits and competitive posture due to this layout decision.

*3. Design a department store layout using the data in the accompanying figure and table. Begin with a schematic and then develop a rectangular floor plan, 60 feet deep by 100 feet across the front.

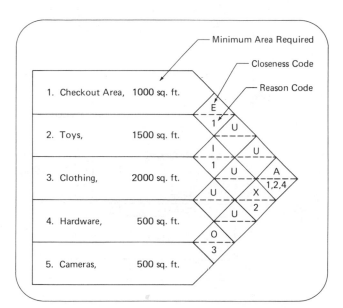

Code	Reason	Code	Closeness
1	Marketing	A	Absolutely necessary
2	Security	E	Especially important
3	Can share personnel	I	Important
4	Frequent contact	O	O.K.
	necessary	U	Unimportant
		X	Undesirable

4. A branch office of a bank[4] has its personnel arranged as shown in the accompanying diagram. The number of trips per day between locations was estimated by the assistant manager, who observed the entire office for one day. The result is shown in the form of a proximity matrix, shown in the second diagram. Using her own wristwatch, the assistant manager also estimated the travel time from the bookkeeper to the loans desk as 8 seconds, or 12 seconds from the bookkeeper to the teller. Thus she estimated that it takes 4 seconds to walk between adjacent desks, and perhaps a little longer to walk diagonally between adjacent desks.

(a) Categorize the proximity requirements as A, E, I, O, U, X, based on number of trips.

(b) Suggest an alternative arrangement that allows the operations manager to act as a teller during peak periods and reduces travel time.

(c) Estimate the daily time savings of your proposed layout. What impact will it have on customer service? On employee morale?

---

[4] This problem is adapted from "Sequoia Bank of California," W. Abernathy and N. Baloff, Graduate School of Business, Stanford University, 1969.

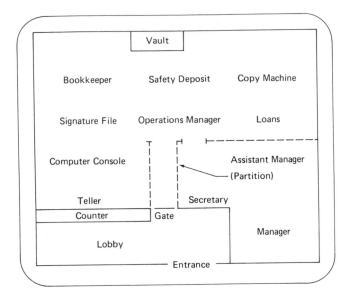

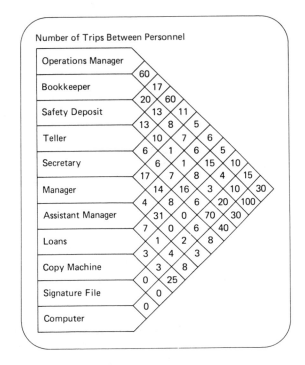

5. Discuss the adequacy of the data-gathering technique in the bank-layout example of Problem 4.

*6. A pipe valve has seven parts, listed below. Prior to final assembly, parts 2 and 3 are combined, as are 4 and 5, into subassemblies. The parts are numbered in order of the assembly operation, and the last step is an inspection. Construct a Gozinto chart for this operation.

1. Body.
2. Bushing.
3. Stem.
4. Packing.
5. Cap.
6. Handle.
7. Nut to secure handle.

7. An assembly line, paced by a single moving belt, has had a history of temporary shutdowns and quality problems. A study showed that of the 54 assembly stations, 51 required only routine, repetitive tasks, but the other 3 required judgment and a varying amount of time. Each of these three stations performed an inspection and touch-up operation, involving tasks such as adjusting doors to fit tightly and repairing small errors in painting.
   (a) How could these three stations be part of the cause of the shutdown and quality problems?
   (b) Suggest a solution.

*8. The production line shown here has been producing an average of 720 items per day. The times given are engineering estimates of the normal production time per item at each station.

Station 1 (25 seconds)	Station 2 (30 seconds)	Station 3 (15 seconds)	Station 4 (20 seconds)

   (a) What is the minimum cycle time (in seconds) possible for this line, according to the engineers? Explain.
   (b) There are currently 7 production hours per day. (i) What is the actual cycle time? (ii) What is the percent balance delay?
   (c) Can one worker be eliminated at the present production rate? If so, how? If not, why not?
   (d) What is the theoretical minimum number of workers for the present production rate?
   (e) What is the maximum production rate possible with the present setup? Explain what you would do *first* if you found it necessary to exceed that rate, without using overtime.
   (f) What is the internal balance delay with the present setup? Why is zero balance delay unattainable?

*9. (a) Use the heuristic described near the end of Section 5-1 to find a first solution to the line-balancing problem for assembly of the jingflopper

(Table 5-2). The target is 20 minutes per workstation to achieve a minimum production rate of 3 per hour. The number of stations need not be 5.

(b) What is the balance delay for this station arrangement?

10. The following is a list of assembly tasks showing sequence restrictions and performance times.

Task	Time (Seconds)	Predecessors
A	5	None
B	4	A, E
C	2	None
D	10	E
E	5	None
F	3	C, D
G	5	H, I
H	7	None
I	8	None
J	4	All

(a) Develop a diagram showing the sequence requirements.

(b) Using the heuristic near the end of Section 5-1, determine a task grouping that does not violate sequence restrictions and has a cycle-time target of 18 seconds.

(c) What is the minimum number of stations needed?

(d) What is the balance delay for the arrangement given by the answer to part (b)?

11. Review the definitions of flexible, automated, responsive, and versatile in Section 5-2. How can a manufacturing system be flexible and automated but not versatile? Responsive but not flexible? Automated but not flexible?

*12. What is the difference between cellular manufacturing and flexible manufacturing? Describe a cellular layout for an outpatient clinic that has 6 doctors, 10 physician's assistants, 6 registered nurses (RNs), 4 licensed practical nurses (LPNs), and 4 receptionist-bookkeeping personnel. Discuss the advantages and disadvantages of your layout.

13. What are the three levels of computer control in flexible manufacturing systems? Briefly discuss the difficulties of implementing Level 3.

*14. The managers of Widget Manufacturing Company (WIMCO) estimate that a flexible manufacturing system for one of their product lines will cost $20,000,000. The life of the system is 10 years. The following cost savings are estimated:

Labor: $2,000,000 per year
Material: $600,000 per year

Inventory: $1,500,000 per year (annual saving-inventory reduction would be much larger)

Added gross margin: $2,000,000 per year (due to increased sales)

(a) Ignoring taxes and using a 14% discount rate, what is the net present value of the investment if only labor savings are included?

(b) If labor and material saving are included?

(c) If all benefits are included?

(d) What other benefits might occur?

*15. Redo Problem 14(c) using a 40% tax rate, an 8% investment tax credit, a 10% after-tax discount rate, and straight-line depreciation over 10 years.

16. A firm is considering dramatically reducing its product line, going from 100 products to a few. What layout implications are there? What are a few of the costs and benefits?

*17. If automation increases wealth and GNP and improves the general economic situation, why might unemployment persist after plants are heavily automated?

REFERENCES

AYRES, R., AND S. MILLER, "Robotics, CAM, and Industrial Productivity." *National Productivity Review,* Vol. 1, No. 1 (1982).

BIERMAN, H., T. DYCKMAN, AND R. SWIERINGA, *Managerial Cost Accounting,* 3rd ed. New York: Macmillan, 1986.

BISHOP, A., AND R. MILLER, "CAD/CAM and the Role of the Industrial Engineer." *Industrial Engineering,* Vol. 13, No. 11 (November 1981).

BLACK, J., "An Overview of Cellular Manufacturing Systems and Comparison to Conventional Systems." *Industrial Engineering,* Vol. 15, No. 11 (November 1983).

BOUCHER, T., AND J. MUCKSTADT, "The Inventory Cost Effectiveness of Group Technology Production Systems." *Annales de Sciences Économiques Appliquées* (Belgium), Vol. 39, No. 1 (1983).

BRADT, L. J., "The Automated Factory: Myth or Reality." *Engineering: Cornell Quarterly,* Vol. 3, No. 13 (1983).

BUZACOTT, J., AND J. SHANTHIKUMAR, "Models for Understanding Flexible Manufacturing Systems." *AIIE Transactions,* Vol. 12, No. 12 (December 1980).

CICHOWITZ, R., "Robots: Who Wants Them and Why?" *Carnegie-Mellon Magazine,* Vol. 2, No. 2 (1984).

COMEPP: Cornell Manufacturing Engineering and Productivity Program, College of Engineering, Cornell University, Ithaca, N.Y., 1982.

DAR-EL, E. M., "MALB—A Heuristic Technique for Balancing Large Single-Model Assembly Lines." *AIIE Transactions,* Vol. 5, No. 4 (1973).

DESAI, D. T., "Parts Coding Using Group Technology." *Industrial Engineering,* Vol. 13, No. 11 (November, 1981).

DUMOLIEN, W., AND W. SANTEN, "Cellular Manufacturing Becomes Major Management Philosophy at One Plant." *Industrial Engineering,* Vol. 15, No. 11 (November 1983).

DUNLAP, G., AND C. HIRLINGER, "Group Technology: The Synergistic Tool." *Industrial Engineering,* Vol. 15, No. 11 (November 1983).

FITCH, J., AND W. BRYCE, JR., "Introducing Automation into the Manufacturing Process." *Industrial Engineering,* Vol. 13, No. 11 (November 1981).

FOULDS, L. R., "Techniques for Facilities Layout." *Management Science,* Vol. 29, No. 12 (December 1983).

FOULKES, F. K., AND J. L. HIRSCH, "People Make Robots Work." *Harvard Business Review,* January–February 1984.

FRANCIS, R. L., AND J. A. WHITE, *Facility Layout and Location: An Analytical Approach.* Englewood Cliffs, N.J.: Prentice-Hall, 1974.

GIGLIO, R. J., *Ambulatory Care Systems,* Vol. II: *Location, Layout, and Information Systems for Efficient Operations.* Lexington, Mass.: D. C. Heath, 1977.

GLENNEY, N., "Material Handling in the Automated Factory." *Industrial Engineering,* Vol. 13, No. 11 (November 1981).

GROOVER, M. P., *Automation, Production Systems, and Computer-Aided Manufacturing.* Englewood Cliffs, N.J.: Prentice-Hall, 1980.

GROOVER, M., AND J. HUGHES, JR., "A Strategy for Job Shop Automation." *Industrial Engineering,* Vol. 13, No. 11 (November 1981).

GROOVER, M., AND E. ZIMMERS, JR., *CAD/CAM: Computer-Aided Design and Manufacturing.* Englewood Cliffs, N.J.: Prentice-Hall, 1984.

GYLLENHAMMAR, P. G., "How Volvo Adapts Work to People." *Harvard Business Review,* July–August 1977.

HAUSMAN, W. H., L. B. SCHWARZ, AND S. C. GRAVES, "Optimal Storage Assignment in Automatic Warehousing Systems." *Management Science,* Vol. 22, No. 6 (1976).

HEGELSON, W. B., AND D. P. BIRNIE, "Assembly Line Balancing Using the Ranked Positional Weight Technique." *Journal of Industrial Engineering,* Vol. 13, No. 6 (June 1961).

HOUTZEEL, A., "Elements of an Effective Computer Assisted Process Planning System." *Industrial Engineering,* Vol. 13, No. 11 (November 1981).

INGRAM, F., "Group Technology." *Production and Inventory Management,* 4th Quarter, 1982.

JENKINS, K., AND A. RAEDELS, "The Robot Revolution: Strategic Considerations for Managers." *Operations Management Review,* Vol. 1, No. 2 (1983).

JOHNSON, R. V., "SPACECRAFT for Multi-floor Layout Planning." *Management Science,* Vol. 28, No. 4 (April 1982).

KAMALI, J., C. MOODIE, AND G. SALVENDY, "A Framework for Integrated Assembly Systems: Humans, Automation and Robots." *International Journal of Production Research,* Vol. 20, No. 4 (1982).

KING, J., AND V. NAKORNCHAI, "Machine-Component Group Formation in Group Technology: Review and Extension." *International Journal of Production Research,* Vol. 20, No. 2 (1982).

KLAHORST, H. T., "Flexible Manufacturing Systems: Combining Elements to Lower Cost and Flexibility." *Industrial Engineering*, Vol. 13, No. 11 (November 1981).

LESNET, D., "Workplace Design for Quick Die Setup." *Industrial Engineering*, Vol. 15, No. 11 (November 1983).

LOFGREN, G., "The Automated Guided Vehicle as a Production System." *Industrial Engineering*, Vol. 13, No. 11 (November 1981).

MASTOR, A. A., "An Experimental Investigation and Comparative Evaluation of Production Line Balancing Techniques." *Management Science*, Vol. 16, No. 11 (1970).

MEREDITH, J., "The Implementation of Computer Based Systems." *Journal of Operations Management*, Vol. 2, No. 1 (October 1981).

OTTINGER, L., "Robotics for the I.E." *Industrial Engineering*, Vol. 13, No. 11 (November 1981).

PERRAULT, M. W., "Facilities Optimization," in *Examination of Case Studies in Health Facilities Planning*. Chicago: Hospital Research and Educational Trust, 1973.

PINTO, P., D. DANNENBRING, AND B. KHUMAWALA, "Assembly Line Balancing with Processing Alternatives." *Management Science*, Vol. 29, No. 7 (July 1983).

POTTER, R., "Analyze Indirect Savings to Justify Robot Implementation." *Industrial Engineering*, Vol. 15, No. 11 (November 1983).

ROTH, B., "Principles of Automation," in *Future Directions in Manufacturing Technology*. London: British Petroleum, 1983.

SAGA, I., "Japan's Robots Produce Problems for Workers." *The Wall Street Journal*, February 28, 1983, p. 19.

SCHONBERGER, R., "Integration of Cellular Manufacturing and Just-in-Time Production." *Industrial Engineering*, Vol. 15, No. 11 (November 1983).

SHORE, R., AND J. TOMPKINS, "Flexible Facilities Decisions." *AIIE Transactions*, June 1980.

SHULTZ, A., "Productivity and Engineering." *Engineering: Cornell Quarterly*, Vol. 17, No. 2 (1982).

SILK, L., "Strange New Robotic World." *The New York Times*, May 4, 1983, p. D2.

STECKE, K., "Formulation and Solution of Nonlinear Integer Production Planning Problems and Flexible Manufacturing Systems." *Management Science*, Vol. 29 (March 1983).

STECKE, K., AND J. SOLBERG, "Loading and Control Policies for FMS." *International Journal of Production Research*, September–October 1981.

STRINER, H., "Regaining the Lead in Productivity Growth." *National Productivity Review*, Vol. 1, No. 1 (1982).

TAYLOR, S., S. SEWARD, AND S. BOLANDER, "Why the Process Industries Are Different." *Production and Inventory Management*, 4th Quarter, 1981.

VEDDER, R., "Robotics and the Economy," prepared for the Joint Economic Committee, U.S. Congress, March 26, 1982.

WANG, T. L., "CAD/CAM in a Distributed Environment." *Industrial Engineering*, Vol. 13, No. 11 (November 1981).

WANG, K. K., "CAD/CAM in Mechanical Engineering." *Engineering: Cornell Quarterly*, Vol. 17, No. 3 (1983).

YANKEE, H. W., *Manufacturing Processes*. Englewood Cliffs, N.J.: Prentice-Hall, 1979.

YOUNG, R., "Software for Flexible Manufacturing Systems." *Industrial Engineering*, Vol. 13, No. 11 (November 1981).

ZIMMERS, E. W., JR., AND L. J. PLEBANI, "Using a Turnkey Graphics System in Computer Integrated Manufacturing." *Industrial Engineering*, Vol. 13, No. 11 (November 1981).

ZISK, B., "Material Transport for Cellular Manufacturing." *Industrial Engineering*, Vol. 15, No. 11 (November 1983).

CHAPTER 6

Measurement and Management of Productivity

Productivity has long been a central focus in the design and management of jobs. However, it is viewed differently by labor and management. One description of the employment situation is that labor sells its services to a company for a price (wage) that is related to the type, quality, and quantity of work to be done. Management may wish to keep this price low, while labor wants the opposite. Productivity is viewed as a bargaining chip in this economic conflict, and it can be used skillfully by both parties.

The long-run benefits of increased productivity has been enormous—widespread prosperity, more leisure time, and inexpensive consumer goods, just to mention a few. But arguments often raised by organized labor against increased productivity are short run—fear of lost jobs, with consequences that are very real and threatening. History has shown that higher productivity in one industry leads eventually to more jobs in many other industries as the result of a chain of economic events that produce lower prices and more overall consumer demand. Nevertheless, labor is often more concerned with the short run, and acts as a force to resist such interindustry shifts in jobs. Consequently, increased productivity can be a goal for both labor and management, but only if substantial and reliable resources are committed to assure equal or improved employment *in the short run* as part of the benefits.

However, these arguments, based on economic conflict, are far too narrow. Wages no longer stand as the unquestioned primary issue:

> [When] a representative sample of 1533 American workers at all occupational levels . . . were asked how important they regarded 25 aspects of work, they ranked in order of importance:

1. *Interesting work.*
2. *Enough help and equipment to get the job done.*
3. *Enough information to get the job done.*
4. *Enough authority to get the job done.*
5. *Good pay.*
6. *Opportunity to develop special abilities [self-development].*
7. *Job security.*
8. *Seeing the results of one's work [feedback and recognition].*[1]

Effective job design integrates this broader view of the desires of workers with the more traditional view of productivity as a technical issue. The goal is to design jobs so that both labor and management gain from the changes.

Certain organizations stand out as examples where labor and management seem to be working together as a team. These organizations cannot be identified by sector, product, or any other physical measure. The difference lies in both the attitudes of workers and managers and the organizational structure that supports and reinforces these attitudes. What constitutes such a structure? How are these attitudes engendered? The study of these questions falls under several academic titles, including organizational theory, industrial relations, behavioral science, and personnel management. Although a single, dominant school of thought has not developed, some answers have emerged from research and experience in these areas. They will be described in a later section.

Somewhat better developed are engineering principles for efficiency: how to get the most output for a given amount of input, *assuming that all the inputs are in management's complete control.* Unfortunately, the assumption of "complete control" is, in the case of the labor input, not accurate. Among the most serious management errors has been the application of the principles of engineering efficiency without proper understanding of the consequences of the failure of that assumption. As a typical example:

> *Through careful study, an industrial engineer was able to streamline a job by eliminating many unnecessary motions. After 3 weeks of practice, the worker was earning twice as much by working twice as fast. Reasoning that the engineer's effort gave birth to the increase in productivity, management cut back the daily wage of the worker to its original level plus 10%. Even though he was better off, the employee felt cheated, and convinced his friends not to cooperate in an experiment to increase productivity.*

This example demonstrates a managerial error. Unfortunately, there are also many examples of purposeful use of "efficiency methods" to obtain more productivity without a fair return to the workers. Such incidents have led to a widespread attitude of *resistance to efficiency methods* on the part of labor.

Of course, productivity improvement involves far more than efficiency. In Chapter 1 we quoted Peter Drucker: "Efficiency is doing things right; effectiveness

---

[1] *Work in America, 1973,* p. 13. The words in brackets have been added by the authors.

is doing the right things." To improve productivity effectiveness is often more important than efficiency. That is, all employees should "work smarter," not necessarily "work harder." Working smarter involves developing improved ways of doing the job and having work, equipment, and materials at the right place at the right time. Good managers plan so that both of these occur. Whether the ideas for improvement come from the workers or from the manager, he or she must establish the atmosphere that facilitates them. Methods for doing so are discussed in this chapter.

Productivity improvements are required if organizations are to compete effectively in worldwide markets. Many different statistics are used to compare productivity of different companies or nations. For example, one can discuss the *rate of growth* of productivity, which makes the United States look bad (Striner, 1982). One can look at output per labor hour, in which case the United States is still near the top, and significantly outperforms Japan. Or one can look at output per dollar invested in labor, and Japan has had an edge (Bullinger and Lentes, 1982, p. 263). The real test, of course, is by individual company, and they must maintain enough productivity to have a competitive cost position.

Society needs productivity improvements to improve the standard of living. Also, there will be few workers entering the U.S. work force during the remainder of this century (Wolfbein, 1982), and we must plan to use less labor content in future products. Thus, improving productivity has many benefits, together with its potential short-term cost to the labor force. We can reduce or eliminate the negative aspects, and we can use the benefits to increase leisure or consumption.

In this chapter we will examine methods for motivating people (Section 6-1), an industrial engineering approach to analyzing work (Section 6-2), and some methods of measuring and managing productivity. The field is far too broad to allow us to extensively treat these topics, but the references can be used to find follow-up reading.

6-1 DESIGNING JOBS AND ORGANIZATIONS FOR PRODUCTIVITY

The design of jobs and organizations is a major influence on how people perform. People must be able to do the work; the organization and managers must facilitate accomplishment. In the introduction, we listed eight important characteristics of work, as seen by workers. Points 2, 3, and 4 all relate to the employee's need to accomplish. Work scheduling, equipment purchases, and other topics in this text can enable workers to get the job done.

However, workers must also want to get the job done. Recent research (Sentry, 1981) shows that, while there is a belief that people care less about their work than previously, most workers believe that productivity is a problem and would like to do something about it. The organization must provide the right setting and incentives for good performance.

Motivation is often used to describe the tendency to want to be productive (see Gibson et al., 1982, and Steers, 1981, for a more complete discussion). When productivity is seen as the best path to achieve an important personal goal, people will want to be productive. The list of eight "good job" characteristics from the introduction gives managers insight into what can be used as *work incentives*.

Characteristics 2, 3, and 4 call upon the manager to manage well. All parties want 2, 3, and 4. Item 1, interesting work, has led to significant changes in some industries, leading to sociotechnical systems, quality-of-work-life programs, job enrichment, job enlargement, semiautonomous teams, and similar approaches. We will discuss those approaches to motivation in the next subsection.

Pay (item 5 in the list of characteristics of a good job) is an obvious incentive. Achieving a bonus or a raise provides short-run satisfaction, but the desire for higher pay continues. (Most of the work force is in a position to appreciate a meaningful pay increase.) According to Niebel (1976, p. 632), most unions oppose the installation of new wage plans (such as piece-rate or group incentives), but paradoxically, will fight to continue and expand existing ones. Perhaps this can be explained by years of struggle in which many bad plans have been eliminated, creating a suspicion of all new plans but leaving in place those plans that were well conceived. Successful plans reward superior performance with higher pay but guarantee decent wages for average performance. Some are designed for very quick feedback, whereas others have monthly or yearly bonuses. They also differ as to whether rewards go to individuals, groups, or the entire company, through some kind of profit-sharing scheme.[2] Successful examples can be cited for each of these approaches, although the nature of the product and the work force strongly influence the appropriate choice of a plan.

The trend in financial rewards above base pay is toward group incentives, for two reasons. First, people have a need to be part of and contribute to a group. Second, small, local goals can be counterproductive. If we are not selling our product, producing more is a negative factor, not even neutral.

One important approach is called *gainsharing*. In these systems, overall goals such as profitability or total cost are used as a basis for gainsharing. Improvements in total cost are shared, say 60% to employees, 40% to the corporation. (These systems have a historic root in *Scanlon plans,* in which productivity improvements were shared by all workers.) Bullock and Bullock (1982) describe two gainsharing operations; see also Fein (1983), for examples and discussion. Changes in management style are sometimes needed to reflect the commonality of interest of all parties. Bullock and Bullock (1982) describe success stories, but they caution that the plans must be evaluated over time rather than immediately. They describe these systems as tackling overall problems, and they say that is the only correct method (a systems approach). "[Managers] do not address major organizational issues because it is smart—we do it because it is easier" (Bullock and Bullock, 1982, p. 407).

[2] For a summary of wage incentives, see Niebel (1976, Chap. 25).

Individual goal setting is also used in many organizations. Individual goals have been very successful in many settings. The goals should be specific (rather than "do your best"), high but achievable, and agreed upon by the employee. Goal setting, together with the difficulties of implementation, are discussed by Gibson et al. (1982, Chap. 5).

Self-development is often thought to be the major motivating factor for some people. The steps of a career ladder present short- to medium-run goals (the next promotion) which are also self-renewing, unless the career path is a short, dead-end street. Unfortunately, many jobs do not have good potential for self-improvement. However, use of self-improvement as an incentive tends to bring talented people to higher positions and therefore to make better use of their talents.

The search for motivating factors has extended beyond those considered above. *Pride and loyalty* are familiar slogans in company campaigns to motivate people. However, it is difficult to convince somebody to be proud of a narrow, repetitive job with no responsibility. Increases in pride and loyalty can be a result of meaningful changes, but exhortations for pride and loyalty are not effective motivators.

Accountability has been found to be a key motivator, but it cannot stand alone. When accompanied by authority, increased accountability for quality and productivity provides a positive stimulus. However, in the absence of authority and access to necessary equipment and information, responsibility for outcomes will not be accepted. Thus accountability encourages productivity when the worker feels that the necessary elements have been provided to do the job well.

Designing Good Jobs

Successful change in the nature of work in a firm is difficult. It requires changes in organization, attitudes, and behavior, and these changes are felt throughout the hierarchy. The following descriptions of actual cases illustrate several job design approaches, including *job enlargement, participative management, job enrichment, semiautonomous teams, quality of work life,* and *sociotechnical systems.* Several other examples are given by Steers (1981, p. 371).

A number of companies have attempted to reorganize work to make it more interesting and to improve the worker's feeling of accomplishment in seeing the results of his or her work (numbers 1 and 8 in the definition of a "good job"). *Job enlargement* means moving away from the high degree of specialization that has evolved through so-called efficiency methods. *Motorola, Incorporated* (see *Work in America,* 1973, p. 101) attacked the undesirable nature of assembly-line work. For one product, each employee was trained to do the complete assembly, and the assembly line was eliminated. The result was 25% more workers needed for the same output, as well as a more costly training program. Nevertheless, the program nearly broke even because of better product quality (resulting in fewer inspections and less repair) and lower turnover and absentee rates. A key element of this program was accountability—the employee's name appeared on each item produced, providing both recognition for good work and instant feedback for poor quality.

Recently, Motorola has continued their efforts to engage the worker. Their *participative management* program attempts to involve workers in decision making in the organization (Simpson, 1983). One key to participative management programs is soliciting and being open to suggestions. If suggestions are to lead to labor saving, workers must feel secure in their jobs. Some Japanese companies (not all) offer lifetime employment. Some U.S. companies guarantee that in addition to bonuses for cost-saving suggestions, current workers will not lose jobs. The work force may, however, be reduced over time by attrition.

Job enrichment and *job enlargement* are sometimes considered the same idea. However, job enlargement is making work more interesting by increasing the size of the task, thereby lengthening the work cycle and reducing the repetitiveness of the job. In contrast, Herzberg (1976, pp. 114–118) defines an *enriched job* by listing eight characteristics not altogether different from the ones we have been using, with the notable addition of accountability for the quality of work. The emphasis is *vertical* job design, in that tasks normally assigned to a supervisor become part of the job. Thus not only are there more tasks, but also new levels of skill and responsibility. These design principles can also lead to a reduction in the number of supervisory personnel and an attendant reduction in red tape.

A very large company (see Herzberg, 1976, pp. 130–134) employed a group of people specifically to handle stockholder correspondence. Despite the importance of this task, the employees' attitudes toward the job were dismal. The following list summarizes the job enrichment program, which resulted in improvements in both performance and attitudes.

Diminish role of supervisor:

1. Less frequent supervisor proofreading.
2. Outgoing mail bypasses supervisor.
3. Experienced workers were designated as subject matter experts, to serve as first-line consultants to the other workers.

Increase authority/accountability:

1. Correspondents sign their own names.
2. More personalized letters encouraged.
3. Accuracy and quality of letters reflect on individual rather than supervisor.

Norsk Hydro Fertilizer company, in Norway, experimented with a design that allowed and encouraged employees to help one another. This was based on a *semiautonomous team approach*. One factory, employing about 50 people, was organized into work areas, with one team assigned responsibility for production in each area, including quantity and working hours. Jobs were rotated among team members to encourage learning new skills. However, workers chose their own learning paces. A bonus system based on output and production cost was designed to be applied to all 50 workers. This firm experienced a 30% decrease in production costs and higher employee satisfaction (measured by a survey).

The term *sociotechnical systems* (STS) (Chase, 1975) has been given to job design that focuses explicitly on the social aspects of work. STS job design typically involves teams (as in the previous example) but with explicit consideration of one's "need" to be a valued team member. Although this brings a new dimension to the issue of job design, the kinds of organizational changes are similar to the ones described previously.

Another phrase that has been used to describe methods of improving the work setting from the employee's view is *quality-of-work-life* (QWL) programs (see Lawler and Ledford, 1982, and Copenhaver and Guest, 1983). These programs change many aspects of a work situation, often beginning with minor annoyances such as insufficient changing or washing space for workers. *QWL* programs are long-term efforts to unlock the employee's abilities for the good of both the organization and the individual. If the program has management commitment, QWL programs lead to more *satisfaction* for the employees. Sometimes, improvement in productivity also occurs, but the link of QWL or satisfaction to productivity remains unclear.

In summary, job design with careful attention to the desires of workers has been shown to benefit both labor and management. However, certain warnings occur repeatedly in the literature.

1. An effective, long-lasting scheme requires changes in attitude as well as behavior.
2. Middle-level management is most likely to cause problems, as job enrichment will be encroaching on their domain. (Their jobs usually can be enriched as well.)
3. Careful diagnosis must precede action. Projects often fail because the wrong problem was addressed.
4. Implementation must proceed slowly, beginning with small projects, to demonstrate (a) what is going on, (b) effectiveness, and (c) long-run management commitment to the new system.
5. Approaching the problem as though attitude change is the major goal is inadvisable, since the program may be dismissed as another public relations gimmick.
6. Even implementation of a small demonstration project must take a system-wide view. The new roles of supervisors, for example, must be carefully spelled out to avoid a continuing tendency to slip back into the old ways.
7. As a result of all of the preceding potential difficulties, top-level management must be solidly behind the program and fully prepared to invest in the new training, equipment, and personnel that will be required for a substantial period of time (possibly years) before positive results will accrue.

One of the key similarities in successful job improvement programs is the redefinition of the role of the middle-level people, particularly foremen and supervisors. Bringing accountability to the worker reduces substantially the role of supervisor as "checker and slave driver." Management's role becomes more supportive of the worker, assuring that the tools, equipment, and information necessary to do the job are available. In addition, the need for training is increased to facilitate self-development; the position of supervisor is ideal for this training function, assuming that superior experience and skill are some of the qualities that lead to promotion to supervisory levels.

Of the production processes described earlier in this chapter, the assembly line is the most resistant to job enrichment. But progress is possible. In Sweden, for example, Volvo has made substantial investments in improving the quality of work life in automobile manufacturing and assembly (Gyllenhammar, 1977). Changes are aimed at environment (e.g., noise) as well as work process. Elaborate transport systems have been installed to replace the production line.

It is important to remember that there are some people who actually prefer repetitive work, and seek only good pay, decent working conditions, and job security. Job enrichment does not work for these people, since they do not want authority, responsibility, and advancement. Given the choice, they will select more pay over any of the other "good job" traits. Job design must recognize individual differences and encourage people to select jobs suited to their preferences.

Review Problem

It is often argued that incorporating job changes to improve worker satisfaction will result in lower productivity as a result of less pressure on the workers, less specialization, and so on. Review some of the broader issues that tend to counter this argument.

Solution

Common sources of savings are:

1. Improved product quality, reducing scrap cost, customer dissatisfaction, and cost of quality control.
2. Reduction in the requirements for personnel whose role is pushing the workers (expediters, certain foremen, etc.).
3. Reduction in employee grievances and/or union difficulties.
4. Reduction in turnover, costs of recruiting, training new workers, and disruption of operations.

6-2 *WORK DESIGN: AN INDUSTRIAL ENGINEERING APPROACH*

Jobs can be made easier, more pleasant, and more efficient through careful attention to detail and proper design and use of equipment. A classical experiment in work improvement was carried out by Gilbreth (Taylor, 1919, pp. 77–85) in the bricklaying trade. The changes were:

1. A helper placed bricks on a newly developed table, with the best edge facing up.
2. A new scaffold was used to keep the worker at the proper height relative to the wall.
3. Mortar was carefully mixed to the proper consistency to avoid the need for excessive tapping of the bricks to properly secure them.
4. Careful observations allowed many motions to be eliminated altogether.
5. Workers were trained to work with both hands at the same time. For example, with proper positioning of materials, one should scoop mortar with one hand while picking up a brick with the other.

The result of this effort was an increase from 120 to 350 bricks laid per worker per hour. Moreover, the bricklayers did not have to work harder, since the new method eliminated the heaviest tasks, such as bending over to pick up bricks and mortar, which requires lifting both the materials and the 150 pounds or more of the worker's own body more than 1000 times per day.

This example illustrates the major elements of task design.

1. Careful observation of the task.
2. Obtaining or designing equipment most suited to the task.
3. Optimal preparation of materials.
4. Design of the workplace to make the task easier and quicker.
5. Training the worker.
6. Providing lower-skilled labor to support and facilitate the work.

The returns from higher productivity have to cover the expenses of the design project as well as the additional labor required for support. The almost trebled output in this case left a substantial surplus, from which the bricklayers were given a large raise.

The theme of this example was improved efficiency. Although bricklaying has been practiced for thousands of years, such a dramatic improvement was made possible through systematic observation by someone who was not a bricklayer! Similar improvements continue to be possible, and should certainly be welcomed, for example, by a work team that has the authority to select work methods and is paid according to the results.

To be proficient in work methods an industrial engineer (IE) must be familiar with a wide variety of processes and machines as well as with the methods for getting the most from each machine. In addition, principles of motion economy have been developed to aid in streamlining a job. A third area is understanding the capabilities of people as they operate on a job, including their interactions with other people and with machines. Effect on the environment is a crucial factor, with regard to both the health and safety of the workers and the impact on the community in which the organization is situated.

Most of these topics are highly technical in nature, and consequently the "efficiency expert" has typically received an education with little emphasis on the organizational and human factors discussed earlier. This has been cited as a contributing factor to labor–management strife over productivity measures. Nevertheless, a well-trained IE can contribute substantially to job design, so we will review briefly a few of the tools of the trade.

The most important part of a work improvement study, *operation analysis,* is observing the process so as to understand the nature and purpose of each operation, constantly making notes on possible improvements and seemingly unnecessary operations. Three examples are:

1. *Paperwork.* The supervisor's signature and proofreading of all letters to stockholders were eliminated in the study cited earlier (Herzberg, 1976, pp. 130–134)
2. *Delays.* Preadmission of maternity and other predictable hospital admissions reduces the waiting time for all patients entering a hospital, since the patient fills out the necessary admission forms at home and mails them to the hospital.
3. *Touch-up.* Improved control over the amount of plastic injected into a mold can eliminate the need for removing the excess from the finished product.

The tools for a systematic operation analysis include many kinds of charts, including some that we have already described (flow diagrams, flow process charts, layout schematics, Gozinto charts, etc.). These devices help to visualize the process in detail and thereby provide a means for working out improvements. At the same time, such a systematic approach minimizes the chances of an unforeseen outcome of a suggested change.

Combining and/or subdividing operations is one place where operation analysis overlaps with job enrichment. (However, combining operations may result in enlargement without enrichment!) Whether in manufacturing or service, combining two steps can save setup time (preparing to do the operation) but requires more skills of the operator, may necessitate more equipment, and results in a workplace that is more difficult to organize.

Motion study was developed around the turn of the twentieth century by Frank and Lillian Gilbreth and others. In its present form (Niebel, 1976, Chaps. 7 and 8) it is an important part of design of jobs and layout of the workplace. Information has been cataloged on human capabilities in terms of the kinds of motions that are easiest (most natural and least tiring are curved, continuous motions), physical capabilities (force that can be applied by a person sitting or standing, pushing or pulling, etc.), and coordination of effort (both hands should begin and end their tasks simultaneously). The kinds of basic hand motions are called therbligs (Gilbreth spelled backward), and include search, select, grasp, reach, and 13 other elements, each of which has a standard abbreviation, color code, and pictorial symbol for use in charting. With these elements, an engineer can describe an existing operation or design a new one. The symbols are used to construct process flowcharts, which describe the task assigned to each hand.

Micromotion study is carried out with videotape or motion pictures, which are viewed one frame at a time to categorize, study, and criticize the elemental motions of an operation. This very expensive form of analysis is not justifiable for most situations, but the fine tuning it achieves can recover the investment for high-volume operations.

Information has also been cataloged relating various work conditions (noise, pace, vibration, rest periods, etc.) to fatigue and performance. The interface between human beings and machines is also approached in part from this point of view. For example, attention span is important in monitoring patients and equipment in an intensive care unit, loads on a municipal electrical system, or flows and heat in a chemical factory. Innovations such as installing warning lights and orienting dials so that the normal position of the indicator is straight up (the 12 o'clock position) have immensely improved the reliability and ease of monitoring.

Time Studies

Time studies have been used for many purposes, including measuring travel times for layout design, measuring task times for job design, setting standards for evaluating worker performance, estimating job times for scheduling production sequence (see Chapters 11 and 12), and estimating the number of personnel needed for scheduling the workforce (see Chapters 9 and 14). Time studies not only require accurate time measurement, but also reliable methods for rating the performance of the person being observed. Ratings and standards will be discussed later.

Stopwatch techniques can be used after careful observation has divided a task into its elements. Once a carefully selected operator has agreed to participate, the observer remains on the site timing elements of the operation without interfering in the actual process. In most cases, it is advisable for the observer to remain inconspicuous, but those parties to be observed *must* be willing, notified participants. Each element is timed repeatedly until the desired accuracy is obtained.

Times can be estimated without a stopwatch through a technique called *work sampling*. In this technique, an observer takes data at preselected times of day. Each observation consists of a notation of what work element was being performed at the preselected instant of time. After a large number of such observations, the fraction of observations that noted "activity *i*" being performed becomes the estimate of the proportion of the day being spent on activity *i*.

To be valid, the preselection of times must be done in a random fashion, using a table of random numbers[3] or some other randomizing method, to avoid the possibility of the observations being taken in a cycle that may coincide with work patterns. For example, observations "on the hour" might be biased because of the pattern of work breaks.

---

[3] There is a list of random numbers in Table 1, Appendix D.

Both the stopwatch method and work sampling require at least a two-phase study, with the first (pilot) phase used to iron out the methods and to estimate the variability of the process elements. From the results of the pilot study, the number of observations required in phase 2 is estimated. Table 6-1 summarizes the formulas used for each method. The first phase is carried out using an arbitrarily chosen sample size, typically around 30 for the stopwatch method and 50 to 100 or more for work sampling. The results are used in the formula for sample size, which determines the extent of the data to be collected in the second phase.

For example, in a pilot study, a work element was timed $n = 30$ times. The average was $\bar{x} = 0.372$ minute, and the standard deviation was $s = 0.123$ minute. For 95% confidence we find that $z = 1.96$ (Table 2, Appendix D). Therefore, the precision of the estimate is

$$\frac{zs}{\sqrt{n}} = \frac{(1.96)(0.123)}{\sqrt{30}} = 0.044$$

which is about 11.8% of $\bar{x}$.

Management desired 2% precision, so the appropriate sample size is

$$n = \left[\frac{(1.96)(0.123)}{(0.02)(0.372)}\right]^2 = 1050$$

TABLE 6-1   SUMMARY OF STATISTICAL FORMULAS FOR WORK MEASUREMENT

Stopwatch	Work Sampling
Estimates	
$\bar{x}$ = average measured time on the activity	p_i = fraction of observations that noted activity i
s = standard deviation of the measurements	n = total number of observations
n = number of measurements taken on the activity	
Approximate precision of estimate (confidence interval)	
$\dfrac{zs}{\sqrt{n}}$	$z\sqrt{\dfrac{p_i(1 - p_i)}{n}}$
z = standard normal statistic[a]	z = standard normal statistic[a]
Approximate sample size needed	
$n \approx \left(\dfrac{zs}{\varepsilon\bar{x}}\right)^2$	$n \geq \left(\dfrac{z}{L_i}\right)^2 p_i(1 - p_i)$
	for all activities i
ε = acceptable error, as a fraction of $\bar{x}$	L_i = acceptable numerical error in p_i

[a] See Table 2, Appendix D, to find a z value for the desired level of confidence. For example, $z = 1.96$ for 95% confidence in a given level of precision. This is only a rough approximation if the sample size is less than 30.

Standards

Most wage incentive systems require some sort of performance evaluation for each worker. Typically, this is accomplished by specifying a standard time in which the operation should be completed. Intense controversy often erupts over the issue of what the standard should be.

Time-study observers are trained to rate their subjects according to their observed work pace. For example, a stopwatch study might result in $\bar{x} = 0.123$ minute for a worker whose pace was rated 110% of normal, so the estimated standard would be $(0.123)(1.10) = 0.135$ minute. The ability of observers to give accurate ratings has been studied. Whereas an average error of less than $\pm 5\%$ is desirable, a study of 599 trained time-study observers by the Society for Advancement of Management (Niebel, 1976, p. 660) showed that 59% of the observers had error rates exceeding 10%, with one person as high as 22%.

The conclusion is that there is no way to be sure of a correct standard. Therefore, standards are themselves open to negotiation. The accuracy of time-study numbers is often substantially overstated, since they must be adjusted for pace using a factor that averages greater than 10% error.

Nevertheless, standard time data have been collected over many years and are available in tables, classified according to type of operation. With reference to these tables, standards can be constructed for jobs that have never been done before, and from these standards, labor costs per item may be estimated for purposes of product planning. Although these must be treated as rough estimates (for reasons that should now be clear), they are better than a seat-of-the-pants estimate, which would be the only other alternative.

Review Problems

1. In the stopwatch method example (above), the observer rated the worker at 80% of normal pace in the pilot study.
   (a) Was the worker faster or slower than normal?
   (b) What is the adjusted estimate of the normal task time? (The observed time was $\bar{x} = 0.372$ minute.)
2. The sample size of 1050 was judged to be unacceptably large (too expensive). What sample size should be used if the allowable error is relaxed to 4%?

Solutions
1. (a) Slower.
   (b) "Adjusted $\bar{x}$" $= (0.372)(0.80) = 0.298$ minute.
2. 263. Notice that reducing the accuracy by a factor of 2 cuts the required sample size by a factor of 4.

6-3 MEASURING AND IMPROVING PRODUCTIVITY

As discussed in the introduction, improvements in productivity can lead to benefits for the individual, the organization, and society. When productivity declines (or fails to increase at a sufficient rate), it is blamed on worker attitudes, management, unions, and government (Sentry, 1981). In short, it is everyone's fault. When productivity rebounds, a new awareness of the problem and general concern get the credit (Anderson et al., 1984).

Productivity is, of course, everyone's business. It is not just for factories, since 75% of the labor force in the United States is in the service sector. Productivity measurement in the service sector is often more difficult, but many articles and books have been written regarding productivity in areas such as banking (Anthony, 1984, Metzger, 1983, and Mundel, 1983), research and development (Rantfl, 1977), offices (Umbaugh and Juliff, 1982, and Gery, 1982), urban transit (Gleason and Barnum, 1982), school districts (Bessent et al., 1982), and white-collar workers in general (Ruch, 1982, and Charon and Schlumpf, 1981). In this section we will discuss both service and manufacturing examples, beginning with *measurement* of productivity.

Measurement

Measuring productivity is simple in concept but difficult in practice. A productivity index in basic form is defined as:

$$\text{productivity index (P.I.)} = \frac{(\text{outputs/inputs}) \text{ in the current period}}{(\text{outputs/inputs}) \text{ in a base period}}$$

For example, suppose that a firm produced 4 units of an item using 2 labor hours, in the base period. In the current period, the firm produces 6 units in 2.5 labor hours. Then the productivity index is

$$\text{P.I.} = \frac{6/2.5}{4/2} = \frac{2.4}{2.0} = 1.2$$

The index shows a 20% improvement in productivity, but the improvement may be illusory. Perhaps the item has been redesigned so that the units are not exactly comparable. Perhaps a capital investment has resulted in the improvement, and the 20% increase does not show whether the investment was justified or not. Perhaps there is a setup time of 1 hour; the labor force produced 4 units in 1 hour after setup in the base period and 6 units in 1.5 hours after setup in the current period.

This example illustrates several important points about productivity measurement. We will highlight each main point below with some examples from Mundel (1978).

First, the quantity to be measured must be selected carefully; it must reflect what the organization wishes to improve. For example, in measuring productivity of hospital nursing staffs, it would seem shortsighted to measure nursing hours per "hospital-patient-day." If more nursing hours can result in more healed patients, productivity has improved; if patient care does not improve, productivity has declined. In measuring the effectiveness of a government agency charged with ensuring compliance with pollution standards, "number of citations issued" per inspector day is inappropriate; inspectors should strive to increase the "fraction of firms in compliance" with the regulation. Productivity measures can be counterproductive unless they are selected carefully. In the two cases cited above, it is easy to see how nursing hours per patient-day might decline or number of citations issued might increase while not improving the real goal of the organization.

A productivity measure must also represent something that is controllable by the people being measured. For example, a weather department was measured using the "number of typhoons tracked"!

Several difficulties plague productivity measurement. For example, how should a productivity ratio handle products that change over time? (Consider how different computers or cars are today than they were 15 years ago.) Also, how can a firm measure the input due to capital equipment? How can a productivity measure for a plant or company be developed when there are many outputs (such as cars, spark plugs, and carburetors) and many inputs (such as unskilled labor, skilled labor, engineers, and capital equipment)?

The difficulties noted above lead to two main points. First, in spite of the fact that productivity may be a measure of physical output, a productivity index for a large organization requires that everything be placed in monetary terms as a common unit. The effects of inflation must be removed. Second, all productivity measures are imperfect and must be used with care. This may mean that several separate indexes are maintained, to study separate effects. In any case, the manager has the final responsibility for interpreting the data.

Productivity measures that attempt to include all inputs are called total factor productivity measures. One such measure for manufacturing firms is given by Taylor and Davis (1978):

total factor productivity = (value added in sales + change in
    inventory + additions, produced by the firm, to plant and
    equipment) ÷ [wages and benefits + (fraction of return on assets in
    base year) × (working + fixed capital)]

Symbolically:

$$\text{TFP} = \frac{(S + C + MP) - E}{(W + B) + (K_w + K_f)F_b \cdot d_f}$$

where
S = sales
E = purchases and other exclusions, so that $S - E$ is value added
C = change in inventory
MP = manufactured plant (adding value to our own facilities)
$W + B$ = wages plus benefits
$K_w + K_f$ = working plus fixed capital assets employed (plant, equipment, inventory, and so on)
F_b = return on assets earned in the base year (against which we are comparing)
d_f = a price deflator to adjust capital assets to base-year values

All parts of the measure are in dollars, and the units would be adjusted for inflation. This measure is a good way to analyze productivity, but it can also lead to misconceptions. For example, if inventory is growing dramatically, our productivity measure can look good, but the company can be in bad shape.

If total factor productivity models can produce misleading results, partial measures, such as labor productivity, can be even worse. As mentioned above, capital equipment (such as a flexible manufacturing system) can make labor several times more productive. But the investment may not be cost-effective. Thus partial measures of productivity should be used with great care. Gold (1982, 1983) discusses the weaknesses of several common productivity measures and proposes a system based on examining a "network of productivity relationships." He gives several problems of measurement of productivity, including (1) changes in the scope of operations, (2) changes in capacity utilization, (3) changes in product design, (4) changes in the production process, and (5) changes in the scale of operations.

In summary, we must measure productivity if we are to improve it, but no one measure of productivity is flawless. Total factor productivity measures allow inclusion of many very different inputs and outputs, but they can be misleading. (See the Review Problems for this section.) Several productivity measures may be needed, but they must be interpreted by a manager who understands the organization being measured. Since productivity measurement, from goal selection to final computation to interpretation, requires management judgment, managers must be aware of both the value and the difficulty of measuring productivity. Managers must routinely be part of the process.

Improving Productivity

Productivity measures have several uses: (1) as evidence of long-run profitability of an organization, unobscured by short-term factors, (2) to control efficiency by making comparisons with an organization's own past or to other (competitive) organizations, (3) forecasting costs (budgeting) based on past trends in productivity, and (4) collective bargaining (Kendrick and Creamer, 1965).

An example of points (2) and (3) is given by Charon and Schlumpf (1981). In IBM, a linear regression model is used to predict the appropriate number of indirect work-force members. For example, for a plant with 2000 direct labor employees, how many secretaries should there be? Of course, the number of direct labor employees does not capture the entire need equation. Thus the resulting number must be questioned. Nevertheless, it provides a starting point for setting a goal. Comparisons to other units give an indication of where productivity improvements might be easily found, but they do not tell the manager how to make the improvements.

There are three major areas for the improvement of productivity:

1. Changing attitudes of managers, government, and workers.

2. Investing in properly selected new capital equipment.

3. Managing the detailed operations of capital and labor more efficiently.

Often mentioned in the first category is cooperation among managers, government, and workers. One key to Japan's success in certain manufacturing areas is that government, workers, and management cooperate to improve productivity and to compete in world markets. That cooperation does not exist in some Western countries; the three groups mistrust each other.

One tangible way, mentioned earlier, in which management can improve trust and cooperation is to guarantee that returns from laborsaving suggestions from workers will be shared and will not result in a loss of pay or jobs. This implies that workers must be heavily involved in any productivity improvement program. A study reported by Fein (1983) bears this out. Government's major challenge is to create an atmosphere in which firms can be competitive in world markets, so that society can profit from their advances. Finally, labor must realize that if the firm does not do well, in the long run everyone suffers. Improving the motivation of all employees within an organization is perhaps the best method of improving productivity.

The second area of productivity improvement involves equipment. The level of capital investment per worker is often given as a reason for the success of Japanese and German industry. Those countries have had a higher level of investment per worker recently than that in the United States. However, simply spending more may not improve productivity sufficiently to justify the expense. Investment in new equipment is discussed in Chapter 5.

In the third area, managers must schedule operations to avoid idle time, reduce assets employed, and still provide the service desired by the customers. Methods for obtaining improvements such as these form the core of this book.

In summary, productivity measurement is commonplace but nevertheless elusive. Careless application of productivity incentives can lead to grave errors. Difficult as measurement is, it is very useful to monitor the effects of managerial or governmental changes. Each of the three areas for potential productivity improvement (attitudes, new equipment, and managing detailed operations) can be very important. The first requires managers to be sensitive to the needs of others while stressing the importance of cooperation. The second and third areas require operations managers to analyze their operations carefully, understanding both the broad view and details of the problem, using techniques discussed in the other chapters in this text.

Review Problems

Refer to the total factor productivity formula in this section. Suppose that a manager wanted to maximize the productivity rating.

1. Why might inventories grow?
2. What other factor might be used to improve the productivity rating?

Solutions

1. If capacity is underutilized, the marginal cost of the next unit of production is probably lower than the average cost. Since inventory additions count as much as sales, the firm's productivity index would go up if we produce extra units, even though they are not needed. (The inventory will increase the numerator more than it increases the denominator.)

2. Several answers are possible here. For example, the firm could add to its plant (MP). If capacity is limited, the productivity rating could be increased by producing only high-margin items, perhaps causing long-term marketing difficulties. For a while, the firm could allow fixed capital to decline, thereby obtaining a short-term productivity increase by borrowing from the future. We are *not* suggesting that managers play games with productivity (or other) measures, but if someone is rewarded using any measurement, the organization is telling them to improve that measure. Performance measures must be selected carefully, and judgment must be used as well.

6-4 Summary

All organizations should try to be more productive. This can mean lower production cost, so that a manufacturing firm is more competitive, or less time spent on routine work so that a social service agency can spend more time in contact with people needing their services. Productivity improvements have been good for our society, dramatically improving our standard of living, and they can often be good for all members of an organization.

Perhaps the most important method of improving productivity is through having jobs, organizations, and management styles that allow people to contribute to the goals of the organization. In this effort, managers must know that all employees respond to both pay and other factors. Many types of organizations that give more authority and control to workers have been successful. Still, there is no magic formula. People are different, and managers must adapt to the situation at hand.

Industrial engineering methods have been used successfully for most of this century. They can be used effectively in modern organizations. An unbiased, analytical view of a job can be very helpful. The use of the tools must be managed so that workers feel that they are being helped rather than hurt. Industrial engineering methods must be viewed as a managerial tool, not a panacea.

Productivity measurement looks at organizations (a plant, for example) rather than at an individual job. There is no productivity measure that captures all key factors in all situations. Managers should use productivity measures, but they must interpret the results using judgment. Improving productivity calls on the manager to use his or her analytical ability, interpersonal skills, knowledge of the particular system being managed, and judgment. Improving productivity is often difficult, but there is no more important management task.

PROBLEMS

*1. Can the semiautonomous team approach, illustrated by the Norsk Hydro case, be best described as job enrichment or job enlargement? What elements were present that are not fundamental to either job enrichment or job enlargement?

2. A work incentive may be thought of as a motivation factor that is at least partially withheld from workers, so that it may be "earned" by workers who perform well. At the beginning of Section 6-2, there is a list of "good job" characteristics. Which of these do you feel are commonly used as work incentives?

3. Support or refute the statements, "Job enrichment is applicable only to nonsupervisory jobs" and "Job enrichment of nonsupervisory jobs will not affect the work of the manager."

*4. (a) What is the fundamental difference between the stopwatch method and work sampling?
   (b) Why are ratings of work pace necessary for both methods?

5. (a) What are the roles of operation analysis and motion study in the design of jobs?
   (b) Why is it that time-and-motion studies are well received by the workers in some settings but not in others?

*6. A work sample is being conducted. The observer randomly samples 60 times in a day and notes that a particular element is performed 12 times.
   (a) Estimate the percentage of the time that workers spend on this element.
   (b) Calculate the precision of the estimate (a 95% confidence interval).
   (c) Determine the appropriate sample size required for a second set of observations if the acceptable numerical error in p_i is 0.02.

7. In a work study, the basic tasks for assembly of a can opener were timed. The raw data are shown in the accompanying table.
   (a) Calculate the precision (95% confidence) of the average task times.
   (b) How many additional observations are needed to reduce the error in the average task time to $\pm 1\%$ for task 6?
   (c) What is the theoretical minimum number of workers required to produce 50 can openers per hour?
   (d) In your answer to part (c), what vital piece of information is missing, and under what circumstances will it change the required number of workers?

Task	Number of Observations	Average Task Time (Minutes)	STANDARD DEVIATION, s	
			Minutes	% of Average Task Time
1	20	0.50	0.04	8
2	100	1.00	0.50	50
3	10	0.70	0.03	4.3
4	20	0.30	0.06	20
5	100	2.00	0.80	40
6	10	1.00	0.04	4
7	20	0.70	0.01	1.4

8. There are five different work groups in a plant, and we want to design a work sampling plan to ascertain what percentage of time is being spent by each worker in each of eight general activity categories. Our prior estimates range from a low of 5% for activity category C to a high of 25% for category F.
(a) What sample size is needed to achieve an accuracy of ± 3 percentage points (or better) for all categories with 95% confidence?
(b) The plan is to visit the work groups at randomly selected times over a 4-hour period, each day, until a sufficiently large sample size is achieved. There will be at least 15 minutes between observations and one worker will be observed in each visit. Show how to randomly assign 15-minute observation intervals among the five work groups, using one die.
(c) How many days will be required to take the sample? Suggest a way to reduce this time.
(d) How many observations would be required to double the accuracy?

*9. How can management successfully solicit laborsaving suggestions from employees?

10. A firm makes nails in 20 sizes. Suppose that a productivity goal is given in (a) number of nails or (b) pounds of nails. What products might they make in each case, and why? (This question is based on an old Russian cartoon about central planning goals.)

*11. The MT company had 50 employees in the base year. In the base year it produced 20 large computers. In the current year, the firm produced 25 computers with 60 employees.
(a) Compute a labor productivity index.
(b) Why might this partial productivity index be misleading?

*12. This problem should be done after Problem 11. Suppose that the MT company, described in Problem 11, makes two models of computer. Product 1 (P1) requires 2 labor years, and product 2 (P2) requires 3 labor years. In the current year they produced 15 P1's and 10 P2's.
(a) Next year they believe they can sell up to 20 P1's and 20 P2's. They

will have 60 employees. How many of each should they produce if they want to maximize the productivity ratio from Problem 11?

(b) Why might the answer to part (a) be bad for the company?

*13. This problem requires information from Problem 12. Suppose that P1 sells for $1,000,000 and P2 sells for $2,000,000.

(a) If the company wants to maximize revenue, what products should they make next year with 60 employees, assuming that they can sell up to 20 of each?

(b) Why might this not be the right thing to do?

14. The company in Problems 11 to 13 (you must read those problems for information) has decided to use a total factor productivity model and to purchase rather than manufacture some subsystems. That is, they will add less value to their products than before. They will not fire people, but they may allow the work force to be reduced over time through attrition. Their capital assets will be unchanged, at least in the short run.

(a) If they produce 15 P1's and 10 P2's next year (as they did this year), describe what will happen to their total factor productivity index, indicating the terms that will cause the change.

(b) If they are going to purchase 60% of the sales value of each product, and if they can now produce P1 with 1 labor year and P2 with 2 labor years, what products should they produce to maximize their value added? (They can sell up to 20 of each product.)

(c) In the TFP formula in Section 6-3, $C = MP = 0$; $W + B = 60$ times $100,000 = \$6,000,000$; $K_w + K_f = \$40,000,000$; $F_b = 0.20$; and $d_f = 1$. Compute the value of TFP projected based on your decision in part (b). Comment briefly on the meaning and validity of the value of TFP.

15. List four reasons why good productivity measurements are difficult to obtain.

*16. Discuss reasons for favoring group incentives. What arguments favor individual incentives?

REFERENCES

ANDERSON, H., M. RESENER, AND C. MA, "A Surprising Surge in Productivity." *Newsweek,* February 6, 1984.

ANTHONY, G. M., "Designing Productivity Standards for White Collar Employees." *Industrial Engineering,* Vol. 16, No. 1 (January 1984).

BESSENT, A., W. BESSENT, J. KENNINGTON, AND B. REAGAN, "An Application of Mathematical Programming to Assess Productivity in the Houston Independent School District." *Management Science,* Vol. 28, No. 12 (December 1982).

BITRAN, G., AND L. CHANG, "Productivity Measurement at the Micro Level," Working Paper, Sloan School of Management, MIT, Cambridge, Mass., 1983.

BULLINGER, H. J., AND H. P. LENTES, "The Future of Work: Technological, Economic and Social Changes." *International Journal of Production Research*, Vol. 20, No. 3 (1982).

BULLOCK, R. J., AND P. F. BULLOCK, "Gainsharing and Rubik's Cube: Solving System Problems." *National Productivity Review*, Vol. 1, No. 4 (1982).

CHARON, K., AND J. SCHLUMPF, "IBM's Common Staffing System: How to Measure Productivity of the Indirect Workforce." *Management Review*, August 1981.

CHASE, R. B., "A Review of Models for Mapping the Socio-technical System." *AIIE Transactions*, Vol. 7, No. 1 (January 1975).

COPENHAVER, L., AND R. GUEST, "Quality of Work Life: The Anatomy of Two Successes." *National Productivity Review*, Vol. 2, No. 1 (1983).

FEIN, M., "Managing Philosophy Affects Productivity Improvement Programs." *Industrial Engineering*, Vol. 15, No. 10 (October 1983).

GERY, G., "Office Technology: Creating Receptivity among Executives and Professionals." *National Productivity Review*, Vol. 1, No. 2 (1982).

GLEASON, J., AND D. BARNUM, "Toward Valid Measures of Public Sector Productivity: Performance Measures in Urban Transit." *Management Science*, Vol. 28, No. 4 (April 1982).

GIBSON, J., J. IVANCEVICH, AND J. DONNELLY, JR., *Organizations*, Plano, Tex.: Business Publications, 1982.

GOLD, B., "Practical Productivity Analysis for Management: Part I. Analytic Framework." *IIE Transactions*, Vol. 14, No. 4 (1982).

GOLD, B., "Practical Productivity Analysis for Management: Part II. Measurement and Interpretation." *IIE Transactions*, Vol. 15, No. 1 (1983).

GYLLENHAMMAR, P. G., "How Volvo Adapts Work to People." *Harvard Business Review*, July–August 1977.

HACKMAN, J. R., "Is Job Enrichment Just a Fad?" *Harvard Business Review*, September–October 1975.

HERZBERG, F., *The Managerial Choice: To Be Efficient or to Be Human.* Homewood, Ill.: Richard D. Irwin, 1976.

KATZELL, R., P. BIENSTOCK, AND P. FAERSTEIN, *A Guide to Worker Productivity Experiments in the United States, 1971–75.* New York: Moffat, 1977.

KENDRICK, J., AND D. CREAMER, *Measuring Company Productivity.* Studies in Business Economics. New York: The Conference Board, No. 89, 1965.

LAWLER, E., III, AND G. LEDFORD, JR., "Productivity and the Quality of Work Life." *National Productivity Review*, Vol. 1, No. 1 (1982).

METZGER, R., "Banking in the 80's: Productivity Improvement on an Exponential Curve." *National Productivity Review*, Vol. 2, No. 1 (1983).

MUNDEL, M., "Measures of Productivity," in *Productivity: A Series from Industrial Engineering*, M. Mundel, ed. Atlanta: Institute of Industrial Engineers, 1978.

MUNDEL, M., "Measuring Productivity by the Box Score." *Industrial Engineering*, Vol. 15, No. 10 (October 1983).

NIEBEL, B., *Motion and Time Study*, 6th ed. Homewood, Ill.: Richard D. Irwin, 1976.

RANTFL, R., *R&D Productivity*, 2nd ed., P.O. Box 49892, Los Angeles, CA 90049, 1977.

RUCH, W., "The Measurement of White-Collar Productivity." *National Productivity Review,* Vol. 1, No. 4 (1982).

SENTRY, *Perspectives on Productivity: A Global View,* A Sentry Study. Stevens Point, Wisconsin, 1981.

SIMPSON, E., "Motorola's Participative Management Program." *National Productivity Review,* Vol. 2, No. 1 (1983).

STEERS, R., *Introduction to Organizational Behavior.* Santa Monica, Calif.: Goodyear Publishing Co., 1981.

STRINER, H., "Regaining the Lead in Productivity Growth." *National Productivity Review,* Vol. 1, No. 1 (1982).

TAYLOR, F. W., *Shop Management.* New York: Harper & Brothers, 1919.

TAYLOR, B. W., III, AND K. R. DAVIS, "Corporate Productivity—Getting It All Together," in *Productivity: A Series from Industrial Engineering,* M. Mundel, ed. Atlanta: Institute of Industrial Engineers, 1978.

ULLMAN, J., "White-Collar Productivity and the Growth of Administrative Overhead." *National Productivity Review,* Vol. 1, No. 3 (1982).

UMBAUGH, R., AND R. JULIFF, "Office Technology, Paperwork, and Productivity." *National Productivity Review,* Vol. 1, No. 3 (1982).

U.S. Department of Health, Education and Welfare, *The Industrial Environment—Its Evaluation and Control.* Bethesda, Md.: National Institute for Occupational Health and Safety, 1973.

WOLFBEIN, S., "Planning for the U.S. Labor Force of the '80s." *National Productivity Review,* Vol. 1, No. 2 (1982).

Work in America, report of a special task force to the Secretary of Health, Education and Welfare. Cambridge, Mass.: MIT Press, 1973.

CHAPTER 7

Capacity and Location Analysis

The Salt Ridge Bakery Company produces relatively expensive breads for sale through supermarkets. The firm's sales have been growing in recent years and are expected to continue to grow. At the same time, the baking industry has been moving to larger bakeries, to achieve economies of scale; this trend has continued in spite of the resulting higher transportation costs.

The Salt Ridge Bakery needs to expand to meet the increased demand for their product. The vice-president for operations, Sharon Westphal, must decide where to place new plants and how large to make them. In reaching a decision she must consider the forecast of sales in each region of the country, the costs of building and operating each size of plant, the availability of work force and transportation, and the capacity and location of the firm's current facilities.

The forecast must be broken down into different product categories, where each category uses a different kind of capacity. (Breads require different mixers than do cookies, for example.) Any major changes in the product line must be predicted. Some of these data must be obtained from sources other than the forecasting group.

In determining the *capacity plan,* Westphal must consider company policies toward their product line and toward financial decisions. For example, should the plant be designed to provide highest quality, no matter what the cost? Should a new plant earn 15%, 20%, or more, or less on the money invested? Should a plant be tightly designed around the current product mix (a low-cost strategy in the short run), or should it be flexible enough to allow changes in the product mix with little or no adaptation?

In determining the location of new facilities the immediate effect upon production and transportation costs must be considered. In addition, how the new plant will fit with future plants must be considered.

For a profit-making organization such as Salt Ridge, capacity and location decisions are important parts of their competitive strategy. Production costs, ability to meet surges in demand, nearness to customers, and distribution requirements are determined by capacity and location decisions. Further, since these decisions are made infrequently, and since they are not easy to reverse, the capacity plan and location decisions must provide flexibility to deal with an uncertain future. Intermediate horizon decisions (such as hiring plans for the next several months and overtime or extra shifts during that same period) and short-term decisions (such as which products to produce in what quantities and in what order, during the current week) are constrained by the capacity plan. The effect on these shorter-range decisions must be considered in developing the capacity plan.

Nonprofit organizations, including service organizations, also face capacity and location decisions crucial to their survival. The Somerton Health Maintenance Organization (SIIMO) discussed in Chapter 4 was an example. Another example is the problem faced by many school boards in the 1980s—excess capacity in the face of declining enrollments. Even with excess capacity, some building may be necessary to replace old facilities. Some facilities will have to be closed, and neighborhood schools may have their service areas redefined. The capacity plan is very important, and the objectives are multifaceted, including, but not limited to, holding down the cost of operating the school system and maintaining its quality.

In this chapter we will discuss several capacity and location situations, beginning with the problem of sizing one productive facility. The use of analytical techniques such as linear programming and computer simulation will be discussed in dealing with capacity and location decisions for multiple facilities. We will see that different considerations are used in locating plants than in locating warehouses, and that the multiplicity of objectives faced by the public sector make their problems even more difficult.

7-1 LOCATING AND SIZING ONE FACILITY

Plant location and service facility location involve different considerations. Most labor costs in a manufacturing organization are incurred at the plant. The customer contact value of a plant is minimal, except that, because of concern regarding pollution, some plants give a negative image to the firm's products.

A customer service warehouse, on the other hand, must be close enough in terms of shipment time to the final customer to facilitate good customer service. A small portion of the firm's labor costs but a large portion of the transportation costs are incurred at such warehouses.

A retail store must be located to attract customers. Convenience and attraction for retail customers is of paramount importance. The same considerations are important in locating satellite health clinics designed to reach many individuals.

Location decisions are frequently analyzed by using "checklists" to see how a potential location performs on several different criteria. The checklist serves as an aid to the decision maker. The same list might be used for locating many types of facilities but, as discussed above, different items become more or less important in different situations. To illustrate this, consider Table 7-1, which lists six items of importance for three different location problems. You are to rank the items as to importance in each of the three situations. (That is, place the numbers 1 to 6 in each of the three columns.)

Because the actual rankings may vary dramatically from one situation to another, we will not attempt to give "correct" rankings for the table. However, certain points are clear. Most warehouses exist to provide speed of service and to reduce transportation cost. Thus for the warehouse column, ranks 1 and 2 probably would appear in rows 1 and 4. In contrast, the typical manufacturing plant incurs heavy labor costs, and access to raw materials is vital. Also, construction is more complex and expensive than for warehouses. Thus items 2, 3, and 5 will probably have the top three ranks for a plant. (As part of labor cost at the plant, management will also consider the attitudes of local unions and the extent of unionization.) Finally, for most retail location decisions item 4 is of prime importance. The decision maker considering a retail location will include some measure of the competition in analyzing the attraction to customers. Item 6, attitude of local governments, can be very important for any location decision, but it is probably most important for a plant, which will have a large presence in the area. In fact, the labor, political, and social situation of the region, community, and even the particular site are very important in selecting a plant location.

Topics such as these are discussed extensively in Heskett et al. (1973), and we will not give a complete discussion here. It is important, though, for us to understand that many considerations are involved. Models that "optimize" the location of one facility typically consider only one or two of the necessary

TABLE 7-1 SOME LOCATION CONSIDERATIONS

	RANK BY IMPORTANCE FOR:		
Item	Warehouse	Plant	Retail Store
1. Transportation and inventory costs	_____	_____	_____
2. Availability and cost of labor	_____	_____	_____
3. Cost of construction, taxes, and land	_____	_____	_____
4. Convenience to and attraction for the final customers	_____	_____	_____
5. Convenience to raw materials	_____	_____	_____
6. Attitude of local and state governments	_____	_____	_____

considerations. Nevertheless, these models can be used by management as a tool. For example, transportation cost minimization may be one key factor. But other factors must be included, probably in a subjective fashion. When we discuss mathematical methods for multifacility location we must keep in mind the factors not included in the quantitative measures.

Once a facility is located, a capacity must be selected. Choosing capacity is a long-term problem, so a long-horizon forecast must be used. In some cases that forecast will be difficult to obtain and it may contain large "ifs," such as "if the product catches on." In addition to managerial judgment, quantitative tools such as decision analysis and time discounting can aid in making such decisions. These are discussed next.

Using Decision Analysis in the Capacity Decision

Salt Ridge is considering the addition of a new product to its product line. The new product would require a capital expenditure, since current capacity is fully utilized and a new type of machine is required. Sharon Westphal is considering expanding one plant and selling the product in that one region. If the product catches on, a capacity of 5000 units per week will be necessary, and the company will make a net profit of $40,000 per week. (Net profit is used here to be sales revenue minus all costs of production *except* the cost of capital tied up in the plant.) If the product does not catch on, a capacity of 2000 units per week will be needed, and the company will make a net profit of $16,000 per week on 2000 units.

A 2000-unit capacity can be built for $800,000. A 5000-unit capacity can be built for $1,500,000. A 2000-unit capacity can be expanded to a 5000-unit capacity for $1,000,000. Either addition will be of no value after 20 years but will perform until that time. Excess capacity is worthless. After 1 year of sales, they will know whether the product has caught on. Westphal has three initial possible choices; they are shown in the *decision tree* in Figure 7-1. The boxes in the figure represent decisions to be made by the firm. The circles represent a state of nature, to be observed after a decision is made. Formulations of this type are discussed in Neter et al. (1982).

A decision tree is useful when there are one or more major uncertainties surrounding a decision problem. We want to see how a decision will perform in each possible situation. A decision may be rejected because it has a small chance of losing a lot of money. On the other hand, if the firm can afford the potential loss, it may choose the decision with the highest expected profit. Westphal believes that Salt Ridge should pick the decision with the largest expected profit.

We first note that the net profits occur over time, so time discounting (discussed in Chapter 2) must be used. Thus we need a discount factor for Salt Ridge. In addition, we need to have a probability of high demand and low demand. Westphal says that the firm wants to earn 25% (before taxes) on invested funds, so the discount rate is 0.25. The probability of high demand, based on

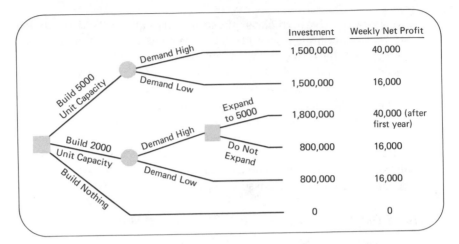

	Investment	Weekly Net Profit
Demand High	1,500,000	40,000
Demand Low	1,500,000	16,000
Expand to 5000	1,800,000	40,000 (after first year)
Do Not Expand	800,000	16,000
Demand Low	800,000	16,000
	0	0

Figure 7-1   Decision tree for the salt ridge capacity problem.

other, similar, new product introductions, is 0.2. The first year's net profits occur, on the average, 1 year after the plant investment is required, for either the original plant or an expansion.

With these data we can complete the analysis of the Figure 7-1 problem. (We will use a 25% before-tax discount rate and ignore taxes here. Taxes are included in one of the problems at the end of the chapter.) First, we consider the *second* decision point: if we find out that demand is high, should we expand? (Such problems are always worked "backwards.") That is, after 1 year, is it worthwhile to invest an additional $1,000,000 to obtain $40,000 per week instead of $16,000 per week for the remaining 19 years of plant life? The additional net profit due to expansion is

$$\text{additional net profit} = \sum_{j=1}^{19} (40,000 - 16,000)(52)\left(\frac{1}{1.25}\right)^j$$

This is an annuity of $(24,000)(52) per year for 19 years. An annuity can be evaluated using the formula given in Chapter 2 or using an annuity table. The formula from Chapter 2 gives us

$$A\left[\frac{1 - (1 + i)^{-T}}{i}\right] = (24,000)(52)\left[\frac{1 - (1.25)^{-19}}{0.25}\right]$$
$$= (24,000)(52)(3.942)$$
$$= \$4,920,000$$

total return above investment = 4,920,000 − 1,000,000 = $3,920,000

The firm should expand if it finds itself with a low-capacity plant and high demand. The expansion will pay for itself.

Now Figure 7-1 can be modified to reflect the fact that we know what the second decision will be. Figure 7-2 shows the modification. The total return above the investment can be calculated for each endpoint of the tree. For example, for the branch "build 2000, demand high," the $800,000 investment returns $16,000 per week for 20 years. In addition, at the end of 1 year, the plant expansion worth $3,920,000 will be undertaken. The net present value is

$$(16,000)(52) \sum_{j=1}^{20} \left(\frac{1}{1.25}\right)^j + (3,920,000)\left(\frac{1}{1.25}\right)^1 - 800,000 = \$5,626,000$$

For "build 5000, demand low," the values are

$$(16,000)(52) \sum_{j=1}^{20} \left(\frac{1}{1.25}\right)^j - 1,500,000 = \$1,790,000$$

The other two values are $6,724,000 for "build 5000, demand high" and $2,490,000 for "build low, demand low."

Finally, we can incorporate our estimate of the probability of high demand. We have used a decision tree to formulate the problem and present-value calculations to evaluate the possible outcomes. Now we can use an *expected-value* calculation (see Neter et al., 1982) by multiplying each dollar outcome by its probability of occurrence and summing the results.

Build 5000:   expected net present value = (0.2)(6,724,000)
                                        + (0.8)(1,790,000) = $2,777,000

Build 2000:   expected net present value = (0.2)(5,626,000)
                                        + (0.8)(2,490,000) = $3,117,200

Build nothing: expected net present value = 0

This analysis suggests that Westphal should use a small capacity initially and expand it after 1 year if the demand is high.

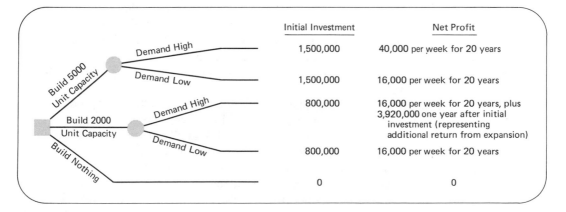

Figure 7-2   Modified decision tree.

Review Problems

1. Since the quantitative analysis above does not contain every consideration, the decision might be either to build 5000 or build 0, in spite of the quantitative analysis. What considerations might cause Westphal to reach those decisions?

2. One important aspect of a good quantitative analysis of a problem is a *sensitivity analysis,* wherein the sensitivity of the decision to possible estimation errors is studied. If the probability of high demand is as high as 0.5, does the decision change?

3. List three factors that are important in locating a new high school that will serve several very small communities.

Solutions

1. If the firm is unable to obtain the necessary capital, they may be forced to build nothing. If they are afraid that the zoning commission may not allow expansion in a year, they might build 5000 units of capacity initially.

2. Build 5000: $(0.5)(6,724,000) + (0.5)(1,790,000) = \$4,257,000$
   Build 2000: $(0.5)(5,626,000) + (0.5)(2,490,000) = \$4,058,000$
   Ms. Westphal would not make the same decision.

3. Possible factors are transportation costs (busing costs, based on where the students are in relation to the possible sites), land and construction costs, nearness of the school to population centers so that the building is accessible for continuing education and other activities, nearness to fire protection, possible political reaction to placing the school in one town (to the exclusion of the others), and so on.

7-2 STRATEGIC ASPECTS OF CAPACITY PLANNING

Determining capacity is one of the most important decisions an organization must face. Capacity planning for the long term is a strategic decision. If capacity is too small, an organization may (1) lose customers, (2) allow competitors to enter the market, or (3) be unable to provide timely service. If capacity is too large, an organization may (1) have difficulty controlling the operations, (2) glut the market and drive down the price, or (3) be unable to pay off a loan obtained to build capacity.

One important capacity planning problem is faced by utility companies. They must plan for future electricity production, given a highly uncertain future (in the United States, consumers are using much less electricity than was predicted a few years ago) and uncertain costs of expansion (nuclear plants cost much more than was predicted a few years ago, for several reasons). Sophisticated quantitative analysis can deal with some of the factors involved. (See Levin et al., 1983, for one approach. See Luss, 1982 and Freidenfelds, 1981, for more references, including references on models of the general capacity expansion problem.) However, policymakers should spend more effort trying to predict utilization of electricity and costs of various technologies for generation of electricity. This capacity expansion problem requires long-range forecasting, quantitative analysis, and judgment.

Many factors are involved in selecting the capacity for both manufacturing and service organizations. In factories, for example, Skinner (1974) argues that a factory should not be so large that it cannot be given a focused set of tasks. That is, a factory should have a mission that is easy to manage. These ideas have caused some managers to artificially separate a plant into multiple parts for organizational purposes. They believe there are some diseconomies of scale in coordinating very large plants. This effect has not been verified using cost data, but it appears to be true in some situations. Thus one strategic question with capacity planning is: Can we manage the new larger facility effectively? If we decide to use smaller factories, the firm still may face the larger capacity question to decide how many to build over the next several years.

The main reason for increasing capacity is to have the capability to satisfy market demand. However, this involves more than just a forecast. In some situations additional capacity is used to enable the firm to respond very quickly to customers or to allow the flexibility to change or modify products to maintain a good product line. Of course, capacity greater than the *average* needed is not really excess if its purpose is to allow a more competitive, service-oriented posture in response to variations in demand.

Some organizations increase capacity to attempt to dominate an industry. Some strategic planning systems (see Chapter 17) stress the value of dominating the market. One way to do that is to have the largest capacity. If the industry now has only 80% of the needed capacity, building a facility that can supply 25% more makes it unprofitable for a competitor to expand. To do so, the competitor would have to cut the price (starting a price war), so that a high return could not be earned. By being first, a company can impose a *barrier to entry*.

Of course, there are risks in selecting capacity strategically. Someone else may have the same idea. For example, in the airline industry (see Braniff, 1974) an S-shaped curve has been used to relate available seats to market share. It is felt that a firm with 60% of the seats on a route between two cities will have more than 60% (say 70%) of the customers. The difficulty is that if all firms know this, they may all add to capacity, systematically ruining their financial health without gaining customers.

Wheelwright (1979) lists an "Eight-Step Process for Capacity and Facilities Planning":

1. Assess company situation and environment.
2. Determine available (existing) capacity.
3. Estimate required capacity.
4. Develop alternative plans for matching required and available capacity.
5. Perform quantitative evaluation of the alternatives.

6. Perform qualitative evaluation of the alternatives.
7. Recommend a course of action.
8. Implement the course of action.

We feel this is a good list, focusing as it does on both quantitative and qualitative analysis, and on implementation. Item 3 is complex. "Estimate" implies a long-range forecast (discussed in Chapter 4), and that is typically difficult. But "required capacity" also involves other factors. We may want excess capacity for marketing purposes or to bar competitors. We may want small capacity so that we can manage it better.

Failure to perform capacity planning can be very costly. The electronics industry was unable to meet demand for personal computers in the first half of the 1980s. But expanding too quickly might cause excess capacity later. The U.S. government supported medical school expansion in the 1960s and 1970s only to face a surplus of doctors in many specialties (an unthinkable idea a few years ago). Organizations must engage in careful capacity planning, and they must consider strategic aspects of that analysis.

Review Problem

Two manufacturing firms in the same industry develop capacity plans. They will each add one plant. Firm A decides to build a plant with capacity less than their forecast of demand and to have it produce only a few products from the line. Firm B decides to build a plant with capacity far in excess of their forecast of demand. How can you explain their plans?

Solution

Firm A may want to have a "focused factory" for managerial reasons. Firm B may want to provide a barrier to entry or provide for long-term growth.

7-3 USING QUEUING ANALYSIS TO DETERMINE SERVICE CAPACITY[1]

Some capacity questions involve the choice of the number of service facilities to have at a location. For example, we may want to determine the number of toll booths, bank tellers, or supermarket checkout counters that should be used. Queuing analysis, discussed in Appendix A, can be used to assist in determining such capacities. We will discuss the use and misuse of these techniques, with several examples.

First, suppose that we want to know how many toll booths to open during peak traffic times. For example, between 4 P.M. and 6 P.M. on the Gotham City

---

[1] This section requires knowledge of Appendix A. It can be skipped here without loss of continuity.

Expressway, cars arrive at a specific outward bound toll area every 7.1 seconds on the average. The service time averages 34.7 seconds and is largely composed of time to drive forward to the booth after the car ahead has pulled out. The analyst believes that the Markov assumption (see Appendix A for a definition) is appropriate, so Table A-2 in Appendix A can be used.

The number of toll booths open must be five or more, since four servers could complete a service every 34.7/4 = 8.675 seconds on the average, which is not sufficient. (Average service time must be less than average interarrival time.) The question is: Should we have six or seven or more toll booths? If the number of cars waiting exceeds 40, traffic jams are caused on access roads. To use Table A-2 in Appendix A we need to know

$$\lambda = \text{arrivals per second} = \frac{1}{7.1} = 0.1408$$

$$\mu = \text{service rate per second} = \frac{1}{34.7} = 0.0288$$

Then

$$\rho = \frac{\lambda}{S\mu} = \text{utilization rate}$$

where

$$S = \text{the number of servers (the decision variable)}$$

$$\rho = \frac{4.889}{S}$$

We will try $S = 5$, 6, and 7. Thus $\rho = 0.98$, 0.81, or 0.70.

Table A-2 gives the average number waiting and the 95th and the 99th percentile of the waiting line. Here we have reproduced the appropriate numbers from that table.

S	Average Number Waiting	95%	99%
5 ($\rho = 0.98$)	46.566	145	225
6 ($\rho = 0.81$)[a]	2.071	10	17
7 ($\rho = 0.70$)	0.702	5	9

[a] As an approximation, $\rho = 0.80$ was used in Table A-2. We could interpolate to obtain a slightly better answer. Those values would be 2.36, 11, and 19; N_q (and perhaps the other values) would be too high since linear interpolation tends to overstate these values.

$S = 5$ is clearly insufficient, since the *average* number waiting exceeds the limit of 40. $S = 6$ is clearly sufficient, since 99% of the time the number waiting will be less than 20. When $S = 6$, the idle time percentage will be $1 - 0.81 = 0.19$, or 19% for each toll booth.

The assumptions used in the foregoing analysis should be investigated briefly. First, the exponential probability law for interarrival time and service time is assumed. That is reasonable here since the most likely times are small, but occasionally a much longer time may result. (For example, someone who has trouble finding change may have a longer service time.) Another assumption made above is that there is a single waiting line. This implies that there would never be an idle server when someone is waiting. Although this is not true, it is close enough, since cars can switch lines and oncoming cars select idle servers.

A more important assumption to question is that of steady state. That is, queuing formulas and tables assume that the system has operated long enough to eliminate any initial effects. If this assumption is not met, and it frequently is not, another form of analysis is necessary. Here, we want to know if steady state can be achieved in a 2-hour time span. The answer is yes; since arrivals occur every 7 seconds, steady state will be reached in a matter of minutes. (If we had a job shop with arrivals every few hours, but jobs are completed so the shop starts empty every day, steady state could not be assumed.)

The second example concerns a set of service representatives who repair large machines such as computers or copying machines. The service office is centrally located within the area served so that the total service time, which consists of travel time plus actual repair time, is likely to be small. Also, the machines seem to need service randomly. Thus, the Markov property can be reasonably assumed. Management believes the system is in steady state. However, there are two kinds of maintenance to be performed: periodic maintenance, every few months, and emergency maintenance when a machine breaks. The emergency maintenance takes priority.

Periodic maintenance jobs arrive every 86 minutes during the business day, on the average. Emergency maintenance jobs arrive every 52 minutes during the business day on the average. Either kind of job can be serviced in an *average* time of 118 minutes, which is composed of 37 minutes of driving time from the representative's present location and 81 minutes of service. An emergency job should have an average waiting time less than 1 hour in the queue, in management's judgment. This waiting time does not include the travel time; travel time is counted as part of the service time. They want to know how many representatives should be assigned to this service area.

The formulas to use in this analysis are given in line IV, Table A-1, Appendix A.

$$\lambda_1 = \text{priority 1 arrival rate} = \frac{1}{52} = 0.01923 \text{ per minute}$$

$$\lambda_2 = \text{priority 2 arrival rate} = \frac{1}{86} = 0.01163 \text{ per minute}$$

$$\mu = \frac{1}{118} = 0.008475$$

Thus

$$\rho_1 = \frac{\lambda_1}{S\mu} = \frac{2.26}{S} \qquad \rho_2 = \frac{\lambda_2}{S\mu} = \frac{1.37}{S}$$

Since $\rho_1 + \rho_2$ must be less than 1.0 (i.e., 100% utilization), we need at least $2.26 + 1.37 = 3.63$ servers to meet the average demand. Since we cannot have a fractional person we will consider numbers of 4 and larger. For $S = 4$:

$$\rho_1 = 0.5650 \qquad \rho_2 = 0.3425 \qquad \rho = \rho_1 + \rho_2 = 0.9075$$

From Table A-1:

$$B_1 = 1 - 0.5650 = 0.4350$$

$$B_2 = 0.4350 - 0.3425 = 0.0925$$

$$A = \frac{\rho/(1 - \rho)}{N_q} \qquad \text{where } N_q \text{ from Table A-2} = 7.09 \text{ at } \rho = 0.90$$

(We could interpolate, yielding $N_q = 8.567$, but linear interpolation overstates N_q and is particularly bad for high ρ values.) Then

$$A \approx \frac{0.9075/0.0925}{7.09} = 1.38$$

and the average number in the queue is

Priority 1: $\qquad \dfrac{\rho_1}{A(1)(B_1)} = \dfrac{0.5650}{1.38(1)(0.4350)} = 0.941$

Priority 2: $\qquad \dfrac{\rho_2}{A(B_2)(B_1)} = \dfrac{0.3425}{(1.38)(0.0925)(0.4350)} = 6.17$

The average waiting time is

Priority 1: $\qquad \dfrac{0.941}{\lambda_1} = \dfrac{0.941}{0.01923} = 48.9 \text{ minutes}$

Priority 2: $\qquad \dfrac{6.17}{\lambda_2} = \dfrac{6.17}{0.01163} = 530 \text{ minutes}$

(These answers are 57.5 and 624 minutes, respectively, if the interpolated value of $N_q = 8.567$ is used.)

Even though there is very little idle time ($0.0925 = 1 - \rho$), and even though regular maintenance waits almost 9 hours (in excess of 1 working day), the limit on average waiting for emergency orders is met. Emergency jobs wait less than 1 hour on the average. The total time before a machine is operative again would be 48.9 plus the service time of 118 minutes, on the average. A broken machine is operative within 3 hours, on the average. The priority system is doing its job, and four servers are sufficient.

Review Problems

In some queuing situations there is a finite number of potential customers. For example, in one of Salt Ridge Baking Company's plants there are 30 mixing machines that frequently need very minor maintenance. In fact, a machine runs for $1\frac{1}{3}$ hours on the average before requiring service, which takes $\frac{1}{20}$ hour on the average. There are finite queuing tables (see Peck and Hazlewood, 1958, for example) which give values that allow you to compute N_q, the average number of nonfunctioning machines in the maintenance queue, and other quantities, such as the average number of running machines and the average waiting time in the queue (T_q). Using such a table to investigate the problem above, Salt Ridge found the following.

S	N_q	T_q (Hours)	Average Number of Working Machines
1	4.41	0.239	24.67
2	0.36	0.017	28.57
3	0.06	0.003	28.86

1. Since a machine breaks down every $\frac{1}{3}$ hours on the average, the arrival rate per working machine is $\frac{3}{4}$ maintenance demands per hour. The service rate is 20 per hour. If there are 30 machines, why is one server able to service the machines even though the arrival rate of $(\frac{3}{4})(30) = 22\frac{1}{2}$ exceeds the service rate of 20 per hour?

2. If the firm had one server for each machine, the machines would never wait in a queue. However, they still would be out of service 3 minutes for every 80 minutes they run, on the average. How many working machines would the firm have on the average?

3. What can you say about the number of servers that might be a reasonable choice? Why?

Solutions

1. The number of machines arriving per hour is $\frac{3}{4}$ times the number of running machines, not $\frac{3}{4}$ times 30. (A broken machine cannot break again until it is fixed.) For one server, 24.67 is the average number of working machines, and $(24.67)(\frac{3}{4}) = 18.5 < 20$. Thus one server can keep most of the machines working.

2. The machines would work 80 of every 83 minutes, or $80/83 = 0.9639$ of the time. $(30)(0.9639) = 28.92$ of the machines would be working on the average.

3. The third server (or servers past the third) does not appear useful (unless each machine generates thousands of dollars of profit every day). However, we cannot choose between one and two servers without knowing the opportunity loss of an idle machine and the cost of an extra repair person.

7-4 SYSTEMS ANALYSIS OF MULTILOCATION PROBLEMS

An organization, such as Salt Ridge, that is considering the location and capacity of several facilities must view the entire system in a holistic way.   Each location's impact on other locations must be analyzed.

Before initiating a multilocation analysis, a manager should determine the objectives of the system.   For Salt Ridge, the objective of the multiplant system may be to maximize the net present value of the firm's profits.   The manager probably has to stay within a budget constraint for new construction in achieving this objective.   Profit-making organizations can consider investments in capacity using present-value methods.   They must also balance short-term and long-term investments to maintain their economic viability through time.

However, nonprofit organizations typically face the additional difficulty of having a nonmonetary objective to be balanced against the cost of reaching that objective.   For example, the managers of a regional health plan must consider the cost–benefit trade-offs of spending additional dollars to provide some additional health care.   Similarly, a plan for locating fire stations must be devised considering the reduction in property damage and loss of life that is attainable by properly allocating extra tax dollars to fire protection.   (In this section we will briefly examine two studies of location problems of this type.)   In such cases there are two levels of decision.   The top-level decision involves the amount of budget allocation for a particular service.   That decision is typically made by political units (city councils, for example) over long periods of time.   The other level is that of the operating manager who decides how to allocate the total available budget to particular locations and services.

In preparation for location decisions, a manager must consider who the customers are and what service they want or need.   For example, some customers may care more about dependable resupply within 2 weeks than about a high probability of immediate resupply, if it is possible to accurately forecast the need for the item.   In that case relatively few warehouse locations, each with adequate inventories, and a dependable transportation system may be an optimal warehousing system.   In a retail situation, if the firm's product has many close competitors, the product can only be sold by making it easily available.   This implies having many locations, close to large populations.   The interaction of the nature of the product or service and the demand for the product or service must be a central part of the analysis.

In locating fire stations, the objectives of reducing damage and injury are met by being able to respond quickly to the alarm.   Research has shown that a few minutes difference can reduce damage dramatically.   The location decision must be based on a knowledge of the type of risks present in each area of a city, and a history of what has occurred in each area.   Different areas must be treated differently.   Certain areas have petroleum tanks, some areas have many false alarms (in large cities at end-of-school time a large fraction of alarms near schools are false alarms), and other areas have high population densities.

In managing a fire department there are many decisions to be made concerning location and capacity. The first is how many locations to have and what capacity (number and type of fire trucks) to have at each. This problem is complicated by barriers to travel, such as lakes, parks, and rivers (see Larson and Sadiq, 1983). Once that decision is made several important decisions remain. Kolesar and Walker (1974) have studied the relocation of units. The fire department must decide what units to send to an alarm. (The answer will depend on the area of the city.) However, the department must also decide whether to send a backup unit to a fire station that has all its units out on call. Doing so, according to an optimum plan, has been found to improve system performance.

Several comments are in order here. First, part of the systems analysis is asking the right question. In the case above, someone thought of the idea of moving firefighting units other than to fight a fire—to position them for maximum coverage. Second, the objective is not completely clear, but it is highly likely that faster response leads to less damage and injury. Thus the objective of reducing response time is appropriate. Third, the amount of movement that occurs can be used to modify the basic fixed facility locations as time progresses. Finally, it makes almost no sense to attack any system other than the entire city's problem, since the units are interdependent in their use.

In the firefighting case, some of the facilities go to the customers. This is also true for ambulance service, visiting nurses, and so on. In other situations, such as locating primary care health facilities for a geographically dispersed population (see Abernathy and Hershey, 1972, and Giglio, 1977, Chaps. 1 to 3) or in locating retail stores over time, within a constrained budget (see Lilien and Rao, 1976), the customers must come to the facility location. In these situations the attraction of customers to the facility is the key variable.

The Abernathy and Hershey study provides another example of planning locations to take advantage of differences in the regions. In their study the population was grouped into several categories by volume of health care demands. (Older people require more health care, for example.) They present solutions for the best single location, pair of locations, and so on. The methodology involves optimizing a chosen criterion using a computerized search routine. The study's results illustrate the importance of choosing a proper objective. Abernathy and Hershey use four different criteria, and the resulting locations are quite different. The four criteria are:

1. *Maximize utilization.* This objective requires data on how many people of a given type will come to a facility that is x miles distant. The objective is to see as many people as possible.

2. *Minimize average distance per capita.* This requires only the location and number of people who may use the facility or facilities. The objective is to minimize the distance to the closest facility, summed over the entire population.

3. *Minimize distance per visit.* This calculates the average distance only for actual customers. People who choose not to use the facilities are not included, and more weight is given to the more frequent users.

4. *Minimize percent degradation in utilization.* This is a measure of lost sales. If we had a facility next door to every individual, we would get a specified amount of utilization. How much less (as a percent) utilization does the current set of facilities obtain?

These four objectives will lead to different locations, as you will discuss in the Review Problem below. One of the main points of this section is that the right question must be asked. That includes using reasonable objectives and considering reasonable alternatives. In the health facilities case, the objective to use is not clear. In the fire protection case, an improvement was made by relocating fire-fighting units away from their home base. It would have been possible to never consider that option.

Good systems analysis also calls for studying the right system. In location–capacity problems, that is usually the entire system. It may be necessary to study the system as it changes over time. In the next two sections, we will study quantitative methods that are used to investigate problems of this type (and return to the Salt Ridge Bakery Company's problems). This section has had the purpose of reminding us that the thought and analysis which occur before a quantitative technique can be used are typically more important than what technique is used.

Review Problem

Pick two of the different criteria suggested in the Abernathy–Hershey study of health facility location, and describe how the two optimal solutions would differ.

Solution

Criterion 1 would concentrate locations near large numbers of distance-sensitive individuals who are likely to use the facility if it is available. Criterion 3 will locate near large numbers of users but will perhaps ignore some individuals for whom distance is a barrier. Criterion 2 treats all individuals as equally likely to use the facility. It acts as if being available to all individuals was the goal, and a solution will put facilities near population centers regardless of the characteristics of the population. Criterion 4 will cause locations similar to those chosen by criterion 1. It is easy to imagine policymakers being concerned about the poor or elderly and using objective 1. It is also easy to imagine policymakers choosing to make health care widely available and selecting criterion 2. Neither approach is right or wrong, but a clear knowledge of objectives will enable managers to better pursue the stated goals.

7-5 *MATHEMATICAL PROGRAMMING FOR CAPACITY AND LOCATION ANALYSIS*[2]

The Salt Ridge Bakery Company has a distribution planning linear program that is used to determine which plants will ship to what market areas. The linear program (LP) is run after capacity changes or when demand patterns have changed enough to warrant a reexamination of the production–distribution pattern. Sharon Westphal would like to know if there are any weaknesses in their current use of the LP and, further, if the LP can be used to help them plan the location and capacity of new plants. In order to facilitate the discussion, the costs and other information about the LP model are given below.

| Plants: | A, B, C | 3 different plant locations |
| Customer areas: | 1, 2, 3, 4, 5, 6, 7, 8, 9, 10 | 10 different customer area locations |

Production costs, in dollars per pound of product, and capacities, in pounds per day, are:

Plant A: $0.347/lb;   capacity = 1,800,000 lb/day

Plant B: $0.326/lb;   capacity = 4,000,000 lb/day

Plant C: $0.351/lb;   capacity = 1,600,000 lb/day

Transportation costs are given in Table 7-2.

TABLE 7-2 TRANSPORTATION COSTS IN DOLLARS PER POUND OF PRODUCT, SALT RIDGE BAKERY COMPANY

FROM PLANT	TO CUSTOMER IN AREA:									
	1	2	3	4	5	6	7	8	9	10
A	0.021	0.024	0.019	0.048	0.037	0.029	0.020	0.041	0.050	0.047
B	0.039	0.029	0.040	0.027	0.024	0.023	0.041	0.034	0.034	0.035
C	0.035	0.034	0.029	0.026	0.032	0.041	0.032	0.019	0.018	0.018

Westphal investigated the basis for these cost figures and believes they are appropriate marginal costs to use in making distribution decisions. (However, we must remember that if adding a new plant or retiring an old plant is being considered, the fixed costs of operation must be included in the analysis.) The cost that is relevant to choosing a plant to use in meeting a certain area's demand is the production cost plus the trai sportation cost. This means we should add 0.347 to each element in the first row of Table 7-2, 0.326 to each element in the second row, and 0.351 to each element in the third row. These figures are shown in Table 7-3.

[2] This section requires a knowledge of linear programming, which is described in Appendix C.

TABLE 7-3 TRANSPORTATION PLUS PRODUCTION COSTS ($/LB), SALT RIDGE
BAKERY COMPANY

FROM PLANT	TO CUSTOMER IN AREA:									
	1	2	3	4	5	6	7	8	9	10
A	0.368	0.371	0.366	0.395	0.384	0.376	0.367	0.388	0.397	0.394
B	0.365	0.355	0.366	0.363	0.350	0.349	0.367	0.360	0.360	0.361
C	0.386	0.385	0.380	0.377	0.383	0.392	0.383	0.370	0.369	0.369

The demands per day are fairly constant. Estimates of the demand rates
are given below (in millions of pounds per day).

	AREA									
	1	2	3	4	5	6	7	8	9	10
Demand (million lb/day)	0.5	0.8	0.5	0.9	0.9	0.8	0.6	0.6	0.8	0.7

There is a total capacity of 7.4 million pounds per day. There is a total
demand of 7.1 million pounds per day. The linear programming formulation that
will solve for an optimal (in terms of production and transportation cost) distribution
plan is given below. It is a transportation type of linear program.

Define

X_{ij} = units, in millions of pounds, produced at plant i and shipped to
area j; $i = A, B, C$ and $j = 1, 2, \ldots, 10$

C_{ij} = cost of 1 unit (million pounds) of product produced at plant i
and shipped to area j; for example, $C_{A1} = \$368,000$, which is
0.368 from Table 7-3, times 1 million pounds per unit.

CAP_i = capacity, in millions of pounds per day, of plant i

DEM_j = demand, in millions of pounds per day, in area j

Then the LP formulation is

minimize
$$\sum_{i=A}^{C} \sum_{j=1}^{10} C_{ij} X_{ij} \qquad (1)$$

subject to
$$\sum_{j=1}^{10} X_{ij} \leq \text{CAP}_i \qquad i = A, B, C \qquad (2)$$

$$\sum_{i=A}^{C} X_{ij} = \text{DEM}_j \qquad j = 1, 2, \ldots, 10 \qquad (3)$$

$$X_{ij} \geq 0 \qquad \begin{array}{l} i = A, B, C \text{ and} \\ j = 1, 2, \ldots, 10 \end{array} \qquad (4)$$

The formulation minimizes total production and transportation costs subject to staying within each plant's capacity and satisfying all demands. The first set of constraints requires that the sum of each plant's total production (the sum of the units shipped to all areas from that plant) must be less than or equal to the plant's capacity. The second set of constraints requires that the total of the units shipped into an area (the sum of the units shipped from all plants to the area) must equal the demand in that area.

The optimal solution to the Salt Ridge Bakery Company problem is as follows:

$$X_{A1} = 0.5 \quad \text{(million pounds)} \quad X_{B2} = 0.8$$

$$X_{A3} = 0.5 \qquad\qquad\qquad\qquad X_{B4} = 0.9$$

$$X_{A7} = 0.6 \qquad\qquad\qquad\qquad X_{B5} = 0.9$$

$$X_{C9} = 0.8 \qquad\qquad\qquad\qquad X_{B6} = 0.8$$

$$X_{C10} = 0.7 \qquad\qquad\qquad\qquad X_{B8} = 0.6$$

Plant B's capacity is fully utilized. Plants A and C have 0.2 and 0.1 million pounds of slack capacity, respectively. No area is served by more than one plant, but that is a coincidence; it will not necessarily happen in an LP of this type.

Having found a solution, Westphal examined the answers to see if the solution changed any of the cost figures. In particular, she feels that a plant operating at less than 80% capacity will have substantially higher costs per pound. In this case the lowest utilization is 0.89, at plant A, and it is safe to use the solution given. The present use of the LP model seems appropriate. The LP could, in practice, be much larger than the one above, since there might be more plants (perhaps 20) and many more market areas (perhaps as many as 1000). Computer solution of such an LP is easily accomplished. We kept the size small only to allow us to present the data and solution in a small space.

Salt Ridge is considering three plans for expansion, since plant C needs to be replaced due to age. Two of the alternative plans are to build a new plant at the plant C site, with either 2 million or 4 million pounds per day of capacity. The other plan is to increase the capacity of plant B, to a total of 6 million pounds per day of capacity. Can LP be used to help management make this decision?

To use LP we need to know the marginal cost of production in each proposed facility. The marginal cost of production is 0.326 at the plant B expansion, 0.320 at the 4 million pound unit at site C, and 0.335 at the 2 million pound unit at site C. The annual fixed costs of operation must be considered. However, these are expected to be the same in each of the three cases, so we can ignore them. (The larger plant would include more automated equipment, so that the annual fixed costs of operation are the same as for the smaller plant.) The investment required is $18,000,000 for either of the 2 million pound capacity units and $34,000,000 for the 4 million pound capacity unit. The firm does have the option of staying with their current capacity. If the old plant *C* is removed, it has a salvage value of zero.

LP can be used for each of the four possible capacity plans separately. The resulting daily costs can be compared, and the improvement due to the investment can be computed. We can see if the improvement is sufficient to warrant the investment of $18 or $34 million.

To illustrate the method, we can initially assume that demand will not change in the near future. Then we have four LPs to run. The capacities would be changed appropriately for each one, and the C_{ij} figures would be calculated using Table 7-2 and the new production cost figures given above. The total cost would be part of the computer output. The four daily costs, the result of four runs, are given below.

LP1	LP2	LP3	LP4
Original capacities	Close plant *C* and expand plant *B*	Build new 2 million pound plant *C*	Build new 4 million pound plant *C*
Daily cost = $2,561,600	Daily cost = $2,547,300	Daily cost = $2,533,100	Daily cost = $2,469,700

Several comments should be made about details not reported in the preceding summary of the solutions. In LP2 and LP3, plant *A* is used only to 55% utilization. In LP4 plant *A* is not used at all. Also, demand for the product may be increasing. If we set those considerations aside momentarily, we can analyze the investment in new plant capacity. Westphal tells us there are 300 working days in 1 year.

Plant *B* expansion (LP2) can be eliminated since the new plant *C* (2 million pounds) costs the same and gives a larger cost reduction.

The 2 million pound capacity plant *C* results in a saving of 2,561,600 − 2,533,100 = $28,500 per day. This is (28,500)(300) = $8,550,000 per year, for an investment of $18,000,000. Even with a discount factor of 40% that is a good investment. (See the discussion in Chapter 2 to refresh your memory regarding time discounting.)

The 4 million pound capacity plant *C* results in a further saving (compared to the 2 million pound capacity) of 2,533,100 − 2,469,700 = $63,400 per day. This is (300)(63,400) = $19,020,000 per year, for an additional investment of $16,000,000. The investment is profitable at any reasonable discount rate. The analysis above thus suggests the LP4 plan, with a new 4 million pound plant *C*.

However, several important considerations were left out of the foregoing analysis. For example, in LP2 and LP3, the 55% utilization of plant *A* would almost certainly increase costs, making those plans less attractive. But those plans are less attractive than LP4 anyway. Before accepting the LP4 plan, Westphal must consider the benefit or loss of closing plant *A*. She must also consider the predicted growth in demand and how the new capacity plan will fare when demand grows. In fact, LP's should be run using a 5- or 10-years-hence forecast. It may be that plant *A and* both 4 million pound plants will be needed. The analysis is far from complete, but it appears that Westphal and Salt Ridge should invest in the new, large plant at site *C*, since demand is expected to grow; we cannot be sure without further analysis, which we will leave to the firm.

Integer Programming and Plant Capacity

Many problems involving mathematical programs have a structure similar to the problem above. A plant is there or it is not. We have 0 or 1 plant of a given capacity at a given site. Such problems can be formulated using *integer variables*, and the technique for solving such problems is called *integer linear programming* (IP). A detailed discussion of integer programming is beyond the scope of the text. However, it is important to know that methods very different from LP are used, and solutions are much more difficult to obtain. Using integer programming in problems of a locational type is discussed by Ross and Soland (1977), Walker (1976), and Geoffrion and Graves (1974). The latter two references illustrate the use of integer programming approaches in large problems. Until recently large integer programs could not be solved, owing to their computational difficulty. Advances in computer technology and IP solution methods are surmounting these problems, and practical use of integer programming is increasing. Some recent research is discussed by Barr et al. (1981) and Crowder et al. (1983).

As an example of a formulation using an integer variable, suppose we consider the possible expansion of plant *B* in the Salt Ridge case to be a new plant, *D*, with the same costs as plant *B*. Define a new variable, δ_D, which is 1 if plant *D* is used and 0 if plant *D* is not used. (δ is the lowercase Greek letter delta.) The integer programming computer code restricts δ_D to be one of these two integers. We can write a new capacity constraint:

$$\sum_{j=1}^{10} X_{Dj} \leq (\delta_D)(2.0) \tag{5}$$

Because δ_D will be 0 or 1, the right-hand side (capacity) is either 0 or 2.0 million pounds. The objective function would have to include the daily equivalent cost of the investment if $\delta_D = 1$. That is, the product (fixed cost)(δ_D) would be added to the objective function. [See capital budgeting texts such as Bierman and Smidt, 1984, for a discussion of equivalent annual (or daily) costs.] We would also constrain:

$$\delta_D = 0 \text{ or } 1 \tag{6}$$

The formulation would be almost identical to the previous one; we would incorporate plant *D* in equations (1) to (4), include equations (5) and (6), and add "daily equivalent investment cost" times δ_D to the objective function (1). The computer would then have the choice of using the new plant if it would reduce production–transportation costs by more than the investment cost. All four possible capacity plans could be included similarly; the IP would need to have three integer variables, one for each method of increasing capacity.

This brief introduction is not intended to leave you with an understanding of the complex area of integer programming formulations and solutions. It is intended only to give you a feeling for how such formulations can be written and when they are appropriate. In this example, integer variables were used to include or exclude the fixed cost of a new plant, depending on whether the program uses any of the facility or not. An attempt to do this with continuous variables would allow *part* of the fixed cost and part of the facility to be included; this would be a serious error in this all-or-nothing situation.

Other mathematical programming formulations have been given to deal with the timing, sizing, and location decisions in a capacity plan (see Rao and Rutenberg, 1977). However, whether advanced techniques such as these or the simpler techniques of decision trees and capital budgeting are used, the analysis must be based on a good long-range forecast and a proper system definition.

Review Problems

1. In the formulation given in equations (1) to (4) there are 30 variables and 13 constraints other than the $X_{ij} \geq 0$ constraints. Using the cost data from Table 7-3 and the demand and capacity information given in the first part of the chapter, completely write out the objective function and each of the 13 constraints. That is, write the formulation without using summation notation.

2. If Salt Ridge wanted to solve the LP using a forecast of demand 5 years hence, which is 40% higher than the current demand rates, and if they wanted to consider using the 4 million pound capacity plant C, what would change from your answer to 1? (Do not write the entire formulation; just say what would change.)

Solutions

1. Minimize $368{,}000X_{A1} + 371{,}000X_{A2} + 366{,}000X_{A3} + 395{,}000X_{A4}$
   $+ 384{,}000X_{A5} + 376{,}000X_{A6} + 367{,}000X_{A7} + 388{,}000X_{A8}$
   $+ 397{,}000X_{A9} + 394{,}000X_{A10} + 365{,}000X_{B1} + 355{,}000X_{B2}$
   $+ 366{,}000X_{B3} + 363{,}000X_{B4} + 350{,}000X_{B5} + 349{,}000X_{B6}$
   $+ 367{,}000X_{B7} + 360{,}000X_{B8} + 360{,}000X_{B9} + 361{,}000X_{B10}$
   $+ 386{,}000X_{C1} + 385{,}000X_{C2} + 380{,}000X_{C3} + 377{,}000X_{C4}$
   $+ 383{,}000X_{C5} + 392{,}000X_{C6} + 383{,}000X_{C7} + 370{,}000X_{C8}$
   $+ 369{,}000X_{C9} + 369{,}000X_{C10}$

   subject to

   $$X_{A1} + X_{A2} + X_{A3} + X_{A4} + X_{A5} + X_{A6} + X_{A7} + X_{A8} + X_{A9} + X_{A10} \leq 1.8$$
   $$X_{B1} + X_{B2} + X_{B3} + X_{B4} + X_{B5} + X_{B6} + X_{B7} + X_{B8} + X_{B9} + X_{B10} \leq 4.0$$
   $$X_{C1} + X_{C2} + X_{C3} + X_{C4} + X_{C5} + X_{C6} + X_{C7} + X_{C8} + X_{C9} + X_{C10} \leq 1.6$$

$$X_{A1} + X_{B1} + X_{C1} = 0.5$$
$$X_{A2} + X_{B2} + X_{C2} = 0.8$$
$$X_{A3} + X_{B3} + X_{C3} = 0.5$$
$$X_{A4} + X_{B4} + X_{C4} = 0.9$$
$$X_{A5} + X_{B5} + X_{C5} = 0.9$$
$$X_{A6} + X_{B6} + X_{C6} = 0.8$$
$$X_{A7} + X_{B7} + X_{C7} = 0.6$$
$$X_{A8} + X_{B8} + X_{C8} = 0.6$$
$$X_{A9} + X_{B9} + X_{C9} = 0.8$$
$$X_{A10} + X_{B10} + X_{C10} = 0.7$$

Even for this small LP, writing out the complete formulation is a pain. That is why we use summation and index notation.

2. The plant C capacity would change from 1.6 to 4.0. All 10 plant C costs in the objective function would be reduced by 0.031 due to the 0.351 to 0.320 production cost reduction. Finally, all demand figures would be 40% higher; the new values would be $(1.4)(0.5) = 0.7$, $(1.4)(0.8) = 1.12$, 0.7, 1.26, 1.26, 1.12, 0.84, 0.84, 1.12, and 0.98.

7-6 MODELS FOR WAREHOUSE LOCATION

Mathematical and computer models have been applied to warehouse location problems with notable success. There are several reasons for this. First, warehouses incur much of the transportation and inventory cost in a firm and very little of the labor cost. The transportation–inventory costs are relatively easy to measure. Thus quantifiable considerations often dominate the warehouse location decision. Second, many companies have 20 to 100 warehouses, so that all possible combinations of the locations of the warehouses cannot be considered in any reasonable way, and the firm may require a computer to aid in the choice. Third, warehouses are inexpensive compared to plants, so a warehouse can be closed or bought or sold without a large loss. The advent of public warehouses (where firms rent space rather than own it) makes it even easier to relocate a warehouse. Thus a company can seriously consider redesigning its warehouse locations more often that it can add a new plant.[3] (There are, of course, large relocation costs involved in shifting warehouse sites, but they are small compared to shifting plant sites.)

The models used fall basically into one of two types: computer simulation,

---

[3] Warehouse location models are also applicable to public agencies. One interesting application, to tax collection in Texas, is given by Fitzsimmons and Allen (1983).

with or without "heuristic" methods, and integer programming approaches. We will not discuss all the models, choosing instead to concentrate on a few. As with most mathematical models, insights can be gained by thinking through the models, and these insights can help a manager deal with the problem.

Simulation[4] models are attractive for warehouse location because, unlike linear programming, they are not limited to linear cost functions. Transportation costs, for example, depend in a nonlinear way on the volume of traffic. The cost of operating a warehouse is an increasing function of the volume handled, but the marginal cost per unit is typically a decreasing (and nonlinear) function of volume. To use a simulation model the manager must specify these functions, but the choice is not limited to linear forms.

The earliest major simulation model for the warehouse location problem was published by Shycon and Maffei (1960). They made a serious effort to incorporate the many real-world complexities involved in managing such systems. The model has been updated since that time. (See Shycon and Sprague, 1975.) The data needs of the model are prodigious. The location of the customers and the anticipated volume of demand must be broken down by type of products used and the typical size of order. For each potential warehouse site management must know the investment required (if any; remember there are public warehouses), the fixed cost of operation, and a variable cost per unit. Transportation cost to the warehouse and local delivery cost to the customer are a function of many items; the relationships must be specified. Finally, the factories must be identified as to their location and capacity for each product.

Prior to using the computer model, large orders that will be filled directly from the plant are selected and eliminated from further consideration. Then, once a set of warehouses is selected, the model uses an LP to plan the plant-to-warehouse shipment pattern, and each customer is served by the nearest warehouse. The cost of operating the entire system is then computed. (The demands are deterministic, not random as in many smaller simulations.)

A set of warehouses is selected in one of two ways. A manager can specify a set of locations to be tried, or a *heuristic* program will search for a solution. The heuristic program is a series of rules that have been programmed to look for improvements in the pattern. We will discuss heuristics further below. The interaction of the manager and the computer is important. Even a complex model cannot incorporate all the real-world considerations. A manager can apply judgment in addition to the cost considerations of the model. The model is used, appropriately, to support the manager rather than to make the decision.

Shycon and Sprague (1975) attempt to incorporate one more real-world factor into the use of the model. It is believed by many marketing people that a warehouse in an area will cause sales to increase because of the firm's *presence* in the market. If that is so, a firm might choose to have more warehouses than the number that would minimize transportation and inventory cost. This effect

---

[4] Computer simulation techniques are discussed in Appendix B.

is very important, and it is very difficult to deal with. Good information from your customers and a feel for your particular industry must be used.

In another early modeling effort, Kuehn and Hamburger (1963) use simulation and allow complex cost relationships. The heuristics they use to generate potentially good solutions to be tested depend on the following ideas:

A. Good locations for warehouses will be near demand concentrations, to reduce local delivery costs. Thus the number of potential sites is drastically reduced.

B. A good set of locations can be derived by adding one warehouse to the set you have, until no new warehouse reduces cost by more than the cost of the warehouse.

C. At each stage the site to be added can be chosen by completely evaluating only a few promising sites.

The procedure to develop a set of locations is as follows:

1. Using only the savings generated by local delivery costs, pick a few promising sites. (This amounts to selecting large demand centers that are not currently near a warehouse.)

2. Analyze the total impact of each of the sites chosen from 1. That is, obtain the simulated cost of the entire system if each new site is added.

3. Add the best site from 2 and return to 1. Stop when no new site improves the total cost.

4. See if warehouses can be moved slightly (to a neighboring city) to improve overall performance. This step is called the "bump-and-shift" routine.

The ideas used to reduce the search are reasonable, but B is the easiest to question. It may not be possible to reach a good solution by adding warehouses one at a time if only a few warehouses are to be acquired. For example, consider five potential sites, along a long road.

1   2   3   4   5

It may be that the best solution is to have two warehouses, one at 2 and one at 4. However, the heuristic would first locate a warehouse at 3, making it unprofitable to add a warehouse at 2 or 4. You should convince yourself that this problem is not as likely to occur if 20 warehouses are to be located in the entire United States. However, in using any heuristic, you should try to conceive of the situations in which it will perform poorly; then you can decide whether or not to trust it in the situation at hand.

Integer programming formulations for warehouse location are more restrictive as to the cost representation than simulation models are. They can allow a fixed cost for having a location plus a linear cost per unit volume handled. However, their strong point is the ability to automatically eliminate and/or evaluate thousands of possible combinations of sites—far more than is feasible with simulation.

Integer programming models for location were discussed briefly in Section 7-4. Geoffrion and Graves (1974) give an example, applied to a large distribution system design. A description of some problems and methods is given by Geoffrion (1975) and by Revelle et al. (1970) for location problems in general. An extensive bibliography of location theory is given by Francis and Goldstein (1974). A discussion of the managerial insight to be gained using location analysis is given by Geoffrion and Powers (1980).

One major problem with location models, including those discussed above, is that they are static models; demand at one point in time is used to design the system. In fact, demand patterns shift, with demand rising in some regions and falling in others, through time. Warehouse location must consider the shifts in demand since warehouses deal directly with the customers. Plant location decisions should also be made considering shifts in demand, but they will have a smaller effect. For location of service facilities, shifts in demand patterns are, again, of prime importance.

One simplistic model of dealing with demand shifts is given in Ballou (1973), based on his own previous work. Lilien and Rao (1976) give a model for planning expansion of the number of facilities over time. Grote (1980), Van Roy and Erlenkotter (1982), and Denardo et al. (1982) use mathematical programming models to analyze dynamic location problems. However, managers can deal with shifting demands by using a one period location model in an appropriate way. First, of course, a forecast of the shifts in demand must be obtained. This is based on major promotional plans as well as shifts in population. Then a manager must obtain a solution that will perform well now, and still perform well (or be changeable so as to perform well) during the life of the facilities. This calls for an interactive use of the model by the manager. Capital constraints, service-level goals, and many other items would also be considered in making final judgments.

Review Problems

1. If a firm wants to locate 20 warehouses at 1000 possible warehouse sites, why can't they just have the computer evaluate all possible combinations?

2. Why is the actual design of a warehouse system even more complex than the problem posed in Review Problem 1?

3. Why is the design of Salt Ridge Bakery Company's system of plants different from a warehouse location problem? Briefly give two important differences.

Solutions

1. Because there are $(1000)(999) \cdots (981)/(20)(19) \cdots (1) = (0.34) \times 10^{42}$ possible combinations. This number of combinations cannot be evaluated, by even the fastest computers, in a distribution manager's lifetime.

2. Because the number of warehouses to have is also a decision variable, and because the optimal pattern of warehouse locations changes over time.

3. Because the plants incur a much larger labor cost and entail more investment

than a warehouse, and because the final customer is a large-scale consumer (a supermarket). Thus there are no "local" delivery costs in the same sense as in many warehouse systems.

7-7 Summary

Capacity decisions typically involve larger investments than any other faced by the organization. Capacity determines the organization's ability to deal with changes in the environment, including changes in demand, product line, and competition. Moreover, the scale of operations frequently affects the ambience of the work situation; large plants may be more automated and less personal, for example. In short, these decisions are of prime importance to the organization, whether it is a profit-making or a nonprofit organization.

Location decisions determine the organization's proximity to customers and, thus, the organization's ability to sell its product or service. Also, many of the organization's employees must live near the facility. (This often includes the person who is choosing the location.) Locations can be selected to reduce and control transportation and inventory costs, which are large for many organizations. Location and capacity decisions are frequently tied together, involving the organization's highest-level policies and policymakers. Managers make capacity decisions for many strategic reasons, including controllability, providing barriers to entry, planning for growth, and ability to respond quickly to customers.

This chapter has discussed a variety of capacity–location problems and ways to approach them. Quantitative techniques have been introduced which deal very effectively with the large-scale problems involved. The very basic tool of present-value analysis is needed because the decisions involve long time horizons. This also necessitates the use of forecasting techniques such as those discussed in Chapter 4. Queuing analysis can be used to help select the capacity of certain service facilities, but the technique must be used carefully; frequently, as discussed in Section 7-3, the necessary assumptions are not met.

Multilocation problems have been analyzed using mathematical programming and computer simulation models, as discussed in Sections 7-5 and 7-6. Mathematical programming models can minimize the production and transportation costs of meeting a specified level of demand. Integer programming can consider the fixed costs of building and operating a new facility. Simulation models are not limited to linear cost relationships (or to any specific form of cost relationships), but they do not guarantee a "best" solution from among the possible alternatives. Both mathematical programming and computer simulation have been used extensively in location–capacity decisions.

The basic warning to be given, though, is that a quantitative technique must be used carefully. Because of the importance of the decisions, qualitative as well as quantitative considerations must be included. Further, a static analysis should be avoided; the effect on future decisions and system performance must be considered and is often the determining factor.

From the outset of any capacity–location analysis, the notions of the systems approach must be used. The appropriate system is typically the entire production–distribution system. A narrower view may lead to errors. Also, the right questions must be asked. What are the goals of the organization—now and in the future? (This varies from industry to industry.) Are there nonquantifiable factors which dominate the decision? If not, mathematical techniques can lead to an excellent set of locations and capacities, but it is also possible to misuse techniques and make matters worse.

PROBLEMS

1. What considerations are important in locating a single facility, such as a warehouse, plant, or retail store?

*2. What considerations are most important in determining the location for a new high school in a city where there are two other high schools that will also be in operation?

3. Table 7-1 gives six "location considerations." Describe a type of facility for which item 1, transportation and inventory costs, might be the most important factor. Then do the same for items 2 to 6.

*4. Figure 7-1 shows the returns from the possible Salt Ridge capacity plans, and the problem is analyzed in a before-tax manner in the portion of Section 7-1 that follows Figure 7-1. Use an investment tax credit of 8% of the investment value, a tax rate of 48%, and straight-line depreciation to year 20 (so the expansion would be depreciated over 19 years).
   (a) Redo the analysis using a 10% discount rate on an after-tax basis. (After-tax analysis is discussed in Chapter 2.)
   (b) The probability of "demand high" was estimated to be 0.2, but the manager is unsure of that estimate. Over what range for that probability will "build 2000" still be optimal? (That is, what is the breakeven probability?)

5. A company has $100,000 available to invest in a new plant. If business conditions remain unchanged, the investment will return 15% per year, but, if there is a mild recession, it will return only 3% per year. Alternatively, the money can be invested in government bonds for a sure return of 5%. What probability must management assign to the condition "recession" before the investment in government bonds is the better choice if they want to maximize the expected return?

6. The president of Aviation Electronics is considering how to approach a proposal for building a vertical-takeoff-and-landing plane for use by the military special forces and navy combat ships. If the company submits a proposal, it may obtain the contract or lose it to a competitor. If it wins

the contract, it must then elect whether to build the plane in a new facility from the start or use its present plant. The new plant would be more costly in the construction phase but less costly to operate than using existing facilities if the final prototype is accepted and a long-run production contract obtained. Of course, it is possible to build a new plant at this time, but it would create delays in meeting orders and a subsequent loss of revenue. The design engineers are at the moment considering three possible designs, only one of which can be submitted. Diagram the decision problem. Denote the final return at the end of each branch of the decision-tree diagram by v_1, v_2, and so on. Indicate those portions of the diagram that are management decisions and those that are chance events. (Assume that the final dollar value of the contract order, if development is successful, is fixed and known. That is, it is a certain number rather than an unknown, as in most real cases.) Are the v_i's uncertain? Why or why not? Indicate for each stage how many different costs or probabilities are involved.

*7. A house painting contractor accepts an average of four jobs per month; the arrival rates are closely approximated by the Poisson probability law. He is able to complete a job in about $\frac{1}{5}$ of a month on the average; the actual times are assumed to follow the exponential probability law, since most jobs take only a few days but some commercial jobs take much longer. Each job contributes $300 to profit, and he has negligible fixed costs. Word-of-mouth advertising by satisfied customers has resulted in an increase in potential customers. If he hires an additional painter for his crew, he could decrease the amount of time to paint a house to $\frac{1}{6}$ of a month, but owing to the inefficiency of the new employee, he figures the profit per house would drop to $250. He is worried that any increase in waiting time for customers could result in losing some customers.

   (a) What is his current average monthly profit and how long, on the average, does a customer have to wait before painting begins?
   (b) To make this expansion in business at least as profitable as it is now, what is the minimum number of contracts per month that he would have to receive, on the average? (Presumably sales would increase due to better service; how much of an increase is necessary?)
   (c) For the following arrival rates, determine the average customer waiting time and average monthly profit, assuming that the new painter is hired: 4.2, 4.8, 5.1, 5.4.
   (d) How desirable is this expansion?
   (e) Can you suggest an alternative to the painter and still increase his profits?

8. A bank, through innovative marketing, had recently increased the number of customers. In a memo to branch managers, the vice-president of branch banking had suggested that queuing theory may be appropriate to ensure that customers do not have to wait too long in line, lest they take their business elsewhere. The vice-president stated that an average waiting time

of over 5 minutes was unacceptable. Otto Lone, a branch manager, collected the following data for his branch for a typical week: a teller could process a customer in 1 minute on the average (with process times following the exponential probability law), an average of 150 customers per hour entered the bank (following a Poisson probability law), and five tellers were employed full time. If a customer arrived and each teller was busy, the customer entered a queue that was serviced by all tellers; that is, there was only one line, not a line in front of each teller.

(a) Calculate the average number in the queue (N_q) and the average waiting time (T_q). Is Otto on the right track?

(b) Otto collected some additional data for the period that was the busiest for the branch. He found that 294 customers per hour arrived during the busy period on the average, and the tellers worked at the same rate as before. Calculate N_q and T_q.

(c) What would happen in part (b) if a sixth teller were added? Is average waiting time less than 5 minutes?

(d) Unfortunately, Mr. Lone's budget for this year does not allow him to hire a sixth teller. How can he solve his problem?

(e) The bank's personnel service offers a teller training program which claims to be able to cut 2 seconds off the average teller processing time. During the busiest period, will five tellers be sufficient to reduce average waiting time to 5 minutes or less?

9. In Problem 8, a bank attempted to reduce the average waiting time to less than 5 minutes. (You need not have done Problem 8 to complete this problem.) They found that with $T_s = 58$ seconds they achieved an average waiting time of 3.4 minutes. (They used $\rho = 0.95$ and $S = 5$ to get $N_q = 16.678$ from Table A-2, Appendix A.) The managers are concerned about the length of the line during the busy periods. What can you tell them about how long the line might be occasionally?

*10. A pediatrician in a community clinic wants to determine how many chairs to have in a waiting room. Most of their patients are "walk-ins," so the patient load can vary dramatically from time to time. Patients arrive according to the Poisson probability law at a mean rate of three per hour (assume that each patient is accompanied by one adult). The doctor is able to examine a patient (with the adult also present in the examining room) in 15 minutes on the average. Service times are governed by an exponential probability law.

(a) How many chairs are needed to accommodate the average number of waiting patients and adults?

(b) If the doctor wants to accommodate his patients 95% of the time, how many chairs are needed?

(c) Calculate the average time spent by the patients in the waiting room and suggest a reason why this doctor should place magazines in the waiting room.

11. A supermarket manager notices that during a busy part of the day, when she has six cash registers working, the average time customers spend in line at the registers is 10.2 minutes, and the average time to check out at a register is 3.5 minutes. (Assume Poisson input, exponential checkout times, and a single queue, so that Table A-2, Appendix A, can be used.) The arrival rate into the system is 97.8 customers per hour.

   (a) Is the single queue assumption reasonable?

   (b) If a seventh cash register is opened, what would be the average waiting time?

   (c) Are there any alternatives other than adding a seventh cash register?

*12. A large film manufacturing company employs a maintenance department to keep things working. The maintenance group handles two kinds of jobs—production-line failures (a production line is inoperative until repair is complete) and routine maintenance. Both types of jobs require one pair of maintenance workers (they always work in pairs) and require an average repair time of 2.0 hours. (No travel time is involved.) Repair time follows the exponential probability law. Production line failures are given first priority and arrive at the rate of 0.1 per hour. The second category (priority two jobs) arrive at the rate of 0.6 per hour. Both follow the Poisson probability law. How many pairs of repair personnel must the firm maintain at all times? How long will a priority one job have to wait before service begins, on the average, if they use the minimum number?

13. In Problem 12, the answer indicates that the priority one jobs spend an average of 38 minutes waiting in the queue plus an average of 2.0 hours in service being repaired. The plant manager says that any priority one job must be repaired in 1 hour or less, since the cost of having an inoperative production facility is exorbitant.

   (a) How might a maintenance group be staffed and managed to make this possible?

   (b) How could we evaluate the effect of the policies in part (a)?

*14. A large dairy-products company is redesigning their truck-fleet maintenance department. They want to keep the trucks on the road as much as possible, and, in fact, many of the trucks average 14 or more hours of usage per day, 365 days per year.

   (a) What might "capacity" of the maintenance facility mean?

   (b) What considerations go into deciding on the appropriate capacity of the maintenance facility?

   (c) If they need 25 operative trucks to make the daily runs, what information do they need to determine how many extras to have over and above the 25?

15. The following LP is from the chapter text.

   Minimize $\displaystyle\sum_{i=A}^{C} \sum_{j=1}^{10} C_{ij} X_{ij}$

subject to

$$\sum_{j=1}^{10} X_{ij} \leq CAP_i \qquad \text{for} \quad i = A, B, C$$

$$\sum_{i=A}^{C} X_{ij} = DEM_j \qquad \text{for} \quad j = 1 \text{ to } 10$$

in which X_{ij} = units produced at i and shipped to j.

(a) Explain how this LP could be used to evaluate the *future* returns from an investment in a *new plant* (denoted plant D) whose location has already been determined.

(b) If there are six potential sites for plant D, how can the LP be used?

(c) What other major factor must be considered that cannot be included in the LP?

*16. Ace Beverage Company produces a regionally sold line of soft drinks. They have two plants (A and B) from which they ship to four market areas. Their sales have been growing dramatically. This year's sales forecast and next year's sales forecast are shown below.

SALES FORECAST
(THOUSANDS OF CASES)

Area	This Year	Next Year
1	2000	2500
2	2000	3000
3	4000	5000
4	2000	2000

The two existing plants each have an annual capacity of 5,000,000 cases (5000 units). The firm has decided to build a new plant that will also have a 5000-unit capacity. Otherwise, they will have insufficient capacity next year. The new plant will be at location C or D. The production and transportation costs anticipated for next year are shown below, also in units of thousands of cases.

PRODUCTION
COSTS ($/UNIT)

Site	Cost
Plant A	$1200
Plant B	$1200
Plant C	$1400
Plant D	$1200

TRANSPORTATION COSTS ($/UNIT)

FROM:	Area 1	Area 2	Area 3	Area 4
Plant A	300	200	300	400
Plant B	500	400	350	250
Plant C	500	400	250	400
Plant D	200	300	450	500

(a) Write the LP formulation that would minimize cost, meet demand, and decide what production–shipping pattern to use if plant site C is used. Indicate the changes that would be necessary to consider the plant D location.

(b) How would you decide which site to use?

(c) Without running an LP, which plant site do you prefer and why? (Assume here that both sites cost the same to build and that cost is the only factor.)

17. In Problem 16, we could use an integer linear programming formulation to simultaneously consider both plant sites. Write that formulation. (Refer to Problem 16 for cost, demand, and capacity data.)

*18. In Problem 16, suppose that site D is preferred to site C by the LP cost analysis.

(a) What factors might cause a manager to accept plant site C in spite of that analysis?

(b) What information would you need to see if the firm should invest in either plant? That is, how would they decide if the preferred site is a good investment?

19. A distribution manager is going to completely redesign the company's warehousing and shipping patterns, using public warehouses. What information would be needed? Which of the items mentioned in your list would be most difficult to obtain?

*20. What is the difference between a simulation and a heuristic program?

21. A special distribution planning problem is that faced by a firm with an expanding sales territory. (The company might be a new company with a new product which was sold regionally initially.)

(a) What difficulties would be encountered in using the Kuehn–Hamburger heuristics to develop a warehouse system in this situation?

(b) What are the advantages of using public warehousing vis-à-vis company-owned warehouses in this situation?

22. To save money, a firm is planning to consolidate their plants and warehouses into fewer of each. They are concerned that they might lose sales because they will have a presence in fewer markets. How might they estimate the presence effect without having to try the new plan to observe the effect?

*23. In the airline industry, the belief has been held that the firm with more capacity (available seats) will have a disproportionate share of the customers.

(a) Why might this be true?

(b) Assume that two companies have equal capacity, with a total of 400 available seats each day. Assume they are both barely profitable. If one firm decides to change its capacity, describe what might happen in the short run and the long run.

REFERENCES

ABERNATHY, W. J., AND J. C. HERSHEY, "A Spatial-Allocation Model for Regional Health-Services Planning." *Operations Research,* May–June 1972.

BALLOU, R., *Business Logistics Management.* Englewood Cliffs, N.J.: Prentice-Hall, 1973.

BARR, R., F. GLOVER, AND D. KLINGMAN, "A New Optimization Method for Large Scale Fixed Charge Transportation Problems." *Operations Research,* Vol. 29, No. 3 (May–June 1981).

BIERMAN, H., AND S. SMIDT, *The Capital Budgeting Decision,* 6th ed. New York: Macmillan, 1984.

Braniff International, HBS Case Services, Harvard Business School, Boston, 1974.

CROWDER, H., E. JOHNSON, AND M. PADBERG, "Solving Large Scale Zero–One Linear Programming Problems." *Operations Research,* Vol. 31, No. 5 (September–October 1983).

DENARDO, E., G. HUBERMAN, AND U. ROTHBLUM, "Optimal Locations on a Line Are Interleaved." *Operations Research,* Vol. 30, No. 4 (July–August 1982).

FITZSIMMONS, J. A., AND L. A. ALLEN, "A Warehouse Location Model Helps Texas Comptroller Select Out-of-State Audit Offices." *Interfaces,* Vol. 13, No. 5 (October 1983).

FRANCIS, R., AND J. GOLDSTEIN, "Location Theory: A Selective Bibliography." *Operations Research,* March–April 1974.

FREIDENFELDS, J., *Capacity Expansion: Analysis of Simple Models with Applications.* New York: North-Holland, 1981.

GEOFFRION, A., "A Guide to Computer-Assisted Methods for Distribution Systems Planning." *Sloan Management Review,* Winter 1975.

GEOFFRION, A., AND G. GRAVES, "Multicommodity Distribution System Design by Benders' Decomposition." *Management Science,* January 1974.

GEOFFRION, A. M., AND R. F. POWERS, "Facility Location Analysis Is Just the Beginning." *Interfaces,* Vol. 10, No. 2 (April 1980).

GIGLIO, R., *Ambulatory Care Systems,* Vol. II: *Location, Layout and Information Systems for Efficient Operations.* Lexington, Mass.: D. C. Heath, 1977.

GROTE, B., "Exact and Heuristic Solution Procedures for the Dynamic, Noncapacitated Facilities Location-Allocation Problem," Ph.D. dissertation, Cornell University, 1980.

HESKETT, J., N. GLASKOWSKY, AND R. IVIE, *Business Logistics,* 2nd ed. New York: Ronald Press, 1973.

KHUMAWALA, B., AND C. WHYBARK, "A Comparison of Some Recent Warehouse Location Techniques." *The Logistics Review,* Spring 1971.

KOLESAR, P., AND W. WALKER, "An Algorithm for the Dynamic Relocation of Fire Companies." *Operations Research,* March–April 1974.

KUEHN, A., AND M. J. HAMBURGER, "A Heuristic Program for Locating Warehouses." *Management Science,* July 1963.

LARSON, R., AND G. SADIQ, "Facility Locations with the Manhattan Metric in the Presence of Barriers to Travel." *Operations Research,* Vol. 31, No. 4 (July–August 1983).

LEVIN, N., A. TISHLER, AND J. ZAHAVI, "Time Step vs. Dynamic Optimization of Generation-Capacity-Expansion Programs of Power Systems." *Operations Research,* Vol. 31, No. 5 (September–October 1983).

LILIEN, G., AND A. RAO, "A Model for Allocating Retail Outlet Building Resources across Market Areas." *Operations Research,* January 1976.

LUSS, H., "Operations Research and Capacity Expansion Problems: A Survey." *Operations Research,* September–October 1982.

NETER, J., W. WASSERMAN, AND G. WHITMORE, *Applied Statistics,* 2nd ed. Boston: Allyn and Bacon, 1982.

PECK, L., AND R. HAZELWOOD, *Finite Queuing Tables.* New York: Wiley, 1958.

RAO, R., AND D. RUTENBERG, "Multilocation Plant Sizing and Timing." *Management Science,* July 1977.

REVELLE, C., D. MARKS, AND J. LIEBMAN, "An Analysis of Private and Public Sector Location Models." *Management Science,* July 1970.

ROSS, G. T., AND R. SOLAND, "Modeling Facility Location Problems as Generalized Assignment Problems." *Management Science,* November 1977.

SHYCON, H., AND R. MAFFEI, "Simulation—Tool for Better Distribution." *Harvard Business Review,* November–December 1960.

SHYCON, H., AND C. SPRAGUE, "Put a Price Tag on Your Customer Servicing Levels." *Harvard Business Review,* July–August 1975.

SKINNER, W., "The Focused Factory." *Harvard Business Review,* May–June, 1974.

VAN ROY, T., AND D. ERLENKOTTER, "A Dual-Based Procedure for Dynamic Facility Location." *Management Science,* Vol. 28, No. 10 (October 1982).

WALKER, W., "A Heuristic Adjacent Extreme Point Algorithm for the Fixed Charge Problem." *Management Science,* January 1976.

WHEELWRIGHT, S., ed., *Capacity Planning and Facilities Choice,* Division of Research, Graduate School of Business Administration, Harvard University, Cambridge, Mass., 1979.

PART III

Managing the Production and Delivery of Goods and Services

In Part III the topics are intermediate- and short-range decisions. As in Part II, we begin with a discussion of the methods of obtaining the information needed for the decisions to be faced. However, Chapter 8 deals with different forecasting techniques than Chapter 4 because of the shorter time horizons of the decisions.

Work-force and production plans are often made on an aggregate basis for a period of months in advance, leaving the details to be fleshed out as the actual production time approaches. Chapter 9 describes some of the techniques used for developing less detailed, intermediate-range plans for production of goods and services, and discusses a hierarchical system of planning which assures that the short- and intermediate-range plans and goals will be commensurate.

Chapters 10 to 14 discuss ways of making detailed decisions in several different settings. Chapter 10 discusses inventory ordering systems that are applicable to both service and manufacturing. Chapter 11 develops a method for scheduling the use of a single facility that produces several items and shows how the resulting schedule can fit into intermediate-range production plans. Chapter 11 also discusses the special problem of scheduling a job shop, where the timing of production is less predictable. Chapter 12 describes the material requirements planning (MRP) and just-in-time (JIT) approaches to coordinating multistage manufacturing systems. JIT, MRP, and other production control approaches are compared. The situations discussed in Chapters 10, 11, and 12 involve similar concepts and trade-offs, but the settings are progressively more complex and require different approaches.

In Chapters 13 and 14 the focus changes to one of providing service.

Chapter 13 discusses the service of moving physical goods from manufacturer to consumer. It describes the trade-off between inventory and availability, pointing out that not only the quantity of inventory, but also its physical location determines the effectiveness of supply. Chapter 14 describes some tools for scheduling personnel, including the problems associated with rotating through several shifts. Of particular interest to service systems is the opportunity to schedule the demand through appointment systems or other means, such as price promotions. Other methods of coordinating the consumers and providers of services are also discussed, such as vehicle route selection.

CHAPTER 8

Information Requirements and Forecasting

To undertake the kinds of decisions and planning processes described in this book, the operations manager needs information on costs, capacities, technology, and demands for the product or service to be offered. Sources for this information are many, as discussed in Chapter 2. For example, cost information is supplied by accounting practices, and the capacities and technology to be available in the future depend a great deal on financial investments, both planned and recently undertaken. Demands hinge not only on the marketing strategy of the firm, but on the competition and the economic climate.

In choosing how to gather information, one must consider the time frame of the decision and the level of detail required. These two issues are very closely related, since the necessary level of detail is substantially less for long-range decisions than for short-range decisions. For example, long-range decisions such as plant capacity may require only an overall estimate of the production output of a plant, without detailed reference to individual products; in contrast, short-range decisions typically require reference to individual personnel (for example, work-force scheduling), or individual products (production sequencing decisions).

This portion of the text (Part III) is devoted to short- and intermediate-range decision making. This chapter revisits some of the concepts from Chapter 4, where the focus was on long-range planning. However, the techniques and principles differ because of the different implications of the shorter time horizon. The first section describes some general concepts of information systems for supporting short- and intermediate-range decision making. The remaining sections are devoted to forecasting with primary emphasis on methods which search for patterns in historical data (time series) and use those patterns in projecting future trends.

8-1 INFORMATION SYSTEMS FOR PRODUCTION AND OPERATIONS MANAGEMENT

The two examples below will illustrate some good and some poor information systems, helping us to focus our attention on how information systems are designed to support management decisions. We will not attempt to cover the very broad and important area of management information systems, leaving that to texts on the subject such as Lucas (1982).

Hugeco Manufacturers has a worldwide transaction reporting system. Every sales-related transaction is reported within 24 hours to the home office computer. This immense data file is stored by a transaction code so that it is easy to find out what has happened to any order. The information is transmitted from overseas operations by communications satellite.

This system was established because the company was having difficulties meeting delivery promises and following up on sales. They also had a problem of inventory accumulation. Several items had growing inventories, and total company-wide inventories had tripled in a period of only about 2 years. The information system was part of an overall redesign of the manufacturing and delivery systems. They hoped that sales follow-up would be better, that delivery would be quicker and more predictable, and that inventories would decline. They also hoped that they could use this system to provide information for use in forecasting their individual product sales.

The company found that while their first two objectives were met, inventories continued to grow and forecasting was as difficult, if not more so, than before. The reason was that the incredible level of detail held in the information system made it impossible to obtain useful management summaries by product. For example, it was too expensive to sort through the transactions file to obtain monthly sales for each product for the past several years. That kind of information would be necessary to develop a good forecast, but the excessive detail made the information system useful only for managing day-to-day operations, and not for future management planning, even for 1 month at a time. In this case the company established a separate system to routinely summarize many items, even though it led to redundant data storage.

Farm Supply Corporation has 250 retail stores and three distribution centers (DCs) that are used to supply the stores. Precise inventory records, up to the minute, are maintained for all inventories at the distribution center level. Since the inventory records are updated every time there is any transaction, the inventory system is referred to as a "real-time" or "perpetual" inventory system. The problem is at the store level, where current records are not maintained for inventory, and there are no sales records by item. Therefore, although the firm knows how many units are shipped into a store from the DC, actual sales can be quite different, since many items are sold in very small quantities compared to the size of shipments. Meanwhile, at the corporate level, copious reports are received from the sophisticated information system maintained at the distribution center level. Yet the firm is unable to answer the basic questions of "How much do we have?" and "How much have we sold?".

These two examples lead us to several conclusions.

1. Different uses require different information. The information system must be designed to assist particular managers. This means that the users of the information should be surveyed before any major information systems design project occurs.

2. Reports should be designed so that they can convey the needed information quickly. This means concise reports, tailored to individual management needs.

3. It is often economical to design files to be redundant. A sale, for example, in Hugeco's case, must be recorded in more than one place—on a daily transactions file, on an item sales record file, and, if the item has been shipped into or out of inventory, on an inventory file. There may be other files that require that information as well. The point is that any information that is frequently asked for in a particular form should be stored in that form, even if it is redundant.

4. An information system should be designed in a compatible way throughout the organization, and the level of complexity should probably be similar throughout as well. The Farm Supply Company could benefit from this principle.

The appropriate amount of money to invest in information systems is never clear. Most small organizations should not buy expensive systems. However, it is not clear that large organizations should. Speed of response costs money. If your organization requires speed of response, as Hugeco did, a large investment is appropriate, since it will pay off in terms of better service and lower inventory costs. The current trend of rapid reductions in computer costs will bring computerized records within the grasp of almost any organization in the near future; increased sophistication will become generally less expensive.

Characteristics of successful decision support systems have been studied by many researchers. For example, Fuerst and Cheney (1982) determined that success depends on characteristics of the managers and of the implementation process as well. They provide an extensive reference list for further exploration of this topic.

Model-Based Information Systems

Many information systems are tied to models used for forecasting, inventory control, and other purposes. Because they provide analytic tools for the manager, in addition to the usual information about sales and other company data, they are called *model-based* systems. In a typical model-based system, a manager can ask the computer for sales records, and then ask the computer to make forecasts of future sales, using methods we will describe later in this chapter. The computer may also be able to help in other ways, such as developing a plan for the necessary seasonal inventory to meet the upcoming peak sales. The most effective systems are designed so that managers can interrogate them, obtaining almost instantaneous response. If properly designed, this tool can make large improvements in a manager's effectiveness. The models range from very simple to complex representations of entire corporations. (For a discussion of the use of large-scale corporate models, see Naylor and Schauland, 1976.)

Many kinds of model-based systems are used in operations management. For example, computer companies sell standard packages that keep track of production and inventory control data. Systems for material requirements planning (MRP, Chapter 12) provide timely information, oriented toward future planning. MRP does not optimize in the sense that some inventory control formulas do. However, it provides an excellent coordination tool for complex manufacturing systems.

Much of the information that is collected about sales is used for two basic purposes—to maintain inventory files and to predict future sales. Sales forecasts are required for production planning, inventory control, marketing decisions, financial planning, and many other purposes. The methods for forecasting that we will discuss in the remainder of this chapter are used mainly in production and inventory control. Other forecasting methods and applications were discussed in Section 4-4.

Review Problem

Explain how a model-based information system is different from other kinds of information systems.

Solution

Data are gathered specifically as input to some kind of mathematical routine which has been designed to make recommendations or predictions for management. In contrast, the usual information system only collects and summarizes data.

8-2 FORECASTS TO FIT THE NEED: A MATTER OF JUDGMENT AND CHANCE

Southnorthern Power Company (SPC) forecasts demand for electricity many years into the future because of the long lead time for approval and construction of power plants. At a recent meeting with the Public Utility Commission, these forecasts were called into question. Figure 8-1 shows the history of per capita power consumption along with the SPC forecast and an alternative forecast prepared by Maria P. Angelo (MPA) from the Utility Commission. The discussion revealed that both forecasts used the same methodology, but SPC put substantial weight on the historical trend, whereas Angelo assumed that the moderation of

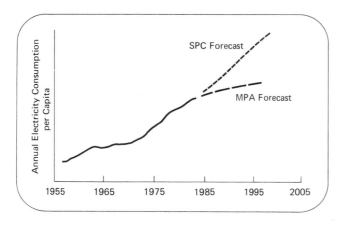

Figure 8-1 Southnorthern Power Company energy forecasts.

this trend in the early 1980s was a new pattern and therefore substantially discounted the pre-1980 data. Each forecasting model showed a very good ability to fit the data.

Podunk Hospital has a call-in system of patient admissions which is intended to smooth out the daily fluctuations of inpatient census. Each afternoon, assistant administrator Martin P. Sand would take out a worksheet (Figure 8-2) and prepare a forecast of patient discharges for the following day. This was subtracted from the current census. Then the admissions scheduled for the next day were added, along with an allowance for emergency admissions and forecast error. The

Daily Census Record			
Day	Disch	Adms	Census
TH			2 50
FR	60	20	210
SA	30	5	185
SU	10	65	240
MO	20	50	270
TU			
WE			
TH			
FR			
SA			

Worksheet: Discharge Forecast for Tuesday

Day	Discharges		Admissions		Census	
	Factor	Product	Factor	Product	Factor	Product
FR	0		.2	4.0	.0214	4.5
SA	0		.3	1.5	0	
SU	./	1.0	.2	13.0	0	
MO	.2	4.0	./	5.0	0	

D Total _5.0_   A Total _23.5_   C Total _4.5_

A Total _23.5_

(Add) _28.0_

D Total _5.0_

(Subtr) _23.0_

Constant _3.0_

Discharge Forecast for Tues.   (Add) _26.0_

Figure 8-2 Podunk Hospital discharge forecasting method.

resulting census forecast was compared to a target, to determine how many patients could be offered the opportunity for an earlier-than-planned admission. A report was then sent to the head nurse, summarizing the expected situation for the next day, to aid in last-minute adjustments in nursing work schedules. Recently, the head nurse has required that a daily census forecast be prepared for each ward, based on the nurses' knowledge of the doctors and patients. A comparison of the statistical forecast and the nurses' forecast revealed that:

1. Neither forecast was always correct.
2. The nurses' reports were better at predicting exceptionally low discharge rates.
3. A combination of the two performed slightly better, overall, than either separately.

These examples point out a number of important principles, which will now be summarized.

Forecasts Are an Integral Part of Decision Making. Accordingly, they must be timely (daily for Podunk Hospital) and dependable. SPC and the Utility Commission are going to have a difficult time making a decision until it is resolved as to which forecast is more reliable.

Forecasts Are Always Wrong! Systems that incorporate forecasts must be designed to allow adjustments to plans and schedules, to allow for imperfect forecasts. This also implies that there is no such thing as *the* best forecasting method. Different forecasting methods may give similar results and may complement one another. Moreover, the same forecasting method may give different results, depending on the assumptions of the forecaster.

Forecasting Methods Should Be Chosen to Fit the Need. That is, use the simplest method that will provide satisfactory forecasts. Podunk Hospital cannot afford to spend days or weeks obtaining and justifying the forecasts, whereas SPC must. A forecasting method can and should be tested by comparing its performance against that of a simpler forecasting method. It is often the case that a very simple model will provide forecasts that are good enough so that even the most complex methods cannot substantially improve the quality of the forecast.

A Forecast Is Often Confused with a Goal. Sales forecasts, for example, are sometimes biased on the high side when they are reported to sales personnel (to encourage them to work hard), and biased on the low side when reported to higher levels of management (so that the actual achievements will appear to have exceeded expectation). This may explain, in part, why the SPC forecast was higher than the Utility Commission's. The former sells power, whereas the latter is charged with (among other duties) energy conservation.

Judgment and Forecasting

All forecasting requires judgment. However, some methods rely more heavily on judgment than others. In Section 4-4, forecasting information is divided into four categories:

1. Grass-roots information.
2. Management judgment and expert opinion.
3. Patterns in past sales records.
4. Other quantitative data, such as economic indicators.

These categories differ not only in the kinds and complexity of data analysis required, but also in the degree of human judgment involved. Strangely, both the simplest and the most complicated methods involve more judgment than do those of moderate complexity. The most straightforward method is to simply ask people to make judgments (or express opinions) and to construct forecasts from that information. In contrast, the most complicated methods use data from several sources, with an assortment of techniques (mathematical or judgmental) to reduce the data to a forecast. In this case, it is the choice of data and procedures that requires a substantial element of judgment. Poor choices can very easily lead to forecasts which are much worse than even the most simple approaches would achieve.

For example, Chatfield and Prothero (1973) displayed a model that gave unbelievably bad forecasts, even though it seemed to be a correct use of the sophisticated methods of Box and Jenkins (1970). In the critical discussion that followed, a number of experts proposed different reasons for the poor performance. The conclusion seemed to be that there is an extreme amount of judgment required to use methods as complex as that of Box and Jenkins, and even the experts will disagree in many situations.

In short- and intermediate-range decision making, it is often desirable to have an automatic forecasting system which, once implemented, requires minimal judgment. Only techniques of moderate complexity are used in automatic systems. With these methods, choice is limited to selection of one or two parameters, and (as we shall see) even these may sometimes be selected and modified automatically. Human judgment is concentrated at two points: implementation and intervention. Implementation requires judgments as to what situations are suitable for use of these methods, and which options are to be used. Intervention is required if forecast accuracy becomes inadequate, at which time a judgment must be made as to the cause of the errors, and the appropriate action. Typically this occurs infrequently, so that the vast majority of forecasts are made without additional judgments.

Human judgment as a basis for forecasting was discussed in Chapter 4. The principles are very similar in short- to intermediate-range forecasting. For example, many manufacturers and distributors routinely collect opinions from their sales force, from which forecasts are constructed. The forecast is not necessarily the sum of the individual projections, however. Management may have additional information, such as a consumer survey, knowledge of an impending strike in a related industry, or plans for an upcoming promotional effort.

It can be very frustrating to try to bring these kinds of information together into a single, quantitative forecast. A reliable, systematic procedure must be established for collecting the opinions. Yet the process must also be rapid, since the usefulness of the information diminishes with age. Chambers et al. (1971) describe several useful procedures under the heading "Qualitative Methods."

A common judgmental method is variously entitled BFE (bold, freehand extrapolation) or SWAG (sophisticated, wild guess). The information contained in these forecasts is substantial, because of the experience of the managers who provided them. They suffer, however, from various human weaknesses such as the tendency to overreact and the dominance of the most forceful presentation (the squeaky-wheel effect). Formal methods such as Delphi (described in Chapter 4) are intended to reduce these effects by careful control of personal contact during a session when forecasts are being elicited. However, such an approach is usually too cumbersome for frequent and repeated use, as is generally required in short-range decisions.

The major advantages of judgmental methods are their relative simplicity and the possibility of predicting rare events. The first advantage explains why these methods are widely used—managers feel comfortable with a method that is straightforward and easily understood. Predicting rare events is sometimes simple for people but impossible for statistical methods. This is because all statistical methods are based on relationships that have been observed in the past. There is, in classical statistics no counterpart to private conversations that transmit information about an impending event which may never have occurred before.

A disadvantage of judgmental methods is the time required. Many firms have thousands of items subject to inventory control and forecasts of usage are very important in preventing shortages. Lawrence (1983) has shown that in an experimental environment, judgmental forecasting can be at least as accurate as "black box" statistical computer programs, and sometimes better. However, Carbone et al. (1983) concluded that judgmental modification of statistical forecasts makes little difference in the accuracy. The best system is probably, nevertheless, a combination of statistical and judgmental, in which the statistical methods are monitored on an exception basis. Rao and Cox (1978) give an extensive review and comparison of quantitative and judgmental forecasting methods.

The remainder of this chapter is devoted to statistical forecasting methods. An important part of the discussion is how to implement an automatic system to detect when human intervention is needed.

1. If forecasts are always wrong, of what use are they?
2. What is a judgmental forecasting method?
3. In what way is judgment used in statistical forecasting?

Solutions

1. Planning requires some estimate of the future. Forecasts are useful if they can be relied on to provide an estimate of the future, within a known level of error.

2. Forecasts derived directly from opinions and judgments of people are said to be judgmental. This could involve a series of brainstorming sessions or consulting expert opinion, for example.

3. Selecting the statistical method to use requires a judgment. Whether or not to believe a forecast and whether to seek additional information are also management decisions.

8-3 TIME-SERIES[1] ANALYSIS AND EXPONENTIAL SMOOTHING

It is possible to prepare a statistical forecast even when there is no apparent pattern in the history of the demand. A simple average with confidence intervals brings a certain amount of order to the decision process by allowing plans to be made in which the risks are explicit. Often, there are patterns in the data that can be quantified and projected into the future to improve the accuracy of the forecast. In this chapter, two of the more common patterns are discussed: seasonal patterns and growth trends (including negative growth). Each of these can be estimated by careful use of methods based on averages. However, the *exponentially weighted average* has two advantages over the simple average:

1. It is easier to calculate.
2. Data are automatically *discounted* as they get older, so that old trends are forgotten as new ones emerge.

The Exponentially Weighted Average

The usual method for calculating an average is to add a series of quantities and divide by their number. This simple method becomes cumbersome when used as a part of an ongoing forecasting system. For example, a 12-month average requires one to look up and sum the previous 11 data points, add the new month's

---

[1] A time series is a list of repeated observations of a phenomenon, such as demand, arranged in the order in which they actually occurred.

data, and divide by 12. This may seem a minor task, but it may be repeated thousands of times in a firm which requires forecasts for most or all of the items it carries in inventory. And remember, the process is repeated periodically to prepare new forecasts based on the latest data. (That is called a *moving average*.)

One way to simplify this calculation is to compute a weighted average of (1) the latest datum and (2) the *previous average*. The previous average carries, implicitly, data from all previous months, so it should count more heavily than the single new observation. This may be formalized by defining S_t as the average calculated in period t, S_{t-1} as the average calculated one period earlier, D_t as the new datum, and the Greek lowercase letter alpha (α) as the weight factor (smoothing parameter). Then the exponential smoothing formula is

$$\text{new average} = (\text{small weight})(\text{new data})$$
$$+ (\text{large weight})(\text{old average})$$

or

$$S_t = \alpha D_t + (1 - \alpha)S_{t-1} \tag{1}$$

For example, if sales averaged 350 units over the previous few months, but the most recent month showed sales of 400 units (we shall use $\alpha = 0.1$ without explanation for the time being), the new average would be

$$(0.1)(400) + (0.9)(350) = 355$$

The formula for S_t not only gives a shorthand rule for the calculation, but also allows us to explore the implications of using this method repeatedly through time. Specifically, we may write down how S_{t-1} was calculated, and S_{t-2}, and so on.

$$S_t = \alpha D_t + (1 - \alpha)S_{t-1}$$
$$\uparrow$$
$$S_{t-1} = \alpha D_{t-1} + (1 - \alpha)S_{t-2}$$
$$\uparrow$$
$$S_{t-2} = \alpha D_{t-2} + (1 - \alpha)S_{t-3}$$

If the expressions for S_{t-2} and S_{t-1} are substituted as indicated by the arrows, the result is

$$S_t = \alpha D_t + (1 - \alpha)\alpha D_{t-1} + (1 - \alpha)^2\alpha D_{t-2} + (1 - \alpha)^3 S_{t-3} \tag{2}$$

Formula (2) is never actually used, since it is equivalent to (1). Notice that the exercise could continue by substituting for S_{t-3} in (2), and so on. Referring to (2), we can see some of the properties of S_t:

1. The new average, S_t, implicitly contains all the data, back to the time when the calculation was first begun. (That is, D_{t-1}, D_{t-2}, etc.)
2. Unlike a regular average, the data are weighted. For $\alpha = 0.1$, the weights are 0.1 for D_t, $(0.9)(0.1) = 0.09$ for D_{t-1}, 0.081 for D_{t-2}, and, in general,

for data that are n periods old, the weight is $\alpha(1 - \alpha)^n$. The weights decrease, because of the exponent n attached to $(1 - \alpha)$; this is why the average is called *exponentially* smoothed or weighted.

3. Because of this exponential discounting of the past, whatever number was originally used for the old average (the first time the formula was used) will receive progressively less weight as time passes. That is, old data are progressively discounted.

Feedback: The Response to Forecast Error

The exponential smoothing formula, equation (1), can be rearranged into an equivalent form in which the role of α becomes more explicit.

$$S_t = S_{t-1} + \alpha(D_t - S_{t-1}) \tag{3}$$

new average = old average + α(forecast error)

This is referred to as a *feedback equation*, because the new average is obtained by "feeding back" part of the discrepancy in the previous forecast. To see this, suppose[2] that S_{t-1} had been used as the forecast of D_t. If S_{t-1} overestimated the demand, the forecast error $D_t - S_{t-1}$ is negative, and equation (3) adjusts the new forecast downward from the old one. The opposite is true if S_{t-1} was too low. Therefore, the magnitude of α determines the degree of responsiveness to forecast error. There are two implications of this observation, and they are in conflict:

1. Response: Larger values of α mean that the new average will change more quickly if the new data are substantially different from the old forecast. Thus, a large α value is desirable because a permanent shift in demand will be incorporated more quickly into the average.

2. Stability: For the same reason, large α values will allow the average to respond when it should not. For example, in a month when sales were low due to a special offered by a competitor, one would not wish the subsequent forecasts to be unduly altered. Thus a large α value also has disadvantages.

The choice of a value for α is therefore a trade-off between responsiveness and stability. A manager who is facing this trade-off will find it helpful to draw a parallel to an unweighted average: The exponentially smoothed average behaves similarly to a regular (unweighted) average of $N = (2 - \alpha)/\alpha$ data points. Thus an α of 0.1 corresponds roughly to a 19-period moving average, whereas $\alpha = 0.5$ is similar to averaging only the last three data points.

$$\textit{Guideline formulas:} \quad N \approx \frac{2 - \alpha}{\alpha} \quad \text{or} \quad \alpha \approx \frac{2}{N + 1} \tag{4}$$

[2] One would only use S_{t-1} as a forecast if no growth or seasonal patterns were evident.

Alpha is used to fine-tune the forecast to the manager's view of the situation. Small values of α (0.1 and lower) are used in periods of stability, when the month-to-month variations are judged to be of no permanent duration. Large values (above 0.3) may be desirable during periods of change, when historical data are of less relevance due to changes in the environment.

A common practice in selecting a value for α is to try several values, using historical data to test for the value that does the best job. There also are methods which automatically adjust α, according to a tracking signal. These methods increase α whenever the accumulated forecast error becomes significant. (See Section 8-6 for further discussion.)

Limitations

The exponentially smoothed average has important advantages in ease of computation and discounting of older data. The smoothing parameter, α, is a very flexible tool for adjusting the sensitivity of the forecast to fluctuations in the data. However, the exponentially smoothed average *by itself* is of very limited use. Just like any other average, S_t is not a good forecast when there is a steady increase or decrease in the data. For example, for the series 10, 12, 14, 16, 18, a logical forecast would be 20, but the average is 14. It is also not logical to compute an average when there are predictable swings in the data due to, for example, seasonality of sales. We now turn to methods to handle both *growth* and *seasonal* effects. In these methods S_t will no longer be the forecast, but it can be part of the forecast.

Review Problems

1. Compute the average of the following numbers: 10, 11, 10, 11, 14, 15, 14, 15.
2. Compute the exponentially weighted average of the numbers in Review Problem 1, using $\alpha = 0.5$. Do this by using equation (1) repeatedly, beginning with the first number, 10, as the old average, and the second number, 11, as the new data.
3. To forecast the next number in this series, which average would you prefer, the answer to Review Problem 1 or 2? Explain.
4. The next number in the series from Review Problem 1 is 14. Compute new averages for Review Problems 1 and 2. Which is easier?
5. Repeat Review Problem 4, using equation (3) for S_t.
6. What value of α would make Review Problems 1 and 2 approximately equivalent?

Solutions

1. $(10 + 11 + 10 + 11 + 14 + 15 + 14 + 15)/8 = 12.50$
2. $S_t = \alpha D_t + (1 - \alpha)S_{t-1}$ and $S_1 = 10$ (given)
   $S_2 = (0.5)(11) + (0.5)(10)$ $= 10.5$

$$S_3 = (0.5)(10) + (0.5)(10.5) = 10.25$$
$$S_4 = (0.5)(11) + (0.5)(10.25) = 10.63$$
$$S_5 = (0.5)(14) + (0.5)(10.63) = 12.31$$
$$S_6 = (0.5)(15) + (0.5)(12.31) = 13.66$$
$$S_7 = (0.5)(14) + (0.5)(13.66) = 13.83$$
$$S_8 = (0.5)(15) + (0.5)(13.83) = 14.42$$

3. That depends on what you see in the data. There was a sudden increase after the fourth number. Is it permanent, or is another jump (up or down) about due? We cannot tell. If we assume that the jump is permanent, $S_8 = 14.42$ is a much more reasonable forecast than the unweighted average of 12.50.

4. Unweighted: $(10 + 11 + 10 + 11 + 14 + 15 + 14 + 15 + 14)/9 = 12.67$. Exponentially smoothed: $S_8 = 14.42$, from Review Problem 2, so $S_9 = (0.5)(14) + (0.5)(14.42) = 14.21$. The exponential calculation is much easier when the initial work (in this case Review Problem 2) has been done already.

5. $S_9 = 14.42 + (0.5)(14 - 14.42) = 14.21$, the same as in Review Problem 4. Thus equations (1) and (3) are equivalent.

6. In Review Problem 1, we averaged $N = 8$ data points. Equations (4) then suggest that $\alpha = 2/(8 + 1) = 0.222$ as approximately equivalent. You may verify that $\alpha = 0.222$ gives $S_8 = 13.02$, which is (as expected) closer to the unweighted average.

8-4 SEASONAL EFFECTS

Many goods and services have a *seasonal demand pattern*. That is, there are predictable rises and falls in demand, because of seasonal influences such as weather, holiday seasons, and so on. The seasonal pattern of demand is often the most important aspect of a forecast. For example, based on a predictable slump in demand, hospitals often schedule renovations in one or more wards, manufacturers schedule a plant shutdown during which substantial maintenance is done, and retailers schedule vacations and inventory counts.

Fortunately, rather simple methods are available to quantify the seasonal pattern. One of the simplest is illustrated in the example below, in which a single product is examined by itself. (The reader should note that more reliable estimates are often obtained by working with groups of products that share a common seasonal pattern. This also reduces the computational task since there may be only a few hundred product groups in a product line with 50,000 items.)

Table 8-1 is a worksheet for computing quarterly seasonal factors for Tomasco Apple Wine sales. Part 1 of the table lists the quarterly sales itself for 3 years. Part 2 contains a series of 1-year "centered averages." The purpose of this calculation is to get an estimate of what sales would have been if there were no

TABLE 8-1 DERIVING SEASONAL FACTORS FOR TOMASCO APPLE WINES

	PART 1. SALES			PART 2. CENTERED AVERAGES			PART 3. SEASONAL RATIOS			PART 4. Average Seasonal Factors
Quarter	Year 1	Year 2	Year 3	Year 1	Year 2	Year 3	Year 1	Year 2	Year 3	
1	504	581	586		544.6	562.0		1.067	1.043	1.055
2	484	523	543		552.8	564.6		0.946	0.962	0.954
3	409	452	454	519.9	556.1		0.787	0.813		0.800
4	644	666	685	534.4	559.3		1.205	1.191		1.198
									Total =	4.007

Sample Calculation for Part 2: second quarter, year 2 ($t = 6$)

$$\text{average} = \frac{0.5D_4 + D_5 + D_6 + D_7 + 0.5D_8}{4}$$

$$= \frac{(0.5)(644) + 581 + 523 + 452 + 0.5(666)}{4} = 552.8$$

Because the number 4 is even (four quarters per year), there is no way to "center" the calculations on a given quarter. The 0.5 factors are used to include a full year (from the middle of period 4 to the middle of period 8 in the sample calculation), so period 6 is in the exact center. This is not necessary if an odd number of periods is used. For example, a year can be defined as 13 four-week "months."

Sample Calculation for Part 3: second quarter, year 2 = 523/552.8 = 0.946, where 523 is from part 1 and 552.8 from part 2.

seasonal effect. (We will see why this is important in a moment.) The centered average covers one complete year to get rid of seasonality; the high seasons offset the low.

The average is centered because of the growth. For example, to estimate the level of sales in the third quarter of year 1 (period 3 in the data set), we compute the average from the middle of period 1 to the middle of period 5, as illustrated in Figure 8-3 by the shaded area. The resulting average is representative of the midpoint, which is period 3. Similarly, as shown in the sample calculation in Table 8-1, the centered average for period 6 runs between the midpoints of periods 4 and 8.

Evidence of seasonality comes to light if we compare the actual sales to the centered average. Because the centered average has no seasonality, if first-quarter sales tend to be consistently above the first-quarter centered average, we may conclude that the first quarter is a high season. Part 3 of the table contains the ratios of actual sales to centered averages (a sample calculation is given). The two first-quarter ratios are 1.067 and 1.043. Although both ratios exceed 1.0, this is certainly not conclusive evidence that the first quarter is a strong one, since it is based on only two observations. One would normally require at least 5 years of data (preferably more) to compute seasonal effects.

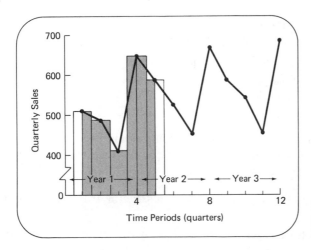

Figure 8-3 Demand for Tomasco Apple Wine: Shaded area is interval for Period 3 centered average.

Finally, Part 4 of Table 8-1 lists the average of the seasonal ratios from Part 3. Averaging several observations tends to cancel random effects, so the average seasonal factors can be used with more confidence than, for example, last year's experience. The four seasonal factors, by quarter, are 1.055, 0.954, 0.800, and 1.198. A factor of 1.0 would indicate no seasonal effect. Therefore, we conclude that the first quarter tends to be seasonally high by $1.055 - 1.0 = 0.055$ or 5.5%, the second quarter is low by 4.6%, and so on.

In summary, the seasonal factors are ratios expressing the proportional variation that we can ascribe to a repeating seasonal pattern. There are many other methods for computing seasonality. All use statistical methods of one sort or another to separate the effects of seasonality from those of growth and randomness. Time periods of any length can be used. Monthly data yields 12 seasonal factors and uses 12-period centered averages. Day-of-week variation uses seven factors (one for each day) and seven-period (weekly) centered averages rather than annual.

Another approach to seasonal patterns is based on a development in the year 1822, when J.B. Fourier proved that many repeating functions can be represented by a sum of sine and cosine terms. The Fourier series has been extended to exponential smoothing to account for seasonal patterns. However, all Fourier methods are more difficult to initialize than the seasonal factor approach described previously, particularly when only a few years of data are available. Nevertheless, this system is often used in practice.

One common question is what to do if there is evidence that the seasonal pattern may be changing. We shall reserve this issue for a homework problem, since some of the ideas in subsequent sections should be brought to bear.

Seasonal factors are used in two ways: deseasonalizing raw data so that other trends are more apparent and seasonalizing forecasts that have been made from deseasonalized data. The following steps may be used with any forecasting system.

1. Observe latest data value D_t.
2. Deseasonalize: $D_t^* = D_t/$seasonal factor (t).
3. Use D_t^* to update exponentially smoothed (or other) forecast.
4. Seasonalize: Forecast for period $t + k$ = (exponentially smoothed forecast) $\times$ (seasonal factor for period $t + k$).

Review Problems

Suppose that the deseasonalized exponentially smoothed average sales for Tomasco Apple Wines has been computed to be 565 through quarter number 11. That is, $S_{11} = 565.0$.

1. Using $\alpha = 0.10$ and the appropriate seasonal factor from Part 4 of Table 8-1, compute S_{12}.
2. Construct forecasts for quarters 13, 14, and 15, using the appropriate seasonal factors.

Solutions

1. Following the four steps, we find $D_{12} = 685$ from Part 1 of Table 8-1, and deseasonalize. Period 12 is the fourth quarter of year 3, so we use the fourth quarter's seasonal factor. $D_{12}^* = 685/1.198 = 571.8$. Using equation (1), $S_{12} = (0.1)(571.8) + (0.9)(565) = 565.7$.
2. The forecast for period 13 (first quarter) is $565.7(1.055) = 596.8$, and for periods 14 and 15 we get $565.7(0.954) = 539.7$ and $565.7(0.800) = 452.5$.

8-5 EXPONENTIAL SMOOTHING WITH LINEAR GROWTH

The growth trend in apple wine sales becomes more evident when seasonal effects are removed by dividing actual demand by the average seasonal factors from the last column of Table 8-1. Figure 8-4 and Table 8-2 display the deseasonalized sales (denoted with an asterisk as D_t^*), which shows rapid growth during year 1, slowing to a more moderate rate which seems to be well established

TABLE 8-2 DESEASONALIZED SALES (D_t^*)
FOR TOMASCO APPLE WINE[a]

Quarter	Year 1	Year 2	Year 3
1	477.7	550.7	555.5
2	507.3	548.2	569.2
3	511.3	565.0	567.5
4	537.6	555.9	571.8

[a] Sample calculation: quarter 1, year 1: (sales)/(seasonal factor) $= 504/1.055 = 477.7$, in which 504 and 1.055 came from parts 1 and 3 of Table 8-1, respectively.

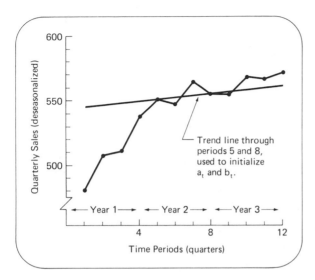

Figure 8-4 Deseasonalized sales for Tomasco Apple Wine.

by year 2. Note that the scale is magnified in Figure 8-4 compared to Figure 8-3. This was made possible by the removal of the large seasonal variations. The moderation of the growth is more obvious in Figure 8-4 than in Figure 8-3, and this leveling off is extremely important in making a forecast.

Management decided to try an exponential smoothing forecast that incorporates growth. The simplest growth model is linear. The linear forecasting equation is

$$\begin{array}{c} \text{forecast for a time} \\ k \text{ periods in the future} \end{array} = \text{intercept} + (k)(\text{slope}) \qquad (5)$$

$$= a_t + kb_t$$

There are now two terms to be estimated—a growth term (b_t = slope) and an average term (a_t = intercept). Each uses an exponential smoothing equation, so there are two α values. To distinguish the growth model from simple exponential smoothing, we use R_A instead of α as the response rate for a_t, and R_B as the response rate for b_t. A technical note, at the end of this section, explains how to choose values for the response rates. Table 8-3 summarizes the steps of exponential smoothing with linear growth.

To compute a new forecast as with simple exponential smoothing, we make use of the previous one. For example, consider the situation at the end of time period 6. The sales $D_6 = 523$ has just been observed, and is deseasonalized to become $D_6^* = 548.2$. Suppose the following values had previously been calculated for time period 5: $a_5 = 550.7$ and $b_5 = 1.7$. These are a_{t-1} and b_{t-1}, respectively, to use in equations (6), (7), and (8) of Table 8-3. To update a_5 and b_5, based on the new information D_6^*, we first compute the error of the old forecast. Using equation (6),

$$e_6 = D_6^* - (a_5 + b_5)$$

$$= 548.2 - (552.4) = -4.2$$

TABLE 8-3 SUMMARY OF PROCEDURE FOR FORECASTING WITH LINEAR GROWTH

To forecast into the future a distance of k periods, calculate the "k period forecast" = $a_t + kb_t$, in which a_t is the intercept at the present time and b_t is the slope or linear growth rate. Both a_t and b_t are estimated by exponential smoothing, using the feedback form of the equations.

Procedure:

1. Observe the latest data value, D_t, and deseasonalize it (divide it by the seasonal factor). Call the result D_t^*.

2. Calculate the error (e_t) of the *old* (previous) one-period deseasonalized forecast.

$$e_t = \text{latest demand} - \text{previous forecast (both deseasonalized)} \qquad (6)$$

$$= D_t^* - (a_{t-1} + b_{t-1})$$

3. Feed back part of the forecast error, to update the intercept and growth.

$$\text{new intercept} = \text{old forecast} + R_A e_t \qquad (7)$$

$$a_t = (a_{t-1} + b_{t-1}) + R_A e_t$$

$$\text{new growth} = \text{old growth} + R_B e_t \qquad (8)$$

$$b_t = b_{t-1} + R_B e_t$$

4. Construct new forecasts for periods beyond the present.

$$k \text{ period forecast} = a_t + kb_t \qquad (9)$$

5. Multiply each forecast by the appropriate seasonal factor for period $t + k$.

The negative forecast error indicates that the old forecast of 552.4 was too high; it exceeded D_6^* by 4.2. Using smoothing constants $R_A = 0.25$ and $R_B = 0.02$ (discussed later), equations (7) and (8) yield the new values, adjusted for the forecast error just observed:

$$a_6 = a_5 + b_5 + 0.25\,(e_6)$$
$$= 550.7 + 1.7 + 0.25\,(-4.2) = 551.4$$
$$b_6 = b_5 + 0.02\,(e_6)$$
$$= 1.7 + 0.02\,(-4.2) = 1.6$$

Then, equation (9) is used to project into the future (beyond period 6). That is, as of period 6 the forecasts for periods 7, 8, and 9 are obtained by using $k = 1$, 2, and 3, respectively, in equation (9).

Period 6 deseasonalized forecasts:

$$\text{for period } 7 = 551.4 + (1)(1.6) = 553.0$$
$$\text{for period } 8 = 551.4 + (2)(1.6) = 554.6$$
$$\text{for period } 9 = 551.4 + (3)(1.6) = 556.2$$

Each of these must be seasonally adjusted by multiplying by the corresponding seasonal factor. For example, period 7 is the third quarter of year 2 (see Table

8-1) so the seasonal factor is 0.800 and the seasonalized forecast for $t = 7$ is $(0.800)(553.0) = 442.4$.

To understand what exponential smoothing has accomplished, it helps to compare the forecasts before and after the period 6 sales information was used. Using the period 5 forecasting information in equation (9), the forecasts for periods 6, 7, and 8 would be as follows.

Period 5 deseasonalized forecasts:

$$\text{for period } 6 = 550.7 + (1)(1.7) = 552.4$$

$$\text{for period } 7 = 550.7 + (2)(1.7) = 554.1$$

$$\text{for period } 8 = 550.7 + (3)(1.7) = 555.8$$

Now compare the deseasonalized forecasts of the period 7 sales from the two different time bases. From period 5 we predict 554.1 but from period 6 we predict 553.0. The forecast was lowered because the period 5 forecast was observed to be too high for period 6. That is, the negative forecast error was incorporated in both a_6 and b_6 resulting in lowered expectations for all periods beyond period 6. That is the philosophy of exponential smoothing. If a forecast is too high, aim lower next time (and vice versa). The smoothing parameters R_A and R_B, being less than 1.0, cushion against overreacting.

The example just given is not quite realistic because we made a forecast for period 7, a time that is actually in the past. Furthermore, in seasonalizing the forecast, we used the factor 0.800 which was computed in the previous section using data before and after period 7. Real forecasting will be illustrated in the review problem.

Getting Started

To use equations (6), (7), and (8), old values must already exist for a_t and b_t. How do we get these values for the first time, in order to begin using exponential smoothing? This is called *initialization*. There are many ways to do this. The one we shall illustrate is quite simple. First, the graph of deseasonalized data is observed to determine whether a constant trend is present. Figure 8-4 indicates that the slope is nearly constant for years 2 and 3, so we ignore year 1 data which seems to have a different slope. Next, we choose some reasonable values for a_t and b_t for the beginning period, which is now period 5. The third step is to apply equations (6), (7), and (8) repeatedly for the rest of the data set, periods 6 through 12. The theory behind this method is that the repeated use of exponential smoothing *discounts* the initial values a_5 and b_5 so that they have very little influence on the forecast after period 12. Furthermore, using exponential smoothing on periods 5 to 12 simulates how the forecast is likely to perform in the future.

This idea is illustrated in Table 8-4. For simplicity, the initial values were obtained by fitting a straight line through D_5^* and D_8^*, which brackets the first year of data. (Homework problems 14 and 15 illustrate another method, using regression.) The intercept of this line at time period 5 is therefore D_5^* or 550.7,

TABLE 8-4 EXPONENTIAL SMOOTHING WITH GROWTH, USING TOMASCO APPLE WINE'S SALES, WITH $R_A = 0.25$ AND $R_B = 0.02$

	DESEASONALIZED DATA		DESEASONALIZED TRENDS			Seasonalized Forecast for
Quarter	Sales, D_t^*	Error, e_t	a_t	b_t	$a_t + b_t$	$k = 1$ Period Lead Time
5	550.7		550.7	1.7	552.4	527.0 for period 6
6	548.2	−4.2	551.4	1.6	553.0	442.4 for period 7
7	565.0	+12.0	556.0	1.8	557.8	668.2 for period 8
8	555.9	−1.9	557.3	1.8	559.1	589.9 for period 9
9	555.5	−3.6	558.2	1.7	559.9	534.1 for period 10
10	569.2	+9.3	562.2	1.9	564.1	451.3 for period 11
11	567.5	+3.4	565.0	2.0	567.0	679.3 for period 12
12	571.8					

Note: $R_A = 0.25$ is equivalent to a seven-period moving average, according to the Technical Note in this section. $R_B = 0.02$ was calculated to be equivalent to Brown's double smoothing, equation (11) in the Technical Note.

and the slope is $(D_8^* - D_5^*)/(8 - 5)$ or 1.7. These are used as a_5 and b_5 in Table 8-4. The table shows the seasonalized forecasts projected one period into the future. Thus, after a_6 and b_6 are calculated, the forecast for period 7 is 553.0 (deseasonalized) and 442.4 when corrected for the expected seasonal drop in the third quarter, as expressed by the factor 0.800 from Table 8-1. To illustrate how well the system is working, deseasonalized and seasonalized forecasts for year 3 are shown in Figures 8-5 and 8-6.

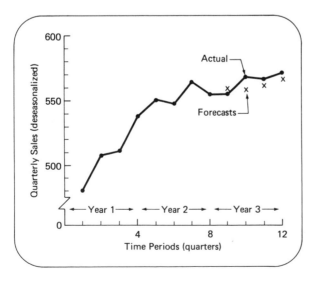

Figure 8-5 The $k = 1$ period lead time forecasts for year 3 of Tomasco Apple Wines' deseasonalized sales.

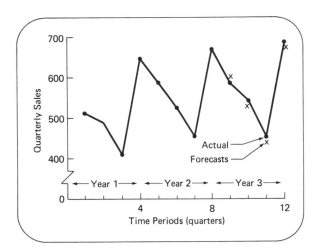

Figure 8-6 The k = 1 period lead time forecasts for year 3 of Tomasco Apple Wine, including seasonal effects.

Technical Note: Setting the Response Rates, R_A and R_B

The magnitude of R_A determines how much the intercept (a_t) will change in response to an observed forecast error. R_B has the analogous effect on the growth or slope term (b_t). There are several methods for deciding on appropriate values for R_A and R_B. The preferred method is to test the model on historical data, repeating the test for several combinations of R_A and R_B. One then chooses the pair that results in the most accurate forecasts on the average. However, sometimes there are insufficient *relevant* data to perform a meaningful test (for example, when a relatively new product is being studied or when a change has recently taken place in the rate of demand). Then R_A and R_B must be chosen on the basis of one's understanding of the situation. The following rules are useful.

1. One can choose R_A in the same way as α was chosen in the no-growth model. That is, the equivalent number of periods of historical data included in the forecast is N, where

$$R_A \approx \frac{2}{N + 1} \qquad \text{or} \qquad N \approx \frac{2 - R_A}{R_A} \qquad (10)$$

2. To choose R_B, two reference points are available.
    (a) Brown (1963) recommends a model that is equivalent to the formulas in Table 8-3 if

$$R_B = 2 - R_A - 2\sqrt{1 - R_A} \qquad (11)$$

    (b) Winters (1960) gives a different formulation, which is also equivalent to our formulas. If his intercept and trend smoothing constants are set equal, the result is the same as if equations (2) and (8) had

$$R_B = (R_A)^2 \qquad (12)$$

The R_B value implied by this equation is larger than the one implied by Brown's formulation.

3. It is tempting to use $R_B = R_A$, a value larger than either the Brown or Winters equivalents. However, a model in which $R_B = R_A$ was discarded by Brown because it performed erratically, far overshooting and undershooting the demand pattern. McClain and Thomas (1973) demonstrated that this effect can occur in models in which R_B is too large relative to R_A.

4. Therefore, if the growth is thought to be constant or nearly so, R_B should be set equal to or below the value specified in (11). On the other hand, if the trend is not well established, a larger R_B such as (12) is appropriate. Extreme caution should be used if (12) is exceeded.

Review Problems

1. In the Tomasco Wine example, if period 11 were the present time (period 12 demand being unknown), what would the forecast be for periods 12, 13, and 14? Use the data in Table 8-4. Be sure to allow for seasonal effects.

2. Carry out the missing calculations for period 12 in Table 8-4.

3. Why is $R_A = 0.25$ a reasonable value to use in this case?

4. Do you think that $R_B = 0.02$ was reasonable? Discuss.

5. What would a negative value of b_t imply?

6. If b_t and R_B are both zero, in what ways are a_t and S_t different?

Solutions

1. Using steps 4 and 5 from Table 8-4, with $a_{11} = 565$ and $b_{11} = 2.0$, we obtain the following:

Quarter	Forecast $(a_{11} + kb_{11})$	Seasonal Factor (Table 8-1)	Seasonalized Forecast
12($k = 1$)	567.0	1.198 (4th quarter)	679.3
13($k = 2$)	569.0	1.055 (1st quarter)	600.3
14($k = 3$)	571.0	0.954 (2nd quarter)	544.7

2. Error $= +4.8$, $a_{12} = 568.2$, $b_{12} = 2.1$; $a_{12} + b_{12} = 570.3$, the deseasonalized forecast for period 13, and the seasonal factor is 1.055 (Table 8-1, first quarter) so the seasonalized forecast is $(1.055)(570.3) = 601.7$ for period 13.

3. According to equation (10) in the Technical Note, $R_A = 0.25$ is equivalent to a seven-period moving average. Therefore, by the end of period 12, the initial guesses for a_5 and b_5 are nearly forgotten.

4. Because the initial estimate of $b_t = 1.7$ may not be very accurate, perhaps a higher R_B such as $R_B = (R_A)^2 = 0.0625$ would be appropriate, as suggested in equation (12). In any case, we would be well advised not to count on the accuracy of b_t until more time has passed.

5. Declining sales.
6. If $R_A = \alpha$, there will be no difference. Make the changes in equation (7) and compare to equation (3).

8-6 *ERROR DETECTION AND AUTOMATIC FORECASTING SYSTEMS*

Lewis (1975) points out that a typical manufacturer, having a large number of products, would be willing to delegate the forecasting responsibility for as many as 70% of those items to an automatic system. This frees management to concentrate effort on other items for which forecast errors are of greater consequence to the firm. However, even an automatic system must have human intervention from time to time. For example, if there is a significant change in the demand pattern, it takes approximately $(2 - \alpha)/\alpha$ periods [or $(2 - R_A)/R_A$ periods, according to equations (4) and (10)] for an exponential smoothing system to fully incorporate the new situation in the forecast. In the meanwhile, serious forecast errors will occur. There are two approaches to dealing with this dilemma: automatic error detection, and self-adaptive methods that provide automatic adjustments in the response rate.

Automatic error detection produces a signal when human intervention and judgment is needed. This would have been very useful to Tomasco, for example, when the growth rate in apple wine sales suddenly changed late in year 1. Errors are detected statistically by looking for a pattern in the forecast error, e_t. [The formula for e_t is equation (6) in Table 8-3.] A measure of expected forecast error is the *mean absolute deviation* (MAD), which may be estimated by exponentially smoothing the forecast errors without regard to sign:

$$\text{MAD}_t = \alpha|e_t| + (1 - \alpha)\text{MAD}_{t-1} \tag{13}$$

in which $|e_t|$ is the absolute value of the forecast error (drop the sign). If the forecast error is normally distributed, MAD is theoretically related to the standard deviation, σ, by

$$\sigma = \sqrt{\frac{\pi}{2}}\,\text{MAD} \approx 1.25\text{MAD} \tag{14}$$

Because of this relationship, about 95% of the time (if demands are roughly normally distributed) the forecast should be within 2 standard deviations, or 2.5MAD, of the actual demand, and within 3MAD about 98% of the time.

Several kinds of errors should be monitored. The first, and probably the most important because it is often neglected, is *spurious data*. If we suddenly get a large forecast error, the first place we should look is at the data itself. It is possible, for example, that last month's sales figures were incorrectly entered into the computer. Or, last month's sales may have been influenced by a heavy, one-time promotion. In either case, the large forecast error is not an indication of trouble with the forecast, and e_t should not be incorporated into next month's forecast unless it is first corrected for the spurious event. A *spurious data filter* can be constructed by establishing a confidence interval for the forecast error:

$$\text{``possibly spurious data'' if } |e_t| > n_1 \text{ MAD}_t$$

The parameter n_1 determines the sensitivity of the filter. Deciding on a value for n_1 will be described after we look at two more filters.

A second kind of error is *forecast bias*. A forecast is biased upward if it tends to be too high substantially more than half of the time. Downward bias is just the opposite. Causes of forecast bias fall into two categories: incorrect model and changed data pattern. If, for example, we are using a no-trend model such as simple exponential smoothing, but there is a downward trend in the data, the forecast will be high on the average. Even if a trend is included in the model, if there is a sudden change in the demand pattern due to a new competitor, the intercept and trend estimates are suddenly incorrect, and biased forecasts will result.

To detect bias requires a look at more than one period. One method is to compute the *smoothed average error*:

$$E_t = \alpha e_t + (1 - \alpha)E_{t-1} \tag{15}$$

The sign does count in this formula, so E_t can be positive, negative, or zero. Trigg (1964) proposed as a *tracking signal* the ratio E_t/MAD_t and included a suggested method for setting cutoffs.

$$\text{tracking signal} = \frac{E_t}{\text{MAD}_t} \tag{16}$$

Then a *forecast bias filter* is

$$\text{``possibly biased forecast'' if } |\text{tracking signal}| > n_2$$

A third kind of error is *forecast variability*. If the forecast error is unbiased, but is large on the average, the forecasts will not be very accurate. One possible cause of variability is use of inappropriate seasonal coefficients (for example, if no seasonal adjustments are made when there really is a seasonal pattern). Other causes cannot be corrected. For example, items with very low average usage rate tend to have long periods of zero demand followed by sporadic usage. A *forecast variability filter* is

$$\text{``possibly variable forecast'' if } \frac{\text{MAD}}{\text{forecast}} > n_3$$

The magnitude of the three filter parameters, n_1, n_2, and n_3, is determined through a combination of theory and experience. The theory given after equation (14) suggests that n_1 should be about 3, but experience may dictate a higher or lower value. Trigg (1964) pointed out that the tracking signal as given in equation (16) is between -1 and $+1$, so n_2 should be less than 1.0. To detect errors for a simple (no trend) exponential smoothing system, Gardiner (1983) recommends that n_2 be set between 0.36 and 0.47 for $\alpha = 0.1$ and somewhat larger for higher α values. However, he also found that larger values of α can lead to poorer performance of this error detector and points out alternative methods.

The appropriate value for n_3 is primarily a judgment, based on experience. This parameter measures the average percentage error in the forecasts. One useful approach is to ignore n_3 while initiating a forecasting system and then separate items into two groups based on the percentage errors achieved. For example, if 90% of the items were able to achieve average forecast errors of 30% or less, then $n_3 = 0.30$ would be a reasonable dividing line indicating hard-to-forecast items.

Self-adaptive methods have been proposed by a number of authors. (See Whybark, 1972, for a summary.) The idea is to increase the response when the forecast seems to be inaccurate, and to quickly reduce it again as the forecast realigns itself. The Trigg and Leach method is the simplest: the smoothing constant α (or the response rate R_A) is set equal to the tracking signal (dropping the sign). Self-adaptive systems such as this have demonstrably improved ability to quickly respond to a sudden change in demand and are therefore worthy of careful evaluation in selecting a forecasting method to incorporate as part of an ongoing management system.

Review Problems

1. Name two ways in which MAD can be used.
2. Explain why the Trigg–Leach method will always respond quickly to sustained forecast errors.

Solutions

1. Confidence intervals on the forecast, and automatic error detection.
2. Normally, the forecast error will tend to be small and will tend to alternate in sign (sometimes positive, sometimes negative). When either a large error or several smaller ones of the same sign occur, the smoothed average error, E_t, will increase (i.e., move away from zero). In the Trigg–Leach approach, this leads to a larger tracking signal and a higher response rate.

8-7 THE BOX–JENKINS METHOD

A more complex time-series-analysis method is that of Box and Jenkins (1970). This approach has both supporters (Newbold, 1975) and detractors (Chatfield and Prothero, 1973). The main arguments of the detractors are that (1) the tools of analysis are difficult to master, sometimes leading to poor forecasts; (2) large amounts of data are required in order to properly use the method; and (3) the data must be transformed to achieve "stationarity" before the forecasting model can be developed. In fact, all the arguments are true, but the highly skilled users of the method are sometimes able to obtain significant increases in accuracy when compared to exponential smoothing (Newbold, 1975).

The major steps in preparation of the model are:

1. Data transformation; if necessary use a function (such as the logarithm or the first difference) to eliminate trends in the average level of demand and in the variability.
2. Model identification; analyze the remaining variability (using some cleverly derived rules of thumb) to determine one or more models that account for the autocorrelation[3] in the transformed data.
3. Parameter estimation; find the optimal values for the unknown parameters in the model(s) selected above.
4. Checking; repeat steps 2 and 3 as many times as necessary until no further improvements are found.

The resulting model bases its forecasts on two sources of information—previous forecast errors and previous values of the data. When no seasonal effects are present, the models typically consist of one to three recent forecast errors and a like number of past data values, each suitably weighted according to the results of the estimation step. These forecasts must then be transformed back to the original scale (reversing step 1) so that growth and other factors are reintroduced. Seasonal effects typically add one or two more terms to the model and require data from the previous year in order to implement the forecast.

As an example, Nelson (1973) gives the following equation for the one-period-ahead forecast for the (natural logarithm of the) monthly number of automobile registrations in the United States:

$$\text{forecast} = D_t + D_{t-11} - D_{t-12} - 0.21e_t - 0.26e_{t-1} \tag{17}$$
$$- 0.85e_{t-11} + 0.18e_{t-12} + 0.22e_{t-13}$$

Thus the forecast for next month's registrations is based on the value just observed this month (D_t), plus the seasonal change observed between the same two months last year $(D_{t-11} - D_{t-12})$, modified by feeding back five different forecast errors, including the most recent (e_t) and one that occurred 13 months previously. In this form (having completed the difficult estimation process) the model is quite easy to use as long as 25 data points are retained for easy access (12 months of auto registration and 13 months of forecast errors). In contrast, a comparable exponential smoothing model would retain 14 data points (12 seasonal factors plus the intercept and slope terms).

Short-range forecasts of hospital occupancy were developed by Wood (1976) using the Box–Jenkins technique. He reports on models for five hospitals which predict with an average error of 1.6% to 3.4% for the next-day forecast, and 3.5% to 5.7% for forecasts 1 week in advance. The typical forecast equation

---

[3] Autocorrelation is a correlation between a variable and its own previous values.

requires eight inputs, including hospital occupancy and forecast errors dating back as much as 1 week.

Recent research has indicated that the Box–Jenkins method is superior when there is low randomness in the data. This is the case with highly aggregated data such as industry-wide statistics. However, both Carbone (1983) and Lawrence (1983) report that greater accuracy was achieved using simpler methods such as exponential smoothing when randomness was a large factor, as is the case with forecasts of single-item demand. Surprisingly, in almost all cases the forecast accuracy achieved in these experiments was almost the same for all methods. Therefore, we are now in the unenviable position of knowing which kinds of methods are best under a variety of circumstances, but being unable to produce substantial improvements with this knowledge. Since this is true, it seems preferable to use less complex models such as exponential smoothing.

8-8 Summary

Information systems are designed to support both daily operations and advance planning. There are several guiding principles in selecting an information system, most notably designing the system according to its intended use, and keeping a consistent level of detail throughout. The advent of relatively inexpensive computers has had a major impact on the effectiveness of information systems, but has also led to the generation of large masses of unused reports. The microcomputer revolution is bringing these benefits and problems to small organizations.

Implementation of an information system requires great care. For example, Lawrence (1983) reports on a survey of selected Australian companies whose forecasting systems have fallen into disuse for a variety of reasons:

1. The users were not the instigators.
2. The users did not maintain data accuracy.
3. Great effort was required to manage the data base, removing extraordinary events.
4. Manual review of computer forecasts was not well thought out.
5. The system was designed to replace the user.
6. Responsibility for forecast accuracy was not established.

The guiding theme of these comments is that an information system must be viewed as part of a larger management system, carefully designed and integrated. Changes in work assignments or responsibilities must be carefully considered so that the new system is seen to support, not compete with, the users.

Forecasting is a model-based information system, and there are many models to choose from. Not only do they differ in techniques but also in effort and cost of implementation. Thus, like other information systems, forecasting methods should be selected to suit the need. Exponential smoothing is one of the simplest quantitative techniques for forecasting from historical data. It is reasonably accurate for short lead times, at least until some significant event causes the underlying pattern to change. After such a change, unless there is human intervention, forecasts will be biased for a time until the old patterns are forgotten, as a result of the discounting inherent in the system. Most exponential smoothing systems currently in use estimate both growth and seasonal trends and have an error-detection system to signal the user whenever human intervention is needed. In addition, some systems are programmed to take corrective action automatically.

The Box–Jenkins method, although far more difficult to implement, is easy to use once the correct model has been identified and parameters have been estimated. Because of its more general form, this method sometimes leads to prediction of the all-important turning point, when an upward or downward trend is expected to change. However, experience has shown that even highly trained forecasters can make significant errors in implementing a Box–Jenkins model.

It is well to remember that forecasts are always wrong. Because of this, it may be difficult to decide among the many alternative forecasting methods. The acid test is to try the candidates, using historical data as though it were just occurring. One should then select the simplest model that does an adequate job. It is often the case that using the next better model yields only a small improvement at a significant additional cost.

It is not an exaggeration to say that most important decisions are based on forecasts, either implicitly or explicitly. Every decision that has an element of planning requires some estimate of what is to be expected in the future. This includes long-range decisions such as capacity and location planning, intermediate-range production and work-force plans, and short-range personnel and other scheduling decisions. The All-Sports caselet (which follows) asks you to estimate the value of a forecasting model for control of inventory in a distribution company.

CASELET: ALL-SPORTS DISTRIBUTION COMPANY

The All-Sports Distribution Company distributes sporting goods to retail stores and schools in a four-county area in Ohio. They cover a basically rural area, with a total population of 450,000. There are several cities in the range of 20,000 to 50,000 population, but no larger cities. All-Sports has about 20% of the market, sharing the market with one larger competitor, and two smaller competitors.

All-Sports has not been using any forecasting techniques. Rather they have relied on yearly average sales and maximum monthly sales to make their decisions on how many units to carry. They have not had a problem with lost sales, but they believe that they are carrying too much inventory. Recently, their warehouse has been full at all times, and some units have been stored in the receiving room, causing some difficulties in handling.

The firm has 120 product lines, and each line has several sizes or styles. They define a line, for example, as "Wilson T-3000, tennis racquet," and there are nine combinations of weight and grip. The mix of the weight-grip combinations is relatively stable; they assume that the mix will continue to be constant, and they can ignore the problem of what weight-grip combinations to order.

They want to study the sales of Wilson T-3000 racquets to see if better forecasting can reduce their inventory sufficiently to warrant the expense.

Costs. An outside company has proposed to operate a forecasting system for All-Sports. The forecasting system would require a computer terminal, at a cost of $120 per month. The computer time and storage is estimated to cost $160 per month. The data necessary are already available in a central location, and it is estimated that the additional time to enter the data and receive the output would be only 3 or 4 hours once a month. The employee who would do that task is paid $8 per hour gross salary, but the office manager feels that the employee can perform that task without affecting other work. Thus they feel there is no additional cost. (It is important to note that no in-house computer expertise is required for this application.) There would be some initial expense, which will be incurred in setting up the system. The firm estimates this expense to be $100 plus 2 days of management time. The management time will be 1 day for the warehouse superintendent plus 1 day for the executive vice-president.

The cost of a T-3000 racquet to distributors is $25. They sell it to their customers at $32, who, in turn, sell it for $48. Since other distributors are available, they do not want to be out of stock. The president of All-Sports says that it is impossible to say what the cost of capital is for the inventory, since the company uses long-term debt, short-term debt, and current receipts to finance its operations.

Current Policy. The company places an order for each product line in each month. They order an amount so that their inventory (on hand plus on order) is equal to the maximum monthly demand last year plus 10 units. The orders arrive very quickly; they do not have a problem with lead time. They began each month in 1984 with $140 + 10 = 150$ tennis racquets, since the maximum 1983 demand was 140 in April.

The firm knows that this policy is too conservative, but they have not had time to make separate monthly forecasts of each product line. They have stated that they believe a policy of ordering up to next month's forecast plus 20 units would yield customer service as good as the present system.

Data. As of the time of this analysis, July 1985, the firm had $5\frac{1}{2}$ years of data available for T-3000. As mentioned above, no breakdown by weight–grip combinations is given or deemed necessary.

	1980	1981	1982	1983	1984	1985
Jan.	72	75	80	78	84	82
Feb.	71	77	78	76	81	81
Mar.	102	110	120	131	124	128
Apr.	115	110	136	140	142	140
May	81	74	78	84	85	91
June	60	68	76	71	75	78
July	58	54	58	61	66	
Aug.	61	64	66	68	72	
Sept.	75	78	74	91	88	
Oct.	92	97	105	101	110	
Nov.	120	124	121	130	145	
Dec.	115	116	117	122	128	

PROBLEMS

1. In what ways do the information needs change as one ascends the ladder of responsibility in an organization? How should this be reflected in an information system? How does this relate to forecasting?

2. The level of detail is an important issue in the design of an information system. Contrast the difficulties faced by Hugeco Manufacturers and Farm Supply Corporation (Section 8-1) in this regard.

*3. What does a model-based information system add in the way of management information, compared to a system that is not model-based?

4. What do the trends in the computer industry imply for the future of management information systems?

5. Describe how forecasts with confidence intervals would be useful for
   (a) Ordering office supplies.
   (b) Planning maintenance of equipment.
   (c) Preparing a budget for a school district.
   (d) Scheduling employee vacations.
   (e) Planning an employee recruitment and training program.

6. Would exponential smoothing be an appropriate forecasting method to supply information for capacity/location decisions? For intermediate range production and work-force planning? Explain your answers, briefly.

*7. Two employees have been having a forecasting contest for the past 12 months. Each has been using no-trend exponential smoothing with $R_A = 0.2$, but George has been calculating his forecasts monthly, whereas Mary updates weekly. Three months ago there was a substantial drop in demand. Prior to that time, demand had been fluctuating around an average of 200 per week, but now it seems to be nearer 100. Who is more likely to have an accurate forecast, given the recent drop? Why?

8. The Amalgamated Battery Company distributes a large-capacity battery that has been used by some industrial processes heretofore. They know that electric cars are now in production and they think that a jump (permanent, one-time increase) has occurred in their demand. They are forecasting by simple exponential smoothing [equation (1) in the text] since there has been no trend. The battery costs $25 to produce. At the end of December, the exponentially smoothed average was 150. The recent demands are: January = 230, February = 250.

   (a) Which of the following values is more appropriate, $\alpha = 0.05$ or $\alpha = 0.30$? Why?

   (b) Incorporate January and February into the exponentially smoothed average, using equation (1).

   (c) Compute forecasts for March and April.

   (d) They are using these forecasts as a basis for deciding on production quantities. What difficulties do you foresee in using this method in this situation?

*9. A manufacturer of commercial upholstery-sewing machines has decided to implement a new method to forecast demand for its finished products. There are four different models of this product. Spare parts for these machines are their only other products. Their production policy for sewing machines has recently changed from "produce only to fill firm orders" to "produce to fill forecasted orders."

   (a) The forecast for one type of sewing machine has been stable at 16 per month with no trend or seasonal. The MAD has been 2.1. The most recent sales figure, since new delivery promises went into effect, was 24. Compute the forecast for next month using exponential smoothing with no trend [i.e., use equation (1) to forecast] and compute the new MAD value. Use $\alpha = 0.3$.

   (b) Describe how the company should forecast sales for the upcoming period. First, if they are going to use exponential smoothing, how should they use it? Second, what other information should they collect?

*10. It is the end of February and Joe Schmoe has been working on a forecast for March. So far, he has calculated

$$a_{\text{Feb}} = 180 \qquad b_{\text{Feb}} = 3 \qquad \text{MAD}_{\text{Feb}} = 10$$

using smoothing constants (response rates) of $R_A = 0.2$ and $R_B = 0.011$, and $\alpha = 0.2$ for MAD.

   (a) What is the forecast for March? (There is no seasonal pattern.) Put a 95% confidence interval around the forecast.

   (b) A month has passed since problem (a) and the March demand turned out to be 200 units. What is the April forecast? The 95% confidence interval?

11. The accompanying table is an excerpt from the records of a company that has been using exponential smoothing for a long time. The data have been deseasonalized. Ignore seasonal factors for this problem.

(a) In month 109, what was the forecast for month 110?

(b) In month 109, what was the forecast for month 112?

(c) In month 110, what was the forecast for month 112?

(d) Explain why the answer to part (c) is lower than the answer to part (b). (What happened in month 110 that would suggest that the forecast should be revised downward?)

(e) It is now the end of month 111. The (deseasonalized) demand in month 111 was 567.9. What is the forecast for month 112?

(f) Put a 95% confidence interval around your answer to part (e).

(g) Calculate a tracking signal for periods 108 through 111.

EXPONENTIAL SMOOTHING ON DESEASONALIZED HISTORICAL DATA

t	Deseasonalized Demand	a_t $R_A = 0.36$	b_t $R_B = 0.04$	$a_t + b_t$	MAD $(\alpha = 0.2)$	E_t $(\alpha = 0.2)$
108	555.3	563.8	8.095	571.9	11.26	−8.10
109	558.3	567.0	7.551	574.6	11.73	−9.20
110	571.7	573.5	7.437	581.0	9.96	−8.00

12. After a new product is introduced a firm believes its sales will follow a pattern of the form shown below.

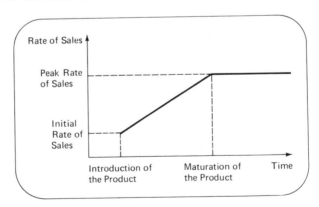

After maturation, the product continues at the same rate of sales for the foreseeable future. (Eventually sales will drop off, but we do not have to plan for that now.) Since there is uncertainty in sales, the firm must use forecasting techniques. They are concerned first about forecasting during the growth phase of the demand pattern.

(a) If, ahead of time, the sales manager guesses that the slope coefficient would be some specific value, say b_o, and that the maturation point would come in approximately 2 years, how should she include this into the forecasting system? (Be sure to answer both parts of the question, b_o *and* maturation point.)

(b) Part way into the introductory period, $a_t = 156$, $MAD_t = 20$, $b_t = 4$, $R_A = 0.19$, $R_B = 0.01$, and $\alpha = 0.1$ for MAD. What is the forecast for the next period's demand?

(c) If D_{t+1} turns out to be 150, find the values of a_{t+1}, MAD_{t+1} and b_{t+1}.

*13. The demand for egg agitators has recently changed dramatically. As shown in the accompanying figure, there has been an upswing in what had been a downward trend in the sales of this nonseasonal item. Using your eyeball (and perhaps a straightedge) you are to determine reasonable values for a_6 and b_6, which are to be used as initial values for an exponential smoothing system of forecasting egg agitator sales.

(a) Given the data for periods 1 to 6 only (forget that you ever saw the data after period 6), what are reasonable values for b_6 and a_6 (intercept at time 6)? Why?

(b) Given what you can see from the entire data set, give reasonable values for a_6 and b_6. Explain.

(c) What values of R_A and R_B would you use to initialize a forecast by exponentially smoothing periods 7 to 12? Why?

(d) Carry out the exponential smoothing for periods 7 to 12, using your answers to parts (b) and (c) to get started.

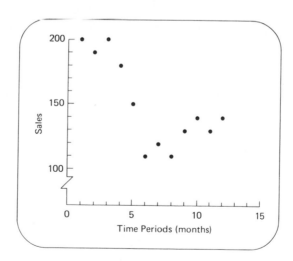

14. Southern Barnesville Distribution Company purchases small gift items in bulk, packages them, and sells them to retail stores. They are conducting an inventory control study of all their items. The following data are for item number 1C-42A, which is not seasonal:

MONTHLY SALES DURING 1980

51,	55,	54,	57,	50,	68,
66,	59,	67,	69,	75,	73

Using linear regression, the function "sales $= a + bt$" was estimated from the data above, with $t = 1$ representing January 1980.

Regression results: $a = 48.3$, $b = 2.1$, and MAD $= 2.8$

(a) Based on the regression results, what are the appropriate initial values for the exponential smoothing terms a_t, b_t, and MAD_t as of December 1980?

(b) Calculate forecasts for the first four months of 1981.

(c) During January, February, and March, the firm expects demand to be 10 units higher than normal, as the result of a promotional campaign. How does this change the forecasts in part (b)?

(d) Suppose January demand turned out to be 80. What forecasts would you make for February, March, and April? Be sure to decide how to make allowance for the "extra" demand of 10 units. Use $R_A = 0.1$, $R_B = 0.01$.

(e) Calculate a confidence interval for the February forecast. Use $\alpha = 0.1$. What can you say about confidence intervals for March and April?

(f) Briefly, what other effects might the promotion have?

*15. (a) The linear regression formulas for the slope b and intercept a are shown below. Treating time as x and sales as y, compute the coefficients a and b from the data in Problem 14 for the Southern Barnesville Distribution Company. (You need not work Problem 14 to complete this problem.)

$$b = \frac{\sum x_i y_i - n\bar{x}\bar{y}}{\sum x_i^2 - n\bar{x}^2}$$

$$a = \bar{y} - b\bar{x}$$

(b) Calculate how accurately the regression line $a + bt$ fits the data. Do this by computing values for $a + bt$ for each month and subtracting them from the sales data above. Ignoring the signs of these deviations, calculate their average. (That is, calculate the unweighted mean absolute deviation.)

16. Demand for Markov Chains (tire chains for traction on snow and ice) follows a seasonal pattern, which has been quantified by calculating a multiplicative factor for each quarter of the year.

Quarter	Seasonal Factor
First	1.1
Second	0.5
Third	0.4
Fourth	2.0

Demand per year has been growing at a rate of about 15%. Last year, total sales were $5 million.

(a) Prepare a numerical forecast for the next eight quarters from the information above. (Do not use regression or exponential smoothing.)

(b) If you were going to forecast quarterly sales with exponential smoothing, with a *linear* growth (or trend) term, what *initial* value should the growth term be given?

(c) Is the linear growth model appropriate here? Explain briefly.

*17. (a) Calculate a seasonal factor for Wednesday using the following data.

	Week 1	Week 2	Week 3	Week 4	Week 5
Sun.	103	95	104	96	105
Mon.	124	118	113	124	116
Tue.	131	125	136	121	137
Wed.	126	118	117	128	118
Thu.	120	115	124	119	127
Fri.	108	96	102	102	106
Sat.	81	74	88	73	85

(b) Suggest a method for computing seasonals that would put greater emphasis on recent data and less on older data.

*18. Two products, frosting mix and cake mix, share the same seasonal pattern but have different trends. We are now at the beginning of September, and the exponential smoothing calculations have been carried out to include August sales, except for the last few steps.

(a) Given the following information, construct forecasts for the next 5 months.

	Seasonal	CAKE MIX		FROSTING MIX	
Month	Factors	Intercept a_t	Trend b_t	Intercept a_t	Trend b_t
Sept.	1.1	90,000	0	51,000	1000
Oct.	1.2				
Nov.	1.4				
Dec.	1.3				
Jan.	0.8				
Feb.	0.7				

(b) Compute a forecast for the final quarter of the year, for each product.

(c) Time passes. It is now October 1, and September sales were 94,000 cases of cake mix and 58,000 cases of frosting mix. Compute new forecasts for October. Use $R_A = 0.1$ for both products, but $R_B = 0$ for cake and $R_B = 0.01$ for frosting.

(d) If these two items share a common seasonal pattern, how should the seasonal factor computation of Table 8-1 take this into account?

19. For two years, Risky Parts Co. has been using an exponentially smoothed forecast, with trend and seasonal factors. They are using smoothing constants of $R_A = 0.05$ and $R_B = 0.05$; they "update" the slope and intercept terms monthly and the seasonal factors annually.

    (a) It is now May 1, and the slope and intercept terms have been updated by the forecasting department with the results shown below. Use this information to forecast demand for May, June, and July.

    Forecasting terms, updated to include April's demand:
    $$a = 178.3$$
    $$b = 1.2$$

    Seasonal factors:

0.90 (April)	0.95 (May)	1.05 (June)
0.85 (July)	1.02 (August)	

    (b) It is now May 31, and May's demand was 205. Use this new information to forecast June, July, and August demands.

    (c) Risky Parts Co. has not been happy with the performance (accuracy) of this forecasting model. Suggest why poor performance might be expected, given the description above, with reference to the Technical Note in this chapter.

*20. The following data are the natural logarithms of the number of U.S. automobile registrations (in thousands) for 14 months beginning in January 1967. Also shown is the Box–Jenkins forecast made in the previous month. Use equation (17) to construct a forecast for March 1968.

Data:	6.42	6.29	6.51	6.67	6.71	6.69		
Forecast:	6.29	6.56	6.55	6.52	6.60	6.67		
Error:	0.13	−0.27	−0.04	0.15	0.11	0.02		
Data:	6.62	6.59	6.31	6.57	6.47	6.60	6.49	6.40
Forecast:	6.79	6.33	6.60	6.47	6.56	6.33	6.47	6.71
Error:	−0.17	0.26	−0.29	0.10	−0.09	0.27	0.02	−0.31

21. Midway Hospital uses a modified exponential smoothing approach to forecast the number of patient meals to be served (the meal census). The required lead time is 2 days. The method used is as follows. The days of the week have a predictable pattern. This is quantified by calculating seven exponentially smoothed averages, S_{Sun}, S_{Mon}, ..., S_{Sat}. However, the patient census 2 days from now is very strongly influenced by today's census, since most of today's patients will still be in the hospital. The average length of stay is 5.0 days. Therefore, today's census is a good indicator of whether the census will be above or below normal in 2 days. The general form of the forecast is

$$\text{census forecast for day } t + k = \text{previous week's average for day } t + k + \beta^k \left(\text{today's census} - \text{previous week's average for day } t \right)$$

Symbolically,

$$\text{forecast}_{t+k} = S_{t+k-7} + \beta^k (\text{census}_t - S_{t-7})$$

In this formula, k is the lead time in days, β is a parameter less than 1.0, and the S terms are the exponentially smoothed averages calculated 1 week previously using the following equation:

$$S_t = \alpha \cdot \text{census}_t + (1 - \alpha)S_{t-7}$$

In this problem, we will use $\alpha = 0.1$ and $\beta = 0.8$. The interpretation of the forecast equations is the goal of this problem. As of Tuesday, January 17, the exponentially smoothed averages were as follows:

S_{Sun}	S_{Mon}	S_{Tue}	S_{Wed}	S_{Thu}	S_{Fri}	S_{Sat}
146	152	155	148	140	130	112

(a) On Wednesday, January 18, the census was 152. Calculate forecasts for Thursday, Friday, Saturday, and Sunday.

(b) Referring to part (a), what role does β play in the model? What would happen if β were decreased from 0.8?

(c) What is the new Wednesday average, S_{Wed}?

(d) Interpret the meaning of S_{Wed} by referring to equation (4), $N = (2 - \alpha)/\alpha$. Then interpret the meaning of $\text{census}_t - S_{t-7}$ in the forecast equation.

(e) Two formulas have been suggested for determining the best value of β. They are $\beta = 1 - (\text{average length of stay})^{-1}$ and $\beta = 1 - \text{average discharge ratio}$. (Discharge ratio is calculated daily as the number of discharges divided by the patient census.) As a manager, how could you decide whether either of these β values is best or whether another would be better?

REFERENCES

Box, G. E., and G. M. Jenkins, *Time Series Analysis*. San Francisco: Holden-Day, 1970.

Brown, R. G., *Smoothing, Forecasting and Prediction of Discrete Time Series*. Englewood Cliffs, N.J.: Prentice-Hall, 1963.

Cadzow, J. A., *Discrete-Time Systems: An Introduction with Interdisciplinary Applications*. Englewood Cliffs, N.J.: Prentice-Hall, 1973.

Carbone, R., A. Andersen, Y. Corriveau, and P. P. Corson, "Comparing for Different Time Series Methods the Value of Technical Expertise, Individualized Analysis, and Judgmental Adjustment." *Management Science*, Vol. 29, No. 5 (1983), pp. 559–566.

Chambers, J. C., S. K. Mullick, and D. C. Smith, "How to Choose the Right Forecasting Technique." *Harvard Business Review*, July–August 1971, pp. 45–74.

Chatfield, C., and D. L. Prothero, "Box–Jenkins Seasonal Forecasting: Problems in a Case-Study." *Journal of the Royal Statistical Society*, A, Vol. 136, part 3 (1973), p. 295.

CHISHOLM, R. K., AND G. R. WHITAKER, JR., *Forecasting Methods*. Homewood, Ill.: Richard D. Irwin, 1971.

FUERST, W. L., AND P. H. CHENEY, "Factors Affecting the Perceived Utilization of Computer-Based Decision Support Systems in the Oil Industry." *Decision Sciences,* Vol. 13, No. 4 (1982), pp. 554–569.

GARDINER, E. S., JR., "Automatic Monitoring of Forecast Errors." *Journal of Forecasting,* Vol. 2, No. 1 (1983), pp. 1–21.

KEEN, P. G. W., AND M. SCOTT MORTON, *Decision Support Systems: An Organizational Perspective.* Reading, Mass.: Addison-Wesley, 1978.

LAWRENCE, M. J., "An Exploration of Some Practical Issues in the Use of Quantitative Forecasting Models." *Journal of Forecasting,* Vol. 2, No. 2 (1983), pp. 169–179.

LEWIS, C. D., *Demand Analysis and Inventory Control.* Lexington, Mass.: Saxon House/Lexington Books, 1975.

LUCAS, H. C., *Information Systems Concepts for Management,* 2nd ed. New York: McGraw-Hill, 1982.

MAKRIDAKAS, S., AND S. C. WHEELWRIGHT, *Forecasting Methods and Applications.* New York: Wiley, 1978.

MCCLAIN, J. O., "Dynamics of Exponential Smoothing with Trend and Seasonal Terms." *Management Science,* Vol. 20, No. 9 (1974).

MCCLAIN, J. O., "Restarting a Forecasting System When Demand Suddenly Changes." *Journal of Operations Management,* Vol. 2, No. 1 (1981).

MCCLAIN, J. O., AND L. J. THOMAS, "Response Variance Tradeoffs in Adaptive Forecasting." *Operations Research,* Vol. 21, No. 2 (1973), pp. 554–567.

NAYLOR, T. H., AND H. SCHAULAND, "A Survey of Users of Corporate Planning Models." *Management Science,* Vol. 22, No. 9 (1976), p. 927.

NELSON, C. R., *Applied Time Series Analysis.* San Francisco: Holden-Day, 1973.

NEWBOLD, P., "The Principles of the Box-Jenkins Approach." *Operational Research Quarterly,* Vol. 26 (1975), pp. 397–412.

RAO, V. R., AND J. E. COX, *Sales Forecasting Methods: A Survey of Recent Developments.* Report 78-119, Marketing Science Institute, Cambridge, Mass., 1978.

TRIGG, D. W., "Monitoring a Forecasting System." *Operational Research Quarterly,* Vol. 15 (1964), pp. 271–274.

WHYBARK, D. C., "A Comparison of Adaptive Forecasting Techniques." *The Logistics and Transportation Review,* Vol. 8, No. 3 (1972).

WINTERS, P. R., "Forecasting Sales by Exponentially Weighted Moving Averages." *Management Science,* Vol. 6 (1960), pp. 324–342.

WOOD, S. D., "Forecasting Patient Census: Commonalities in Time Series Models." *Health Services Research,* Vol. 11, No. 2 (1976), p. 158.

CHAPTER 9

Intermediate-Range Planning and Scheduling

The goal of intermediate-range planning is to arrive at overall production and work-force decisions for a number of months to come. The importance of these plans cannot be overstated. For example, policies concerning the use of overtime have an effect on the national unemployment level. Brennan et al. (1982), studying this issue in the European Economic Community, pointed out that reduced use of overtime could create jobs but would also lead to increased capital costs. At the individual company level, the intermediate-range plans determine the ability to respond to opportunities in the marketplace, as well as influencing the delivery lead time of manufactured products. The quality of a firm's intermediate-range planning has a substantial effect on its competitive position.

Intermediate-range plans provide guidelines for detailed scheduling decisions in the immediate future, and therefore they must satisfy certain criteria. The overall plans must (1) meet demand requirements, (2) be within capacity restrictions, (3) be consistent with company policy, (4) leave the firm in a good position at the end of the plan, and (5) minimize costs.

The planning process consists of three phases. Anticipating future requirements is the first phase; it consists of forecasting demand month by month over the planning period and setting safety margins to allow for the possibility of forecast error. Seasonality of demand and future economic trends are usually important in intermediate-range forecasts.

In the second phase, work-force and production plans are made on an overall, or aggregate, basis for the entire operation (firm, division, etc.). This process begins with a search for potential production and capacity bottlenecks. A detailed study of production/work force plans is then carried out over a future span of time (the *planning horizon*) trading off the costs of the various alternatives, such as work-force changes, subcontracting, overtime, and the use of inventory. Of particular importance is whether to plan seasonal work-force layoffs corresponding to seasonal demand patterns. In the second phase, production planning for service industries differs from planning for manufacturers, in that it is usually impossible to produce a service in advance of demand, whereas a physical product may be stored in inventory. (See Chapter 1 for a discussion of situations in which services can be inventoried.) It is also common for manufacturers of expensive and/or perishable goods to produce only when orders have been received. Make-to-order producers, like most service organizations, do not include inventory in their intermediate-range plans.

The third phase is implementation of the plan, when preparations are begun for planned future changes and the immediate plans are disaggregated into detailed work-force and production schedules, product by product.

Intermediate-range plans must be coordinated with both short- and long-range decisions. The time scale of intermediate range planning is usually measured in months, and the production plans are made in aggregate production units. Longer-range decisions, with the time scale measured in years, include capacity planning and product design. Both of these longer-range decisions interact with intermediate-range planning by placing restrictions on it, including capacity restrictions and production requirements. At a lower level, with a time scale in days or weeks, are the scheduling decisions for individual items and decisions involving the individual workers. The intermediate-range plan acts as a restriction on the short-range decisions by specifying the overall level of production and work force.

Intermediate-range planning is facilitated by aggregating the many products of a company into a single unit of output, referred to as the *aggregate production unit*. Some companies aggregate their sales and production levels on the basis of a common output measure such as barrels in the oil industry. Others use dollars, worker-hours, or machine-hours. When correctly implemented, plans for this aggregate product can be disaggregated at a later date into detailed plans for individual products. The advantages of aggregation include more accurate forecasting and simplification of the planning process. That is, aggregation allows one to work with many restrictions on future plans, without the additional complication of simultaneously considering hundreds or thousands of different items of production. Bitran and Hax (1977) have proposed a scheme for aggregating production units:

1. *Items* are the final products to be delivered to customers.
2. *Families* are groups of items that share a common manufacturing setup.
3. *Types* are groups of families whose production quantities are to be determined by an aggregate production plan. Items within a type share a common seasonal demand pattern.

Under this scheme there are several aggregate products (the types) rather than just one. This added complexity is not serious, however, since the Bitran–Hax scheme (discussed further in Chapter 15) includes a method for automatically generating the aggregate production plans for each product type, using linear programming (to be discussed later). The major advantage of using this multilevel approach is the natural way in which the aggregate plans (for types) may later be broken down into specific production schedules for families, and for items.

Production smoothing means avoiding large changes in the overall production level. There are several reasons for wanting to smooth production. A steady production rate allows a constant work force without major layoffs. Moreover, it avoids use of large amounts of overtime or subcontracting and avoids the costs of setting up or shutting down a new operation to meet peaks in demand. These costs of changing production levels can be avoided in two different ways. The first way is through the use of inventory, which represents production in advance of demand. The second way (the only way available to service industry and make-to-order manufacturers) is through modification of the demand pattern itself (Sasser, 1976). This can be accomplished by several means, including promotional effort to encourage demand during slack periods and deliberate underproduction during peak demand, resulting in backlogs and possible loss of sales. Some companies, including American, European, and Japanese firms, allow long-term capacity shortages to exist as a way of obtaining smooth growth and uniform labor requirements. Of course, these means of achieving production smoothing are costly, and the aggregate production planning problem may be viewed as searching for the optimal trade-off of the cost of changing production levels against the cost of avoiding the changes.

Before explaining the techniques used to develop aggregate production and work-force plans, two additional concepts should be understood—rolling schedules and frozen horizon. The term *rolling schedule* recognizes that the aggregate plans are by no means final. That is, the methods we are about to study must be repeated monthly, even if the aggregate plans extend many months into the future. The reason for this is that demand, being difficult to predict, will often turn out to be different from the forecast; this leaves the company in a different inventory position than had been planned. Consequently, after the first period, the entire problem is rolled forward one period, and new aggregate plans are made. The sequence of first period aggregate plans is referred to as a rolling schedule.

Frozen horizon refers to the fact that it may already be too late to modify the plans for the first month, or maybe 2 or 3 months, due to lead times for acquiring material, scheduling personnel, and so on. Periods that cannot be changed are referred to as the frozen horizon and need not appear in a production planning chart. Throughout our discussion, period 0 refers to the end of the frozen horizon and period 1 refers to the first month in which plans can be changed.

In this chapter, we shall follow the case of the Smooth Products Company through two planning phases (anticipating requirements and developing work force/production plans). The last section of the chapter will present a linear programming version of aggregate production planning. Detailed scheduling will be the topic of subsequent chapters.

The Smooth Products Company

The Smooth Products Company has recently initiated several projects to improve efficiency and cut costs. One of these efforts involves a study of the possibility of cutting inventory by use of seasonal layoffs. In this study, production was measured in aggregate units equivalent to 100 worker-days of labor. That is, the regular-time production capacity is 0.01 aggregate production unit per worker per day. This can be increased by up to 10% by scheduling overtime, but overtime production costs $2000 (per aggregate unit) more than regular time. There are currently 450 production workers, resulting in a regular time production rate of 4.5 aggregate units per day.

The maximum daily production rate is 7.0 aggregate units, owing to physical limitations. This limit applies to total daily output, so it may not be exceeded by use of overtime. However, additional production can be subcontracted to another firm, at a cost that is $3500 higher per aggregate unit than regular-time production.

The average cost of hiring and training a worker is $400, whereas reducing the work force costs $200 per worker laid off. By company policy, a minimum of 400 workers is always retained.

It costs $10,000 per year to hold, in inventory, products equivalent to one aggregate unit of production. Currently (at the end of December) there are 80 aggregate units on hand. The annual demand is 1200 aggregate units. The seasonal demand pattern (column (2) of Table 9-1) has peaks in late spring and in December. There is an annual 2-week shutdown in July, a slack month.

9-1 ANTICIPATING REQUIREMENTS

Required production consists of two elements—demand and inventory requirements. Demand is anticipated through forecasting methods such as those described in Chapter 8. It is significant that aggregate forecasts are more accurate than forecasts for individual items. This is because the randomness in the demand for individual items is somewhat reduced when the items are aggregated. However, because forecasts are not perfectly accurate, there is a need to specify a margin of safety. In the case of manufacturing, this is done by specifying a required minimum level of inventory referred to as *safety stock*. In addition to meeting all the demands, production must be sufficient to keep inventory at or above the safety stock level.

There is often another inventory requirement, referred to as *cycle stock*.

TABLE 9-1   CUMULATIVE PRODUCTION REQUIREMENTS
FOR SMOOTH PRODUCTS COMPANY

(1)	(2)	(3)	(4)	(5)	(6)	(7)
		Cumulative		Cumulative		Cumulative
	Demand	Demand,	Minimum	Requirements	Production	Production
Period,	(Forecast),	$\sum\limits_{i=1}^{t} D_i$	Inventory,	[(3) + (4)],	Days,	Days,
t	D_t		MI_t	CR_t	$DAYS_t$	CD_t
0. Dec.			40	40		0
1. Jan.	70	70	15	85	22	22
2. Feb.	50	120	10	130	18	40
3. Mar.	100	220	30	250	22	62
4. Apr.	200	420	40	460	21	83
5. May	150	570	35	605	22	105
6. June	50	620	10	630	21	126
7. July	50	670	10	680	12	138
8. Aug.	50	720	10	730	22	160
9. Sept.	90	810	30	840	21	181
10. Oct.	90	900	30	930	21	202
11. Nov.	100	1000	30	1030	20	222
12. Dec.	200	1200	40	1240	18	240

For example, if all items reach their safety-stock levels at the same time, there is no way to schedule production which can avoid some items falling below their safety-stock levels and perhaps even incurring shortages. Consequently, the inventory requirement will usually be above the safety-stock level. (See Chapter 11 for a discussion of production cycles.) The minimum inventory (MI_t) for a time period t is the sum of safety stock, cycle stock, and any other required inventory.

We will now formalize the concept of requirements. At the end of period t, the *cumulative requirement* (CR) is defined as the minimum allowable ending inventory for that period plus the cumulative demand through period t. This is summarized in equation (1), in which D_j is the forecast of demand during period j:

$$CR_t = MI_t + \sum_{j=1}^{t} D_j \qquad (1)$$

Demand and minimum inventory levels are given in columns (2) and (4) of Table 9-1 for the Smooth Products Company. The cumulative demand is shown in column (3). Cumulative requirements in column (5) is simply the sum of columns (3) and (4).

The reason for calculating cumulative requirements is to place a lower limit on production. As we consider alternative production plans, we are only interested in plans that meet or exceed CR_t, so that demand can be met with at least the extra margin of inventory given by MI_t. Of course, if production exceeds requirements, the inventory will exceed MI_t. Although excess inventory represents a cost to the company, production that exceeds requirements during part of the planning horizon may have advantages such as a more constant production rate leading to less overtime or reduction in hiring or layoffs.

For purposes of illustration, a cumulative production plan is plotted in Figure 9-1 together with cumulative requirements and cumulative demand. Note that at time $t = 0$ the production curve is at a level of 80 units. This is the initial inventory I_0, which represents leftover production from the past. The production rate in this plan is 3.87 per day through day 62, increases to 6.63 until day 105, then is 4.07 until day 202, and finishes the year at a rate of 6.32 per day. These values are represented by the slopes of the top line.

A general relationship between inventory and production is

$$\begin{array}{ccccc} \text{inventory} & = & \text{initial} & + & \text{cumulative} & - & \text{cumulative} \\ \text{in period } t & & \text{inventory} & & \text{production} & & \text{demand} \end{array} \qquad (2)$$

$$I_t \quad = \quad I_0 \quad + \quad \sum_{j=1}^{t} P_j \quad - \quad \sum_{j=1}^{t} D_j$$

in which P_j is production during period j. That is, inventory is the difference between the cumulative production (including initial stocks) and cumulative demand. In the graph, this difference is the vertical distance from the cumulative demand to the cumulative production. Therefore, if the cumulative production graph dips below the cumulative requirements, inventory is less than MI_t, indicating

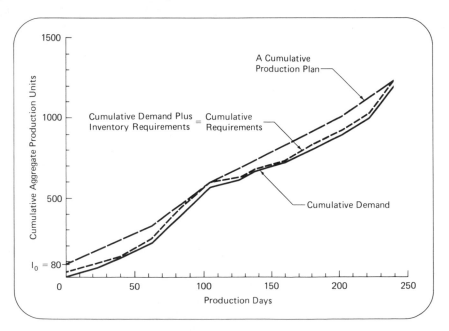

Figure 9-1 Demand and inventory requirements for the Smooth Products Company.

an unacceptable plan. That is, *the cumulative requirements represent a minimum for cumulative production plus initial inventory*.

Backlogging Demand

Make-to-order and service organizations can use these same concepts with a slight modification. In these firms, production occurs at the same time as or later than demand. When production lags behind, demand is said to be backlogged, and the amount of the backlog is equal to the difference between the cumulative demand and the cumulative production. That is, backlog equals negative inventory.

If the minimum inventory MI is a negative number, it represents the *maximum* allowable backlog. Equations (1) and (2) still hold, but we require inventory to be negative.

For example, in Table 9-1, if $I_0 = -80$ and all the MI_t terms were given negative signs, it would mean that we currently have a backlog of 80 aggregate units of demand, but our goal would be to cut the backlog to 15 by the end of January, 10 in February, and so on. In this case, the rationale for allowing the backlog to grow again (as high as 40 in April) would be that a larger backlog during high-demand months may allow us to avoid drastic changes in the work force.

Allowing a backlog changes the relationship of the lines in Figure 9-1. The cumulative requirements curve will be below the cumulative demand curve, as may be seen in equation (1) with MI_t negative. Also, if inventory is not allowed, the cumulative production curve must lie below the cumulative demand, which places it between the demand and requirements curves. Because of this, a company with demand that is as seasonally varying as the Smooth Products Company would have to face wide fluctuations in production rate unless the allowable backlogs were larger than (the negative of) the MI_t numbers used in Figure 9-1.

Some manufacturers use both inventory and backlogging (during slack and peak months, respectively). In a month when backlogging is allowed, MI_t will be negative, but it can be positive during slack demand months. Likewise, the inventory variable I_t represents a backlog when it is negative and inventory when positive.

Interpreting negative inventory as backlogged demand allows us to use equations (1) and (2) for all the situations we have discussed. However, for sake of simplicity, backlogging of demand will not be allowed for the remainder of this chapter. The calculations are very similar to the ''inventory only'' model, as will be seen in the problems at the end of the chapter.

Review Problems

1. If the Smooth Products Company continues at 450 workers with no overtime or subcontracting, what will the inventory be at the end of January, and at the end of February? (Use the data in Table 9-1, and recall that there are 80 units of inventory currently on hand.)

2. What is the first period in which inventory will not meet the required MI at this production rate?

Solutions

1. 450 workers produce 4.5 units per day, and there are 22 working days in January (see Table 9-1). Therefore, $P_1 = (22)(4.5) = 99$ units produced. $I_1 = I_0 + P_1 - D_1 = 80 + 99 - 70 = 109$. Similarly, $P_2 = (18)(4.5) = 81$, so $I_2 = 80 + (99 + 81) - (70 + 50) = 140$.

2. Continue the same calculation. In April, inventory is 6.5 units below the required level of 40.

9-2 PLAN DEVELOPMENT BY THE GRAPHICAL METHOD

In Figure 9-1, any curve that starts at 80 on the vertical axis and remains above the cumulative requirements curve is a potential production plan. It is useful to narrow the choices somewhat. In the case of the Smooth Products Company, the minimum daily production rate is 4.0. On a cumulative graph, a production rate translates to the *slope,* so any portion of a production plan that has a slope less than 4.0 is not realistic. We were also given a maximum production rate of 7.0 per day, so a slope steeper than 7.0 is also not allowed, unless a subcontract is let to augment production.

The MCP (Minimum Constant Production Rate) Production Plan

Upper and lower limits of production still leave many possibilities. One alternative that may be attractive is to adopt a constant daily production rate. Figure 9-2 shows two production plans that have constant rates. The lower of these two lines is more economical because it has less inventory. (Remember that, on the graph, inventory is the distance between production and requirements curves.) Furthermore, no *constant-rate* production plan can be lower in inventory than the one labeled minimum constant production rate plan (MCP), since to do so would put it below requirements at day 105 (the end of May). Therefore, MCP is a fitting label.

After May, the MCP stays above the requirements curve. Perhaps a change to a new constant rate would be desirable at that time. That question will be left for later.

The production rate of the MCP is easily calculated because we know two points on the MCP, and it is a straight line. MCP passes through 80 at time zero and equals the CR of 605 at the end of May, day 105. Therefore, the daily production rate is $(605 - 80)/(105 - 0) = 5.00$ per day.

Table 9-2 illustrates another way of determining the MCP production rate. (Please note that this table is a continuation of Table 9-1, and the columns are numbered accordingly.) Column (8) contains the same calculation we just per-

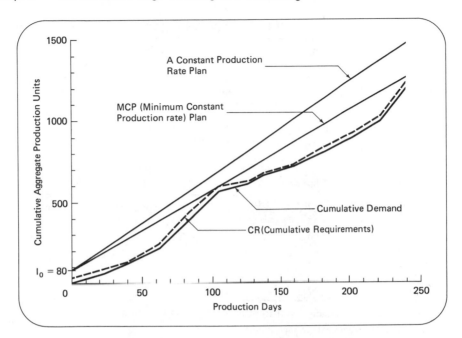

Figure 9-2   Cumulative Production Plans with constant daily rates of production.

formed, but repeats it for all the months rather than just for May. The MCP rate stands out as the largest of these "average requirements" because the MCP line is tangent to the "high point" of the cumulative requirements curve, as viewed from the initial inventory position of 80 units.

Before discussing other production plans, some additional evaluation of the MCP plan is in order. Table 9-2 illustrates how to compute the inventory on a monthly basis. The cumulative production in column (11) begins at 80, the initial inventory, and each month's production is added at the rate of 5 units per production day, using the production days per month from Table 9-1. Inventory is calculated as the difference between column (11) and column (5) from Table 9-1. This is simply carrying out equation (2). The calculations stop at May, for reasons to be discussed later.

To complete the evaluation, consider how the production plan could be implemented. The current rate of production at Smooth Products Company is 4.5 per day. To achieve the MCP rate of 5 per day, there must be either hiring or overtime until May. It appears from the graph that a slowdown after May might be desirable, so some of the newly hired might be laid off again. Nevertheless, some hiring must take place, since the maximum amount of overtime was given as 10%, which would increase the current rate to 4.95. To complete the evaluation, one would have to specify how the production rate would change, and apply the appropriate costs.

As an example, suppose that the entire increase is by hiring. (Refer back

TABLE 9-2 CALCULATING THE MCP (MINIMUM CONSTANT PRODUCTION) PLAN

(1) Period	(8) Average Requirements[a]	(9) Production Rate[b]	(10) Production[c]	(11) Cumulative Production Plus I_0	(12) Inventory[d]
				$80 = (I_0)$	
Jan.	0.23	5	110	190	120
Feb.	1.25	5	90	280	160
Mar.	2.74	5	110	390	170
Apr.	4.58	5	105	495	75
May	5.00	5	110	605	35
June	4.37		Beyond the natural horizon		
July	4.35				
Aug.	4.06				
Sept.	4.20				
Oct.	4.21				
Nov.	4.28				
Dec.	4.83				

[a] Average requirements = $(CR_t - I_0)/(CD_t - CD_0)$, all from Table 9-1.

[b] Choose the largest average requirement.

[c] Rate times DAYS ("DAYS" is column 6, Table 9-1).

[d] Inventory = cumulative production plus I_0 minus cumulative demand (from column 3, Table 9-1).

to the description of the Smooth Products Company just before Section 9-1.) The costs through May are as follows.

> INVENTORY: Monthly cost is $10,000/12 = $833.33 per aggregate unit. Total unit-months of inventory = 120 + 160 + 170 + 75 + 35 = 560 at $833.33 per unit = $466,667.
>
> HIRING: Increasing production by 0.5 aggregate unit requires addition of 0.5/0.01 = 50 workers at $400 per worker for hiring and training = $20,000.
>
> OVERTIME PREMIUMS: Zero.
>
> SUBCONTRACTING PREMIUMS: Zero.
>
> LAYOFFS: Not clear yet, but probably some after May.
>
> NORMAL COST OF PRODUCTION: Not a variable cost. It will be the same under all plans because we account separately for additional costs (i.e., premiums) due to overtime and subcontracting.
>
> TOTAL VARIABLE COST THROUGH MAY: $486,667.

Plans With Varying Production Rates: Some Restrictions

If the production rate remains at 4.5 rather than 5.0 for a while, the total inventory will be reduced. Eventually, production must increase, however, so that the increased demands of April and May can be met and the minimum inventory levels satisfied. Since the MCP rate of 5.0 was just enough to meet the May peak, it stands to reason that if the 4.5 rate is maintained for a month or more, a rate above 5.0 must be achieved to make up the difference.

Figure 9-3 shows two plans of this sort. Both plans retain a rate of 4.5 during the first 3 months. Plan X increases the production rate substantially at that point, whereas plan Y increases production more modestly, only enough to achieve the May requirements. We can see that the graphs of both plans are steeper after March than the MCP, confirming that the production rates are both in excess of 5.

Rather than carry out a numerical evaluation of these plans, consider the following arguments.

Plan X has more hiring costs, because it is steeper during April and May.

Plan X has more inventory costs because it is either the same or above plan Y in the diagram.

Both plans will require layoffs after May to avoid overproduction, unless demand after the end of the horizon (day 240) is very high. Plan X, having the higher production rate, requires a greater layoff.

It is easy to see from these arguments that plan Y dominates plan X unless there is a dramatic increase in demand beyond day 240. If no such increase is expected, we can drop plan X from consideration without checking the exact costs. In fact, by a similar argument:

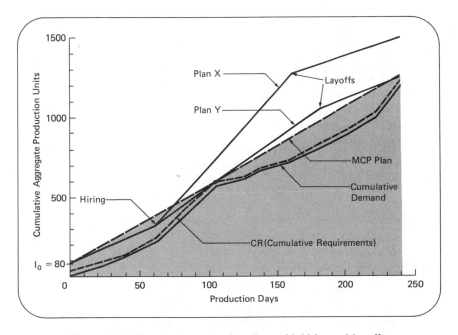

Figure 9-3 Cumulative production plans with hiring and layoffs.

If the objective is to minimize costs within the planning horizon, we can drop any plan that has any segment above the MCP.

This idea is extremely important. We can now restrict our attention to production plans whose graphs fall between the cumulative requirements curve and the MCP (inclusive).

The Natural Planning Horizon

The point where the MCP touches the cumulative requirements curve is called the *natural planning horizon*. (Homework problem 6 suggests the reason for this label.) We need not concern ourselves with any production plan that does not pass through this point. A plan passing below that point does not meet requirements. A plan passing above the natural horizon can be ruled out by an argument similar to that in the preceding paragraphs.

Now the reason why the calculations of Table 9-2 stopped at the end of May is clear. The "after May decisions" can be separated from the "before May decisions," since every "before May plan" must lead to the same point, the natural planning horizon.

In the next section, guidelines that use the costs of inventory, overtime, hiring, and firing are described.

Review Problems

1. Use equation (2) to calculate the inventory at the end of the first 2 months of the MCP.
2. When May arrives, given the data we have, what will the new MCP be, and when will the next natural planning horizon occur?

Solutions

1. January production = 22 days at a rate of 5 per day or 110 units. Starting with 80 units, the January ending inventory is $80 + 110 - 70 = 120$. February production = $(18)(5) = 90$, so inventory is $80 + (110 + 90) - (70 + 50) = 160$.

2. Using Figure 9-2, starting from the CR curve at May, a straight line tangent to CR in December represents the next MCP. The production rate will be $(1240 - 605)/(240 - 105) = 4.70$ units per day. Unless more data beyond December change this picture, December will be the next natural planning horizon.

9-3 DEVELOPING ALTERNATIVE PLANS—ECONOMIC GUIDELINES

In this section, we shall study how to develop and evaluate good plans using principles that are based on the relevant costs. As always, an anlaysis based entirely on costs is narrow in scope, and management may wish to use additional criteria to finally decide on a plan. For example, many firms believe that the long-term cost of firing people is so high in terms of loss of morale that they will do almost anything to avoid firing.

Research has resulted in a set of rules that are useful in the search for a minimum-cost plan. The rules we shall use apply only to linear costs, but more general forms are given in the original papers (Kunreuther and Morton, 1973, and McClain and Thomas, 1977). Careful use of these rules leads to very good plans, but does not guarantee that the least-cost plan will be found. Table 9-3

TABLE 9-3   RULES FOR AGGREGATE PLANNING

DEFINITIONS

C_H = cost of increasing production by hiring one worker

C_F = cost of decreasing production by firing one worker

C_O = overtime premium per unit (i.e., additional cost of producing one aggregate unit in overtime)

C_I = cost of holding one aggregate unit in inventory for 1 month

n = average number of production days per month

p = productivity, or daily output of aggregate units per worker

m^* = largest integer less than $-0.5 + [0.25 + 2(C_H + C_F)/(npC_I)]^{1/2}$

l^* = largest integer in $(C_H + C_F)/(npC_O)$

k^* = largest integer in C_O/C_I

seasonal layoff = reduction in work force for which the next scheduled work-force change is an increase (hiring)

RULES

1. Two seasonal layoffs should be at least $2(m^* + 1)$ months apart. Therefore, if $2(m^* + 1)$ > 12 months, seasonal peaks should not be met through planned layoffs and hiring.

2. Inventory should be at the minimum level at least once in every $2(m^* + 1)$ periods. If a plan violates this rule, it can be improved by an immediate layoff, with hiring at some future time. An exception to this occurs when the work force is currently at its minimum level.

Layoffs

3. Work-force reductions should only occur in period 1 (i.e., immediately) or when inventory is at the minimum level MI (e.g., at the end of a peak season).

4. After a layoff, do not use overtime within $k^* + 1$ months or hiring within $m^* + 1$ months. (If necessary, a smaller layoff should be planned to avoid such premature increases in production.)

Hiring and Overtime

5. Temporary production increases of l^* or fewer months' duration should be accomplished through overtime. For longer time spans, temporary hiring (i.e., followed by layoff) is cheaper.

6. After hiring people, do not plan a layoff within $m^* + 1$ months, or use overtime within k^* months. Avoid these by hiring sooner. (This does not apply to first period hiring, since hiring sooner is impossible.)

Timing of Production

7. Within the restrictions above, produce as late as possible to minimize inventory costs.

---

contains a summary of the rules and of the symbols used for costs and time periods; this should be carefully read before continuing.

The easiest rules to understand involve temporary production increases—should one use overtime or would temporary hiring be better? Suppose that a production plan requires the use of overtime for L consecutive months. It might be more attractive to hire a worker for the same time span, thereby reducing the amount of overtime needed. The cost of processing the temporary worker into and out of the work force is $C_H + C_F$. This worker produces p units per day for n days per month for L months, which reduces the required overtime costs by $L \cdot n \cdot p \cdot C_O$. Temporary hiring would be worthwhile if the costs $(C_H + C_F)$ are less than the savings $(L \cdot n \cdot p \cdot C_O)$, or if $L > (C_H + C_F)/npC_O$. The last ratio is called l^*, and we have just derived rule 5.

Another very useful result is the inventory/overtime trade-off used in rules 4 and 6. Suppose that a production plan called for hiring in the third month, but the number of people to be hired was not large enough to avoid overtime during a peak demand month that occurs K periods later. Would it be worthwhile to move some or all of the hiring one period earlier? If one person is hired in month 2 instead of month 3, there will be np more units in inventory at the end of month 2. These units can be carried for K months and then used to satisfy some of the peak demand, thereby reducing the overtime required by np units.

Therefore, hiring earlier is worthwhile if the added inventory cost of $K \cdot n \cdot p \cdot C_I$ is less than the savings in overtime premium of $n \cdot p \cdot C_O$, which is true if $K < C_O/C_I = k^*$. We have just derived part of rule 6. Rule 4 also refers to k^*, and that relationship is obtained similarly.

Notice that these rules suggest certain things you should or should not do in developing a plan. They do not guarantee that you will find the best plan, but they do help eliminate many alternatives.

The other rules involve m^*. It is considerably more difficult to explain how they are derived. Instead, we shall return to our example and consider production plans for the entire year.

For the Smooth Products Company, there are 240 production days per year, so the average is $n = 20$ days per month. The costs and other parameters are summarized in Table 9-4. By rule 1, since $m^* = 2$, the use of a seasonal layoff is economically feasible. Therefore, we should consider when to schedule a layoff.

The natural planning horizon at the end of May is a good time to schedule a layoff, because every plan of interest has inventory at the MI level in May, and rule 3 says that this is a precondition for a planned layoff. Review problem 2 from the preceding section suggests that December is also a natural planning horizon, so we might consider a layoff there as well. However, one of these two layoffs can be ruled out. Since $2(m^* + 1) = 6$, and there are only 5 months from January to May, rule 1 prohibits scheduling both of these layoffs. The interval from May to December is longer, and therefore a layoff at the end of May is more attractive than one in January.

Even if there is no layoff in January, there must be some hiring before

TABLE 9-4 PLANNING PARAMETERS FOR THE SMOOTH PRODUCTS COMPANY

$n = 240/12 = 20$ working days per month

$p = 0.01$ aggregate unit per worker per day

$C_H = \$400$ per worker hired

$C_F = \$200$ per worker fired

$C_O = \$2000$ per unit produced in overtime

$C_I = \$10,000/12 = \$833.33$ per month per unit of inventory

$m^* = $ integer less than 2.23, or 2 months

$l^* = $ integer part of 1.5, or 1 month

$k^* = $ integer part of 2.4, or 2 months

$I_O = 80$ units of inventory on hand

$W_O = 450$ workers currently on the payroll

$MCP = 5.0$ units per day through May (105 days), or 525 units total

May. We know this because the average production rate through May is 5.0 (the MCP rate), which cannot be achieved with the present work force because of the 10% limit on overtime (4.5 plus 10% is 4.95). Furthermore, rule 5 prohibits using overtime in more than one consecutive month.

Based on these observations, two plans have been proposed.

Plan 1. Allow 10% overtime in May, and hire immediately (in January) the smallest number of workers to meet the May peak. Since May has 22 days, we have 2.2 overtime days and 105 regular time days to achieve 525 units of production $(CR_5 - I_0)$. The daily rate must therefore be $525/107.2 = 4.897$ units per day. With a daily productivity of 0.01 unit per worker, 4.897 may be achieved with 490 workers, so 40 must be hired immediately. We assume they will be laid off after May.

Plan 2. Postpone hiring as long as possible under rule 6, and use 10% overtime in May. Because of the layoff at the end of May, rule 6 requires us to hire at the beginning of March (or earlier) so that the workers are retained at least $m^* + 1 = 3$ months. Therefore we will have 450 workers (the present level) through February and 514 through May. (You may verify this using the same method as in plan 1.) The reader should be able to predict which plan will be best by reviewing rules 5, 6, and 7.

Table 9-5 shows the calculation of inventory for plan 1, and the costs of both plans are summarized in Table 9-6. By hiring more temporary workers later in the year, plan 2 achieved lower overall cost because the increased hiring/firing is more than offset by decreased inventory.

Review Problems

1. Modify plan 2 by hiring 2 fewer people (lower daily production by 0.02) in March, replaced by hiring those 2 plus 1 more person in April. Layoffs occur at the end of May, as before. Compare the new plan to plan 2.

TABLE 9-5 INVENTORY FOR PLAN 1

Period	Work Force	Days	Regular[a]	Overtime[b]	Cumulative Production Plus I_0	Cumulative Demand[c]	Inventory[d]
	$450 = (W_0)$				$80 = (I_0)$	0	
Jan.	490	22	107.8		187.8	70	117.8
Feb.	490	18	88.2		276.0	120	156.0
Mar.	490	22	107.8		383.8	220	163.8
Apr.	490	21	102.9		486.7	420	66.7
May	490	22	107.8	10.5	605.0	570	35.0
June	450 (assumed)					Total =	539.3

[a] Regular time production = (work force) · (productivity) · (days) in which productivity is 0.01.
[b] Overtime ≤ 10% of regular time, just enough to satisfy requirements in May.
[c] Cumulative demand from Table 9-1.
[d] Inventory = cumulative production + I_0 − cumulative demand. Note that inventory is measured in aggregate production units, or 100 worker-days worth of product.

2. Modify plan 2 by hiring 3 people in February, and reducing the March-to-May work force by 1. Evaluate the new plan. (Be careful. The March hiring is reduced by 4 people, since the 3 hired in February will remain on the job.)

3. Presuming that a subcontract is for at least 1 month, why should production never be subcontracted unless in-house production is already at capacity of 7.0 per day?

Solutions

1. Compared to plan 2, March inventory drops by 2 workers' output, or $(2)(0.01)(22) = 0.44$ aggregate unit; the extra person replaces 0.21 unit in April, leaving the April inventory $0.44 - 0.21 = 0.23$ unit below the plan 2 level. By the end of May, the inventory is back to plan 2, with 0.22 unit produced by the extra person and 0.01 produced at overtime. Since C_I is $833.33 per month, the saving in inventory cost amounts to $(0.44 + 0.23$

TABLE 9-6 COSTS FOR PLANS 1 AND 2

Source	Cost per Unit	PLAN 1		PLAN 2	
		Units	Cost	Units	Cost
Inventory	$ 833.33	539.3	$449,415	498.1	$415,082
Hiring	400	40	16,000	64	25,600
Firing	200	40	8,000	64	12,800
Overtime	2000	10.5	21,000	10.9	21,800
Subcontracting	3500	0	0	0	0
Total			$494,415		$475,282

+ 0)(833.33) = \$558.33. The cost of hiring and laying off the extra person is \$600, which more than outweighs the saving, even without including the 0.01 unit of overtime. This change is therefore not desirable.

2. The February inventory goes up by $(3)(0.01)(18) = 0.54$, but this excess is reduced to $0.54 - 0.22 = 0.32$ in March, 0.11 in April, and is eliminated at the end of May, so inventory cost increases by $(0.54 + 0.32 + 0.11 + 0)(833.33) = \$808.33$. Plan 2 hires 64 in March, but the new plan hires 3 in February and 60 in March, for a total of 63 hired, so both hiring and firing drop by 1 person, saving \$600. Therefore, the change is not worth it.

3. To hire 1 worker for a month and then fire costs \$600, for an average of 20 days of production, or 0.20 unit. To subcontract for the same amount would cost $(0.20)(3500) = \$700$.

9-4 AGGREGATE PLANNING BY LINEAR PROGRAMMING

The calculations required to analyze aggregate plans using the graphical technique may be done on a computer, giving the manager instantaneous feedback on the cost of various alternatives. With slightly more sophisticated programs, the computer can make suggestions, and actually find minimum-cost solutions, within whatever limitations you care to specify. In this section, a linear programming (LP) formulation is used as an example. It should be no surprise that the formulation is rather lengthy, considering all the options and calculations we have been through in Section 9-3. (You should have read the material in Appendix C on linear programming before proceeding with this section.)

The complete LP formulation is shown in Table 9-7. The first equation is the cost over the T months of the planning horizon. The terms C_H, C_F, and so on, are the per unit costs of the variables representing hiring, firing, and so on, which will now be described.

The work-force variables, at the beginning of each period, are number of workers (W_t), number hired (H_t), and number fired (F_t). Equation (4) accounts for the hiring and firing by increasing or decreasing W_t compared to the previous period's work force (W_{t-1}).

The production variables during each period are total "within-firm" production (P_t), overtime production (O_t), and undertime (U_t), which is the amount by which production falls short of the normal amount of regular time ($n_t p W_t$) for the given work force. Equation (5) forces the LP to pay an overtime premium or an undertime opportunity cost if production is above or below $n_t p W_t$, respectively. Production subcontracted to an outside firm (S_t) is added to the within-firm production in equation (6), to be discussed next.

Inventory at the end of each period (I_t) is the remaining set of variables, and equation (6) adjusts the inventory between periods by the difference between

TABLE 9-7 AGGREGATE PLANNING LP

Minimize $\sum_{t=1}^{T} (C_H H_t + C_F F_t + C_O O_t + C_U U_t + C_S S_t + C_I I_t) + C_H H_{T+1} + C_F F_{T+1}$ (3)

subject to the following constraints for each period $t = 1, 2, \ldots, T$

Work force

$W_t = W_{t-1} + H_t - F_t$ (this equation also holds for period $T + 1$)   (4)

minimum work force $\leq W_t \leq$ maximum work force

$0 \leq H_t \leq$ allowable monthly hiring

$0 \leq F_t \leq$ allowable monthly firing

$W_0 =$ current work force (period 0 only)

$W_{T+1} =$ required ending work force (period $T + 1$ only)

Production

$P_t = n_t p W_t + O_t - U_t$ (5)

$0 \leq P_t \leq n_t \times$ (daily plant capacity)

$0 \leq O_t \leq (n_t p W_t) \times$ (allowable fraction of overtime)

$0 \leq U_t \leq (n_t p W_t) \times$ (allowable fraction of undertime)

$0 \leq S_t \leq$ available subcontracting

Inventory

$I_t = I_{t-1} + P_t + S_t -$ (demand in period t)   (6)

(safety + cycle stock) $\leq I_t \leq$ storage capacity

$I_0 =$ inventory currently on hand

$I_T =$ required ending inventory

Note: In these equations, n_t is the number of productive days available in period t and p is the daily worker productivity (aggregate production units per worker per day). Both of these are constants. The other variables are defined in the first several paragraphs in the text of this section.

total production (both within firm and subcontracted) and demand. (Note that this period-by-period adjustment gives exactly the same result as subtracting *cumulative* demand from *cumulative* production, as in the preceding section.)

The rest of the formulation consists of more-or-less self-explanatory restrictions. Note that every English phrase in Table 9-7 represents a number that must be obtained before the LP can be run. They are a mixture of hard facts (such as daily plant capacity) and softer numbers, representing policies that may be flexible (such as allowable hiring or firing).

The two variables I_0 and W_0 tie the LP to the current status of the firm, expressed as actual inventory and work force at the present time. The variables I_T and W_{T+1} represent the desired status of the firm (targets) after the T periods have expired. Normally, their values are unimportant to the period 1 decision, since a natural planning horizon is likely to exist between periods 1 and T. However, it is advisable to perform a sensitivity analysis on these target values. If they have no effect on the first-period decisions, a horizon has been encountered somewhere in the planning period. One way of dealing with these targets when a planning horizon does not exist has been described by McClain and Thomas (1977).

Many different computer packages exist for solving linear programming problems. However, research has shown that the aggregate planning LP can be solved with algorithms that are more efficient than the usual simplex method. Posner and Szwarc (1983), for example, developed a one-pass method for solving this problem. Moreover, their algorithm applies when backorders are allowed (at a cost), which is a more difficult version of the aggregate planning LP. Nevertheless, aggregate planning LP models, with or without backorders, are easily solved using standard LP packages.

Using LP for Aggregate Planning

In order to use the LP, demand forecasts must be obtained, along with each of the cost coefficients of equation (3), the productivity factor p, working days n_t, and the upper and lower limits shown in Table 9-7. For a 12-month model, this could amount to a sizable task. Fortunately, only the demand forecasts and initial inventory and work force will change each time the model is used; there will be only occasional changes in the other parameters. Consequently, only 14 numbers are needed as a regular input, and the LP will find a minimum-cost plan.

A word of caution is in order. The solution recommended by the LP minimizes the cost equation (3), which is not necessarily an accurate reflection of the actual costs. Thus, although the solution is *optimal for the model,* there may be solutions which are better in that they achieve lower actual costs or because the LP solution does not meet some qualitative requirements that could not be expressed in the constraints. Four of the expected difficulties are discussed below.

Costs Are Not Linear. Fortunately, in aggregate planning, costs are usually either linear or U-shaped (increasing marginal cost or diseconomies of scale). If the curvature of the cost function is not extreme, the linear functions are often satisfactory approximations. Methods are available to improve the accuracy of the model by approximating the curve with a series of straight-line segments. In LP texts, this is referred to as "separable programming" or "piecewise linear approximations."

Productivity of Workers Changes with Time. For new employees, learning while on the job causes an increase in productivity. This is sometimes represented by using a learning curve (Ebert, 1976). However, disruptions caused by breaking in new workers can degrade performance of experienced employees. The combination of these two effects can remove aggregate planning from the realm of LP. Khoshnevis and Wolfe (1983) describe a method that will handle such a situation.

Production Rates Cannot Always Be Changed Continuously. This presents a more difficult problem. Usually, small variations in production can be achieved through overtime or hiring and firing, but large changes are accomplished by adding an entire work shift. Thus H_t and F_t may be restricted to a few discrete values. There are two approaches to this problem: (1) interact with the computer, varying the lower and upper bounds on work force among possible values until a satisfactory solution is obtained; or (2) use a more expensive computer code which will restrict some variables to discrete values (see the discussion of mixed-integer LP in Hillier and Lieberman, 1980).

The Effects of Other Company Decisions Are Not Recognized in the Standard LP Formulations. For example, advertising may change the demand pattern. Also, financial considerations such as cash budgeting are related to employment, production, and inventory patterns, since these are the largest users of cash in many companies. Models that attempt to tie these different planning areas together in an LP are given by Thomas (1971).

Review Problems

1. In equation (5), explain what $n_t p W_t$ means, and say the equation in English. Also explain the two constraints that follow (5).

2. How would the formulation change if there were three aggregate products [e.g., three types, in the terminology of Bitran and Hax (1977) discussed in the introduction]?

Solutions

1. W_t is the work force, p is the regular time daily production output per worker, and n_t is the number of days in time period t, so $n_t p W_t$ is the regular time production capacity in period t. For time t, equation (5) reads "production equals regular time capacity plus overtime production minus undertime production." The last term accounts for reduced output if production is set below the normal output of the work force. The next constraint keeps production between zero and the monthly plant capacity. In the next constraint, the right-hand side is the regular time capacity multiplied by the fraction of overtime allowed by policy. The constraint therefore keeps overtime production between zero and the maximum allowed by company policy for the time period.

2. In each period, there would have to be three inventory, three production, and three subcontracting variables. Equation (6) would also be repeated for each product. Equation (5) would be modified so that total production of the three products was covered by the work force, with adjustments for overtime and undertime.

9-5 Summary

The techniques available for intermediate-range planning are suitable for either hand computation (using graphs such as Figure 9-4) or computer-assisted planning. The computations are complicated by the existence of many options in meeting requirements, multiple time periods, and restrictions handed down from higher-level decisions. Using graphs helps to visualize differences between production plans, and may suggest good alternatives. The alternatives must then be analyzed for their cost performance and effect on company policies. Using an optimizing scheme such as linear programming takes the process one step further by isolating a plan that minimizes a cost model.

To use the graphical method, products must be aggregated into a single measure of output. With more advanced methods such as linear programming, several aggregated product types may be used. After aggregate plans have been determined, the first period becomes the basis for the short-range, detailed plans of individual products. That is, the plan's first period is disaggregated. At the conclusion of that period, aggregate plans may be reconsidered using new forecasts and recognizing the amount by which actual experience deviated from the plan. Thus the most recent experience may affect plans over the entire planning horizon. Plans made in this manner are called rolling schedules.

A substantial portion of this chapter has been devoted to presenting rules and principles for constructing aggregate plans. A cost basis for justifying actions such as layoffs was presented. Of course, decisions such as these are not based on short-run cost minimization alone. The company's commitment to its work force or its position in the community may overrule the cost-based policies, for example. Methods such as those presented in this chapter should be used not as the sole decision criteria, but rather for generating some very valuable information.

Regardless of the method used for finding and comparing alternatives, one of the problems of implementation is obtaining the needed data. The costs and demands are estimated by commonly available cost accounting and forecasting methods. However, many of the planning restrictions are subjective, but at the same time very important to future labor or community relations. It is important to include as many realistic restrictions as possible in developing alternative plans.

The function of a medium-range plan is to anticipate upcoming changes in work force and production, and to set overall output rates that may be translated into a detailed schedule at least for the first planning period. It is important, therefore, to use the best information available in setting these plans. For example, more elaborate (and expensive) forecasting methods are justified for aggregate planning than for individual product decisions.

The Handicraft Jewelers caselet (which follows) requires one to make an informed judgment about what kind of product mix will be held in inventory. It also provides an example where the structure of the work force is somewhat different than in the Smooth Products example.

CASELET: THE HANDICRAFT JEWELRY COMPANY

The Handicraft Jewelry Company makes four handmade items on a fairly large scale. The items are all 24-carat gold, so inventory is expensive. Their demand forecast is:

Period	Item 1	Item 2	Item 3	Item 4
March	800	1000	1000	600
April	800	800	600	800
May	1200	1400	500	1000
June	1200	1600	500	1500
July	400	400	500	1000
August	800	1000	500	400

Items 1, 2, and 3 are rings (class, wedding, and other), and they each take 1 hour to produce. Item 4 takes 2 hours to produce. Items 1, 2, and 3 have a unit variable cost (direct labor plus materials) of $20 each, while item 4 costs $76.00. Monthly inventory cost is 1% of the value of the items in inventory.

The regular work force consists of highly skilled artisans who have worked for the company an average of 22 years. Accordingly, the use of seasonal layoffs has been totally ruled out. This results in a regular work-force capacity of 4000 worker-hours per month at $16 per hour, with the possibility of up to 800 overtime worker-hours at $24 per hour.

There is, in the community, a cadre of people who are pleased to work for part of a year, to supplement family income. Over the years, 15 people have received enough training to qualify for this short-term employment. When such a person is hired, he or she is always employed full time for full calendar months. In the first month, productivity is only 50%, compared to a regular worker, increasing to 75% in the second month, and 100% thereafter. For temporary workers, the month is 160 hours long, and no overtime is allowed. The pay is $12 per hour. The total cost of hiring and eventually laying off each temporary worker is $800, including a certain amount of catch-up training. (The training cost is in addition to the lower productivity in the first 2 months.)

Operating policy has been to produce only as necessary to meet each month's demand. Hiring decisions are postponed to the last possible date. Recently, Handicraft began serious consideration of smoothing out the production process by building up inventory in anticipation of peak demands.

With very little promotional effort, June demand can be increased by 400 units for item 1. However, this has not been done because the month of June is already quite hectic due to the high sales rate. Passing up opportunities such as this is one of the main reasons for considering the use of inventory.

Required
1. Convert the demand forecasts into an aggregate measure, month by month.
2. Find the MCP solution, and determine its inventory.
3. Determine at least one work-force plan to achieve the MCP production rates.
4. Compare the cost of your MCP plan to the current plan.
5. Determine at least one plan that is better, and evaluate its cost.
6. Modifying your plan from 5, evaluate the cost of meeting the increased June demand, and compare that to the cost under current policy.

PROBLEMS

1. What is production smoothing? In what ways is it desirable? What problems can it cause?

*2. How can production smoothing be accomplished in a service organization?

3. What kinds of organizations are not likely to use inventory in intermediate-range planning?

4. Is forecasting accuracy enhanced or lessened by the aggregation of products for intermediate-range planning? Explain.

*5. The Red Wine Producers face a demand pattern with a peak in December. All their wine is produced within a few weeks after the autumn harvest. It is stored in vats until it is needed for the bottling process. Currently, their bottling policy is to run one shift from January to September, and add a second shift for the 3 months in advance of the December peak, to build enough inventory to avoid shortages. They are considering the possibility of smoothing out the bottling process to a uniform rate for the entire 12 months with one shift.
   (a) Make a list of the costs that would be incurred if they went to the 12-month "level-production" bottling system, but which are not currently incurred.
   (b) List the costs they are incurring now that would be avoided or reduced by the level-production system.
   (c) What new risks would be incurred under 12-month level production?
   (d) What risks would be reduced or eliminated?

6. Mentally place yourself into Figure 9-2. You are standing at time zero and your height is 80 aggregate production units. The dotted-line cumulative requirements curve represents a hillside you must climb. From where you stand, what is the farthest point you can see? (Remember, the ground is opaque.) What does this have to do with the concepts we have discussed?

*7. In Figure 9-2 and Table 9-2, the natural planning horizon occurs in May (at day 105), but the MCP very nearly meets the requirements curve again in December (day 240).

(a) How much higher can the December forecast be before December becomes the natural horizon?

(b) Because the requirements curve is plotted on a cumulative basis, increases in June's forecast will increase cumulative requirements for June and each month thereafter. Show that an increase of 50 in June's forecast will shift the planning horizon to December.

(c) How much higher can the August forecast be before the natural horizon is no longer in May? If such an increase occurs, when will the natural horizon be?

(d) Suppose that several of the forecasts were changed at the same time. What impact would the following combination of forecast changes have on the period 1 (January) production rate? June = down 20, July = up 40, October = down 10, and December = up 20.

8. Smooth Products Company is considering a constant production rate of 4.90 per day. Calculate inventory at the end of each month through July. (The Smooth Products data are given in Table 9-1.) What is the maximum inventory? Is there any backlogging?

*9. Alprodco uses 4-week "months" for its aggregate planning time periods, and each month has 20 working days (ignore holidays for this problem). The monthly demands in aggregate units are 110, 110, 140, and 100 for the next 4 months, and will then remain at or below 110 for the rest of the year. Inventory is currently 20 aggregate units, and this is the minimum level allowed by company policy.

(a) Using months (rather than days) as the time unit, plot the cumulative requirements.

(b) Their production plan is 115, 130, 115, and 100, for the next 4 months, respectively. Will this meet requirements?

(c) What costs would change if 5 units of production were shifted from month 2 to month 3? Will this be an improvement?

*10. The accompanying graph shows a cumulative requirements curve and a cumulative production plan for 10 months. (Notice that cumulative demand has not been drawn.)

(a) What time period has the highest planned production rate? How do you know?

(b) What is the production rate for month 1?

(c) Find the natural planning horizon by plotting the MCP with a straightedge.

(d) Suggest a production plan that will save money, compared to the one shown in the graph. (*Hint:* Try to cut down on the inventory in month 6 without increasing other costs.)

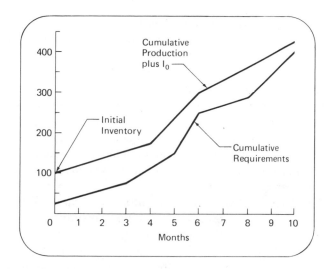

11. Farmer Milton McSnarf grows rutabagas, selling some immediately and storing others in his root cellar. They can be stored indefinitely, and he has one growing season per year. Because of the increasing popularity of rutabaga milkshakes, he predicts the following demands:

Year	Forecasts of Demand (Thousands of Bushels)
1	100
2	120
3	200
4	250
5	300

Workers are hired for at least 1 year. He currently has 3 workers. He had 110,000 bushels of rutabaga production last year, and he has a total of 20,000 bushels in inventory. He makes no attempt to maintain a minimum inventory. Workers are paid only for work actually done. (They are not compensated for undertime.) Overtime costs $1 per bushel more than regular time. Inventory cost is assumed to be $0.10 per bushel per year. Hiring one person costs $1000, and one person can produce 30,000 bushels per year in regular time and 10,000 bushels per year in overtime.
   (a) Find the MCP solution and evaluate its total cost (over and above the regular time wages) over the natural planning horizon, without using overtime.
   (b) The solution to part (a) requires some hiring. Consider the timing of the hiring decisions, and suggest a better plan, still without using overtime.

Explain why your plan is better. (This can be answered with no calculations. However, you may use numbers if you wish.)

(c) Does overtime look like an attractive alternative in this case? Why or why not?

12. (This problem is based on Milton McSnarf's farm, Problem 11, but you need not have completed Problem 11.) The crop of year 1 proved to be quite rewarding for Farmer McSnarf. He planned to produce 190,000 bushels, but the crop was actually 220,000. Rutabaga milkshake popularity also exceeded expectations, and demand for rutabagas was 150,000 bushels. McSnarf has adjusted his forecasts upward by 25%, and forecasts 400,000 for year 6.

(a) Calculate his starting inventory for year 2. Why should it be different from the *planned* year 1 ending inventory?

(b) Find the MCP production rate.

*13. Fancy Furniture, Inc., has a small production facility that has been characterized as machine-limited. That is, the production output cannot be increased by adding personnel because the furniture is assembled and finished on a production line with a fixed number of workstations. However, they do have the capability of adding a second shift, or of working overtime to meet demand in the peak summer months. If a new shift is added by hiring workers, production capacity is doubled, and the new workers must be retained for either 2 months, 4 months, or permanently. Fancy Furniture never produces at reduced capacity. The production rate is 5000 units per shift per month. Demand forecasts for the first 8 months of 1981 are shown in the accompanying table along with other necessary information.

(a) Find the MCP solution, and find its cost.

(b) Evaluate the cost of a solution that hires a second shift for months 6 and 7.

(c) Being careful to account properly for the fact that the two plans above will have different ending inventories, which one would you recommend and why?

The data are:

inventory holding cost = $40 per unit per month

regular-time pay = $80,000 per month per shift

overtime pay = 50% more than regular time pay

fringe benefits = $30,000 per month per shift

hiring cost = $10,000 to hire a new shift

firing cost = $40,000 to lay off an entire shift

monthly production capacity = 5000 units per shift

monthly overtime capacity = 1250 units per shift

minimum inventory = constant at 500 units

inventory entering first period = 1500 units

Month	1	2	3	4	5	6	7	8
Demand (thousands)	5	5	4	4	7	7	8	8

14. The Knudsen Boltz Company produces three high-quality fabricated parts for the automotive industry. Their main customers are companies that produce expensive cars, so their sales have not been hurt by economic slowdowns as much as some other firms in the industry. Some data concerning the firm are given in the accompanying table.

SALES FORECASTS (THOUSANDS)

	YEAR 1 (CURRENT YEAR)			YEAR 2				YEAR 3
Quarter:	2	3	4	1	2	3	4	1
Item 1	40	50	55	50	80	90	80	60
Item 2	35	35	40	35	50	60	50	40
Item 3	20	15	15	20	20	20	25	25

Based on their experience and the data, the firm notes that quarter 3 (July, August, and September) is usually their highest sales period, but that the industry is expected to enjoy a large increase in sales beginning late this year. Item 3 is sold as a spare part through independent dealers, while items 1 and 2 are sold to the automotive companies for assembly and to both the automotive companies and independent dealers as spares. Each item is sold in several different styles, and the figures given are totals for each type of item. Each of the three items requires 0.10 hour of labor per unit.

The firm has a policy of not using layoffs or overtime in their aggregate plans. They currently have 11,000 person-hours per month capacity, and the plant is capable of using up to 15,000 hours per month. (To exceed 15,000 hours, the firm would have to add new facilities, since 15,000 would require three shifts, 7 days per week.) Inventory cost is 20% of the item value per year. The unit values are $10, $8, and $4 for items 1, 2, and 3, respectively. The cost of hiring is $2000 for the first 1000 worker-hours hired in a quarter. They currently have an aggregate inventory equivalent to 5000 worker-hours, and they feel the optimal MI, inventory to have during the entire 2-year planning horizon is 4000 person-hours.

(a) Compute the aggregate demand forecast, by quarter, using 1000 worker-hours as the unit of measure.

(b) When they are producing to build up an aggregate inventory, which item(s) should they be producing for inventory?

(c) Given your answer to part (b), what should one use for the per unit cost of holding aggregate inventory?

(d) Calculate the MCP solution and evaluate its total cost, using $C_I =$ \$3000 per aggregate unit of inventory per quarter.

(e) They are considering hiring 500 worker-hours in each of quarters 2 through 7, so that they will have labor hours (in thousands) of 11.0, 11.5, 12.0, 12.5, 13.0, 13.5, 14.0, 14.0 in the eight quarters of the planning horizon. Calculate the aggregate inventory of this option. Evaluate the total cost over the eight quarters.

(f) Compare the MCP to the plan proposed in part (e). Show how the differences in costs arise. Which plan do you recommend?

(g) If the firm had a natural attrition of employees (because of resignations, retirements, etc.) of 200 worker-hours each quarter, discuss how this would change your recommended work-force levels.

*15. The U.R. Truckin Company produces 38 types of shirts for sale to organizations. Their forecasts for the next 6 months, in aggregate form, are as follows:

Month	1	2	3	4	5	6
Forecast	4000	5000	4000	8000	5000	4000

After month 6, demand will remain at the 4000 to 5000 level until next year's peak (month 16).

All shirts take exactly the same time to produce. With their 10-person work force, they have a regular time capacity for 5000 shirts per month, and overtime capacity for 1000 shirts per month. Each shirt costs \$2 to produce in regular time, including \$1 labor and \$1 material. Overtime labor is \$1.50, so a shirt costs \$2.50 to produce in overtime. They can hire people at a cost of \$200 each and each person can produce 500 shirts per month in regular time and 100 in overtime. New workers are paid the same amount as regular workers, and the \$200 cost of hiring includes training cost so they are as efficient as regular workers. It costs \$200 to fire someone. They want to always meet demand, and they think the carrying-cost rate for inventory is 2% per month. No minimum inventory has been specified, and they are currently out of stock (have no inventory). First, Truckin managers want to decide whether to use seasonal hiring and layoffs as an ongoing policy.

(a) Show that a seasonal hiring/layoff cycle is economically justifiable for U.R. Truckin, using rule 1, Table 9-3. During which month would a seasonal layoff take place?

(b) If they lay off people in month 4, how soon should they consider adding to the work force again?

(c) When they hire seasonal workers, how long should they be kept?

(d) Given the previous answers, only one seasonal hiring/layoff schedule should be considered. When should hiring occur?

Truckin has decided on a seasonal layoff after period 4, adding again to the work force in period 11. Now they want to focus on what to do right now, considering the current inventory and work force situation. Workers are available to be hired immediately, and they expect this situation to prevail indefinitely.

(e) Show that the present work force cannot meet demands without using overtime or hiring more workers.

(f) What is the most economical way to increase production: overtime or hiring and then firing later? You may wish to use the rules in Table 9-3.

(g) Truckin management is considering hiring workers at the beginning of period 4. What is your advice to them?

(h) Calculate the total costs over a 4-month horizon of each of the three following plans. Don't forget the cost of layoffs at the end of period 4.

	PLAN 1		PLAN 2			PLAN 3		
Month	Regular-time Production	Over-time Production	Regular Time	Overtime	Hiring	Regular Time	Overtime	Hiring
1	5000	0	5000	0	0	5000	0	0
2	5000	0	5000	0	0	5000	0	0
3	5000	0	5500	0	1	5000	0	0
4	5000	1000	5500	0	0	5500	500	1
			(layoff)		−1	(layoff)		−1

(i) The personnel manager is arguing that temporary help should not be hired for a period of less than 6 months, since it is too expensive to train such a person, and short employment may give the company a bad name in the community. How much will it cost the company to go along with personnel's advice, based on your answer to part (h)?

16. (a) Formulate Problem 15 as a linear program (LP). Assume that pay is on a "per shirt produced" basis.

(b) Suppose that on the average 1 person per month resigns, retires, or is fired for poor performance. Show how to include that in your LP.

(c) What do you think the effect might be of having no cost of undertime in the objective function?

*17. A company that produces fire trucks follows a make-to-order policy. That is, no trucks are produced until a firm order has been received. They currently have orders for 10 fire trucks, and they desire to keep the backlog between 5 and 15 trucks. They currently have 100 workers and can produce

10 trucks per month. Their demand forecasts are shown below, using 4-week months.

Month (4-week period)	1	2	3	4	5	6
Forecasts	10	5	9	13	15	9

(a) What constant production rate would bring the backlog to its maximum level at the end of 6 months?

(b) Show that the production plan in part (a) does not meet their backlog policy.

(c) Following the method used in Table 9-2, except using months in place of days, calculate the MCP solution. Note that the maximum backlog of 15 corresponds to a minimum inventory of $MI_t = -15$. Does the MCP stay within the backlog limits?

(d) Would you recommend that they adopt the MCP plan or stay with the current rate of 10 trucks per month? Why?

18. The medical-surgical department in City Hospital occupies eight floors. They desire to schedule a complete shutdown of one floor for maintenance, which will require 2 weeks. The maintenance needs to be done within the next 8 weeks.

Demands for hospital beds are measured in patient-days. A patient who stays 6 days has consumed 6 patient-days. Each floor can produce up to 100 patient-days per week. The demand forecast for patient days is shown in the accompanying table. Of course, a patient-day may not be inventoried, but can be backlogged within limits, since 40% of the patients are admitted for elective procedures, which can be delayed.

Experience has shown that the efficiency of production is reduced when the backlog of patient-days is low, simply because empty beds are more likely to remain unfilled due to mismatches among the schedules of the physicians, patients, and operating rooms. As a guide, 100 patient-days can be produced per floor per week if the average backlog is 50 or more patient-days per floor (400 total), but production drops to 95 if the average backlog is between 1 and 50 patient-days per floor. (The average backlog is: beginning of the week backlog plus ending backlog divided by 2.) When there is no backlog, production does not exceed 90 per week. The present backlog is 500 patient-days, which is considered quite high.

The current plan is to shut down the floor right after the peak demand, so that it would be closed in weeks 4 and 5.

Weeks	1	2	3	4	5	6	7	8
Forecast of patient-days demanded	700	800	1000	700	700	800	600	700

(a) Evaluate their plan.

(b) Suggest and evaluate an alternative.

(c) What will the production rate be in week 9 of their plan if demand is 700?

REFERENCES

BAKER, K., "An Experimental Study of the Effectiveness of Rolling Schedules in Production Planning." *Decision Sciences,* Vol. 8, No. 1 (1977), pp. 19–27.

BITRAN, G., AND A. HAX, "On the Design of Hierarchical Production Planning Systems." *Decision Sciences,* Vol. 8, No. 1 (1977), pp. 28–55.

BRENNAN, L., J. BROWNE, B. J. DAVIES, M. E. J. O'KELLY, AND A. R. GAULT, "An Analysis of the Overtime Decision." *International Journal of Operations and Production Management,* Vol. 2, No. 3 (1982), pp. 19–36.

EBERT, R. J., "Aggregate Planning with Learning Curve Productivity." *Management Science,* Vol. 23 (1976), pp. 171–182.

HILLIER, F. S., AND G. J. LIEBERMAN, *Introduction to Operations Research,* 3rd ed. San Francisco: Holden-Day, 1980.

KHOSHNEVIS, B., AND P. M. WOLFE, "An Aggregate Production Planning Model Incorporating Dynamic Productivity" (in 2 parts). *IIE Transactions,* Vol. 15, Nos. 2 and 4 (1983).

KRAJEWSKI, L., AND L. RITZMAN, "Disaggregation in Manufacturing and Service Organizations." *Decision Sciences,* Vol. 8, No. 1 (1977), pp. 1–18.

KUNREUTHER, H. C., AND T. E. MORTON, "Planning Horizons for Production Smoothing with Deterministic Demands, I." *Management Science,* September 1973.

MCCLAIN, J. O., AND L. J. THOMAS, "Horizon Effects in Aggregate Production Planning with Seasonal Demand." *Management Science,* Vol. 23, No. 7 (March 1977), pp. 728–736.

POSNER, M. E., AND W. SZWARC, "A Transportation Type Aggregate Production Model with Backordering." *Management Science,* Vol. 29, No. 2 (February 1983), pp. 188–199.

SASSER, W. E., "Match Supply and Demand in Service Industries." *Harvard Business Review,* November–December 1976, pp. 133–140.

SCHWARZ, L., AND R. JOHNSON, "An Appraisal of the Empirical Performance of the Linear Decision Rule for Aggregate Planning." *Management Science,* Vol. 24, No. 8 (April 1978), pp. 844–849.

THOMAS, L. J., "Linear Programming Models for Production–Advertising Decisions." *Management Science,* April 1971.

CHAPTER 10

Inventory Control: Ordering Systems for Independent Demand

Zero inventory became a common phrase in the mid-1980s. Although it is not an attainable (or even desirable) goal, it does represent a shift in attitude; it emphasizes all the bad things that inventory can do. In this and subsequent chapters, we describe some of the beneficial functions of inventory as well as the costs. As an introduction, it is instructive to consider why people work toward zero inventory.

Inventories held in the United States exceed $500,000,000,000 in value (see *Survey of Current Business*). That is, one-half trillion dollars are tied up in goods stockpiled for one reason or another. If even half of these dollars could be freed for investment, a modest return of 10% would yield $25 billion annually. It is no wonder that reduction of inventory is sometimes viewed by managers as a potential source of capital.

Companies differ dramatically in their use of inventory. The *turnover rate* is a common measure, being defined as annual cost of sales divided by the average value of inventory. As an example of the contrast, Toyota achieves 70 turns per year compared to 8 for General Motors (see the annual reports for Toyota and GM). Although the turnover rate can be criticized as a measure, it is clear that such a large difference must reflect greatly differing methods of operation. Indeed, Toyota's just-in-time production system has become a model for study and imitation by other firms. Methods used in this and other inventory-lean systems are described in Chapters 5, 6, 11, and 12.

Contrasts such as this lead people to believe that perhaps a sizable portion of our half-trillion dollar investment in inventory can be eliminated. Reduction in inventory is never without cost, however. In the automotive example, investments in new production techniques, robots, facility layouts, vendor contracts, and even reorganization of work-force management are required. Even at the micro level, controlling cost is not the same as minimizing inventory. For example, consider the quantity discount. If you have to buy more than immediate requirements to obtain a cost-saving discount, then inventory increases. This and other inventory-related trade-offs are described in this chapter, including methods for controlling the associated costs.

Inventory is an important part of every system that produces goods or services. Its greatest role is in promoting smooth operations. Chapter 9 described how aggregate inventory is used to smooth production and work-force levels over a period of months. In this and subsequent chapters, we will study inventory of individual items (i.e., not aggregated), and its role in coordinating operations. This chapter concentrates on inventories of items to be sold or used at one location, without further transformation. In a manufacturing setting this will include finished goods and some materials but not partially finished items or items in transit. The accumulation of partially finished and finished goods is discussed in Chapters 11 and 12, and the logistics of controlling goods in transit in multilocation systems is the topic of Chapter 13. In nonmanufacturing situations, such as hospitals or retail stores, the methods of this chapter are widely used. In order to clarify when these methods can be applied, we introduce the concepts of *independent* and *dependent* demand.

Independent and Dependent Demand

When there are plans and schedules that are either under your control or known to you for some other reason, the demand for supplies is said to be *dependent* on those plans and schedules. In this situation, the demand can be accurately anticipated in both amount and timing. An example of a dependent demand is the required raw materials for manufacture of an item that has been scheduled for a production run from June 3 to June 20. Materials requirements planning (MRP) is appropriate for this kind of situation, and is the subject of Chapter 12.

An example of *independent* demand is retail sale of waterproof boots. Demand is highly seasonal for this product, but the exact quantity needed for any given week or month is not perfectly predictable. Demand arises from many sources, each of which has its own plans or schedules which are unknown to you.

The difference between dependent and independent demand is important because it suggests a different approach to management of the inventory system. Independent demand requires a statistical forecast, such as the ones described in Chapter 8, whereas dependent demand is estimated by working backward from the known schedule. Incorrectly using the statistical methods of independent demand can be very expensive. This is because a safety margin of extra inventory is usually kept for the independent demand situation, much of which can be eliminated when the demand schedule is known.

It is sometimes practical to use independent demand models even when demand could be calculated from known schedules. This is the case when demand arises from a large number of known schedules, requiring a substantial amount of calculation to predict the demand by working backward from the schedule. If this results in a moderately steady average usage rate, it may be more appropriate to treat the demand as independent, and use a statistical forecasting method. This is particularly so when there are likely to be changes in many of the schedules which give rise to the demand.

Independent demand describes only a part of the inventory of a manufacturing firm, but it predominates in service-oriented firms such as hospitals, many distributors, and even retailers. In this chapter we shall discuss materials management for independent demand.

Functions of the Materials Manager

Materials management is a combination of ordering, receiving, and supply operations. The goal of a materials management system is to make sure that the items are available when and where they are needed, and that the total cost associated with the supply system is kept to a minimum. This requires familiarity with sources of supply, price negotiations, methods of shipment, bulk discounts, budgeting, physical handling and record keeping, and inspection of shipments. In addition, an integrated system is required to coordinate all these functions. There are statistical and economic principles which can be applied to this problem of coordination, and it is on these principles that this chapter concentrates.

Inventory control systems can be and are circumvented by employees. Unofficial inventory is a label given by Rakowski (1981) to quantities that have been issued by a stockroom but have not yet been used. This applies to materials in the nursing supply cabinets of a hospital, or many other analogous circumstances. Knowledge of the quantity and location of these supplies can substantially reduce the need for stock in other locations. The advent of computerized materials management systems (see Shore, 1981, for example) makes multilocation inventory coordination increasingly common.

Reduction and control of costs is an important part of the material manager's job. However, under normal circumstances, the rate of usage of an inventory item is not under the material manager's control. Instead, it is dictated by those who use the materials. Among the exceptions to this rule are antiwaste campaigns and standardization efforts (an attempt to eliminate some items by substituting one that is similar and perhaps less expensive). However, for the most part, annual usage will be estimated through some kind of forecasting method. The three costs that we shall concentrate on in this chapter are, to a certain extent, unavoidable: the cost of holding inventory, the transaction cost associated with ordering supplies, and the cost of shortages. It is the material manager's job to minimize these costs.

Sometimes it is not possible to specify all the costs. For example, shortages may cause bad feelings, which are difficult to measure in dollar terms. We will explore several approaches to this kind of problem, and show how the trade-offs can be presented to management in an informative manner.

10-1 INVENTORY CONTROL: THE A-B-Cs OF INVENTORY

Prior to the advent of computerized inventory systems, it was common practice to categorize the inventory items into several classes, with one class identified as the major target of careful control. High-speed data processing has, for many firms, eliminated the need for this kind of scheme, since the marginal cost of extending computer control to the entire inventory is very low once a computer system is in place.

Nevertheless, what has become known as the A-B-C system of inventory classification is a useful learning concept, and is still widely used to separate items into groups that are controlled differently. The basis of this scheme is the recognition that the total variable cost, associated with inventory control of a given item, is primarily a function of its annual dollar volume, $D^\$$ (unit price times annual demand). Therefore, the greatest cost reductions may be achieved by concentrating inventory control efforts on items with high $D^\$$ (category A) while building slack in the system to avoid problems for other items (categories B and C).

The great practical nature of this scheme becomes clear by the following observation. If one goes down the list of stock-keeping units (SKU, or item names) and picks off those with the highest $D^\$$, by the time the top 20% of the SKUs have been tallied, about 80% of the annual cash outlay will have been accounted for. Thus we have identified category A as the minority of stock-keeping units that cause the majority of cash-flow headaches. Similarly, category C comprises about 50% of the items that account for only 5% of the sales, and B items are the remainder. This concept will come up repeatedly in this chapter.

It is important to understand how items in inventory are counted. Tax laws require annual (or more frequent) physical counts. This can be done all at once or by *cycle counting,* whereby SKUs are counted in an annual sequence to minimize disruptions and smooth the workload. *Event-based* cycle counting is a further refinement. If counting is initiated by an event such as placement of a replenishment order, total work may be reduced since inventory is typically near its lowest levels when an order is placed. The reason for physical count is that there are often discrepancies between stock on hand and stock on record. The count is needed to set the record straight. Reasons for discrepancies vary from record-keeping errors to theft, and efforts to reduce these discrepancies are an important part of inventory control.

As mentioned earlier, turnover rate is a measure of inventory. How often the inventory turns over depends on how long the average item remains in inventory. This measure is applied both to individual stock-keeping units and to an organization's total inventory. The conventional wisdom is that a high turnover rate is good and a low one is bad. Although it is true that low turns might indicate an excessive amount of stock on hand, one must recognize the trade-off as the turnover rate is increased—shortages may increase, and more frequent handling may be required due to smaller order quantities. Therefore, the turnover rate should be used with caution. Many companies have made management errors because of a mandate to achieve a specific number of inventory turns.

Inventory Replenishment Policies

The most obvious method of inventory control is to count stocks at the end of a fixed period of time and to order enough to increase the supply on hand to a level that will meet the needs until the next inventory. This *periodic review* system[1] is used widely, but has several limitations: (1) lack of positive control between reviews; (2) requirement for large safety cushions of extra inventory because of possible surges in demand between reviews: and (3) variability in order quantity, which sometimes precludes the negotiation of certain quantity discounts. However, this kind of system will continue to be used to control items for which these limitations are of little consequence, because it allows freedom from continuous monitoring and reporting.

Perpetual inventory systems require more record keeping. In the most common perpetual system, every item withdrawn from inventory is recorded, and the resulting inventory tally is checked against a reorder level R. A new order is triggered when stock on hand *plus* stock previously ordered but not yet received *minus* stock backordered (promised to someone, but not yet delivered) falls below R. In contrast to the periodic review policy, the order is for a fixed amount Q, alleviating the variability in order quantity mentioned above (problem 3 in the preceding paragraph). Surges in demand automatically trigger the order sooner (by drawing inventory below the reorder point), eliminating problem 2. Problem 1 is certainly addressed in this system, but periodic physical counts are still necessary to correct the tally for breakage, pilferage, and record-keeping errors.

The paperwork involved in perpetual inventory systems is its major disadvantage. This has been addressed in some firms by attaching machine-readable tags to items as they are received. Then with the brush of an electronic pen, or the flash of a laser, the inventory tally is made automatically when the item is withdrawn. Such a system can be programmed to produce a purchase order, addressed to the appropriate supplier, when the reorder point is reached. An example of this kind of system is the laser bar-code readers found in many supermarkets.

---

[1] Another version of this system does not place an order each period, but instead waits until inventory is below a reorder level. Once the reorder level is reached, inventory is replenished to its original level. The advantage of this system is the elimination of small orders.

Standing-order systems are becoming more widespread in both manufacturing and service industries. Rosenshine and Obec (1976) describe a scheme in which a contract with a supplier guarantees delivery of an order of size Q on a regular schedule. This eliminates the portion of the transaction costs attributable to placing orders. More important, an annual contract gives more leverage to negotiate for discounts and preferential treatment in promptness of delivery.

There are two new costs that are introduced by standing orders. The first stems from the need for a special method to protect against running short when the forecast turns out to have been low. Since one may neither request early delivery nor increase the order quantity, Rosenshine and Obec's model assumes that shortfalls are handled by placing an emergency order (at extra cost) when inventory drops below a prespecified level. (Perhaps this should be called the panic reorder level.) The second new cost is incurred if the long-range forecast proves to have been too high, resulting in an oversupply; the contractual nature of the deliveries specifies that a penalty will be incurred when unused items are returned. Alternatively, the excess supply can be sold, presumably at a net loss.

Standing orders do not eliminate the need for monitoring inventory levels. Indeed, both emergency orders and item returns are triggered by unanticipated changes in amount of stock. Either periodic or continuous review of inventories may be used.

In general, a standing order is likely to be preferable when usage is highly predictable, so that the emergency measures described above need not be used very often. Also, if it becomes difficult to obtain supplies within a *reliable* lead time, the preferential treatment of a standing-order customer would be worth considering.

Information Requirements and Cost Trade-offs

Information required for inventory control includes more than just the inventory tally. We have already mentioned the need for information on suppliers, discounts, and so on. Effective inventory control also requires (1) forecasts of usage trends, (2) knowledge of the reorder lead time, and (3) accurate knowledge of the three basic costs (holding, transaction, and shortage). Forecasting methods such as those discussed in Chapter 8 are included in most of the various commercially available inventory control computer programs. The reorder lead time will be discussed later, in conjunction with safety stocks. The costs must be carefully defined, as we shall see in the following paragraphs.

Inventory holding costs accrue from several sources. Most significant is the opportunity cost of capital invested in the inventory. This is usually specified as a required rate of return on investment,[2] and serves to assure that capital is put to its best use throughout an organization. In addition, there are costs of storage, including operation and depreciation (or rental) of the warehouse, taxes,

---

[2] Sometimes called a *hurdle rate*.

insurance, obsolescence, breakage, pilferage, and any special costs such as refrigeration. This is summed up in the symbol C_I, which is the annual holding cost per unit of inventory. This differs across items, owing primarily to differing unit price. Although it is not strictly correct to do so, inventory holding cost is often expressed as a percentage of the per unit purchase price of an item, resulting in what we shall term F_I (fractional holding cost). That is, F_I equals C_I divided by unit price. This term has been quoted as being anywhere from 10 to 40%, with opportunity cost of capital usually the primary component.

Inventory can be viewed as a hedge against inflation. That is, capital invested in inventory may hold its worth as the value of the dollar drops. To account for this, an estimate of the annual rate of inflation should be *subtracted* from the cost of capital in computing C_I. In economic terms, we should use the real cost of capital, corrected for inflation of the cost of the items. This adjustment is explained in Bierman and Thomas (1977).

In estimating C_I, it is important to follow the principles of *fixed* versus *avoidable costs*. For example, much of the cost of owning and operating a warehouse is fixed, not affected by the quantity of inventory. However, if inventory is growing, C_I must eventually reflect part of these fixed costs, or else inventory, being underpriced, will grow until a new warehouse cannot be avoided. However, the manager must be careful to exclude any costs that will be fixed no matter what inventory level is chosen.

F_I is often overstated because firms include fixed costs and use a hurdle rate that is too high. As stated above, the hurdle rate should be close to the borrowing rate net of inflation. On the other hand, obsolescence rates can be quite high, particularly in high-technology industries. The obsolescence rate is a function of the size of the inventory and is, therefore, not constant, but a constant rate is always used as a matter of practicality.

A similar principle applies to C_T, *the cost associated with the transaction of a single replenishment order, independent of the order quantity*. This includes avoidable costs such as paperwork in ordering and receiving the item, but does not include costs that are a function of annual volume of usage. For example, the cost of attaching machine readable tags to each item should not be included in C_T, because changing the frequency of replenishment transactions will not change the number of tags per year.

The cost of a transaction depends in part on the technology employed. Computer-assisted ordering, for example, may substantially affect the cost. It is important to be able to allocate avoidable costs of administrative use of a computer to include as part of C_T. On the other hand, if labor is a fixed cost over the entire possible range for number of orders, labor cost should not be included in the analysis. (In some cases, an implied cost or shadow price of labor can be used to represent the effect of a constraint on the number of replenishments per year as discussed in Chapter 2.)

Shortage costs are more difficult to measure. If estimated at all, they are often subjective (i.e., guesswork). This issue will be discussed more thoroughly in the section concerning safety stocks. The cost of a shortage occurs when an item is needed, but unavailable (out of stock). There are two common responses: the item may be *backordered* (delivery promised as soon as possible, perhaps at the cost of a rush order), or else the request may be canceled (which may represent a *lost sale,* with a corresponding opportunity cost). The symbol used is C_B, *which refers to the per unit cost associated with either backordering an item when it is not in stock, or losing the sale.*[3] In the literature on inventory control, there are two ways to specify this cost. Some models assume that the shortage cost is proportional to the duration of the shortage. However, in this chapter, the other view is taken: C_B does not include a time factor. It denotes a one-time cost accrued at the time of the shortage, and assumes that the duration of the shortage is irrelevant. These two approaches can give very different results. Time-weighted measures are discussed in Chapter 13. Refer to texts such as Love (1979) for development of models with time-weighted backorder cost.

Inventory control is achieved by a trade-off of these costs. For example, two major categories of inventory in a supply system are cycle stock and safety stock. *Cycle stock* refers to the inventory generated by ordering in quantity. Increasing the order quantity (Q) (and with it the cost of holding cycle stock) decreases the frequency of replenishment orders (reducing the transaction cost); large orders may also achieve a quantity discount. *Safety stock* is an identifiable quantity kept to protect against unexpectedly high demand or long lead times. Increasing the reorder level (R) results in larger quantities of safety stock (increasing holding cost) while improving the service provided (reducing shortage costs). The next section explores these trade-offs in detail and examines just how the ABC classification scheme is useful in cost control.

Review Problems

1. A fixed order quantity, Q, is used in both perpetual and standing-order inventory systems. Why do standing-order systems require special measures not normally encountered under perpetual control?
2. Why are better prices often available for standing orders?
3. Explain how it is possible for category C to constitute as many as 50% of the items, yet only 5% of annual dollar volume.
4. A manager computed the fractional holding cost as $F_I = 0.40$ (or 40%) per dollar invested in inventory per year. However, the 10% rate of inflation was not factored in. What adjustment should be made to F_I?

Solutions

1. The perpetual system is self-adjusting. If demand slows down, new orders are automatically delayed, since inventory falls more slowly toward the

---

[3] Theoretically, the cost model for lost sales is different from the backordered demand model. However, in most cases a shortage is a rare event, and the two models are, for practical purposes, the same.

reorder level R. In contrast, a standing order would continue to build inventory until some special action is taken to change the contract. A similar argument applies if demand increases.

2. A smooth delivery schedule is easier for the vendor.

3. Each category C item has a small annual dollar volume, either due to low price or low usage (or both). Most organizations have a wide variety of such items in stock.

4. F_I should be reduced by the inflation rate, so $F_I = 0.30$.

10-2 *THE ECONOMIC ORDER QUANTITY*

One of the oldest (1915) methods of scientific inventory control, the *economic order quantity* (EOQ) has endured because of its ability to balance some major costs and to be very flexible and adaptable for many situations. The EOQ is the major focus of this chapter, not only because of its wide use, but also because the relatively simple analysis brings out the nature of the trade-offs that must be faced in any inventory system.

All the important terms and formulas used in the following discussion (as well as in Sections 10-3 and 10-5) have been collected in Table 10-1 for handy reference. The reader may wish to attach a paper clip to this page, as the table will be used many times.

The key aspects of the EOQ system are shown in Figure 10-1. The decision variables are Q (the number of units ordered) and R (the reorder level). Inventory is controlled by placing a replenishment order of size Q whenever inventory falls below R units. This leads to the seesaw pattern exhibited in the figure.

When to Order?

The reorder level R serves two functions. It triggers a replenishment order with enough lead time (LT) so that the inventory usually will not run out before the goods arrive. If demand were steady and lead time always constant, the reorder policy would be simple: Place an order when there is just enough inventory to last until the shipment arrives. In this case, the reorder level would be equal to the *average lead time demand, $\overline{U}$*. (Three examples of lead time demand are labeled U_1, U_2, and U_3 in Figure 10-1.) However, because of fluctuations in lead time and/or demand, a safety stock (SS) is the second component of R, to provide a safety margin against stockouts in all but the most extreme cases. As Figure 10-1 shows, when the shipment is received, part of the safety stock may have been used, and must be replenished from the new order. In a properly designed system, the likelihood is very small that all the safety stock will be used.

The trade-off between service and cost is faced squarely in deciding on the quantity of safety stock. High-quality service depends on having stock on hand

TABLE 10-1   SYMBOLS AND FORMULAS FOR INVENTORY CONTROL[a,b]

I. Inventory Quantities

D = annual[c] usage (demand in units per year)

$D^\$$ = annual[c] dollar volume (\$ per year) = (unit price) · (D)

d = daily usage (demand)

U = usage during replenishment order lead time

LT = length of the lead time (lag until order is actually received)

n = number of replenishment orders placed each year[c] for an item

Q = quantity of each order = D/n

$Q^\$$ = dollar value of the order = (unit price) · (Q)

R = reorder level, or quantity on hand when an order is placed

SS = safety stock to protect against stockout in case of unexpected increase in lead time usage, U. By definition, $SS = R - \bar{U}$

P = probability of running out of stock before Q arrives (per reorder cycle)

SO/yr = average number of times per year[c] that inventory reaches zero (a stockout condition). By definition, $SO/yr = nP$

II. Per Unit Costs

C_I = annual[c] cost of holding 1 unit in inventory. Cost of capital, insurance, obsolescence, storage, etc.

F_I = fractional holding cost = C_I divided by the unit purchase price of the item

C_T = transaction cost for each replenishment order placed and received; this includes paperwork and handling, but excludes the cost of the item

C_B = backorder cost, incurred each time an item is needed but out of stock (as noted in the text, this may be the opportunity cost of a lost sale)

III. Economic Order Quantity Formulas

TVC = total annual[c] variable cost

A. Order Quantity (Sections 10-2 and 10-3)

$$TVC = C_I Q/2 + C_T D/Q + C_B SS$$
$$= F_I D^\$/2n + C_T n + C_I SS \tag{1}$$

$$Q^* = \sqrt{2DC_T/C_I} = D/n^* \tag{2}$$

$$n^* = \sqrt{C_I D/2C_T} = D/Q^*$$
$$= \sqrt{(F_I/2C_T)(D^\$)} \tag{3}$$

B. Statistics of Lead-Time Demand (Section 10-5)

$$\bar{U} = \bar{d}\,\overline{LT} \text{ where } \bar{U} \text{ denotes the average of } U \tag{4}$$

$$\text{Var } U = (\text{Var } d)(\overline{LT}) + (\text{Var } LT)(\bar{d})^2 \tag{5}$$

$$\sigma_u = \sqrt{\text{Var } U} \tag{6}$$

C. Safety Stock When Backorder Costs Are Unknown

$$P^* = (\text{desired } SO/yr)/n \tag{7}$$

z = value from normal table to achieve P^* $\qquad(8)$

$$SS^* = z\sigma_u \tag{9}$$

$$R^* = \bar{U} + SS^* \tag{10}$$

Implied backorder cost (Section 10-5)

$$C_B \text{ (implied)} = C_I/(\text{desired } SO/yr) \tag{11}$$

D. Safety Stock When Backorder Costs Are Known

$$\text{Optimal } SO/yr = C_I/C_B \tag{12}$$

$$P^* = (\text{optimal } SO/yr)/n \tag{13}$$

R^* = same as equations (8), (9), and (10) $\qquad(14)$

E. Stockout Protection When a Reorder Level Is Prespecified

$$SS(\text{actual}) = R - \bar{U} \tag{15}$$

$$z(\text{actual}) = SS(\text{actual})/\sigma_u \tag{16}$$

$P(\text{actual})$ = value from normal table given $z(\text{actual})$ $\qquad(17)$

$$SO/yr(\text{actual}) = nP(\text{actual}) \tag{18}$$

[a] Equations (8) and (16) assume demand has a normal probability distribution.

[b] An asterisk indicates the optimal value. Thus Q^* is the optimal order quantity, and n^* is the number of orders placed annually if Q^* is the order quantity.

[c] One year is used as the measure of time in this table. Any other period could be used (e.g., 1 week), but the *same* time period must be used for D, C_I, F_I, n, SO, and TVC.

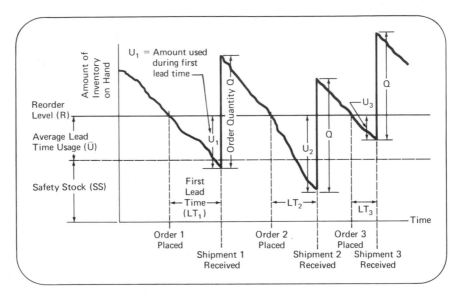

Figure 10-1   Level of inventory through time in a perpetual (continuous review) system, with replenishment order quantity Q and reorder level R.

when needed. Increasing the safety stock improves the service but ties up capital and storage space. Practical methods for setting safety stocks will be discussed in a later section.

How Much to Order?

Study of Figure 10-1 reveals that the safety stock (SS) is the average low point of inventory.[4] The high point is Q units higher, resulting in an average inventory of SS + $Q/2$, for an average annual cost of (C_i)(SS + $Q/2$). This equation shows that inventory costs may be reduced by ordering in small quantities, since the cycle stock, $Q/2$, is changed proportionately. However, ordering in small quantities necessitates more frequent order transactions to keep up with demand (usage). The annual number of orders placed (n) must satisfy the annual demand (D); therefore, $n = D/Q$ and the annual transaction cost is nC_T or $(C_T)(D/Q)$. A company that reduces its order quantities will therefore suffer increased transaction costs, primarily due to the need for more people to process and receive orders.

The cost trade-off between cycle stock and transaction frequency is more tangible than the safety-stock problem, although the two costs often affect different departments within an organization. The economic order quantity determines the best trade-off between holding and transaction costs.

---

[4] There are R units on hand when the procurement order is placed, and $\overline{U}$ units are used (on the average) by the time the shipment arrives. The remaining inventory therefore averages $R - \overline{U}$, which is the safety stock.

The total variable cost is, by the preceding discussion, the annual cost of holding inventory plus the annual transaction cost [equation (1) in Table 10-1]. The minimum cost may be found by calculus.[5] The economic order quantity ($Q*$) achieves the minimum cost by taking on a square-root relationship with annual demand [equation (2) in Table 10-1]. For example, if demand for an item were to double, one would increase the order quantity, but not double it.[6] Accordingly, to keep up with demand, the order frequency (n) must also increase. Therefore, inventory and transaction costs remain in balance, both having increased somewhat.

It is instructive to contrast the EOQ to another order quantity rule, "days of supply." In this rule, a common target value of t days of supply is used for a group of items, and applied by setting Q = (daily demand rate) times (t). With this rule, order quantity is directly proportional to demand, in contrast to the EOQ's square-root relationship. Therefore, a days-of-supply system does not minimize holding plus transaction cost. Nevertheless, it is widely used for other reasons. For example, coordination of orders can be accomplished by such a rule, and this can lead to quantity discounts. That notion is pursued in Section 10-4.

Review Problems

1. Demand for widgets occurs at an absolutely constant rate totaling D = 10,000 units per year. No safety stock is kept. C_I = \$5 per unit per year and C_T = \$9.25 per order. Evaluate the cost of the current policy of ordering batches of 1000 units, and compare it to the optimal policy.

2. How important is it to follow the optimal policy precisely? For example,

---

[5] The formula for the total variable cost is in section III of Table 10-1:

$$\text{TVC} = \frac{C_I Q}{2} + \frac{C_T D}{Q} + C_I \text{SS}$$

Taking the first derivative,

$$\frac{\partial \text{TVC}}{\partial Q} = \frac{C_I}{2} + C_T D \left(-\frac{1}{Q^2} \right) + 0$$

If $\partial \text{TVC}/\partial Q = 0$, then

$$\frac{C_I}{2} = \frac{C_T D}{Q^2}$$

Therefore,

$$Q* = \sqrt{\frac{2DC_T}{C_I}}$$

$$\frac{\partial^2 \text{TVC}}{\partial Q^2} = C_T D \left(+\frac{2}{Q^3} \right)$$

which is greater than zero, so $Q*$ is the minimum cost value of Q.

[6] If demand goes up by a factor of 2 (100%), the EOQ formula says that the order quantity should increase by a factor of $\sqrt{2}$ (only 41.4%). Therefore, since the order size does not fully reflect the increased demand, orders must also be placed more frequently.

what happens to TVC if Q is 50% above or below optimal in Review Problem 1?

Solutions

1. From equation (1) in Table 10-1,

$$\text{TVC} = \frac{C_I Q}{2} + \frac{C_T D}{Q} + C_I \text{SS}$$

$$= (5)(500) + (9.25)(10) + 0 = \$2593 \text{ per year}$$

From equation 2, each order should be for

$$Q^* = \sqrt{\frac{2DC_T}{C_I}} = \sqrt{37{,}000} = 192.4, \text{ or } 192 \text{ units}$$

Using equation (1), the optimal cost is TVC = \$962 per year. Thus using the optimal ordering policy should save about 63% of inventory related costs.

2. Try $Q = 288$ and $Q = 96$ in equation (1). The result is TVC = \$1041 and TVC = \$1204, which are different from the optimum by only 8% and 25%, respectively.

10-3 USING EOQ WITH ROUGH COST ESTIMATES

Podunk Hospital orders supplies from many different distributors. Order quantities have been determined with very little thought to cost trade-offs. Table 10-2 shows current policy for a random sample of items from Podunk's inventory.

The hospital administrator had read about inventory control several times in recent journals. Those sources suggested that annual holding costs for hospital supplies are generally between 15 and 30% of the unit cost of an item, mainly due to the opportunity cost of capital.

An investigation to determine the transaction cost met with some difficulty. Careful study pointed out that the major portion of the costs was salaries, but the allocation of the salaries among the many functions performed by the person-

TABLE 10-2 SUMMARY OF ORDERING POLICY FOR A SAMPLE OF PODUNK'S INVENTORY

Item	Current Order Quantity	Annual Usage	Price	Annual Volume
A	500	1000	$30	$30,000
B	30	360	5	1,800
C	72	432	50	21,600
D	10,000	5000	0.42	2,100
E	600	1800	3	5,400
			Total	$60,900

nel was, at best, a guess. The transaction cost was estimated to be somewhere between $1 and $10 per order placed.

Question 1 Can we do anything at all, given such rough cost estimates?

Analysis Do the analysis with midrange values for the costs. Then do a sensitivity analysis. Use F_I = 20% and C_T = $3.50 initially. Table 10-3 summarizes the results.

Sensitivity Analysis The suggested new policy (Q^*) cuts gross inventory from $12,375 to $1413 by increasing orders per year from 23.5 to 82.1. Since the number of orders was increased and the inventory decreased, we can make the new policy look its worst (relative to the old policy) by using the lowest inventory cost (15%) and highest transaction cost ($10). That would change the result to TVC(Q^*) = (0.15)(1413) + (10)(82.1) = $1033 compared to $2091 for the present policy, a savings of about 50%.

Conclusion If F_I = 20% and C_T = $3.50 are correct, variable costs (associated with order quantities) may be reduced by about 75% (from $2557 to $570) for this sample. More important, the savings are still 50% even if these cost estimates are incorrect in the worst possible way.

Question 2 Switching to Q^* would more than triple the number of orders per year, according to the preceding analysis. This may not be feasible over the next few years, because it would require a large staff increase in the ordering and receiving departments. Can we achieve any savings without adding personnel?

Analysis Adjust all the Q^* values upward until n drops to its original value of 23.5 per year for the sample. (This method is discussed in Plossl and Wight, 1967). Q^* implies 82.1 orders per year, which is 3.49 times larger than the desired value

TABLE 10-3 VARIABLE COSTS USING PODUNK'S EOQ AND CURRENT Q

Item	Q^*	COSTS USING Q^* (Price) × (Q^*/2)	$D/Q^* = n^*$	COSTS USING OLD Q (Price) × (Q/2)	$D/Q = n$
A	34	$ 510	29.4	$ 7,500	2
B	50	125	7.2	75	12
C	17	425	25.4	1,800	6
D	645	135.5	7.7	2,100	0.5
E	145	217.5	12.4	900	3
Totals		$1,413	82.1	$12,375	23.5
Multiply by:	F_I =	0.20 C_T =	$3.50	F_I = 0.20 C_T =	$3.50
Costs		$282.6	$287.4	$2475	$82.3
TVC		$570		$2557	

TABLE 10-4 VARIABLE COSTS USING PODUNK'S Q^+

Item	$Q^+ = 3.49Q^*$	(Price) $\times$ ($Q^+/2$)	$D/Q^+ = n^+$
A	119	$1785	8.4
B	175	437.5	2.1
C	59	1475	7.3
D	2253	473.1	2.2
E	507	760.5	3.6
Totals		$4931	23.6
Multiplied by:	$F_I =$	0.2	$C_T =$ $3.50
Costs		$986.2	$82.6
TVC		$1068.8	

of 23.5. Therefore, we multiply all Q^* by 3.49. The new Q values will be denoted by Q^+ and are shown in Table 10-4.

Sensitivity Analysis (same method as before)

$$\text{TVC (at } F_I = 15\% \text{ and } C_T = \$10) = \$975.7$$

Conclusion The Q^+ policy costs $1068.8 compared to $2257 for the current policy, a saving of 53%. Even if the unit costs are erroneous, variable costs would decrease from $2091 to $975.7, a 53% saving. And Q^+ accomplishes this without changing the work load in the ordering department.

Question 3 What happens if we round off the order quantities to make more natural order sizes?

Analysis There are many ways this could be done. For illustration, consider the following set of order quantities, all of which are within 20% of Q^*: A = 30, B = 50, C = 20, D = 600, E = 150. You may show that TVC = $574, a trivial difference. If one tries the same kind of analysis for Q^+, the result may be different. Specifically, if the round off results in more than 23.6 orders per year, you may have a *lower* cost than Q^+ since you have moved toward Q^*.

Conclusions on the Use of the EOQ

The example has illustrated several important points about the economic order quantity. Perhaps most striking is the success of the Q^+ policy, which appears to be a very arbitrary modification of the EOQ. It is instructive to compare the last two columns in Table 10-4 to the "old Q" portion of Table 10-3. The major differences occur in items A and B. Q^+ achieves its savings by reducing the order quantity of item A which has by far the greatest cycle stock ($7500). A smaller order quantity means more frequent orders, so item A's transactions increase from 2 to 8.4 per year. Item B only has $75 tied up in cycle stocks and is ordered 12 times per year under the old policy. Q^+ increases B's cycle stock at very little cost and achieves a reduction in annual transactions from 12 to 2.1. This offsets the change in item A.

In short, the Q^+ policy is efficient because it breaks up high-dollar-volume items into very frequent orders, and does the opposite for low-dollar-volume items. This property is shared by the EOQ. Therefore, the idea of multiplying all EOQ values by a constant is not as arbitrary as it first appears. In fact, it is the most efficient method to achieve a target for annual transactions (as in the example) or a target for cycle stock. A Review Problem and homework problem 23 pursue this point further.

The following notes summarize the conclusions from the example.

Robustness. The EOQ formula gets you in the right ballpark, even with shaky cost estimates. Within that ballpark, deviations of up to 20% in order quantities will cause only small cost penalties, owing to the fact that marginal transaction costs and holding costs are balanced at Q^*. Figure 10-2 summarizes how TVC varies as the order quantity changes; it shows that oversized orders are a less serious error than ordering too few.

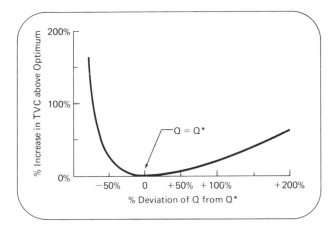

Figure 10-2 Total Variable Cost (TVC) expressed as a deviation from the optimal value.

Annual Dollar Volume. According to the A-B-C idea, $D^\$$ is the key to costs, and therefore to cost reduction. Table 10-5 illustrates that the Q^* and Q^+ policies explored in the example share the following property: The annual ordering frequency (n), the dollar value of the order ($Q^\$$), and the costs (TVC) are all highest for items of high annual dollar volume.

Practicality. The second analysis (developing Q^+) showed that a straightforward modification of the EOQ can significantly reduce costs without imposing major changes on the current system. The secret is that the dollar value of the order ($Q^\$$) should be proportional to the square root of annual dollar volume ($D^\$$).

Other practical modifications can be made, based on EOQ. Several are described in the next section, and other versions of the Q^+ modification are considered in the problems at the end of the chapter.

TABLE 10-5 RELATIONSHIP BETWEEN $D^\$$ AND OPTIMAL ORDERING POLICY

Item	Annual Volume $(D^\$)$	n^*	$Q^{\$*}$	TVC	n^+	$Q^{\$+}$	TVC$^+$
A	$30,000	29.4	$1020	$205	8.4	$3570	$386
C	21,600	25.4	850	173	7.3	2950	321
E	5,400	12.4	435	87	3.6	1521	165
D	2,100	7.7	271	54	2.2	946	102
B	1,800	7.2	250	50	2.1	875	95

The robustness property is really what makes this material worth studying, since the assumptions underlying EOQ are almost never totally realistic. For example, demand rates are often random, and may vary seasonally. Or, in the other extreme, demand may be totally predictable but lumpy (rather than uniform) over time. The latter is often faced when the supplies are to be used in a scheduled production process. This will be considered extensively in Chapters 11 and 12, where it will be seen that EOQ still plays an important role.

Keying on annual dollar volume is the basis of the A-B-C analysis discussed earlier. We have now seen that A items will be ordered more frequently than others, which is part of the additional effort we are willing to undertake to keep these items under tight control.

Review Problems

1. Are the potential savings for Podunk Hospital due to reduced inventory or fewer transactions? How do you know? What is the implication for personnel?

2. The last inventory count revealed that Podunk had $8 million tied up in supplies. If the EOQ policy were implemented in the entire supply system, what would the inventory level be? State your assumptions.

3. Suppose that Podunk wanted to achieve a reduction of 70% in the cash tied up in cycle stocks but would prefer to change its annual order transactions as little as possible. How should they compute order quantities?

Solutions

1. The analysis in Table 10-3 showed that, if the optimal quantities (Q^*) were used, inventory would drop in dollar value from $12,375 to $1413, and annual transactions would increase from 23.5 to 82.1. This change would require substantial increases in the work load of those involved in ordering and receiving. The modified policy Q^+ achieved its savings from inventory alone.

2. Using Q^*, the drop in dollar value of inventory would be 88.6% in the sample of five items. If the sample is representative and if the latest inventory count is accurate and representative of the usual situation, we could expect an overall reduction of 88.6% of $8 million, or $7.1 million. Using 20% as

the holding cost, the savings due to lower inventory would be $1.42 million per year. Against this savings would be a 250% increase in annual replenishment transactions.

3. Target cycle stock = 30% of $12,375 = $3712.50. The EOQ has a cycle stock of $1413, so multiply each EOQ by 3712.5/1413 = 2.627. This will achieve 82.1/2.627 = 31.2 transactions per year.

10-4 *ADAPTING EOQ TO FIT THE REAL SITUATION*

Quantity Discounts

If a lower price is offered for buying an item in larger quantity than the EOQ, a very simple analysis will show whether it is worthwhile to order the larger quantity. Simply calculate the increase in TVC due to ordering the price-break quantity, and compare it to the annual savings due to the discount.

Suppose that item A of the Podunk sample has been purchased at a $1 discount, which will disappear if Q falls below its current value of 500. Using $F_I = 20\%$ and $C_T = \$3.50$, first note that C_I will go up if we no longer get the quantity discount: currently, $C_I = (0.2)(30) = \$6$ per unit per year, but it will become $C_I = (0.2)(31) = \$6.20$. Therefore, our previous calculation of Q^* was in error. However, the small difference is lost in rounding off, and Q^* is still 34. We now calculate the overall cost of ordering $Q^* = 34$ at a time, and compare it to ordering in lots of 500, to obtain the discount. The calculations show that ordering the EOQ of 34 is appropriate in this case, since the potential savings with the discount are more than offset by higher costs. Note that a safety stock of 100 units is included in the calculation. This is important since the change in price affects the holding cost of safety stock as well as cycle stock, as noted by Aucamp (1981).

TVC CALCULATION AT $Q^* = 34$ WITH SAFETY STOCK SS = 100

Q	Price	C_I	$C_IQ/2$	C_TD/Q	C_ISS	TVC
500	$30 (discount)	$6	$1500	$ 7	$600	$2107
34	31	6.20	105	103	620	828

Increased TVC = 2107 − 828 = $1279 per year

Annual savings = (discount)(annual demand)

= ($1)(1000) = $1000 per year

If Podunk Hospital's discount had applied only to the additional items above the break point, it would be called an *incremental discount*. Then the first 500 items would cost $31 each, regardless of how large the total purchase is. In this case there is no incentive to order ''just enough'' to obtain the discount, in strong contrast to the situation described above. Potential savings are much smaller in this case, and the computations, described by Johnson and Montgomery (1974) are more complicated.

Announced Price Increases

If the price of item B is about to increase by $1, permanently, how much more than the EOQ should we order? Each unit added to the order will incur inventory holding costs until it is eventually used. If we order Q units, the last one will be used $t = Q/D$ years from now, so the holding cost of the last item used is $(C_I)(t) = C_I Q/D$. The main saving on that last item is $1 by avoiding the price increase. (Some reduction in the number of setups is also achieved, but it is usually a small saving.) Should we have bought that last unit? Or should Q have been smaller? The marginal costs and benefits of the last unit will offset each other if $1 = C_I Q/D$, so the optimal one-time order quantity is $Q = (\$1)(D/C_I)$. For item B, the order will be placed at the $5 price, so $C_I = (0.2)(5) = \$1$, and $Q = (1)(360/1) = 360$ units, compared to an EOQ of 50 under the old price and 46 under the new price.

The result, stated in general terms, is

$$Q = (\$ \text{ price increase})\left(\frac{D}{C_I}\right) \text{ or EOQ, (whichever is larger.)} \qquad (19)$$

This simple formula is quite different from the EOQ, and is included here both to increase your arsenal of handy tools and to show clearly that a permanent price change is different from a constantly available quantity discount. A complete, more complicated analysis is given in Love (1979).

Multi-Item Orders

Often, many items are supplied by the same vendor. For items that are ordered with similar frequency, it may be beneficial to combine them on one order. The savings that accrue include a smaller transaction cost per item (placing three items on one order takes less time than writing three separate order forms) and possibly a quantity discount based on the dollar value of the order. The difficulty arises because the three items will not necessarily hit their reorder levels simultaneously, resulting in excess inventory for those which are ordered prematurely.

A simple method to determine joint order quantities is to conceptually combine all the items into a single entity and compute its optimal ordering frequency, n^*. The correct method is to add together the annual dollar volumes $D^\$$ and use the square-root formula for n^* [see Table 10-1, equation (3)]. For example, Podunk Hospital's items B and D have annual demands of 360 and 5000, and prices of $5 and $0.42, respectively (Table 10-2). If they are ordered in a single transaction, the annual cash outlay is $D^\$ = 1800 + 2100 = \$3900$.

Suppose that ordering two items instead of one only adds $0.50 to the $3.50 transaction cost. Then $C_T = \$4.00$, and using $F_I = 0.2$, we obtain

$$n^* = \sqrt{\left(\frac{F_I}{2C_T}\right)D^\$}$$

$$= \sqrt{\left(\frac{0.2}{8}\right)(3900)} = 9.9$$

Using $n^* = 9.9$, we can compute

$$Q = \frac{D}{n^*} = \frac{360}{9.9} = 36 \text{ for item B}$$

$$= \frac{5000}{9.9} = 505 \text{ for item D}$$

Excluding safety stock, the total variable cost for joint ordering [equation (1) in Table 10-1] is

$$\text{TVC} = \frac{F_I D^\$}{2n} + C_T n = \$79 \qquad \text{(excluding safety stock)}$$

Compared to the TVC of $50 for B and $54 for D when ordered separately (Table 10-3), this is a saving of $25 per year.

In dollar terms, the joint order quantity is $(\$5)(36) = \$180$ for B and $(\$0.42)(505) = \$212$ for D, for a total of $392 per order. If this is not large enough to merit a quantity discount, the analysis should proceed exactly as described in the earlier discussion. That is, consider increasing the size of the order to achieve the discount, and compare the increase in TVC to the discount savings.

Review Problem

When Items B and D are jointly ordered, a quantity discount of 5% is available if the order size is $1000 or more. Should they increase their order to $1000 to obtain the reduced price?

Solution

If the order size is $1000 instead of $392, the order quantities are multiplied by $1000/392 = 2.551$, and the transaction frequency is divided by the same number. Therefore, the average inventory is $1000/2 = \$500$, representing a cost of $(0.2)(500) = \$100$ per year. There are 3.9 transactions per year at $C_T = \$4$ each. Therefore, the total variable cost is $\text{TVC} = \$100 + \$15.6 = \$115.6$. Compared to $79, which was the TVC at Q^*, this is an increase of $36.6 per year. The annual savings is 5% of the $3900 nominal annual dollar volume, or $195. If we include SS in the calculation, the savings would be even greater with the discount, so it is certainly worthwhile to deviate from the optimal quantities in order to achieve the savings.

10-5 SAFETY STOCKS

The economic order quantity is useful in a variety of situations. However, the discussion so far has made no reference to the possibility of running short of stock. This issue will now be addressed through the use of safety stocks, which are extra buffers of inventory kept on hand in case (1) delivery of the order is delayed or (2) demand exceeds expectations during the lag between placing and receiving the order.[7]

There are two difficult issues with safety stocks. (1) "What is the optimal level of protection?" Or, stated another way, "How often will we tolerate running out of stock?" This is a theoretical issue, based on the trade-off between holding costs and shortages. (2) "What reorder level should we set to achieve this theoretically optimal protection?" This is a practical question and is handled through statistics. Because the discussion of each of these issues is complex, they are handled one at a time, beginning with the practical one.

Practical Methods for Setting Safety Stocks

In this section, we must assume that a criterion has been set for an acceptable quality of service. One way to do this is to determine the acceptable average number of stockouts per year (SO/yr). This criterion is often specified through the intuition and experiences of management; a cost analysis will be discussed later. Once SO/yr has been specified, the problem focuses entirely on the lead time (LT), its variability, and the demand that occurs during lead time.

The lead time begins when inventory hits the reorder level R, and ends when a new order for Q items arrives on the shelves, ready for use. During the lead time are numerous opportunities for delay. The critical events are: (1) the discovery that inventory is at or below R, (2) an order is placed, (3) the supplier receives the order, (4) the supplier ships the order, (5) the shipment is received, and (6) the stock is on the shelf. *Control of these events often pays handsome dividends, since unreliability in any of these stages translates directly into the need for extra safety stock.* The word *unreliability* deserves special emphasis. The goal is not only to minimize lead time, but also to minimize the variability in lead time. To see why, consider suppliers X and Y, each of whom averages 5 weeks delivery time. Supplier X always delivers in exactly 5 weeks, but Y randomly varies from 4 to 6 weeks. We need at least 6 weeks' supplies on hand when we place an order with Y, of which 0 to 2 weeks' supply will still be on hand when the order arrives. If X is our supplier, we can order 1 week later, and the order will arrive just when it is needed. Therefore, inventory can be reduced by 1 week's supply, on the average.

---

[7] Strictly speaking, when shortages are included in the analysis, the EOQ should be reexamined, since larger Q means less frequent ordering and therefore fewer times per year when inventory is near the stockout level. However, because of the robustness of EOQ, the resulting increase in the optimal order quantity usually has negligible effects on total costs. Johnson and Montgomery (1974) describe an algorithm that allows for this effect.

Even if lead time does not vary, there is still a need for safety stock because of fluctuations in the rate at which supplies are used. Suppose that the usage of an item is between 60 and 80 per working day, averaging 70. Then if we use supplier X, lead time is 5 weeks, the average lead time usage $\overline{U}$ is (5 weeks) (5 days per week) (70 units per day) = 1750 units. To this we must add the safety stock, in case there are more high-usage days than low-usage days during the lead time. (Safety stock is discussed further below.) This discussion is encapsulated in the following formula, which is equation (8) in Table 10-1.

$$\text{reorder level} = \begin{array}{c}\text{average} \\ \text{lead-time} \\ \text{demand}\end{array} + \begin{array}{c}\text{safety} \\ \text{stock}\end{array}$$

$$R \quad = \quad \overline{U} \quad + \quad \text{SS}$$

A few details from Figure 10-3 will help to fix this relationship firmly in mind. The term $\overline{U}$ is the average depletion of inventory during lead time. (In Figure 10-3, U_1, U_2, and U_3 represent actual depletion during the three lead times shown in the figure). The safety stock is an excess built into R, to protect against heavy depletion (such as during lead time 2 in the figure) due to an unexpectedly long lead time or an unusually heavy usage rate.

The *worst-case method* is to set the reorder point equal to the largest lead time demand ever experienced for the item in question. If an item has never stocked out, quick savings may be attained by scanning the inventory records, finding the *lowest* inventory level over the past few years, and reducing the

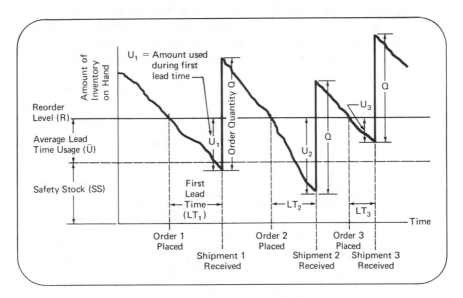

Figure 10-3 Level of inventory through time in a perpetual (continuous review) system, with replenishment order quantity Q and reorder level R.

reorder level by that amount. (Caution and judgment must be used, as always, when basing your decision on data that are several years old. There may have been changes in usage, suppliers, or even in safety stock.) If data on lead time demand (U) is available, the worst-case method would set R equal to the largest U encountered in the relevant history.

The *n*th *worst-case method* applies if a criterion has been specified for an acceptable number of stockouts per year (SO/yr). Suppose that we have data on 30 reorder cycles spanning 6 years, and the criterion was to allow one stockout per 2 years. Then the reorder level should be set somewhere between the third and fourth largest lead time demands encountered over the 6 years. (That would have resulted in three stockouts in 6 years = one in 2 years.)

Theoretical distributions are often useful, especially if only limited relevant information is available on lead-time demand. We present, for your toolbox, two formulas [equations (5) and (6) from Table 10-1] that will be used shortly in an example.

$$\overline{U} = \overline{d}\,\overline{LT}$$

$$\text{Var } U = (\text{Var } d)(\overline{LT}) + (\text{Var } LT)(\overline{d})^2$$

As before, U refers to lead-time demand, LT to lead time (working days), and d to daily demand. "Var" is an abbreviation for the statistical variance, which is the square of the standard deviation.

The first formula states the obvious: Average lead time demand is the product of average demand rate and average lead time. The second formula takes us back to our earlier discussion of unreliability in lead time. If $\text{Var}(d)$ (the variance of daily demand) is not zero, that is the same as saying that the daily demand is not always the same. Similarly, $\text{Var}(LT)$ measures the unreliability of lead time. The formula shows that both of these uncertainties combine to give the variance in lead time demand, $\text{Var }(U)$, against which the safety stock is to protect.

These formulas are important because they help one estimate the two components of the reorder level R. In particular, *safety stock (SS) is directly proportional to the standard deviation of lead time demand* (σ_u). That is,

$$\sigma_u = \sqrt{\text{Var } U}$$

$$\text{SS} = z\sigma_u$$

in which z is a constant of proportionality, to be defined below. Therefore, the formula that relates the reorder level R to lead time demand is

$$R = \overline{U} + z\sigma_u$$

which is equation 8 in Table 10-1.

The *normal probability law* is sometimes used as an approximation for the probability distribution of lead-time demand. When this is done, the constant z is taken from the normal tables (Table 2, Appendix D). The value is chosen to achieve a prespecified service level criterion (illustrated below).

Poisson and *exponential* are two other probability laws that are sometimes used in inventory control. Carlson (1982) combines these two distributions for items with short and variable lead times, and derives simple formulas for order quantities and safety stocks. Regardless of the probability distribution, one cardinal rule is to test the resulting reorder levels carefully, against old data if possible, and in actual use. It is not too difficult to determine, for example, whether stockouts are occurring more often than planned, if one observes the performance over many items.

Safety Stock Example

Podunk Hospital is changing suppliers for item G, which has a per unit holding cost of $C_I = \$1$ per year. They plan to continue ordering it four times per year, and have specified a service level of one stockout per 3 years (SO/yr = 0.33). The history of reorder lead times (based on Podunk's experience on other items purchased from this new supplier) is shown in Table 10-6. A similar table (not included here) compiled daily demands during the last 6 months. From that table, it was calculated that $\overline{d} = 40$ units per day, and Var(d) = 30 (units/day)^2.

TABLE 10-6   LEAD TIMES FOR SIMILAR ITEMS OBTAINED FROM THIS SUPPLIER

Order placed (date):	1/7	2/3	3/16	4/6	5/2	6/2
Order received:	1/18	2/21	4/20	4/28	5/20	6/23
Lead times						
Calendar days	11	18	35	22	18	21
Working days	7	12	25	16	14	15

Question   What is the appropriate reorder level, R?

Analysis   Referring to equations (5) through (9) in Table 10-1, we see that the average and variance of lead time are needed. They are calculated as follows:

$$\overline{LT} = \frac{7 + 12 + 25 + 16 + 14 + 15}{6} = 14.83 \text{ days}$$

$$\text{Var}(LT) = \frac{(7 - 14.83)^2 + (12 - 14.83)^2 + \cdots}{6 - 1} = 34.97 \text{ (days)}^2$$

These numbers, with $\overline{d}$ and Var(d) (given above), are substituted in equations (4) to (10) as follows:

$$\overline{U} = (40)(14.83) = 593.3 \text{ units demanded per lead time} \tag{4}$$

$$\text{Var}(U) = (30)(14.83) + (34.97)(40)^2 = 56{,}397 \tag{5}$$

$$\sigma_u = \sqrt{56{,}397} = 237.5 \text{ units per lead time} \tag{6}$$

desired SO/yr = 0.33 (as stated above)

order cycles/year = 4 (given) = n

$$P^* = \text{desired probability of stockout per order cycle} \qquad (7)$$

$$= \frac{\text{SO/yr}}{n} = \frac{0.33}{4} = 0.083$$

From Table 2, Appendix D, $P = 0.083$ corresponds to $z = 1.39$ (8)

$$\text{SS}^* = (1.39)(237.5) = 330.1 \qquad (9)$$

$$R^* = 593.3 + 330.1 = 923.4 \qquad (10)$$

Conclusion   Assuming that these data are representative of what we can expect in the future, orders should be placed whenever inventory drops to 923 units of item G. This allows for the average usage of 593 units, plus a safety stock of 330.

Sensitivity Analysis   Should we be concerned with the unreliability of lead time in this case? Suppose that Var(LT) could (somehow) be eliminated. Repeating the calculations, Var(U) is substantially reduced, and the resulting safety stock is only 29 units, compared to 330 above. The reorder level is reduced from 923 to 622, and therefore the inventory is lowered by 301 units, on the average. Because C_I is \$1 for this item, the annual saving is \$301. In addition, we would presumably reap similar savings for the other items ordered from this supplier. Consequently, it may be worthwhile to expend some effort to improve reliability of lead time.

Optimal Stockout Frequency and Implied Backorder Costs

Most safety stock decisions are based on a more-or-less arbitrary level of protection. The following analysis shows how to minimize costs by considering the costs and savings of a 1-unit change in the reorder level.

Suppose that we considered reducing the reorder level by 1 unit for a given item. *What will it save?* Referring to Figure 10-3, if R is lowered, the entire graph moves down, indicating a lower average inventory. The saving is therefore C_I dollars per year for each 1-unit reduction in R. *What will it cost?* The answer depends on the number of times per year we are out of stock (SO/yr). Each time we were out of stock last year, if R had been lower, we would have had greater shortages. Thus lowering R by 1 unit will cost us 1 more unit of shortage for each out-of-stock condition, and so the average cost per year is

$$(1 \text{ shortage}) \cdot (\text{average SO/yr}) \cdot (\text{cost per item short, } C_B)$$

If the costs are less than the savings, we should reduce R. If costs exceed savings, R should be higher. Therefore, at the optimal R, costs of a marginal change should equal savings, or

$$(\text{SO/yr}) (C_B) = C_I$$

From the analysis above (rearranging the last equation) the reorder level R must be set in such a way that the average annual number of stockouts is numerically equal to C_I/C_B, or

$$\text{optimal SO/yr} = \frac{C_I}{C_B}$$

This is equation (12) in Table 10-1.

To apply this result, suppose that item G is estimated to have a shortage cost of $10 at Podunk Hospital, because of the scrambling that must take place to procure the item if it is needed when out of stock. As before, $C_I = \$1$, $\overline{U} = 593.3$ units demanded during lead time, $\sigma_u = 237.5$, and $n = 4$ replenishment orders per year.

Question 1   What is the optimal reorder level R?

Analysis $C_I/C_B = \$1/\$10 = 0.10$, so the optimal reorder policy should average 10 years between stockouts (one-tenth stockout per year). The service level specified in the preceding example was one stockout in 3 years, which is too frequent according to this analysis. (Refer to Table 10-1 for the following equations.) The reorder-level calculations are:

$$\text{optimal SO/yr} = \frac{C_I}{C_B} = \frac{\$1}{\$10} = 0.10 \tag{12}$$

$$P^* = \frac{\text{SO/yr}}{n} = \frac{0.10}{4} = 0.025 \tag{13}$$

$$\left.\begin{array}{l} z = 1.96 \text{ (from the normal probability table, for } P = 0.025)\\ R^* = 593.3 + (1.96)(237.5) = 593.3 + 465.5 = 1058.8 \end{array}\right\} \tag{14}$$

Conclusion   The optimal reorder level is 1059. This is 132 units higher than the $R = 926$ that we calculated earlier, based on the value 0.33 SO/yr, specified subjectively by management.

Question 2   The inventory manager is adamant, claiming that it is a waste of money and storage space to increase R above 926, which was the level that achieves one stockout per 3 years. Can this dispute be mediated?

Analysis   Knowing that $C_I = \$1$, suppose we assume that the optimal SO/yr really is 0.33, as the manager is insisting. What value of C_B is implied? Solve equation (12) for C_B:

$$\text{SO/yr} = \frac{C_I}{C_B}$$

$$0.33 = \frac{\$1}{C_B}$$

$$C_B = \frac{\$1}{0.33} = \$3$$

or, in general terms,

$$\text{implied } C_B = \frac{C_I}{\text{desired SO/yr}}$$

Conclusion The dispute comes down to the correct valuation of a shortage. Unless C_B is substantially lower than \$10, the inventory manager is wrong; that is, allowing 0.33 stockout per year is optimal only if $C_B = \$3$. However, perhaps the manager has some less expensive method of dealing with shortages. If so, an increase in safety stocks is not appropriate. The argument can be resolved by finding out whether \$10 or \$3 more realistically represents all the tangible and intangible costs of being short of item G by 1 unit.

A caveat: The method just described for setting optimal safety stocks is an approximation. Porteus (1983) describes situations in which far better results can be obtained using more complex models. In general, the equations developed here can be trusted when the backorder cost C_B is very high relative to the inventory cost. However, we assumed that inventory status is continuously monitored and that orders can be placed at any time. If these events take place only once per week, or once per month, serious errors can be incurred by using this model. Porteus (1983) gives examples of several models that are designed for periodic review inventory control and compares their effectiveness.

Safety Stocks and A-B-C

The A-B-C concept may be summarized by reviewing the equations in Table 10-1, as follows. High-dollar-volume ($D^\$$) items are ordered most frequently [high n^*, equation (3)]. But a high n^* necessitates a low stockout probability per cycle [low P^*, equations (7) and (13)] to keep the frequency of stockouts at its optimal annual level. This, in turn, requires extra safety stock. The conclusion that high-dollar-volume items will have high safety stocks confirms the idea that effort spent on controlling lead time, or anything else to make possible lower safety stocks, should be concentrated on the A items, in order to obtain the biggest saving per time spent.

A practical concern that Podunk Hospital must face has often been expressed in the question: "Should a lifesaving item ever be considered a C item?" The answer is: "Definitely yes, if it has a low annual dollar volume." A lifesaving C item may achieve stockout protection at very little cost through increased safety stock. Of course, some lifesaving items may have high $D^\$$ and therefore belong in category A. In that case, more elaborate methods of avoiding shortages may be employed, in order to cut down on the safety stocks. This could be done through a sharing agreement with another firm, or a hot line to the supplier, for example.

As with order quantities, the largest safety-stock-related costs are incurred by high-dollar-volume items. We have studied two approaches to controlling these costs: statistics and economics. The statistical method begins with management's specification of a reasonable number of stockouts per year, and sets a reorder level through analysis of average lead times and demands and their variability. The economic analysis can supply an optimal level for the stockout criterion if an accurate value of backorder costs is available. When backorder costs are not well defined, one may ascertain whether management's target stockout level is in the right ballpark by calculating the backorder cost *implied* by the current policy.

10-6 *OTHER INVENTORY CONTROL SYSTEMS*

The *periodic review system* for consumables was briefly described early in this chapter. The key variables are T, the *review period* (fixed time between reviews of inventory records), and TI, the *target inventory level* on which orders are based. Figure 10-4 summarizes the operation of a *forced ordering* periodic review system, so called because an order *must* be placed at the end of each review period. Each review period is exactly T days long; at the end of this period, an order is placed for a quantity sufficient to replenish inventory to the target level, TI. After the reorder lead time (LT), the shipment arrives and goes into inventory. The order quantities are different each period, being calculated as Q = TI − inventory on hand − previous orders not yet received. The formula for TI for a fixed interval T is as follows:

$$\text{TI} = \begin{matrix}\text{average} \\ \text{review-} \\ \text{period} \\ \text{demand}\end{matrix} + \begin{matrix}\text{average} \\ \text{lead-time} \\ \text{demand}\end{matrix} + \text{safety stock} \qquad (20)$$

$$= (T)(\bar{d}) \quad + \overline{U} \qquad + z\sqrt{(T)(\text{Var }d) + \text{Var }\overline{U}}$$

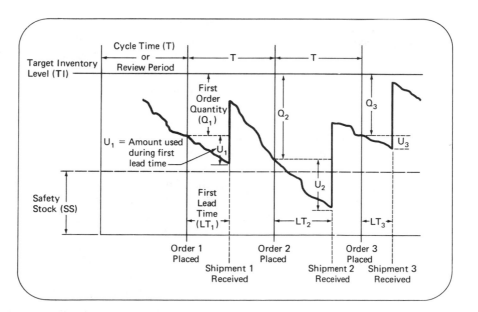

Figure 10-4 Level of inventory through time in a periodic review system: Order quantity = target inventory − inventory on hand.

In comparison to a continuous-review reorder-level system (such as the one studied in the preceding section) the periodic forced ordering system requires more safety stock. The clue to understanding this statement is in the comparison of equation (20) to equation (9) in Table 10-1. This is explored in Problem 17.

Perishable supplies and obsolescence present a new set of problems. The most important rule in inventory management of perishables is "first in, first out." That is, the first item to arrive should be used first. Sometimes this is difficult to enforce. For example, a blood bank may be required to supply their freshest blood for certain surgical procedures in which the quantity of blood needed is high and/or the patient is in very poor condition. In the retail grocery business, dairy and baked goods will often be selected on a "freshest first" basis by the customer, contrary to desires of the grocer.

The primary method for reducing spoilage is to *share the risk* with other users. Thus there will be a smaller percentage of spoilage in a blood bank that serves three hospitals than if each hospital had its own. Unfortunately, this leads to the need for somewhat complex organizational arrangements, and the types of models we can present in this book do not apply. Further reading and references on this problem can be found in an article by Nahmias (1982).

There are two simple approaches that work for some situations. An EOQ model with a reorder level may be used if the shelf life is of the same order of magnitude as the turnover time, $(Q + SS)/\bar{d}$. In this approach, a factor is added to the inventory cost C_I to reflect the average amount of spoilage that has been experienced. This results in somewhat smaller Q^* and SS, and therefore less spoilage, at a cost of more frequent orders and higher likelihood of shortage.

The other approach is referred to as the *newsperson problem*. This is useful when spoilage or obsolescence is almost immediate, so that there is no inventory carried over between orders. End-of-season ordering is another important application, encountered in automobiles, clothing, chocolate Easter bunnies, and many other markets. In this model, the size of the order is based on the probability that it will be entirely used.

The newsperson model may be developed by examining the costs and savings of a 1-unit change in the order quantity Q. If we order one unit less than Q, and if demand (d) subsequently is greater than or equal to Q, we have lost the net revenue of that unit, and we have incurred the cost of one shortage (perhaps loss of goodwill). Thus the expected loss is (net revenue + shortage cost) times the probability that ($d \geq Q$). On the other hand, if demand turns out to be less than Q, the reduction of the order quantity represents a savings equal to the cost of the item less its salvage value.

If the expected cost and expected saving are equal, there is no incentive to change the order quantity. Therefore, Q is optimal if

$$(\text{net revenue} + \text{shortage cost})[\text{Prob } (d \geq Q)]$$
$$= (\text{cost} - \text{salvage value})[1 - \text{Prob } (d \geq Q)]$$

The optimal probability of stockout (rearranging the foregoing equation) is the *newsperson formula*:

$$\text{optimal stockout probability} = \text{Prob}\,(d \geqslant Q) \qquad (21)$$

$$= \frac{\text{cost} - \text{salvage value}}{\text{net revenue} + \text{shortage cost} + \text{cost} - \text{salvage value}}$$

in which all these costs are on a per unit basis. The optimal policy, therefore, is to set the order quantity just high enough to achieve this stockout probability. The usefulness of this result is limited by the ability to specify the shortage cost, which, as in the EOQ analysis, is partly intangible (e.g., loss of customer good will). Therefore, another useful form of this equation is obtained by solving for the implied shortage cost.

implied shortage cost   (22)

$$= \frac{\text{cost} - \text{salvage value}}{\text{stockout probability}} - \left(\genfrac{}{}{0pt}{}{\text{net}}{\text{revenue}}\right) - \text{cost} + \text{salvage value}$$

The managerial use of this kind of formula (implied shortage cost) was described in the previous section (safety stocks).

Reusable supplies are often more akin to production processes than the other situations considered here. For example, when and how quickly to clean and resterilize surgical equipment depends on the sterilization equipment available, the work force, and the stock of clean items on hand. The inventory consists of cycle stock of clean equipment (to allow batching of the cleaning process), safety stocks for obvious reasons, stock of equipment in use, and cycle stock waiting to be reprocessed. Therefore, one major trade-off is capital tied up in the supplies versus frequency of reprocessing, with more frequent (and smaller) batches leading to smaller cycle stocks. The appropriate batch size may be obtained through an EOQ approach, with C_T interpreted as a setup cost for the reprocessing run.

Review Problems

Christmas tree retailers must place their orders 3 months in advance of the holiday season. The average cost of a tree is $8, and they sell for an average of $12. It costs $1.00 to dispose of each leftover tree.

1. What is the optimal ordering policy in terms of planned stockout probability?
2. If demand has the normal probability law, and the forecast is for 500 trees (with a standard deviation of 50 trees), how many should be ordered?

Solutions

1. The salvage value is negative (i.e., $-$1.00) because of the disposal cost. Net revenue = $12 $-$ $8 = $4. Using equation (21), the stockout probability should be

$$P = \frac{8 - (-1.00)}{4 + \text{shortage cost} + 8 - (-1.00)}$$

If there is no cost assigned to running short (other than the lost profit), this is $P = 9.00/13.00 = 0.692$, or 69.2%. Therefore, one should carry *fewer* trees than the expected value of demand.

2. From the normal probability table (Table 2, Appendix D), to have a stockout probability of 69.2%, we must have $z = -0.5$. Therefore, $Q = 500 + (-0.5)(50) = 475$ trees.

10-7 Summary

Inventory has been viewed as a service function in this chapter. The goal has been to provide an acceptable level of service (availability) at a minimum cost. The level of service is adjusted through safety stocks, and the costs are minimized by ordering in the proper quantity. When costs are balanced at the margin, surprisingly large deviations may be taken from the optimal order quantities at very little cost penalty. This property of robustness is due to the fact that increases in holding costs (as Q increases) are almost exactly offset by decreases in transaction costs when Q is near Q*.

There is a major interaction between this aspect of operations management and both finance and marketing. The financial aspect of these models requires careful attention to the allocation of fixed costs. For example, the cost of a new warehouse may be avoidable if there are major shifts in inventory policy. In this situation, therefore, the fixed costs of warehousing must be allocated to the holding cost C_I. Furthermore, inventory, just as all other uses of capital, must show an acceptable return through cost reductions and service. This is assured by including the cost of capital (hurdle rate) in C_I. In many operations, there will be an additional restraint in the form of a budget which effectively limits the overall inventory investment. Methods of managing an overall inventory investment are discussed further in Chapters 13 and 17.

Forecasting demand is but one interaction of inventory management with marketing. Of particular importance is the coordination of supplies with sales promotion schemes. The marketing department should provide information concerning customers' plans and competitors' schemes that will affect demand and therefore inventory. These observations join the growing list of reasons why it is important that the operations manager establish and maintain close ties with other areas of management.

There are squirrels in most organizations, whose instincts require them to fill closets with supplies in case the central supply system fails. One consequence of this is that there is more safety stock around than management is aware of. However, capital is tied up in these stocks, and their protection against damage and pilferage is less than ideal. Further, they often contribute to general disarray and clutter. Consequently, one of the major goals in inventory control is to install a system that can be relied on, and implement it in such a way that the users believe in it. Then (and only then) can the squirrels' nests be eliminated. The dollar benefit of this is difficult to measure, but this kind of tidying up is often considered as a major improvement.

Major cost savings come from getting a good handle on lead time and lead-time demand. Monitoring late deliveries is a very important materials management function. The mathematical models we have presented allow us to carry out sensitivity analyses (such as the example in Section 10-5) to pinpoint major sources of inventory cost. Decreasing the procurement lead time substantially reduces the safety stock required, for example. A quantitative estimate of these savings is useful in deciding whether to pursue new vendor contracts, or whether to hire an order expediter. Major savings are also achieved through elimination of low-use items, concentration on multiuse items, and reduction of duplicate purchasing (go to a single brand when possible). A good information system is very important for this aspect of operations management, allowing rapid access to the data needed for the kinds of analyses we have discussed.

Most computer manufacturers and many other firms sell software packages that are designed for inventory control in various situations. The advantage of dealing with these people is that they bring experience from other implementations, and, of course, we avoid reinventing the wheel. The disadvantages are the cost and the fact that no prepackaged routine ever fits a situation completely. Nevertheless, a well-implemented computerized inventory control system goes a long way toward minimizing the major cost sources such as orders placed late, out-of-date stock quantities, and time-consuming manual order processing.

CASELET: VENERABLE DISTRIBUTORS

"Twenty million dollars of inventory is simply too high! We are getting only 3 turns per year while our competitors are getting from 4 to 10. As I see it, there are two ways to reduce our inventory of supplies. One way is to order in smaller quantities, and the other is to cut down on safety stocks. Ms. Place, both purchasing and inventory control report to you. I want you to find ways to increase our inventory turnover."

Apparently finished, Mr. Topp sat back in his chair and puffed on his unlighted cigar. Ms. Place thought for a moment and then replied, "I've been telling you for months that my departments are understaffed. We need more personnel if we are to control inventory more carefully. Suppose we reduced the size of every order by half. Then we would have to process twice as many orders."

"True," replied Mr. Topp, "but I think there may be some avenues you have not yet explored. I want you to have a chat with Mr. Byte in the data processing department and see if there is any way that your ordering operation can be made more productive by using the computer more effectively. Maybe you should get a microcomputer. I want you to increase turnover without adding to your budget. I'm sure you can find ways to control inventory more efficiently.''

After the meeting, Ms. Place went to see Ms. Dee Olds, her predecessor as VP for materials management. ''Vendor control,'' said Olds. ''That's the secret. Our biggest reason for safety stock is to cover for late deliveries. If the vendors were more reliable with lead time, we could save a bundle. I had dinner with Charlie Young over at Consolidated the other day and he told me about the deal he had worked out with one of his best vendors. He called it 'favorable status.' Charlie explained that from now on vendors would be evaluated on delivery reliability as well as price and quality. Vendors with good delivery records would be more likely to be chosen. Consolidated expects to reduce substantially the number of vendors they deal with.''

''Much to his surprise, Charlie found out that the vendor liked the idea. They worked out a deal that covered a large number of items. I didn't get all the details, but he did say that by putting all the items into a single package they were able to work out some favorable prices.''

''In addition, they agreed on a different delivery arrangement. Rather than waiting for an order from Consolidated, the vendor delivers items on a weekly basis, although slow-moving items are delivered less frequently. Charlie set up limits so that if an item gets too low or too high, its order is modified. The change is guaranteed to be implemented on the next delivery. Now, most of the deliveries occur with virtually no transaction cost. The paperwork is standardized so only the changes require any special attention.''

''It sounds like Charlie killed three birds with one stone,'' said Ms. Place. ''But tell me, Dee, how much time and expense went into making all these arrangements? Does he have to set up a unique agreement with each vendor, or is there one system that fits all?''

''I don't have a good answer. All I know is that he has been working on it for a year already and is still ironing out the details with some of his vendors.''

Required

1. What are the ''three birds'' that Charlie bagged? Discuss how they relate to Ms. Place's problem.

2. How much of a reduction in inventory does she have to achieve? Given what you know about the cost of holding inventory, how much will the annual saving be if she succeeds?

3. Describe in detail how Ms. Place could estimate the reduction in cycle stock if she adopted Consolidated's ''favored vendor'' idea.

4. How does Consolidated's delivery schedule arrangement affect the calculation of safety stock? Make reference to the equations in the

chapter, and describe how Ms. Place could evaluate the potential savings.

5. The purchasing manager is evaluated on the basis of costs, including cash outlays for purchasing as well as wages and other operating expenses. How might this manager react to including reliability of delivery as a criterion for vendor selection?

PROBLEMS

1. What determines the time at which an order is placed and the quantity ordered in
   (a) Periodic-review forced ordering systems?
   (b) Perpetual-inventory systems?
   (c) Standing-order systems?

2. Under the A-B-C classification, comparing the A and C categories, which has
   (a) The greater number of types of items?
   (b) The greater capital tied up in inventory per SKU?
   (c) The greater physical quantity of inventory?

3. A company has a warehouse for storing the supplies purchased for company use. The warehouse is typically one-half to two-thirds full. In deciding on values of the unit costs to be used in setting inventory control policies, the manager was having difficulty with certain items. Decide how to allocate the costs listed below between the parameters C_I and C_T, defined in Table 10-1. Indicate which costs should not be included in either of the two parameters.
   (a) The cost of heat and lights in the warehouse.
   (b) Wages paid for the annual physical count of inventory.
   (c) Wages paid for inspecting the quality of items when they are received.
   (d) Janitorial wages.
   (e) Wages of the materials handling crew (warehouse and receiving dock).
   (f) Wages paid for paperwork involved in ordering and receiving.

4. Scan the equations in Table 10-1 and point out where forecasts must be used, including a measure of forecast accuracy such as the standard deviation.

*5. An inventory system for supplies (independent demand) has been using a perpetual inventory (Q, R) system, but with arbitrarily defined order quantities. Recently, the paperwork due to order transactions has begun to increase, and the boss is looking for a way to control (minimize) this trend. One suggestion was an across-the-board increase in order quantities of 25% for all items.

(a) Explain briefly why this will reduce the paperwork.

(b) Explain briefly why this will increase inventory.

(c) Suggest a method for reducing the paperwork due to transactions *without* increasing total inventory costs.

6. Both of the following situations could be characterized as dependent demands, but situation I is a suitable application for the methods of this chapter, whereas situation II is not.

(a) Explain why, by noting a very simple ordering policy for situation II which is a substantial improvement over the reorder quantity/reorder level (Q, R) system.

(b) What is it about situation II that allows this improvement?

> SITUATION I: A production line is devoted to one product, and operates at a steady pace all year (excluding nights, weekends, etc.). One of the raw materials is ordered with $Q = 200$, $R = 200$. The average usage of raw material is 175 units per 4-week period.
>
> SITUATION II: A production line is used for many products. Product A is manufactured once every 4 weeks, and the production run requires 1 day. One of the raw materials for A is also used in six other products, but their production schedules are occasional and sporadic. The raw material is ordered using $Q = 200$ and $R = 200$, and 150 units of it are used in each product A run. The average total usage of the raw material in the other six products is 25 units per 4-week period.

*7. An aircraft company uses rivets at an approximately constant rate of 5000 pounds per year; rivets cost $2 per pound and it costs $20 to place an order. The annual carrying cost of inventory is 10% of the price of the item, and the cost of storage is negligible. Assume zero safety stock for this problem.

(a) What is the economic order quantity (EOQ) for rivets?

(b) Another item, a titanium alloy, costs $40 per pound. Demand is also 5000 pounds per year, and other costs are the same as above. Calculate its EOQ, $D^\$$, TVC, and n.

(c) Explain why it is best to order titanium more frequently than rivets in this problem.

8. A retailing firm has a constant demand rate of 70 units per month for a certain product. They have established the fact that ordering cost is $14 per order, and they use 1% per month as the cost of capital. The cost of capital is the only relevant inventory cost, since this product takes very little storage space. The purchase cost is $10 per unit up to a quantity of 200 and $9.90 per unit if 200 or more units are purchased. Safety stock is 80 units. Management wants to know how many units to order.

*9. Find an order quantity that minimizes annual cost, given the following information.

$$\text{annual inventory holding cost} = 20\% \text{ of item price}$$

cost of placing an order $= \$3.00$

price of the item $= \$20$ each in lots < 200

$\quad\quad\quad\quad\quad\quad\quad\quad \$19.50$ in lots $\geqslant 200$

forecasted annual usage $= 50,000$ items

10. Using the following table of discounts, what is the best order quantity, and why? (The EOQ numbers were calculated using the corresponding prices.)

Quantity	Price per Unit	EOQ
0–99	$10.00	490
100–499	9.80	495
500 and up	9.40	505

*11. You are the manager of the supplies department of a manufacturer. The annual usage of part MB014 is 4000 cases, compared to 16,000 for part XZ201. They come from different manufacturers, and each is used in many different assembly operations in your company. The cost of placing an order is the same for both items, and their prices are very nearly equal. Each is ordered in quantities of 400. They are *not* substitutes for each other.
   (a) Show that this ordering policy is not consistent with the principles of EOQ.
   (b) Does this imply that one or the other (or both) order quantities should be changed? Why or why not?

12. Parts MB014 and MB213 are ordered from the same supplier at prices of $1 and $4 per case, respectively. The transaction cost of placing an order is $0.75, but if both items are ordered at the same time, the transaction cost is only $1 instead of $1.50. Annual holding cost is 20%, and annual demands are 4000 cases for each item.
   (a) Calculate an EOQ for each item.
   (b) How many orders per year would there be for MB014 using the EOQ? For MB213?
   (c) If you order them both *every time an order is placed,* which one should have the larger order quantity? Explain your answer.
   (d) What is the optimal number of orders per year if they are ordered jointly as in part (c)?
   (e) What are the order quantities and the TVC corresponding to your solution in part (d)?

*13. A $20 item has a usage rate of 500 per year and is normally ordered in quantities of 40. A 10% price increase is expected in 6 weeks. The holding cost is 20% per year. How much should we order and when?

14. The city of Harpo has a small department devoted to ordering supplies. The clerks in that department are fireproof (cannot be fired). Because they

are only working at about 60% of their capabilities, morale is sagging. They would like to be busier, but their job definitions do not allow them to accept work from other departments. A similar situation prevails in the receiving department. A study of the items ordered in this department showed that quantity discounts are not available for most items. Economic order quantities and the current order quantities are shown in the accompanying table for a random sample of items.

(a) What order quantities should be used?

(b) Would savings be obtained by ignoring EOQ but scaling down the current order quantities?

| | | ORDER QUANTITIES | |
Item	Annual Demand	Current	EOQ
1	20,000	5,000	3,487
2	14,000	7,000	2,521
3	27,000	1,000	5,112
4	2,340	2,340	206
5	576	1,000	200
6	40	10	5
7	4,521	500	567
8	5,000	1,000	392

*15. An item is used in an assembly operation at a constant rate of 16 per day (5 days per week, 50 weeks per year). This item is procured from an outside vendor at a cost of $12.50 each. The unit holding cost is $2.50 per year, and the transaction cost is $50 per transaction.

(a) What is the optimal order quantity?

(b) How many transactions will there be per year?

(c) Lead time is normally distributed with a standard deviation of 3 days. How much safety stock should be maintained for 99% protection against stockouts, per order cycle?

(d) What is the annual cost of this safety stock?

(e) How much could be saved by reducing the average lead time by 50%? By reducing the standard deviation of lead time by 50%?

16. Weekly demand has been forecast, using exponential smoothing, for an item with independent demand. The forecast indicates an average demand of 300 per week, 52 weeks per year, and the MAD of the forecast is 20. (As we learned in Chapter 8, $\sigma \approx 1.25$MAD.) The item is purchased from a vendor with a lead time of exactly 2 weeks. Orders are placed about twice per year.

(a) What is the standard deviation of weekly demand?

(b) What are the mean and standard deviation of lead-time demand?

(c) What should the reorder level be to achieve an average of one stockout in 10 years? (Assume the normal probability law.)

(d) How much safety stock is included in the answer to part (c)?

(e) How much reduction would there be in safety stock if the average lead time were reduced by 50%?

(f) How much reduction would there be in safety stock if the forecast error (MAD) were reduced by 50%?

(g) What significance do the answers to parts (e) and (f) have for a manager?

17. (Problem 16 should be done in conjunction with this one.) Management is considering a periodic-review forced ordering system for the item described in Problem 16, ordering twice per year on the first days of January and July.

(a) Compute the appropriate target inventory level (TI), assuming $z = 1.645$ for a 95% level of protection against stockouts.

(b) Using the new policy, what would the order quantity be if inventory is 1000 at the time the order is placed? At the average rate of demand, when would inventory (including this order) be depleted?

(c) What is the safety stock associated with this policy? Why must the safety stock be larger in this problem than with a (Q, R) system as in Problem 16?

*18. An item with annual demand of 10,000 is ordered 10 times per year, on the average. An order is placed whenever inventory falls below 600. The item is used in a production line, so the daily usage is always the same, 50 weeks per year, 5 days per week. However, the delivery time varies, averaging 10 working days with standard deviation 2 days. C_I is $2 per year.

(a) How often should a stockout be expected?

(b) After considerable heated argument, it was determined that the backorder cost of this item should be between $200 and $500, owing to its importance in the production process. Is the current reorder level reasonable? If not, suggest a better one.

19. There are 30 raw materials used at Wacko Manufacturers. The service level has been specified—an average of one stockout per year is acceptable for the entire system (i.e., $1/30 = 0.033$SO/yr for each raw material). The inventory holding cost is $1 per unit per year for all raw materials. It costs a premium of $2.50 per unit to special order raw materials, and the lead time for a special order is 2 days.

(a) Compute the implied backorder cost.

(b) Compare part (a) to the $2.50 special-order charge. Is it possible that this difference can be justified? Explain.

*20. The Happy Grocery receives baked goods twice each week, on Monday and Thursday. They sell the items as day-old if they remain on the shelf on the afternoon before the new shipment arrives. Day-old items sell at 10% below the wholesale cost and all day-old items are sold very quickly. Markup on all items is 30% above wholesale.

(a) Assuming that this is a newsperson problem with zero shortage cost, find a rule for determining order quantity. The rule is independent of the actual wholesale cost.

(b) Demand for pumpernickel bread averages 10 loaves per order cycle, and the Poisson probability law is applicable. How many should be ordered? Wholesale cost is $0.40 per loaf.

(c) Is this really a newsperson problem? What is the most questionable assumption of the newsperson problem as applied to this situation?

21. The aggregate and detailed production plans for Hurtin Shoe Manufacturer are based in part on the annual style change in a large number of their products. During most of the year, the plans are based on a forecast of demand plus a safety stock. The actual demand seems to vary from the forecasts according to a normal probability law, with a standard deviation that is approximately 80% of the square root of the forecast [e.g., if the forecast is 100 units, the standard deviation is 80% of $\sqrt{100}$ or $(0.8)(10) = 8$]. Items not sold during their style year are sold at a discount during the annual end-of-season sale. These sales yield a return that is 5% below cost. In contrast, normal sales return 50% above costs. Inventory holding cost is 25% of item cost (per unit per year) and setup cost is $50 per production run.

(a) What should the size of the *final production order* be for an item that costs $20 with demand forecasted to be 4900 units during the remainder of the model year?

(b) How should this be modified if current inventory on hand consists of 1000 units plus a safety stock of 200 (for a total of 1200 on hand)?

*22. The accompanying table gives a record of actual daily demands of a stock item at Central City Hospital for a 6-week period. Inventory on hand at the beginning of week 1 is 600 units.

(a) Estimate what value of D should be used in an EOQ formula.

(b) Construct an inventory and backorder record assuming that a perpetual inventory system was in use with $Q = 550$ and $R = 550$. Assume that the lead time was 1 week for the first order, 2 weeks for the second, and 3 weeks for the third. $I_o = 600$.

(c) Repeat part (b) using a forced ordering system with review period 2 weeks (every second Monday, beginning in week 1) and TI = 1100.

	Week 1	Week 2	Week 3	Week 4	Week 5	Week 6
Mon.	33	42	39	21	33	41
Tue.	27	39	33	44	69	43
Wed.	41	33	21	42	39	27
Thu.	15	26	18	33	42	36
Fri.	61	44	65	51	22	66
Sat.	38	48	41	68	38	62
Sun.	39	50	40	18	40	21

(d) Using the average demand rate from part (a) and an average lead time of 2 weeks, how much safety stock is there for the policies in parts (b) and (c)?

23. The example of Section 10-3 computed two ordering policies, Q^* and Q^+. The Q^+ policy simply multiplied each Q^* by 3.49 in order to decrease the annual number of orders placed from 82.1 if Q^* were implemented to 23.6 for Q^+.

    (a) Using the same approach, what multiplier would be used to achieve 20 orders per year? 40? 60? 80?

    (b) Compute the dollar value of inventory for each answer in part (a) and plot a trade-off curve of dollar inventory against orders per year when a Q^+ type of policy is used. Join the points with a smooth curve.

    (c) Now plot a single point that describes the current operating policy (before EOQ or Q^+ was considered).

    (d) Which section of the curve represents changes that would be easiest to sell to management as improvements?

    (e) Suppose that we want to have about 50 orders per year. What should the order quantities be for each item A, B, C, D, and E? You may wish to use your graph from part (b) to help you.

24. In Section 10-3, the Q^+ order quantities were 3.49 times Q^*. Verify that the same result would be obtained by multiplying the transaction cost by $(3.49)^2$ and using the result in the EOQ formula. Compare this idea to the implied backorder cost concept.

25. The derivation of the EOQ (see footnote 5 in Section 10-2) is only an approximation to a complete economic analysis. Let r be the discount rate and i be the inflation rate, so that all costs incurred at time t are discounted by e^{-rt} and inflated by e^{it}. Let C_H be the inventory holding costs excluding the cost of capital, and p be the price of the item.

    (a) Write an expression for the present value of the cost of using an EOQ system (ignoring safety stocks).

    (b) Take the first derivative to find the condition for an optimal solution.

    (c) Use the approximation $e^x = 1 + x + x^2/2 + \cdots$ to derive the EOQ from part (b).

    (d) Show that the EOQ is a reasonable formula if $C_I = C_H + (r - i)(p)$ and if $(r - i)Q/D$ is not too large.

REFERENCES

AMMER, D. S., *Purchasing and Materials Management for Health Care Institutions.* Lexington, Mass.: Lexington Books, 1975.

AUCAMP, D. C., "A Caveat on the Inventory Price-Break Model." *International Journal of Operations and Production Management,* Vol. 2, No. 2 (1981).

BIERMAN, H., AND L. J. THOMAS, "Inventory Decisions under Inflationary Conditions." *Decision Sciences,* Vol. 8, No. 1 (1977), pp. 151–155.

CARLSON, P. G., "An Alternate Model for Lead-Time Demand: Continuous-Review Inventory Systems." *Decision Sciences,* Vol. 13, No. 1 (1982), pp. 120–128.

JOHNSON, L. A., AND D. C. MONTGOMERY, *Operations Research in Production Planning, Scheduling, and Inventory Control.* New York: Wiley, 1974.

LOVE, S. F., *Inventory Control.* New York: McGraw-Hill, 1979.

NAHMIAS, S., "Perishable Inventory Theory: A Review." *Operations Research,* Vol. 30, No. 4 (1982).

PORTEUS, E. L., "Inventory Policies for Periodic Review Systems." Research Paper 650 Rev., Graduate School of Business, Stanford University, 1983.

PLOSSL, G. W., AND O. W. WIGHT, *Production and Inventory Control.* Englewood Cliffs, N.J.: Prentice-Hall, 1967.

RAKOWSKI, J. P., "Unofficial Inventory." *Journal of Purchasing and Materials Management,* Vol. 17, No. 3 (1981), pp. 8–11.

ROSENSHINE, M., AND D. OBEC, "Analysis of a Standing Order Inventory System with Emergency Orders." *Operations Research,* Vol. 24, No. 6 (1976).

SHORE, B., "A Micro-computer Based Purchasing Information System." *Journal of Purchasing and Materials Management,* Vol. 17, No. 2 (1981), pp. 8–12.

SPECHLER, J. W., *Administering the Company Warehouse and Inventory Function.* Englewood Cliffs, N.J.: Prentice-Hall, 1975.

CHAPTER 11

Production Scheduling: Lot Sizing and Job-Shop Control

In the introduction to Chapter 10, we saw that profits could be greatly increased by controlling costs of procurement. In the manufacturing setting, this potential extends to production scheduling. Although the fundamental trade-offs are the same, there are many complicating factors in production that are not present in procurement. For example, a machine has limited capacity, whereas any number of items can be simultaneously ordered from the outside in any quantity. Production lots may become available one unit at a time as they are finished, but procured lots usually arrive all at once. Finally, manufacturing management must constantly coordinate the efforts of diverse workers and facilities of which procurement may be a part.

This chapter and Chapter 12 describe complexities introduced in some manufacturing settings. Sections 11-1 to 11-3 examine a single facility with several products. One approach is described that establishes a schedule based on a repeating cycle of products. Although no attempt is made to describe the entire field of single-facility scheduling methods, several other approaches are briefly summarized. In all these examples, schedules are based on *independent demand* deriving from sources outside the control of management.

These methods can apply even in a plant consisting of several facilities. For example, if all items follow more or less the same path through a plant and management prefers to schedule each item to completion without interruption by other items, then for scheduling purposes the plant can be treated as a single facility. Another common application is when one facility in a plant can be identified as a bottleneck and the other facilities' schedules are driven by the bottleneck's. An application of this idea is to *master schedule* final assembly, and derive from that the schedules for procuring, manufacturing, and assembling the required components. This idea is formalized in Chapter 12.

Section 11-4 introduces the idea of coordinating multiple facilities within a job-shop plant. Problems of control are extremely complex in this example because different products may follow different but overlapping paths through the shop. Emphasis is placed on the need for an integrated system of control that takes into account the behavior of personnel in this environment. The section concludes with a discussion of some problem areas that have been successfully addressed through the mathematical tool of integer programming.

The discussion of production in a multilevel facility is continued in Chapter 12, in which manufacturing resources planning (MRP) and just-in-time (JIT) systems are described. These are examples of schedule-derived or *dependent demand,* since the schedule at one level is the source of the demand at the preceding stage.

Production scheduling at the individual-item level (sometimes called *detailed scheduling*) occurs at the bottom of a hierarchy of manufacturing planning problems. Capacity planning (Chapter 7) and aggregate production planning (Chapter 9) come above it, as shown in Figure 11-1.

The upper-level decisions constrain the ability of the production manager to schedule production, as signified by the downward arrows in Figure 11-1. Information from detailed scheduling and actual production is often required for upper-level decisions, as represented by the arrows on the left-hand side of Figure 11-1. An example is information on capacity requirements as one input to aggregate planning decisions. We will discuss overall management in hierarchical production systems such as this in Chapter 15.

Manufacturing operations can be divided into three different types: continuous, batch, and one-shot production (see Chapter 1 for more discussion). Detailed scheduling for one-shot projects is the subject of Chapter 3. Continuous production,

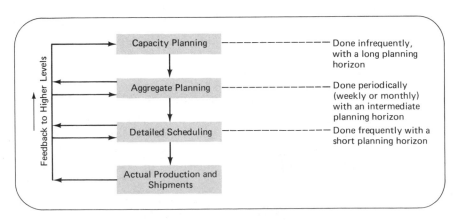

Figure 11-1 The place of detailed scheduling.

an assembly line for example, poses unique problems. First, if several products share one assembly facility, batch production will be used, with changeovers from one product to another. In that case, production is not really continuous, and some of the methods of this chapter can be used. On the other hand, if only one product is being made, the scheduling decisions are essentially an aggregate planning problem: At what *rate* does the firm want to produce its finished product? Automobile manufacturers, for example, change the assembly rate very infrequently. The firm still has the problem of supplying materials to support the continuous production (Chapter 12), of managing inventories at the many stocking locations after production (Chapter 13), and of planning the aggregate production rate (Chapter 9). But the detailed scheduling problem does not occur for finished goods in many continuous production situations.

This chapter, then, deals with batch-production situations. Facilities are limited, and there are competing uses for productive facility time. We will deal with two different production situations: production of units to be put into stock, and production of units for a specific order (job shop operation). Production to stock implies that there is an established product line, and that the sales of each item can be forecast at least in a statistical sense. This is the setting for Sections 11-1 and 11-3. Job shops, discussed in Section 11-4 are characterized by unique jobs, each produced to order; thus finished product demand typically cannot be forecast, even statistically. However, since all the organization's products use some of the same productive facilities and raw materials, it is often possible to forecast material or facility usage, aggregating over finished products. In developing detailed schedules for completed items, the problem is one of sequencing many dissimilar jobs through all their required operations.

11-1 SINGLE-ITEM PRODUCTION QUANTITIES

National Carpet (NC) makes three categories of product: wool carpet, artificial-fiber carpet, and carpet backing. They produce one type of backing and many types of both categories of carpet. The types differ with regard to colors and patterns. The production control manager, Margaret Gill, has been charged with investigating the production scheduling for NC. Recently, they have had difficulty meeting delivery dates, since the factory has been operating at 100% capacity. Gill believes that too much time has been lost in changing over from one product to another.

The EPQ

"Why should we produce in batches that are so large? Look at all the finished goods inventory sitting around waiting to be shipped!" The answer to a question like this depends on the same kind of reasoning used in developing the economic order quantity (EOQ) in Chapter 10. Larger batches reduce the annual outlay for processing transactions while increasing the inventory cost. The optimal trade-off between these costs, when demand is constant, is referred to as the EPQ (economic production quantity).

Production batches tend to be larger than purchase order quantities because the transaction cost is larger. It includes not only the paperwork of placing the order, but also the *setup cost* needed to initiate a production run. This cost includes the payroll cost of people working to change the production process from one item to another (unless they are underutilized on the average), the cost of scrap as the first items come out (until the bugs are worked out of the process) and the opportunity cost of lost production time during the setup.

The formulas for the EPQ look almost the same as the EOQ formula:

$$Q^* = \sqrt{\frac{2DC_T}{C_I(P - D)/P}}$$

in which P is the production rate (units per period) and the rest of the terms are the same as in Chapter 10. See Table 11-1 for a summary. We will refer to Table 11-1 throughout Sections 11-1 to 11-3. The difference is in the term

TABLE 11-1   DEFINITIONS AND FORMULAS FOR LOT SIZING

Individual items

i	= subscript denoting an item (sometimes deleted)
Q_i	= production quantity (lot size, batch size) per setup
T_i	= production cycle time (between production starts)
D_i	= average demand rate[a]
P_i	= production rate[a]
$C_{I,i}$	= inventory holding cost per unit per period[a]
$C_{T,i}$	= transaction (or setup) cost per batch
TVC_i	= average setup plus holding cost per period[a]

Families of items

f	= subscript denoting a family
N	= number of items in a family
$C_{T,f}$	= major setup cost for family f
$FTVC_f$	= average family setup plus holding cost per period[a]
FT_f	= family cycle time (between major setups)
FD_f	= family average demand rate[a]
FP_f	= family production rate[a,b]
ROT_f	= family runout time
ST_f	= safety runout time (in excess of cycle time)
AT_f	= accumulation time for production smoothing

Facilities

$TMAX$	= facility cycle time
PT_f	= average production time for family f during TMAX
m_f	= number of setups for family f during TMAX (called production multiples)

TABLE 11-1   (continued)

Lot size formulas

$$\text{TVC}_i = C_{I,i}(Q_i/2)(P_i - D_i)/P_i + C_{T,i}D_i/Q_i \tag{1}$$

$$Q_i^* = \sqrt{2D_iC_{T,i}/[C_{I,i}(P_i - D_i)/P_i]} \quad \text{(the EPQ)} \tag{2}$$

$$T_i^* = Q_i^*/D_i = \sqrt{2C_{T,i}/[D_iC_{I,i}(P_i - D_i)/P_i]} \tag{3}$$

$$\text{POQ}_i = \text{(demand forecast for } T_i^* \text{ periods)} - \text{(stock on hand)} \tag{4}$$

Family cycle formulas

$$\text{FTVC}_f = (\text{FT}_f/2) \sum_{i=1}^{N} D_iC_{I,i}(P_i - D_i)/P_i + (1/\text{FT}_f)(C_{T,f} + \sum_{i=1}^{N} C_{T,i}) \tag{5}$$

$$\text{FT}_f^* = \sqrt{2\left(C_{T,f} + \sum_{i=1}^{N} C_{T,i}\right) \Big/ \left(\sum_{i=1}^{N} D_iC_{I,i}(P_i - D_i)/P_i\right)} \tag{6}$$

$$\text{ST}_f = (\text{FT}_f)(\text{safety factor}) \tag{7}$$

$$\text{AT}_f = \text{(target inventory for family } f)/\text{FD}_f \tag{8}$$

$$\text{ROT}_f = \text{FT}_f + \text{maximum } (\text{ST}_f, \text{AT}_f) \tag{9}$$

$$Q_i = \text{(demand forecast for ROT}_f \text{ periods)} - \text{(stock on hand)} \tag{10}$$

Facility cycle formulas

$$\text{TMAX} = \text{largest FT}_f^* \text{ on facility (rounded for convenience)} \tag{11}$$

$$m_f = \text{TMAX/FT}_f^* \text{ rounded to integer value} \tag{12}$$

$$\text{PT}_f = (\text{TMAX})(\text{FD}_f)/(\text{FP}_f) \tag{13}$$

[a] Any time period can be used (days, weeks, years), but it should be the same for D, P, C_I, FD, FP, and variable costs.

[b] Assumed equal for all items in the family.

$(P - D)/P$, which accounts[1] for the fact that the maximum inventory is less than the order quantity because some of the supply is being used during the time production takes place. Figure 11-2 illustrates the resulting sawtooth pattern of inventory.

For the NC case, Gill has supplied the following data for carpet backing. (Note that the time period is a week.)

$$D = 15,000 \text{ square meters per week (demand)}$$

$$P = 35,000 \text{ square meters per week (production)}$$

$$C_T = \$650 \text{ per setup}$$

$$C_I = \$0.016 \text{ per square meter per week (inventory)}$$

[1] To produce Q items at rate P per week requires Q/P weeks. During that time, demand will be $(D)(Q/P)$ units. Therefore, at the end of the production run, when inventory is at its maximum, the inventory is $Q - DQ/P = Q(P - D)/P$. The average inventory is half of this, and the TVC formula in Table 11-1 follows, using the same logic as with the EOQ in Chapter 10. The EPQ is derived by setting the first derivative equal to zero and solving. The formula is quite different if items cannot be used to satisfy demand until after the entire batch is produced.

$$Q^* = \sqrt{2(15,000)(650)/[0.016(20,000/35,000)]}$$

$$= 46,182 \text{ or about } 46,200 \text{ square meters per production run}$$

Thus, if demand is constant, the optimal lot size for carpet backing is 46,200 square meters. That is enough to satisfy the 15,000 per week demand rate for $46,200/15,000 = 3.08$ weeks.

Many other methods have been proposed for computing lot size. The reason other solutions may be better is because there are many situations in which demand is not constant. For example, there may be periods when demand is zero, followed by several intervals with varying quantities needed. When demand is known over a definite period in the future, the *dynamic lot-size algorithm* developed by Wagner and Whitin (1958) gives the optimal timing and quantities of production batches using the method of dynamic programming. The substantial computations needed by this algorithm have hindered its implementation, but that is becoming less of a burden with the ever-increasing availability of low-cost, high-speed computers. The algorithm is described in more advanced texts, such as Peterson and Silver (1979).

Other lot-sizing methods are referred to as heuristics because they do not guarantee finding the lowest-cost solution. A number of these have been developed and can be studied in texts on production control. One of these, called the *period order quantity* (POQ), is based on the EPQ. To use the POQ, we first compute the EPQ, then divide by the demand rate to get a time interval that represents how long the EPQ would last if demand were constant. The period order quantity heuristic says to add up the expected demand over that interval.

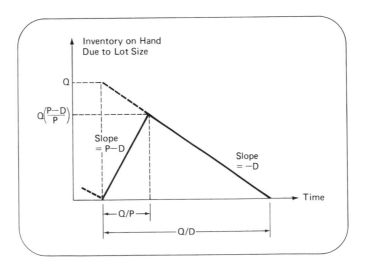

Figure 11-2 Inventory holding pattern for production situations.

That is,

POQ = (demand forecast for the next T^* periods) − (stock on hand)

where

$$T^* = \frac{Q^*}{D}$$

For our example, $Q^* = 46,200$ and $D = 15,000$ per week, on the average. Suppose that inventory on hand = 10,000 units and the weekly shipment schedule for the next 3 weeks = 21,000, 17,000, and 24,000. Then the POQ is computed as follows:

$$T^* = \frac{Q^*}{D} = 3.08 \text{ or } 3 \text{ weeks}$$

POQ = (21,000 + 17,000 + 24,000) − 10,000 = 52,000 square meters

Notice that the POQ in this example is larger than the EPQ because the upcoming demand is higher than the average of 15,000 per week. Presumably, there will also be times when demand is below average, reducing the POQ accordingly.

Review Problems

C_I was determined by Gill to be 0.4% per week times a unit cost of $4 per square meter for carpet backing. C_T included the opportunity cost of the lost production due to the 1 hour it takes to change over to producing carpet backing ($610) and the $40 cost of labor and materials to implement the change. The $610 represents the average gross margin of 1 production hour's worth of carpet products. Gill thinks this is appropriate, since NC has been turning away business due to lack of capacity.

1. Is NC's value for C_I reasonable?
2. One of Gill's assistants feels that C_T should include only the $40. Another feels that C_T should include the $610, the $40, and the cost of idle labor. (Workers are idle during the changeover, but they are, of course, paid for the time.) Whom do you agree with, and why?
3. If D were 34,999 in the example above, what would the optimal Q^* be? What does such an answer mean?

Solutions

1. The C_I value is reasonable since 0.4% per week is 20.8% per year, well within the usual range of 10 to 40%. It is also appropriate to use cost (as NC has done), not selling price, in determining C_I.
2. Any cost that occurs as a result of a setup should be included. If possible business is being turned away, and if larger lots would allow NC to obtain some of that business, Gill is correct to use the $650 figure. $40 would be

too low. (They must expect this condition to continue in the future to make $650 appropriate.) Counting idle labor cost *and* opportunity cost would be double counting. Idle labor cost is often included in place of the opportunity cost of the lost production time, but doing so implies that the cost of labor equals its value. Here Gill is apparently assuming that idle labor has opportunity cost in excess of its cost.

3. $Q^* = \sqrt{\dfrac{2(34,999)(650)}{0.016(1/35,000)}} = 9,976,392$

This Q^*, which is more than 5 years' worth of demand, indicates that if demand nearly equals productive capacity, you will dedicate a facility to that one product and operate in a continuous mode.

11-2 LOT SIZING AND GROUP TECHNOLOGY: THE FAMILY CYCLE

Group Technology was introduced in Chapter 5. When items are carefully grouped, economies of production ensue. For example, the situation for NC's carpet products is more complicated than the preceding section indicated. A major setup is required to change from or to wool carpet, artificial-fiber carpet, or backing, but only a minor setup is required to change color or pattern within the same category of carpet. A major setup costs $650, while a minor setup costs only $120.

A group of products that share a major setup is called a *family* by Hax and Meal (1975). Once a major setup occurs, it is a common policy to schedule most or all the items in that family. The exceptions are usually items that have very low demand, which are produced only occasionally. NC has such a policy. They have 10 types (color–pattern combinations) of carpet that they produce to stock in each carpet category. They have hundreds of color–pattern combinations that they will produce on special order. They receive an average of two special orders per week in each carpet category.

Family Cycle Times

Group Technology offers the opportunity of avoiding large setup costs by timing production so that entire product groups or families are produced together. In contrast, if we follow the EPQ or other lot-sizing rule, items of a given family will have different cycles, so that the major family setup cost will be incurred every time any item in the family is produced. The key is to define a *family cycle time* (FT) and assign lot sizes to individual family members that fit this single cycle. Then, when one family member is produced, we produce them all while incurring the family setup only once.

The total variable cost for an entire family f with family cycle time of FT_f is given[2] by (see Table 11-1)

$$FTVC_f = \frac{C_{T,f} + \sum_{i=1}^{N} C_{T,i}}{FT_f} + \frac{FT_f}{2} \sum_{i=1}^{N} D_i C_{I,i} \frac{(P_i - D_i)}{P_i}$$

and the optimal value of the cycle time is

$$FT_f^* = \sqrt{\frac{2(C_{T,f} + \sum_{i=1}^{N} C_{T,i})}{\sum_{i=1}^{N} D_i C_{I,i}(P_i - D_i)/P_i}}$$

These formulas are not as complicated as they look. For example, the term $(C_{T,f} + \sum_{i=1}^{N} C_{T,i})$ is the total setup cost when the entire family sequence is run with no other families interrupting the major setup. The other summation term is an inventory cost per unit time. In fact, if $N = 1$ (only one item per family) the formula for FT_f^* is the same as Q^*/D, where Q^* is the EPQ from the preceding section.

As an example, we will consider wool carpets for NC.

$C_T = \$650$

$C_{T,i} = \$120$ for each item

$P_i = 35,000$ square meters per week

$C_{I,i} = \$0.12$ per square meter per week

$N = 10$ (initially, they want us to consider only the standard stock items)

$D_1 = 3000$ square meters per week

$D_2 = 2000$ square meters per week

$D_3 = 2000$ square meters per week

D_4 to D_{10} each equal 1000 square meters per week. Thus total family demand equals 14,000 square meters per week. To apply the family cycle equations, we first need

$$C_{T,f} + \sum_{i=1}^{N} C_{T,i} = 650 + \sum_{i=1}^{10} 120 = \$1850$$

---

[2] The cost $FTVC_f$ is obtained from equation (1) of Table 11-1 by noting that when all items are produced every FT_f periods, the production quantity for item i must be $Q_i = (D_i)(FT_f)$ on the average. This is substituted for Q_i in equation (1). Adding over all items in the family and inserting the family setup cost gives the family cost. The optimal value FT_f^* is obtained by setting the first derivative equal to zero.

$$\sum_{i=1}^{N} (D_i)(C_{I,i}) \frac{P_i - D_i}{P_i} = (3000)(0.12)\left(\frac{35,000 - 3,000}{35,000}\right)$$

$$+ \cdots + (1000)(0.12)\left(\frac{35,000 - 1000}{35,000}\right)$$

$$= 329.1 + 226.2 + 226.2 + 116.6 + 116.6$$

$$+ 116.6 + 116.6 + 116.6 + 116.6 + 116.6$$

$$= 1597.7 \approx 1598$$

Substituting into equation (6), we find that

$$FT_f^* = \sqrt{\frac{2(1850)}{1598}} = 1.52 \text{ weeks}$$

NC should produce wool carpet every $1.52 \approx 1.5$ weeks. On the average they will produce $D_i FT_f^* = D_i(1.5)$ square meters of each product: that is, 4500 square meters for product 1, 3000 square meters for products 2 and 3, and 1500 for products 4 to 10, for a total of 21,000 square meters. The exact order quantities are discussed next.

Equal-Runout-Time Heuristic for Production Quantities

If the wool carpet family is to be produced every 1.5 weeks, how much of each item should be produced? This is a natural application of the period order quantity heuristic, which suggests that we add up the expected demands for the next week and a half, adjust for stock on hand, and produce the resulting quantity. However, uncertainty in the forecasts plays havoc with such a rule. If one item has a larger-than-expected demand, it could run out before 1.5 weeks and cause the entire family to be set up too soon. A safety margin is often added to the cycle time for this reason. Furthermore, for reasons of production smoothing (see Chapter 9) it may be desirable to have a larger lot size to build inventories in advance of a peak in demand. This is usually expressed as target inventories for the family.

The equal-runout-time heuristic is one method of coordinating a family's production to achieve safety margins and target inventories. The simplest form of this heuristic assumes that the family demand rate is constant and that the production rate is the same for every item in a family. We will only explain the simple version here to exemplify the procedure. Modifications for unequal production rates and varying demands are straightforward.

The goals of safety margin and target inventory are first expressed as safety time and accumulation time:

$$ST_f = (FT_f)(\text{safety factor}) = \text{safety time for family } f$$

$$AT_f = \frac{\text{target inventory for } f}{FD_f} = \text{family } f \text{ accumulation time}$$

in which the safety factor is a percentage safety allowance for the family cycle time. The safety factor would be set (based on past experience) to assure a low probability of shortage for every item. NC desires a 20% safety margin for the wool carpet family. If that family has $FT_f = 1.5$ weeks, then $ST_f = 1.5(0.2) = 0.3$ week. No target inventory has been specified by NC, but suppose that a target of 28,000 was desired. The family demand rate is 14,000, so $AT_f = 28,000/14,000 = 2$ weeks. However, we need not add both the 2-week accumulation time and the 0.3-week safety time, since having an extra 2 weeks of stock for production smoothing will provide the stockout protection as well. To achieve this, define the *family runout time*, ROT_f, as

$$ROT_f = FT_f + \text{maximum } (ST_f, AT_f)$$

Order quantities are computed for each item in a manner similar to the period order quantity:

$$Q_i = (\text{item } i \text{ demand forecast for the next } ROT_f \text{ periods})$$
$$- (\text{item } i \text{ stock on hand})$$

Using these formulas, the wool carpet family would have $ROT_f = 1.5 + \text{maximum}$ (0.3, 2.0) = 3.5 weeks. The production quantity for item 1 would be $Q_1 = (3000)(3.5) - (\text{stock on hand})$ or 10,500 square yards less actual stock on hand when the family run begins. Similar calculations give the quantities for the other items in the wool family.

This method is summarized by equations (7) to (10) in Table 11-1. As we shall see, the desired production quantities to meet the safety and accumulation margins may not be possible when the facility is shared with other families.

Review Problems

Suppose that NC were to drop products 4 to 10 in the wool carpet family due to low demand, and that the demands for the three remaining products became 10,000 square meters per week, 6000 square meters per week, and 4000 square meters per week, respectively. All costs and P_i values remain the same.

1. Compute the new ideal family cycle times FT_f^*.
2. There are no production smoothing inventory targets, but a 40% safety margin is desired for runout time. Product 2 has 500 square meters in stock. What should its production quantity be?

Solutions

1.
$$C_T + \sum_{i=1}^{N} C_{T,i} = 650 + 120 + 120 + 120 = 1010$$

$$\sum_{i=1}^{N} D_i(C_{I,i}) \frac{P_i - D_i}{P_i} = (10,000)(0.12)\left(\frac{35,000 - 10,000}{35,000}\right)$$

$$+ (6000)(0.12)\left(\frac{35,000 - 6000}{35,000}\right)$$

$$+ (4000)(0.12)\left(\frac{35,000 - 4000}{35,000}\right) = 1879$$

$$T^* = \sqrt{\frac{2(1010)}{1879}} = 1.036 \text{ weeks}$$

2. Rounding FT_f^* to 1.0 week, $ST_f = (1.0)(0.4) = 0.4$ weeks, so $ROT_f = 1.0 + 0.4 = 1.4$ weeks. $Q_2 = (D_2)(ROT_f) -$ (stock on hand) $= 6,000(1.4) - 500 = 7900$ square meters.

11-3 SCHEDULING WITH LIMITED CAPACITY

NC cannot implement the family cycle method without further development. The reason is that the three product families (wool carpet, artificial fiber carpet, and carpet backing) must take turns on a single facility, but the family cycles interfere with one another. In Figure 11-3, timing of the family production runs is illustrated. The family cycle times of $FT_f^* = 1.52, 2.62,$ and 3.08 were rounded to 1.5, 2.5, and 3.0, yet it is clear that the second run of wool will have to be delayed beyond 1.5 weeks, because at week 1.5, backing will be in the middle of a run.

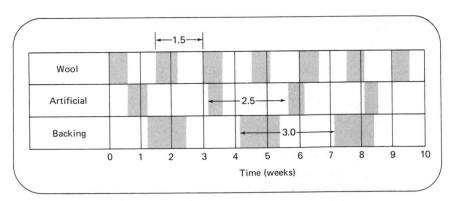

Figure 11-3 National Carpet's production-run spacing.

The problem is scheduling. Capacity is sufficient. The family demand rates are 14,000 for wool, 6000 for artificial fiber, and 15,000 for backing, totaling 35,000 square meters per week, which equals the production rate. Admittedly, it is difficult to operate at 100% capacity, but we should at least be able to come up with a nonoverlapping schedule. NC will probably require some overtime to compensate for unscheduled maintenance, changeovers, and so on.

The Facility Cycle Scheduling Method

From the point of view of the manager, a repeating production cycle is very desirable. Procurement of raw materials is simplified when production runs are scheduled on a regular basis, and supervision of changeovers and production is facilitated. One method for establishing a facility cycle builds on the family cycle method. *The idea is to establish a cycle time for the entire facility and to schedule each family to one or more production runs within the cycle.* The family cycle times are modified to fit the facility cycle. The objective is to keep each family run close to its ideal family cycle time. Because the family cycle method was based on a cost model similar to the EOQ, we know that modest deviations from the ideal family cycles will not greatly increase cost. Robustness of the EOQ guarantees that (see Chapter 10). This is discussed for family scheduling by Maxwell and Singh (1983).

Because the facility cycle will contain at least one production run of every family, it is logical to choose the facility cycle equal to the longest of the family cycles, rounded to the nearest managerially suitable number. (Try to avoid strange cycle times such as 1.4142 weeks.) Each family is then assigned an *integer multiple m_f* representing its number of runs during one facility cycle. In selecting m_f we are changing the family cycle time from FT_f^* to $TMAX/m_f$, so we let $m_f = TMAX/FT_f^*$ (rounded off) to keep the family cycle time near its ideal value. (For an extensive discussion of the reasoning involved and more complex ways of dealing with this problem, the reader can refer to Elmaghraby, 1978, and Delporte and Thomas, 1977.) To summarize the method:

1. Calculate the ideal cycle time FT_f^* for each family. Set TMAX equal to the largest of these FT_f^* values.
2. Round TMAX to a convenient value for scheduling production. TMAX is now the facility cycle time.
3. Compute $TMAX/FT_f^*$ for every family and round these to integer values, to be used as production multiples. Let m_f be the multiple for family f.
4. Also form an alternative set of multiples by rounding each number from step 3 to the nearest power of 2. (Note: 1.0 is a power of 2.)
5. Compute average total production time for each family, per complete facility cycle. The formula is $PT_f = (TMAX)(\text{total demand for family } f)/P_f,$

where P_f is the production rate for items in family f, assumed here to be the same for all items in the family.

6. Using a chart such as Figure 11-3, form a sequence as best you can. For each family, use its "production multiple" to schedule m_f setups during the facility cycle. The multiples from step 3 will be easier to use than those from step 2.

7. For each family that has a multiple greater than 1, distribute its total production time, PT_f, among its setups.

For example, in the National Carpet case, carpet backing has the largest family cycle value at $FT_f^* = 3.08$ weeks, so we set TMAX = 3 weeks (steps 1 and 2). The ratios are $TMAX/FT_f^* = 3/1.52 = 1.97$ for wool carpet, $3/2.62 = 1.15$ for artificial-fiber carpet, and $3/3.08 = 0.97$ for backing. Therefore, the multiples for step 3 are 2, 1, and 1. (The same multiples result from step 4.) In summary, we have a facility cycle of 3 weeks, and the new family cycles are 1.5 weeks for wool and 3 weeks for the other two families.

In step 5, the wool demand rate is 14,000 square meters per week and the production rate is 35,000, so the average production run time devoted to wool in each 3-week facility cycle is $PT_f = (3)(14,000)/35,000 = 1.20$ weeks. For the other two families, we obtain $PT_f = 0.5$ week for artificial-fiber carpet and $PT_f = 1.3$ weeks for carpet backing. Using the 2, 1, 1 multiples found above, we need to have a cycle with two runs for wool carpet, totaling 1.2 weeks, and one run of backing 1.3 weeks in length and one of artificial-fiber carpet 0.5 week in length. A possible production cycle is shown in Figure 11-4.

The two batches of wool need not have the same size, although we have drawn them that way in Figure 11-4. Given the spacing between wool productions, it appears that the first run of wool carpet should be between two and three times the length of the second run. For example, the changeover times might become 0.8, 2.1, 2.5, and 3.0, giving planned runs for wool carpet of length 0.8 and 0.4 week. Even though we have rounded and modified in several instances, these production-run lengths would come close to minimizing setup and inventory costs since we started with the EPQs.

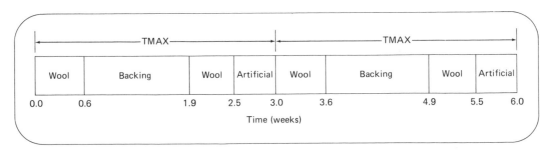

Figure 11-4 Schedule for NC's production, by family, for two cycles.

This exercise has developed a workable sequence of production which approximates the ideal family cycle times. These are typically very good schedules, even though there is a great deal of rounding off and trial and error in the process. Methods have been proposed (Delporte and Thomas, 1977) to optimize production quantities, but they require substantially more sophisticated analysis and typically yield only small improvements. The reason is that the cost functions are fairly flat near the optimal solution, so that approximate solutions have a good chance of doing well.

The facility cycle was established by changing the family cycle times. Consequently, the family production quantities will also be modified. The equal-runout-time heuristic described in the preceding section can still be applied. There are two differences, however. First, the family cycle time FT_f will be the time between setups in the derived schedule (see Figure 11-4) rather than the ideal time given in equation (6). For the wool carpet family, if the cycle of Figure 11-4 is implemented, then two FT_f values will be used. The first wool run must last $FT_f = 1.9$ weeks, and the second must last $FT_f = 3.0 - 1.9 = 1.1$ weeks. In each case, safety margins and target inventories would be dealt with as before.

The second difference is that there may not be enough production time available for all families to achieve the desired safety and smoothing inventory targets. The runout times must be decreased when this occurs, or else capacity must be increased by some means such as overtime.

Capacitated Lot-Size Heuristics

Production planning with limited capacity is not easy, even with constant demand rate as in the NC example. There are many situations in which facility cycles are desirable even though demand is not constant. If management has specified inventory targets to achieve a smooth output level, for example, the effect on production schedules is the same as if demand were constant. Automobile production is a case in point. Demands are highly seasonal, but production smoothing is common.

However, in other situations demand may be quite erratic. Several products (or families) may have different seasonal patterns, for instance, yet share the same equipment. A production schedule that changes over time will be more desirable in that case. Optimal allocation of productive capacity among competing activities has been studied for many years. In fact, linear programming (Appendix C) was invented for such a problem. Unfortunately, when all-or-nothing costs are present, such as a setup cost, the efficient methods of linear programming do not apply.

There is a large body of literature in this area, which has become known as the multi-item capacitated lot-size problem. A paper by Dixon and Silver (1981) puts the field into perspective: "An exact solution to this complex problem is out of the question. Most of these techniques either cannot guarantee the generation of a feasible solution or are computationally prohibitive.'' In fact, an optimal algorithm does exist. The computations are far more extensive than with the dynamic lot-size algorithm mentioned in Section 11-1. As an alternative, heuristics such as Dixon and Silver's (1981) and Lambrecht and Vanderveken's (1979) have been developed and tested. Application of these methods does not yet appear to be widespread. We will have more to say about capacity and scheduling in the next chapter.

Review Problem

Assuming zero allowance for safety and accumulation stocks, calculate the four production quantities if the changeover times in Figure 11-4 were 0.8, 2.1, 2.5, and 3.0. How many square meters of wool carpet must be in inventory at time 0.8 if the inventory is to last until the next production run for wool at 2.1? Remember that the demand for the wool carpet family totals 14,000 square meters per week.

Solution

The production quantities will be equal to 35,000 (the production rate) times the length of the production run. That is, the four runs will be for $(0.8)(35,000) = 28,000$ square meters, $(1.3)(35,000) = 45,500$ square meters, $(0.4)(35,000) = 14,000$ square meters, and $(0.5)(35,000) = 17,500$ square meters. The first and third quantities are for wool carpet. The inventory of wool carpet at time 0.8 must last 1.3 weeks. Thus it must be equal to (or greater than) the demand rate of 14,000 square meters per week times 1.3 weeks. The inventory must be at least $(14,000)(1.3) = 18,200$ square meters.

11-4 *PLANNING THE USE OF SEVERAL PRODUCTIVE UNITS*

Coordinating production in multistage manufacturing is the topic of the next chapter. The methods described in this section are fundamental for understanding the complexities when items move through a facility, incur both assembly and fabrication steps, and have many opportunities to interfere with each other. The first tool, the Gantt chart, represents one of the earliest techniques of modern production scheduling. This discussion is followed by job-shop scheduling, an area where computer simulation has been used heavily to study alternative management methods in an exceedingly complex environment. Finally, a brief discussion of integer programming applications points the way to the near future of production scheduling.

Gantt Charts and Scheduling

Many productive facilities can be treated as a single facility. If all the products use essentially the same production steps in the same way, the facility can be looked at as if it were a single, large machine. When different products use different parts of the productive capacity, as is true in a machine shop, we must plan each unit separately.

One basic tool for doing so is the *Gantt chart,* developed by Henry Gantt shortly after the turn of the century. The Gantt chart is simply a visual aid that helps a manager view the jobs and facilities on a time scale. A simple example is given below, using three jobs (J1, J2, and J3) and three machines (M1, M2, and M3). The data are as follows:

Job	Must Follow the Machine Sequence:	OPERATION TIME (DAYS) ON MACHINE:		
		M1	M2	M3
J1	M1, M2, M3	2	4	4
J2	Any sequence	3	3	0
J3	M3, M2, M1	1	6	3

Two Gantt chart schedules are shown in Figure 11-5.

Gantt charts can be physical representations, made of reusable materials such as plastic strips, to show facility usage. They can also be printed by a computer as part of an interactive scheduling session with a manager. In either case, they effectively help the manager visualize the situation and explore alternative schedules.

It is instructive to view Figure 11-5 to see if we can determine which of the two schedules is better. (Take a minute to examine the two schedules before continuing to read.) It is tempting to say that schedule 2 is better because it

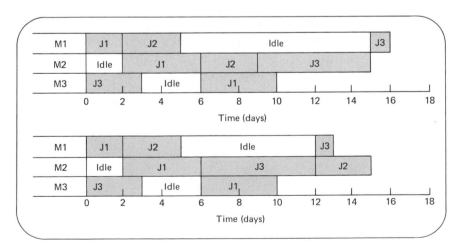

Figure 11-5 Two schedules for three jobs on three machines.

finishes sooner and has less idle time before completing the jobs. However, we cannot decide which schedule is better without knowing when the jobs are promised to the customers, what penalties are involved with being late, and what other jobs await these machines. We need more data, and we need to know the objective function.

The objective function is unclear in situations like this. In the long run, idle time reduces the productivity of the plant, so minimizing idle time is one objective. However, jobs have due dates, so minimizing total lateness is another objective. If a known set of jobs is at hand, it may be appropriate to minimize completion time of the last job (called *make-span*). These objectives may conflict at a given point in time. Several other objectives can also be given, and different solutions may be appropriate for each objective. The choice of an objective is, as always, crucial.

Use of the Gantt chart is a skill bordering on an art form. Much of the research on scheduling uses as a criterion: "Can the computer beat an experienced scheduler?" This becomes particularly important when the production schedule must be changed frequently due to changes in orders, machine breakdowns, and so on. It is very difficult to program a computer with the kind of flexibility in problem solving that human beings exhibit. The advent of computer graphics has allowed Gantt charts to move to a new plateau. The computer can draw new charts so rapidly that the human scheduler, interacting with the computer, can try out many alternatives in the time available. Thus, learning how to use a Gantt chart can now be turned into a computer game. A review problem will illustrate how you can reschedule when new jobs arrive.

Job Shops

A job shop is a facility composed of several machines (or other work centers), each of which performs some operations required by some of the finished items. However, unlike an assembly-line operation, each of the finished items may follow a different path through a job shop. One job may require a sequence of machine A, then B, then C, while another job may require a sequence of C, then B, then A. The job shop must be designed to be flexible, allowing different types of jobs to flow through the shop efficiently.

One job shop might consist of a set of lathes, drill presses, and screw machines. A computer center is a job shop that might consist of a mainframe computer, input–output units and consultants. The job shop may produce items for individual customer orders or for inventory. A "process layout" is used in the facility, grouping similar machines together.

If the product line is standard, an inventory of finished items may be maintained and orders will be based on a forecast. From these individual item forecasts, the firm can obtain a forecast of the total usage of each machine, since each product requires a known amount of time on each machine. These totals can be used to see if the planned capacity is sufficient, to develop a staffing plan (including overtime), and to develop the detailed schedule using methods such as Gantt charts.

However, many job shops operate only on firm customer orders. In this case, inventories of finished items are not maintained and individual items cannot be forecast. Detailed scheduling must then be a reaction to firm orders. Nevertheless, the aggregate usage of each machine (or machine group) can be forecast even though the individual items cannot. That is, a firm can predict that approximately 400 hours of lathe time will be needed during the next month, even though it does not know for what items the time will be used. This information can be used to schedule worker-hours for the upcoming month or months, leaving detailed item scheduling until later (perhaps even paying little attention to it, using dispatching rules discussed below).

Scheduling, Dispatching, and Information Flow in Job Shops

A *job* is defined to be a complete order requiring time on several of the machines (or other work centers) in the job shop. A *task* is defined as an individual operation on one of the machines; that is, a job is a set of tasks, to be done in a specified sequence. Given a firm set of items to be produced, *scheduling* is the process of assigning a starting time for each job on each machine. Usage of a machine must not exceed the available time. To properly schedule a set of jobs, a manager needs to know sequencing and operation time requirements, the due date, and how expensive (not necessarily in monetary terms) it is to be late, for each job.

Gantt chart methods are used for static job shop scheduling. However, we must remember that a static schedule is usually inappropriate. New jobs arrive making the old schedule obsolete in many cases. One method of managing such a changing environment is to maintain a *rolling schedule;* periodically, all current jobs are scheduled, but only the immediate part of the schedule is implemented, since new information will soon lead to a new schedule. The rest of the schedule is only for planning purposes. The Review Problems illustrate a changing schedule due to the arrival of a new job.

An alternative to rolling schedules is a combination of planning aggregate facility usage and *dispatching.* Once the aggregate usage of each facility has been established, a firm may choose to delegate sequencing to machine operators, using dispatching rules. A *dispatching rule* chooses what task to perform next from among the set of tasks waiting at that machine. (One such rule would be: Select the easiest job first. Other rules are discussed in the next subsection.) In a very large job shop it may be necessary to use an aggregate facility usage plan coupled with dispatching rules due to the size of the scheduling task. This approach has the disadvantage that it is more difficult for management to know when a job will be finished; information systems designed to help predict completion times are discussed next.

A job shop can be thought of as a set of waiting lines. Each machine has its own set of jobs waiting. When a job is finished at one machine, it joins another waiting line or moves to the finished item area for delivery. Waiting lines, and thus job shops, are relatively easy to model using a simulation.[3] The simulation can tell the manager how long it should take, including waiting time, to complete a particular new job. This can be used to make delivery promises or schedule overtime (if the waiting time is too long).

Simulation should be used in conjunction with an information system that keeps track of the current situation in a real-time manner. That is, all breakdowns, long or short processing times, and decisions to expedite any job are recorded by the computer information system immediately. Management can then see where any job is, when it is expected to be completed, and see if expediting is necessary. Coupled with dispatching rules for routine "what next" decisions, such a system can enhance management control in even very large job shops.

Dispatching Rules for Job Shops

Dispatching rules have been studied by many researchers with fairly consistent results. See Blackstone et al. (1982) and Conway et al. (1967). There are several objectives that have been used to evaluate dispatching rules, including minimizing average idle time of the machines, minimizing the average lateness of jobs, maximizing the fraction of jobs completed on time, and minimizing the standard deviation of completion tardiness. (This last objective is designed to keep a few jobs from being very late to allow the bulk of the jobs to be completed early.)

There are many possible dispatching rules. Blackstone et al. include a list of 34. Some important ones are given below.

1. FCFS (first come, first served). This rule selects the first job to arrive at each work station, from among those waiting.
2. SOT (shortest operation time). This rule always selects the task with the shortest time requirement on the machine, from among those waiting.
3. TSOT (truncated shortest operation time). This rule selects according to the SOT rule, unless a job has been waiting longer than a specified *truncation time,* in which case that job goes to the front of the waiting line. If several jobs are past the truncation time, some tie-breaking rule, such as FCFS, must be used within that group.
4. DS/RO (dynamic slack per remaining operation). For each job waiting, this rule computes the DS/RO value as the amount of slack remaining (time until due minus remaining processing time on all machines including the current machine), divided by the number of operations remaining, including

---

[3] Simulation is discussed in Appendix B.

the current operation; the job with the lowest DS/RO value is chosen to work on first.

5. CR (critical ratio). Dynamic slack (due date minus date now) is divided by the estimated lead time required to finish the job (processing + transfer + waiting). Lowest ratios are chosen first. There are many different forms of this rule, since the estimate of lead time depends on a shop load forecast for the remaining waiting time in the system.

6. COVERT (cost over time). This rule computes the ratio of expected cost of tardiness divided by operation time and selects the largest. A job that has nearly enough work yet to be done to fill the time to the due date and that can be done quickly at its current machine will move to the head of the line. The formulas used are given in Baker (1974).

One very surprising result has emerged from the research. The SOT rule seems to dominate all others in a wide variety of simulated circumstances. For example, even though SOT has nothing to do with due dates, it seems to maximize the number of jobs completed on time. According to Blackstone et al. (1982), the exception to this rule occurs when the work load of the job shop averages 80% or less and due dates are relatively loose, in which case DS/RO, CR, and COVERT perform well. The clue to understanding this result is that SOT works well when due dates are unrealistically tight. By processing the shortest jobs first, the throughput (jobs per hour) of each machine is maximized. The largest possible number of jobs is processed, resulting in the smallest average lateness. Pity the long jobs, however, for they might wait forever. (That is why TSOT was invented, to move long jobs through.)

In practice, variants of the critical ratio (CR) are commonly used. As long as due dates are assigned intelligently (that is, with some attention paid to the current shop load projection) this is a very reasonable choice. Baker and Bertrand (1981) report a limited simulation confirming that when due dates are set with a small allowance factor for shop load, SOT is the best rule, whereas due-date-based rules are best when the allowance factor is large enough.

In conclusion, it is important to note that many job shops are characterized by chaos, with jobs usually late, large quantities of work-in-process inventory (WIP) congesting the work areas, and schedules that are constantly rearranged through a bargaining process between production supervisors and expediters. Cost reduction in such a situation accrues by implementing a system that controls all three of these elements. The keys are (1) setting realistic due dates, (2) controlling the release of jobs, (3) tracking jobs to keep them on schedule, and (4) minimizing the number of exceptions to the plan. Achieving these goals often requires a major change in the method of operation, including reassignment of responsibilities, reduction in the amount of dispatch discretion, and reassignment of expediters. With a good information system, alternate job routings through the shop can lead to reduced congestion (WIP) and better on-time delivery performance.

Integer Programming and Multifacility Production Scheduling

Another approach to solving this kind of problem is the use of integer programming. The setup of an item is represented as a variable that equals zero when the facility is not set up for this item and equals 1.0 to signify that the setup has occurred. Setup cost is included in the objective function, multiplied by the zero–one setup variable. Billington et al. (1983) describe this formulation and discuss some methods to make it possible to implement in real situations. Successful applications have appeared in the literature in special cases, where the computational burden of integer programming can be reduced. Scheduling of electric power generation among a variety of facilities was described by Muckstadt and Koenig (1977). Production of radioisotopes for use in manufacturing, medical therapy, and food processing is scheduled by integer programming, according to Economides and Crawford (1982).

Injection-molded plastic pipes and fittings are produced in facilities that make many different products, with a number of machines available. Each product requires that a particular tool be mounted on a machine, although more than one machine may be compatible with the tool. Brown et al. (1981) describe a large-scale application of integer programming that determines tool-to-machine assignments and production quantities per month for a year. Standard solution methods could not handle a problem of this magnitude, but through some mathematical wizardry they developed an algorithm that gives solutions within 2% of optimum for a problem with 52,000 variables, of which 12,000 are required to be zero or one. This enormous task is accomplished in 3 minutes on a high-speed computer.

Flexible manufacturing systems (FMS) add another level of complexity to the problem, and at the same time simplify it. The simplification comes from the reduction in setup costs by introduction of computer-controlled equipment capable of changing fixtures quickly and automatically. When setup costs are sufficiently small, it is economical to produce small batches, even individual items. The complexity arises from the same source. Because a number of small batches are being conveyed through the system, each with its own path from facility to facility, the choices available in scheduling are vastly increased. Instead of three batches to run in a given day, a machine center may face 500. Mathematically, more choices means a harder problem. Stecke (1983) describes an integer programming algorithm for machine loading of FMS facilities. Her approach does not deal with individual items, but rather assigns a type of operation to a group of machines.

These examples indicate the diversity of production problems that can be addressed by integer programming. With the trend toward faster, less expensive computers, application of integer programming is increasingly common.

Review Problems

1. In the Gantt chart example of Figure 11-5 (with data preceding Figure 11-5), suppose that any lot can be split (performed in two half-runs), by having another setup that requires 1 day. Thus job J1 on machine M1 will take 3 days instead of 2 if it is split. Form a schedule, by splitting a lot, that will get all jobs done sooner than either schedule in Figure 11-5. (Use the second schedule from Figure 11-5 as a starting point.) Do you see another schedule that can finish as soon without splitting lots?

2. In the second schedule in Figure 11-5, suppose that a new job (J4) arrives at time unit 4. It requires 4 days on machine M3 followed by 5 days on machine M1, followed by 1 day on machine M2. Modify the schedule to incorporate the new job.

3. The number 4 milling machine in Elmer's job shop had no jobs in the waiting line at 7:59 A.M. The machine operates 24 hours per day. The following jobs arrived during the next several hours.

Job	Operating Time (Hours)	Arrival Time	Hours Until Deadline (Measured from 8 a.m.)	Number of Operations after No. 4 Milling	Total Time Required by Operations after No. 4 Milling
A	3	8:00 a.m.	24 (8 a.m. tomorrow)	2	16
B	2	10:15 a.m.	20 (4 a.m. tomorrow)	3	14
C	4	11:10 a.m.	7 (3 p.m. today)	0	0
D	3	11:45 a.m.	40 (midnight tomorrow)	9	27
E	4	12:02 p.m.	10 (6 p.m. today)	1	8
F	1	2:15 p.m.	20 (4 a.m. tomorrow)	0	0

Schedule these jobs as they would be scheduled through time. For example, at 8:00 A.M. only job A is in the waiting line, so any rule will schedule it to start then. The next job to arrive is B, at 10:15. Use the following dispatching rules:

(a) SOT, with FCFS used to break ties.

(b) TSOT with a truncation time of 3 hours, with FCFS used to break ties if more than one job has passed the truncation time.

(c) DS/RO.

Solutions

1. J2 must be begun earlier. It can be placed on machine M2 at time zero. J2 on machine M1 is unaffected, but it has room to slide if necessary. Since 2 days' work is done on J2 before it is thrown off, there are 2 more days remaining. When J2 starts again at time 12, it will be finished by time 14. Without job splitting, we can put all of J2 on machine M2 starting at time zero, push J1 back 1 day, and finish all jobs by time 14. These two schedules are shown in Figure 11-6a and b.

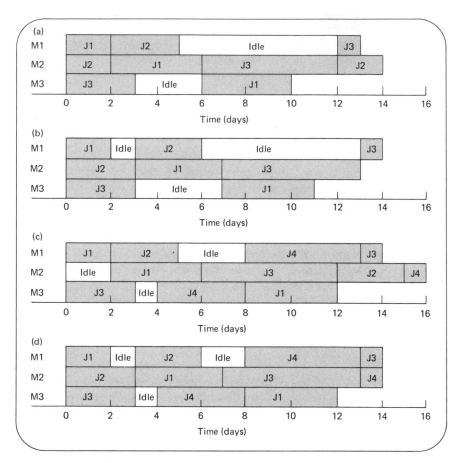

Figure 11-6   Modifications of the Figure 11-5 schedules.

2. The new job can begin on M3 right away (time 4), pushing J1 back. It continues at time unit 8 on machine M1, pushing J3 back. It moves to machine M2 at 15. The schedule is shown in Figure 11-6c. If we had used the second schedule mentioned in the solution to Review Problem 1 (shown in Figure 11-6b) as a starting point, all jobs could be done 2 time units sooner with very little idle time. This is shown in Figure 11-6d, and it illustrates the value of minimizing idle time, to avoid scheduling conflicts caused by new arrivals.

3. The solution is given by writing what happens for each rule, through the day. The final sequences are given at the end.

Time	Rule	Action
8 a.m.	All	Each rule selects job A, which finishes at 11 a.m.
11 a.m.	All	Only job B is waiting, so each rule selects job B, and it finishes at 1 p.m.
1 p.m.		Jobs C, D, and E are waiting, and none of them has passed the truncation time.
	SOT and TSOT	Both SOT and TSOT will select the task with the shortest processing time, task D, which will finish at 4 p.m.
	DS/RO	For DS/RO we need to make three calculations, one for each of the three jobs (C, D, and E). Remember that the hours until deadline given above are measured from 8 a.m., and it is now 5 hours later, 1 p.m. For example, job C is 2 hours from its deadline. Job C has 4 hours on No. 4 milling and no requirements thereafter. Thus DS/RO for job C will be $(2 - 4)/1$.

C: DS/RO $= (2 - 4)/1 = -2.0$
D: DS/RO $= (35 - 30)/10 = 0.5$
E: DS/RO $= (5 - 12)/2 = -3.5$

The smallest value (the most negative in this case) is -3.5, so the DS/RO rule selects E, which finishes at 5 p.m.

Time	Rule	Action
4 p.m.		The SOT and TSOT rules must choose from among jobs C, E, and F.
	SOT	SOT chooses job F since it has the shortest task time. It finishes at 5 p.m.
	TSOT	TSOT chooses job C, since both C and E are past truncation time, and FCFS is used to select between them. Job C finishes at 8 p.m.
5 p.m.	DS/RO	The DS/RO rule must choose from among jobs C, D, and F. The DS/RO calculations are now:

C: $(-2 - 4)/1 = -6.0$ (job C is already 2 hours past due.)
D: $(31 - 30)/10 = 0.1$
F: $(11 - 1)/1 = 10.0$
Job C is selected. It is finished at 9 p.m.

Time	Rule	Action
5 p.m.	SOT	SOT must choose between C and E. There is a tie, so job C is selected using FCFS. It will finish at 9 p.m., at which time job E will be scheduled.
8 p.m.	TSOT	TSOT must choose between E and F. Both are past their truncation time, so E is selected using FCFS. At midnight, job F will be scheduled.
9 p.m.	DS/RO	DS/RO must choose between D and F. The DS/RO calculations are now:

D: $(27 - 30)/10 = -0.3$
F: $(7 - 1)/1 = 6.0$

Job D is selected. At midnight, job F is scheduled.

1. SOT sequence: A, B, D, F, C, E
2. TSOT sequence: A, B, D, C, E, F
3. DS/RO sequence: A, B, E, C, D, F

11-5 Summary

This chapter contains methods for production scheduling in several different manufacturing settings. The economic production quantity (EPQ) and period order quantity (POQ) of Section 11-1 are variants of the EOQ, designed for calculating the lot size that minimizes the sum of setup and inventory costs. Defining the unit costs is not always straightforward, since opportunity costs may be included in the setup cost.

Sections 11-2 and 11-3 discuss the complexity involved in fitting several products' lot sizes into a schedule. The logic of EPQs is retained in computing the time between family production runs, but the times must be modified to allow a manageable, repeating production sequence. At the most detailed level, individual item decisions can be made fairly easily using equal runout times. This is appropriate if the cost to change from one product to another within a family is small compared to the major setup cost to begin the family's production run.

One of the oldest production management techniques in use today is the Gantt chart. As with some newer management tools, one of the Gantt chart's main uses is to present information to a manager in a useful and timely way. The complex problem of scheduling several jobs on several machines, dynamically through time as new jobs arrive and breakdowns occur, is, at the moment, best handled by developing good sources of information (including mathematical and computer models as one source).

In job shops, the scheduling task is never complete, owing to the large number of changes that occur. Thus, either after scheduling is done or in place of it, management must be able to take quick action without losing control of the operation. Knowing what the current status is and how the plant will react to new jobs or other changes facilitates good control. This may allow a manager to rely on a dispatching rule for most of the detailed "what next" decisions.

Particularly in job shops, but also in other settings, a question arises as to who in the organization is charged with solving the detailed scheduling problems. The supervisor on the factory floor knows the people and the machines, but a production control staff can be more aware of the entire system and the overall workload. As with nearly all important questions, there is not one answer that is correct in all situations. However, we feel that the production control staff should schedule jobs and release them to the factory at the appropriate time. In addition to obtaining an overall view, this approach has two main advantages. First, the investment in work-in-process inventory is reduced because some material and labor costs are not incurred until the job is released. Lower work-in-process inventory also means that the factory floor is less cluttered, reducing the chaos.

The second advantage of centralized scheduling is that the variability of lead time can be reduced. With only a few jobs in the factory, a job's progression to completion is more predictable than if there are many jobs. If all the jobs are released at once a few may be completed quickly, but others may have to wait while one particularly long job is completed. In fact, a supervisor's job is easier when long jobs can be assigned, since the supervisor need not return to that person or machine for a long time. Supervisors are most likely to make such assignments at the busiest times, when the consequences are worst. (Many jobs will be waiting.) Note that expected time to completion is not affected by releasing a few jobs at a time since the jobs are waiting in paper form back in production control. But the variability of completion time is reduced and management is more able to decide which jobs are finished first. The suggested procedure does not eliminate the scheduling problem, but the problem is moved off the factory floor and into the production control office. Papers are shuffled rather than pallet loads of material.

In any of the production settings discussed here, designing the information system to allow ease of updating and control is essential. The reason for the complexity of the detailed scheduling task is that there are many (often thousands per month) decisions to be made and the problem won't hold still. For that reason many of the techniques try to help a manager bring order to the system in a rational, cost-effective way.

PROBLEMS

*1. A manufacturer uses screws at the rate of 400 per day. The firm makes all its own screws, and they are capable of producing 100 screws per hour. Setup cost is $30 and the carrying cost of a screw is $0.02 per year. Assume an 8-hour day and 365 days per year.
   (a) What is the EPQ?
   (b) How long would it take to produce the EPQ?
   (c) How many days between setups would there be if the EPQ were used?
   (d) Recalculate parts (a), (b), and (c) assuming a production rate of 1000 screws per hour. Compare the production quantity to the quantity determined using the EOQ formula from Chapter 10.

2. A production scheduler has been starting the production of a certain part every second month in quantities just sufficient to meet 2 months' demand. The setup cost is $100, and holding cost is $50/year. If the production rate is 2500 per year, and the demand is 1000 per year, what annual cost savings would result from using the EPQ over the scheduler's method?

*3. Implementing the suggestions of a famous consulting group, the Bland Chard packing company has increased the length of their production runs, with fewer production changeovers per year. As a result, two production supervisors were able to take on additional tasks in the time that was made available by the reduction in changeovers. The consultants, having anticipated an increase in the supervisors' idle time, had not included any opportunity cost for the supervisors' time spent on changeovers in their calculations.

(a) The consultants have made an error in the costs. Explain what the error is and how you know it is wrong.

(b) If this error is corrected, will there be an increase or decrease in the *length of production runs?* Explain.

4. A manager of a machine shop that specialized in aerospace fabrication jobs is concerned over the production run spacing for a family of two similar products. The production rate is 100 per year for both products, and the demand rates are 10 and 5 per year. The use of rare metals causes the holding costs to be $1000 per year per item. The intricate machining requirements cause many trials to be made before good output will be produced, but once that is accomplished the similarity of the two pieces allows rapid changeovers from one piece to the other. The result is a major family setup cost of $10,000 but a minor setup cost of $50 for each of the two items.

(a) To minimize total cost, determine the time between production runs assuming both items are always produced in the same run.

(b) How many units of each product will be produced in one run?

(c) After seeing your answers to parts (a) and (b), the manager objected to the large production run and long time between runs. He was concerned about the high holding costs that would result. Explain why your answers are intuitively sound.

(d) Why should both products be produced each time a run is made for the family?

*5. A manufacturer produces three items, A, B, C, in one family. The major setup cost is $200. Other information is provided below.

	ITEM		
	A	B	C
Minor setup cost ($)	10	20	30
Holding cost ($/week)	2	3	1
Weekly demand (units)	300	200	100
Production rate per week (units)	2000	2000	2000

(a) Determine the time, in weeks, between production runs to minimize total cost if each item is produced any time the family setup occurs.

(b) How many units of each product will be produced in one run?

(c) What will be the length of time to complete one production run?

6. A corrugated board manufacturer uses a single facility to produce two families of board, double and triple thickness. Each family can be produced in 4- or 6-foot widths.

	DOUBLE		TRIPLE	
	4	6	4	6
Minor setup cost ($)	50	50	50	50
Holding cost ($/linear-foot year)	0.02	0.02	0.02	0.02
Weekly demand (linear feet)	50,000	25,000	13,000	7,000
Production rate (linear feet/week)	144,000	144,000	144,000	144,000

Family setup cost is $1000 for either family. There are 50 working weeks per year.

(a) Find the time between production runs for each family to minimize costs; you need not consider scheduling conflicts.

(b) How many units of each product would be produced in one run?

(c) What would be the length of time to complete one production run for each family?

(d) Would a conflict between the families arise?

7. (In this problem, if an answer cannot be derived precisely from the information given, give a numerical estimate and explain briefly.) In the accompanying diagram, production runs for families A, B, and C are shown. How long is:

(a) The production cycle time?

(b) The production run time for family A?

(c) The runout time for family A?

| A | B | C | B | A | B | C | B | A | B | C | B |

Time 0   1   2   3   4   5   6   7   8   9   10 11   12
(weeks)

8. The following information is for a manufacturer of four items in two families that are produced on a single facility. Family A has an ideal cycle time of FT = 6 weeks, whereas B has FT* = 14 weeks.

Family:	A		B	
Item:	1	2	3	4
Demand, weekly	70	20	30	20
Production rate, weekly	150	150	150	150

(a) Using the seven-step method in Section 11-3, calculate the total production time for each item for a complete production cycle.

(b) Draw a sequence chart showing the production of the four items for one complete production cycle.

9. The following data pertain to production of a finished item.

$$C_I = \$2.50 \text{ per year}$$

$$C_T = \$200 \text{ per setup}$$

Annual demand = 750 units

Daily demand = 3 units (250 days/yr)

Daily production rate = 25 units

(a) How often should this item be produced, and in what quantity?

This item shares a production facility with 11 other items. The facility cycle is 25 days, during which there are three setups of this item, as follows:

Day 1:   produce 25

Day 11:   produce 25

Day 21:   produce 25

(b) Prove that initial inventory cannot be zero if we are to satisfy demand, using the schedule above.

(c) Modify the production quantities so that demand can be satisfied without initial inventory. (Do *not* change the times of the setups.)

(d) Should the item be produced according to your modified schedule in part (d)? Why or why not?

*10. Consider the following data for a plant producing five families of items.

Family	Annual Demand	FT* (Years)	Daily Production Rate	NUMBER OF RUNS PER CYCLE	
				Plan 1	Plan 2
A	10,000	0.1000	500	1	1
B	30,000	0.0333	500	3	3
C	50,000	0.0400	500	3	2
D	40,000	0.0375	500	3	3
E	20,000	0.0500	500	2	2

(a) Show that plans 1 and 2 are both reasonable for a facility cycle of 0.1 year.

(b) (i) Develop a production sequence for plan 1.
(ii) Develop a production sequence for plan 2.

(c) Assume that a complete facility production cycle takes 0.1 year (30 working days) and that there is no idle time. Put your production sequences from part (b) on a time scale, showing each item's production time in days.

11. Craters of the Moon, Inc., packs fruit into wooden crates. The production rate is 2000 crates per day at full output, and only one product can be

crated at a time. There are five families of fruit, and the optimal cycle times for each family are shown in the following table.

Family	Current Inventory (Crates)	Daily Demand (Crates)	FT$_i^*$ (Days)
A	5700	640	8.0
B	4100	400	8.7
C	1800	160	13.4
D	1500	160	11.5
E	1200	240	26.9

There are 5 days per week and 260 days per year.

(a) What percent of the time will the packing facility be idle?

(b) If a facility cycle time (TMAX value) of 25 days is used, how many days of production should be devoted to each family during each 25-day cycle on the average?

(c) How many setups would you recommend for each family in the 25-day facility cycle?

(d) The planned inventory target for family E at the end of the next cycle is 2000 crates. What runout time should be used if we are required to have a safety stock of 15% of the demand for the 25-day cycle?

(e) Repeat part (d) for inventory targets of 0, 500, 1000, and 1500. Explain what is different in the range 0 to 1000 than above that range, and why it should be this way.

(f) Given your answer to part (d), how many days of production should be devoted to family E for the upcoming cycle? (Assume that the table above describes the situation as production of E is about to begin.)

(g) How long can we delay the start of production for family A and still avoid running out?

(h) Suppose that part (f) of this problem has been done for all families and the total production time exceeds the 25 days of the cycle. Discuss the alternative actions and their consequences.

*12. Among its many products, Cavity Candy Company produces four flavors of gum (all numbers are in thousands):

	Fruity	Wintergreen	Spearmint	Bubble Gum
Weekly demand (packs)	150	900	800	400
Inventory (packs)	450	1200	1100	600

These products constitute one family. Management has imposed a limit of 2500 packs for the upcoming production run of this family. If the run begins immediately:

(a) How long will the resulting stock satisfy the demand?

(b) Using your answer to part (a) as a runout time, calculate the production quantity for each flavor using the equal-runout-time approach.

(c) Given the wide range of demand rates in this family, why might management wish to use an unequal-runout-time heuristic?

13. A glass manufacturer produces three different shapes in a family of soft drink bottles. The following information was available at the beginning of a week when production of the family was scheduled.

	Short	Regular	Huge
Inventory	1,000	15,000	18,000
Weekly demand	7,000	10,000	3,000

Total available production for this setup is 100,000 bottles. The firm always uses 1-week-long production runs, and they can produce 100,000 bottles in that time.

(a) Calculate the family runout time, assuming a 1-week run of this family is just beginning, for 100,000 bottles.

(b) Calculate the production quantity for each item for this production run.

(c) In what order should the items be produced?

14. Repeat parts (a) and (b) of Problem 13 assuming that the production rates are 120,000, 100,000, and 80,000 per week for short, regular, and huge bottles, respectively. You need to refer to Problem 13 for data, but you need not have done Problem 13 before doing this one.

*15. Consider the following Gantt chart for two jobs on two machines.

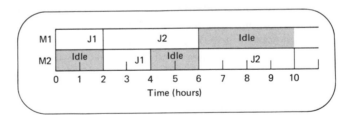

(a) If both jobs have sequence requirements so that the machine 1 operation must come first, could the makespan be reduced? If so, draw a new Gantt chart. If not, why not?

(b) If sequencing is not important, could makespan be reduced? If so, draw a new Gantt chart. If not, why not?

(c) If a job can be split with no loss of time, what is the minimum makespan? That is, assume that job J2 could be done on machine 2 in two separate 2-hour time segments, for example.

16. Here are two Gantt charts for two jobs on two machines. Both jobs must be processed first by machine 1.

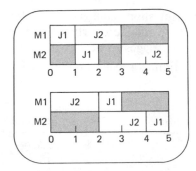

Since both charts have makespan of 5, what factors may influence a choice of one over the other?

*17. A scheduling problem with the following jobs and sequencing requirements is discussed in the review problems of Section 11-4 and shown in Figure 11-6c and 11-6d.

			OPERATION TIME (DAYS) ON:		
Job	Arrival Time	Machine Sequence	M1	M2	M3
J1	0	M1, M2, M3	2	4	4
J2	0	Any sequence	3	3	0
J3	0	M3, M2, M1	1	6	3
J4	4	M3, M1, M2	5	1	4

(a) The production manager says that job J4 is unusual, but J1, J2, and J3 are common jobs that occupy most of the machine center's time, in roughly equal proportions. If the manager has approval to buy another machine (an M1, M2, or M3), what type should it be? Why?

(b) On day 6 the new machine chosen in part (a) and another J1, J2, and J3 all arrive. Use the Figure 11-6d schedule for day 0 to day 6, then use your own schedule thereafter. How soon can all these tasks be complete? Show the Gantt chart.

18. A print shop has the following information available at 7:00 A.M.

Job (In Order of Arrival)	Time To Run On Machine 1 (Hours)	Time To Run On Machine 2 (Hours)
A	3	1
B	4	3
C	1	4

All jobs must start on machine 1. The shop stays open until all jobs are completed, and no other jobs arrive during the day.

(a) For the following rules, determine the sequence for the three jobs and the time of completion for each job: (i) FCFS, and (ii) SOT.

(b) If the print shop manager wants to complete the last job as early as possible (to reduce overtime) and using your answer to the SOT rule as a start, suggest a new sequence.

*19. Bicycle Boutique's repairman has the following repair jobs. It is now 10:00 A.M.

Job (In Order of Arrival)	Estimated Time To Complete Repairs (Hours)	Completion Time Promised To Customers
A	2.0	11:00 a.m.
B	1.5	4:00 p.m.
C	0.5	4:00 p.m.
D	1.5	6:00 p.m.
E	2.5	1:00 p.m.

(a) Using each of the following rules, determine the sequence for the jobs, the number of jobs completed late, and the amount by which each late job will be late: (i) FCFS, (ii) SOT, and (iii) DS/RO (there is only one remaining operation for each job).

(b) If the repairman wanted to minimize the total number of customers for whom jobs would be late, which rule should he choose?

(c) If he wanted to minimize the total number of late jobs as in part (b), and then minimize total late time as a way to break the tie, which rule should he choose?

(d) If total late time (summed over all jobs) were to be minimized, which rule should he choose?

(e) Are the answers in parts (b), (c), and (d) likely to hold in general, or do they just apply to this set of jobs?

20. The two jobs below are waiting to be processed at the same machine center. Assuming that we work 7 days per week, with no holidays, and the current date is November 10, which job would be next, using

(a) First come, first served (FCFS)?

(b) Shortest operating time (SOT)?

(c) Truncated SOT with $T = 6$ days?

(d) Dynamic slack per remaining operation?

	Job A	Job B
Deadline	November 30	November 30
Arrival date	November 5	November 3
Processing time on this machine	5 days	6 days
Next task processing time	2 days	6 days
Next task processing time	3 days	Finished
	Finished	

*21. (This problem requires a knowledge of queuing models from Appendix A.) Joe's Jobbers have a machine shop that is organized into 25 centers. Each center has several identical machines, each staffed by an operator. Jobs arrive at each machine center and are either partly finished (and sent to another center for further processing) or are completed. Machine center A has five machines. During a 5-week period when the shop was very busy, there was always a waiting line of jobs and the total output of center A was 10 jobs per day.

(a) Estimate the service rate parameter (μ) for a queuing model of this center.

(b) What would be the average inventory of waiting jobs if the arrival rate of jobs to the center averaged 9.5 per day over a 1-year period, with no weekly or seasonal cycles?

(c) List the assumptions used in obtaining the answer to part (b).

(d) If Joe's Jobbers use the SOT heuristic, what would their inventory be, compared to part (b)? Why?

22. The facility cycle method is one of many approaches to production scheduling. Different manufacturing settings may require modifications of the methods given here, but the general approach can be adapted to many situations.

(a) Describe the situation in which the methods of Sections 11-1 to 11-3 best apply.

(b) Describe a modification that might be needed in some situation.

23. The STAZO corporation makes a series of handmade items in a job shop setting. Their machine shop layout is shown below. WIP stands for a work-in process inventory, and M^c stands for a machine and its operator.

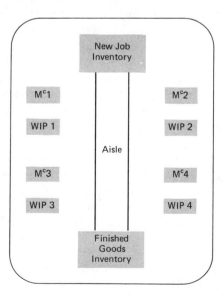

For example, after M^c1 finishes a task, the item is placed in WIP 1. Then the operator examines the new job inventory and each of the WIP inventories to find either a critical job or the job with the shortest expected operating time. When a job is complete, it is moved to finished goods inventory, where it eventually is shipped to the customer. A job, upon arrival, is assigned expected times at each machine, as well as the path that it must take. An example of this type of information would be (M^c1: 2 hours), (M^c3: 1 hour), (M^c4: 3 hours), (M^c2: 1 hour), indicating that the sequence is 1, 3, 4, 2.

The problem is that completion times are random variables due to the complicated nature of the work, and some of the jobs can require several times the expected duration.

(a) Very briefly, suggest improvements in the method of operation and/or their layout.

One type of job that commonly occurs has the following requirements, in order.

First operation on M^c2:   time required = 2 or 6,
                                  (probability of 0.7 that t = 2)

Second operation on M^c4:   time required = 4

Third operation on M^c1:   time required is normally distributed,
                                  $\mu = 3, \sigma = 1$

                      M^c3:   is not used on this job type

(b) The shop manager feels that the job type above should get lower priority on machine 2 than a job with the same expected value (3.2) but lower variance. Does that rule make sense? Why?

(c) Briefly state a dispatching rule that would force a job with a high variance to wait, as suggested in part (b).

(d) This problem requires a knowledge of simulation, which is discussed in Appendix B. At the present time there are, in the shop, only jobs of the preceding type. There is one such job in the new job inventory, and one each at WIP's 2 and 4. Each machine is empty at the moment. Remember that the one job in WIP 2 has been finished at M^c2 and is ready to go to M^c4, and the job in WIP 4 is ready to go to M^c1.

  (i) Generate activity times for all tasks required to finish these three jobs. Six task times are necessary (two of them are not random). Use the random numbers 0.27412, 0.89304, 0.27085, and 0.81016. Use the first random number to generate the task time for the only job waiting to be done by machine 2.

  (ii) Using an event-step simulation, show the timing of job movements through the system until each of the three jobs moves to the finished goods inventory. Number the jobs J1 (new job), J2 (in WIP 2), and J3 (in WIP 4).

REFERENCES

BAKER, K. R., *Introduction to Sequencing and Scheduling.* New York: Wiley, 1974.

BAKER, K., AND J. W. M. BERTRAND, "An Investigation of Due-Date Assignment Rules with Constrained Tightness." *Journal of Operations Management,* Vol. 1, No. 3 (February 1981), pp. 109–120.

BILLINGTON, P. J., J. O. McCLAIN, AND L. J. THOMAS, "Mathematical Programming Approaches to Capacity-Constrained MRP Systems: Review, Formulation and Problem Reduction." *Management Science,* Vol. 29, No. 10 (1983).

BLACKSTONE, J. H., JR., D. T. PHILLIPS, AND G. L. HOGG, "A State-of-the-Art Survey of Dispatching Rules for Manufacturing Job Shop Operations." *International Journal of Production Research,* Vol. 20, No. 1 (1982), pp. 27–45.

BROWN, G. G., A. M. GEOFFRION, AND G. H. BRADLEY, "Production and Sales Planning with Limited Shared Tooling at the Key Operation." *Management Science,* Vol. 27, No. 3 (1981), pp. 247–258.

CONWAY, R., W. MAXWELL, AND L. MILLER, *Theory of Scheduling.* Reading, Mass.: Addison-Wesley, 1967.

DELPORTE, C., AND J. THOMAS, "Lot Sizing and Sequencing for N Products on One Facility." *Management Science,* June 1977.

DIXON, P. S., AND E. A. SILVER, "A Heuristic Solution Procedure for the Multi-item, Single-Level, Limited Capacity, Lot-Sizing Problem." *Journal of Operations Management,* Vol. 2, No. 1 (1981), pp. 23–40.

ECONOMIDES, S. C., AND W. T. CRAWFORD, "Radioisotope Production in a Nuclear Reactor." *Decision Sciences,* Vol. 13, No. 3 (1982), pp. 501–512.

ELMAGHRABY, S., "The Economic Lot Scheduling Problem (ELSP): Review and Extensions." *Management Science,* February 1978.

HADLEY, G., AND T. WHITIN, *Analysis of Inventory Systems.* Englewood Cliffs, N.J.: Prentice-Hall, 1963.

HAX, A., AND H. MEAL, "Hierarchical Integration of Production Planning and Scheduling," in *TIMS Studies in the Management Sciences,* Vol. 1: *Logistics,* M. Geisler, ed. New York: North-Holland/American Elsevier, 1975.

LAMBRECHT, M., AND H. VANDERVEKEN, "Heuristic Procedures for the Single Operation, Multi-item Loading Problem." *AIIE Transactions,* Vol. 11, No. 4 (1979), pp. 319–326.

MAXWELL, W. L., AND H. SINGH, "The Effect of Restricting Cycle Times in the Economic Lot Scheduling Problem." *IIE Transactions,* Vol. 15, No. 3 (1983).

MUCKSTADT, J. A., AND S. A. KOENIG, "An Application of Lagrangian Relaxation to Scheduling in Power-Generation Systems." *Operations Research,* Vol. 25, No. 3 (1977), pp. 387–403.

PETERSON, R., AND E. A. SILVER, *Decision Systems for Inventory Management and Production Planning.* New York: Wiley, 1979.

STECKE, K. E., "Formulation and Solution of Nonlinear Integer Production Planning Problems for Flexible Manufacturing Systems." *Management Science,* Vol. 29, No. 3 (1983), pp. 273–288.

WAGNER, H. M., AND T. M. WHITIN, "Dynamic Version of the Economic Lot Size Model." *Management Science,* Vol. 5, No. 1 (1958), pp. 89–96.

CHAPTER 12

Multistage Manufacturing Systems

Coordinating manufacturing when there are several different stages of production and storage requires tools different from those in Chapters 10 and 11. The organization controls the rate of progress through the system, at least to some extent, and therefore the demand at intermediate stages is not completely random. Several approaches are available to deal with this complex coordination problem. In this chapter we will discuss *material requirements planning* and *manufacturing resource planning* (both referred to as MRP), the *just-in-time* (JIT) system, and some research models.

Material requirements planning (MRP) is a method for coordinating detailed production plans in multistage production systems that involve many products, subassemblies, components, and materials. The basic idea of MRP is simple. One begins with a *master schedule* for the end products and works backward to determine when and how much of each component will be needed. Because the requirements for subassemblies, components, and raw materials are calculated from the production schedule of the end product, they are said to have *dependent demand*. That is, the prior-stage demand depends on the final-stage production, and we can anticipate these demands with great accuracy.

The inventory control methods discussed in Chapter 10 are applicable to situations with independent demand. They apply when there are many small orders arriving at random times for an item. One of the most significant errors in the use of quantitative approaches to operations management has been the use of the Chapter 10 methods to control items with dependent demand.

To illustrate this, suppose a firm produces an end item that is assembled using 100 components. (Many items are more complex than this.) The components are also used in other end items. If we treat the 100 components as if they had independent demand, we will need safety stock. Suppose enough safety stock is maintained that the firm has a 98% chance of having the component in sufficient quantity to begin a batch. We will have a large amount of safety stock, but nevertheless we will often experience delays. With a 2% stockout probability per item, one or more of the 100 inputs will usually be out of stock.

Alternatively, MRP will plan to have the exact amount needed of each component when it is time to begin a batch, thereby reducing work-in-process inventories and improving efficiency. MRP provides a method not only for controlling the work-in-process inventories due to these items, but, more important, it provides a priority planning system which helps management to allocate time on the productive facilities in an organized and effective manner.

Another method of dealing with independent demand is the just-in-time (JIT) system, in which an end item order causes a succession of cards to be sent back through the factory to *pull* the necessary inputs to the end item through the factory. The system is very simple, and it has been effective at reducing lead times and work-in-process inventory. We will discuss the JIT system, including where it is and is not appropriate, in Section 12-5. In Section 12-6 we will discuss some other methods of dealing with the dependent demand found in multistage manufacturing systems.

The KB Company

As an example of dependent demand we will consider the KB Company (KBC), whose president and founder is Knudsen Boltz. KBC produces several products for sale to other manufacturing companies. Among their products are steering assemblies and other similar assemblies for the automobile industry. The products involve several manufacturing steps, including raw-material procurement, component production, and final assembly. Figure 12-1 shows the production process for three of KBC's products, which we will refer to as *end items*. The three diagrams contained in the figure are called *product structure diagrams*.

Figure 12-1 shows that, for example, 5 units of RM1 are required *for each* unit of COMP1. In turn, 2 units of COMP1 are required for each unit of FA1. Four units of RM1 are needed for each unit of COMP4, and 2 units of COMP4 are needed to produce 1 unit of COMP3. One unit of COMP3 is needed for each FA1. In total, 18 units of RM1 are needed for each FA1, 10 that are used in making 2 units of COMP1 and 8 that are used in making 2 units of COMP4.

Figure 12-1 does not depict a common form of display in practice, because in a real factory one could not display the entire production process for several items; it would not fit on one page. Rather, Figure 12-1 is intended to help you visualize the process and to aid us in our explanations.

KBC has a contract with their major customer that calls for a flexible

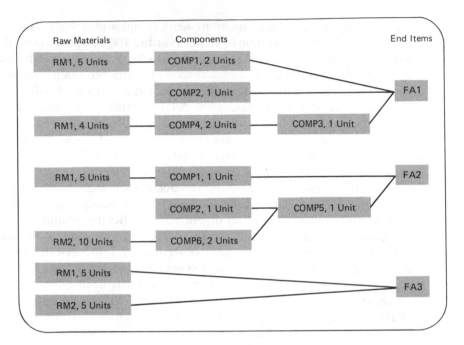

Figure 12-1   Product structure diagrams for three products.

production rate of finished products. They have just received notice of an increase in the requirements for FA1, FA2, and FA3, to 10,000 units of each per week. This rate of requirements is expected to hold for the next 6 months. The firm currently has finished assembly inventories of 70,000, 120,000, and 210,000 units for FA1, FA2, and FA3, respectively. Boltz has determined that the firm should assemble these three end items in batches of 100,000, which can be assembled and shipped in 2 weeks if the required inputs are available. The assembly facility is used for other products, but enough slack is available that they can almost always schedule a batch so that it can be shipped within 2 weeks.

All components except COMP2 are produced in a facility that makes only those components (COMP1, COMP3, COMP4, COMP5, and COMP6). COMP2 is purchased from an outside vendor, as are RM1 and RM2. The component facility is capable of producing up to 100,000 components per week. (For simplicity in this example, all components are assumed to require the same amount of productive capacity.) Since the facility is usually busy and a batch may have to wait, KBC plans production assuming a 3-week lead time is needed for a component order. A 1-week lead time is used for the purchase of COMP2, RM1, and RM2. They have no inventory of components or raw materials at the present time.

Boltz would like us to schedule production and procurement for the next few months. His process is one that can be managed using MRP.

12-1 *REQUIREMENTS COMPUTATION*

If we know the production schedule for a finished product, component and material demand may be computed directly. No statistical forecast is necessary. The demand computation is based on the *bill of materials* and the *master production schedule* for all end items. In the master schedule the end items do not have to be completely finished. There may be options (such as color or fabric, for example) that await a firm customer order, or the product may be only an input to another system. In any case, the master schedule is the top level of the MRP system. The master schedule for KBC is simply to produce batches of 100,000 for each finished item, beginning 2 weeks before inventory would become negative.

The Bill of Materials

The bill of materials (BOM) gives the ingredients for a product. It does not explain the process or list the required tools. That information is kept in other files. The BOM file lists an item's inputs and their quantities. Six examples are shown in Figure 12-2. It can also contain *where used* information, so that we can examine all the uses of a particular component. Other methods of representing the data include an *indented BOM* which gives the same information as shown for these products in Figure 12-1, *summarized BOM* and a *matrix BOM*. The definitions of each of these terms are given in Wallace (1980), as are hundreds of other definitions used in production and inventory control. The details of the data processing will not be covered here (see Vollmann et al., 1984, for more discussion).

Using sequential processing, an MRP system explodes the bills of materials to obtain the complete requirements that result from end item demand. Many manufactured items involve explosions much more complex than the ones we will use for examples. (The term *explosion* arises because each level tends to create more requirements than the previous one.)

In *level-by-level processing* the computer starts with the master schedule, at the top (end item) level, denoted as level 0 of the MRP system. From this schedule the requirements for level 1 are calculated and a production schedule is formed for that level. The system then repeats this process for level 2 and

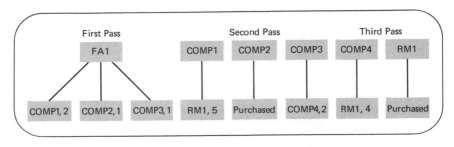

Figure 12-2 Bills of materials for FA1 and its inputs.

all prior stages. To implement level-by-level processing, each component must be assigned to only one level. Otherwise, the total requirements for a component cannot be considered all at once, in light of the total inventory for that item. *Low-level coding* is used to avoid incorrectly assessing the need for production. That is, a component that is used on level 2 and level 3 will be designated as a level 3 component. Thus when level 3 is processed (after level 2), all requirements for that component can be considered simultaneously.

Figure 12-3 displays KBC's product structure using low-level coding. As before, the numbers after a comma indicate the number of units of a component or material used to make 1 unit of the immediate successor. To illustrate low-level coding we can examine COMP2 and RM1. COMP2 goes directly into finished product FA1, but it is also required by COMP5 as part of FA2. Thus it must be coded as a level 2 item. RM1 is used on level 1 (for FA3), level 2 (for FA2 and FA1), and level 3 (as part of COMP4 in FA1). Thus it must be coded as a level 3 item.

A complete and accurate bill of materials is needed if an MRP system is to be used effectively. The task of initially organizing these data frequently involves a large amount of effort from engineers, systems analysts, and management, in spite of the fact that the required information must be available and in daily use to operate the production process with or without MRP. We will not discuss all the potential difficulties, leaving those to texts on MRP (such as Orlicky,

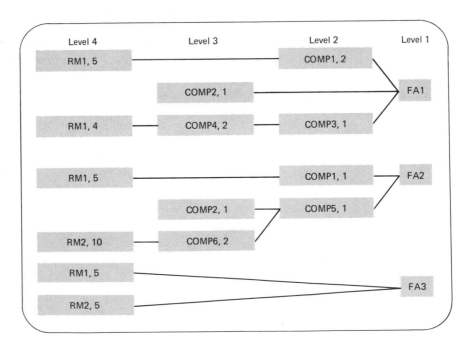

Figure 12-3 Low-level coding for FA1, FA2, and FA3.

1975) and to your future experience. However, we will mention two problems that occur.

First, different levels of detail may have been used by different design engineers, making the bills inconsistent and hard to use for overall planning. Second, the same part frequently has several different numbers in the same company (a number was assigned each time it was used in a new location or product). Renumbering can be a difficult task, although at first it may seem easy. This is true because people are accustomed to the current system, and it may be hard to find all duplications in a large plant. Unless management is willing to invest the effort to produce a complete and accurate bill of materials, without such weaknesses, the MRP system will not perform up to its full potential.

Demand Computation—Time Phasing

In MRP, only independent demands are forecast statistically. A production plan for finished products is developed in the master schedule (Section 12-4) using forecasts as one input. The MRP system uses the bills of materials to compute the resulting net demands on the system. In this subsection we will examine the mechanics of this process. Difficulties in implementation are discussed later in the chapter.

An MRP system computes not only how many units of an item are needed, but when they are needed. Units can be ordered or produced so they arrive only when needed, rather than carrying the units in inventory and withdrawing them when needed. To facilitate this, computer records are maintained in *time buckets,* which are the small periods of time for which production plans are made. They are typically of length 1 day or 1 week. For KBC, the time-bucket size is 1 week, since they produce end items in large batches that are planned to take 2 weeks to complete, and since all lead times are 1 or more weeks in length.

For all products the time bucket contains four kinds of information: *gross requirements, scheduled receipts, projected available inventory balance,* and *planned order releases.* We will illustrate these concepts by examining product FA1, whose time buckets are shown for a 12-week planning horizon in Figure 12-4.

The *gross requirements* are the total amount needed during each period (each week for KBC). For FA1 the weekly requirement is 10,000 units, as specified by their major customer. For level 1, the gross requirements are derived from level 0 production plans. For components, gross requirements equal the sum of the requirements in a period, summed over all user items and including any independent demand, such as for spare parts sales. (*Net requirements* are explained below.)

Scheduled receipts are recorded only when firm production plans are made and the order is released. The production order then implies a scheduled receipt for the date of the order release plus lead time. Figure 12-4 shows that no firm production plans exist as yet for FA1.

0	1	2	3	4	5	6	7	8	9	10	11	12	Week Number
	10	10	10	10	10	10	10	10	10	10	10	10	Gross Requirements
													Scheduled Receipt
70	60	50	40	30	20	10	0	90	80	70	60	50	Projected Available Inventory
						100							Planned Order Release

a Time is viewed at the midpoint of the week indicated. All numbers except the week number are given in thousands of units.

Figure 12-4   Time buckets for FA1.[a]

Projected available inventory balance is the quantity of the item expected to remain after the production and demand have occurred for a period. In Figure 12-4, there are 70,000 units on hand at time zero, and they will all be gone by week 7. The calculation of expected inventory on hand allows us to anticipate the need for a production or purchase order, in the form of a planned order release.

The *planned order release* is generated by moving backward from the anticipated negative level for inventory. This is called *time phasing*. To be received during the period in which the inventory level would become negative, the order release must precede that period by the lead time. For FA1, a receipt would be needed in week 8, and, since the lead time is 2 weeks, the planned order release must occur during week 6. As previously stated, the batch size has been set at 100,000 units for finished goods such as FA1. Thus when we reach week 8, the planned order release of 100,000 units will cause a scheduled receipt of 100,000 units, and inventory is expected to be 90,000, not $-10,000$, in week 8. Finally, if a longer planning horizon were used, a second planned order release would occur in week 16, and a third in week 26.

We are following the *midpoint convention* for determining order release dates. All receipts and requirements are assumed to take effect in the middle of the time bucket. Inventory is measured in the middle of the time bucket. Thus, if inventory was 5 units last period and there are receipts of 10 and requirements of 12, the new inventory is 3. The receipt would be caused by an order release that occurred some time ago. If this is period 6 and lead time is 2, a receipt in the middle of period 6 is caused by an order release in the middle of period 4. If significant errors might occur due to lumping all record keeping at one point in the period, a smaller time bucket is appropriate.

Net requirements are computed by allocating inventory to gross requirements. If 100 are needed in period 1 and 40 units are in inventory, there is a net requirement of 60 units. Planned order releases must cover net requirements.

Then planned order releases are exploded back to determine gross requirements for the inputs.

Once level 0 products have been analyzed, the bills of materials are put to use. Order releases for FA1 and other level 0 products generate the gross requirements for level 1, and planned order releases are computed, as to both time and quantity, in the manner used above. For example, the production order for 100,000 units of FA1 to be released in week 6 causes an order release for 200,000 units of COMP1 in week 3, since component manufacture requires a 3-week lead time and since 2 units of COMP1 are used in each FA1. Because the releases have been time phased to allow for lead times, the level 1 orders are earlier than the level 0 orders, and each subsequent level is earlier still. The *planning horizon* must be long enough to ensure that there is time to obtain all materials and produce all components before a planned order release for finished items. As we will see, the 12 week horizon used in Figure 12-4 is not long enough.

The MRP system allows management input at any stage. For example, Mr. Boltz has determined the lot sizes to be used in the master schedule. He can also group level 1 order releases into batches. Those batches, in turn, cause gross requirements at level 2, which can be grouped into batches. The MRP system will report a suggested production schedule, and batching rules can be changed if necessary. *Lot sizing* is one major decision in a production setting; in an MRP environment it consists of grouping some of the discrete demands that are placed on the system. Lot-sizing methods are discussed in Section 12.3.

For now, we know the lot sizes to be used by KBC at level 0. Boltz further indicates that any component or material requirement of 100,000 or more should be handled by itself, not grouped with requirements from other time buckets. Since all components and materials will be needed in multiples of 100,000 (the level 0 batch size), this means that each gross requirement at levels 1, 2, and 3 will cause a planned order release. Knowing these decisions allows us to give an overall view of the operation of this system through time. Assuming that all planned order releases become actual order releases and then scheduled receipts, Figure 12-5 illustrates the operation of the system through week 23.

In Figure 12-5, the order release for 100,000 units of FA1 in week 6 causes projected available inventory (shortened to "inventory" in Figure 12-5) to equal 90,000 in week 8. It also causes a scheduled receipt for COMP1, COMP3, and COMP2 to occur in week 6, since there is a gross requirement at that time and no inventory. The order releases for COMP1 and COMP3 occur in week 3, time phased 3 weeks earlier than their scheduled receipts to allow for the 3-week component lead time. The order release for COMP2 can occur in week 5, since it is a purchased part with a 1-week lead time. The reader should trace the effects of each of the end item production runs in Figure 12-5, using Figure 12-3 to obtain the inputs needed at each level. For example, consider RM2. The receipt of 2000 units in week 5 is needed because of the order release of 200 COMP6 units in week 5.

Figure 12-5 Operation of the KBC requirements planning system through time.

Level	Item		0	1	2	3	4	5	6	7	8	9	10	11	12	13	14	15	16	17	18	19	20	21	22	23
Level 0	FA1	Requirements	10	10	10	10	10	10	10	10	10	10	10	10	10	10	10	10	10	10	10	10	10	10	10	10
		Receipt									100										100				100	
		Inventory	70	60	50	40	30	20	10	0	90	80	70	60	50	40	30	20	10	0	90	80	70	60	50	40
		Order release							100										100							
	FA2	Requirements	10	10	10	10	10	10	10	10	10	10	10	10	10	10	10	10	10	10	10	10	10	10	10	10
		Receipt														100										100
		Inventory	120	110	100	90	80	70	60	50	40	30	20	10	0	90	80	70	60	50	40	30	20	10	0	90
		Order release												100										100		
	FA3	Requirements	10	10	10	10	10	10	10	10	10	10	10	10	10	10	10	10	10	10	10	10	10	10	10	10
		Receipt																							100	
		Inventory	210	200	190	180	170	160	150	140	130	120	110	100	90	80	70	60	50	40	30	20	10	0	90	80
		Order release																					100			
Level 1	COMP1	Requirements							200					100					200					100		
		Receipt							200					100					200					100		
		Inventory							0					0					0					0		
		Order release				200					100					200					100					
	COMP3	Requirements							100										100							
		Receipt							100										100							
		Inventory							0										0							
		Order release				100										100										
	COMP5	Requirements												100										100		
		Receipt												100										100		
		Inventory												0										0		
		Order release							100										100							

368

			Week columns →				
Level 2	**COMP2**	Requirements		100 / ⟨100⟩		100 / ⟨100⟩	
		Receipt		100 / ⟨100⟩		100 / ⟨100⟩	
		Inventory					
		Order release	100	100	⟨100⟩		
	COMP4	Requirements	200 / 200		200 / ⟨200⟩		
		Receipt	200 / 200		200 / ⟨200⟩		
		Inventory	200				
		Order release	200		⟨200⟩		
	COMP6	Requirements		200 / 200		200 / ⟨200⟩	
		Receipt		200 / 200		200 / ⟨200⟩	
		Inventory	200				
		Order release	200	⟨200⟩			
Level 3	**RM1**	Receipt	800	500 / 800 / ⟨800⟩	1000 / ⟨1000⟩	500 / ⟨500⟩	500
		Order release	1000	500	⟨1000⟩	⟨500⟩	500
	RM2	Receipt	2000		2000 / ⟨2000⟩		500
		Order release	2000		⟨2000⟩		500

a Most zeros are omitted.

b Only receipt and order release are reported for raw materials.

c Circled numbers refer to the second runs for FA1 and FA2, and to the inputs required for those production runs.

d All numbers except the week number are given in thousands of units.

e The labels on the right-hand side have been shortened. See the text for complete definitions.

It should be emphasized that this 23-week plan would not stay unchanged for 23 weeks. A key advantage of MRP is the ability to change the production plan easily when there are demand changes, scrap, lost days of production, or other changes.

Review Problems

1. Examine the lower-level requirements caused by the first demand for FA1. Are there any requirements that cannot be satisfied? What might be done about any infeasibilities that you see?

2. On the average, is a daily production rate of 100,000 enough capacity in the component facility?

3. Even though capacity is sufficient on the average, short-term capacity problems could arise due to a temporarily heavy load. How does this relate to lead-time planning?

Solutions

1. 800,000 units of RM1 must be available by week zero (i.e., now). That is infeasible unless they were ordered last week. The order can probably be expedited to take less than 1 week, and the successor components can perhaps be scheduled in less than the 3-week lead time, using overtime if necessary.

2. In total, KBC needs to produce 90,000 components each week, 50,000 for assembly into FA1 and 40,000 for FA2. (Remember that COMP2 is purchased.) Thus the 100,000 per week capacity is sufficient on the average.

3. The actual lead time is a function of the current load on the facility. If we lengthen planned lead times to accommodate the maximum we might need, in most situations the components will be produced too soon. This problem is discussed briefly in Section 12-3. Here we note only that a manager can use the requirements obtained from the MRP system to help plan changes in capacity and lead times and to foresee trouble points.

12-2 SOME MANAGEMENT OPTIONS IN MULTISTAGE SYSTEMS

Lot-Sizing Techniques

The economic order quantity, $Q = \sqrt{2DC_T/C_I}$, assumes that demand is arriving in a continuous stream. That is not the case in an MRP environment, where it is typical to have large and unequal chunks of demand occur at irregular time intervals. In this situation a lot size will consist of a few of these chunks, and the batch will be timed to arrive so that one of the chunks is never carried in inventory.

For example, suppose that an end item for KBC is required, for shipment to customers, according to the following pattern:

				PERIOD				
1	2	3	4	5	6	7	8	9
Net requirements								
100	0	200	100	0	0	300	0	100
Cumulative requirements								
100	100	300	400	400	400	700	700	800

A batch size of 100, 300, 400, 700, or 800 would be considered for the initial batch, but no other value is appropriate (unless periods beyond period 9 are to be included). A batch size of 150, for example, will cause higher inventory than a batch of 100, but a new setup will still be needed in period 3. If we produce 100 in week 1, the next batch should be planned for exactly week 3, so that there is zero inventory after week 1 until week 3.

Lot-sizing methods must be included in the MRP program since the batch size at level 0 affects the timing and amount of requirements at level 1, and so on. Thus all lot-size decisions on a given level must be made before passing to the next level. The lot size for an item can be changed at any time until production has actually begun on some of the item's predecessors. We will examine only a few of the many lot-sizing techniques.

Lot-for-lot scheduling was used by KBC for all components. Each batch of 100,000 units of FA1, FA2, or FA3 translated into a batch of components or materials. Each lot and its predecessors were scheduled separately, with no grouping of orders. This method is easy to implement and control, but it may lead to inefficient use of the production facility because of excessive setup time.

Production setups are analogous to placing an order in a simple ordering situation (Chapter 10). We will use the same symbol for setup cost as for ordering or transaction cost, C_T. However, production setup cost includes things such as time to clean and adjust machinery, initial waste if the first few units are (usually) rejects, and other labor costs that occur due to the beginning of a production run; thus setup costs are much larger than ordering costs. Thus it often is important to balance setup and holding costs in some way, as we did in deriving the economic order quantity in Chapter 10.

Balancing setup and holding costs is difficult in multistage production systems because it is often unclear what those costs are. For example, a labor group may be maintained to do setups. They represent a fixed cost; if they are not fully occupied, the marginal cost of labor for a setup may be zero. Thus setup cost can be overstated by looking at the average cost. On the other hand, a setup for a subassembly may cause several of its inputs to be set up as well, so that the local setup cost may be only a fraction of the effective setup cost. Similarly, the effective inventory cost may vary. If all the inputs are available only the value added at this stage contributes to inventory cost. If no inputs are available, we must build the item from scratch, and the cost of building the item and *all of its inputs* contributes to inventory cost.

Since the appropriate costs to use are uncertain and may change over time, any lot-sizing method based on one level at a time may be wrong. However, lot-sizing methods can be useful in many situations. Two methods that are used, period order quantity and Wagner–Whitin algorithms, are discussed in Section 11-1. References to and discussions of other methods are given in Vollmann et al. (1984).

Blackburn and Millen (1982) describe ways of modifying the costs to obtain better inputs for techniques such as the Wagner–Whitin algorithm. They are able to improve performance. Some other lot-sizing heuristics are based on mimicking, in one way or another, the behavior of the EOQ, while still taking advantage of the discrete nature of demand. Since they examine the problem one level at a time, they can perform poorly on the system as a whole. Lot-sizing methods that consider the entire system are discussed in Section 12-6. Changing the cost structure so that lot-for-lot scheduling is appropriate is discussed in Section 12-5.

Safety Stock and Safety Time

Even though MRP uses a dependent demand calculation rather than a forecast, some provision must be made for uncertainty. However, in a multilevel system, safety margins at one level buffer against variations at other levels as well. Therefore, it is not correct to carry safety stock at all levels of an MRP system; that will cost a lot and it may not protect the firm. Safety stock should not be compounded but, rather, placed at selected points to protect against uncertainties.

For example, suppose that a firm fabricates and assembles a single product using several hundred materials, components, and subassemblies. The value is added fairly evenly during the different stages of manufacture. Purchased items are available with a short lead time and there are no large scrap rates. Finally, customer demand is erratic and immediate service is required. In such a situation, safety stock should be carried only at the finished product level. The master schedule must maintain that safety stock, but components will need no safety stock. The finished product safety stock would also protect against minor disruptions in production.

In some situations safety stock is needed at carefully selected points, other than the finished goods level, because of uncertainties not associated with the finished products. If, for example, raw materials sometimes arrive in batches that do not match the amounts ordered, some safety stock may be advisable. If a particular production facility often has a high fraction of rejects, safety stock immediately following that stage of the process may be useful.

Whybark and Williams (1976) have pointed out that the need for safety margins arises when there is uncertainty in (*i*) supply timing, (*ii*) supply quantity, (*iii*) demand timing and/or (*iv*) demand quantity. Uncertainties (*ii*) and (*iv*) are related to quantity and therefore give rise to a need for a reserve of extra units (i.e. *safety stock*). The location of the units depends on the location and degree of the uncertainty. A manager should *not* keep safety stock in all locations. On the other hand, uncertainties (*i*) and (*iii*) are related to timing and give rise to a need for an extra margin of planned lead time. Planned lead times include actual production time, expected time waiting for a turn on the production facility, and some *safety time* margin. This time margin leads to earlier production, with an attendant increase in the time inventory is held. This is the counterpart of safety stock.

In selecting where to put safety stock or time, the manager must consider several factors. First, buffering before and after machines that are capacity constrained can ensure that they are fully utilized and that they do not cause work stoppage downstream. If many items move across such a machine, the safety stock should be maintained in items with stable demand. Second, safety stock or safety time after an assembly point can protect against uncertainty up to that stage with less total stock. The *value-added profile* (cost at each stage) is another factor. Recently, analytical work by Lambrecht et al. (1982) has included some of these factors.

Often companies sell components to outside customers (as spare parts, for example). In that event they have components that are subject to both *dependent* and *independent* demand. If the dependent demand is predominant, an MRP system is appropriate and the independent demand will be made to fit into that system. This is accomplished by including in each order for a component a quantity to meet expected spare-parts demand until the next production run and safety stock to cover that same period of time. Then gross requirements arise not only because of finished items to be produced according to the master schedule, but also to meet the independent demand.

Planned Lead Times

Lead times are incorporated in production plans for three reasons. First, time must be allowed for the production process to be carried out. Second, there is often a queue of jobs competing for a facility's time, so waiting time must be expected. Third, both production and waiting time may be highly variable due to breakdowns, interruptions for higher-priority work, and so on, so safety time may be needed to make sure that an item is produced by the time it is needed.

As a product moves through a typical plant, well over half and often 90% of its time is spent waiting. During this time, money is tied up in work-in-process inventory. Properly setting planned lead times in MRP systems (and in other production systems as well) can help to reduce that inventory and yield other benefits. The preceding subsection argued that safety stock and safety time should be placed in a very few, selected points in the production process. For other locations and products, planned lead times should be kept small.

Consider the case of a billion-dollar manufacturing firm. In a 16-stage production process, the average lead time had grown from 1 week to 3 weeks.

The shorter lead times had been inflated because they had occasionally been insufficient. But as total planned lead time moved from 16 weeks to 48 weeks, work-in-process inventory tripled, the factory floor became cluttered with stock waiting to be processed, and huge amounts of money became tied up. Worse yet, the firm found it could make very good 4-month forecasts, but very bad 12-month forecasts. Thus when the total lead time is nearly a year, they often started the wrong amounts of the wrong products. Then the necessary changes in production plans exacerbated their capacity problems. It is surprising, but true, that often a 16-week production cycle is easier to maintain than a 48-week cycle. Long planned lead times become self-fulfilling and actual lead times will be longer than necessary.

Keeping actual lead times and thus the total production cycle as short as possible is one of the most beneficial things a manufacturing firm can do. In MRP systems this is done by minimizing the use of safety time and reducing capacity-caused delays by careful scheduling. The connection between lead times and capacity planning is discussed further in Section 12-3 and by Billington et al. (1983). Lead times are examined in detail by Kanet (1982).

Review Problems

The gross requirements for one component, based only on the master schedule for finished items, are given below. There is no inventory on hand for this item.

Period	1	2	3	4	5	6	7	8
Requirements	400	0	800	400	0	0	1200	0

The setup cost, C_T, for this component is $36, and the inventory carrying cost is $0.02 per period.

1. What production quantities might be considered if you wanted to try all possible appropriate order quantities?
2. What production quantity does the period order quantity suggest as the initial lot size? Use D = average period demand = 350.
3. In addition, there is a spare-parts demand for an average of 40 units per period, with a standard deviation equal to the square root of the expected spare parts demand. [Thus the spare parts demand for 3 periods would average $\mu = (3)(40) = 120$ and have a standard deviation of $\sigma = \sqrt{120} = 10.96 \approx 11$.] Using your answer to question 2, how much extra should be added to the production quantity to cover spare parts demand (including safety stock) if you use $\mu + 2\sigma$ to provide adequate safety?
4. Why do companies use fixed planned lead times when the actual lead times are variable? Why do the planned lead times get inflated?

Solutions

1. Only 400, 1200, 1600, and 2800 would be possible, ignoring safety stock.

2. $$Q = \sqrt{\frac{2(D)36}{(0.02)}} = \sqrt{\frac{2(350)(36)}{0.02}} = 1122$$

$$\frac{Q}{D} = \frac{1122}{350} = 3.2 \text{ periods} \approx 3$$

   Thus the period order quantity suggests covering the first three periods, and the lot size is $(400 + 0 + 800) = 1200$ units.

3. Since they have no inventory on hand, they must add the spares demand of $\mu + 2\sigma$ to 1200. For three periods of spares demand, $\mu = 120$ and $\sigma = 11$, as computed in the question. Thus $\mu + 2\sigma = 142$, and the lot size that must be received in period 1 is $1200 + 142 = 1342$.

4. It is too difficult to anticipate lead times exactly. A fixed lead time is set large enough to cover most situations. Inflation occurs when, on occasion, the plant cannot meet planned lead time.

12-3 MANAGEMENT PLANNING IN MULTISTAGE SYSTEMS

Capacity Planning

Capacity planning occurs on several levels in organizations. With a long planning horizon, firms decide whether to build new, major facilities. With a medium planning horizon they decide whether to recruit new personnel. In the short run, firms try to anticipate which facilities will have capacity difficulties and authorize overtime or modify the production plan. This detailed planning, called *capacity requirements planning,* is the subject of this subsection. In Section 12-4 we will examine MRP-II and how the several types of capacity planning can be included.

Using a computerized MRP system, a manager can select key productive units, such as the component facility for KBC, and have the computer print out a *load projection* or *capacity requirements plan* (CRP) for that unit. This is done by examining orders that are currently in production or planned. The result is a summary of the future activity of the productive unit that allows the manager to look forward in planning the capacity. (Capacity is then "planned" by scheduling overtime, extra shifts, subcontracting, or modifying the production plan for example.)

Some industries plan for very long periods of time, and therefore the plan may include *expected orders,* which are orders that may materialize. These can be listed as planned orders in developing a load projection, but expected orders

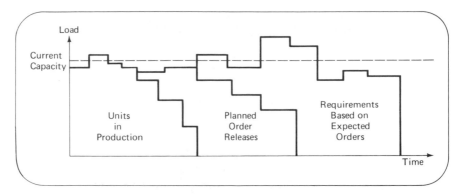

Figure 12-6 Capacity usage (or "load") projection for one productive unit.

should be removed from the system after the projection is made, to maintain the system's validity. This information might be reported as shown in Figure 12-6. Such a picture helps management to see when a capacity problem is coming. The detailed scheduling tool (MRP) feeds into the higher-level problem of capacity planning. (An example of capacity load projections is given in the Review Problem for this section.)

In the intermediate run, managers face the aggregate production work-force planning problem discussed in Chapter 9. The load projection feeds back to that plan to indicate how subunits are faring within the overall aggregate plan. Prior to that, the aggregate plan was used as input to the MRP system in two ways. First, the work-force decisions set the capacity level shown as current capacity in Figure 12-6. Second, seasonal inventory plans lead to large lot sizes to build up the required seasonal inventory. The MRP system responds to this in the same way it responds to any demand. This two-way interaction allows the coordination of the aggregate plan and the detailed MRP.

Finally, there is an interaction between the capacity in a unit and the lead time required. If there is excess capacity, planned lead time can be set close to actual production time, in that waiting time will be small. However, during peak demand periods when capacity is fully utilized, actual lead times will frequently be much larger than production time. This makes the selection of planned lead times difficult. A low planned lead time will occasionally be insufficient, and a large planned lead time will cause excessive work-in-process inventories. A manager may choose to invest in some additional capacity in the long run to avoid this problem. In addition, capacity usage (load) projections such as Figure 12-6 can be used to predict and plan for production bottlenecks and the associated temporary increase in lead times. (As previously discussed, these increases in lead times should not be permanent.)

It is possible to use linear or integer programming methods to plan lead times and stay within capacities, including the potential use of overtime. The use of mathematical programming is explored in several problems at the end of the chapter, and it is discussed in Section 12-6.

Reject Allowance

Lower levels of an MRP system receive dependent demand for components, independent demand for spare parts, and demand for *reject allowances*. Reject allowances are needed when only a fraction of a lot will be useful. Thus, if 100 units are required as input to the next level, 150 units may be produced. MRP systems can handle this by having a reject allowance multiple for each component. Thus, if 1.5 is the multiple, a requirement of 100 causes a production of 150. The inventory would be kept valid (eventually) by a receipt equal to the actual number of good items. The multiple must be determined considering the cost of extra units of inventory (and the potential scrap, mess, and handling cost they entail, as well as the capital tied up) against the cost of having to schedule a second batch to meet the upper-level requirements or to ship a partial order. If the multiple is chosen carelessly, the MRP system will lead to high production costs and/or high work-in-process inventories.

However, there are industries where the rejection rates are both very high and unpredictable (certain operations in the electronics industry have this problem). If lead times for customer orders are very long in the industry, it may be possible to use MRP with long lead times, to allow time to test items and to produce until enough good items are obtained. However, if lead times are short, management may decide to maintain work-in-process inventories for several commonly used components. The reject allowance problem can be severe enough that MRP is not the appropriate way to control production. This decision would depend on many factors, notably the industry practice on customer service. The value of MRP as an information system should be considered, even though some of its advantage of reducing work-in-process inventory would be lost.

Selecting the Appropriate Level 0 for MRP

Level 0 of an MRP system is not always the final assembly or finished item. In the KBC example, the two coincided because of the structure of the bill of materials. In particular, several components or materials funneled down to finished products. As an alternative, suppose that each finished assembly comes with any one of 500 option packages. In that case, the production process would be as pictured in Figure 12-7 for FA1.

Predicting the demand for each option package would be extremely difficult, making it hard to derive a master schedule based on completed items. In this situation, it is likely that MRP should be used with a master schedule based on items without options. Then 1 unit of FA1 would have the options added (have the assembly completed) for a particular customer order. Some finished items

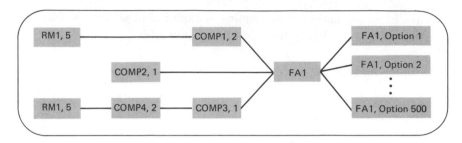

Figure 12-7 FA1 with options.

with popular option packages might be stocked in finished form, but these would just be part of the demand placed on the master schedule.

The advantages of consolidating orders for all option packages is that the total inventory requirement will be dramatically reduced, since the total of all FA1 orders is easier to forecast than are individual option packages. One can then avoid the problem of a shortage of green units and leftover red ones. The disadvantages are that completely finished items are not ready for customers and/or excess final assembly capacity must be maintained to respond quickly to customer demands.

There are other reasons for only performing MRP up to a semifinished product. For example, in the furniture industry, not only are chairs covered with many different fabrics, but semifinished chairs are much less damage-prone. Thus carrying semifinished items reduces deterioration. Some firms produce several basic components then assemble many combinations from those components. This type of situation leads to a *finish-to-order* or *assemble-to-order* approach as opposed to either *make-to-order* or *make-to-stock*. The proper method depends on the cost and on the customer service required in the industry.

MRP is not well adapted to systems that explode at the last step (into many options or colors). In such situations the manager will pick a lower level as the top level for MRP, and manage the final assembly in some other way.

In some situations, a *master scheduling level* (level 0) beyond finished products is used. A bill of materials called a *super bill* can be used. For example, a master schedule might call for 1000 cars to be made, and the firm must begin immediately, without knowing the exact option package for each car. Based on historical data, the firm can begin to build 1000 statistical cars. That is, the average car has 0.6 automatic transmission and 0.4 standard transmission. Thus we start 600 automatic transmissions and 400 standard transmissions. Similarly, the firm begins building other components. As the end of the planning period approaches, we get data on which cars are to have a specific set of options, such as automatic transmission, six-cylinder engines, green paint, and bucket seats. Due to the uncertainty of the option mix, we may start a few extra of each long-lead-time item and include less and less safety stock as we refine our forecast (see Miller, 1980).

The master schedule may even be based on demands outside the factory. In *distribution requirements planning* (DRP), sales at the end of a distribution chain (retail stores, for example) are predicted as level 0. Notice that a distribution system usually has a few plants, more warehouses, and many retail outlets. Thus a picture of the process looks like disassembly. There is a lower percent variation in total demand at a plant than there is in the demand at a retail store. We may know how many items to produce, but not where to ship them. As time progresses and the units are moved through the system, forecasts are refined. Then the allocation can be made.

DRP logic is the same as MRP. Thus we will not describe details. (See Stenger and Cavinato, 1979, for an example.) But DRP should be applied only when forecasts are reasonably good. This will be true for fairly high demand items. For low-demand items such as spare parts, other approaches are needed. These are discussed in Chapter 13. Like MRP, DRP forms a good way to keep track of the massive amounts of data involved. It does not help with allocation when demand is highly uncertain.

MRP as MIS

In Section 8-1 we discussed management information systems (MIS). In that section, we discussed the need to summarize the many details that are available about an organization in some manner that allows a manager to comprehend and control a situation easily. It is also required that the information be available on a timely basis.

MRP is well designed to provide such information, if the appropriate inputs are available. MRP can provide a forward-looking production plan and capacity usage (load) information. This load projection can be used to help the manager determine work-force and other capacity variables, and thus to feed back to the MRP system and change the capacity load in the short to intermediate term. The production plan can be used to isolate trouble spots of meeting delivery schedules, material procurement, and so on, and thus allow management to expedite (or take other action) to avoid the problem. In both cases MRP can help to pinpoint future problems and allow the manager to act in time.

MRP systems should not make production decisions automatically; they are designed to accept management's decisions and plans and to reflect their likely impact on the production system. Production schedules can be changed; lead times can be modified; capacity can be modified. MRP's greatest value is the information it can provide. An MRP system can be used, for example, in a simulation mode. If a large order is anticipated, the manager can see how the system will be able to respond, if the order materializes.

An MRP system cannot function unless it has accurate bill-of-material files, inventory files, and a master schedule. As input to the master schedule, forecasts for all independent demand items will be required, along with an inventory plan (lot size, seasonal accumulation, and safety stock) for those items. Managers, in turn, use information from the MRP system to plan the lot size and seasonal accumulation policies, using the capacity plan as part of the analysis. A simplified version of the information flow around the MRP system is summarized in Figure 12-8.

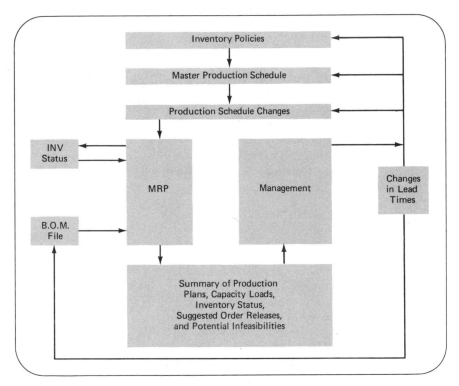

Figure 12-8   MRP as an information system.

In Figure 12-8, MRP's role as input to management decisions is emphasized. The manager controls the master production schedule, inventory policies, and detailed MRP decisions. However, the myriad of details is reduced for the manager by the MRP system, and if there is no intervention, the MRP system will proceed to make production decisions.

Review Problems

1. In Figure 12-5, a production plan for the next 23 weeks is given for KBC. Assume that each order release for COMP1, COMP3, COMP4, COMP5, and COMP6 is accomplished in equal thirds during the week of and each of the 2 weeks following the order release. (COMP2 is purchased rather than produced.) Develop a capacity usage (load) projection for the first 20 weeks. Use only information given in Figure 12-5, and you need not dis-

tinguish between released orders and planned releases. Add the planned production quantities for these five components for each of the first 20 weeks.

2. Assuming that we can begin to produce components immediately, prepare a better production plan than the method in Review Problem 1 yields. *Suggestion:* Work backward from week 21 (the deadline for the last order) and prepare a crash schedule, producing as late as possible, but always at the full capacity of 100 per week. Then modify the crash schedule to smooth out production during slack times.

3. Why might we not be able to begin producing components immediately?

Solutions

1. All components require the same amount of productive capacity, and the capacity is enough for 100,000 units per week. The order releases during the first 20 weeks are, from 0 to 19 in thousands of units: 200, 0, 0, 300, 0, 200, 0, 0, 200, 0, 200, 0, 0, 300, 0, 200, 0, 0, 200, and 0. If one-third of each week's requirements are performed during that week and each of the next 2 weeks, there will be $(\frac{1}{3})(200,000) = 66,667$ produced in weeks 0, 1, and 2, and $(\frac{1}{3})(300,000) = 100,000$ produced in weeks 3 and 4. There will be $(\frac{1}{3})(300,000) + (\frac{1}{3})(200,000) = 166,667$ produced in week 5. (This requirement exceeds the capacity of 100,000.) All 20 weeks are shown in Figure 12-9.

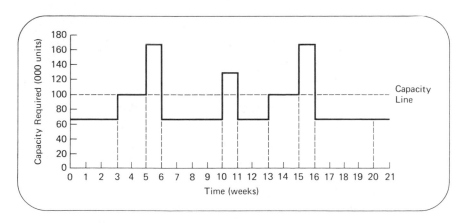

Figure 12-9 Capacity load for KBC component facility.

2. The crash schedule is shown in Figure 12-10. Each block contains the scheduled release time, the deadline (3 weeks later), and the total order quantity. Thus block (18, 21, 200) denotes an order for 200,000 units that must be delivered by week 21. We can begin that order in week 19 and produce at full tilt for 2 weeks to obtain the 200,000 units. Figure 12-11

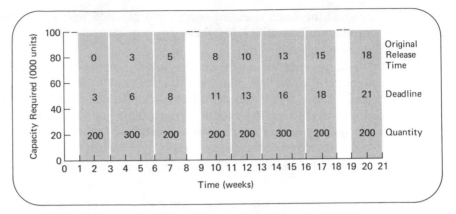

Figure 12-10   "Crash" schedule for KBC component facility.

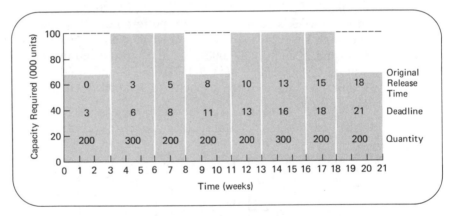

Figure 12-11   Relaxation of the Figure 12-10 schedule.

shows a relaxation of the crash schedule, filling in the slack times to smooth production. Note that there are three batches which begin after their planned release times.

3. Raw materials may not be available. One week would then be needed to obtain materials.

12-4 MASTER SCHEDULING AND MRP-II

Material requirements planning allows good management control of plant activities. It can be used as an information system to use in planning the business. Manufacturing resource planning (MRP-II) is a system of business planning for manufacturing companies, using MRP. At the heart of MRP-II is the *master schedule,* which is a plan for the next few periods of what end products the firm will produce. One of the key ideas in master scheduling is that *marketing, production, and finance must all have the same plan!* Many companies have been led astray by poor coordination among these three areas. In MRP-II, a common saying is "plan the work and work the plan." This implies that all parties agree on what will happen in the next few periods. Then they all work to see that the plan is followed. If the plan is not followed for unforeseen reasons, adjustments are made to the next plan. *The master schedule must reflect a realizable goal. Everyone in the organization should be working with the same set of numbers.*

Master scheduling should be the responsibility of one person, a *master scheduler,* who interacts with top management, other management functions, and the factory. He or she should know the business well. Inputs to the master schedule include a demand forecast, but forecasts are not automatically accepted into the master schedule. Instead, a meeting is held periodically with all interested parties to develop and approve the master schedule. This meeting should occur even if computerized routines develop much of the plan. Production, marketing, and finance all sign off, indicating their agreement to abide by the plan.

Time Fences for Planning and Scheduling

One policy input to master scheduling is a set of *time fences*. These describe the time intervals over which various actions will be considered. The first is the *frozen fence*. Before this time, the production plan will be changed only for emergencies (which should be rare). The frozen fence allows the plant to know what it is doing in the immediate future. The frozen fence is typically short, with production wanting a longer frozen period and marketing wanting a shorter one. The *planning fence* is the time to which the system looks ahead. This fence should be at least equal to the maximum cumulative lead time to make products, including raw material procurement. (If raw material procurement time is highly variable, materials may be maintained on an order point, order quantity basis, so that the planner can assume materials availability.) The planning fence may be longer if the firm builds up seasonal inventory. Firms often maintain a fence between frozen and planning fences, to load in specific demands for finished products. The specific name and use depends on the nature of the business. This fence may be called a *demand fence* or *scheduling fence*.

Information Requirements

In forming a master schedule to drive the MRP system, the information system must collect all the required information inputs. The following is a modification of the list of data sources given by Orlicky (1975, p. 237).

1. Customer orders.
2. Forecasts.
3. Safety stock requirements.

4. Seasonal inventory plans.

5. Orders placed by other parts of our own organization, including orders for interplant shipment and orders for company-owned dealers and distributors.

6. Service-part requirements.

These six sources have varying levels of importance for different companies. Companies that work to backlog (where all customer orders are accepted for future delivery) may deal almost entirely with customer orders in forming the master schedule. A firm that produces to and sells from inventories will base a master schedule mainly on sources 2, 3, and 4.

In some organizations type 5 orders (within the organization) are the same as customer orders. In other organizations a central planning group determines what these orders will be, so the level is known in advance. Finally, service-part requirements or spare parts (item 6) are independent demands for lower-level products. An example would be replacement compressors sold to persons who previously bought a refrigerator. This demand will be entered as a planned requirement at the appropriate level.

Closed-Loop MRP

The basic idea of *closed-loop MRP* is that the master schedule must be a feasible plan throughout the system. Capacity usage must be fed back to the master schedule as must the details of how the plan is (or is not) carried out on the shop floor. The MRP system must feed back any requests that cannot be completed during the lead time allowed. As things change, the master schedule should be changed so that it remains feasible.

Figure 12-12 illustrates how the elements fit together as a planning system. The arrows labeled "modify" are examples of the feedback portion of the loop, showing explicitly that the MRP system is used to evaluate alternative master schedules until a satisfactory plan is achieved. The same feedback loop is used for capacity management in response to last-minute deviations from plan.

Another view of the inputs into the master scheduling process is given by Berry et al. (1978) and reproduced in Figure 12-13. This figure highlights (1) the three levels of capacity planning (resource planning, rough-cut capacity planning, and CRP or capacity requirements planning), (2) demand *management,* and (3) feedback from the shop floor. It also points out the possibility of having an aggregate *production plan* and a separate *final assembly schedule.* We shall discuss each of these.

Production planning refers to a plan, in aggregate units such as sales value of production (SVP), and *resource requirements planning* checks to see whether the plant can be expected to produce that amount. If not, plans for additions to capacity can be made. This plan is made with a relatively long time horizon, without much detail. *Rough-cut capacity planning* interacts with the master schedule to predict which facilities represent potential capacity problems for the

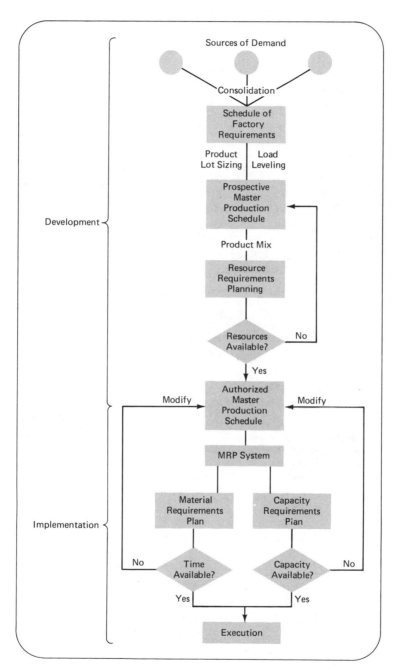

Figure 12-12   Master production schedule development and implementation. Source: Joseph Orlicky, Material Requirements Planning (New York: McGraw-Hill, 1975); used with permission of McGraw-Hill Book Company.

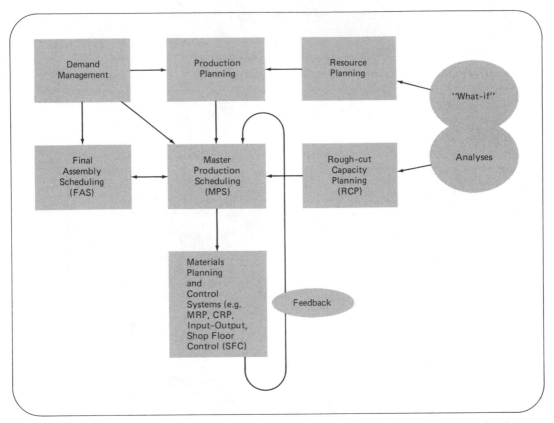

Figure 12-13 Relationship of master production scheduling to other manufacturing planning and control activities. Source: Reprinted with permission, American Production and Inventory Control Society, Inc., W. Berry, T. Vollman, and C. Whybark, *Master Production Scheduling: Principles and Practice*, 1979, p. 8.

particular schedule. *Capacity requirements planning* (abbreviated CRP in the diagram) looks at the MRP schedule in detail and generates load projections. Problems at this level will also be fed back to the master production scheduling activity.

Demand management refers to deciding what demands will be accepted into the master production schedule. Forecasts are not entered automatically. Order promising should be tied to the MRP-II system, so that promises can be kept and one set of numbers is available to everyone. *Final assembly scheduling* (FAS) reminds us that some MRP systems assemble to order, while a master schedule is done at a level below the finished product. FAS will not exist for some firms.

Scheduling problems do not end with the master production schedule. For example, despite the best planning efforts, there still are likely to be disruptions that keep the firm from following the plan exactly. At any point in time, a facility may have several jobs from which a next job must be selected. MRP provides due dates to help in this decision and release dates so that the number to choose among will be small. Job-shop scheduling rules, discussed in Chapter 11, can be used in the selection process.

The relation of master scheduling and MRP to these details, referred to as *shop floor control,* is described by Galligan and Hazarika (1982). The factory produces units based on MRP as driven by the master schedule. Feedback from shop floor control is essential because the plan probably will not be followed exactly. Future plans must take this into account.

In summary, the master schedule and the MRP bill of materials explosion are central elements in a closed-loop MRP-II planning system. When implemented with feedback in the areas of capacity and resources, demand management, and shop floor control, MRP-II is an interactive management tool that helps coordinate the operations of a manufacturing firm. Management's effective use of this tool is dependent on understanding the system, commitment to cross-departmental cooperation, accuracy of data, and timely feedback.

The forecasting, aggregate planning, lot-sizing, and scheduling techniques discussed in Chapters 4, 8, 9, 10 and 11 can be used to help form the master schedule, and they can even automatically generate a trial schedule. However, since there are so many possible factors, and since the overall production plan for a plant is so important, both to cost performance and customer satisfaction, managerial judgment must routinely be used in developing the master plan.

Review Problems

1. Consider a large U.S. automotive manufacturer such as General Motors or Ford. Which of the six items listed in this section as inputs to the master schedule would be most significant? Explain your answer.

2. Marketing departments often want to expedite an order to satisfy a large customer. For example, when backlogs are 5 to 6 weeks in length, they may want to place an order into the master schedule for completion in 3 weeks. How can an MRP system be used to determine if this is appropriate?

Solutions

1. All six items are potentially important, in different parts of the company. Customer orders are important for final assembly. Forecasts, which lead to a stable production plan for a long period of time, would be important for most operations. Each of the six items is an important part of developing some master plan in the company.

2. The MRP system can be used in a simulation mode. If we schedule the item as requested, is there available capacity to meet all orders? If not, what products will have to slip, and how far? Then the marketing department or senior management can determine, based on judgment, if the disruptions caused to the plant *and* other customers is compensated for by delivering for this one customer.

12-5 *THE JUST-IN-TIME (JIT) PRODUCTION SYSTEM*

The *just-in-time* production system (JIT) was made famous by Toyota (see Monden, 1981). It is sometimes referred to as the *kanban* system or the Japanese manufacturing system. The just-in-time system allows large inventory reductions and smooth production. It has been hailed as the best way to manage manufacturing. In this section we will answer three questions related to JIT. First what are the mechanics and underlying philosophy of JIT? Second, how is JIT related to MRP-II? Third, when are JIT, MRP-II, and other approaches appropriate for production control?

The Mechanics of JIT

Just-in-time production is typically described with a kanban system. We will follow this convention, although a JIT system is possible without kanban.

In a JIT system, small batches are used, with an ideal of reducing batches to a single unit. The small batch of a component is produced only when a kanban (a card requesting that parts be produced or moved) is received. Control of production is handled by these kanbans. In a *dual-card kanban system* there are two different types of cards: *production kanbans* and *conveyance kanbans*. When an order to produce a finished product is issued to the plant, the workers withdraw the components from a small storage area on the floor and build the product. The boxes with the parts have conveyance kanbans on them. The conveyance kanban is used as authorization to go to the predecessor stage and retrieve another box of parts. That box has a production kanban on it, which is used as authorization to produce another box of parts. The flow of the process is shown in Figure 12-14, reproduced from Schonberger (1983).

This system is notable for its simplicity. The batch is the size of a box, and it is kept small by management decision. The number of boxes at inventory points is also a management decision and is kept to a minimum. Both of these points will be discussed further in the following subsection. Computer control is unnecessary; parts are never produced until just before they are needed, and the kanbans are manually displayed to control the system. Complex computer control is avoided by designing the factory to respond very quickly to a "pull" for needed parts, signaled by a kanban. This is in contrast to a "push" system, where demands are anticipated and pushed through according to a schedule.

The kanban system is often implemented so that all workers can view the kanban, thereby seeing what their tasks are. The system even extends to the vendors, who may be required to deliver products when a kanban is seen at the loading dock (see Rice and Yoshikawa, 1982).

The Underlying Philosophies of JIT

The JIT system cannot work if setup times are long because that makes small batches impractical. Thus a setup time (and cost) reduction program must be an initial step. This requires substantial investment in engineering research and

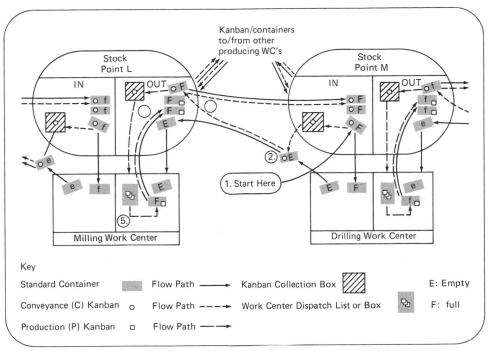

Figure 12-14

The dual-card kanban and container flow pattern for two work centers: a milling work center supplying milled heads to a drilling work center that drills holes in them. Stock point L serves milling (and other nearby work centers); stock point M serves drilling (and other nearby work centers). The flows of parts containers and kanban between milling and drilling are labeled in upper case.

The natural starting point in a pull system is with the pulling (using) work center, in this example, drilling. Parts for drilling are obtained as follows:

(1) "Start here," pointing to a full parts container about to be moved into drilling. Its C-kanban is detached and placed in a collection box for stock point M.

(2) A C-kanban from stock point M is attached to the container most recently emptied in drilling.

(3) The empty with the C-kanban is taken to stock point L (in another part of the plant), where its C-kanban is detached and reattached to a full container, which is taken back to stock point M.

This last act also triggers production activities through the use of production kanban (P-kanban), as follows:

(4) The full container just taken had a P-kanban attached to it. Before it left stock point L, its P-kanban was detached and placed in a collection box.

(5) P-kanban (that apply to milling) are taken to milling every hour or so, where they go into the dispatch box and become the list of jobs to be worked on next. They are worked on in the order of receipt from stock point L.

(6) Parts for each completed job go into an empty container taken from stock point L, the P-kanban is attached, and the full container is moved to stock point L.

Source: Schonberger, R., "Applications of Single-Card and Dual-Card Kanban," *Interfaces*, Vol. 13, No. 4, August, 1983. Reproduced with permission of the publisher.

new equipment. Moreover, when setup time and cost are low, inventory can be dramatically reduced by cutting batch sizes. JIT is based on the philosophy that setup cost should be reduced, not balanced against inventory cost. Notice that the idea of balancing setup cost and inventory cost is not repudiated. Rather a different problem is solved; setup cost is reduced so that the proper trade-off leads to small batches.

This philosophy leads to a second benefit. The simple computerless control system is appropriate only if items can be pulled through quickly. Short setup times and small batches fulfill this requirement. The efficiency of such a simple control system reduces manufacturing overhead.

A second JIT philosophy is that safety stock is a bad thing. It costs money and hides problems such as inefficient production methods. As inventory is reduced, problems become obvious because they disrupt production. For example, a machine that has frequent breakdowns or produces low-quality output can be replaced rather than buffered with safety stock. Once a problem is solved, inventory can be reduced further to find the next problem that keeps production from flowing smoothly and quickly. The goal is zero inventory. This goal is thought important enough by the American Production and Inventory Control Society that they recently announced the "zero inventory crusade," as the successor to the "MRP crusade" that has been under way for nearly two decades (see Hall, 1983a).

A third JIT philosophy is that productivity and quality are inseparable. JIT is not possible if poor-quality components are produced. The firm will not be able to test, rework, and deliver products in a timely fashion. Thus JIT requires not only small batches, low inventories, and quick production, but also a very high level of quality. The goal is 100% good items at every step. (Quality will be discussed at length in Chapter 16.) Often, quality is monitored automatically. In Toyota, this is called *autonomation* or automatic checking (Monden, 1981). Defects are stopped immediately, and the process is corrected.

The three goals of batches of size 1, zero inventory, and 100% quality are based on a belief that the pursuit of those goals is economic in the long run. The goals are not separable. For example, as the first two goals are approached, there is no apparent slack in the system; any quality problem or any other disruption can stop the entire plant. When this happens, the problem must be isolated and solved. A fourth JIT philosophy is that each such occurrence is an opportunity to improve the operation. The impact of the JIT philosophy extends beyond the company. Vendors are also required to meet the quality and timing standards, for example.

Some slack is built into individual jobs in some instances. For example, in Toyota (Monden, 1981), each operation must take a prescribed amount of time. At the end of the allotted period, workers who have not finished signal that they need assistance. Other workers who are finished (implying that some slack exists) come to their aid. If the job still cannot be finished, the line stops until the job is ready to move. This system requires careful engineering of each job so that (1) help can be useful (imagine someone trying to help you cook an omelette), and (2) just the right amount of slack is present on the average. The system also requires extensive cross-training of the work force and a team attitude.

Lifetime employment has been touted as an important difference in Japanese industry. The JIT system does not require lifetime employment, and many Japanese workers do not have this benefit. (For example, women typically work for short and variable portions of their lives, and many companies do not have lifetime employment at all.) The keys to successful JIT implementation are management dedication to the JIT principles and a well-trained work force operating as a team.

JIT, MRP-II, or Something Else?

In theory MRP is a just-in-time system. A master schedule for a finished product calls for inputs to begin with just enough lead time to arrive before the finished product assembly, if lot-for-lot scheduling is being used. However, lead times commonly grow in an MRP system to allow for manufacturing and procurement uncertainties and delays. As a result, forecasts far into the future are needed to develop the master schedule. These forecasts may be poor, so the plant may produce the wrong products, or make quantity or timing errors, as indicated earlier in this chapter. On the other hand, in complex, multistage operations MRP-II with careful lead-time control provides better management information and better control for business planning.

The JIT system using kanbans is best suited to a discrete-parts, highly repetitive manufacturing environment, such as automobiles. JIT tends to perform less well if:

1. Setup times and costs are high (cannot be reduced).
2. Quality is poor or scrap rates are high.
3. The diversity of the product line or the complexity of the product structure is great.
4. The variation in demand throughout the year is high.
5. Worker flexibility is low.

Each of the points above either (a) causes the production cycle to be long, (b) causes the load on a work center to vary significantly, or (c) limits the system's ability to respond. Japanese automobile manufactures have reduced setup times and improved quality. They have simpler product lines than those of U.S. manufacturers. Demand has been steady for long periods of time because they have imposed limits. Worker flexibility is common. Attempting to force the JIT system into situations that lack these attributes can cause difficulty.

A diverse product line need not eliminate the possibility of using JIT, if the factory is designed for flexibility. Flexible manufacturing systems, described in Chapter 5, allow a wide variety of parts to be produced quickly, in small batches. The JIT system is often implemented using automated equipment. The effect on plant layout requirements is also discussed in Chapter 5.

Shonberger (1983) believes that the significant factor governing choice of a system is the ease with which one can associate parts requirements with a specific item in the end-product schedule. For example, if yields are very low, a firm may have to produce that item to stock. A particular unit cannot, at the time of production, be associated with an end-item schedule. The association also becomes more difficult when a part is used in many end items. Schonberger sees a range from continuous operations to systems that should use reorder point methods. Continuous process industries could use MRP-II for business planning, but their system is automatically a just-in-time system. JIT systems are used when discrete-part demands can be easily associated with end-product schedules. Next, as complexity increases, MRP becomes more appropriate. Finally, if uncertainties govern everything, and they cannot be driven out (note that this premise would be rejected by the JIT philosophy), reorder-point methods should be used.

Other comparisons are given by Krajewski et al. (1983) using simulation analysis and by Rice and Yoshikawa (1982). In comparing the systems, two points must be remembered. First, the list above indicates where JIT is most and least appropriate. Second, the JIT system is based on changing the situation so that JIT is appropriate. Instead of managing the system as given, setup times can be reduced, quality can be improved, and other causes of uncertainty can be eliminated. Then the firm can use JIT. In other words, if possible, change the question before answering it. There will be times when this approach will yield great benefits and others where the system cannot be changed sufficiently.

There are other systems for managing production, and we cannot discuss them all. One such method is given by Maxwell et al. (1983) and other references discussed in the next section. A commercially available system, OPT (optimized production timetables), is described by Goldratt (1980) and discussed by Jacobs (1983).

OPT includes two major components: a data processing system that allows a detailed description of the production process and a set of optimization-based heuristics for developing detailed production plans. As with MRP and unlike JIT, a large amount of data must be gathered, but the system does allow for flexibility in the nature of the description. The heuristics are based on several key ideas. First, the bottleneck work centers are few and can be used as a place to begin to develop schedules. OPT rejects the standard costs at these centers because they are understated; they neglect the fact that bottleneck centers constrain the entire plant. Second, lot sizes should vary based on external demand and the total load on the facility. Third, a small amount of safety stock can be effectively allocated to a few locations to provide necessary buffers.

Several management policy decisions are required as input. The OPT system is designed to generate detailed schedules, giving better machine utilization and lower inventory. It can handle large production problems and tends to do better when no one job requires a large fraction of the total time. The details of the system are proprietary.

Review Problems

1. A company produces a few products with several stages of manufacture. They have large setup time and costs. The product is expensive, so inventory is expensive. Demand is fairly stable. What must they change if they are to use the JIT system?

2. A company produces a wide variety of products that require different machinery steps. Demand by item is unpredictable, but aggregate demand is stable. Products must be made in a short period of time to meet customer needs. If the JIT system is to be used, what type of automated equipment would be appropriate?

3. Discuss how portions of the JIT philosophy can be used to improve an MRP system.

Solutions

1. Setup time and cost must be reduced.

2. Flexible automation (a flexible manufacturing system).

3. Nearly all the points about a JIT system would improve an MRP system. The major exception is the simplified manual control scheme, which would be difficult to apply in a firm with a highly varying product mix.

12-6 *SOME RESEARCH ON MULTISTAGE MANUFACTURING*[1]

In MRP systems there are some fundamental, unresolved issues. How do we choose production quantities when lot sizes on one level of the bill of materials may cause trouble on others? Lead times are often made far too long in practice because occasionally a capacity-constrained facility may need the extra time. How can we adjust lead times to change temporarily, only as needed? The opportunity cost of production time on a constrained facility varies dramatically depending on the current load. How can this be estimated? How should that affect the production schedule? Finally, when JIT does not apply, and some uncertainty must be planned for, how can an overall system of management control be developed? We will briefly describe some recent research on these topics in this section.

Multistage Lot Sizing

Many authors have dealt with the problem of properly lot sizing a multistage production system. One special case is assembly systems, in which each component is used in at most one successor. By definition, end products have no successors.

---

[1] This section discusses some recent research and can be skipped without loss of continuity.

In assembly systems with constant demand and without capacity constraints, a component will always be ordered in an integer multiple of the lot size of its successor (see Problem 27). Finding optimal lot sizes with constant or time-varying demand has been discussed by many authors, including Schwarz and Schrage (1975), McClain and Trigeiro (1983), and Afentakis et al. (1984). (Additional references are given in these papers and in Billington et al., 1983, and Maxwell et al., 1983.) The Afentakis et al. paper gives the most computationally efficient scheme to date for time-varying demand. The McClain–Trigerio paper presents an easy-to-use method for constant demand.

Commonality, where an item is used in more than one successor item, is allowed in the papers by Blackburn and Millen (1982), Graves (1981), and Maxwell and Muckstadt (1983). These papers also do not allow capacity constraints.

Capacity constraints are included in Billington et al. (1983) in an integer linear programming formulation. This solution method incorporates the difficult-to-solve capacity planning problem. It also computes tight, time-varying lead times, adding waiting time only when necessary to balance the load on a capacity-constrained facility. Thus lead times are based on the anticipated load. Lot sizes can also vary with the anticipated load. The mathematical program gives the opportunity cost of using constrained facilities through shadow price information. This cost varies through time according to the facility load. Standard accounting costs do not contain the opportunity cost information that is necessary for good management in this situation. Finally, Billington et al. discuss ways of reducing the problem size to focus on the key, capacity-constrained facilities. This *product structure compression* allows the manager to focus on scheduling the key facilities (with or without mathematical programming). Then other facilities follow directly. (Problems 25 and 26 present the pieces of a linear programming formulation. The complete formulation is in the solutions manual.)

Each of the articles above works with deterministic demand, treating setup cost or time as important. If setup cost or time is (or can be made) low, the JIT system may be appropriate. If uncertainties are large, the method must explicitly allow for it. A modeling framework suggested by Maxwell et al. (1983) suggests that a deterministic view such as that of Billington et al. (1983) should be used to determine the lot timing and overall work level for a long horizon. This is phase I. In phase II, a small amount of safety stock should be strategically placed to *protect* the phase I plan. Yield problems, constrained facilities, and uncertainty in final demand should be buffered so that the plan can be implemented as closely as possible. Finally, in phase III, the day-to-day scheduling problems should be solved (1) considering the details of yields, broken machines, and so on, and (2) using the plan for overall production and safety stock as a goal. The cost of deviating from the plan can be obtained as a shadow price from the mathematical program in phase I.

The modeling framework combines master scheduling, MRP, and capacity planning into phase I, for a long time horizon. Shop floor control is accomplished by phase III, which can have better cost information on which to base detailed, short-term decisions. Phase II explicitly recognizes the need to carefully buffer uncertainties that cannot be eliminated. This system allows the manager to connect planning and implementation, taking an overall system viewpoint.

12-7 Summary

Neither MRP nor JIT is an "optimal" system. They do not provide a unique, best answer to any problem. MRP does provide excellent information to a production manager, and it does reduce a massive amount of information to comprehensible form. It can bring order out of chaos, reducing the work-in-process inventories and helping management to allocate production time. It usually replaces an informal production control system that has failed to keep track of all the interactions involved in the multistage production system. MRP provides tentative production schedules as well as input into the capacity planning, aggregate production planning, and inventory policy systems. It is an excellent management tool for dealing with problems that are too complex for us to find optimal solutions at the present time.

The basic ideas of MRP are very simple. By specifying a master schedule for end products, we can obtain the quantity and time requirements for each of the preceding production stages. It may be difficult to tie down the master schedule, but by doing so, we gain stability in running the plant. Further, if the master schedule must change, MRP provides the information to manage this change.

Finally, MRP does not apply to every situation, but it is widely and appropriately used in many complex, multistage production systems. MRP fits best if there are several stages to the production process under the firm's control. It fits best if reject allowances and independent demand for spare parts are relatively small compared to the dependent demand for finished items. MRP will work most effectively if lead times are not highly variable and if forecasts of finished item sales are good enough that a stable master production schedule can be developed. However, even in some situations where these conditions are not met, MRP may allow better control of production than alternative approaches. Its value in providing timely management information must be considered in making this determination.

The basic ideas of JIT are also very simple. An order for a finished product pulls components through the production system using a visual control system. The simplicity allows management to concentrate on other issues, such as quality and quick response time.

JIT requires low setup time and cost. Most of the uncertainties should be removed before using it. Then it replaces complex computer systems with visual control. Inventories will be very low. The system must be prepared for JIT by having high quality, stable demand, a small product line or flexible automation, reliable suppliers, and a dedicated work force, in addition to low setup times. When JIT fits, the benefits can be great. As with MRP, JIT does not fit everywhere.

The correct system to use depends on the situation: the extent to which design changes can be made to make JIT appropriate, the extent to which the product line can be simplified without losing customers, the extent to which the computer control and business planning possible with MRP-II is necessary or desirable, and so on. Management must assess the important problems, whether they are in design or ongoing management, and use a system that will help to solve those problems. MRP and JIT have both proved very effective when used in the right situation with top-management commitment to making it work.

PROBLEMS

1. What is the difference between dependent and independent demand? Why can the inventory levels be significantly lower in a dependent demand situation?

*2. MRP can often reduce work-in-process inventories significantly in a manufacturing situation, but its main function is in establishing a production schedule. It is used as a priority planning system to assist in the allocation of production time to different items. Briefly, how does it do this?

3. What is level-by-level processing, and why does it require low-level coding?

*4. (a) What is the time-related counterpart of safety stock in an MRP system?
   (b) How else can a safety stock of components arise in an MRP system?
   (c) In an MRP system with random demand for finished items, should safety stock of finished items be maintained? Why or why not?

5. (a) How should the length of the time bucket be chosen in MRP systems?
   (b) How is time phasing accomplished in MRP?

6. (a) Why shouldn't the EOQ formula be directly used in an MRP system?
   (b) What modification makes the solution obtained using the EOQ reasonable?

*7. Why might level 0 of an MRP system not correspond to the finished item? State the conditions and give examples.

8. The production process for automobiles involves many stages, components, and subassemblies. The finished assembly rate is constant over significant periods of time. Is MRP appropriate? Why or why not?

*9. State the conditions under which MRP works best. How many of those conditions are met by the automotive example discussed in Problem 8?

10. A cosmetic company makes products that are manufactured using a one-stage process. The lead times for raw-material procurement are long and highly variable. The production process is fast, and excess production capacity is maintained to avoid lost sales. Forecasts of finished item sales are hard to produce and subject to large errors; the company maintains a large finished-goods inventory as a result. They have only one inventory

point, since they sell directly to stores from their single plant. Is MRP appropriate? Why or why not?

11. (a) In determining the amount of reject allowance to have, what tradeoffs are involved?
    (b) If the reject rate for each of 100 components varies between 0 and 5% (and has never exceeded 5%), how much reject allowance is necessary if we want to be reasonably sure that we will have the necessary amount of each of the 100 components required for an assembly? Why?

*12. The assembly of a finished item requires four TM75's and six TM112's. TM75 and TM112 are subassemblies. The lead time to produce the subassemblies has been 1 to 3 months, with an average of 2 months. The two subassemblies each require 4 units of raw material RM-1 per unit. It has taken from 1 to 4 months to obtain the raw material, with an average of 2 months.
    (a) Using maximum lead times, derive the order releases required by finished-item order releases of 25, 35, 40, 40, and 40 in periods 1 through 5; include demand for times prior to the present. Compute the inventory that must be on hand or on order at time zero if we are to follow that plan.
    (b) The raw-material supplier says that the lead time for that item will henceforth be exactly 3 months. That is both good news and bad news. Why?

13. Whiffen, Inc., manufactures a variety of items. Their most successful and steady seller is a fireplace bellows, sold under the name Whiffenpoofer. A component of a poofer is the nozzle. Nozzles are produced at the rate of 200 units per day. Having been scheduled under an MRP system, the average production run has been 2 days in length, and 10 runs have been scheduled per year. A year is 250 production days. Lead time is normally distributed with standard deviation of 3 days.
    (a) How many days should be allocated as a safety margin for lead time, in order to achieve 99% protection against late delivery of nozzles (per order)?
    (b) How much inventory will be held on each day during this extra lead time?
    (c) If C_I = $2.50 per item per year, what is the average annual inventory cost due to the nozzle-lead-time's variability?

*14. The accompanying table gives a bill of materials for items A to F. For example, to manufacture 1 unit of C requires 1 unit of B and 2 units of F.
    (a) Using low-level coding, how many levels are required, and which items are on each level?
    (b) To make 100 units of A, how many units each of B to F are needed?
    (c) Each item has a 2-week lead time. Production of A is scheduled for

week 10, and the quantity to be produced is 100. When must item E be ordered, and in what quantity, in order to meet the production schedule for A while avoiding any unnecessary inventory?

Product	Manufacturing Requirements (Name, Quantity)		
A (finished good)	(B, 2)	(C, 4)	(D, 1)
B	(E, 3)		
C	(B, 1)	(F, 2)	
D	(E, 1)	(F, 3)	
E	Purchased		
F	Purchased		

15. A frozen dessert maker wishes to use MRP. Each frozen dessert requires two wooden sticks (with a 2-day lead time) and 2 ounces of flavored water (with a 1-day lead time). Sales of a constant 100 units per day are forecast. Frozen desserts are produced and packaged in batches of 300 and take 2 days to process and ship. (An order is released 2 days before inventory would be negative.) There are currently 500 frozen desserts on hand and no inventory of sticks or flavored water.
   (a) Determine the production schedule and order-release days and quantities for frozen desserts, sticks, and flavored water for the next 10 days. Use lot-for-lot scheduling for the inputs.
   (b) It is now the middle of day 3. Engineering has determined that a third stick is required to prevent the dessert from falling apart while being eaten. If the production schedule for desserts is not altered, and additional sticks are ordered on the next stick order release, when will be the first day that three-stick desserts will be sold?
   (c) Management, in an economy move, has decided to decrease the quantity of flavored water in each dessert to 1.5 ounces immediately. If it is now the end of day 3, what impact will that decision have on the MRP schedule as determined in part (a)?
16. MRP is said to provide better management information than other systems. What types of information are obtainable, why are they useful, and what must the manager give to the MRP system to allow it to work?
*17. The Apartment Protection Company (APCO) produces two security systems designed for apartments. They sell the completed systems and spare parts for the units. The composition of the two systems is shown in the diagram. COMP3, COMP4, RM1, RM2, and RM3 are purchased from outside vendors.
   (a) Determine the level of each item, using low-level coding, and draw a bill of materials figure for APCO, analogous to Figure 12-3.
   (b) How many RM1's are used in producing one SYS1?
   (c) Is this problem more or less complex than most actual MRP problems?

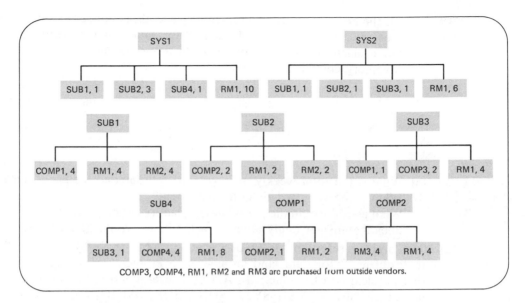

COMP3, COMP4, RM1, RM2 and RM3 are purchased from outside vendors.

*18. APCO, the firm described in Problem 17, has independent demand for SYS1, SYS2, SUB1, SUB2, SUB3, and SUB4. (Refer to Problem 17 for bill-of-materials information. This problem can be done without having done Problem 17, however.) They have long-term contracts to supply several discount stores; the total amounts in units per week are:

SYS1:	100	SUB2:	8
SYS2:	200	SUB3:	6
SUB1:	10	SUB4:	3

They currently have an inventory of 1500 units of SYS1, 1000 units of SYS2, and 40 units of each subassembly (SUB1, through SUB4). All production and procurement lead times are 2 weeks. When an order is released for any item, the firm produces enough to last for 10 weeks.

(a) Using only the six items for which demand rates are given above, give the complete time buckets for the next 15 weeks. That is, show inventory on hand, requirements, planned order releases, and receipts for the two level 1 items (SYS1 and SYS2), the three level 2 items (SUB1, SUB2 and SUB4), and the one level 3 item (SUB3). Do not show receipts unless orders have been released in time period zero or before. This is different from Figure 12-5; otherwise, Figure 12-5 can be used as a model to answer this problem. In your answer, inventory will be negative 2 weeks after the first order release for any item, and thereafter.

(b) How would the answer to part (a) change if each finished system had a steady reject rate of 10% and each subassembly had a reject rate of 20%?

*19. APCO, the firm described in Problems 17 and 18, is concerned about their lot sizes. (Refer to Problems 17 and 18 for data, but you need not have worked Problem 17 or 18 in order to do this problem.) The transaction and inventory costs are as follows:

	C_T ($)	C_I ($/Week)		C_T ($)	C_I ($/Week)
SYS1	150	0.50	SUB2	60	0.20
SYS2	120	0.30	SUB3	50	0.25
SUB1	60	0.20	SUB4	50	0.30

(a) What is the total weekly average expected demand for each item?

(b) What is the standard EOQ for each item?

(c) What period would the period order quantity cover for each item? What does the answer imply about how the items would be managed?

*20. This problem refers to APCO, described in Problems 17, 18, and 19. (Refer to Problem 17 for data, and an answer to Problem 18 is required before this problem can be done.) In APCO, one production facility is devoted to manufacturing SYS1, SYS2, SUB1, SUB2, SUB3, and SUB4. Each subassembly requires 1.4 labor-hours and each system requires 1.8 labor-hours.

(a) How many labor-hours are needed in each week to complete all these items, using the production schedule from Problem 18? That is, develop a capacity (load) projection for these items. Assume that a released lot is equally divided between the order-release week and the week following.

(b) Describe a manner in which they can develop a better schedule for capacity usage.

(c) Can the firm operate over this period of 15 weeks with a capacity of 2400 labor-hours for these six items? How much average capacity do they need for these units in the long run?

21. Describe the numerical changes that would occur in the answers to Problems 18 and 20 if the firm used the lot sizes found in Problem 19. To complete this problem, answers to Problems 18, 19, and 20 are required.

22. The KB Co. is described in the introduction to this chapter, and a summary of their expected production schedule is shown in Figure 12-5. The firm has just obtained a major new contract for FA2 and FA3, raising their demand rates to 20,000 units per week beginning in week 1.

The final assembly facility has ample capacity for the new demands, so its 2-week lead time and 100,000 unit lot sizes remain unchanged. The capacity of the component facility will be doubled, becoming 200,000 per week, by adding an extra shift. Consequently, management has reduced the planned component lead times (for all components except COMP2, which is purchased with a 1-week lead time) from 3 weeks to 2 weeks, which still leaves a margin of safety. Other lead times are 2 weeks (final assembly) and 1 week (procurement) as before. Lot-for-lot scheduling is used for all components.

(a) Redo Figure 12-5 to reflect the changes noted above.

(b) Describe any infeasibilities that occur.

23. This problem requires an answer to Problem 22. A capacity plan for the component facility of KB Co. is given in Review Problems 1 and 2. Remembering that COMP2 is purchased rather than produced, redo that analysis using the new situation described in Problem 22. Give only two capacity plans: one splitting each batch between the order-release week and the next week and one that improves upon that plan.

24. Suppose that a component has a period order quantity of 12 weeks and that a negative inventory position has just been reached. If the next 12 demands are (4, 0, 4, 0, 4, 0, 4, 0, 4, 0, 4, 200), what order quantity does the period order quantity imply? Suggest a better order quantity and argue for its superiority.

25. This problem and the next require a knowledge of linear programming, which is described in Appendix C. Let

R_{it} = requirements for item i in period t

D_{it} = external (independent) demand for item i in period t

P_{jt} = number of units of item j produced in period t (this is a decision variable)

a_{ij} = number of units of item i used in 1 unit of item j ($i = 1, \ldots, N$ and $j = 1, \ldots, N$)

There are N items (finished items and components) and T periods in the planning horizon.

(a) Write an equation defining $R_{i,t}$ in terms of the other variables.

(b) Let

$I_{i,t}$ = number of units of item i in inventory at the end of period t

F_i = scrap rate of a batch of item i (assumed known and constant)

Write an equation defining $I_{i,t}$ in terms of $I_{i,t-1}$, $P_{i,t}$, F_i, and $R_{i,t}$. Assume all lead times are zero. Once a unit is required ($R_{i,t}$), we assume it is no longer in inventory.

(c) Two other constraints might be

$$I_{i,t} \geqslant 0$$

$$\Sigma \, b_i P_{i,t} \leqslant \text{capacity of facility K}$$

(The sum is taken over all items produced in facility K; there could be more than one such constraint.)

Lead time is left out of the first constraint above ($I_{i,t} \geqslant 0$). Why is it left out? In the second constraint above, what is b_i?

26. Refer to Problem 25 for definition of symbols.
    (a) If lot-for-lot scheduling is used throughout the system and batch sizes are prescribed for finished goods, setup costs will be fixed and need not be considered. Then, what objective function is approprate in conjunction with the constraints listed in Problem 25? Write it, defining any new symbols. If we minimize this objective function subject to the constraints in Problem 25, is the model a linear program?
    (b) If lot-size decisions (other than lot for lot) are to be made by the mathematical program, can ordinary linear programming be used?
    (c) Comment on the size of the mathematical program described in Problems 25 and 26(a).

27. An end item has one input. The lead times for the end item and its input are both zero. The only costs are for setup and inventory. Capacity is not constrained. If the finished item will be produced in batches of 100, once per week, what lot sizes might be appropriate for the input item? Why? Does this logic carry over if there are several inputs? Why or why not?

28. Describe the cost, demand, and production process characteristics that make JIT the appropriate choice for a control system.

*29. The Boxit company makes a variety of products. Their plant has only two machines (A and B) but both are quite flexible. Changeover time between products is small. Every product is manufactured in two steps, with step 1 occurring at machine A and step 2 at B. Inventory of semifinished product (having step 1 completed) is maintained in boxes that hold exactly 10 units, and a 10-unit batch size is enforced for each production run. There are four boxes for each product, of which two are maintained at A to receive semifinished units and two more are at B. Boxit uses the JIT system with conveyance and production kanbans. When machine B is set up to produce an item, say item X, 10 semifinished units are withdrawn from one box and the box is taken (empty, with a conveyance kanban) to A. A full box of the same item is then sent from A to B. The production kanban on the empty box at A is a signal to produce 10 more semifinished units of item X.
    When this control system was established, Boxit made only two products, so only eight boxes were needed. Now they make 12 different items and are planning to expand their product line. The unit cost of semifinished items is approximately $10.00 (the same for all items).
    (a) When they made two products, how much work-in-process (semifinished) inventory did they have? How much will they have if they expand to 100 products?
    (b) What management decisions related to inventory have been made by the company? How might these be changed to reduce inventory?

30. How is slack built into JIT systems like Toyota's? Why is training and worker flexibility important in such systems?

*31. What is the ultimate goal in JIT for lot size, inventory, and quality?

REFERENCES

AFENTAKIS, P., B. GAVISH, AND U. KARMARKAR, "Computationally Efficient Optimal Solutions to the Lot-Sizing Problem in Multi-stage Assembly Systems." *Management Science,* Vol. 30, No. 2 (February 1984).

BERRY, W., T. VOLLMANN, AND C. WHYBARK, *Master Scheduling: Principles and Practice.* Falls Church, Va.: American Production and Inventory Control Society, 1978.

BILLINGTON, P., J. MCCLAIN, AND J. THOMAS, "Mathematical Programming Approaches to Capacity-Constrained MRP Systems: Review, Formulation and Problem Reduction." *Management Science,* October 1983.

BITRAN, G., D. MARIENI, AND J. NOONAN, "Introduction to Multi-plant MRP." Sloan School of Management, MIT, Working Paper 1486-83, October 1983.

BLACKBURN, J., AND R. MILLEN, "Improved Heuristics for Multi-stage Requirements Planning Systems." *Management Science,* Vol. 28, No. 1 (January 1982).

DAVIS, E. W., ed., *Case Studies in Material Requirements Planning.* Falls Church, Va.: American Production and Inventory Control Society, 1978.

GALLIGAN, S., AND P. HAZARIKA, "Shop Floor Control in a Continuous Production Flow Environment." *Production and Inventory Management,* Vol. 23, No. 4 (1982).

GOLDRATT, E., *OPT—Optimized Production Timetable.* Milford, N.Y.: Creative Output, 1980.

GRAVES, S. C., "Multi-stage Lot Sizing: An Iterative Procedure," in *Multi-level Production/ Inventory Systems: Theory and Practice,* L. Schwarz, ed. New York: North-Holland, 1981.

HALL, R., "Zero Inventory Crusade—Much More than Materials Management." *Production and Inventory Management,* Vol. 24, No. 3 (1983a).

HALL, R., *Zero Inventories.* Homewood, Ill.: Dow Jones–Irwin, 1983b (with American Production and Inventory Control Society).

JACOBS, F. R., "The OPT Scheduling System: A Review of a New Production Scheduling System." *Production and Inventory Management,* Vol. 24, No. 3 (1983).

KANET, J., "Toward Understanding Lead Time in MRP Systems." *Production and Inventory Management,* Vol. 23, No. 3 (1982).

KRAJEWSKI, L., B. KING, AND L. RITZMAN, "Kanban, MRP and Shaping the Production Environment," working paper, Academic Faculty of Management Sciences, Ohio State University, 1983.

KROPP, D., AND R. CARLSON, "A Lot-Sizing Algorithm for Reducing Nervousness in MRP Systems." *Management Science,* Vol. 30, No. 2 (February 1984).

LAMBRECHT, M., J. MUCKSTADT, AND R. LUYTEN, "Protective Stocks in Multi-stage Production Systems." Technical Report 562, School of Operations Research and Industrial Engineering, Cornell University, Ithaca, N.Y., 1982.

MAXWELL, W., AND J. MUCKSTADT, "Establishing Consistent and Realistic Reorder Intervals in Production-Distribution Systems." Technical Report 561, Cornell University School of Operations Research and Industrial Engineering, Ithaca, N.Y., 1983.

MAXWELL, W., J. MUCKSTADT, J. THOMAS, AND J. VANDEREECKEN, "A Modeling Framework for Planning and Control of Production in Discrete Parts Manufacturing and Assembly Systems." *Interfaces*, Vol. 14, No. 6 (December 1983).

MCCLAIN, J., AND W. TRIGEIRO, "Production Setup Patterns in Assembly Systems." Graduate School of Management, Working Paper 8301, Cornell University, Ithaca, N.Y., 1983.

MILLER, J., "Hedging the Master Schedule." Graduate School of Business Administration, Harvard University, Cambridge, Mass., 1980.

MONDEN, Y., "What Makes the Toyota Production System Really Tick?" *Industrial Engineering*, Vol. 13, No. 1 (January 1981).

ORLICKY, J., *Material Requirements Planning*. New York: McGraw-Hill, 1975.

PROUD, J., "Controlling the Master Schedule." *Production and Inventory Management*, Vol. 22, No. 2 (1981).

RICE, J., AND T. YOSHIKAWA, "A Comparison of Kanban and MRP Concepts for the Control of Repetitive Manufacturing Systems." *Production and Inventory Management*, Vol. 23, No. 1 (1982).

SCHONBERGER, R., "Applications of Single-Card and Dual-Card Kanban." *Interfaces*, Vol. 13, No. 4 (August 1983).

SCHWARZ, L. B., AND L. SCHRAGE, "Optimal and System Myopic Policies for Multi-echelon Production/Inventory Assembly Systems." *Management Science*, Vol. 21, No. 11 (July 1975).

STENGER, A., AND J. CAVINATO, "Adapting MRP to the Outbound Side—Distribution Requirements Planning." *Production and Inventory Management*, Vol. 20, No. 4 (1979).

TAYLOR, S., S. SEWARD, S. BOLANDER, AND R. HEARD, "Process Industry Production and Inventory Planning Framework: A Summary." *Production and Inventory Management*, Vol. 22, No. 1 (1981a).

TAYLOR, S., S. SEWARD, AND S. BOLANDER, "Why the Process Industries are Different." *Production and Inventory Management*, Vol. 22, No. 4 (1981b).

VOLLMANN, T., W. BERRY, AND C. WHYBARK, *Manufacturing Planning and Control Systems*. Homewood, Ill.: Richard D. Irwin, 1984.

WALLACE, T. F., *APICS Dictionary, Fourth Edition*. Falls Church, Va.: American Production and Inventory Control Society, 1980.

WHYBARK, D. C., AND J. G. WILLIAMS, "Material Requirements Planning Under Uncertainty," *Decision Sciences*, October, 1976.

CHAPTER 13

Multilocation Distribution Systems

Physical distribution, moving goods from one location to another, has become increasingly important. As manufacturing cost has declined to less than half of GNP in the United States, distribution cost has grown to over 20% of GNP. Roughly half of the 20% cost is involved in transportation, and half in warehousing and inventory cost. Less than 5% of the 20% cost is spent on managing these activities. Citing several sources, Lambert and Stock (1982) indicate that distribution accounts for 14% of the jobs in the United States (compared to 20% for manufacturing) and 21% of the sale price of goods; transportation accounts for 25% of all energy consumed in the United States. Large cost-saving potential exists in properly managing these costs. Also, since physical distribution delivers the product to customers, sales can be generated by giving better customer service.

Inventory plays a variety of roles in an organization. Chapter 10 discussed ordering-cycle or lot-size stock and safety stock. In service settings (such as retail stores, hospitals, and a university bookstore) and in some industrial purchasing situations these types of inventory are most important. Chapters 11 and 12 discussed methods of dealing with work-in-process (WIP) inventories and ways of scheduling final assembly lot sizes in a production facility. In some manufacturing companies these types of inventories are most important. In fact, many manufacturing firms have over one-half of their total inventory value tied up in work-in-process inventories. Chapter 9 dealt with seasonal inventories, built up to allow organizations to meet peak demand without having to increase productive capacity. In organizations with strongly seasonal demand, this type of inventory is likely to be the most important.

In this chapter we will discuss another type of inventory—*pipeline inventory*.

405

Pipeline inventory occurs because a multilocation organization must have some inventory at each location, and some inventory in transport between locations, in addition to manufacturing inventories (if any) and units to be sold to final customers. Just like a physical pipeline, which must be filled to allow water or oil to flow, a distribution system must have inventories to allow a smooth flow of units from producer to consumer. A one-location organization frequently does not own the inventory that is in transit to or that is being produced for the organization. They do not bear the cost of pipeline inventory directly, but they pay for it in the price of the item. A multilocation distribution system owns the pipeline stock and must pay the associated inventory cost.

Sears, the U.S. Navy, and the A & P supermarket chain are examples of large distribution systems with inventories produced largely by other organizations. Distribution is really a service function, and many nonmanufacturing organizations operate large distribution systems. Firestone, Xerox, and Corning Glass each have a large distribution system containing mostly inventories they produced themselves. Many other organizations, both large and small, are part of a large production–distribution network.

This chapter will concentrate on inventory control in multilocation production–distribution systems. Some of the key concepts will be used in Chapter 15, which discusses production planning in multilocation production systems.

13-1 PRODUCTION–DISTRIBUTION SYSTEMS

Many physical goods are produced at one or more plants, shipped through one or more distribution centers, and finally delivered to a final customer. Farm Supply Corporation, discussed in Chapter 2, was an example. A schematic representation is shown in Figure 13-1, including the flow of materials from suppliers of raw material to the final destination for finished goods. When one organization is in control of the distribution center (DC) and either the plant or the retail level or both, it is said to have a *multiechelon* distribution system.

When the distribution center function is filled by a different organization

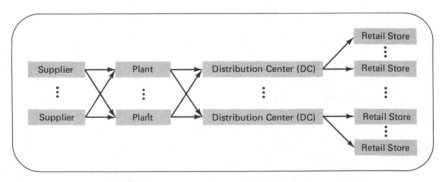

Figure 13-1 Production–distribution system.

than either the plant or the retail store, the pejorative term *middlemen* is used to describe the distributors. The question is often asked: Why do middlemen exist? Consider 100 plants that produce products sold in 1000 retail stores. If each plant is in contact with each retail store, (100)(1000) = 100,000 transportation links must be maintained, and each will have low volume, implying a high transportation cost. If, instead, one middleman serves the entire system, there will be 100 transportation links from the plant and 1000 transportation links to the retail stores, a total of 1100, and each one may have higher total volume. Of course, not all links are equally costly to maintain, but the example shows why intermediate levels can be cost-effective.

Even if an organization owns the entire system, they may want to take advantage of bulk shipment rates. To do so, a DC may be established near several (perhaps hundreds of) retail stores. Cheap shipment, in full railcars, for example, to the DC covers most of the miles. The savings can more than pay for the DC and its inventory. Transportation cost savings cause many firms to have multiechelon systems. As we shall see, inventory systems can take advantage of this structure.

Research on physical distribution has taken several different viewpoints. For example, Lesser and Roller (1983) examine the efficiency of the DC (or warehouse) level in grocery-chain distribution systems. Harrison and Wills (1983) use mathematical programming, discussed in Appendix C, to optimize production and distribution operations. Gross et al. (1981) use mathematical programming to optimize the design of the system, considering facility cost and inventory cost. Williams (1983) presents some simple models that optimize production and distribution schedules given known demands. In this chapter we will examine the effects of random demand on design and management of these systems. When demand is random, the time lags through the system are of crucial importance.

The total time lag from supplier to retailer is often large, running into several months or even years. There may be more layers in the system; for example, there may be several plants involved in sequentially making the product rather than several plants in several locations making the same product, as shown in Figure 13-1.

The time lag between supplier and plant is sometimes called the *procurement cycle*. It includes time to identify the need, group items for an order, communicate the order to the supplier, assemble the items for shipment at the supplier, transport the items, and receive the items. The *replenishment cycle* is the time lag between the plant and the distribution center. It includes time while items are batched at the plant for (say) truckload orders, time for order communication, time to produce, purchase or retrieve the order from stock, time to assemble the order for shipment, transportation time, and time to receive the order. The *order cycle* is the time lag between the DC and the retail store. It includes time to identify the need for an item, group orders, communicate the orders, check credit of the retailer (and other information-processing steps), and to assemble, transport, and receive the order.

Each of these cycle times represents somebody's *lead time*. If an organization is to avoid stockouts most of the time, it must have inventory sufficient to cover sales during the lead time. *Pipeline stock* includes the expected demand during each of the cycle times above. If a firm owns the plant, DC, and retail store, pipeline stock includes units to be used during the order cycle and replenishment cycle. The pipeline stock will include inventory in transit, which is often a significant part of the total. *Safety stock* is the extra inventory carried over and above the pipeline stock, to increase the protection against stockouts.

As an example, Farm Supply Corporation owns plants, DCs, and retail stores. They must have pipeline stock to cover expected demand during the order cycle and the replenishment cycle. Table 13-1 gives the average length of those two cycles for Farm Supply.

The numbers in Table 13-1 are averages, as indicated. An individual order might have an order cycle time or replenishment cycle time that is significantly different. For example, if the DC is out of stock, the order cycle time might be several weeks or even months. The replenishment cycle time might be reduced to around 14 days if the plant has the item in stock, but it might be 100 days if

TABLE 13-1 ORDER CYCLE AND REPLENISHMENT CYCLE FOR FARM SUPPLY CORPORATION

	Average Time Required (Days)
Order cycle	
Identify need	1
Group orders	2
Communicate orders to DC	0
Obtain items from stock[a]	$\frac{1}{2}$
Assemble order at DC	$\frac{1}{2}$
Transport order	3
Receive order	$\underline{1}$
	8
Replenishment cycle	
Identify need	0
Batch orders	1
Communicate orders	0
Produce, purchase or retrieve items	25
Assemble orders for shipment	2
Transport order	7
Receive order	$\underline{1}$
	36

[a] If the DC is out of stock, which occurs about 6% of the time, this step takes much longer. The item may be "emergency ordered" from a plant or a supplier, depending on the particular item involved.

the next scheduled production run is 3 months from the present. Protecting against the variability in lead time is the function of safety stock. Variability can also be dealt with by procedures for expediting important orders.

Many trade-offs are possible regarding pipeline inventory. For one example, Farm Supply may have purchased telecommunications equipment so that zero days of time are involved in communicating orders. This does not affect the pipeline stock directly because inventory enters the pipeline only after the order is received. However, it does reduce the amount of safety stock because there are fewer days of uncertain demand to be faced between order and receipt.

For another example, suppose that the firm were to increase their truck fleet so that a 3-day reduction in transportation time became possible for their replenishment cycle. In this case the units would be in the system (on the trucks) 3 fewer days. Three days of demand for each product would be cut from the pipeline stock. In addition, safety stocks can be reduced for the same reason as the preceding example. Reducing the cycle time almost always leads to a reduction in safety stocks needed, because of the reduction of the variability of lead-time demand. An additional decrease in inventory is possible if we reduce the length of time physical units *owned by our organization* are in the pipeline, unavailable for use. These examples show that different savings can result depending on how a cut in the cycle time is achieved (see Problem 2).

Reducing the order cycle and replenishment cycle also has the benefit of allowing the organization to react to changes in the demand pattern more quickly. An oscillation in demand at the lowest level usually leads to a much larger swing in the demand seen by the upper levels. This is so because all retail units are likely to place large orders soon after the upswing in retail demand, and their inventories will carry them for a longer time during the downswing. Reducing the cycle times will reduce the magnitude of this effect. The oscillation is illustrated in Figure 13-2.

These cycles, induced by information lags, have been blamed for exacerbating recessions. Beman (1981) contrasts the 1974 and the 1980 recession. In the 1974 recession, inventories continued to grow after sales had turned down, and the inventories delayed the rebound. In 1980, inventories were relatively much lower and manufacturers kept them from growing dramatically during the decline. Beman argues that the better control minimized the length and severity of the recession.

Using smaller batch sizes and reducing the order cycle can help management cope with inventory cycles. In addition, detailed information should be maintained on what is happening to retail level sales. This information can help the firm to plan its production schedules in advance and avoid the huge swings shown in Figure 13-2. This planning is easiest when the entire system is under one organization's control. Many firms do not control the final selling point of their products. Industries such as the electronic components industry have often had dramatic changes in production levels caused by more modest changes in retail

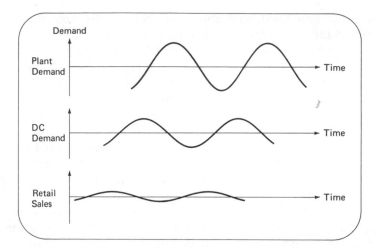

Figure 13-2 Effect of swings in retail demand.

demand. In that situation, the plant can pay for information and/or offer incentives for long-term contracts. In the case where the final sales point is owned, routine collection of information can allow better management control of the entire system.

Review Problems

Farm Supply Corporation has a total daily demand rate of $3,000,000. If they want to fill the pipeline, they must have inventory equal to the sum of the order and replenishment cycle times, multiplied by the daily demand rate. Some of this stock is at the store level and some at the DC level.

1. Estimate the amount of inventory they need to fill the pipeline.
2. They are considering more frequent shipments. The transport time in both the order cycle and the replenishment cycle would be reduced to 1 day. The new system will cost $2,400,000 more per year than the previous system. (This includes the annual equivalent cost of investment in trucks.) Should they change to the new system?

Solutions

1. (44 days) × ($3,000,000 per day) = $132,000,000
2. A reduction from 3 + 7 transport days to 1 + 1 transport days results in an inventory reduction of (8)(3,000,000) = $24,000,000. The annual saving would be the inventory carrying cost rate (F_I) multiplied by the inventory reduction of $24,000,000. If F_I is greater than 10%, the firm should use the new system. Common F_I values are in the 15 to 40% range, so the firm probably should use the new system.

13-2 POLICIES AND INCENTIVES

Multilocation inventory systems share many of the problems of other large-scale operations. For example, there is often a diffusion of the responsibility for results. Also, it is difficult to establish service-level goals for upper echelons (as we will see). Finally, it may be true that the incentives faced by individual managers in the system cause them to make decisions that are not good for the entire organization. Dealing with problems such as these is frequently necessary before beginning an analysis of the inventories themselves.

Organization and System Design

Why does an organization choose to have a multiechelon (many-layered) inventory system, with plants shipping to DCs, which in turn ship to the final customer? One reason stated above is that transportation costs can be reduced by using inexpensive bulk shipment (train carloads, for example) from plants to the DCs, then using more expensive shipment for the local delivery. Another reason is that the DC is physically closer to the market, and therefore a more effective backup stocking point, thus allowing quicker response to stockouts at the bottom level.

Once it is determined to have a multiechelon system, the designer must decide how many layers to have and how many facilities to have in each layer. The number and location of facilities was discussed in Chapter 7, and we will not add to that discussion here. The number of layers to have depends on how many final customer locations there are, and how close a support warehouse should be. If there are thousands of lowest-level inventory points (such as repair inventories held by service representatives for computers or copying machines) and if they require close support to provide proper service, close to 100 support warehouses may be necessary. Then it is possible that another layer can be justified between the support warehouses and the plants, based on transportation cost savings. However, the existence of more than three layers is uncommon, and it occurs when there are special reasons for it. (One other example of a several layer system is the U.S. Navy, which has stock on board each ship, in supply ships, in ports, and in large distribution centers that receive shipments from suppliers' plants.)

Once a system is designed, there are organizational questions to be answered. For example, what authority does the manager of each location have? To what extent should control of the distribution system, including all inventories, be centralized?

The extent of centralization of control is a crucial question with no obvious answer. Many important savings are possible if the distribution system is viewed and controlled in its entirety. Total inventory can be reduced and system-wide trade-offs can be made involving transportation, location, production scheduling, and inventory. (The extent of potential inventory savings is examined in Section

13-5.) These savings have led some companies to adopt a system for overall control of materials throughout the organization. A Director of Logistics (or similar title) would be created to perform this function.

The argument against centralization of the distribution function is that local managers know things that a central manager cannot. Totally centralized control removes one competitive weapon—inventory levels—from division, sales, or product managers. In a profit center, a manager who is responsible for profit must have control over the relevant variables. Some companies feel that establishing responsibility will lead to better management and offset the lost cost-reduction potential of central decision making. There are, of course, intermediate solutions where staff support is available to local managers on a voluntary basis.

Service Policies

Inventories are used to provide service to the customer. The extent of the inventories is largely governed by the level of service the organization wishes to provide. A policy statement on service might say: "85% of all demands at the retail level will be satisfied immediately, and 13% of the remaining 15% will be satisfied within 2 days." Another might be "A demand for a spare part will be satisfied quickly enough that the average downtime due to spares requisition is less than 2 hours."

A statement of service policy must consider standard practice among competing firms in the industry. In addition, it should consider the cost of meeting the specified level. This is discussed further in Section 13-4, using "trade-off curves." Finally, in a multiechelon distribution system, the service policy must specify more than a retail service level. There must also be an incentive for upper echelons to quickly support the retail level in an out-of-stock situation. This is discussed further in Section 13-3.

It is important to recognize that service measures differ greatly with the situation. Many books concentrate on "percent off-the-shelf service" as a measure. That is, what fraction of the demands are satisfied immediately? In many industries there is no off-the-shelf service; providing the product within 4 weeks may be considered to be excellent service. The mathematical approaches must be molded to the service measure used, not the reverse. Lalonde and Zinszer (1976) discuss customer service at length, and they give dozens of examples of what industry managers mean by customer service. The variety is astonishing.

Accounting in Inventory Management

Several cost accounting[1] questions are crucial to inventory management. We will discuss three of these. First and foremost, what value of the inventory cost

---

[1] We will not discuss other accounting issues related to inventories, such as LIFO versus FIFO. We will leave those subjects to accounting texts, since they have little effect on the management of the inventories.

is appropriate? C_I is the carrying cost, defined in Chapter 10; it is the item value times F_I, the carrying-cost rate. Second, what ordering or setup cost, C_T, is appropriate? Finally, what procedures are appropriate for dealing with obsolete inventory?

F_I includes a cost of capital, cost of theft, the marginal cost of physical storage, cost of obsolescence, and any other costs that vary with the amount of inventory. In a multilocation system, these costs vary from location to location, and different F_I values should be used. The cost of obsolescence differs dramatically from item to item, and this difference should be reflected. The cost of obsolescence may vary by location as well. Inventory is more likely to become obsolete the farther out in the system it goes. While centralized, it can be shipped to satisfy demands in many locations and is therefore likely to move out of the system sooner. Finally, the item's value is increased at the lower levels, since transportation cost has been added to the value. This cost may be unimportant in some cases, but it is a large portion of the value for items, such as certain spare parts, that are low in cost but relatively expensive to ship.

C_T, the ordering or setup cost, tends to be much larger at plants than at DC's or retail stores. Pure ordering situations involve a small amount of clerical time and computer time to process an order. Thus orders at the retail and DC level tend to be sized to cover a short period of time. (Exceptions to this are caused by price breaks and anticipation of a price increase or a shortage.) For manufacturing, C_I must also include the cost of starting a new production run, so a batch may be sized to last several months.

Rules for determining obsolescence are often a source of argument in manufacturing firms, and the topic leads us to another type of inventory. In addition to lot-size, safety, seasonal, work-in-process, and pipeline inventories, there is *dead stock*. Dead stock is obsolete inventory that is unlikely to be sold. Once inventory items are recognized to be dead stock they can be written off, meaning that inventory assets are reduced by the book value of the inventory. In a company that is making profit, this results in a reduction of income and, therefore, income tax. A company with a 40% tax rate saves $40 in taxes by writing off $100 of dead stock. The money to be saved by writing off inventory can be substantial. It should be noted that the amount of this tax write-off is the same as the tax deduction for cost of goods sold. Therefore, it is never profitable to build inventory that is expected to become obsolete.

The reason for arguments over rules for declaring inventory obsolete is that individual managers have a reduced profit if their inventory is written off. (The corporation, not the division, gets the tax saving.) Thus managers do not want to write off inventory.

The key to resolving such conflicts lies first in using a charge for holding inventory, F_I per dollar, including a required return on capital and an estimated cost of obsolescence; the total inventory cost is subtracted from divisional profits. However, division managers often move on within a few years, before inventory costs would exceed the item's value. Thus policies for declaring items obsolete are also necessary. They must be clear and followed routinely, with exceptions kept to a minimum.

The precise rule to be followed depends strongly on the industry. A company with a dynamic product line will want to declare items obsolete quickly. A slow, but steady sales item should not be declared obsolete quickly. One company has a rule that declares items obsolete once they are held in inventory for 6 weeks. Another has a rule that declares as obsolete only inventory in excess of five times last year's sales. The rules are different, but both may be appropriate.

System Performance

The points in this section are discussed at more length in Muckstadt and Thomas (1983). They give four policy questions related to productivity of distribution inventories. These are:

1. How is service defined, and what level of service is the standard in the industry?
2. Where will the organization locate inventory, and what mode of transportation will be used?
3. Who's in charge?
4. What measure of inventory performance should be used?

The correct answers depend on the situation, but an organization cannot be efficient if management fails to clearly answer the questions. Our opinion on question 4 is that financial measures should be used. The cost of inventory is subtracted from a manager's profit measure, and the benefit of carrying the inventory (increased sales, lower production cost, and so on) should accrue to the same individual.

Review Problems

1. A manager has $400,000 of inventory in an item built precisely to one customer's specifications. The items are of zero value to anyone else. The customer has reduced his order to $200,000, but he will take the remaining $200,000 in 3 years. (Assume there is no doubt about the future sale or its timing.) The company uses $0.40 = F_I$, where the cost of capital is 0.15, the cost of obsolescence (on the average) is 0.15, and the physical costs of storage are 0.10. (All three values are on a before-tax basis. The after-tax cost of capital is 0.09.) Since 0.40 per year times 3 years is 1.20 (i.e., more than 100%), the manager feels that the items should be scrapped now and new items should be built in 3 years. Is he right? Why or why not? (Use an after-tax analysis with a tax rate of 0.48. You can assume that there will be no inflation. Remember that if they keep the items now, they still get a tax deduction in 3 years.)

2. Summarize the arguments for and against centralization of all distribution system functions.

3. In order to resolve conflict between marketing and production, the controller suggests that marketing be charged with making forecasts that production must meet, and that finished-goods inventory costs be charged to marketing's budget. If a last-minute change in the forecast is necessary, marketing would be charged for any additional production costs. Production would be responsible for material, work-in-process inventories, and costs incurred if they overproduce or are unable to meet the forecast. Is this breakdown reasonable? Why or why not?

Solutions

1. Since the $200,000 cannot be recovered immediately, applying the cost of capital to the full amount is inappropriate. (It was appropriate before the production decision was made.) Also, since we have been assured that the items will not be obsolete, the 0.15 cost of obsolescence is irrelevant. Thus the only marginal cost is the 0.10 physical storage cost. The other costs are sunk. Thus, if the firm keeps the items, there will be only an (0.10)(200,000) = $20,000 cost per year, for physical storage. If the firm scraps the items, they receive $96,000 now, but they must pay $200,000 to build the items in year 3. If they keep the items, they receive a $96,000 tax benefit in year three. The $20,000 and $200,000 costs must be multiplied by (1.0 − 0.48) to put everything on an after-tax basis. Thus the cash flows are:

		YEAR		
Action	0	1	2	3
Scrap	96,000	0	0	− 104,000
Keep	0	− 10,400	− 10,400	− 10,400 + 96,000

The revenue from the sale of the items is not considered since it is common to both plans. We want to select the larger of the two discounted cash flows. Discounting to time zero using the 9% after-tax cost of capital, we obtain $15,693 and $47,805 for scrap and keep, respectively. The firm should keep the items.

2. Centralization is appropriate because large savings are possible by viewing the entire distribution system. On the other hand, individual managers inevitably lose some of their discretionary authority, and the company loses the benefits which that authority can achieve.

3. Yes, since the group in charge of the forecast is also in charge of the consequences of the forecast (finished-goods inventory). Production is charged with meeting that forecast as efficiently as possible.

13-3 DETERMINING INVENTORY LEVELS

Objectives

A *stockout incidents* objective is one in which the number of stockouts that occur at the lowest level is to be minimized, regardless of how quickly the system could satisfy the unsatisfied demand. A *backorder incidents* objective counts the *amount* of demand that cannot be satisfied immediately due to a stockout, assuming that the sale is not lost (the customers allow the item to be backordered). If the sale is lost, the percent of *lost sales* can be measured. The complement of backorder incidents or lost sales is the *fill rate,* which is the percent of demand satisfied immediately, off the shelf. All these objectives ignore the duration of the shortage from the consumer's point of view. A *time-weighted backorders* objective is one that considers the length of time before a demand is satisfied; in such a system one item backordered for 2 weeks is assumed to be as costly as two items backordered for 1 week. In either system stockout costs can vary from one item to another, depending on factors such as the gross margin of the item.

The main reason for wanting to avoid stockouts at the upper echelons is that they can lead to a series of stockouts at the organization's lower levels. Of course, the upper levels need pipeline stock and safety stock so they can ship orders promptly, thus reducing the chance for stockouts at the bottom level. However, most multiechelon systems have 10,000 or more SKUs (stockkeeping units), and most of these are not carried at the lowest level, owing to low demand. In that situation, a stockout incidents objective is counterproductive, because every one of these items is "stocked out" at the lowest level, and quick response to an order would not be recognized as valuable. Unless time weighting is used, there is no incentive to carry these low-demand items at any level in the system. This situation and other similar observations argue for a time-weighted type of objective in a multiechelon system. Mathematical methods for implementing two different time-weighted objectives are discussed in Muckstadt and Thomas (1980), along with empirical results.

Schwarz et al. (1984) use a *fill rate* objective. They show that safety stock should be concentrated at the retail level in a two-echelon system, even to the point of having negative safety stock at the DC. (Negative safety stock can occur when we place an order at a stock level we expect to be insufficient to cover demand during lead time.) If fill rate is an appropriate objective, this research seems to indicate that a firm should not maintain large amounts of safety stock at the DC. However, fill rate is not an appropriate objective for systems with thousands of SKUs with very low demand. Such items are not cost-effective to carry at the retail locations, as discussed in the paragraph above.

Several systems in practice use a stockout-incidents type of objective with an arbitrary level of service set for the upper levels. Thus a system might have a goal of satisfying 95% of the demands at the retail level and 90% of the demands at the DC level. The problem with such an approach is discussed below. In this discussion we will refer to only two levels, a retail level and a DC level.

One formula that can be used to set service levels optimally (for one item at one location) was described in Chapter 10:

$$\text{optimal probability of stockout during lead time} = \frac{C_I}{C_B} \frac{1}{\text{orders per year}} \tag{1}$$

The reorder level (expected demand during lead time, plus safety stock) is set to the level that accomplishes equation (1). (Refer to Chapter 10 for a discussion of the calculations.) C_I is the cost of inventory per unit per year and C_B is the cost of being out of stock or backordering 1 unit. A cheap item that is ordered several times a year will have a much lower probability of stockout, optimally, than an expensive item that is ordered once a year, if C_B is the same in both cases. In general, the formula shows that the probability of stockout and the level of safety stock *should be different* from item to item. To achieve an average service level of 95% of the demands satisfied off the shelf at the retail level, some items should have nearly 100% service and some should have almost none.

This logic is true when applied to a single location, but it falls apart if it is applied to *each level* of a multiechelon system. The low-service-level items will be the low-demand items, for the most part, at both the retail level and the DC. The high-demand items will have safety stock in large quantities at both the retail level and the DC. Thus there will be excess safety stock (double protection) for some items and no support for other items.

These points can be emphasized as follows.

1. In a one-location system, service levels should vary among items.
2. In a multiechelon system, the upper level has the task of supporting the lower level. Thus it should carry the safety stock and pipeline stock for items that do not have a high service level at retail outlets. It should not provide excess safety stock for items that have an excellent retail service level. (The DC should carry pipeline stock in these items.)
3. Applying one-location methods to a multiechelon system will lead to decisions counter to point 2. Some system-wide approach must be used.
4. The service level that is appropriate at the retail level depends on the annual demand and its variability, as well as the values for C_I and C_B.
5. There are ways to modify single-location methods to act as discussed in point 2. These are described next.

Modifying Single-Location Methods

In modifying single-location methods for a multilocation system, we must take advantage of the system structure in locating safety stocks. One crucial point is that less total safety stock is needed if it is held at the DC level. This is true since a high demand at one retail outlet can be offset by a low demand at another when stocks are held at a central location, but this cannot occur if each location must protect itself. This phenomenon leads to the establishment of regional blood banks, for example, because the demand for some rare types of blood is low on the average in all locations, but occasionally high at some location. Much less blood will be needed if most of the safety stock is centralized. Based on experience with many kinds of demand data, the following formula is sometimes used to approximate the amount of safety stock required.

$$\text{safety stock needed} = kD^a \qquad (2)$$

where k = safety factor, determined considering C_I and C_B; this will
                   be different for different products

D = total expected demand during lead time

a = exponent, $0.5 < a < 1.0$

If $a < 1.0$, safety stock can be decreased by centralizing stocks. For example, if $a = 0.5$, and we are considering centralizing stocks for two locations that each have $D = 100$, we obtain: safety stock $= k(100)^{0.5} = k(10)$ for each of the two locations, for a total of $(k)(20)$ at the pair. In comparison, safety stock $= k(200)^{0.5} = k(14.4)$ if the stock is centralized. The reduction from $20k$ to $14.4k$ is significant.

The implication of an a value between 0.5 and 1.0 is that a facility covering several demand areas will have less safety stock than would be required in total to cover the areas with several facilities. Magee (1968) states that "the degree of relationship must be examined for each product line; a number of actual cases have indicated that the magnitude of variation increases with the 0.6 to 0.9 power of item demand."

Another issue in centralization of stocks is correlation among demands at different locations. Statistically, high correlation has the same effect as high a values in equation (2)—the advantage of centralization is reduced. The authors have observed correlation among demands of different retail outlets of from 0.3 to 0.6. Such studies should examine "residual correlation" after removing common explainable terms such as trend and seasonal factors. As long as correlation is not perfect, incentives for centralization exist. (Models that allow correlation among retail units have been studied, for example, by Ehrhardt et al., 1981.) Thus centralizing safety stocks is appropriate where it is possible, if it does not lead to loss of sales due to stockouts at the retail level. Better safety can be purchased more cheaply at a centralized facility.

However, better safety may not mean better service if the product will arrive later. Customers may expect delayed service in some industrial settings but in other settings delays may not be acceptable. The statistical savings (described above) provide the manager with one side of the trade-off. With centralized inventory we can be as sure (or even more sure) of providing the product, but it will arrive later. If immediate service is needed, we may choose not to centralize.

Inventory can be centralized without owning a central warehouse. This occurs when central stock is held by the vendor. The customer consolidates orders from all its DCs to obtain quantity discounts. Shipments are sent directly to the DCs as needed. The cost of this service is included in the vendor's price. This problem is studied by Eppen and Schrage (1981) and by Federgruen and Zipken (1984).

One common way of determining inventory levels in multilocation systems is to carry a specified number of days of supply in each item at each location, and ordering so as to maintain those levels. This does not recognize differences in costs and demand and can have very poor cost performance. The single-location methods discussed in Chapter 10 account for differences in costs and demand, but they do not take advantage of a multiechelon structure. One approach to this problem has been called a *dual distribution system* by Heskett et al. (1973).

Items can be grouped by both demand and cost considerations; they are often grouped using demand times cost, in an A-B-C classification. The top-selling items, by dollar volume, are called A items. In this system, as commonly used, the top 20% of the items often account for 80% or more of the total sales. The lowest-selling items (50% of the items may account for only 5% of the dollar sales) are called C items. Other items are called B items. An organization may choose, then, to have no C items at the retail level. The DC must carry pipeline stock *and* safety stock for these items. The organization might choose to have a high service level (say 95% satisfied off the shelf) for A and B items at the retail level. The DC should carry pipeline stock but little or no safety stock in these items.

However, dollar demand does not optimally separate the items into groups for this purpose. An expensive item with low demand is the very best candidate for centralization, and it might turn out to be a B item because of its cost. For this reason, an A-B-C breakdown based on unit demands is preferable for the purpose at hand to A-B-C categories based on dollar sales. (For other purposes, dollar sales is more useful.) An even better method would be to form categories of (high unit demand, low cost) and other such demand-cost groups. A perfect breakdown is difficult to obtain, but some attempt at using the structure of the distribution system can reap large benefits. With some breakdown of this type, single-location methods, such as those discussed in Chapter 10, can be used to manage a multiechelon system.

The methods to be discussed in Section 13-5 can optimally make inventory decisions in some situations. Since they are complex and relatively expensive to implement, modifications of single-location methods still will be used in some multiechelon systems. The manager must blend a knowledge of the Chapter 10 methods with an understanding of how to take advantage of the multiechelon structure of the system.

Consider the following example, from a real situation. A salesperson took an order for 50 units from a German customer. However, the local warehouse had only 30 units, so they could not satisfy the order. Their standard order quantity was 200 units, which they ordered from the European central warehouse in Great Britain. The British warehouse had 150 units, so they could not satisfy the request. They ordered their standard 1000 units from the U.S. worldwide distribution center. The U.S. distribution center had 500 and ordered 5000 from the plant. The plant had 2500, so they scheduled a manufacturing run of 20,000 units, which they produced 2 months later. This example illustrates that to manage a multilocation system properly, some*one* must (1) have an information system that gives the status of the entire system (so that the German customer could get the product), and (2) have authority to apply common sense.

Review Problems

Suppose that one DC supports 100 identical retail outlets. We are considering two items. Each has $C_I = 1$ and $C_B = 10$. Item 1 is ordered once a year and item 2 is ordered 10 times a year, at the retail level. Item 1 has lead-time demand at each retail outlet of 10 units, while item 2 has lead-time demand of 1000 units at each retail outlet. The lead time is the same at the DC as at the retail level, so the DC has lead-time demand of $(100)(1000) = 100,000$ units for item 2 and $(10)(100) = 1000$ units for item 1.

1. What probability of stockout would be appropriate for each item using the one-location formula given in equation (1)?
2. Using equation (2), $k = 2.0$ [for both items, in spite of the answer to Review Problem 1] and $a = 0.5$ (so that $D^{0.5} = \sqrt{D}$ is used), how much safety stock is needed for each item if safety stock is held at the retail outlets? At the DC?
3. Why might the firm not centralize all safety stock for all items?

Solutions

1. Probability of stockout $= \dfrac{C_I}{C_B} \dfrac{1}{\text{orders per year}}$, which is $(\frac{1}{10})(\frac{1}{1}) = 0.1$ for item 1 and $(\frac{1}{10})(\frac{1}{10}) = 0.01$ for item 2.
2. At each retail store, safety stock $= kD^a = (2)(D)^{0.5}$. This is $2(10)^{0.5} = 6.32$ for item 1 and $2(1000)^{0.5} = 63.2$ for item 2. The total at all 100 retail units will be $100(6.32) = 632$ for item 1 and $100(63.2) = 6320$ for item 2.

   If safety stock is held at the DC only, D will be 100 times as large. Then we obtain $2(1000)^{0.5} = 63.2$ for item 1 and $2(100,000)^{0.5} = 632$ for item 2. As we can see, the total safety stock is reduced significantly. (It is reduced by a factor of $\sqrt{1/100} = 1/10$.)
3. It may be unacceptable to depend on the DC for safety stocks. By the time the stock arrives, it may be too late. Locating stock in a multiechelon setting requires a trade-off between reducing inventory by centralizing stock and providing fast service for the customer, to avoid loss of sales.

13-4 *TRADE-OFF ANALYSIS FOR INVENTORY MANAGEMENT*

Trade-Off Curves

In Chapter 2 we derived a trade-off curve for Farm Supply Corporation, computed in Table 2-3 and shown in Figure 2-2. Figure 2-2 is reproduced below as Figure 13-3. This curve shows that management can buy total protection against unfilled demands, for the one item represented, by investing in 20 units of inventory, 7 more than expected demand. This may be too expensive when all the items (5000 or more SKUs) are considered. In fact, in a one-location system, in order to properly make the trade-off, a curve that represents the total number of unfilled demands versus total inventory is necessary.

 With this type of information, a manager can make a decision as to how many millions of dollars to invest in inventory in the entire system. In a one-location system, we can obtain a trade-off curve as discussed below.

 The optimal number of unfilled demands or backorders to allow depends crucially on C_B, the cost associated with each unit of shortage. (A *backorder* is an *unfilled demand* that will be filled, but later than desired. In many multiechelon inventory systems, all unfilled demands are backordered. We will use both terms in our discussion.) Because this cost is difficult to specify, we are going to try a range of C_B values. If backorders are thought to be equally costly for all items, we proceed to try the range of values with no adjustment. If some backorders are worse than others, an importance index can be assigned to each item so that its backorder cost is C_B, $2C_B$, $3C_B$, or some other value. Alternatively, we might estimate all costs of a backorder except ill-will cost, so that C_B = other costs + ill-will cost. Then ill-will cost could be varied over a range.

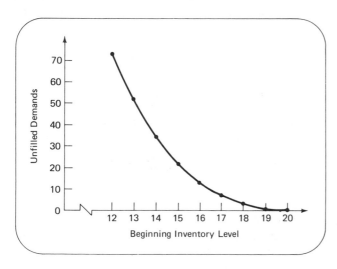

Figure 13-3 Pictorial representation of inventory versus out-of-stock trade-offs for one item.

Once a range of C_B values has been determined, we use equation (12) in Chapter 10 to determine the average number of times there is a stockout per year for each item. We use equations (13) and (14), Chapter 10, to determine R^* (the reorder level) for each item. Total inventory is estimated as $Q^*/2 + R^* - \overline{U}$, where Q^* is the order quantity and $\overline{U}$ is the expected lead-time demand. Then we have, for each item, the number of stockouts and the average inventory. This is summed over all the items. Then we start all over with a new C_B value, and each repetition gives one more point to be plotted on the trade-off curve.

Before doing an example, two points must be made. First, in our example, for reasons of simplicity, we will use stockout incidents per year as the service measure. As mentioned above, stockouts per year is not the same as backorders per year. Each stockout occurrence may lead to several unsatisfied requests which remain backordered until the stock is replenished. The second major point is that a sample of a few hundred items can be used to adequately represent up to 50,000 items. Items are chosen to represent different demand and cost situations. This sampling procedure saves thousands of computations. To predict total performance, the stockouts and inventory for each item are multiplied by the number of similar items.

As an example, suppose that we use only two products to represent a total inventory system. (The small number of items is used so that we can report the arithmetic in a limited space. A much larger sample would be used in practice.) Item 1 has a demand rate of 10,000 per year and is similar to 500 products. Item 2 has a demand rate of 100 per year and is similar to 5000 products. Both items have a value of $5 per unit, $C_I = \$1$ per year, $C_T = \$50$, lead time is equal to $\frac{1}{4}$ year, and the standard deviation of demand is equal to the square root of expected demand, over any period of time. The items have normally distributed demand. (See Appendix D for the table of the normal distribution.) Calculations are given below, using formulas discussed in Chapter 10 and using $C_B = \$10$ as the initial value.

Item	Q* Value	Choose R* Such That:
1	$Q^* = \sqrt{\dfrac{2(10,000)(50)}{1}}$ $= 1000$	Probability of stockout $= \dfrac{QC_I}{C_B D} = 0.01$ so $z = 2.32$ (see Table 2, Appendix D) in the $\overline{U} + z\sigma = R^*$ formula.
2	$Q^* = \sqrt{\dfrac{2(100)(50)}{1}}$ $= 100$	Probability of stockout $= \dfrac{QC_I}{C_B D} = 0.10$ so $z = 1.28$.

During the lead time, expected demand is one-fourth of annual demand, which is 2500 and 25, respectively. The standard deviation of lead time demand is $\sqrt{2500} = 50$ and $\sqrt{25} = 5$, respectively. This results in:

Item	R^*
1	$R^* = \overline{U} + z\sigma = 2500 + (2.32)(50) = 2616$
2	$R^* = \overline{U} + z\sigma = 25 + (1.28)(5) = 31.4 \approx 31$

The number of stockouts per year is, at the optimal values, $C_I/C_B = 0.1$ for both items. Finally, we can compute the values of total inventory and number of stockouts per year.

Item	Inventory (Units)	Stockouts/Year	ADJUSTED FOR NUMBER OF ITEMS REPRESENTED	
			Dollars in Inventory	Stockouts/Year
1	$\dfrac{Q^*}{2} + R^* - \overline{U} = 616$	0.1	($5)(500)(616) = \$1,540,000$	$500(0.1) = 50$
2	$\dfrac{Q^*}{2} + R^* - \overline{U} = 56$	0.1	$(5)(5000)(56) = \$1,400,000$	$5000(0.1) = 500$
			$\$2,940,000$	550

This one point on the trade-off curve is shown in Figure 13-4 as part of the entire trade-off curve, with several other points indicated as well. Each C_B value leads to one more point, using the same calculations as the example just completed. The Review Problem below asks you to verify one of the points on the trade-off curve, and the next section discusses trade-off curves for multiechelon inventory systems.

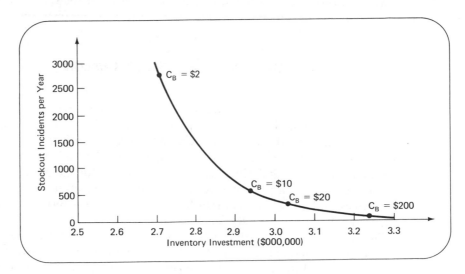

Figure 13-4 Trade-off curve.

Review Problem

Using $C_B = 2$, find the exact value of inventory investment and stockouts shown in Figure 13-4.

Solution

When C_B is changed, Q^* values are unchanged. We should choose R^* so that the probability of a stockout is $(QC_I/C_BD) = [1000(1)/2(10,000)] = 0.05$ for item 1 ($z = 1.65$) and $[100(1)/2(100)] = 0.50$ for item 2 ($z = 0$). Then $R^* = 2500 + 1.65(50) = 2582.5 \approx 2582$ for item 1 and $R^* = 25 + 0(5) = 25$ for item 2.

The optimal number of stockouts per year is $C_I/C_B = 0.5$ for both items. Then:

| | | | ADJUSTED FOR NUMBER OF ITEMS REPRESENTED | |
Item	Inventory (Units)	Stockouts/Year	Dollars in Inventory	Stockouts/Year
1	$\frac{Q^*}{2} + R^* - \overline{U} = 582$	0.5	(5)(500)(582) = \$1,455,000	(0.5)(500) = 250
2	$\frac{Q^*}{2} + R^* - \overline{U} = 50$	0.5	(5)(5000)(50) = \$1,250,000	(0.5)(5000) = 2500
			\$2,705,000	2750

Therefore, the point labeled $C_B = \$2$ has an inventory of \$2,705,000 and 2750 stockouts per year. Other points on the curve include (\$3,022,500 with 275) for $C_B = \$20$ and (\$3,237,500 with 27.5) for $C_B = \$200$.

13-5 RESEARCH ON TRADE-OFF CURVES FOR MULTIECHELON SYSTEMS

In a multiechelon system, pipeline inventory is largely determined by the length of the order cycle and the replenishment cycle. Lot-size inventory may or may not be determined by the use of an economic order quantity. In fact, in many systems, most orders are for 1 unit at a time, and they are used to replenish inventory after each sale. (In a spare-parts system, for example, demand for many of the parts is low, and a replenishment occurs after each.) Assuming that pipelines and lot-size inventories have already been determined, we are left with a trade-off between safety stock and backorders.

This problem can be formulated using a technique called the *method of Lagrange multipliers*. There is an objective of minimizing a time-weighted back-order measure, and there is a single budget constraint on total system inventory. The trade-off curve is generated by trying different levels of the budget constraint.

minimize: time-weighted backorders at the bottom level   (3)

subject to: $\displaystyle\sum_{i=1}^{n}\sum_{j=0}^{m}$ (cost of item i)(stock level at location j)   (4)

$\leq$ budget constraint

The zeroth location ($j = 0$) refers to a distribution center, so two levels are considered simultaneously. The formulation uses one DC with m retail stores. Each DC and the stores that report to it are treated as an independent system. The system described by (3) and (4) and an application are discussed by Muckstadt and Thomas (1980). (A Lagrange multiplier method is necessary because it allows us to solve separately for each item. This greatly reduces the computational task.)

The foregoing type of approach, simultaneously considering both levels, extends the logic of the dual distribution system. Very low demand/high cost items will be centralized at the DC. Service levels will be very high at the retail level for high demand/low cost items. However, the mathematical approach will analytically divide the items into these groups, whereas guesses will frequently be in error. (The Review Problems at the end of this section will give you a chance to try your hand at guessing.)

To illustrate the importance of using a multiechelon approach (either based on managerial judgment or a mathematical method in a multiechelon setting) we will reproduce a pair of trade-off curves from an actual inventory system, given in Muckstadt and Thomas (1980). The system studied was a spare-parts supply system with low demand for most items. Thus all orders placed were for 1 unit; an order was placed each time a demand occurred. This is reasonable in a system with low demand and low ordering cost.

In addition to the multiechelon approach of equations (3) and (4), a single-echelon approach was tried for comparison. Each level (retail and DC) was examined separately. Several different service levels were used for each of the two levels of the system. Retail service levels of 60, 75, 85, and 95% were coupled with DC level service levels of 50, 60, 75, 85, and 95%, for a total of 20 combinations. The service levels were averages, and individual item service levels were optimally chosen to minimize total investment at that level. This method, however, does not take advantage of the multiechelon structure of the system.

The service-level objective was stated in terms of backorder days per demand. Thus an 0.50 value implied that on the average, each item demanded had to wait for 0.50 day. (Of course, most items waited for zero days and some waited much longer.) The trade-off curve given in Muckstadt and Thomas (1980) is given in modified form here as Figure 13-5. The higher of the two lines represents the best we can do using the single-echelon approach.

The savings from using a multiechelon approach are huge. At any level of backorder days (the service-level measure) the single-echelon approach requires

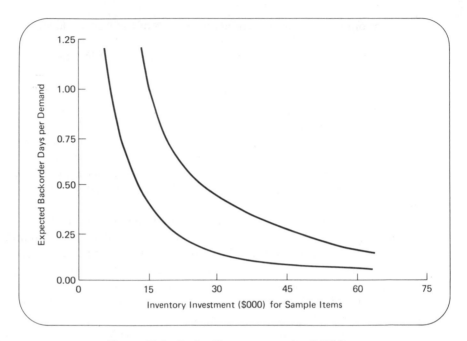

Figure 13-5   Trade-off curves—sample of 418 items.

about *twice as much* inventory investment. For example, there is a saving of from $31,000 to $15,000 while maintaining average backorder days of 0.4.

Part of the saving could be achieved by modifying single-location methods as discussed previously. To illustrate this, consider Table 13-2, which contains data on eight items. The Review Problems ask you to test your ability to predict the items that will be centralized.

There are many other models that can effectively manage complex inventory systems. For example, Nahmias (1981) reviews the large body of research on repairable items (such as jet engines). Hausman and Scudder (1982) examine the major effect that maintenance scheduling has on such systems. Finally, the collection edited by Schwarz (1981) contains many good articles and an extensive list of references.

Review Problems

At one budget level, the optimal solution centralized three of the eight items described in Table 13-2. It carried 1 unit of one item at each of the 15 locations in the retail level and 3 units of another at each location in the retail level. The other three items had stock levels of 2 at the retail level. (In preparation for answering the problems, you may wish to compute the expected lead-time demand for each item. You will note that expected demand is low.)

TABLE 13-2 COST AND DEMAND DATA FOR SAMPLE ITEMS

Item	Average Retail Level Daily Demand Rate	Unit Cost	Order Cycle Time (Days)	Notes
1	0.04077	$ 69.85	41	Highest unit demand
2	0.00380	1.10	41	Low unit demand, lowest cost
3	0.00787	9.88	41	Low unit demand, medium cost
4	0.03289	5.32	41	High unit demand, low cost
5	0.00207	78.24	41	Low unit demand, high cost
6	0.03409	1376.00	41	High unit demand, highest cost
7	0.02622	15.30	41	High unit demand, medium cost
8	0.00198	34.24	41	Lowest unit demand

1. Which three items do you think were centralized? Why?
2. Which item do you think had the retail stock level of 3? Why?

Solutions

The expected lead-time demands are found by multiplying the order cycle time of 41 days by the daily demand rate. The results are 1.67, 0.16, 0.32, 1.35, 0.08, 1.40, 1.07, and 0.08.

1. Items 5, 6, and 8 are centralized. Items 5 and 8 are the lowest two unit demands, and item 6 is so expensive that the investment in retail inventory is not warranted. Even though demand is low for item 3, its relatively low cost makes the investment for 1 unit at each store worthwhile.

2. Item 4 has 3 units at the retail level. It is not the item with the highest demand, but it does have high demand and relatively low cost. From these examples we see that unit demand is a good place to start in determining which items to centralize. After that, a high cost makes us want to centralize.

13-6 Summary

There are many kinds of inventories: lot-size, safety, work-in-process, seasonal, pipeline, and dead. Any of these can be important in a given situation, and, in fact, each constitutes the majority of the inventory investment in some systems. It is important to understand the different purposes served by each of these and how to approach the analysis of each one.

In multilocation inventory systems, pipeline inventories may be large. A trade-off exists between inventory investment and speed of order processing and of transportation.

The allocation of safety stock throughout a multiechelon multi-item system cannot be handled well using one-location methods. One-location methods will tend to have too much safety stock for some items and too little for some others. The upper echelon should be used to back up the bottom level, not duplicate its pattern of stocking. Some items, at least including items with very low demand and relatively high cost, should be centralized to gain the savings available. High demand items with relatively low cost should have excellent service at the bottom level; the service at the distribution center need not be as good. Some items should have fair service at the bottom level with good service at the upper echelon to provide backup.

Single-location methods can be modified, using the ideas in the preceding paragraph, to gain some of the advantage available to a multiechelon system. There are ways to mathematically optimize such systems, however, and the increased saving is often significant. The benefit from using a multiechelon approach instead of a straight single-echelon approach can be huge.

Finally, before any analysis is done, questions relating to policies and incentives must be answered. Inventory charges and rules for obsolescence can be used to encourage individual decisions that are good for the overall organization. The degree of centralization of authority (and the savings potential from viewing the overall system) must be balanced against the degree of autonomy that is desirable for individual profit-center managers. Service policy statements must be appropriate for the industry, and, if possible, trade-off analysis can be used in establishing those goals.

Multilocation distribution systems require sound managerial judgment, good system design, and detailed analysis that is often complex. The potential benefit is worth the effort.

PROBLEMS

*1. Define procurement cycle, replenishment cycle, and order cycle.

 2. Why does a reduction of transportation time lower pipeline inventory more than a reduction in order transmittal time?

*3. A firm that sells $1,000,000 per day of product is considering two proposals for reducing pipeline inventory. The retail-store level carries safety stock equal to three times the square root of lead-time demand, and the current lead time (the order cycle) is 14 days. The two proposals are to reduce transportation time by 2 days at an annual cost of $400,000 and/or to reduce order transmittal time by 2 days at a cost of $20,000. If they use $F_I = 0.25$ as a carrying-cost rate (including a 0.15 cost of capital), should they accept one, both, or neither of the proposals?

 4. Why would a firm have a multiechelon inventory system? Based on your

answer, characterize the type of firm for which a multiechelon system would perform best.

*5. Are the following statements true or false? Why?
   (a) F_I may vary dramatically from item to item.
   (b) An item's value (as used in making inventory decisions, for example) should not change as it moves through a multiechelon system.
   (c) Dead stock never has any value.

6. A firm is using a before-tax inventory-holding-cost rate of $F_I = 0.30$ per year, where the cost of capital is 0.12, the cost of obsolescence is 0.12, and the physical cost of storage is 0.06. The after-tax cost of capital is 0.072 per year. The tax rate is 0.48. (Note: $0.072 > 0.12 (0.48)$; see page 42.) One product is selling steadily at the low rate of 10 per month. They believe demand will continue at that rate for 10 years or more. They have 1500 units on hand in inventory and the unit cost is $1.
   (a) Their current policy, which applies uniformly to all items, is to declare obsolete any items that are in excess of 5 years' forecast of demand. Based only on economic considerations, evaluate the cost of holding one item for 5 years (ignoring sunk costs) and compare that to the cost of scrapping the item and rebuilding it in 5 years. Use an after-tax analysis. Remember that if they keep the item, there is a tax benefit at the time of sale.
   (b) Again based only on economic considerations, and ignoring the five-year rule, how many should they throw away? Either use trial and error to find (approximately) the time at which the two cost formulas are equal or derive a formula to give the answer.

*7. Are the following statements true or false? Why?
   (a) Centralizing inventories for all low-demand items is always appropriate.
   (b) Centralizing responsibilities for all distribution system functions will always be financially beneficial to a firm, even though some managers may not like it.

8. (a) In a multiechelon inventory system with many items, why should some items be carried only at the levels above the retail level?
   (b) If a high-demand item has a high level of service at the retail level, should the upper levels have zero inventory for that item? Why or why not?
   (c) What do parts (a) and (b) have to do with using a time-weighted objective function?

*9. A firm has a DC that supports 70 retail outlets. One product has $C_I = \$0.42$ per year and $C_B = \$2.55$, and it is ordered once per month. The annual demand at each retail store is 1200 units, and lead time is 1 month for orders placed by retailers and 2 months when the DC places an order.
   (a) What probability of stockout would be appropriate at the retail outlets, using equation (1)?

(b) Given your answer to part (a), if demand is normally distributed, what k factor would be appropriate for use in equation (2)?

(c) If $a = 0.7$ in equation (2), how much safety stock is needed if the item is carried at each retail store? If the item is carried only at the DC? Use the k factor calculated in part (b) for both situations.

10. The Review Problem at the end of Section 13-3 asks you to use $k = 2.0$ "in spite of the answer to Review Problem 1."

(a) What k factor is appropriate, assuming that the demand is normally distributed and using the probabilities of stockout, calculated to be 0.1 and 0.01?

(b) Using the new k factors (for both the retail outlets and the DC), compute the inventory reduction that would occur if each item is centralized at the DC.

*11. The Review Problem at the end of Section 13-4 calculates one point on a trade-off curve, the point corresponding to $C_B = \$2$. The point for $C_B = \$10$ is calculated in the text of the section. Values are given in the solution to the Review Problem for $C_B = \$20$ and $C_B = \$200$. Verify those two points. For a stockout probability of 0.0005, $z = 3.29$ is used.

12. How might a trade-off curve involving F_I and inventory investment be constructed? What complications might arise?

13. A manufacturing firm is using three products to represent their total investment—an A item, a B item, and a C item. All three items have a unit value of $10, $C_I = \$2.50$ per year, $C_T = \$40$, a lead time of 1 month, and a standard deviation of lead-time demand equal to the square root of expected lead-time demand. The three demand rates are 2000, 300, and 2 per month, and the items are representative of 40, 200, and 5000 items, respectively. Assume that demand is normally distributed.

(a) Try $C_B = \$10, \$40$, and $200, and plot a trade-off curve similar to Figure 13-4.

(b) If they currently use $C_B = \$10$, what one-sentence information might you give them regarding a reduction in the number of stockouts?

*14. **(a)** Describe the type of item that is most appropriate for having centralized stocking in a multiechelon inventory system.

(b) What trade-offs are involved in the decision to centralize an item's inventory? That is, what is gained and lost in centralizing the inventory?

15. (This problem is only intended for students who have an understanding of the method of Lagrange multipliers.) Describe how equations (3) and (4) would be solved using a Lagrange multiplier. Why would the problem be separable by item for each Lagrange multiplier value (λ), and what would be the interpretation of the λ value that causes all the budget to be used?

*16. A one-product firm is considering consolidating its three regional DCs into one. They have calculated that by paying $400,000 more for faster transportation, they would be able to provide the same service to customers, if they keep the same probability of stockout as before.

Their lead time to either the regional DCs or the consolidated DC is one month. The means and standard deviations of monthly demand are as follows (figures are in millions of dollars):

	Mean	Standard Deviation
DC1	2.0	0.5
DC2	3.0	0.6
DC3	4.0	0.7

If the demands are independent, the sum of the means and variances will equal the mean demand and variance for the new DC. Thus we can find

$$\sigma_{1+2+3} = \sqrt{\sigma_1^2 + \sigma_2^2 + \sigma_3^2} = 1.05 \text{ (million dollars)}$$

(a) The firm was keeping two standard deviations of demand as safety stock, and they would do the same in a centralized DC. How much safety stock can they save by centralizing?

(b) Is the inventory saving sufficient to justify the additional transportation cost if the carrying-cost rate of inventory is 0.20?

(c) If the demands at the three regional DCs were positively correlated, might that change the answer to part (b)? Why or why not?

REFERENCES

BEMAN, L., "A Big Payoff from Inventory Controls." *Fortune,* July 27, 1981.

BIERMAN, H., T. DYCKMAN, AND R. SWIERINGA, *Managerial Cost Accounting,* 3rd ed. New York: Macmillan, 1986.

EHRHARDT, R. A., C. R. SCHULTZ, AND H. M. WAGNER, "(*s, S*) Policies for a Wholesale Inventory System," in *Multi-level Production/Inventory Control Systems: Theory and Practice,* L. Schwarz, ed. New York: North-Holland, 1981.

EPPEN, G., AND L. SCHRAGE, "Centralized Ordering Policies in a Multi-warehouse System with Lead Times and Random Demand," in *Multi-level Production/Inventory Control Systems: Theory and Practice,* L. Schwarz, ed. New York: North-Holland, 1981.

FEDERGRUEN, A., AND P. ZIPKEN, "Approximations of Dynamic, Multilocation Production and Inventory Problems." *Management Science,* Vol. 30, No. 1 (January 1984).

GROSS, D., C. E. PINKUS, AND R. M. SOLAND, "Designing a Multi-product, Multi-echelon Inventory System," in *Multi-level Production/Inventory Control Systems: Theory and Practice,* L. Schwarz, ed. New York: North-Holland, 1981.

HARRISON, H., AND D. WILLS, "Product Assembly and Distribution Optimization in an Agribusiness Cooperative." *Interfaces,* Vol. 13, No. 2 (April 1983).

HAUSMAN, W., AND G. SCUDDER, "Priority Scheduling Rules for Repairable Inventory Systems." *Management Science,* Vol. 28, No. 11 (November 1982).

HESKETT, J., N. GLASKOWSKY, AND R. IVIE, *Business Logistics,* 2nd ed. New York: Ronald Press, 1973.

LALONDE, B., AND P. ZINSZER, *Customer Service: Meaning and Measurement.* Chicago: National Council of Physical Distribution Management, 1976.

LAMBERT, D., AND J. STOCK, *Strategic Physical Distribution Management.* Homewood, Ill.: Richard D. Irwin, 1982.

LESSER, W., AND V. ROLLER, "Explaining Productivity Differences in Grocery Warehouses," in *Productivity and Efficiency in Distribution Systems,* D. Gautschi, ed. New York: North-Holland, 1983.

MAGEE, J., *Industrial Logistics.* New York: McGraw-Hill, 1968.

MUCKSTADT, J., AND L. J. THOMAS, "Are Multi-echelon Inventory Methods Worth Implementing in Systems with Low Demand-Rate Items?" *Management Science,* Vol. 26, No. 5 (May 1980).

MUCKSTADT, J., AND L. J. THOMAS, "Improving Inventory Productivity in Multilevel Distribution Systems," in *Productivity and Efficiency in Distribution Systems,* D. Gautschi, ed. New York: North-Holland, 1983.

NAHMIAS, S., "Managing Reparable Item Inventory Systems: A Review," in *Multi-level Production/Inventory Control Systems: Theory and Practice,* L. Schwarz, ed. New York: North-Holland, 1981.

SCHWARZ, L., ed., *Multi-level Production/Inventory Control Systems: Theory and Practice.* New York: North-Holland, 1981.

SCHWARZ, L., B. DEUERMEYER, AND R. BADINELLI, "Fill-Rate Optimization in a One-Warehouse N-Identical Retailer Distribution System." *Management Science,* forthcoming (1984).

WILLIAMS, J., "A Hybrid Algorithm for Simultaneous Scheduling of Production and Distribution in Multi-echelon Structures." *Management Science,* vol. 29, No. 1 (January 1983).

CHAPTER 14

Scheduling Personnel and Service Systems

One of the unique characteristics of the service industry is the immediacy of demand. The service is produced when both consumer and provider are present. This gives rise to many problems of coordination, particularly when more than one customer (e.g., the automobile and its owner) or more than one provider (e.g., a general mechanic and an automatic transmission specialist) are involved. The first two sections of this chapter focus separately on the provider and the consumer. The third section deals with examples where these two elements are integrated.

Personnel scheduling systems require a recognition of patterns of future work requirements. Alternative methods of meeting these requirements are evaluated according to how well they meet the needs of the workers and the consumers. In addition, the predictions of demand are never perfect, so devices such as a float pool of personnel are included to allow for last-minute changes. These are the topics of Section 14-1.

Consumer scheduling is often accomplished through an appointment system. Section 14-2 introduces the principles of design for simple appointment systems and follows this with two complex examples (passenger reservations and hotel/hospital scheduling). Selecting school bus or delivery van routes requires that the timing of both the producer and consumer be in the control of management. This and other examples are discussed in Section 14-3.

14-1 PERSONNEL SCHEDULING SYSTEMS

Intermediate-range plans provide an overall guide for personnel scheduling. As described in Chapter 9, these plans use forecasts prepared for many months in the future, and account for predictable rises and falls in the requirements. For example, Lamont (1975) shows how this kind of reasoning applies to nurse staffing, making use of slack periods to schedule both vacations and maintenance of hospital units.

Converting forecasts into staffing levels is a tricky business. There are often many types of staff that have overlapping capabilities, so there is some degree of substitutability. There is also a problem of disaggregating the forecasts. For example, in nurse scheduling a forecast of the total number of patients in a hospital must be separated according to type of patient and severity of need for nursing time.

This requirement for detail makes accurate forecasting difficult except in the short range. Therefore, personnel planning is often done in three stages— annual budgeting, schedule planning (several weeks in advance), and daily assignment. The annual plan is made on an aggregate basis (as described above), whereas the schedules are developed for individual workers or groups of workers, and based on more up-to-date forecasts. Last-minute adjustments are made on a daily basis, in order to meet needs created by unplanned absences and variations from the forecasted requirements.

Several methods are in common use for daily adjustments, including a *float pool* (a group of people who work where and when they are needed), *call-in personnel* (part timers who are available at short notice), *overtime,* and *reassignment* of regular staff to balance the work load. Examples include part-time bank tellers (Maebert and Raedels, 1977) and float nurses (Trivedi, 1976).

Adjusting personnel assignments on short notice is not desirable for several reasons: part time, float, or transfer personnel may not be as well qualified as regular staff; the time and effort required to accomplish a major rebalancing of workers can be substantial; constant, large-scale reshuffling of personnel can be upsetting to the work situation, particularly in a setting such as a hospital, where continuity of care is important. Therefore, it is important to achieve a good staffing assignment through careful budgeting and scheduling, so that daily reassignment is kept to a minimum.

A systematic approach is needed to tie together the three stages (budgeting, scheduling, daily assignment). Kelley and McKenna (1976) describe an integrated nurse staffing system, which includes the required data-gathering elements for forecasting, scheduling, and daily assignment. One important aspect of the system is daily projection of the level of work required in each unit of the hospital. This is accomplished through an evaluation and classification of the patients into four types, according to the intensity of care required. These requirements are converted to nurse staffing levels through a set of standards, expressed as a table. The system is designed to call attention to variances between the planned and actual staffing levels, an important element of any management control system.

The remainder of this section concentrates on personnel scheduling methods. This is a vital issue in personnel planning, since it is the means whereby the budget decisions are implemented, and its adequacy determines whether elaborate or simple methods will be used for last-minute personnel changes. We will begin by describing methods for scheduling a single work shift, and then discuss the situation when there is more than one shift per day.

Sundays Off

Detailed scheduling of personnel has two basic objectives: provide an adequate work force to meet daily operating requirements; and provide suitable recreation clusters (days off) for the personnel. For example, the New York City Sanitationworkers (Beltrami, 1977, Chap. 2) all have Sunday off, and must average 2 days off per week. The garbage load on Monday is therefore much heavier than average, and more work crews would ideally be operating on Monday than on other days. However, for 40 years, the crews were divided equally among six different recreation clusters, which are shown in Table 14-1. These assignments were rotated each week, so a crew would have Sunday–Monday off one week, then Sunday–Tuesday off the following week, and so on. This rotating schedule repeats itself every 6 weeks, and does not allow a heavier work schedule on Monday.

TABLE 14-1   SIX-WEEK ROTATING SCHEDULE OF DAYS OFF

Week	Mon.	Tue.	Wed.	Thu.	Fri.	Sat.	Sun.
1	×						×
2		×					×
3			×				×
4				×			×
5					×		×
6						×	×

One solution is to have enough workers in each of the six work groups to meet Monday's load, and let the other days be easy days. Such overstaffing would be quite expensive. Instead, one could allow part of the garbage to remain uncollected for several days, an unsavory solution, indeed! A third solution is to divide the work crews into smaller groups. This would result in a larger number of groups (compared to six at present), but the manager could assign fewer groups to the Sunday–Monday days-off pair.

Table 14-2 gives a possible schedule for 30 work groups. Each group follows the same cycle (rotation), but group 1 begins with the week 1 schedule, group 2 begins with the week 2 schedule, and so on. The bottom row of Table 14-2 shows that Monday occurs as a day off only twice in the cycle, so the average number of crews not working on Monday is 2/30 = 6.7% of the work force. In contrast, 7/30 = 23.3% of the work force is off on Saturday.

In this example, the solution to the problem came through modifying a 40-

TABLE 14-2 THIRTY-WEEK ROTATING SCHEDULE OF DAYS OFF

Weeks	Mon.	Tue.	Wed.	Thu.	Fri.	Sat.	Sun.
1–2	×						×
3–5		×					×
6–9			×				×
10–16				×			×
17–23					×		×
24–30						×	×
Total days off:	2	3	4	7	7	7	30

year-old idea by dividing the work force into smaller groups, but utilizing the familiar days-off pairs. This can be formulated as a linear programming problem, which allows inclusion of any desired set of recreation clusters, including 3-day weekends, for example. See Beltrami (1977) for a discussion of how this was done in the Sanitationworkers example.

Days-Off Pairs

Telephone exchanges, airline reservation systems, and hospitals are staffed at all times. This rules out a schedule where everyone has the same day off. Another approach is to form schedules based on "days-off pairs" so that everyone has two nonworking days per week. Table 14-3 shows all such schedules for which days off are consecutive. The advantage of these schedules is that employees would have two uninterrupted days away from work, even though they may not coincide with a normal weekend.

TABLE 14-3 CONSECUTIVE-DAYS-OFF SCHEDULES

Schedule	Mon.	Tue.	Wed.	Thu.	Fri.	Sat.	Sun.
1	×	×					
2		×	×				
3			×	×			
4				×	×		
5					×	×	
6						×	×
7	×						×

One way to determine work schedules is to use linear programming (LP), a mathematical method described in Appendix C. Rothstein (1973) gave an example of scheduling hospital personnel. His approach assumes that the number of full-time workers N is already known, and that forecasts of work load have been prepared and converted into daily personnel requirements, R_k. The difference $N - R_k$ then represents the number of workers who can have a day off on day

k. That is,

$$N = \text{number of available full time personnel}$$

$$R_k = \text{number of personnel required on day } k$$

$$n_k = N - R_k = \text{number of days off available on day } k$$

If n_k is negative, this indicates that N workers is insufficient on day k so either N must be increased, or part-time or overtime help must be used to decrease R_k. R_k can also be made less than N by shifting some of the work assignments from day k to another day.

The available days off must be numerous enough so that each of the N employees can have at least two. If the seven different n_k values sum to less than $2N$, then again either N must be increased or R_k decreased. (Reassigning work among days will not help in this case.

Once these decisions have been made, an LP can be formulated to schedule the work force. However, because the pattern of requirements varies over the week, it may not be possible to assign consecutive days off to everyone. Hence two kinds of variables are needed:

$$x_k = \text{number of personnel assigned to the } k\text{th day-off}$$
$$\text{schedule in Table 14-3}$$

$$u_k = \text{number of personnel assigned to an unpaired}$$
$$\text{(nonconsecutive) day off on day } k$$

There are three kinds of constraints needed. The first is

$$x_1 + x_2 + u_2 \leqslant n_2$$

$$x_2 + x_3 + u_3 \leqslant n_3$$

$$\vdots \tag{1}$$

$$x_6 + x_7 + u_7 \leqslant n_7$$

$$x_7 + x_1 + u_1 \leqslant n_1$$

In English, the first constraint in (1) focuses on Tuesday, day 2, since x_1 represents Monday–Tuesday off, x_2 represents Tuesday–Wednesday off, and u_2 represents unpaired Tuesdays off. Thus the constraint assures that the Tuesday work requirements are met by assigning no more than n_2 Tuesday days off.

Constraint (2) makes sure that there are enough days off—two per worker:

$$\sum_{k=1}^{7} 2x_k + u_k \geqslant 2N \tag{2}$$

The third type of constraint is more complicated:

$$u_1 \leqslant \quad u_2 + u_3 + u_4 + u_5 + u_6 + u_7$$

$$u_2 \leqslant u_1 \quad + u_3 + u_4 + u_5 + u_6 + u_7 \tag{3}$$

$$\vdots$$

$$u_7 \leqslant u_1 + u_2 + u_3 + u_4 + u_5 + u_6$$

The first constraint in (3) guarantees that unpaired Mondays off, u_1, are not too numerous. We have to give everyone 2 days off, and if Monday had more unpaired days than the rest of the week combined, someone would require 2 days off on Monday, which is impossible.

Objectives   Several are possible. The manager must choose one that is appropriate for the situation at hand. Two examples are

$$\max \sum_{i=1}^{7} x_i \qquad \text{(maximize consecutive days off)} \qquad (4)$$

$$\max x_5 + x_6 + x_7 \quad \text{(maximize consecutive days off which involve Saturday or Sunday)} \qquad (5)$$

Table 14-4 summarizes the solution to Rothstein's example, which was for the 31-person trash removal crew in a hospital, using objective function (5). The left section shows the uneven daily availability of days off. The center section shows the optimal solution, and the right section summarizes how this solution meets the requirements. Thus the LP recommends use of only 4 of the consecutive-days-off schedules, with one worker having Tuesday–Wednesday (i.e., $x_2 = 1$), 8 having Friday–Saturday, and so on. On Wednesday, there are $u_3 = 9$ unpaired days off, compared to 8 on Friday and 1 on Saturday. Therefore, eight workers have Wednesday and Friday off, and one will get Wednesday and Saturday.

In order to use an LP such as equations (1) to (4), a manager must supply three things: a set of feasible work schedules, such as Tables 14-1 or 14-3, commensurate with the number of work groups; an objective such as equation (4) or (5); and the allowable numbers of days off. In return the LP delivers two things: a feasible assignment of days off, and shadow prices (see Appendix C) to evaluate possible changes in the work requirements. For example, the shadow price associated with constraint (1) would tell the manager how much the objective function would change if management were to alter n_2 (available Tuesday days

TABLE 14-4   DAYS OFF FOR HOSPITAL TRASH REMOVAL WORKERS

INPUT DATA		OPTIMAL SOLUTION			DAYS OFF SCHEDULE		
Day	Available Days Off	k	x_k	u_k	Day	Unpaired	Paired
MO	12	1	0	0	MO	0	$12 = x_7 + x_1$
TU	1	2	1	0	TU	0	$1 = x_1 + x_2$
WE	10	3	0	9	WE	9	$1 = x_2 + x_3$
TH	0	4	0	0	TH	0	$0 = x_3 + x_4$
FR	16	5	8	8	FR	8	$8 = x_4 + x_5$
SA	10	6	1	1	SA	1	$9 = x_5 + x_6$
SU	13	7	12	0	SU	0	$13 = x_6 + x_7$

off) by adding or deleting part-time personnel. This would change the utilization of the full-time personnel, and must therefore be done as a part of overall employment planning.

Additional constraints might be imposed on the LP. For example, if it is desired to have at least 8 Saturday–Sunday days off pairs, the constraint $x_6 \geq 8$ could be included in the formulation.

There is usually no guarantee that an LP will yield a whole number (integer) solution. However, Rothstein's (1973) formulation has been shown to always result in an integral solution, so that management need not concern itself with methods for rounding off the answers. Wagner (1975, Chap. 6) describes another employment scheduling program which also has this integer property, and explains an integrality theorem that applies to many similar problems.

Implementing Personnel Scheduling Systems

Other examples of personnel scheduling applications include check encoders in banks (Davis and Reutzel, 1981 and Krajcwski et al., 1980), telephone operators for betting (Wilson and Willis, 1983), bank tellers including part-time staff (Maebert and Raedels, 1977), and telephone traffic exchange operators (Henderson and Berry, 1977). Each of these is based on a formulation similar to the LP described earlier. First, the personnel requirements are forecast. Then a list of schedules is prepared (similar to Table 14-3, but usually far more numerous). Variables x_k are defined to be the number of employees assigned to schedule k, and constraints are formulated so that the solution will satisfy work requirements and policies. Finally, some method is employed to choose integer values for the x_k variables. Heuristics are often employed to allow manual assignments or to speed up computer solution.

How does one determine which person is given which day-off schedule? The Sanitationworkers followed a rotating schedule, so that everyone had the same number of Saturday–Sunday pairs, in the long run. However, it may not be desirable to have such an equal allocation. Some people may have different preferences than others, and therefore unequal assignments may make all parties more satisfied. Arthur and Ravindran (1981) and Miller et al. (1976) describe nurse scheduling procedures that allow the nurses to express preferences for different work schedules, and allocate work assignments in a way that equalizes the nurses' satisfaction in the long run. One method is to construct an *aversion index* for each nurse, which incorporates how well a nurse's schedules have matched his or her preferences in the past, so that a nurse who accepts a bad schedule actually builds up points toward a better schedule in the future.

Developing around-the-clock schedules is based on the same ideas as the LP we have explained earlier, but the number of alternatives and constraints is very much greater because of the need to deal with several classes of workers, several shifts per day, and rotation among shifts as well as choice of days off. The algorithms mentioned above are not linear programs. Instead, they are based on heuristics to find good feasible schedules and to choose the best combinations from a cost and worker-preference point of view.

Many service (and manufacturing) organizations operate on more than one shift per day. If each shift is staffed independently, then a three-shift operation could be scheduled with three LP's of the kind we have discussed. However, there are two other possibilities—shift rotation and overlapping shifts. In the case of shift rotation, each shift can be viewed as a separate "day," (so a seven-day week is viewed as 21 days) but care must be taken in designing work schedules, to avoid requiring a person to work two consecutive shifts with no rest. This can be accomplished by leaving such schedules out of the set of alternatives, much as we left out 3-day weekends in Table 14-3. The number of feasible schedules becomes very large when shift rotation is included, so it is important to choose very carefully which ones to include as alternatives to choose among.

Overlapping shifts are useful when the requirements vary according to a pattern over a 24-hour period. For example, the police reduce their staffing level some time during the night, but not necessarily at 5 P.M. Glover et al. (1984) describe a heuristic scheduling procedure that operates on a personal computer. This condenses about 8 hours of manual work into 20 minutes to develop weekly work schedules for 100 employees. The method allows for work requirements that vary within a day, overlapping shifts, breaks, lunch periods, requested days off, and limits on available part-time personnel. The automatic scheduler is described as a managerial robot because it actually replaces a manager, freeing him or her for more interesting work. A Review Problem shows the similarity between overlapping shifts and the consecutive-days-off problem.

Review Problems

1. The number of policemen needed varies according to the hour of the day. The requirements for one city are shown below.

	A.M.			P.M.		
Hour	2–6	6–10	10–2	2–6	6–10	10–2 A.M.
Staff required	10	40	30	35	15	20

   (a) Construct a table similar to Table 14-1 or 14-3, showing all possible 8-hour shifts, using × to denote time on duty (rather than days off, as in previous tables).

   (b) Write an equation that will assure that the requirements for the 6–10 A.M. interval are met.

2. In the hospital trash crew example, Table 14-4, each of 31 people are assigned days off. There are 8 Friday–Saturday pairs, 12 Sunday–Monday pairs, 8 Wednesday–Friday pairs, and one each of the pairs Tuesday–Wednesday, Wednesday–Saturday, and Saturday–Sunday. One possible

31-week rotating schedule is shown in the next table, and includes one 3-day weekend. The numbers in the body of the table indicate which of the 31 weeks a given day off corresponds to. For example, the first row has Wednesday and Saturday off as the week 1 pair, and Sunday off as the first part of the week 2 holiday.

(a) Find the 3-day weekend.

(b) Identify the work periods that are longer than 5 consecutive days.

(c) What kinds of difficulties might one have in trying to implement weeks 15 to 30?

THIRTY-ONE-WEEK ROTATING SCHEDULE

Week	Days Off	M	T	W	T	F	S	S
1	WS			1			1	2
2	SM	2						3
3	SM	3						4
4	SM	4						5
. . .				(Repeat SM until week 13)				
13	SM	13						
14	TW		14	14				
15	WF			15		15		
16	FS					16	16	
17	WF			17		17		
18	FS					18	18	
. . .				(Repeat WF–FS until week 30)				
29	WF			29		29		
30	FS					30	30	
31	SS						31	31

3. Each of the scheduling methods assumes that we know how many personnel are needed.

(a) Where would this information come from?

(b) What management tools are used to respond to errors in this information?

Solutions

1. (a)

Schedule	A.M.			P.M.		
	2–6	6–10	10–2	2–6	6–10	10–2 A.M.
1	×	×				
2		×	×			
3			×	×		
4				×	×	
5					×	×
6	×					×
	10	40	30	35	15	20

(b) The requirements for the 6–10 A.M. interval can be met through a combination of schedules 1 and 2, so we would write

$$x_1 + x_2 + u_2 = 40$$

in which u_2 represents the number of police who are called in for a split shift from 6 to 10 A.M.

2. (a) Saturday–Sunday–Monday at the end of the first week.

(b) Week 13 has 7 consecutive workdays beginning on Monday and ending with a day off the following Tuesday. There are 6-day work periods beginning on Thursday of week 14, and Saturday of 15, 17, 19, 21, . . . , 29, and Sunday of week 30. These are interspersed with short weeks, with split days off.

(c) This part of the schedule requires a change every week. This might be viewed as undesirable and confusing. This is all the more important because people rotate through the schedule individually rather than in groups like the New York Sanitationworkers. Can you imagine trying to arrange a car pool with this schedule?

3. (a) Careful forecasts of work requirements are used to prepare the work schedules.

(b) Float pools, call-in personnel, and reassignment of regular staff are three common tools.

14-2 SCHEDULING THE CONSUMER

There are many ways to mold the pattern of consumer demand to suit the availability of a service. Pricing and rationing are the most common. Rationing is often accomplished through an explicit system of appointments or reservations so that customers do not have to wait in line for service. Discounts are often used to attract consumers to times when excess service capacity is available. This section is primarily devoted to the reservation approach.

Appointment Systems

Appointment systems can be beneficial to both the consumer and the provider of a service. To be efficient, providers must not incur excessive idle time. Unfortunately, this often means that the consumer must accept a delay while waiting for service. Queuing theory models, such as the ones described in Appendix A, are sometimes useful in exploring the trade-off between consumer and provider delays. However, a well-designed appointment system has the capability of reducing delays for both parties or, alternatively, increasing the productivity of providers with no increase in consumer waiting times.

There are many variables that affect the design of an appointment system. A list of the most significant ones is shown in Table 14-5. Experimentation on alternative appointment systems has relied on both field trials and computer

TABLE 14-5 FACTORS IMPORTANT IN DESIGNING AN APPOINTMENT SYSTEM

Customer characteristics
  Punctuality of customers
  Cancellations
  No-shows (cancellation without notice)
  Walk-in rate (no appointment)
  Call-in rate (last-minute appointments)
  Categories of customers
  Priorities among categories
  Properties of arrival rate and service time (variation by time of day, day of
    week, customer category, etc.)
Provider characteristics
  Alternative providers
  Punctuality
  Service capabilities
  Need for breaks
  Need for consultation
  Absenteeism
System characteristics
  Number of services
  Appointment interval (every 15 minutes, for example)
  Appointment loading (how many customers are given the same appointment
    time?)
  Type of appointment (customer given a time and a server, or only a time and
    takes first available server)
  Priority system (who's next?)
  Follow-up visits
  Availability of facilities

---

simulation. Fortunately, the results are fairly easy to grasp and implement, although their development was a long and difficult task.

Behavioral characteristics of consumers and providers under different appointment systems is a crucial factor. For example, Rockart and Hofmann (1969) report that both physicians and patients act more responsibly (more punctual, fewer no-shows) when the appointment system is more personal (customer given definite appointment time, or customer assigned a particular server rather than first available). This is particularly significant because many researchers have found that punctuality and no-show rate have a very significant influence on the effectiveness of an appointment system (Fetter and Thompson, 1966).

The United Hospital Fund of New York (1967) recommended a six-step procedure for designing an appointment system.

1. *Establish the appointment interval.* This is based on the average time spent by the server on each consumer, including all matters directly connected with the service being provided, but excluding coffee breaks and the like. Be sure to allow for follow-up visits occurring later in the same day.

2. *Make allowance for nonarrivals.* Calculate an average percentage of cancellations and no-shows, and overbook to allow for this. Strongly consider overbooking the first appointment of the day, since without this redundancy, a no-show or late arrival at this time is guaranteed to leave a server idle.

3. *Establish the number of appointment slots per day.* From the number of server-hours per day, deduct time for breaks and other interruptions, and deduct an estimated amount of time (if any) to be devoted to walk-in customers (those without appointments). Divide the remaining time by the chosen appointment interval to establish how many appointments to make.

4. *Make appointments for the full day.* If properly designed, there will be adequate allowances to avoid overcrowding near the end of the day. Vary the number of appointments by time of day to allow for periods when large numbers of walk-ins are expected, and to allow for same-day follow-up visits.

5. *Maintain appointment order.* Do not use a first come, first served rule, as it will encourage people to arrive excessively early, and thereby increase congestion.

6. *Maintain the system.* Management must review system performance, make sure the rules are being followed, and adjust the system as necessary. Without maintenance, the system can fall apart.

The effect of all these rules is to balance the flow of customers with the capabilities of the providers, and to substantially reduce the random fluctuations in work load which lead to both congestion and idle periods.

In many situations, walk-in arrivals and no-shows occur in a pattern. Rising et al. (1973) found both a time-of-day and a day-of-week pattern for walk-in patients at a university health clinic. They therefore decreased the number of appointment intervals during the heavy walk-in times, and increased appointments at other times, to achieve a balance. To do this, it was necessary to count the walk-in arrivals during each hour of each day for several weeks, in order to establish the pattern. Careful collection and analysis of data are fundamental to both design and control of an appointment system.

Computers are widely used in large-scale appointment and reservation systems. This has been particularly useful in the airline industry, and also in health clinics, as exemplified by the paper by Rising et al. (1973). The main advantages of the computer systems are the ease of locating available appointments and making changes, and the capability of generating reports for management on a regular basis, with a minimum clerical effort.

Scheduling Passenger Service

Air, bus, and train passenger systems have three elements to schedule—crews, equipment, and passengers. Unlike an office-based service, these elements physically move. Coordination that involves *where* as well as *when* makes this problem different from professional services such as medical and legal. However, we shall see that some of the elements previously described are still useful.

Competition and regulation are key elements in passenger transportation. One aspect of the scheduling decision is to determine the degree to which customer purchasing behavior may be influenced by changing the price structure (special fares for low-travel times) or the service offered (routes, times, movies, etc.). Government regulation makes some of these changes more complicated.

The three elements (crews, equipment, and passengers) usually have different destinations. Typically, a crew will be routed so as to have a round trip of short duration (1 or 2 days) with appropriate rest periods. The vehicle may have a longer round trip, involving several different crews and very little time off, until scheduled maintenance is due. The passengers may spend a shorter or longer time with a given vehicle than does the crew; this will generally vary among passengers, depending on their destinations and which other carriers they use on their trips.

Vehicle schedules are based on type of equipment and its reliability. For example, it is desirable (and perhaps necessary) to avoid landing large-capacity aircraft in low-traffic areas. It is important to have good information readily available, in order to allow rapid decision making in the event of equipment failure. It may be necessary to reassign several aircraft, for example, in order to take one out of service in Denver, when the nearest spare is in Seattle.

Crew assignments are typically based on seniority. Designing a system of round-trips that cover an entire network is very difficult. There are nearly unlimited combinations, and it is inevitable that some will be less desirable than others. It is sometimes necessary to transport crew members in passenger seats in order to complete a cycle. However, because of the regularity of the schedule, it is possible to rotate work assignments in a manner similar to the systems described in Section 14-1.

The computer has been a blessing to the passenger reservation system. Careful programming and engineering have made it possible to ascertain almost instantly the alternative ways to get from point A to point B, the cost, and the availablility of seats. One of the difficulties of passenger booking, as with any other appointment system, is last-minute cancellations. This is countered by deliberate overbooking,[1] which, unfortunately, sometimes leads to passengers being bumped because there are fewer seats than passengers.

The CAB requires airlines to compensate passengers who are bumped due to overbooking. A policy has been instituted whereby airlines ask for volunteers who will accept a fixed compensation in exchange for a change in their tickets. This allows the inconvenience due to cancellations to be transferred to individuals who are not on a tight schedule.

Just as in the health clinic, different categories of consumers can be used

---

[1] See Schlifer and Vardi (1975). A similar problem in hotel overbooking has been studied by Liberman and Yechiali (1978).

to fill in the low-demand times. Standby passengers have a lower fare but no guarantee of a seat. Their likelihood of obtaining passage is higher if they travel at a time when the carrier has a low load factor. The number of reduced fare tickets to be sold is limited by the carrier. Glover et al. (1982) describe a system for determining the number of special fare seats to make available on each segment of 600 Frontier Airline flights. Their system successfully dealt with 30,000 different passenger itineraries.

Scheduling Extended-Stay Customers

Hotels, hospitals, nursing homes, and other such facilities have a scheduling problem that is unique because most of the customer's time in the system is not in the direct presence of the producer of the service. In fact, it is often convenient to conceptualize a server as a bed, or perhaps a room, rather than the personnel who staff the facility. When this is done, the same scheduling principles apply as in the short-stay situations described previously. Unfortunately, this may overlook one or more of the primary functions of an institution. For example, a resort hotel provides a room, recreational programs, meals, entertainment, and perhaps transportation. A scheduling method that concentrated only on rooms might be disruptive to some of the other functions.

The epitome of this situation is the hospital. Many surgical procedures are not urgent, and may be scheduled. This leaves room to schedule for the convenience of patients, doctors, operating room staff, regular nursing staff, recovery room staff, admitting department, X-ray, laboratory, and so on. Unfortunately, these various points of view conflict. For example, surgeons like to schedule several operations in a block, so as to minimize disruption of their other activities. Using a less rigid schedule could require the surgeon to make many trips back and forth between office and operating room while office patients sit and wait.

Operating room staff also need a regular schedule. The key to this problem is to schedule operations so that utilization of the operating room is fairly uniform. This reduces idle time of staff and facilities, so that the required procedures can be done without excessive overtime.

Many surgical patients are placed in a recovery room until they have regained consciousness and their physical condition has stabilized. Kwak et al. (1976) simulated an operating and recovery room system to investigate the effect of five different scheduling strategies. They estimated that a simple strategy could reduce the daily duty time of recovery room personnel by about 2.4 hours. The best strategies gave priority (surgery early in the day) to patients who are expected to require use of the recovery room, and to patients whose surgery is expected to take a long time. Unfortunately, it was not reported what such a priority scheme would imply for the schedules of the surgeons. It would seem that any system which does not focus on the surgeon's time would tend to spread his or her patients throughout the day and week.

A hospital admission scheduling system, which has been described by Hancock et al. (1976), anticipates the variation in admissions in several ways. Surgical scheduling gives rise to a day-of-the-week fluctuation in admissions and discharges. Beds must be held empty on Saturday to allow for the expected excess of admissions over discharges which occurs on Sunday, Monday, and Tuesday. An additional allowance is made for the expected number of emergency patients plus a safety margin to assure that all emergencies can be handled. Figure 14-1 shows that there are many types of patients, and that they can be transferred among departments (units) of the hospital, sometimes for convenience (due to a full unit) or because of medical necessity. For example, the intensive care unit has an interchange of patients with the medical-surgical unit.

This kind of system gives fixed quotas of admissions to various categories of patients (with the exception of emergencies). It can also incorporate a call-in list of patients who have agreed to be flexible in their date of admission in exchange for an earlier admission. The result is a more reliable pattern of facility utilization than can be achieved with an unplanned admissions program. With proper fine-tuning, admission scheduling can bring about several kinds of improvements. For example, it can increase the uniformity of patient census through the week, and reduce the variation from planned or expected levels. Both of these achievements make it easier to obtain low-cost work schedules for hospital personnel, using methods such as those described in the previous section. Hancock et al. (1976) describe interactive computer programs which may be used for this fine-tuning, and also for training personnel in the use of the admission scheduling procedures.

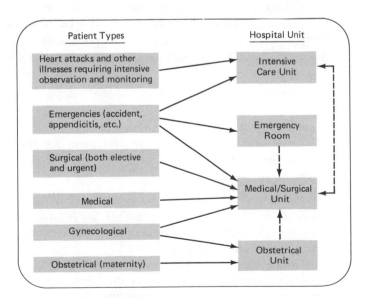

Figure 14-1 Patient types and hospital units. Admissions are shown by solid arrows and transfers by dashed arrows.

Similar principles can be applied in hotels, nursing homes, and so on. One of the important aspects of a scheduling system is simplicity of operation. The system described above is straightforward to use, without the aid of a computer. (The computer was used only to design a system and train personnel.) It is vital that the rationale behind the system be understood by those who use it. A hotel manager and a desk clerk, for example, must understand why it is important to retain some empty rooms prior to an unexpected influx such as a convention. If not, they will not use the scheduling system as intended, and the desired improvements will not be achieved.

The key to consumer scheduling consists of good data on when and what kinds of demands will be made, and how long it takes to serve the customers. With these data at hand, simple scheduling systems can be devised which reduce customer delay and increase provider efficiency.

Review Problems

Joe's Barbershop offers only three services: shaves, haircuts, and razor cuts with blow-dry. Two years ago, Joe established an appointment system at the request of some of his long-time customers. Now, about 50% of the customers call for an appointment. There are three barbers, and they work 7 hours per day, after lunch and other breaks are deducted. During a 1-week period (5 days), careful note was taken of the number of customers served and the idle time of the barbers. There were 220 customers served, and 30% of the workday was idle time, for each barber.

1. From these data, what is the average service time per customer? Is this an appropriate service interval to use in scheduling customers?

2. Of the customers who call for an appointment, 10% do not keep their appointments. How many appointments should be scheduled (at most) for a given day?

3. How should these appointments be distributed through the hours of the day?

4. Draw a parallel between the barbershop appointment system and a hospital admission scheduling system. In particular, for the hospital, what is the counterpart of (a) the appointment interval? (b) the walk-in customer? and (c) the waiting line?

Solutions

1. There were 35 work-hours per barber, or 105 for the week, but only 70% were actually used, or 73.5 hours. Over 220 customers, this averages 0.334 hour, or 20 minutes per customer.

   Since there are three categories of service, one could refine the appointment interval to depend on the work desired. For example, if the appointment interval were 15 minutes, two intervals could be assigned to the razor cuts. One would need more specific service time data to do this.

2. If the appointment interval is 20 minutes, a barber can serve 3 per hour, so the shop can handle 63 per day. If the past is any indication, half of these 63 would be walk-ins, and we would like the other half to be by appointment. Allowing for a 10% no-show rate, we would make up to $(0.5)(63)/(0.90) = 35$ appointments.

3. If there is any pattern to the walk-in arrivals, the appointments should be concentrated in periods when walk-ins are fewer. Also, one might wish to give more than one appointment per barber at opening time, in case a customer is late or cancels. However, with only a 10% no-show rate, this seems undesirable.

4. (a) The patient's length of stay in the hospital.
   (b) Emergencies, and other unscheduled admissions.
   (c) The barber's waiting line has several counterparts: emergency patients temporarily held in the emergency room; patients in the admitting office, waiting to go to their rooms; and patients who have been placed on a call-in waiting list, who will take the first available bed.

14-3 JOINTLY SCHEDULING CONSUMERS AND PRODUCERS

The examples of personnel scheduling in Section 14-1 assumed that work requirements were known and fixed. In Section 14-2 consumer demands were molded to provider availability. When both consumer and provider are subject to management, scheduling can take into account preferences and availability of each. This section gives examples that fall into two categories: route selection and conflict avoidance.

Route Selection

Choice of routes can have major cost and revenue effects. In the passenger service sector, establishing a new link between two cities can affect the traffic on all other links. The new link could lure more traffic from competitors by providing more convenient connections, but it could lower traffic in some parts of the system by providing an alternate route.

School bus routes are assigned partly on the basis of cost of equipment and labor. Although covering a smaller geographical area than airlines or other commercial carriers, the problem is nevertheless very complicated because of the large number of locations for passenger pickup and the desire to keep the time spent on the bus to a minimum. Gochenour et al. (1980) describe a simple heuristic used in selecting school bus routes. Thomas and Wells (1980) report on a transport system designed to relieve the housing shortage at the University of Manitoba by making larger areas of the city accessible for apartment dwelling students.

Meals on Wheels is a volunteer service organization that provides hot meals to persons who live at home but cannot cook for themselves. Bartholdi et al. (1983) describe a method of rapidly assigning clients to drivers and establishing a route. The system is based on two Rolodex files and a clear overlay for the city map. Although it is not optimal, the method is quick, easily used, and cuts travel distance by 13%. Adding and deleting clients is a simple matter with this system, in contrast to most optimizing methods in which any change requires a totally new solution.

A number of computerized routing methods have been developed. Stacey (1983) describes VANPLAN applied to a problem with 10,000 to 20,000 customers, 100 to 400 orders per day, and daily rescheduling. Fisher et al. (1982) describe ROVER, an interactive package with color graphics. It was applied to schedule delivery of consumable supplies to customers of DuPont. The supplies are for use with automatic clinical analyzers, and the customers are located in more than 1000 cities. ROVER determines delivery routes so that each customer can get a shipment every month.

Scheduling to Avoid Conflict

College exams and on-campus employment interviews are examples of services that are scheduled on a one-time basis. (Did you ever consider an exam to be a service?) They differ from appointment systems in that there is a distinct period of time in which all activity is to take place, and the consumer has far less say in the time chosen. All the requirements are known before the schedule is set, and the consumer must accept the assignment. Many other examples exist with similar properties. The general problem is to assign people with the right attributes to perform a set of tasks in a way that optimizes some measure of performance.

In the case of employment interviews, Hill et al. (1983) describe the problem as a network with two sets of nodes (see Figure 14-2). One set represents students

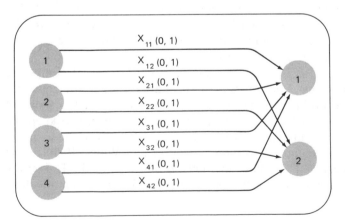

Figure 14-2 The assignment problem as a network.

seeking jobs and the other set represents interviewers. The arcs (arrows) represent possible assignments, and the notation (0, 1) on the arcs indicates lower and upper limits on the flows. The total flow out of a "person node" represents the number of tasks (interviews) assigned to that person. Similarly, the number of people assigned to task j is the flow into its node. The advantage of a network formulation is that it can be solved much faster than a standard LP.

One mathematical formulation of this type of problem uses the variables

$$X_{ij} = \begin{cases} 1 & \text{if person } i \text{ is assigned to task } j \\ 0 & \text{otherwise} \end{cases} \tag{6}$$

Parameters used in the formulation include

U_{ij} = utility (benefit) associated with assigning i to j

t_i, t_i' = lower and upper limits on the number of tasks person i can perform, respectively

p_j, p_j' = lower and upper limits on the number of people who can be assigned to task j, respectively

r_{jk} = number of people with attribute k required to carry out task j

People's characteristics are described by the parameters a_{ik}:

$$a_{ik} = \begin{cases} 1 & \text{for every attribute } k \text{ possessed by} \\ & \text{person } i \\ 0 & \text{if attribute } k \text{ is not possessed by} \\ & \text{person } i \end{cases}$$

The formulation is

$$\max \sum_i \sum_j U_{ij} X_{ij} \tag{7}$$

subject to

$$t_i \leq \sum_j X_{ij} \leq t_i' \qquad \text{for all people } i \tag{8}$$

$$p_j \leq \sum_i X_{ij} \leq p_j' \qquad \text{for all tasks } j \tag{9}$$

$$\sum_i a_{ik} X_{ij} \geq r_{jk} \qquad \text{for all tasks } j \text{ that require attribute } k \tag{10}$$

$$X_{ij} = 0 \text{ or } 1 \tag{11}$$

The utilities U_{ij} of employment interviews can be obtained by requiring each student to rank the companies according to the desirability of obtaining an interview. The parameters t_i and t_i' assure that a student (i) is neither shut out of the schedule nor given too many interviews. Each interviewer (j) can specify a minimum and maximum number of interviews using p_j and p_j'. If interviewers specify certain traits, these can be accommodated by equation (10). For example, one r_{jk} might specify a requirement that a certain number of students must have at least 2 years of work experience.[2] Equation (10) could also be used if an interviewer wants to speak only with business majors.

The interview assignment situation requires a great deal more than a mathematical model. Great care must be given to collecting accurate information in a timely fashion without an inordinate amount of work. Hill et al. (1983) described methods for data collection, error checking, and output reporting that are crucial for successful use of their system. To understand the scope of the effort, consider that they needed 15,000 variables X_{ij} in their model, and each one must have a preference or utility value U_{ij}. To collect such a large volume of data is not difficult. To avoid errors in transcribing the data into the computer is practically impossible. To say the least, implementation of a formal task assignment method that incorporates preferences requires careful management.

A second example of conflict-avoidance assignment is final examination scheduling. Here the primary objective is to minimize the number of students who have conflicts such as two exams at the same time or too many exams on the same day. Anderson and Bernhardi (1981) describe a method to develop minimum-conflict schedules based on a mathematical formulation that is very similar to the employment interview problem. Two heuristic (i.e., quick but not optimal) solutions were also tried for comparison. An interesting finding was that the heuristics could quickly generate a good starting point for the optimization, making the latter much faster than it otherwise would be.

The preceding examples are all special situations where the interdependence of consumer and producer schedules is apparent. Reflecting on the first two sections, it is worthwhile to consider how the producer-oriented Section 14-1 and customer-oriented Section 14-2 would be used in practice when both points of view must be adopted. Certainly, some benefits should accrue by taking a broader view than either of those sections implies.

In practice, scheduling consumers and scheduling servers are often separate responsibilities, and coordination between them is loose or missing altogether. One reason for this is that either one alone is extremely complex, and viewing them simultaneously is too difficult. In other cases, the reason is simply tradition: "That's the way we have always done it!"

As an example of a benefit to be gained by coordination, consider vacation scheduling. There are several times of the year when employees prefer to take their vacations. To grant everyone their desired vacation, overtime or part-time hiring may be needed to retain an adequate work force. If it is possible to shift demand away from such intervals, these extra expenses may be avoided. In some European countries the culture takes care of shifting demand by having August be everyone's vacation time (except for resort workers, of course). From the other viewpoint, if employees can be encouraged to vacation when demand

---

[2] Equations (8), (9), and (10) can be solved by a network algorithm only if the traits (k) are mutually exclusive. Incorporating the traits in the network changes Figure 14-2 substantially. See Problem 19.

is low, similar benefits accrue. Thus joint determination of consumer and producer schedules can be done at the margin even if the responsibilities are separate, and the overall goals of the operation can be better achieved as a result.

Review Problems

1. How are consumer preferences accommodated in selection of school bus routes? Producer preferences?

2. Consider the network representation of the assignment problem in Figure 14-2. How would the following requirements be stated in terms of flow through the network?
   (a) Person 1 should not be given more than one task.
   (b) Task 2 should not be assigned to more than three people.

3. In what ways is scheduling a patient for a physical exam different from scheduling a student for an on-campus employment interview?

Solutions

1. Short bus rides are preferred by both consumers and providers since they minimize both transportation cost and early rising. Routing to minimize bus mileage will tend to address both concerns. In doing so, there may be one bus route assigned to outlying regions. This bus may take a very long time to complete its tour. The scheduler may wish to introduce a constraint that no one spends longer than a certain amount, while minimizing the average distance of a traveler. (Other answers are possible.)

2. (a) The flow out of "person node 1" should be 1 or less.
   (b) The flow into "task node 3" should be 3 or less.

3. The employment interviewers only come once, for a limited time, so students cannot have all the interviews they may desire. In contrast, the physical exam can take place at any time, providing that the patient is willing to wait. Other contrasts exist.

14-4 Summary

Production and delivery of a service often requires the simultaneous presence of a provider and consumer. We have discussed the elements of scheduling systems which make it possible to arrange such meetings in an orderly manner, efficient to both parties. However, design of such systems inevitably requires that a balance be struck between consumer and provider points of view. It is often possible to improve both the work schedule and the convenience to the consumer by instituting a scheduling system, but the final decisions of how a given system will operate requires a trade-off between such variables as provider idle time and consumer waiting time.

Both personnel and consumer scheduling systems have three components, ranging from daily to annual decisions. Work-force planning requires looking at annual demand patterns, working out vacations and planning changes in the number of employees, usually on an aggregate basis. On the other hand, consumer demand may be scheduled on a long-run basis by marketing policies such as price promotions.

At the other extreme are the day-to-day decisions which involve last-minute changes in work assignments, perhaps using a float pool, and last-minute modification of the consumer schedule, involving cancellations and/or calling in wait-listed customers.

Between these extremes are the scheduling methods such as those which we have discussed. They often must address a multitude of objectives, but their general function is to work within the annual plans and provide an easily used method which minimizes the amount of last-minute readjustments.

To accommodate the needs of the consumer, work must often be performed at hours that are undesirable for personnel. The rotating work schedule is used to share this misfortune equally. More sophisticated systems have been developed that allow workers to rate the relative desirability of each work schedule. Rather than rotating on an equal basis, this approach attempts to equalize the desirability of work assignments in the long run. Therefore, if one worker prefers nights to weekends, and another has different preferences, both can be better off with a preference-based system than with a rotating schedule.

The methods for designing a work schedule range from trial and error (requiring substantial time and effort, and based on rules of thumb and judgment) to sophisticated, computer-based models (easy and inexpensive to use but expensive to develop and implement). We have described a linear programming approach that is useful in some situations and provides the basis for some of the more sophisticated programs.

Scheduling the consumer requires attention to fundamental details such as expected service time, punctuality, cancellations, and arrival of unscheduled customers. Fairly simple rules were given to incorporate these details. However, the situation becomes much more complicated when the consumer schedules must be merged with the schedules of several categories of providers. We have discussed airlines and hospitals as two illustrations of these difficulties.

Assignment methods are useful for one-time situations, as illustrated by employment interviews and exam scheduling. In these two examples the complete schedule can be laid out in advance, and both employers and consumers are required to accept it. Consumer preference and availability of employees can both be accounted for in these situations, but management has the final say in making the assignment. Most situations are not this clear cut, but the advantages of coordinating consumer and producer schedules can be substantial.

Behind every scheduling system is an information system, which supplies the data to analyze and forecast demand patterns, and provides other information needed by the personnel who are operating the scheduling system. Airline reservation systems, for example, provide rapid access for ticket agents to information concerning availability of seats, fares, timing, routes, and so on. They should also be designed to provide management with data on types and timing of customer demands, to use in exploring schedule changes. This degree of sophistication is not required for every situation, but advancing technology may soon bring computerized scheduling within the reach of units as small as a lawyer's office.

PROBLEMS

1. There are many ways to deal with variations in the rate of demand for a product that cannot be inventoried. Contrast the following three: float pools, rotating schedules, and appointment systems. Do they deal with the same aspects of the demand variations? In what ways do they complement one another?

2. In a grocery store, many of the workers operate as float personnel. Cite two examples.

*3. In an appointment system, why is it important to discourage consumers from arriving excessively early for an appointment?

4. Joe's Barbershop has been accepting appointments for haircuts. Most appointments are given during times of day when walk-in customers are infrequent. Customers are served on a modified first come, first served basis; all customers with appointments are served before any walk-in customers. Discuss the advantages and disadvantages of this scheme.

5. The arrival of emergency patients to a hospital is very well described by the Poisson probability law. Suppose a goal is to make sure that enough beds are available to accommodate all emergency patients with 99% probability, and the average arrival rate of emergency patients is six per day on Wednesday, when the hospital reaches its peak occupancy. How many beds should be allocated for emergency arrivals on Wednesday?

*6. A large hardware store currently has 14 full-time workers. Management has calculated that 15 workers will be needed on the average during the next 3-month period, but they found that the peak in weekly demand will be too high to be handled by a work force of that size. The data are shown in the accompanying table. Full-timers work 5 days per week. Part-time help can be obtained and trained for this kind of work.

Day	Mon.	Tue.	Wed.	Thu.	Fri.	Sat.	Sun.
Workers needed	9.5	12	16	10	10.5	8	8

(a) Compare the number of worker-days available from the present work force of 14 people to the amount needed. How many worker days of part-time help would be needed each week to avoid hiring another full-timer?

(b) How many part-timers must be trained to allow for the Wednesday peak with 14 full-timers?

(c) Where else during the week would it be logical to use part-timers?

(d) Suppose that two part-timers work all day on Wednesday, and part-time help is used to cover the half-days on Monday and Friday. One more part-time day must be assigned to some day of the week. What are the advantages and disadvantages of assigning a third part-timer to work a full day Wednesday?

(e) Management decided to assign two part-timer days to Wednesday, 1 to Tuesday, and 0.5 each to Monday and Friday. Calculate how many days off are available for the full-timers each day of the week, and in total for the week.

(f) The union says part-timers are welcome as long as the number of full-timers is 15. How does that change your previous answers?

*7. In the Sanitationworkers example of Tables 14-1 and 14-2, suppose that Spokane, Washington, wishes to form a rotating schedule of the same type. Their weekly trash load is 3500 tons, generated in equal amounts of 500 tons each of the 7 days of the week. Each collection crew can handle 50 tons per day and works 5 days per week. There are 16 trucks in the fleet but only 15 are available each day because of a rotating maintenance schedule.

(a) How many crews are needed?

(b) Given your answer to part (a), how much uncollected trash will there be for each day of the week if the collection crews have no days off on Monday, Tuesday and Wednesday?

(c) Devise a rotating schedule that minimizes uncollected trash, using your answer to part (a) and the approach of Table 14-2. Not all the days-off pairs need be used in your answer.

(d) Propose an alternative schedule that has one 3-day weekend but also follows the approach of Table 14-2.

(e) Compare the amounts of uncollected trash in parts (c) and (d).

8. (This problem requires a solution to Problem 7.) A new neighborhood has been added to Spokane, and their trash of 150 tons is collected on Friday. Part-time workers have been suggested as one way to increase the system capacity by 150 tons per week to adjust to the new demand. However, as noted above, there are only 15 trucks available. Trash can only be collected during the normal working hours.

(a) Suggest a method for using part-timers without increasing the amount of uncollected trash, compared to the solution of Problem 7(c).

(b) Suggest a schedule that requires only one part-time crew, working more than 1 day, but which allows the full-timers to have Monday off.

9. Legal Associates, Incorporated (LAI), is staffed by three lawyers and 15 full-time paralegal personnel (PLPs). The PLPs provide service directly to customers in many situations that involve common transactions and standard

forms. They also do certain research and other tasks for the lawyers. PLPs work 5 days per week, and the office is open 6 days per week (closed Sunday). The demand for PLP services is shown below. Each PLP can handle an average of eight clients per day.

Day	Mon.	Tue.	Wed.	Thu.	Fri.	Sat.	Sun.
Clients	130	100	116	90	144	60	0

Other legal offices provide similar services, so LAI tries to satisfy all demands, to avoid losing customers to their competitors. This sometimes requires that the lawyers take some of the PLP clients.

(a) Analyze the demand pattern and show how many full-time PLPs are required each day of the week. How much PLP work is being done by the lawyers?

(b) Making assumptions as necessary, decide on how many days off can be taken each day of the week. Remember that PLPs work only full days, 5 days per week.

(c) Devise a day-off schedule like Table 14-2 for the PLPs. Not all day-off pairs need be used in your answer.

10. The accompanying table shows the days off available for the 14 employees of a hardware store.

Day	Mon.	Tue.	Wed.	Thu.	Fri.	Sat.	Sun.
Days off	5	3	0	4	4	6	6

(a) Formulate an LP that will choose among the schedules in Table 14-3 so as to maximize the number of days-off pairs that are consecutive for the hardware store employees.

(b) Add a constraint that will assure that the Saturday–Sunday pair will be used at least five times in the schedule.

(c) What is wrong with the solution that assigns x_4 = Thursday–Friday = 4, x_6 = Saturday–Sunday = 8, x_1 = Monday–Tuesday = 3, u_1 = Monday (unpaired) = 2 and all other variables equal to zero?

11.

Week	Sun.	Mon.	Tue.	Wed.	Thu.	Fri.	Sat.
1	×	×					
2		×	×				
3			×	×			
4				×	×		
5					×	×	
6						×	×
7	×						×

(a) There are two 3-day weekends in this schedule. Find them.

(b) How many uninterrupted intervals of workdays are there in this 7-week schedule, and how many days are in each one?

(c) How many groups of workers will be on duty each day of the week if this schedule is applied on a rotating basis to seven work groups?

*12. Multiple shift rotating schedules can be made from the table given in Problem 11. (You need not do Problem 11 to answer this one.) Suppose there are 21 work groups and three shifts.

(a) Devise a rotating schedule whereby each group works 7 weeks of day shift (D), 7 of evening (E), and 7 of night (N).

(b) How many work groups will be on duty each shift?

*13. A brokerage firm wants to establish an appointment system that applies to customers who telephone as well as those who visit the office. Appointive telephone consultations would be carried out by the broker returning the client's call at the appointed time. The appointments would be limited to people who call for advice and discussion (consultation). Buy and sell orders would still be accepted as they arrive.

The average office visit of a new customer lasts 50 minutes, whereas office visits by established customers average 20 minutes in duration. Phone calls for consultation average 10 minutes' duration for all customers. Buy/sell orders require 1 minute of the stock broker's time on the average, with the balance of the call handled by a clerk. These 1-minute calls do not interrupt office or phone consultations, since the broker usually need only approve the clerk's work. If the client wishes to speak to the broker, the call is returned when the broker is free. New customers constitute 40% of office visits, 20% of phone calls for consultation, and no part of buy/sell orders.

There are five brokers in the firm, and the percentages quoted above vary among the brokers depending on their seniority with the firm, since the more senior brokers have more permanent clients. Office hours are 9 A.M. to 6 P.M. with 1 hour off for lunch.

There are 150 demands for broker service on the average day, of which 25% are office visits, 25% are phone calls for consultation, and 50% are buy/sell orders.

(a) They wish to establish an appointment interval that can be used for phone consultations, with several intervals assigned for each appointment. What is the appropriate appointment interval?

(b) How many appointment intervals should there be per day? Be sure to allow for buy/sell calls and for personal time.

(c) How much idle time will there be per day?

(d) What is the maximum number of "new customer" office visits you would recommend scheduling for a given day?

(e) Qualitatively, how should the new customer appointments be distributed over the hours of the day? (Should they be concentrated at any particular hours? Are there times to avoid?) How should they be distributed among the five brokers?

*14. There are 160 certified medical-surgical (MS) beds in Central Hospital, although up to 165 patients can be accommodated. Half of the patients are surgical cases, and the other half are admitted for other medical reasons. In each case, half of the patients stay 3 days and half stay 6 days. One-fourth of all MS patients are classified as emergencies, having problems too urgent to delay admission, whereas the remainder can wait for up to 2 weeks for an opportune admission appointment.

Currently, among medical patients, only emergency patients are admitted on Saturday and Sunday, and the admission pattern is heaviest in the early part of the week. This gives the doctors a better opportunity to minimize their weekend hospital rounds. The surgical admissions follow a similar pattern, except that Friday and Saturday are lowest in admissions, whereas Sunday is a popular day, so that patients may be worked up for Monday surgery.

The hospital administrator has been concerned by the low occupancy on weekends and is trying to convince the doctors to admit more medical patients on the low-admission days. The current and proposed admissions patterns are shown in the first two tables, along with the current status of patients who are in the hospital right now, a Thursday.

(a) Calculate how many patients will be in the hospital on each of the next 7 days using the current admissions pattern. The first day's calculations are shown in the patient status table.

(b) Do the same for the proposed patterns. (The new pattern starts tomorrow.)

(c) Study the results of part (a) and criticize the current admissions pattern.

(d) Does the proposed pattern allow the hospital to increase its intake of surgical patients? Discuss.

CURRENT ADMISSIONS PATTERN

	Sun.	Mon.	Tue.	Wed.	Thu.	Fri.	Sat.	Total
Medical (scheduled)	0	20	20	18	16	10	0	84
Medical (emergency)	4	4	4	4	4	4	4	28
Surgical (scheduled)	20	20	18	16	10	0	0	84
Surgical (emergency)	4	4	4	4	4	4	4	28
	28	48	46	42	34	18	8	224

PROPOSED ADMISSIONS PATTERN

	Sun.	Mon.	Tue.	Wed.	Thu.	Fri.	Sat.	Total
Medical (scheduled)	10	14	14	12	12	12	10	84
Medical (emergency)	4	4	4	4	4	4	4	28

(The remainder is the same as the current pattern.)

PATIENT STATUS TODAY (A THURSDAY) AND
PROBABLE STATUS TOMORROW

	NUMBER OF PATIENTS		
		Friday	
Days Remaining in Hospital	Thursday (Today)	Admissions	Total
6	17	9	9
5	21		17
4	23		21
3	41	9	32
2	35		41
1	27		35
Total = census	164		155
Discharges	33		27

15. The Central Hospital problem (Problem 14) asked you to do a manual simulation of 1 week. What would you do to make that simulation more realistic?

16. (Central Hospital is described in Problem 14. It is desirable to have solved Problem 14 before doing this one.) The surgeons at Central Hospital wish to keep their admissions pattern unchanged, allowing them to perform most of their surgery Monday through Thursday. At the time admission is scheduled, a surgeon can predict with fair accuracy (about 75%) whether the patient will have a 3-day or a 6-day stay. Suggest how the surgeons could reduce the peak census (Thursday's) and increase the weekend census.

*17. In the set of schedules shown here, each of nine work groups follows the pattern from Problem 11 (consecutive days off), but they rotate between shifts at different points in the schedule.

    (a) How many work groups are on duty on each shift during each day of the 7 weeks?

    (b) Show that the groups do not have equal work assignments.

    (c) What managerial advantages and disadvantages does this schedule have?

```
         WEEK 1ᵃ     WEEK 2      WEEK 3      WEEK 4      WEEK 5      WEEK 6      WEEK 7
Group   S M T W T F S  S M T W T F S  S M T W T F S  S M T W T F S  S M T W T F S  S M T W T F S  S M T W T F S

  1         D D D D D  D       D D D D  D D     D D D  D D D     E E  E E E E     E  E E E E E        N N N N
  2     D     E E E E  E E     E E E  E E E       N N  N N N N     D  D D D D D    D D D D D        D D D D D
  3     D D     D D D  D D D     D D  D D D D     E  E E E E E     E E E E E      N N N N N  N     D D D D
  4     E E E     E E  E E E E     N  N N N N N    D D D D D        D D D D D    D     D D D D  D D     E E E
  5     D D D D     D  D D D D D    E E E E E      E E E E E      E     N N N N  N N     D D D  D D D     D D
  6     E E E E E    N N N N N      D D D D D    D     D D D D  D D     D D D  D D D     E E  E E E E     E
  7       D D D D D      E E E E E  E     E E E E  E E     N N N  N N N     D D  D D D D     D  D D D D D
  8       N N N N N  N     D D D D  D D     D D D  D D D     D D  D D D D     E  E E E E E        E E E E E
  9     N N     D D D  D D D     D D  D D D D     D  D D D D D      E E E E E        E E E E E  E     N N N
```

ᵃ D, day shift; E, evening shift; N, night shift; a blank represents a day off.

*18. The MBA class at Corinth University consists of eight students. Three recruiters have agreed to come to campus for employment interviews, but they each have time enough for only four interviews. The placement office wishes to be fair and to please everyone; they want to schedule interviews accordingly. The interviewers have read the résumés of all eight students and have indicated which students they would prefer to interview. Student preferences have been gathered by asking each student to rank the interviewers with rank = 1 indicating the most preferred.

  (a) Write down the constraints of an assignment-type formulation for this problem, following the model of equations (8) to (11). Some judgment is required to obtain numbers for some of the parameters, such as t_i and p_i. Use your judgment and explain your logic.

  (b) Several objective functions could be used. Describe at least two and discuss the implications of their use.

19. In the network diagram of Figure 14-2, suppose that each task has a requirement of at least one left-handed and at least one right-handed person. People 1 and 2 are lefties, whereas 3 and 4 are righties. Modify the diagram to include these requirements. You will need to add nodes to do this. Indicate a minimum and maximum flow between two nodes by inserting the two numbers in parentheses on the corresponding arrow.

REFERENCES

ANDERSON, J. M., AND R. H. BERNHARDI, "A University Examination Scheduling Model to Minimize Multiple-Examination Days for Students." *Decision Sciences,* Vol. 12, No. 2 (1981).

ARTHUR, J. L., AND A. RAVINDRAN, "A Multiple Objective Nurse Scheduling Model." *AIIE Transactions,* Vol. 13, No. 1 (1981).

BARTHOLDI, J. J., III, K. PLATZMAN, R. L. COLLINS, AND W. H. WARDEN III, "A Minimal Technology Routing System for Meals on Wheels." *Interfaces,* Vol. 13, No. 3 (1983).

BELTRAMI, E., *Models for Public Systems Analysis.* New York: Academic Press, 1977.

DAVIS, S. G., AND E. T. REUTZEL, "Joint Determination of Machine Requirements and Shift Scheduling in Banking Operations." *Interfaces,* Vol. 11, No. 1 (1981).

FETTER, R. B., AND J. D. THOMPSON, "Patients Waiting Time and Doctors' Idle Time in the Outpatient Setting." *Health Services Research,* Summer 1966.

FISHER, M. L., A. J. GREENFIELD, R. JAIKUMAR, AND J. T. LESTER III, "A Computerized Vehicle Routing Application." *Interfaces,* Vol. 12, No. 4 (1982).

GLOVER, F., R. GLOVER, J. LORENZO, AND C. MCMILLAN, "The Passenger-Mix Problem in the Scheduled Airlines." *Interfaces,* Vol. 12, No. 3 (1982).

GLOVER, F., C. MCMILLAN, AND R. GLOVER, "A Heuristic Programming Approach to the Employee Scheduling Problem and Some Thoughts on Managerial Robots." *Journal of Operations Management,* Vol. 2, No. 4 (1984).

GOCHENOUR, D. L., JR., E. L. FISHER, AND J. BRYD, JR., "Bus Scheduling Revisited: The Monongalia County Experience." *Interfaces*, Vol. 10, No. 2 (1980).

HANCOCK, W. M., D. M. WARNER, S. HEDA, AND P. FUHS, "Admission Scheduling and Control Systems," Chap. III.2 in *Cost Control in Hospitals*, J. Griffith, W. Hancock, and F. Munson, eds. Ann Arbor, Mich.: Health Administration Press, 1976.

HENDERSON, W. B., AND W. L. BERRY, "Determining Optimal Shift Schedules for Telephone Traffic Exchange Operators." *Decision Sciences*, Vol. 8, No. 1 (1977).

HILL, A. B., J. D. NAUMANN, AND N. L. CHERVANY, "SCAT and SPAT: Large-Scale Computer-Based Optimization Systems for the Personnel Assignment Problem." *Decision Sciences*, Vol. 14, No. 2 (1983).

KELLEY, T., AND W. MCKENNA, "An Integrated Nurse Staffing System," *Proceedings of the Seventh Annual Conference of the Hospital and Health Services Divisions, AIIE, NCS HME*,[3] 1976, pp. 113–133.

KRAJEWSKI, L. J., L. P. RITZMAN, AND P. MCKENZIE, "Shift Scheduling in Banking Operations: A Case Application." *Interfaces*, Vol. 10, No. 2 (1980).

KWAK, N. K., P. J. KUZDRALL, AND H. H. SCHMITZ, "The GPSS Simulation of Scheduling Policies for Surgical Patients." *Management Science*, Vol. 22, No. 9 (1976), pp. 982–989.

LAMONT, G. "Census Forecasting: An Answer to Nursing Unit Staffing and Bed Utilization Problems." *Examination of Case Studies in Nurse Staffing*, NCS HME,[3] 1975, pp. 130–143.

LIBERMAN, V., AND U. YECHIALI, "On the Hotel Overbooking Problem—An Inventory System with Stochastic Cancellations." *Management Science*, Vol. 24, No. 11 (July 1978), pp. 1117–1126.

MAEBERT, V. A., AND A. R. RAEDELS, "The Detail Scheduling of a Part-Time Workforce: A Case Study of Teller Staffing." *Decision Sciences*, Vol. 8, No. 1 (1977).

MILLER, H., W. PIERSKALLA, AND G. ROTH, "Scheduling Nursing Personnel According to Nursing Preference—A Mathematical Programming Approach." *Operations Research*, Vol. 24, No. 5 (1976).

RISING, E., *Ambulatory Care Systems*, Vol. I: *Design and Evaluation for Improved Patient Flow*. Boston: D. C. Heath, 1977.

RISING, E. J., R. BARON, AND B. AVERILL, "A Systems Analysis of a University Health Service Outpatient Clinic." *Operations Research*, Vol. 21, No. 5 (1973), pp. 1030–1047.

ROCKART, J. F., AND P. B. HOFMANN, "Physician and Patient Behavior under Different Scheduling Systems in a Hospital Outpatient Department." *Medical Care*, Vol. 7, No. 6 (1969), pp. 463–470.

ROTHSTEIN, M. "Hospital Manpower Shift Scheduling by Mathematical Programming." *Health Services Research*, Spring 1973.

SCHLIFER, E., AND Y. VARDI, "An Airline Overbooking Policy." *Transportation Science*, Vol. 9 (1975), pp. 101–114.

[3] National Cooperative Services for Hospital Management Engineering, 1200 East Broad Street, Box 36, MRV Station, Richmond, VA 23298.

STACEY, P. J., "Practical Vehicle Routing Using Computer Programs." *Journal of the Operational Research Society,* Vol. 34, No. 10 (1983), pp. 975–981.

THOMAS, R. S. D., AND J. M. WELLS, "Multiple-Origin Single-Destination Transit Routing." *Interfaces,* Vol. 10, No. 2 (1980).

TRIVEDI, V., "Daily Allocation of Nursing Resources," Chap. III.4 in *Cost Control in Hospitals,* J. Griffith, W. Hancock, and F. Munson, eds. Ann Arbor, Mich.: Health Administration Press, 1976.

United Hospital Fund of New York, *Systems Analysis of Outpatient Department Appointment and Information Systems,* Training, Research and Special Studies Division, 3 East 54th Street, New York, NY 10022, 1967: 95 pages.

WAGNER, H., *Principles of Operations Research.* Englewood Cliffs, N.J.: Prentice-Hall, 1975, Chap. 6.

WILSON, E. J. G., AND R. J. WILLIS, "Scheduling of Telephone Betting Operators—A Case Study." *Journal of the Operational Research Society,* Vol. 34, No. 10 (1983), pp. 991–998.

PART IV

Making It Work

Robert Burns wrote that "the best laid plans of mice and men g'ang aft aglie." Since plans do go awry, operations managers must develop ways of integrating separate plans into a consistent set, and of monitoring progress to see that the plans are followed as closely as possible. Part IV discusses ways of organizing diverse efforts in pursuit of overall goals and following up to see what actually happens, so that future plans can be modified to keep the organization "on target."

Chapter 15 extends the Chapter 2 discussion of systems analysis by describing methods of ensuring that components in a hierarchical organization act in a manner consistent with the organization's goals. An extensive example, the Chris Tull Glass Company, is included to illustrate the techniques, which include quantitative analysis and management judgment based on the specific situation. Chapter 15 also discusses ways of organizing to allow ease of management evaluation of system components and ease of follow-up procedures.

In many organizations the most important follow-up procedures involve quality assurance. Chapter 16 describes organizational issues affecting quality as well as several quantitative methods that are used as part of quality control. The important ideas of quality circles and "quality is free" are examined.

Policy decisions in the operations area cannot be made without considering the entire organization. Furthermore, these decisions are of great importance because of the strategic position of operations among the functional areas of most organizations. Chapter 17 discusses the reasoning behind these two statements and methods for establishing guiding policies for operations management decisions. In doing so, some formal strategic planning methods are examined. Chapter 17 also takes a look at the likely future of operations management.

CHAPTER 15
Coordination, Implementation, Evaluation, and Follow-Up

In Chapters 1 to 14 we have described many different management problems and ways of planning for those problems. Without managerial effort, these plans will not direct the organization to work in concert toward overall goals. Separate but interrelated plans are made with different time horizons, by different managers, and at different levels of detail. For example, long time horizons are necessary for decisions relating to capacity, location, product design, and so on. Workforce plans must be made for several months ahead. Short-term plans, such as detailed schedules for machines or people, often use a very short time horizon (a few days or weeks). All these plans must be made to fit together.

In this chapter we will investigate ways of *implementing* plans and *following up* to provide corrective action if necessary. We will also investigate methods of *coordinating* plans within a complex organization so that the parts of the organization work together, rather than at cross purposes. Finally, we will discuss ways of *evaluation* of the organization's performance, both against the plans and against industry standards.

15-1 COORDINATION OF OPERATIONS IN LARGE, MULTILOCATION ORGANIZATIONS

All large organizations must deal with problems of coordination among the different parts of the organization. Somehow, the different components of the organization must act in such a way that the overall goals are met. For example, the components of a hospital must operate together to provide health care to the patients. Any one patient may place demands on the laboratory, surgery, pharmacy, food service, and the residential floors. In a large manufacturing organization, several different plants and warehouses must coordinate their efforts to ensure that nationwide customer demands are met. In a large city, the fire stations must be coordinated, both to cover fires in progress and to be prepared to respond quickly to the next fire that may occur.

Designing the organization so that coordination occurs is the task of top management. Some tools that can be used in this process include job descriptions, cost accounting, and information systems.

Information systems must be designed to summarize and pass appropriate information from one group to another. For example, sales personnel must know the length of the production backlog, so that their promises to customers and demands on the production system can be realistic.

Cost accounting methods (discussed in Chapter 2) include transfer prices (the amount paid by one component of an organization for the products from another part) and incentive systems, such as basing managerial bonuses on profit earned. These accounting techniques are designed to coordinate diverse efforts. Each manager's reward structure is supposed to encourage actions consistent with the goals of the organization. For example, establishing a charge (say 20%) for dollars tied up in inventory should cause a manager to balance the cost of money to the firm against the cost of running out of stock. However, the charge will have this effect only if the division manager also is credited with the revenue from sales, since this gives the manager the cost *and* benefit of inventory.

Job descriptions contribute to coordination in several ways. First, a manager's job description should include a phrase such as "coordinate the efforts of (those who report to the manager) so as to implement company policies and achieve company goals." It is important to explicitly state that a key function for each level of management is coordination of the next lower level. Job descriptions can also be used to make sure that all necessary tasks are completed. Each manager's responsibilities should be clearly indicated, and descriptions should be reviewed to see that all the bases are covered. The organization chart can serve as a path for reviewing the descriptions from the top down and level by level.

Several firms have found that fewer levels of management makes coordination of effort easier. However, the advantage of having many levels is that clear lines of authority exist and each manager has a smaller *span of control* (number of people reporting to him or her). The appropriate organizational design, of course, depends on the situation. Further discussion on organizational design is given by Galbraith (1977) and Hax and Majluf (1981).

A manager's job description can never be complete, since one role of management is to respond to unanticipated events. The U.S. government has received some negative publicity due to the requirement of completely specifying jobs in the description. Items not included may not get done. It is preferable to think of job descriptions as a tentative statement; each individual should be given some freedom to modify a job through time. However, the discipline required in trying to describe each job can help to ensure that organizational coordination is achieved.

A manager may also choose to achieve coordination by delegation, assigning specific coordination efforts to the managers on the next lower level. For example, production and marketing may be expected to work through most problems regarding production and delivery schedules without recourse to the higher-level manager. Coordination can also be achieved by using a "matrix organization," in which an individual manager reports to two (or more) bosses, so that competing goals within the organization must be considered and balanced by the lower-level manager. For example, a quality control manager might report to a marketing manager and a production manager. Matrix organizations are explained in Galbraith (1977).

Finally, coordination of a productive system is achieved by assigning responsibilities and routinizing the timing and type of decisions and information flows. Managing a company-wide system of several plants and warehouses, for example, requires a seasonal inventory plan, a capacity plan, a distribution plan, inventory policies, detailed production decisions, and several other items. The manager in charge of the overall system must assign responsibility for each task, select the frequency of replanning (perhaps yearly for capacity planning and daily for detailed production scheduling), and see that the appropriate information flows are established to allow the system to act in a coordinated fashion. It is often more important to have a good overall system view than to have optimal decisions for any one component. An example of such a decision system is discussed in depth in the next section.

Major commitment of resources in an organization typically requires aggregated data (not forecasts for each of 100,000 items, for example) and a long time horizon. This decision must consider the effects on future, detailed decision making. In turn, the detailed decisions must be made within the resources generated by the aggregated decisions. More generally, detailed decisions must act in concert with the organization's overall goals and policies, and management must see that this happens.

Concepts involved in coordinating large production–inventory systems have been described by Hax and Meal (1975). Other recent research on these ideas include Bitran et al. (1981, 1982), Dempster et al. (1981), Caie and Maxwell (1981), and Maxwell et al. (1983). Hax and Meal (1975) structure the production–inventory decisions in their example using a hierarchical system. (See Chapter 2 for a brief discussion of systems analysis and hierarchical systems.) Problems are solved from the top down and sequentially, with each level of decision placing constraints on the next lower level. Hax and Meal give the reasoning for this approach:

We decided upon a hierarchical system, one which makes decisions in sequence, with each set of decisions at an aggregate level providing constraints within which more detailed decisions must be made. We did this because we found that we could not, with available analytic methods and data processing capability, develop an optimization of the entire system. However, even if the current state of the art allowed solution of a detailed integrated model of the production process we would have rejected that approach because it would have prevented management involvement at the various stages of the decision-making process. A model that facilitates overall planning can only become effective if it helps in establishing, at the various organizational levels, subgoals which are consistent with the management responsibilities at each level. The model should allow for corrections to be made to these subgoals by the managers at each level, and for coordination among the decisions made at each level. This is the essential characteristic of hierarchical planning.

Coordination is achieved by the sequencing of decisions and the information flows. Equally important, the individual lower-level managers are allowed to use their specialized knowledge of the local situation. They are given guidelines so that their production plans will fit with the overall system.

The sequence of steps suggested by Hax and Meal (1975) for their example is: (1) plant/product assignment, (2) seasonal planning, (3) product family scheduling, and (4) item scheduling. In plant/product assignment, families of products (a family is a group of products that share a major setup cost, as discussed in Chapter 11) are assigned to the set of plants, considering the fixed cost of tooling up to produce a family and the variable cost of production and distribution. A family may be produced at one plant or several plants. This part of the procedure can be used in two ways. Initially, an integer mathematical program to assign products to plants is run without capacity constraints. This initial solution can be used to determine which plants need to be expanded or contracted in the long run. Second, the cost of producing at any plant whose capacity is exceeded is increased until the capacity constraint is met. This solution is used to provide the plant/product assignment for the coming year.

The seasonal planning portion of the system divides the products into "types" which share the same seasonal pattern. Then, using an aggregate planning LP as discussed in Chapter 9, a seasonal inventory accumulation plan is developed. The LP recommends which types should be produced to inventory, but the manager must select the individual products to be used in building the seasonal inventory.

The family production-run lengths are determined using the EPQ discussed in Chapter 11, computed with the nonpeak demand rate. Seasonal inventory is added to the appropriate family run lengths before the peak, according to the seasonal plan, making sure that inventory is not overstocked to more than needed to meet the peak sales. Finally, individual items within a family are produced to have equal runout times (discussed in Chapter 11). This pushes the next setup for a family of items as far into the future as possible. The overall decision system is summarized in Figure 15-1.

The Hax and Meal article is illustrative of a general approach to system coordination. However, the formulas given in the article would not be used in every situation. In fact, different steps might be needed in the process. Never-

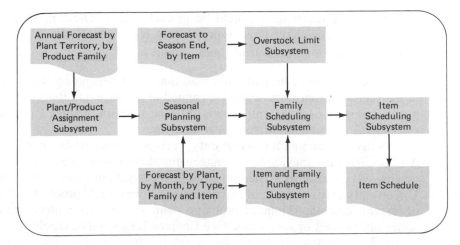

Figure 15-1   Decision sequence in planning and scheduling.

Source: A. Hax and H. Meal, "Hierarchical Integration of Production Planning and Scheduling," in Studies in the Management Sciences, Vol. I, Logistics, Murray Geisler, ed. (New York: North-Holland/American Elsevier, 1975).

theless, the general approach is important, and it can be transferred to other situations. To illustrate this, examples, with different steps in the process, are given in this and the next section. In both the upcoming examples and the Hax and Meal article the reader will see places for potential improvement. Such improvements should be made, of course. But if the overall approach is sound, improvements in the details will lead to small cost saving compared to the saving attributed to the hierarchical planning approach.

In establishing a hierarchical planning system we are essentially determining *boundaries* for each manager's problem. How large a view should be taken? What information flows in and out of each subsystem? And how does the entire system fit together? (Problem boundaries are discussed for problems of planning and design by Volkema, 1983, who also gives a list of references to problem formulation in planning systems.) To complete this section we will discuss an article that describes hierarchical planning approaches to managing large, complex manufacturing systems. Maxwell et al. (1983) discuss a system for making decisions, down to detailed daily production, in a multilevel (MRP-type) manufacturing system. The Hax and Meal (1975) approach is appropriate if production can be thought of as consisting of a single level.

Maxwell et al. (1983) describe a three-stage system: stage 1—master production planning, stage 2—planning for uncertainty, and stage 3—real-time resource allocation. Stage 1 consists of an aggregated, large-scale mathematical program to determine for a long (say, 18-month) horizon:

(a) What products should be produced on which facilities using which process.

(b) What capacities (of labor, for example) should be in which facility.

    (c) What the batch sizes should be in each stage. These may be very small if setup times have been appropriately reduced.

    (d) What the production lead times should be.

The novel ideas in stage 1 are that lead times will depend on the predicted load in the factory rather than being determined in advance and that batch sizes need not be constant over the entire horizon. The solution to stage 1 provides a plan for stage 2 to protect and stage 3 to aim for.

    Stage 2, planning for uncertainty, recognizes that while uncertainty is bad, it is occasionally inevitable. Management should first direct their attention to driving out uncertainty. Then, in stage 2, management deals with what remains. Uncertainty exists because of machine breakdowns, yield problems, absenteeism, order cancellation, shipment problems, and so on. To protect against those, some *safety stock* or *safety time* (see Chapter 12) should be carefully determined. Some firms mistakenly have placed safety stock everywhere. It gets in the way and is usually insufficient. Instead, placing a small amount of safety stock before and after a bottleneck machine (to see that it always can work and does not delay downstream production), after a low-yield process, before a large value-added step (so that we can reliably start that process only when we are sure it is needed) will help to *protect* the stage 1 plan. Safety stock should be held in products with stable demand so that they will be useful in saving machine time. Protecting the stage 1 plan is appropriate because it has minimized the largest manufacturing costs and should be followed to the extent possible.

    Finally, real-time resource allocation models would consider local and current information (one work center, for example) regarding available work and capacity. But these models would use those data to make decisions consistent with stages 1 and 2. The model would always try to end the week (say) in line with the stage 1 plan for production and inventories as well as the stage 2 safety levels. Stage 2 goals are of secondary importance because those buffers are there to be used if necessary to protect stage 1.

    The set of management problems fits together. Lowest-level managers can use detailed information but still consider the effect on the overall, longer-term plans. More detail is given in Maxwell et al. (1983), and individual models are described in the references in that article. In the next section we will examine a concrete example of hierarchical planning.

Review Problems

    1. What forecasts would be needed by each of the four steps described by Hax and Meal? At what level of aggregation and for what time horizon would they be?

    2. How often would each of the four steps be necessary?

    3. What manager would be directly responsible for each of the four steps? (For example, a company-wide executive vice-president would be responsible

for capacity planning and a plant manager would be responsible for a seasonal inventory plan.)

Solutions

1. The plant/product assignment phase would require total company-wide sales for at least the next year, by family. For capacity planning a 5-year or longer forecast might be needed. For seasonal planning the forecast must be broken down by months or weeks, by type, and by plant. A forecast for at least a year would be necessary. For family and item scheduling we would need the seasonal planning forecast to set EPQs, and a detailed short-term (next few months) forecast to establish precise run quantities.

2. The plant/product assignment phase would be run once a year, or more often if there were dramatic changes. The seasonal planning routine probably would be updated monthly to make small changes in the yearly plan. (A rolling schedule would be used, as discussed in Chapter 9.) The family and item-run-length decisions would be made frequently, whenever a run for a family is necessary.

3. Each of these progressively lower-level decisions is strongly constrained by the less frequent but broader scope decisions of higher-level management. Thus the executive vice-president (or other top-level manager) would be responsible for plant/product assignment and the associated capacity planning. Each plant manager, with help from central staff for forecasting, would be responsible for seasonal planning. Lower-level managers within the plant probably would be responsible for the detailed run-length decisions.

15-2 *EXAMPLE OF HIERARCHICAL PLANNING—THE CHRIS TULL GLASS COMPANY*

The Chris Tull Glass Company (CTG) manufactures six categories[1] of glass containers. They have three plants, each of which is capable of producing all six product categories. CTG distributes its products to stores and small companies through five regional warehouses. A few customers are served directly from the plants because of the large size of their orders, but this does not constitute a large fraction of CTG's business.

The firm has four large glass furnaces at each plant, and they have found that their capacity is larger than necessary during most of the year. Jerry Walker, the corporate staff vice-president for manufacturing services, has been charged with the task of reviewing CTG's nationwide production–distribution operations. The review is to include methods of planning aggregate and detailed production and inventory decisions for all locations.

---

[1] These numbers are smaller than is actually the case for a company of this type. The numbers are small to allow us to complete the example in reasonable space.

Prior to beginning the analysis Walker obtained forecast and cost data for the system. Forecasts were obtained by product and by warehouse service area for the upcoming year. Costs were obtained for production, distribution, changeover from one product to another, and for furnace startup and operation.

Data

A furnace costs $15,000 per month to keep operational, whether it is used for production or not. A furnace can be completely shut down, but a shutdown and startup costs a total of $120,000, since a large amount of product is lost in the process. Until now, all furnaces had been maintained in an operational mode. The resulting excess capacity meant that CTG never carried seasonal inventory; peak demand could be met by using more furnaces.

The forecasts for the next 12 months, nationwide by product category, are given in Table 15-1. The units are thousands of tons of product, a common unit used by CTG for aggregate planning.

Each furnace can produce 4.0 thousand tons of product per month. Demand is equally distributed among the five warehouses, each accounting for 20% of the sales in each product category. The variable cost of production per ton of product averages $310 at plant 1 and $320 at each of the other two plants. However, a plant must have two or more furnaces operating or the cost increases by $40 per ton. The inventory carrying cost rate is 12% per year, or 1% per month, for CTG.

The transportation costs are given in Table 15-2.

The final category of cost information relates to changeover costs. Minor setups, for example to change labels within one product category, are a negligible cost and can be ignored. To change from one category to another costs from $8400 to $9200, depending on the changeover involved.

TABLE 15-1 FORECASTS (THOUSANDS OF TONS) FOR EACH PRODUCT CATEGORY FOR CTG

Product Category	MONTH											
	1	2	3	4	5	6	7	8	9	10	11	12
1	8.4	7.5	6.0	5.1	4.5	4.0	4.5	4.5	6.7	9.2	10.7	9.0
2	3.5	4.1	4.9	5.8	6.1	6.2	6.2	6.0	5.5	5.5	5.7	4.4
3	2.1	2.4	2.8	3.1	3.3	3.4	3.3	3.6	2.9	3.0	2.6	2.2
4	0.8	1.0	1.0	1.1	1.5	1.7	1.7	1.7	1.6	1.4	1.3	1.1
5	9.4	9.0	7.9	7.0	6.4	6.0	6.4	6.0	9.1	11.2	13.4	10.7
6	3.5	3.4	3.0	2.7	2.3	2.0	2.2	2.1	3.1	4.0	4.9	3.9
	27.7	27.4	25.6	24.8	24.1	23.3	24.3	23.9	28.9	34.3	38.6	31.3

TABLE 15-2 TRANSPORTATION COSTS (DOLLARS PER TON) FROM PLANT TO WAREHOUSE WITHIN CTG

	TO WAREHOUSE					
From Plant:	1	2	3	4	5	6
1	$30	$37	$36	$49	$51	$75
2	44	41	35	41	49	56
3	74	72	61	57	48	34

Problem Analysis

In the analysis that follows, numbers are given that are the result of calculations not given here. The calculations for level production plans and economic production quantities, for example, are not given, to keep the example from becoming too large. The numbers can be verified by the reader, but you do not need to do so. Knowing what was done, based on previous chapters, and how the numbers are used here is sufficient.

Walker initially wanted to make all decisions centrally, but the company had a philosophy of decentralization. Thus he thought that a hierarchical planning approach could provide system-wide savings and allow decentralized management.

The first step is to see where the significant potential savings are. The major cost categories are (1) variable production cost, (2) transportation cost, (3) changeover cost, (4) inventory cost, and (5) costs of maintaining or restarting furnaces not currently in use.

Walker discovered that while changeover costs were significant, the precise sequence of products made very little difference in that cost. Further, the production scheduling unit at each plant was quite adept at figuring out sequences. Since the sequencing problem was the most difficult to solve mathematically and since very little improvement was possible, Walker was glad to leave detailed sequencing to each plant. The other costs must be dealt with centrally to some extent.

The $40 per ton penalty for operating a plant with only one furnace is so high that no plant will do so. There is a question as to whether or not an entire plant should be closed. Walker's first try at a solution procedure does not consider that possibility.

Since glass production is a capital-intensive operation, labor-force planning is not a key problem. Further, once a furnace is running, they try to run it 24 hours per day; overtime is not possible. Thus the aggregate planning problem is to balance inventory cost against the cost of keeping extra furnaces "warm." The question is: Should CTG use a level-production plan, keep extra furnaces warm to respond to the peak demand rate, or start extra furnaces during peak months?

A level production plan, with production equal to 27.85 thousand tons in each month, would have a total inventory of 111.10 thousand-ton-months. Production cost is \$310 to \$320 per ton, so the cost of holding inventory is roughly $(111,100)(320)(0.01) \approx \$350,000$ per year. (The value is approximate, since production cost per thousand tons will be less than \$320,000 on the average.) Since the production rate of each furnace is 4000 tons per month, a total of $27.85/4.0 \approx 7$ furnaces will be needed.

Alternatively, if 10 furnaces are kept warm, the peak rate of 38.6 thousand tons can be met without any inventory. Keeping the average of three unnecessary furnaces warm for the year would cost $(3)(15,000)(12) = \$540,000$. Starting and stopping three extra furnaces even once would cost \$360,000, and some warming costs would also be incurred. The analysis indicates that a plan that uses seasonal inventory and nearly level production is appropriate.

As a final preliminary, Walker computed some economic production quantities. If demand were evenly divided among the three plants, the EPQs would, according to his calculations, range from 6 to 15 weeks' worth of demand. Average lot-size inventory $(Q/2)$ would be less than 2 months (8 weeks) of demand. Thus the lot-size inventory cost would be less than 2% of the product cost, and the total setup cost would also be less than 2% of the product cost, for a total of less than 4%. Walker calculated that at most an improvement of $1\frac{1}{2}\%$ (from 4% to $2\frac{1}{2}\%$) of the product cost would be made possible by centralizing the production of an item to obtain larger lot sizes.

Since shipping from a plant other than the cheapest one implies an average loss of about \$8 per ton, or $2\frac{1}{2}\%$ of the product cost (see Table 15-2), Walker decided that it would not be worthwhile, in general, to produce some items at only one plant. Walker was aware of the rough nature of his calculations, but since the implication seemed impervious to minor changes in the figures, all plants will be used to produce all products.

Decision System

The preliminaries discussed above helped Walker reach the following definition of a decision system, consistent with the ideas of hierarchical planning.

First, assign warehouses to plants using a linear program with minimum and maximum capacity constraints. The LP will use the average monthly demand, summed across all products, within each region. The LP formulation, nearly identical to one given in Section 7-4, would be as follows:

$$\text{minimize} \sum_{i=1}^{3} \sum_{j=1}^{6} C_{ij} X_{ij}$$

$$\text{subject to} \quad \sum_{i=1}^{3} X_{ij} = \text{DEM}_j \qquad j = 1, \ldots, 6$$

$$8.0 \leq \sum_{j=1}^{6} X_{ij} \leq 16.0 \qquad i = 1, 2, 3$$

where X_{ij} = units shipped during an average month from plant i to warehouse j, thousands of tons of product

C_{ij} = cost of 1000 tons of product manufactured at plant i and shipped to warehouse j; for example, C_{11} = \$320,000 + \$30,000 = \$350,000 for 1000 tons (see Table 15-2 for transportation costs)

The constraints on plant capacity are that at least two furnaces must be used and no more than four are available, each with a capacity of 4.0 thousand tons. Demand must be met.

If the solution calls for a fractional number of furnaces at more than one plant, the executive vice-president's staff will try to modify the capacity to include an integer number of furnaces at all plants but one. The LP will then be rerun with the modified capacity constraints. Some warehouses will be serviced by two plants, and this is acceptable.

Second, lot sizes are developed using the slack season rate of demand for each product at each plant. Third, the plans for seasonal inventory are developed so that production will exceed demands by that amount. The seasonal inventory plan will be based on a year-long forecast for the warehouses served and a level production rate, at each plant. The lot sizes of selected products will be increased as the high-demand periods approach to allow this inventory buildup. In any plant that is allocated a fractional number of furnaces (say $3\frac{1}{2}$), management will use the seasonal plan to determine which fraction (say $\frac{1}{2}$) of the year to use the furnace. Whether the furnace will be started for the fraction of a year or will be kept warm all year depends on the size of the fraction.

Fourth, the detailed production sequences and shipping schedules will be left to local and lower-level plant management. The sales force in each warehouse region will determine warehouse inventory levels, customer shipments from inventory, and direct customer shipments from the plant.

The individual plant managers will be required to report weekly on their performance against the seasonal production plan. (Because of forecast errors, the plan is not followed exactly.) The report will contain a statement regarding large orders to be shipped directly to customers. The executive vice-president can shift these orders from one plant to another to balance facility usage within the constraints of the plan for furnace capacity. It is felt that the additional transportation cost is justified to avoid the cost of changing the capacity plan or not satisfying a large customer. Changes in furnace capacity (by starting a cold furnace) at any plant must be approved by the executive vice-president, but plant managers can change a furnace from warm to active status.

Finally, at each stage of the planning, if difficulties are encountered, a modification in the plan for the higher-level problem can be considered. A summary of the decision system is given in Figure 15-2.

The decision system forces the organization to act in a cohesive, coordinated manner. The executive vice-president is able to make changes that do not make sense if examined from one subunit's viewpoint, if these changes are for the

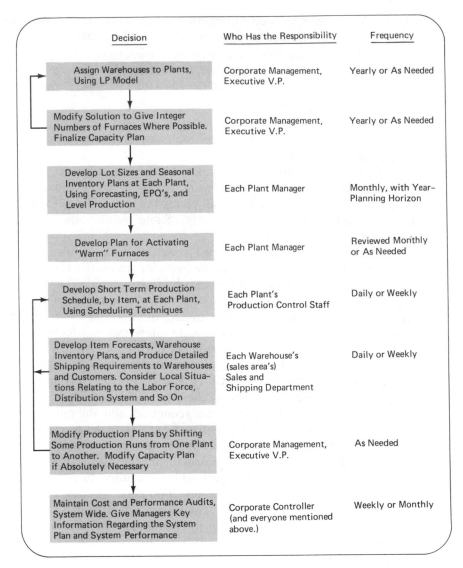

Decision	Who Has the Responsibility	Frequency
Assign Warehouses to Plants, Using LP Model	Corporate Management, Executive V.P.	Yearly or As Needed
Modify Solution to Give Integer Numbers of Furnaces Where Possible. Finalize Capacity Plan	Corporate Management, Executive V.P.	Yearly or As Needed
Develop Lot Sizes and Seasonal Inventory Plans at Each Plant, Using Forecasting, EPQ's, and Level Production	Each Plant Manager	Monthly, with Year–Planning Horizon
Develop Plan for Activating "Warm" Furnaces	Each Plant Manager	Reviewed Monthly or As Needed
Develop Short Term Production Schedule, by Item, at Each Plant, Using Scheduling Techniques	Each Plant's Production Control Staff	Daily or Weekly
Develop Item Forecasts, Warehouse Inventory Plans, and Produce Detailed Shipping Requirements to Warehouses and Customers. Consider Local Situations Relating to the Labor Force, Distribution System and So On	Each Warehouse's (sales area's) Sales and Shipping Department	Daily or Weekly
Modify Production Plans by Shifting Some Production Runs from One Plant to Another. Modify Capacity Plan if Absolutely Necessary	Corporate Management, Executive V.P.	As Needed
Maintain Cost and Performance Audits, System Wide. Give Managers Key Information Regarding the System Plan and System Performance	Corporate Controller (and everyone mentioned above.)	Weekly or Monthly

Figure 15-2   Summary of CTG's production–inventory decision system.

overall good of the organization. On the other hand, the thousands of detailed scheduling and shipping decisions are made by managers who have specialized knowledge of the local scene. Further, since local managers are an important part of the system, they are more likely to be committed to its success.

Modeling the entire system in one, huge model would be difficult and, more important, inappropriate. Many different techniques are used here, but they are used to support individual managers' decisions, and the decisions are forced to fit together.

The general approach of forming an overall decision system is not limited to manufacturing organizations, as mentioned before. The Review Problem below asks you to consider a nonmanufacturing example.

Review Problem

In a large city fire department there is a city-wide superintendent, several precinct captains, and many unit commanders. Using a hierarchical planning framework, briefly describe a decision system for managing firefighting operations.

Solution

There are, of course, many ways to answer a general question such as this. One possible response is shown in Figure 15-3. There are many more decisions and actions taking place in such a system than we can list here. Also note that the precinct captain does not make the detailed dispatching decisions or change the location of equipment. He or she is responsible, but those decisions are made by lower-level personnel in the precinct office, based on policies determined city wide. Finally, just as in the CTG example, there will be cases where policy must be overridden. A fire may be large

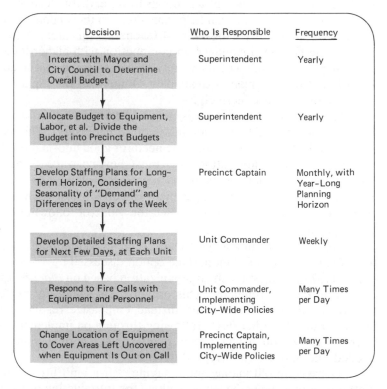

Decision	Who Is Responsible	Frequency
Interact with Mayor and City Council to Determine Overall Budget	Superintendent	Yearly
Allocate Budget to Equipment, Labor, et al. Divide the Budget into Precinct Budgets	Superintendent	Yearly
Develop Staffing Plans for Long-Term Horizon, Considering Seasonality of "Demand" and Differences in Days of the Week	Precinct Captain	Monthly, with Year-Long Planning Horizon
Develop Detailed Staffing Plans for Next Few Days, at Each Unit	Unit Commander	Weekly
Respond to Fire Calls with Equipment and Personnel	Unit Commander, Implementing City-Wide Policies	Many Times per Day
Change Location of Equipment to Cover Areas Left Uncovered when Equipment Is Out on Call	Precinct Captain, Implementing City-Wide Policies	Many Times per Day

Figure 15-3 Hierarchical plan for firefighting operations.

enough that a decision to leave a portion of the city unprotected is made. That decision would be made by some manager on the scene, who has authority granted by the superintendent or precinct captain.

15-3 IMPLEMENTATION, EVALUATION, AND FOLLOW-UP

Implementation

Implementation in operations management is the process of making, shipping, providing, and storing goods and services. Without implementation the organization does not achieve its objectives. Implementation comes at the end of a chain of plans; goals have been set and long-term plans and short-term plans have been made. It is the short-term plans that are actually implemented, although seldom exactly as envisioned. First-level operations managers (shift supervisors, for example) implement short-term plans as best they can and feed back variations from the plan so that the next short-term plan can be modified.

At the implementation level, the dependability and capabilities of individual workers, the weather, how people feel on a given day, and many other factors must be considered. Courses and books in supervision, leadership, the behavioral sciences and related fields can help individuals to think about effective management style, but experience is still the best teacher in this area. However it is accomplished, the first-level manager, in conjunction with higher-level managers, must see that plans are followed as closely as possible and that accurate feedback on deviations from the plan is available. Otherwise, the higher-level goals of the firm cannot be met effectively.

The process of managing is never certain, and plans are used to keep the organization on target. Replanning is often necessary. This is certainly true in most organizations, and it makes the need for good information flow of paramount importance. This information flow must be two way. Supervisors must feed back deviations from the plan, as mentioned above. However, it is equally important for higher-level management to convey how each unit fits into overall plans, so each unit's manager can see the value of following the plan to achieve overall goals.

Sometimes, planning systems become an end in themselves. Organizations must focus on implementation. One option discussed by several authors, including Weick (1979), is to establish an organization based on *reacting* quickly to external cues from the environment. This organization would not place much emphasis (if any) on planning, but would instead emphasize regular data collection and quick action. In either case, following through on implementation is important. If the organization reacts rather than plans, a formal planning system is not needed and may be counterproductive.

There is an old management saying, ''If it ain't broke, don't fix it.'' New methods of managing a system, such as the introduction of quantitative methods for planning operations, run the risk of breaking something that was functioning, albeit functioning imperfectly. One way to avoid this is to implement major changes in management control "in parallel" with the old system. That is, when the new system is ready, put it in operation to see what it would do, but allow the old system to make the actual decisions. Scrutinize the new system's results to see if there are flaws (there often are).

Parallel implementation has been criticized strongly by some managers because it can indicate less than full confidence in the new system and can impose an impossible work load on the employees who are forced to do many tasks twice (the old way and the new way). Whether a system is implemented in parallel or installed cold turkey, the importance of careful testing using historical data and extensive training cannot be overstated. A system that is full of bugs or poorly understood by its users is doomed.

The user of the new system should be included in the design from the beginning, and the design (or redesign) should continue during the implementation. The user will then find inadequacies that could not be predicted before implementation. Changing the system in response to the user's suggestions enhances the probability of eventual success because the user will gain a feeling of commitment to the final form of the system.

Finally, implement the new system when you are convinced that it will improve the situation, based on watching its decisions on the actual system. In other words, "If it ain't broke, fix it only after you're sure an improvement will result."

Evaluation and Follow-Up

Information concerning the success or failure of plans is generated largely by the accounting system in an organization. *Budgets* are established for a department's overall expenditures for a month or a year, for example. Then actual costs are obtained and a *variance* is reported as the difference between the budgeted and the actual cost. A *standard cost* is determined by an industrial engineer for how much a unit should cost to produce or how much a service should cost to perform. Again, the actual cost is obtained by the accounting system and a *variance* is reported. These topics are discussed at length in texts on managerial and cost accounting such as Bierman et al. (1986).

Budgets, or more appropriately goals, can also be established for items that are not measured in monetary units. Service level or sales goals can be established, and deviations should be routinely reported. In fact, proper evaluation of day-to-day operations requires periodic information on the system's functioning vis-à-vis the budgets, goals, and standards both for costs and for some nonmonetary quantities. That information can be used to *follow up,* to see if changes can be made to improve the operations of the organization. How often to obtain the information varies from one organization to another, depending on the cost of the information and the potential cost of allowing a system to get out of control. Also, as we have argued in many places in this text, goals for portions of the organization (such as inventory turns for a division) must not be allowed to hurt the organization. Performance should be measured against goals for information, but managers must apply their judgment to the results.

In addition to regular weekly and/or monthly evaluation and follow-up of the type described above, there must be major evaluations of the operations area of an organization. These will occur annually or whenever a major problem exists.

For example, once a year all profit-making organizations are required to reconcile the actual level of inventory with what the record-keeping system says is present. That is, there must be a "physical inventory" count. This may be done for all items at one time, and an adjustment is made to the inventory record to correct the inventory level. Alternatively, the organization maintains a "perpetual inventory" system in which up-to-date records of inventory levels are constantly maintained; the firm may spread the physical inventory process over the year, doing one item at a time. They make each correction as they find it, and the process starts again as soon as all items have been reconciled. This latter system involves less disruption of the production process.

Sometimes a manager either knows, or wonders if, a system is out of control—costs may be too high for the functions performed or quality may be too low given the market performance of other products. To investigate, a major audit of the system may be necessary. If a major redesign of an operation is contemplated, management needs to specify what the area should be doing, and then see how well it is doing. Total cost of sales, a detailed value-added structure of the products, percent cost of overhead, total inventory level, inventory turnover, and many other items are of interest. Perhaps more important, the change in these variables from year to year should be examined. The manager will also want to compare unit cost of sales, inventory turnover, service level, and other variables against the performance of other organizations in the same industry. This comparative information is obtained from annual reports and industry associations, and it can be very important in assessing a firm's competitive position. There is a danger that, since methods of accounting vary, the external and internal numbers may not be directly comparable. Even so, some attempt at such comparisons is necessary. One example of such *diagnostic analysis* is given by Hax et al. (1980).

Review Problem

In providing fire protection, implementation of plans involves sending equipment in response to calls. Budgets or goals can be set for labor cost, equipment usage, response time, and so on. Very briefly describe some data you would like to have to evaluate the firefighting operations and the type of follow-up procedures that might be appropriate.

Solution

Monthly or weekly accounting variances on costs incurred, labor used, and equipment usage would be needed. Average response time would also be obtained frequently. Too slow an average response might lead management to change some operating policies or to redesign its emergency call system.

Comparative figures from other cities would be obtained occasionally. These figures could also be used to directly compare loss of life and property per capita to see if the higher-level goals are being met, as well as the lower-level goals and budgets.

15-4 Summary

Coordination of the operations function of an organization requires a top-down approach. Each manager from the top to the bottom must know the tasks in his or her domain and how they fit into the whole system. To enhance coordination, interdepartmental charges for goods or services should be designed to encourage behavior consistent with the overall goals of the organization.

In assigning tasks in a complex organization, such as the multiplant, multiwarehouse system of the Chris Tull Glass Company (Section 15-2), a hierarchical planning approach should be followed. The system-wide plan is derived first, and this constrains lower-level decisions. The system can be managed by centralizing some key problems and determining a plan for those, then allowing each local manager to work out assigned problems within the constraints imposed by central plans, using knowledge of the local scene.

Mathematical models can be used at each organizational level, to help solve the manager's problem, but it is often inappropriate to try to solve the entire system-wide problem using a huge mathematical model. The decision system for CTG, described in Figure 15-2, has a sequential structure with models used in several places. All tasks are assigned, feedback is provided for in key places, and the resulting solution will fit together. Even though the problems faced by other organizations will be different, as the Review Problem for Section 15-2 illustrates, the overall approach of coordinating large-scale operations using hierarchical planning is useful in many settings.

All the plans are for nought if they are not implemented. First-line supervision must understand their part in achieving organizational goals. The information system must feed back deviations from the plan to those doing the planning so that the organization can be kept on target. Some organizations may choose to react to the environment rather than plan. In either case, behavioral science, management accounting, proper information flow, sound managerial judgment, and common sense must be used to manage the day-to-day operations so that they help achieve the organization's goals and satisfy the needs of the managers and the labor force.

PROBLEMS

*1. How are job descriptions, cost accounting, and information systems used to achieve coordination in an organization? Give an example of how each of the three might be used.

2. Write a brief job description for a vice-president of logistics who is charged with making decisions regarding material procurement and finished-goods distribution for several divisions in a manufacturing company.

*3. What is the basic idea of a matrix organization? In your opinion, what are the advantages and disadvantages of such an organization?

4. What is the basic idea of hierarchical planning, as described by Hax and Meal (1975)? What is their argument against using a large, integrated model to solve an entire company's production–distribution problems? Finally, give your reasons for either agreeing or disagreeing with the general approach.

5. Describe the function of the following subsystems from Figure 15-1.
   (a) Plant/product assignment subsystem.
   (b) Seasonal planning subsystem.
   (c) Overstock limit subsystem.
   (d) Family scheduling subsystem.
   (e) Item scheduling subsystem.

*6. In Section 15-2, it is stated that "the $40 per ton penalty for operating a plant with one furnace is so high that no plant will do so." Show some brief calculations to verify this statement.

7. In Section 15-2, inventory cost of a level-production plan for CTG is given as being "roughly $(111,100)(320)(0.01) \approx \$350,000$." Verify the 111,100 total inventory figure.

8. In Section 15-2, a decision system is given for CTG. If inventory costs were five times as high, that system would be dramatically different. Giving supporting calculations and discussion where necessary, describe:
   (a) The type of seasonal inventory plan that would be appropriate.
   (b) The LP that could be used to assign warehouses to plants.
   (c) The changes that would be necessary in Figure 15-2.

*9. Redo Problem 8 assuming that inventory costs are the same as in Section 15-2 but the cost of keeping furnaces warm is one-tenth the amount given in Section 15-2.

10. A developing nation has a commissioner of rural health who must seek outside grants for support as well as administer the use of an allocation of tax dollars from her government. The nation is divided into eight geographic regions, each with a regional director. Each region has several clinics as well as mobile operations (visiting nurses, for example) that are attached to the clinics for a home base. The system must react to standard, ongoing needs and to crises. Crises may involve all the mobile units in a region or may even involve units from all regions. Following the pattern in the solution to the Section 15-2 Review Problem, give a hierarchical plan for managing rural health operations.

11. Give an example of an organization that should, in general, react to the environment rather than plan. (They may do some of both, of course.) Justify your example.

*12. Give an example in which each of the following might be used to evaluate and follow up on system performance. In each case what would the purpose of the information be?

(a) Budgets or goals for items measured in nonmonetary units.

(b) Standard costs and variances from standard costs.

(c) Distribution audit.

13. A rural health system is described in Problem 10. (Refer to Problem 10 for a description.) Briefly describe the data you would like to have to evaluate the system and the type of follow-up procedures that might be appropriate. Comment on the problem of replanning after a crisis.

*14. Why should a new system be implemented in parallel with the old one? Are there any disadvantages to doing so?

15. Describe the trade-off involved in determining how often to obtain cost reports from a manufacturing operation.

REFERENCES

BIERMAN, H., T. DYCKMAN, AND R. SWIERINGA, *Managerial Cost Accounting,* 3rd ed. New York: Macmillan, 1986.

BITRAN, G., E. HAAS, AND A. HAX, "Hierarchical Production Planning: A Single Stage System." *Operations Research,* Vol. 29, No. 4 (July–August 1981).

BITRAN, G., E. HAAS, AND A. HAX, "Hierarchical Production Planning: A Two Stage System." *Operations Research,* Vol. 30, No. 2 (March–April 1982).

BITRAN, G., D. MARIENI, AND J. NOONAN, "Introduction to Multi-plant MRP." Working Paper 1486-83, Sloan School of Management, MIT, Cambridge, Mass., October 1983.

CAIE, J., AND W. MAXWELL, "Hierarchical Machine Load Planning," in *Multi-level Production/Inventory Systems: Theory and Practice,* L. Schwarz, ed. New York: North-Holland, 1981.

DEMPSTER, M. A. H., M. L. FISHER, L. JANSEN, B. J. LAGEWEG, J. K. LENSTRA, AND A. H. G. RINNOOY KAN, "Analytical Evaluation of Hierarchical Planning Systems." *Operations Research,* Vol. 29, No. 4 (July–August 1981).

GALBRAITH, J., *Organizational Design.* Reading, Mass.: Addison-Wesley, 1977.

HAX, A., AND N. MAJLUF, "Organizational Design: A Survey and an Approach." *Operations Research,* Vol. 29, No. 3 (May–June 1981).

HAX, A., N. MAJLUF, AND M. PENDROCK, "Diagnostic Analysis of a Production and Distribution System." *Management Science,* Vol. 26, No. 9 (September 1980).

HAX, A., AND H. MEAL, "Hierarchical Integration of Production Planning and Scheduling," in TIMS *Studies in the Management Sciences,* Vol. 1: *Logistics,* M. Geisler, ed. New York: North-Holland/American Elsevier, 1975.

KRAJEWSKI, L., AND L. RITZMAN, "Disaggregation in Manufacturing and Service Organizations: Survey of Problems and Research." *Decision Sciences,* January 1977.

MAXWELL, W., J. MUCKSTADT, J. THOMAS, AND J. VANDEREECKEN, "A Modeling Framework for Planning and Control of Production in Discrete Parts Manufacturing and Assembly Systems.'' *Interfaces,* Vol. 13, No. 6 (December 1983).

VOLKEMA, R., ''Problem Formulation in Planning and Design.'' *Management Science,* Vol. 29, No. 6 (June 1983).

WEICK, K., *The Social Psychology of Organizing,* 2nd ed. Reading, Mass.: Addison-Wesley, 1979.

CHAPTER 16

Quality
of Goods
and Services

One of the major achievements of the industrial revolution has been the ability to mass produce goods of uniform quality. The automobile is an outstanding example. Most American cars can be expected to operate reliably for 50,000 to 100,000 miles or more. "Made in USA" is a label that has long been associated with high quality.

However, in recent years poor quality has been causing problems and embarrassment in American industry. It is not just a rumor. Manufacture of air conditioners is a case in point. Garvin (1983) visited every Japanese manufacturer of room air conditioners and all but one of their American counterparts. He found several interesting facts. First, the product failure rates were between 500 and 1000 times higher for some manufacturers than for others. Compared to American plants, the *average* Japanese assembly-line defect rate was 70 times lower, and the first-year service call rates were "nearly 17 times better." Most embarrassing is the finding that "the poorest Japanese company typically had a failure rate less than half that of the best U.S. manufacturer" (Garvin, 1983, p. 66).

A second example is the Quasar Electronic Company, which acquired a U.S. television manufacturer and within a short period lowered the defect rate to 15 per 100 sets, which is 10 times better than the American average. Quasar is owned by Matsushita Electronics, and the Japanese average is 1 defect in 200 sets. In describing this case, Smith (1979) points out that the methods used in this turnaround were not fancy or revolutionary. The following were their actions:

1. Did a thorough life-cycle test of components.
2. Used a pilot production line for planning.

3. Described the process and instructions in detail and in writing.

4. Designed work stations to minimize operator error.

5. Separated lines that use similar parts, to avoid the error of using the wrong item.

6. Screened critical components before assembly.

Attention to fundamentals was all that was needed. None of these ideas is new. They all exist in American industry, and many of them originated in this country. Someone else is making better use of them.

Quality is an economic problem. Rework is an example. If 20% of items fail an inspection step and must be reworked, the economic cost is substantial. Direct expenses include the salaries of the workers and the additional resources needed to perform the rework, including machines, energy, and raw materials. Indirect costs can be even greater. Examples include missed deadlines, destroyed production schedules, and items sitting in inventory awaiting parts that are being reworked. At a third level there are the costs of the inspection program. All the reworked items must be reinspected. Moreover, a process that is in control needs less inspection to begin with.

Quality and productivity go hand in hand. Although authors disagree on the best way to improve quality, they agree that a company that is in control of quality will have greater manufacturing efficiency and productivity. "Quality is free," declares Crosby (1979), "but it is not a gift." This statement sums up the opinion that effective, permanent quality improvement is difficult to achieve, but more than pays for itself in increased productivity.

Quality has many dimensions that make it elusive to define. One aspect is *reliability,* the ability to perform without failure. Quality also refers to the *grade* of a good or service, such as the U.S. Department of Agriculture grades for meat products (prime, choice, good, etc.). *Safety* and quality are closely related in most people's minds, and safety standards are set by federal agencies such as the Consumer Product Safety Commission and the Food and Drug Administration. *Consistency* is also valued by consumers, as variation in quality level can cause confusion and disappointment. The reader can list several additional dimensions, some of which are specific to the particular good or service.

When it comes to measuring quality, the multiplicity of definitions becomes a major stumbling block. A simple solution is to define quality as *conformance to requirements.* If a good or service lives up to expectations, it is of high quality. This places a heavy burden on product specifications. If a component meets specifications but fails to perform adequately, the specifications are at fault. Deciding on requirements is a major determinant of quality.

It is vital to have a workable definition of quality, and "conformance to requirements" has the advantage of bringing the issue to a practical level. According to this definition, adding an extra fine finish or using materials that are far stronger than required *does not add quality* to an item unless it somehow causes the item to conform better to requirements. Quality is defined relative to use, rather than general characteristics that may be intangible.

A common mistake is to view quality as the sole responsibility of the department that produces the good or service. Lack of conformance can also be a problem of design or advertising. For example, an income tax service that is designed to aid people with average tax situations would get a low quality rating if it were misadvertised as offering advice to everyone. As a second example, consider the manufacture of manual automobile transmissions. If the gears are improperly designed, the transmissions will fail despite the best efforts of manufacturing.

Quality begins at the product concept stage and extends throughout the development, production, delivery, and use of a good or service. Causes of poor quality can occur any place in the organization, from top management to janitorial staff, in accounting, production, sales, service, or any of the functional areas, including the quality control function itself. Some quality problems have roots outside the organization, such as defective supplies from a vendor or incorrect specifications from a customer.

The first section of this chapter describes how quality issues permeate an organization and discusses briefly some organizational design issues as they affect quality. Several quality-improvement programs are described that have found acceptance in practice. The remaining sections describe some statistical techniques commonly used to monitor quality of goods and services.

16-1 ORGANIZATION FOR QUALITY ASSURANCE

Quality assessment is an investigation of the level of quality being achieved. *Quality control* begins with assessment, and includes actions taken to eliminate unacceptable quality. The typical quality control program is based on periodic inspection, followed by feedback of the results and changes or adjustments where necessary. *Quality assurance* includes quality control, but it also refers to emphasis on quality in the design of the products, processes, and jobs, and in personnel selection and training.

Quality assurance is an ancient idea, influencing the development of apprenticeships and guilds, for example. Systematic inclusion of quality assurance throughout an organization is a twentieth-century product, and statistical methods in quality control, first proposed by Shewhart in 1924, were not in wide use in the United States until World War II, when military procurement was (and still is) guided by published quality control procedures. Intensive training courses were provided by the government to explain statistical quality control to contractors, suppliers, and government workers. These courses and published standards were the major factors that established quality control as a way of life in American industry.

Beginning in the 1950s, statistical methods were introduced to Japanese manufacturers (Deming, 1982). Instruction in these methods supplements the training of the workers in the air-conditioner plants studied by Garvin (1983), described in the introduction of this chapter. All the Japanese plants relied heavily on process control charts. In contrast, only one U.S. plant had made a "comparable effort," and it was the one with the lowest defect rate.

In addition to statistical methods, other programs have been invented to deal with the quality problem. Zero defects and value engineering are examples. The quality control circle (or quality circle) is a Japanese import aimed at the same goal. Each of these ideas has merit and has proved successful in some places and not in others.

The major problem in implementing quality assurance programs seems to be the urge to achieve a "quick fix." Ideas painstakingly worked out in one setting have been transplanted, but too often the visible but superficial elements take on an identity of their own. For example, zero defects programs (Halpin, 1966) put great emphasis on signs, slogans, and progress charts to motivate employees. However, by themselves these elements do not bring about permanent change. Zero defects worked well at the Martin Company, but programs that try to implement zero defects without fundamental organizational change are doomed to failure.

Quality control in health care received a boost in the mid-1960s by a federal requirement for *utilization review,* a formal program of evaluation to determine whether hospital resources are being wasted. This has been extended to the practice of medicine itself, and the decade of the 1970s saw the introduction of the Professional Standards Review Organization (PSRO), formalizing and centralizing quality control in medicine. However, this has proved to be a much tougher problem than in manufacturing, since the product is a very complex service, not fully understood by its practitioners, and beyond the comprehension of most of the public. Thus, in medicine, quality assurance consists of high-quality training, certification examinations (with recent emphasis on periodic recertification), and review or inspection with feedback of the findings.

Reducing the Cost of Quality

The term *cost of quality* (COQ) is a misnomer. COQ is a measure of the cost to the firm of a *lack* of quality. It is very difficult to measure, especially in a firm that is just beginning to explore quality improvement.

Crosby (1979) describes what happens to the COQ measure of a firm as it progresses through five stages of understanding. In his example, the actual COQ is 20% of the cost of sales, but management has no idea of its magnitude because it has never been estimated. After a few months of investigation, COQ improves to 18%, but management thinks it is about 3% because they do not realize that more than the cost of the quality control department is involved. For example, the manufacturing department has many people that inspect, test, adjust, and perform other quality control functions. In addition, COQ includes the cost of rework and the additional equipment required to perform it, warranty costs, cost of consumer affairs, cost of implementing engineering changes and communicating them to customers, and many others.

In this example, the *estimated* COQ increases as management progresses in its understanding of how great the potential savings are for doing things right. In later stages, a system-wide view identifies major sources of COQ and problem-solving mechanisms are established to deal with them. The actual COQ is finally known, and it begins to decrease substantially. The final stage has a COQ of 2.5% of the cost of sales, and management has a complete view of the sources of quality problems and mechanisms for detection and prevention.

What actually happens to bring about such dramatic cost reduction through quality improvement? What is the best way to go about it? There are many different approaches, and some of the recommendations conflict. For example, Deming (1982) and Garvin (1983) emphasize the importance of statistical methods, whereas Smith (1979) states that "most people do not understand statistics"; and "Never use statistics when you don't have to." As a second example, Crosby (1979) supports the idea of a zero defects day, whereas Deming (1982) recommends: "Eliminate numerical goals, slogans, pictures, posters, urging people to increase production, sign their work as an autograph, etc. . . . Zero Defects is an example." He refers to these as "management's lazy way out."

Nevertheless, there are many points of agreement.

1. Quality is not only free, it is profitable. Most of the cost of quality is waste.

2. A major commitment must be made by top management, and it must be visible to the employees. One method to achieve this is to create a quality assurance department that reports directly to top management. Constant involvement in and support for quality improvement efforts is vital to their success.

3. Problems are viewed differently at different levels.
   (a) *Importance*. Management might consider a suggestion about the employee cafeteria to be trivial, but quality of work life (see Chapter 6) affects workers' attitudes and performance. (What if someone removed the coffee pot in the executive suite?)
   (b) *Causes*. Supervisors may think the workers are not as careful as they used to be, but the workers may lay the blame on the variability of the materials they receive or improper instructions.
   (c) *Solutions*. Management might see more training as necessary, whereas supervisors might realize that giving inspectors and workers the same specifications would eliminate the problem.

4. Major quality problems often cross departmental lines, so barriers to system-wide actions must be permanently removed, and quality improvement activities must be established as positive efforts rather than as blame assignment.

As an example, engineering changes that are not promptly translated to clear, complete manufacturing directions lead to increased rework. Clearing up this communication channel allows both departments to do their jobs better.

5. Quality problems can have causes outside the organization. Vendor control, for example, is as important as any other element of quality improvement.

6. Accurate information is necessary for effective problem solving. Because of points 3 and 4, this can be very difficult. Problem solvers must have a broad view. Detailed understanding of more than one area and level of the firm is very useful.

7. Attitudes toward quality are important but attitude change programs alone are a waste. All employees (including top management) must understand how important and productive quality improvements are. But it is impossible to change attitudes without changing the way work is done. In the absence of tangible, permanent change a program will be dismissed as just another passing fad.

8. Training is the key. If the use of statistics is to be emphasized, employees must be taught how to use them effectively. If problem identification and solution teams are formed, they must be trained how to find and solve problems. Most important, training in job performance is the key to doing it right the first time.

In any organization, the success of quality assurance depends on how it is implemented. If management views it as a one-time project, focused on improving employee attitudes and pride, the results will be much more limited than if quality assurance is formally integrated into the organization. One structure that accomplishes this integration has a department of quality, equal in position with marketing, finance, manufacturing, and so on. This separation of function has the advantage of creating an identifiable line of authority and responsibility.

However, conflict is common between the quality department and the others, since quality is viewed as the responsibility of outsiders who constantly interfere with the normal flow of work. An alternative is to make each department responsible for its own quality, with occasional audits from outside. The problem with this design is the difficulty of coordinating quality assurance programs across departments. However, job enrichment is facilitated by placing responsibility at the lowest levels, and this responsibility can have a powerful effect on pride and morale of the work force.

A compromise to the preceding two approaches is to establish quality assurance as a separate functional area, but one that has a service rather than policing role. If successful, this organizational scheme allows quality assurance to cross boundaries and yet avoid the barriers that mistrust raises. To achieve this ideal, fear must be eliminated as an element of quality control. If people fear that they will look bad whenever a quality improvement is needed in their area, the quality assurance department will be the enemy, not the servant.

Production Control and Quality

Plant layout and production control methods and philosophy can have a distinct impact on quality. A case in point is the just-in-time system described in Chapter 12. Cross training of employees for several jobs is an important part of this system because of its emphasis on keeping the process going without inventory buffers. If there is a slowdown or stoppage in one work area, help is available from neighboring workers because they are stopped too and they are trained to do both jobs. This affects quality in two ways.

1. Cross training employees improves insight into problems that cross departmental boundaries. The workers become better problem solvers.
2. The philosophy is: "Don't pass an item on until your task is properly done, even if you cause a work stoppage." In other words, do the job right the first time, and get help if necessary. This philosophy reduces manufacturing defects.

Monden (1981) describes how this philosophy is put into action at Toyota by prominently displaying a board with a schematic diagram of the work areas. If a worker does not finish his task in the allotted time, the production process is stopped and a light on the board indicates the area that needs help. The same idea is implemented for fully automatic machines by including automatic inspection with the capability of shutting down the process. They call this *autonomation* because of the autonomy granted to the inspection machine.

Quality control also has an effect on production. Of course, if defective items are found and production is stopped, quality control *can be said to have* slowed down production. (What has really happened is that it has stopped out-of-control production but probably did not reduce the output rate of acceptable items.) More to the point, feedback from quality control measurements can be used to fine-tune the production process.

Deming (1982) describes how this occurred at the Nashua Corporation in the manufacture of carbonless paper. At first, quality control was having a negative effect. The operator of the machine that applied the coating was over-compensating for the variability of the process. By adjusting the flow rate too often, he added to the process variability rather than controlling it. When statistical methods were introduced, the overcompensation ceased. Adjustments were made only when the operator had statistically sound evidence that the machine had strayed from its proper setting. This had the effect of reducing the variability of the process and allowed the machine to be set to apply a lower amount of coating on the average. Savings in coating material were $800,000 per year.

In the health area, statistical methods are used to detect unusual patterns of patient care. For example, diagnosis related groupings (DRGs) categorize patients according to their medical problems, procedures, and other relevant characteristics such as age and sex. Averages and variability of outcome variables such as length of stay and cost of services are collected and used to identify unusual patterns such as a hospital that over- or undercharges, or a physician that keeps his or her patients in the hospital for an unusually long or short period. Information gathered from inquiries based on these statistics sometimes leads to changes in medical practice or pricing of services.

The conclusion of these and other examples in manufacturing and service is inescapable. Quality control and production control are inseparable. Low-quality production does not conform to the customer's requirements and therefore is not really production at all. Increasing quality is increasing *real* production.

Quality Circles

Although originally conceived in Japan as quality control circles, the American version is broader in scope. Werther (1982) views quality circles as productivity and worker participation programs, and provides a long list of major U.S. corporations that use them successfully. Ingle and Ingle (1983) describe applications in service industries such as health care, government, department stores, and education. The basic philosophy is that employees have valuable insights and want to participate in management.

A quality circle is a group of employees whose assignment is to identify problems, formulate solutions, and present their results to management with suggestions for implementation. Although simple in concept, successful implementation of a quality circles program requires a massive effort on the part of management. The support structure usually consists of a steering committee of top management officials, facilitators, circle leaders, and circle members.

> *Steering Committee.* They provide overall guidance, suggest problems for the circles to address, receive recommendations from the circles, and follow up on implementation. The steering committee must make sure that the circles receive the support they need to be effective.
>
> *Facilitators.* One facilitator is assigned to several circles. They provide training for the leaders and support the training programs for the members. When the circle requests information, the facilitator's responsibility is to provide it. A facilitator must be well connected in the organization and requires strong backing from top management.
>
> *Circle Leaders.* Often an area supervisor, a leader has responsibilities that include training the circle members in problem identification and solution methods, and preparing an effective presentation to management. This is considered excellent preparation for someone who is likely to be promoted since they become indoctrinated in the philosophy that a manager's function is to facilitate the tasks of the workers.
>
> *Circle Members.* These are volunteers from the regular work force. They are given one hour of company time weekly to carry out their discussions and projects. Trained in techniques of brainstorming and identifying causes, they keep the facilitator busy by requesting information about various problems

of their choice. Based on preliminary findings, the group focuses on a problem and works out a solution and a strategy to implement it. If the recommendation is accepted by the steering committee, the circle is kept posted on its progress. If the recommendation is rejected (a fairly rare occurrence if the circle leader and the facilitator have done their jobs well), it is the responsibility of the steering committee to explain in detail why it was rejected.

Establishing a quality circle program takes time and effort. It embodies ideas from many other quality assurance programs and requires care to be done well. However, once the structure has been established and several successes have been scored, the process accelerates. More people volunteer as skepticism diminishes.

At Hughes Aircraft, Kohler and Wells (1982) report that over 500 circles have been established, and the president encourages middle managers to "make this a top priority of their job." Among the cases described in that article, there are certain results that seem general.

1. Increased information sharing among employees.
2. Problems are less identified with individuals.
3. People feel less cut off from the company.
4. Departmental interface issues are commonly selected by circles.
5. Personal satisfaction when solutions are adopted.
6. Increased understanding of problems faced by management.
7. Better employee/supervisor rapport.

Is the quality circle another fad? Schonberger (1983) states that the Japanese have not adopted them in their American operations. The important question of whether quality circles can address the "important few" issues rather than the "trivial many" is also raised. For example, could a quality circle ever recommend a complete renovation of a plant and a change in its production control philosophy such as was done at the American Kawasaki plant? Probably not. But many companies have reported great success with quality circles. They are firmly grounded in behavioral science principles and seem popular with employees and management.

Review Problems

1. How does the just-in-time manufacturing system contribute to quality improvement?
2. Why is higher reliability different from higher quality?
3. In the Nashua Corporation example, why could the amount of coating be reduced when statistical control was established?

Solutions

1. There is little inventory between workstations, so the workers are very dependent on each other. There is great emphasis on mutual support, so a worker will ask for help rather than pass on a defective item.

2. An example helps. A bearing that will last for 1 million miles without failure is highly reliable. However, on an automobile designed to last 100,000 miles it is of no greater quality than a bearing designed for 200,000 miles.

3. When the normal process variation was documented and abnormal deviations were detectable through statistics, a smaller allowance was needed for process variation.

16-2 ACCEPTANCE SAMPLING

It is often convenient to inspect items in batches. For example, when a shipment arrives, one may wish to determine if the shipment should be accepted or returned to the supplier. A batch is described by its size (N items in a batch) and the fraction f of defective items. Although N may not always be known (there may be counting errors or a short shipment), for this discussion we will assume that it is. The goal is to find out whether the unknown fraction defective f is small enough to be acceptable.

The idea of acceptance sampling is to inspect only part of the batch, and then decide either to accept or reject the entire batch, based on the sample findings, or (perhaps) to continue inspecting if the findings are inconclusive.

Acceptance sampling is in common use today. However, a goal of zero defects implies that no value of f greater than zero is acceptable. Taken literally, this would eliminate sampling as an inspection strategy. However, zero defects is usually a goal, and sampling can be used to assure that the goal is being achieved, or nearly so, in practice.

The simplest procedure is *single sampling,* in which the accept/reject decision is always determined from the results of one sample of n items from the batch of N items. Each of the n sample items is inspected and categorized as either acceptable or defective.[1] If the number of defective items in the sample exceeds a prespecified cutoff level, c, the entire batch is rejected. (Depending on costs, a rejected batch may be scrapped, 100% inspected, or returned to the manufacturer.) Since a finding of c or fewer defective items in the sample implies accepting the batch, c is often referred to as the *acceptance level*.

The sampling plan is supposed to separate good batches from bad batches;

---

[1] Some sampling plans have several levels of errors, with "critical defect" being the worst. It is also possible to base a sampling plan on one or more measurements on each item, without necessarily judging the item defective or acceptable. These plans, known as acceptance sampling by variables, will not be discussed here.

by definition, the actual fraction of defective items (f) is low in a good batch and high in a bad batch. However, a *sample* from a batch might not be representative, which means that errors will occur; a few good batches will be rejected and a few bad batches will be accepted. How often these errors occur depends on how large the sample (n) is and how the acceptance level (c) is chosen. There are many kinds of sampling plans, but the possibility of error is never eliminated. Our next topic is the operating characteristics curve, which displays the probability of error graphically.

The Operating Charactistic Curve

The formulas and tables of statistical control can be awesome. Before studying the details of finding a sampling plan (i.e., values for n and c), it is useful to have a simple picture that allows us to compare sampling plans—how will they react to a variety of batches, with *unknown*, varying fraction defective? The answer is provided by the *operating characteristic* (OC) *curve,* which displays the probability of accepting a batch with any given fraction defective.

Figure 16-1 shows OC curves for two single sampling plans ($n = 35$, $c = 1$, and $n = 150$, $c = 6$). For example, suppose that a batch with $f = 10\%$ defectives is considered to be a bad batch and $f = 2\%$ is good. Figure 16-1 has

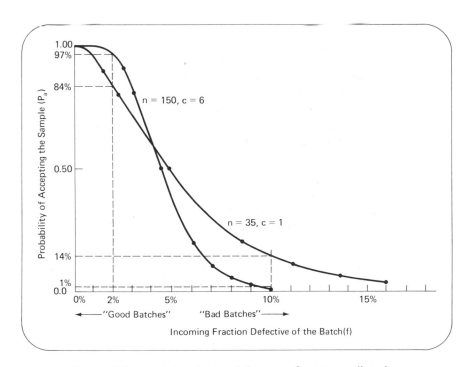

Figure 16-1   Operating characteristic curves for two sampling plans.

a vertical line at $f = 10\%$, helping us to see that the smaller sample of 35, drawn randomly from a batch of this quality, would stand a 14% chance of being accepted. The same unfortunate error can occur with the large sample, drawn randomly from the same batch, but the likelihood is less than 1%. The large sample is also better at *not* rejecting good batches; if $f = 2\%$, the larger sample has a much higher probability of acceptance.

It is not surprising that a larger sample does a better job of discriminating between good and bad batches. It has more information. However, the price for increased accuracy is higher inspection costs.

All sampling plans have an OC curve. Dodge and Romig (1959) devote an entire section of a book to these visual displays, allowing the user to see quickly whether a plan under consideration is suitable. We will learn how to determine the operating characteristics of simple plans, as the discussion continues.

Finding Single Sampling Plans by the OC Approach

We want to find a sampling plan (n, c) which has an OC curve that meets certain prespecified requirements. The criteria, defined below, are related to the probability of making either of two possible errors: accepting a bad batch or rejecting a good batch. The criteria are established subjectively, and the method for translating them into a sampling plan is explained in the next few pages.

1. AQL and α
   (a) The user of the items specifies an *acceptable quality level* (AQL)—the fraction defective that the user considers acceptable. Thus, if a batch were known to have a fraction defective equal to AQL, it should not be rejected.
   (b) Since the accept/reject decision is based on a sample, there is some chance for error. The producer's risk, denoted as α, is defined as the largest allowable probability of rejecting a good batch (by mistake). A value for α is specified subjectively at the same time that a good batch is defined. α is often chosen to be 5%.

2. LTPD and β
   (a) The user also specifies a *lot tolerance percent defective* (LTPD) as the fraction defective that defines a bad batch, or one that should be rejected. Of course, AQL is less than LTPD, and LTPD is usually less than 10% (often far less).
   (b) The consumer's risk, β, is the largest allowable probability of mistakenly accepting a bad batch. The β value, specified along with LTPD, is often chosen to be 10%.

Mugwump Assemblers purchases parts and components from several vendors and assembles mugwumps. One of the purchased items, which comes in batches of 1000 units, sometimes has an unacceptably high percentage of defectives. It would be very expensive to inspect all items in every batch, and wasteful as well because only a small percentage of bad-quality batches has been received. However, when the occasional high-defect batch arrives, production rates are lowered as the assembly testing stations reject items. Rework increases, and production is insufficient to meet demand.

There is no hard-and-fast rule for determining what AQL and LTPD should be, but Mugwump was accustomed to batches with 2% defectives or less. As a first cut it was decided to use 2% as an acceptable defect rate (AQL = 0.02) and that 10% is unacceptable (LTPD = 0.10). Between these values, management is not pleased with the defect rate, but it can be handled without slowing production excessively.

To be on the safe side, a small β value of 0.01 was chosen so that the sampling plan would be 99% sure to spot bad batches before they hit the assembly line. A more modest value of α = 0.05 was used only because it is customary. Mugwump wants a sampling plan that meets these criteria.

One way to find a sampling plan that meets the AQL, α, LTPD, and β criteria is to search through a book of OC curves. For example, we determined from the OC curve in the preceding subsection that for batches with f = 2% (which is now our AQL), the sampling plan n = 35, c = 1 has an 84% acceptance probability, so the chance of error is 16%. (When f = AQL, rejecting the batch is an error.) This is too high to meet the goal of α = 0.05. For bad batches, f = LTPD = 10% and the error probability is 14%. (Accepting is an error when f = LTPD.) This misses the goal of β = 0.01 by a wide margin. Hence we conclude that n = 35 is not a large enough sample. Only more data (larger n) can reduce both of the error probabilities.

The other sampling plan (n = 150, c = 6) does meet the criteria. Its OC curve shows a 97% acceptance probability for f = AQL, whereas α = 0.05 means that 95% would be high enough. And at f = LTPD the error probability is below the required 1%. Mugwump could use this plan to reduce by 99% the occurrence of bad batches reaching the assembly line. Inspecting 150 units, randomly selected from an incoming batch, they would accept the entire batch if 6 or fewer defective items were found, and reject it if there were 7 or more.

Rather than searching through a book of OC curves, n and c can be found with a few calculations and Table 16-1, or by using a *Thorndike chart*, which is a graphical version of this table. (These numbers are based on the Poisson probability distribution, which is an accurate description of random sampling when f is fairly small and n is a small portion of the batch.) Accompanying the table are instructions for three ways to use it. We will illustrate the first two, leaving the third for a review problem.

Instruction 1 tells how to obtain the data to plot an OC curve. Using the plan n = 150, c = 6, we divide the numbers in the column under c = 6 by 150. The result is an f value for each acceptance probability listed on the left. For instance, the first row has probability of acceptance = P_a = 0.01, and we compute f = 14.5706/150 = 0.097. So if Mugwump received a batch with 9.7% defective (unknown to them) and used the sampling plan n = 150, c = 6, there

TABLE 16-1 OPERATING CHARACTERISTICS OF SINGLE SAMPLING PLANS

	Acceptance Probability, P_a	ACCEPTANCE NUMBER, c										
		0	1	2	3	4	5	6	7	8	9	10
		$\mu = nf$ = expected number defective in the sample										
β rows, entries denoted μ_β	0.010	4.6052	6.6383	8.4059	10.0450	11.6046	13.1085	14.5706	16.0000	17.4027	18.7831	20.1447
	0.025	3.6889	5.5716	7.2247	8.7672	10.2416	11.6683	13.0595	14.4227	15.7632	17.0848	18.3904
	0.050	2.9957	4.7439	6.2958	7.7537	9.1535	10.5130	11.8424	13.1481	14.4346	15.7052	16.9622
	0.100	2.3026	3.8897	5.3223	6.6808	7.9936	9.2747	10.5321	11.7709	12.9947	14.2060	15.4066
	0.200	1.6094	2.9943	4.2790	5.5150	6.7210	7.9060	9.0754	10.2325	11.3798	12.5188	13.6507
	0.500	0.6931	1.6783	2.6741	3.6721	4.6709	5.6702	6.6696	7.6692	8.6690	9.6687	10.6685
$(1-\alpha)$ rows, entries denoted μ_α	0.800	0.2231	0.8244	1.5350	2.2968	3.0895	3.9037	4.7337	5.5761	6.4285	7.2892	8.1570
	0.900	0.1054	0.5318	1.1021	1.7448	2.4326	3.1519	3.8948	4.6561	5.4325	6.2213	7.0208
	0.950	0.0513	0.3554	0.8177	1.3663	1.9701	2.6130	3.2853	3.9808	4.6952	5.4254	6.1690
	0.975	0.0253	0.2422	0.6187	1.0899	1.6235	2.2019	2.8144	3.4538	4.1154	4.7954	5.4912
	0.990	0.0101	0.1486	0.4360	0.8233	1.2791	1.7853	2.3302	2.9061	3.5075	4.1302	4.7712

1. To plot an OC curve for a given sampling plan (n, c):
   (a) Find the column for your c value.
   (b) Divide each number in that column by n. The results are the f values for the horizontal axis.
   (c) The P_a values, for the vertical axis, are in the far left column.
2. To find a single sampling plan:
   (a) Find c for which $\mu_\beta/\mu_\alpha \leqslant$ LTPD/AQL.
   (b) Then choose any n between $n_\beta = \mu_\beta$/LTPD and $n_\alpha = \mu_\alpha$/AQL.
3. To find the acceptance probability for a given n, c, and f:
   (a) Multiply $(n)(f)$.
   (b) In the appropriate c column, find values above and below nf.
   (c) In the P_a column read upper and lower limits for P_a in the two rows from step (b) (interpolate, if you wish.)

is only a 1% chance that the batch would be accepted. If we repeated this computation for the rest of the $c = 6$ column and plotted f versus P_a, the result would be the $n = 150$, $c = 6$ curve in Figure 16-1.

The second instruction tells how to find n and c given AQL, α, LTPD, and β. Following instruction 2(a), we locate the "β row" (where $P_a = \beta$) and the "$1 - \alpha$ row" (where $P_a = 1 - \alpha$). These are the top row and the ninth row for Mugwump. Step 2(a) says to find the column where μ_β/μ_α (the ratio of the "β row" to the "$1 - \alpha$ row") drops to LTPD/AQL ($= 0.10/0.02 = 5.0$) *or less*. At $c = 0$ the ratio is $4.6052/0.0513 = 89.0$, and at $c = 1$ it is $6.6383/0.3554 = 18.7$, and so on. The first ratio less than or equal to 5 is 4.44 at $c = 6$. This completes step 2(a) and we know that $c = 6$ will be the cutoff level.

Step 2(b) gives us two limits on the sample size. The lower limit is $n_\beta = \mu_\beta/\text{LTPD} = 14.57/0.10 = 145.7$ and the upper limit is $n_\alpha = \mu_\alpha/\text{AQL} = 3.29/0.02 = 164.5$. To conclude, Mugwump can use a sample size of 146 or 164 or any number in between and still achieve probabilities of error no greater than specified. So, as we already knew from Figure 16-1, $n = 150$, $c = 6$ will do the job. If Mugwump chooses the lower value of 146 to minimize inspection, the risk of bad batches getting through is higher than with a larger sample, but still no greater than the specified value β.

In this section, sampling plans were found using the OC approach, exclusively. After a few review problems, several other methods will be explored.

Review Problems

1. The plan $n = 35$, $c = 1$ shown in Figure 16-1 has $\alpha = 0.16$ and $\beta = 0.14$, both too large for Mugwump.
   (a) What would happen to α and β if c were increased but n remained at 35? If c decreased?
   (b) What would happen if n increased with c constant? If n decreased?
   (c) Why do we need to increase both n and c to lower both α and β?

2. Find a single sampling plan for AQL $= 0.8\%$ (or 0.008), $\alpha = 5\%$, LTPD $= 10\%$, and $\beta = 10\%$.

3. If a batch contains 8% defective items, what is the probability that it would be rejected by the plan $n = 40$, $c = 1$? (See instruction 3 at the bottom of Table 16-1).

Solutions

1. (a) Increasing c relaxes the criterion for accepting a batch. Both β and $1 - \alpha$ are acceptance probabilities, so β goes up and α goes down. Decreasing c has the opposite effect.
   (b) Larger samples mean more chances to find enough defectives to reject the batch; so β goes down and α rises. Lower n has the opposite effect.
   (c) Larger n gives us more information about the batch. The cutoff level has to be chosen relative to n; we are concerned with *fraction* defective which is measured by c/n.

2. Using instruction 2 in Table 16-1:

    (a) LTPD/AQL $= 0.10/0.008 = 12.5$; the "β row" is row 4, and the "$(1 - \alpha)$ row" is third from the bottom. The ratios of these two rows are $2.30/0.051 = 45.1$ for $c = 0$ and $3.89/0.355 = 11.0$ for $c = 1$. Here we stop because $11.0 < 12.5$. Therefore, we conclude that $c = 1$.

    (b) $\mu_\beta/\text{LTPD} = 3.89/0.10 = 38.9$

       $\mu_\alpha/\text{AQL} = 0.355/0.008 = 44.4$

    The plan $n = 40$, $c = 1$ will, therefore, do the job as would $n = 39$, $c = 1$ or $n = 44$, $c = 1$.

3. Using instruction 3 in Table 16-1:

    (a) $(n)(f) = (40)(0.08) = 3.2$

    (b) In the $c = 1$ column, the values 3.89 and 2.99 surround 3.2.

    (c) Therefore, P_a is between 0.10 and 0.20. Linear interpolation yields about 0.18, or 18%. Therefore, the rejection probability is about 82%.

16-3 ACCEPTANCE SAMPLING: OTHER METHODS

There are many ways to do acceptance sampling. The preceding section described the OC approach and single sampling plans. Extensions go in three directions: multiple sampling, sampling plans that change with experience, and methods other than OC to determine sampling plans. Examples of each are discussed in this section.

Double, Multiple, and Sequential Sampling Plans

The total amount of inspection can often be reduced by designing a plan that takes a sequence of small samples rather than taking one large sample. The savings accrue whenever an early decision is possible as a result of exceptionally good (or bad) results.

Wald (1947) proposed a plan that has two stopping rules: after each item is inspected, (1) stop and reject the batch if the cumulative number of defectives falls above a certain limit (see Figure 16-2); or (2) stop and accept the batch if defectives fall below a second limit. If neither limit is violated, another sample item is drawn and the process is continued. It has been estimated that sequential sampling may reduce the average number inspected by approximately 50%, by stopping earlier than a single sampling plan. Thus sequential plans make more efficient use of the information in the sample.

In a *double sampling plan,* after the first sample (of n_1 items) has been inspected, there are three choices, depending on the number of defective items found: (1) reject the batch, (2) accept the batch, or (3) draw a second sample (of n_2 items). If choice (3) is made, the final accept/reject decision is made on the combined sample of $n_1 + n_2$ items. Thus it operates much like a sequential

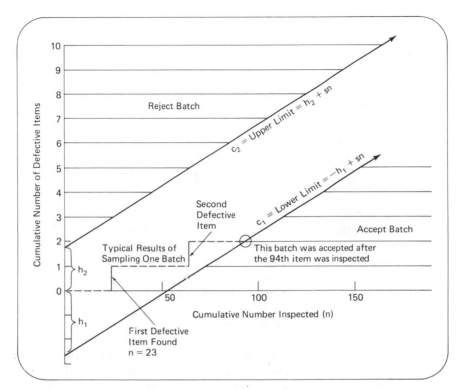

Figure 16-2 Sequential sampling plan[a] for Mugwump assemblers, with AQL = 0.02, α = 0.05, LTPD = 0.10, β = 0.01.

[a] *Formulas for sequential sampling limits shown in Figure 16-2:* First, calculate the factor X, where $\ln$ = natural logarithm and

$$X = 1/\ln\,[\text{LTPD}(1 - \text{AQL})/\text{AQL}(1 - \text{LTPD})] = 0.5901$$

Then, calculate

$$h_1 = X \ln\,[(1 - \alpha)/\beta] = 2.687$$

$$h_2 = X \ln\,[(1 - \beta)/\alpha] = 1.762$$

$$s = X \ln\,[(1 - \text{AQL})/(1 - \text{LTPD})] = 0.0503$$

plan, except that the stopping rules are only applied twice rather than after each item is inspected. A multiple sampling plan works the same way, but with more than two samples.

Double sampling plans reduce inspection costs because many accept/reject decisions are made based on the first sample which is smaller than with single sampling. Sequential sampling reduces inspection to a minimum but is more complex to use. In practice, single and double sampling are most common. The details of how to find a double or multiple plan may be found elsewhere (Duncan, 1974).

Mil. Std. 105d

This approach, explained in detail by Duncan (1974), is an international military standard. It provides tables that lead the user to a sampling plan based primarily on the acceptable quality level (AQL). It also provides a tightened inspection plan (to be used when two of five consecutive lots have been rejected by the normal plan) and a reduced plan (to be used when 10 batches in a row have been accepted). Thus the vendor is rated according to accumulated experience, and the sampling plan is adjusted accordingly.

Cost Minimization

The cost per unit inspected is defined as C_{ins}, and the cost of each undetected defective item is C_{def}. The goal is to find the n and c that minimize the average cost of inspection plus the average cost of undetected defective items. This is best implemented by a special-purpose computer program. So-called "optimal plans" are hard to compute and a prior estimate as to how many defectives are present is required. Problems 17 and 18 illustrate one approach. However, we can note two rules to determine whether sampling is economically practical.

First, if the cost of inspecting an item is less than the *expected* cost of its being defective, then 100% inspection of the entire batch is appropriate, and sampling is ruled out. For example, suppose that inspection cost is $0.50 per item. If the fraction defective has never been below 5% and the cost of outgoing defectives is $11, the expected cost of defectives is at least $(0.05)(11) = \$0.55$ per item. This exceeds C_{ins}, so all items should be inspected. Thus, letting f_{min} represent the lowest fraction defective that ever comes from a given supplier or process:

$$\text{Rule 1:} \qquad \text{If } C_{ins} < f_{min}C_{def}, 100\% \text{ inspection is optimal.} \qquad (1)$$

Second, suppose that f_{max} is the worst fraction defective that ever comes from a given supplier or process. Then:

$$\text{Rule 2:} \qquad \text{If } C_{ins} > f_{max}C_{def}, \text{ "zero" inspection is optimal,} \qquad (2)$$

where "zero" inspection means that only occasional monitoring is needed, but a regular sampling program would not pay. For example, if $C_{ins} = \$0.50$, $C_{def} = \$2$, and $f_{max} = 15\%$, then outgoing defectives cannot cost more than $(0.15)(\$2)$, or $0.30 on the average, compared to a $0.50 cost of inspection. Therefore, it is cheaper to accept the burden of the defectives than to sample any items.

If C_{ins} falls between $f_{min}C_{def}$ and $f_{max}C_{def}$, a sampling program is appropriate to monitor quality and protect against the possibility of relatively high fraction defective.

Quality After Inspection—Average Outgoing Quality

The inspection process has two direct effects on quality—batches with a high fraction defective are rejected, and the sampling process uncovers some of the defects even if the batch is accepted. These effects can be quantified, and the *average fraction defective after inspection* (i.e., in outgoing batches) is the usual measure.

Several formulas are available, depending on what is done with defective items and rejected batches. The following formulas assume that we are using *rectifying inspection,* which means that (1) rejected batches are fully inspected (and therefore are perfect after inspection) and (2) all defective items found (both in sampling and in 100% inspection) are replaced with good items. (Note that this also assumes that inspectors do not make mistakes.)

By assumption 2, all outgoing batches contain N items, the same as incoming batches. However, there are two kinds of outgoing batches—accepted and rejected. (Remember assumption 1 for rejected batches.) Suppose a batch has incoming fraction defective f. If it is accepted, $N - n$ items remain uninspected; we therefore expect that $(f)(N - n)$ are defective. In contrast, if it is rejected (100% inspected and rectified), there are no remaining defectives. Thus, if P_a is the probability that the sampling plan will accept the batch,

$$\begin{array}{c} \text{outgoing fraction} \\ \text{defective} \end{array} = \frac{(P_a)(f)(N - n) + (1 - P_a)(0)}{N} \qquad (3)$$

$$= P_a f \frac{N - n}{N}$$

A plot showing how the outgoing fraction defective depends on the incoming fraction defective (f) is called an *average outgoing quality* (AOQ) curve. Figure 16-3 is the AOQ curve for the sampling plan ($n = 150$, $c = 6$) derived in the preceding section for Mugwump Assemblers. This curve has a surprising property—when faced with increasingly worse batches (i.e., as f increases) there comes a point (labeled f_c in Figure 16-3) at which the outgoing fraction defective actually begins to improve. The reason for this is that the sampling plan rejects most bad batches (high f), and they are rectified through 100% inspection.

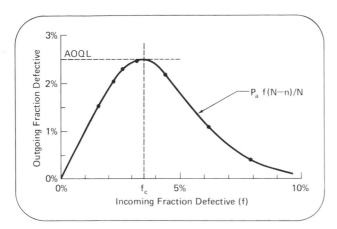

Figure 16-3 Average outgoing quality (AOQ) curve for the sampling plan $n = 150$, $c = 6$ applied to batches of $N = 10,000$.

The most "critical" incoming fraction defective, f_c, gives the worst outgoing quality, on the average, in the long run. The value of f_c is not very important, but the corresponding outgoing fraction defective, denoted AOQL for *average outgoing quality limit*, is extremely useful. No matter what the incoming fraction defective is, the *long-run average* outgoing fraction defective will not be worse (higher) than AOQL. In Figure 16-3, the peak value of the outgoing fraction defective appears to be AOQL = 2.5%.

In general, it is rather laborious to draw an AOQ curve just to find the peak value. Fortunately, a simpler method is available—look up the "AOQL factor," y, in Table 16-2, and multiply by $(1/n - 1/N)$. For example, the Mugwump sampling plan has $c = 6$, so $y = 3.8120$; if the samples of $n = 150$ are drawn from batches of $N = 10,000$, then AOQL $= (y)(1/n - 1/N) = 3.8120(1/150 - 1/10,000) = 0.0250$, or 2.5%.

Many managers prefer to use AOQL as a criterion for designing a sampling plan, rather than trying to decide on values for AQL, α, LTPD, and β. Dodge and Romig (1959) present tables that are designed for this purpose. They are used by selecting a value of AOQL, and a value for the normal process average fraction defective. The tables then give a sampling plan that meets the specified AOQL and minimizes the expected number of items inspected per lot when the process is in control (i.e., when the fraction defective is at the normal value).

The outgoing quality concept (with different formulas) also applies for sequential and multiple sampling, and for different handling of defectives and rejected batches. Duncan (1974, Chaps. 16, 17) describes several of these alternatives, and discusses their similarities and differences.

TABLE 16-2 AOQL FACTOR, y, USED IN THE FORMULA AOQL $= y(1/n - 1/N)$

Acceptance Number, c	AOQL Factor,[a] y
0	0.3679
1	0.8400
2	1.3711
3	1.9424
4	2.5435
5	3.1682
6	3.8120
7	4.4720
8	5.1457
9	5.8314
10	6.5277

[a] Achieved by locating the maximum value of μP_a, using the Poisson probability law for P_a, with mean $= \mu$. See Dodge and Romig (1959) for a discussion and a more extensive version of this table.

Comparing the AOQL and the OC Approaches

The goal of each approach to acceptance sampling is to obtain a reliable judgment of whether batch quality is acceptable, based on inspection of part of the batch. The OC approach protects the consumer against receiving bad batches, with a certain specified probability of error. The AOQL approach guarantees an *average* quality level to the consumer but with no specified probability of error.

Protection for the producer is also different. The AOQL plans offered by Dodge and Romig (1959) are designed to minimize the number of items inspected, whereas the OC approach achieves an acceptably small probability of rejecting good batches. There are several other approaches which use different design criteria. Choice among them is a matter of personal preference. However, regardless of the approach, all sampling plans have both an OC curve and an AOQ curve, so the principles we have discussed in Sections 16-2 and 16-3 can be used to evaluate any acceptance sampling plan.

Review Problems

1. If inspection costs $0.20 per item and each undiscovered defective item requires a special delivery order costing $10, how large must the process average fraction defective be to justify 100% inspection?

2. True or false? "If AOQL = 3%, no batch will have more than 3% defective items in it, after rectifying inspection." Explain your answer.

3. The Ace Supply Company's primary customer is Mugwump Assemblers. For each batch of 10,000 a rectifying acceptance sampling plan of $n = 40$, $c = 1$, is being used at Ace.
   (a) Using Mugwump's definition of LTPD = 0.10, what consumer's risk (probability of accepting a bad batch) is achieved by this sampling plan? (You will need to use instruction 3 in Table 16-1 to do this.)
   (b) What is the AOQL?
   (c) How will Ace's plan affect Mugwump's quality control program?

Solutions

1. 100% inspection is justified if $C_{ins} < f_{min}C_{def}$, or $0.20 < (f_{min})$ ($10), or $f_{min} > 0.2/10 = 0.02$, or 2%. Thus, if all batches have at least 2% defective, sampling part of each batch is not appropriate. All batches should be fully inspected.

2. False. It is possible that a bad batch will yield a good sample (an unlucky draw). However, in the long run, averaging over many batches, there will be 3% or fewer defective items after the acceptance sampling process (with rectification), regardless of how large the incoming fraction defective (f) is or how it varies over time.

3. (a) Using instruction 3 in Table 16-1, $nf = (40)(0.10) = 4.0$. Under $c = 1$, 4.74 and 3.89 surround 4.0. Therefore, P_a is between 5% and 10%.

(b) In Table 16-2, for $c = 1$, $y = 0.8400$, so AOQL $= y(1/n - 1/N) =$ $0.84(1/40 - 1/10,000) = 0.0209$, or about 2.1%.

(c) Although it does not satisfy Mugwump's criterion for consumer's risk, Ace's inspection plan will guarantee that Mugwump will not receive more than 2.1% defective items in the long run. It is also noteworthy that Ace's AOQL of 2.1% is lower than the 2.5% achieved by Mugwump (as displayed in Figure 16-3), even though the Mugwump plan uses a much larger sample.

16-4 PROCESS CONTROL

In order to provide rapid feedback to an ongoing production process, methods somewhat different from acceptance sampling are appropriate. Samples are taken as soon as they are available rather than waiting for completion of a batch. This affords the opportunity to detect unplanned changes in the production process shortly after they occur, and to take quick action, such as adjusting a machine, talking to a worker, or switching to a new batch of raw materials.

The most common device in process control is the *control chart*. First introduced by Shewhart (1931), the control chart is a visual display of the results of an inspection process, incorporating carefully derived limits to indicate unusual behavior. The details of this kind of chart are the subjects of this section.

As was true with acceptance sampling, a control chart can be based on either a categorical measurement such as a good/defective decision for each item (termed inspection by *attributes*) or a quantitative measurement of a quality-related variable, such as length, weight, hardness, and so on (inspection by *variables*). The difference between the two approaches is that the latter, requiring more precise measurement, is usually more time-consuming but also yields more information about the process. For example, knowing that a box of sugar has the incorrect weight is not as useful as knowing what its weight is, when one wishes to adjust the box-filling mechanism.

Process control statistics are used by firms that have adopted the goal of zero defects, even if they have rejected the idea of acceptance sampling. Frequent inspection of small samples ensures that changes in the process are detected quickly so that adjustments can be made before any defective units result, or at least before large numbers of defects have occurred. Statistical process control is very common in Japan, according to Deming (1982), in both manufacturing and service industries.

Process Control by Variables—X̄ and R Charts

All products and services have a certain amount of natural variability, because of variations in the input (different patients for a hospital laboratory or different raw materials for a manufacturer) as well as imperfections in the process (small

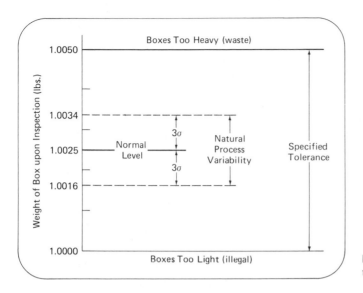

Figure 16-4   Process variability and tolerance.

variations in quantities of added chemicals, heat, motor speed, etc.). This *process variability* may be measured by the *process standard deviation* σ, which indicates how much the products will vary even if the process is in control.

Products also have to meet *specified tolerances,* imposed by their intended use. Accordingly, in designing or selecting a production process, the natural variability must be substantially smaller than the specified tolerance. This is depicted in Figure 16-4, in which the central line is the desired average of the process, the dashed lines are the "3 sigma" limits representing the natural process variability,[2] and the solid lines represent the tolerances (or standards) specified by the intended user of the product.

Within the specified tolerances, a certain amount of process variability is to be expected. However, it is the goal of statistical process control to determine when process variability is getting out of hand, so that corrective action can be taken, preferably before the required tolerances are violated. The method used is based on the idea that an average of a sample of several items will tend to cancel out the normal process variability, so that undesirable changes in the process will be more visible. We shall see how this works through an example.

The Sweet Sugar Company uses an automatic machine to fill 1-pound boxes of sugar. The tolerances are specified at 1.000 pound on the low side (a legal requirement) and 1.005 on the high side (they don't want to waste much sugar). Since the spread is only 0.005 pound, they selected a machine that has a natural

---

[2] It can be shown that variations of more than 3σ from the process average are very unlikely (less than 5%) for most processes, whether or not they can be described by the normal probability law. (See the Camp–Meidel extension of Tchebychev's inequality, in Duncan, 1974, Chap. 4. This depends on the probability law being unimodal.) For the normal distribution, this probability is about one-fourth of 1%.

process variability of $\sigma = 0.0003$ pound. The 3 sigma limits of the machine are therefore $(3)(0.0003) = 0.0009$ pound above and below the mean. The spread between these limits is 0.0018 pound, which is narrower than the specified tolerance. They adjust the machine to fill boxes with an average of 1.0025 pounds, halfway between the tolerance limits.

However, the machine needs periodic readjustment in order to perform within its stated capability, so a control chart was set up to detect when the machine goes out of control. In order to reduce the natural process variability, samples of $n = 5$ boxes were weighed, and the average weight per box, $\overline{X}$, was recorded for each sample. Figure 16-5 shows the control chart used for this machine, and the four points plotted on the chart represent the $\overline{X}$ values from four samples (a total of twenty 1-pound boxes). We shall now examine the details of the chart.

There is an apparent trend in $\overline{X}$; the samples seem to be getting progressively heavier. However, appearances notwithstanding, the trend in Figure 16-5 may be due to random fluctuations in the process. It is for this reason that we must incorporate the concept of *statistical significance* in our discussion.

The standard deviation of the sample average is expressed through the formula

$$\sigma(\overline{X}) = \frac{\sigma}{\sqrt{n}} \tag{4}$$

Therefore, the averages of $n = 5$ boxes of sugar should have a standard deviation of $\sigma(\overline{X}) = \sigma/\sqrt{n} = 0.0003/2.236 = 0.000134$ pound. The control limits in Figure 16-5 represent 3 sigma limits and are therefore $(3)(0.000134) = 0.000402$ pound above and below the intended average box weight of 1.0025 pounds. If a sample

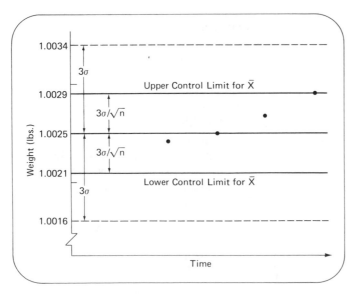

Figure 16-5 $\overline{X}$ control chart, for average weight of five 1-pound boxes of sugar.

TABLE 16-3 WEIGHTS (POUNDS) OF TWENTY 1-POUND
BOXES OF SUGAR

Box	Sample 1	Sample 2	Sample 3	Sample 4
1	1.00218	1.00266	1.00266	1.00306
2	1.00298	1.00242	1.00290	1.00266
3	1.00210	1.00258	1.00223	1.00234
4	1.00226	1.00250	1.00250	1.00322
5	1.00258	1.00234	1.00301	1.00322
Average	1.00242	1.00250	1.00266	1.00290
Range	0.00088	0.00032	0.00078	0.00088

average falls outside these control limits, the deviation from the process average
is statistically significant.[3]

The fourth sample average in Figure 16-5 falls on the 3 sigma upper control
limit. Consequently, there is strong statistical evidence that more sugar is being
put into the boxes than was intended, so the machine should be adjusted.

Table 16-3 lists the weights of the 20 boxes that were inspected and the
averages that were plotted in Figure 16-5. It is noteworthy that not a single box
falls outside the normal process variability range of 1.0016 to 1.0034 pounds;
even so, by taking averages over these samples (subgroups) of five boxes, a
significant trend was made visible.

There are other statistical tests commonly used to interpret a control chart.
Duncan (1974, p. 392) lists the following commonly applied out-of-control criteria:

1. One or more points outside the limits on a control chart.
2. One or more points in the vicinity of a warning limit. This suggests the
   need for immediately taking more data to check on the possibility of the
   process being out of control.
3. A run of 7 or more points. This might be a run up or run down or simply
   a run above or below the central line on the control chart.
4. Cycles or other nonrandom patterns in the data. Such patterns may be of
   great help to the experienced operator.
5. A run of 2 or 3 points outside of 2 sigma limits.
6. A run of 4 or 5 points outside of 1 sigma limits.

Rule 3, for example, indicates that we do not have enough data in Figure 16-5
to test for a significant upward trend using the "runs" test.

---

[3] It is customary in the United States to use 3 sigma limits in quality control whether or not
the process variability is governed by the normal probability law. However, the central limit theorem
assures us that the variation of sample averages is well approximated by the normal distribution,
and experience has shown this to be true, even for samples as small as four or five items. Therefore,
3 sigma limits on an $\bar{X}$ chart correspond to a Type I error probability of approximately one-fourth
of 1%. Of course, z values other than $z = 3$ could be used. For example, if $z = 1.96$, the Type
I error probability is 5%.

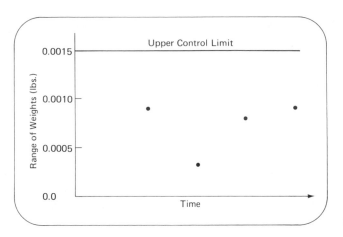

Figure 16-6 R control chart for the difference in weight between the heaviest and lightest of five 1-pound sugar boxes.

If one consistently applies a battery of criteria (such as the six rules listed above), the probability of early detection of a process change is enhanced, but so is the probability of a false alarm. In fact, Hilliard and Lasater (1966) describe a small but common set of rules that lead to a false alarm rate of 25%. This suggests that one should be careful in applying a battery of tests. Strong evidence should be required before shutting down a process for adjustment.

The *R chart* (range control chart) is also commonly used in control by variables. The range of a sample is the largest value minus the smallest (e.g., heaviest weight box of sugar minus the lightest). An *R* chart is appropriate if the process sometimes goes out of control in a way such that items become more inconsistent but with little or no change in the process average. This could result, for example, when fatigue limits the capability of a worker who is required to do a highly precise task. The *R* chart used by the Sweet Sugar Company is shown in Figure 16-6; the points on the graph are the ranges of the four samples (five boxes per sample) whose averages were plotted in Figure 16-5.

Tests for runs, cycles, and so on, can be applied to *R* charts as well as $\overline{X}$ charts. The control limits are somewhat different, however. There is typically no need for a lower control limit, since the smallest possible range is zero, and small ranges do not indicate a need for process readjustment. Table 16-4 is useful in setting an upper control limit for an *R* chart—the factor D_2 from the

TABLE 16-4 UPPER CONTROL LIMIT FACTOR, D_2, FOR RANGE CONTROL CHARTS. "3 SIGMA UPPER CONTROL LIMIT FOR *R*" = $D_2\sigma$

Sample Size	D_2	Sample Size	D_2
2	3.686	6	5.078
3	4.358	7	5.203
4	4.698	8	5.307
5	4.918	9	5.394
		10	5.469

table is multiplied by the process standard deviation, σ. The Sweet Sugar R chart therefore has an upper control limit of $D_2\sigma = (4.918)(0.0003) = 0.00148$ pound for a sample of $n = 5$ boxes of sugar. (More extensive tables with other useful factors are available for R charts. See Duncan, 1974, Table M.)

Determining the sample size, n, is an important decision. It is common to use $n = 4$ or 5 in order to obtain fast, low-cost feedback to the production process. However, larger samples are necessary if the process standard deviation is large compared to the specified tolerance of the product. As a general rule, $n = 5$ is satisfactory for detecting shifts in the process average of 2σ or more, whereas $n = 15$ to 20 is required if process shifts as small as 1σ are important.

Let us see whether Sweet Sugar's samples of 5 are large enough. When the filling machine is operating properly, most boxes fall in the range $1.0025 \pm 3\sigma$ or from 1.0016 to 1.0034 pounds. Now $n = 5$ is satisfactory for detecting shifts of 2σ or more in the process average, which, in this case, would move the entire range by $(2)(0.0003) = 0.0006$ pound. Suppose that the sugar filler shifts upward by 2σ. Then the sugar boxes would range between 1.0022 and 1.0040 pounds, which is still within Sweet Sugar's specified maximum of 1.005 pound. Since the sample of $n = 5$ will allow us to detect this 2σ shift, we can expect to discover a drift in process average before boxes are being filled beyond the tolerable weight. (A similar analysis holds for a downward shift.)

Frequency of sampling, together with sample size, determines the cost of the sampling program. This must be balanced against the expected cost of allowing an out-of-control condition to continue during the time interval until a sample is taken. The frequency of sampling should therefore be proportional to the average frequency of out-of-control conditions. However, the arguments become fairly complex as one attempts to define rules for optimal sampling. Further discussion may be found in Duncan (1956) and Meske (1976). Convenience often plays an important role in establishing the sampling frequency.

Process Control by Attributes

Inspection may not result in a quantitative measure such as weight. For example, a shirt might be classified as either defective or acceptable, depending on the seriousness of errors in its manufacture. There are several kinds of sampling plans available when only the attribute ''defective/acceptable'' is measured. We shall describe the control chart approach.

The *p chart* is based on the fraction defective, p, in a sample of n items. If p_0 represents the normal process fraction defective (i.e., when the process is in control), then the 3 sigma control limits are

$$3 \text{ sigma limits} = p_0 \pm 3 \sqrt{\frac{p_0(1 - p_0)}{n}} \qquad (5)$$

(This is based on the observation that the number of defectives has the binomial probability law.) The control chart is used just like an $\overline{X}$ chart, except that the fraction defective p is calculated rather than $\overline{X}$ for each sample of n items, and a lower control limit is often omitted.

Sample sizes are typically larger for p charts than for $\overline{X}$ charts. In fact, the required sample size can be computed from a formula. In the formula, p_0 is the normal process fraction defective, and p_1 is a specified fraction defective that is unacceptable. (That is, p_0 is like AQL in acceptance sampling, and p_1 is like LTPD.) The required sample size n is approximately[4]

$$n = \left[\frac{1.645\sqrt{p_1(1 - p_1)} + 3\sqrt{p_0(1 - p_0)}}{p_1 - p_0} \right]^2 \qquad (6)$$

For example, the Extra Shirt Company has found that 4% of its shirts are defective when the manufacturing process is in control, and they want to be able to detect a shift to 12% defectives on the basis of one sample of n items. Then $p_0 = 0.04$, $p_1 = 0.12$, and the formula suggests a sample size of 197. The upper control limit would be $p_0 + 3\sqrt{p_0(1 - p_0)/n} = 0.0819$, or 8.19%.

Samples as large as this may preclude rapid feedback to the production process. The upper control limit of 8.19% defective corresponds to 16 defective shirts out of the sample of 197, and the plan is therefore more like acceptance sampling than process control. Consequently, process control plans by attributes are often more complex than the simple p chart. For example, defects may be categorized into major and minor, and very strict control of major defects can be instituted, with a careful investigation whenever a major defect is found and an increase in the frequency of sampling until the source has been found and corrected.

Review Problems

One of the important functions of a hospital laboratory is to perform tests on blood samples. The quality of this process is tested periodically by selecting five blood specimens and dividing each specimen into two equal parts. Approximately $\frac{1}{2}$ hour after the first batch of five has been processed, its twin is submitted and the results are compared. (This procedure is sometimes used to test quality control inspectors, too.) The following data were taken at four different times over one 8-hour shift.

PERCENT DIFFERENCE BETWEEN READINGS ON TWO IDENTICAL BLOOD SAMPLES

	Batch 1 (9:30 A.M.)	Batch 2 (11:00 A.M.)	Batch 3 (2:00 P.M.)	Batch 4 (4:00 P.M.)
	1.2	0.6	0.6	2.1
	1.8	0.3	1.5	0.6
	1.5	0.3	1.0	0.6
	0.9	0.0	0.0	2.7
	0.3	0.6	1.9	2.7
$\overline{X}$ = averages	1.14	0.36	1.00	1.74
R = ranges	1.50	0.60	1.90	2.10

[4] This is based on the normal approximation to the binomial probability law. It assumes that the probability of Type II error is to be 5% and the allowable Type I error is set by a 3 sigma limit.

1. Calculate upper and lower 3 sigma control limits for this process, assuming that the normal process average is 0.9%, and the normal process standard deviation is $\sigma = 0.5\%$.
2. What upper control limit would be used for a range chart?
3. Does the process seem to be in control?

Solutions

1. $\sigma(\overline{X}) = \sigma/\sqrt{n} = 0.5/\sqrt{5} = 0.223$. Therefore, the control limits are 0.9 $\pm$ 3(0.224), or 0.23% (lower) and 1.57% (upper).
2. From Table 16-4, $D_2 = 4.918$ for $n = 5$, so the upper control limit is $D_2\sigma$ = 4.918(0.5) = 2.46%.
3. The last batch of five specimens, which was submitted near the end of the day, falls above the control limit on the $\overline{X}$ chart. It would be worthwhile to determine whether operator fatigue is a factor.

16-5 Summary

Quality is conformance to requirements. Using that definition leads to many opportunities to improve both quality and productivity simultaneously. This observation has encouraged many firms to undertake massive campaigns to improve quality. The most successful programs bring about permanent changes in attitude, organizational structure, and work methods; and they heavily involve top management. Missing any of these elements is likely to lead to temporary improvements that are lost in the long run.

Many quality problems have causes that cross departmental boundaries or even come from outside the organization. Methods such as quality circles are intended to uncover this type of problem and find implementable solutions. Cross training of employees in more than one job increases the likelihood that such problems will be found and corrected.

Any quality control program requires information. Statistical methods are important in this regard because they are designed to separate random variations from real assignable causes of deviation from normal. However, statistics can be complicated and confusing. Substantial training is required for all employees that are expected to make appropriate use of statistical control.

Inspection serves both a statistical purpose and a behavioral one. In addition to detecting errors, an inspection system may be designed to assure that workers continue to produce acceptable units. Accordingly, recognition and rewards for good performance are as important as negative feedback for control.

Acceptance sampling is inspection of part of a batch to form a judgment about the entire lot. Several methods are available for finding an acceptance sampling plan. One valuable tool is the operating characteristic (OC) curve, used to evaluate the likelihood of erroneous judgments. When the quality of a batch is altered by sampling (rectifying inspection), the average outgoing quality limit (AOQL) provides a useful measure of the long-run impact that the sampling program has on the fraction of products that are defective.

Quality control charts display the results of inspecting a continuous process. This provides convenient and rapid feedback, suggesting when adjustment, overhaul, or retraining may be needed.

The statistical methods discussed in this chapter are widely used in manufacturing and service industries, as well as in auditing of financial information and other applications. Furthermore, they are the basis for many of the commonly used, but more complex, schemes described in our references.

The amount of quality control an organization engages in is a policy-level decision. The image a firm desires, the selling price, and the customer it wishes to attract depend strongly on product quality. Successful quality assurance programs must therefore have a long-range focus and be a permanent part of an organization.

Quality and productivity are closely related. Quality improvement programs often more than pay for themselves in the long run by reductions in the cost of quality and increases in the real output rate. Proper evaluation of COQ is difficult because it contains such elements as lost market opportunities. Nevertheless, learning how to evaluate COQ and how to estimate productivity increases are necessary parts of quality assurance. Without this understanding, the benefits of quality improvements are always understated.

With a clear understanding of the broad impact of the quality of goods and services, avenues are opened for savings that may be as great as 20% of the cost of sales, better market image, and a leaner, healthier operation. Quality assurance is certainly one of the most important tasks in operations management.

CASELET: THE COMPUTER PRINTER DIVISION

The Computer Printer Division (CPD) manufactures printers for sale to another division of the same company. The printers are used in several types of systems sold to small to medium-sized firms. The printer is a small part of the total cost of the systems they sell, but an important and visible part of how the product is perceived.

CPD has had quality problems; up to 5% of the printers have proven to be defective when received by customers. Given the high quality of some competitors' products, this level of quality is unacceptable. Mary Smith, a recent MBA from a local university, was given the job of improving the monitoring and reporting of quality. In her investigation of the current system, she found that the production process was very simple. The components are purchased from outside vendors. Assembly was done by groups of five individuals. During assembly each unit was passed back and forth among all the workers. It was thought to be impossible to check quality during this process. The assembly workers' performance evaluations were primarily based on the number of units completed, without consideration of defects.

Quality was monitored by a group of four quality inspectors, after the product was completed. They did some simple tests on each unit, and extensive tests on a sample. The simple tests were not perfect, leading to the failure rate found later in systems using the printer. The procedure was also tedious, and inspection steps were often omitted. The quality inspectors had a goal of turning back as many units as they could, and found satisfaction in stopping the process when defects were too frequent. Ms. Smith noted that relations between the assemblers and the quality control workers were terrible. In addition, no one was responsible for the level of quality; 95% sounded pretty good, even though the competitors had over 99% quality. No long-term data were available to identify trends or causes for defects.

When finished items were received by the other division of the company, a sample was inspected to see whether to pass or to reject the batch. If the batch was rejected, 100% inspection was used, and bad items returned to CPD for credit. The user division was very concerned about quality since they thought their reputation in their markets was slipping. They had threatened to go to another vendor.

Defective items were found to be due to purchased materials 40% of the time, manufacturing or assembly 50% of the time, and poor design 10% of the time. The cost of purchased materials comprised 50% of the transfer price paid by the user division to CPD. A sample of the purchased materials was inspected. Automated inspection, which was common in other products in the company, was not seen as viable for the printers.

Mary posed several questions which she thought should be investigated.

1. What could be done to improve relations between assembly and quality control personnel?
2. Since purchased materials comprise such a large fraction of the value of the product, should some inspection be done before assembly?
3. How could the two divisions cooperate to solve the quality problems?
4. How could they work with the vendors on the quality of purchased materials?
5. How can the competitive pressures faced by the client division be internalized by CPD? Should the user division be allowed to solicit an outside vendor?

In developing solutions, Ms. Smith was to avoid suggesting additional quality control expense. Also, she needed to do something quickly. Some short-run expense would be allowed, as long as it was clear that total costs would not increase in the long run.

Required   Write a report containing suggestions for Ms. Smith. You should deal with a short-run solution and a long-run quality program. Include comments on each of Ms. Smith's five questions.

PROBLEMS

1. Argue pro and con:
   (a) The facilitator is the key to success or failure of a quality circle program.
   (b) It is important to inspect the inspector.

2. Sum up what the Quasar experience tells you about quality assurance.

3. Explain the following ideas.
   (a) As a quality improvement program begins to take hold, the cost of quality increases.
   (b) Quality is free, but it is not a gift.

4. (a) What is the fundamental difference between the use of acceptance sampling plans and process control charts?
   (b) In which situation (acceptance sampling or process control) is the quality control inspector more likely to be in close contact with the people whose work is being examined?
   (c) Under what circumstance is inspection by sampling from completed batches not a good idea?

5. List two or three causes of product variation for each of the following products.
   (a) Baked goods.
   (b) Vaccinations.
   (c) Street cleaning.
   (d) Bookkeeping.

6. Why are averages of small samples used in control charts rather than individual readings or large sample averages?

*7. A recent graduate was asked to look over the quality control program at his new company. The first thing he noticed was that the quality control charts were labeled as 99% confidence limits, but that 4% of the points plotted on them fell outside the limits. He claimed the limits should be moved out until only 1% of the points fell outside. *But he is wrong*. Explain why you might expect more than 1% of the points to fall outside the 99% control limits, even in the long run.

8. In setting up an $\overline{X}$ chart for the weight of 1-pound boxes of sugar, an argument arose. The question concerned the correct method for determining the central line of the control chart. The two contenders were (i) the long-run average weight, and (ii) the desired weight of 1.002 pounds. Discuss both of these alternatives and explain the situations in which each is appropriate.

*9. An automobile manufacturer buys roller-bearing subassemblies in large batches for use in assembly. Each bearing unit is inspected as it is being installed. However, if there are too many defectives, the assembly line must be slowed down. Therefore, management has decided to inspect a sample from each batch upon receipt. The foreman has estimated that the assembly-line slow-down is likely to occur if there are more than 5% defective parts. When the batch has 1% or fewer defective bearings, the pressure on the assembly line is considerably relieved. Because of the economics of sampling versus slowing down the line, they want to reject a bad batch with probability 0.975 or higher, but are willing to reject a good batch 10% of the time.

(a) Design a sampling plan (n, c).

(b) With the sampling plan you have just defined (i.e., with your values of n and c), what is the acceptance probability of a batch with 2% defectives? Draw a rough operating characteristic curve.

(c) If your sampling plan is used, what can you say about the average fraction of defective items in batches as they reach the assembly line? Batches consist of 5000 subassemblies.

10. A manufacturing company produces a small product in lots of 10,000. They want to be 90% sure of accepting a lot with a fraction defective of 0.01 and 95% sure of rejecting a lot with a fraction defective of 0.08. The use of Table 16-1 is beyond their abilities currently, so they are eyeballing a sampling plan. They have begun with a sample size of 100, although this may be changed at a later time. They reasoned that $c = 4$ should be used since accepted samples would have 4/100 or 4% defective or less, and rejected samples would have 5/100 or 5% defective or more. This seems reasonable because 4% and 5% are centered between the acceptable and unacceptable fraction defective.

(a) Does their plan achieve their goals?

(b) With $n = 100$, would either $c = 3$ or $c = 2$ achieve their goal?

(c) Suggest a plan better than either ($c = 2$, $n = 100$) or ($c = 3$, $n = 100$).

(d) What are the AOQL values for these plans? Discuss briefly.

*11. Mugwump Assemblers used AQL $= 0.02$, $\alpha = 0.05$, LTPD $= 0.10$, and $\beta = 0.01$ in the example used in the chapter text. They arrived at the sampling plan $n = 150$, $c = 6$. However, it was observed that only 3% of batches were as bad as LTPD, so a β of 1% meant that 3 batches out of 10,000 reaching the assembly line would be bad.

(a) What will the savings be in number inspected if β is raised to 5%? 10%?

(b) What happens to AOQL with these changes? (Remember that $N = 10,000$ per batch.)

12. The Mortimer McSnarf Manufacturing Co. (the M^3 Co.) makes balloons for promotional purposes in lots of 1000. Mortimer McSnarf founded the company in 1971 and his son, Milton McSnarf, is the plant manager. He says the cost of inspection is $0.01 per item, and the per unit contribution to fixed cost and profit is $0.02. He also says that he wants to be 95% sure of accepting a lot that has a fraction defective of 0.01. The sales manager, Lowd Roar, says that he wants to be 90% sure of rejecting a lot with 0.025

fraction defective. The controller, Hierman Bass, says that they must make an average of $0.015 per balloon to cover their fixed costs, after subtracting sampling costs from contribution. The personnel director, Marilyn McCool, says that an inspector should not be assigned a task of inspecting more than 200 per lot due to boredom problems. (At present they have one inspector.)

(a) Find a sampling plan, if possible, to satisfy both McSnarf and Roar.

(b) Are the constraints by Bass and McCool met? Show your computations and state your reasons.

(c) What do you suggest they do?

13. A transistor manufacturing firm has found that the cost of inspection of each transistor is $0.021. The cost of an undetected defect is $7.00. They know that the process is in one of two states, in control with $f = 0.005$, or out of control with $f = 0.020$. They currently use a sampling plan with $n = 100$, $c = 1$. They believe that the process is in control most, but not all, of the time, and it is never in any state other than $f = 0.005$ or $f = 0.020$.

(a) How can they improve the sampling inspection scheme?

(b) What value of α and β (producer's risk and consumer's risk) does their plan achieve? If they desire $\alpha = 0.10$, $\beta = 0.20$, have they achieved both these goals?

*14. The XYZ Corporation produces widgets in lots of 1000. They know beyond a shadow of a doubt that their fraction defective is between 0.01 and 0.08, and their costs of inspection and of an undetected defect are $1 and $20, respectively.

(a) Can they argue that either 0 or 100% inspection is optimal? Why or why not?

(b) Further study disclosed that fractions defective above 4% almost never occur, with only 1 out of the past 1000 batches exceeding this level. What kind of quality sampling plan do you suggest?

15. (a) Plot the operating characteristic curves for the three sampling plans $n = 100$, $c = 3$; $n = 100$, $c = 4$; and $n = 78$, $c = 3$.

(b) From the OC curves, in part (a), estimate α and β for each of the three sampling plans if AQL $= 1.6\%$ and LTPD $= 8\%$.

(c) Study the results of parts (a) and (b) in order to answer the following. Suppose that you already have a sampling plan in operation but it has been determined that β is too high and α is lower than required; what change would you suggest in the sampling plan? (Change n or change c? Up or down?)

(d) Calculate the cutoff ratio $(c + 0.5)/n$ for each plan. Two of the plans have almost identical cutoff ratios. What can you say about the changes in α and β as n is changed but the cutoff ratio does not change?

16. Use the data in your solution to Problem 15 to plot an AOQ curve for the

plan $n = 100$, $c = 3$, if the batch size is $N = 10,000$. Estimate the AOQL from your figure.

*17. An automobile supplier produces headlight dimmer switches. In order to maintain adequate customer relations, she must maintain an average outgoing quality of 2% or less in lots of 1000 switches. She currently uses an acceptance sampling plan with sample size $n = 100$ and acceptance number $c = 2$. The AOQ curve for the plan is shown in the accompanying figure.

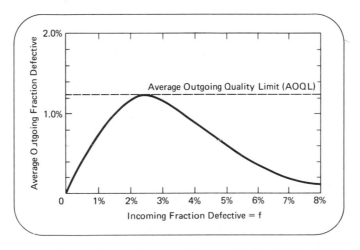

(a) What is the worst average outgoing quality performance her sampling plan will allow?

(b) The past 20 batches were 100% inspected to determine how the fraction defective varies. The following table describes the result:

Incoming fraction defective	0.01	0.03	0.05	0.07
Number of times observed	3	8	8	1

Make an estimate of the long-run average outgoing fraction defective.

(c) Compare your answers to parts (a) and (b), and discuss.

18. (Problem 17 should be completed before this one.) The cost of inspecting a headlight dimmer switch is $0.10, and the cost of sending out a defective switch is estimated to be $3.00.

(a) Should a sampling plan be used at all?

(b) Estimate the long-run average cost of defectives present in outgoing batches, assuming that the sampling plan $n = 100$, $c = 2$ is used as in Problem 17.

(c) Suppose that $f = 0.03$ and is not changing. What is the expected value of the inspection cost per batch, assuming that if a batch is rejected, all items in the batch would be inspected? (You will have to work out a formula to answer this.)

(d) Suppose that f takes on the values 0.01, 0.03, 0.05, and 0.07 with the frequencies given in Problem 17. What is the long-run average inspection cost per batch?

(e) Describe briefly how one could find a sampling plan that minimizes cost of inspection plus cost of outgoing defectives. Would a computer be useful for this?

*19. Which of the following statements can be said to be true, based only on the average outgoing quality curve shown in Problem 17? (A solution to Problem 17 is not required to do this one.)

(a) The average outgoing quality is 1.23% defective.

(b) The outgoing quality of *each and every batch* is better than 1.23% defective.

(c) The most likely incoming fraction defective is about 2.3%.

(d) Incoming fraction defective is very unlikely to be above 7%.

(e) Incoming batches with 2% defectives yield worse outgoing quality than batches with 5% defectives, on the average.

(f) An incoming batch with 5% defectives is less likely to be rejected than one with 2% defectives.

20. The Red Canners Corporation is concerned about the quality of their whole canned tomatoes. They produce tomatoes in batches, and one batch contains 10,000 cans, each of which sells to the wholesaler for $0.20. Unfortunately, to inspect a can of tomatoes, they must destroy the can and its contents. (They open the can to check the percent of grade A tomatoes. A defective item is one that contains too few grade A tomatoes. The process guarantees no bacterial content, and we are not concerned here with that question.)

Since they can sell any cans they are able to produce, the quality control manager, Mack Cann, says that the cost of inspection is the selling price ($0.20) plus the labor cost of inspection ($0.10). Thus he says sampling cost is $0.30 per can. The cost of shipping a defective is deemed to be high, but they are unwilling to specify a value.

(a) Is Cann's cost of inspection value reasonable? Why?

(b) If the firm knew for sure that the true fraction defective were 0.02 or lower, they would not inspect any items, but if it were 0.10 or higher, they would inspect every item (thus reject the batch). What can you say about their implied cost of shipping a defective?

(c) Suppose that AQL $= 0.002$, LTPD $= 0.05$, $\alpha = 0.10$, and $\beta = 0.10$; does the sampling plan $n = 50$, $c = 0$ satisfy all these values?

(d) A formula for outgoing fraction defective was given in equation (3). Why does this formula not apply for destructive testing? Give at least two reasons.

(e) Derive a formula for outgoing fraction defective with destructive testing.

21. (a) Using the formulas accompanying Figure 16-2, calculate the parameters h_1, h_2, and s for a sequential sampling plan with AQL $= 0.02$, $\alpha = 0.05$, LTPD $= 0.10$, and $\beta = 0.05$.

(b) In drawing a diagram of the sequential plan in part (a) (see Figure 16-2), what values would the upper limit line (c_2) have when the cumulative number inspected is $n = 0$? $n = 100$?

(c) Repeat part (b) for the lower limit line.

(d) Using this plan, what is the smallest sample that might lead to acceptance of a batch?

(e) How many defectives must be found in order to reject a batch based on the first 10 items inspected?

*22. Figure 16-2 shows a sequential sampling plan that fits the same OC criteria as the single sampling plan $n = 150$, $c = 6$. The accompanying table tabulates the results of the inspection process for several different batches. For example, in the first batch, the tenth item was defective, as were the twentieth, thirtieth, and so on. You are to determine

(a) Which batches would have been rejected by the single sampling plan $n = 150$, $c = 6$.

(b) Which batches would have been rejected by the sequential plan.

(c) The average number inspected per batch under each plan, assuming that rejected batches are returned to their manufacturer without further inspection.

Batch	Number Defective in Sample	Item Numbers of the Defectives Discovered in the Sample						
1	6	10	20	30	40	50	60	
2	3	10	50	100				
3	0							
4	4	40	80	120	140			
5	7	20	40	60	80	100	120	140

*23. In a factory the number of production labor-hours lost each day because of accidents is a normally distributed random variable with mean = 30 and standard deviation = 8. The firm desires a weekly control chart on which it plans to plot the average number of production labor-hours lost daily because of accidents.

(a) How would you construct a weekly $\overline{X}$ control chart with appropriate limits? What would the limits be? (Assume 5 working days in a week.) What assumptions do you have to make in order to use the data given above in setting up an $\overline{X}$ chart?

(b) Would it be possible in this case to have a daily control chart? If so, how would it be constructed?

(c) Suppose now that the number of labor-hours lost each day is not normally distributed. Could you use a weekly $\overline{X}$ control chart in this case? How would you obtain the appropriate limits? Could you use a daily control chart in this case?

24. The consistency of a manufacturing process is being investigated. The following data were taken at four different times of day. Each time, five

finished items were removed from the conveyor and the "specific gravity" was measured for each one.

Sample 1	Sample 2	Sample 3	Sample 4
1.025	1.036	1.011	1.022
1.042	1.016	1.029	1.027
1.013	1.028	1.031	1.046
1.027	1.023	1.021	1.033
1.018	1.025	1.019	1.034

(a) Calculate mean and standard deviation of each sample.

(b) Calculate the averages of the four means and of the four standard deviations.

(c) Set up a (95% confidence) quality control chart based on your answer to part (b), and plot the four samples on it.

(d) Discuss whether any changes should be made to the control chart.

(e) Based on your answer to part (b), estimate the proportion of items that will have specific gravity of 1.000 or less when the process is in control.

*25. The diameter of roller bearings must be within a tolerance of ± 0.010 millimeter of the designated diameter. A production process is selected that has a normal process standard deviation of 0.003. Is a sample size of 5 sufficient to reliably detect a shift in the process mean that is large enough to produce significant numbers of out-of-tolerance bearings?

*26. The process standard deviation in the manufacture of roller bearings is 0.003 millimeter.

(a) What should the upper control limit be for an R chart when the sample size is 6?

(b) Why should a roller-bearing manufacturer be interested in an R chart?

27. [This problem is based on the solution to parts (a) and (b) of Problem 24.] From the data given in Problem 24, set up an R chart and plot four points corresponding to the four samples.

*28. Equations (6) and (5) are sometimes used to design sampling plans, using p_0 = AQL and p_1 = LTPD. In equation (6) the number 1.645 achieves β = 0.05, and the number 3 achieves α = 0.0013, assuming that only an upper control limit is used. Mugwump Assemblers found that n = 150, c = 6 was just right for AQL = 0.02, α = 0.05, LTPD = 0.10, and β = 0.01. In the normal tables (Table 2, Appendix D) we find that z = 2.33 corresponds to a probability of 1%.

(a) Put the appropriate z values in equation (6) in place of 1.645 and 3 to achieve β and α, respectively, as specified by Mugwump.

(b) What would the upper control limit be for fraction defective in the sample, again using the appropriate z value in place of 3?

(c) Use your results from part (b) to find a cutoff level c. Then calculate a sample size n from Table 16-1. Compare this to part (a) and to the plan $n = 150$, $c = 6$ (which we found for Mugwump while illustrating the use of Table 16-1) and comment.

REFERENCES

BARRA, R., *Putting Quality Circles to Work.* New York: McGraw-Hill, 1983.

CROSBY, P. B., *Quality Is Free.* New York: McGraw-Hill, 1979.

DEMING, W. E., "Improvement of Quality and Productivity through Action by Management." *National Productivity Review,* Vol. 1, No. 1 (1982).

DODGE, H. F., "A Sampling Inspection Plan for Continuous Production." *Annals of Mathematical Statistics,* Vol. 14 (1943), pp. 264–279.

DODGE, H. F., AND H. G. ROMIG, *Sampling Inspection Tables—Single and Double Sampling.* New York: Wiley, 1959.

DUNCAN, A. J., "The Economic Design of $\overline{X}$ Charts Used to Maintain Current Control of a Process." *Journal of American Statistical Association,* Vol. 51 (1956), pp. 228–242.

DUNCAN, A. J., *Quality Control and Industrial Statistics.* Homewood, Ill.: Richard D. Irwin, 1974.

GARVIN, D. A., "Quality On the Line." *Harvard Business Review,* September–October 1983.

HALPIN, J. F., *Zero Defects.* New York: McGraw-Hill, 1966.

HILLIARD, J. E., AND H. A. LASATER, "Type I Risks When Several Tests Are Used Together on Control Charts for Means and Ranges." *Industrial Quality Control,* August 1966.

INGLE, S., AND N. INGLE, *Quality Circles in Service Industries.* Englewood Cliffs, N.J.: Prentice-Hall, 1983.

KOHLER, M. T., AND E. R. WELLS, "Quality Circles at Hughes Aircraft." *National Productivity Review,* Vol. 1, No. 3 (1982).

MESKE, H., "A Management Standard for Economic Inspection." *Quality,* January 1976.

MONDEN, Y., "What Makes the Toyota Production System Really Tick?" *Industrial Engineering,* January 1981.

SANIGA, E. M., AND D. C. MONTGOMERY, "Economical Quality Control Policies for a Single Cause System." *AIIE Transactions,* Vol. 13, No. 3 (1981).

SCHONBERGER, R. J., "Work Improvement Programmes: Quality Control Circles Compared with Traditional Western Approaches." *International Journal of Operations and Production Management,* Vol. 3, No. 2 (1983).

SHEWHART, W. A., *Economic Control of Quality of Manufactured Product.* New York: Van Nostrand, 1931.

SMITH, M. R., *Qualitysense.* New York: AMACON, 1979.

Statistical Research Group, Columbia University, *Sequential Analysis of Statistical Data: Applications.* New York: Columbia University Press, 1947.

WALD, A., *Sequential Analysis.* New York: Wiley, 1947.

WERTHER, W. B., JR., "Quality Circles and Corporate Culture." *National Productivity Review,* Vol. 1, No. 3 (1982).

CHAPTER 17

Integrating Operations into the Strategy of the Organization

In most organizations the operations area is where the action is, in that most of the organization's money is both spent on and made by the goods and services produced there. Also, most of the firm's assets are tied up in operations. Even though this is true, some top managers think of strategic decisions in financial or marketing terms exclusively. As a result, Skinner (1969) has found that "top management unknowingly delegates a surprisingly large portion of basic policy decisions to lower levels in the manufacturing area."

Throughout this book we have argued that operations, marketing, finance, and other areas of the firm should be integrated to obtain the benefits of a systems view of the organization. Further, overall goals should be formed at the top of the organization from which policy guidelines should be developed to mold operational decisions. This chapter will review ways of accomplishing integration of functions and the development of guiding policies. It is particularly appropriate to discuss these questions here, at the end of the text, where we have an opportunity to integrate many of the topics we have studied.

17-1 THE STRATEGIC IMPORTANCE OF OPERATIONS

To illustrate the strategic importance of operations, let us first consider a few service examples: fire departments, banks, mail-order stores, and fast-food chains. The fire department has the objective of minimizing loss of life and property due to fire and related incidents. It tries to achieve those objectives through its operations. Therefore, the operating policies that govern daily activities are life and death decisions. For example, consider a question involving resource allocation.

Sending a second hook and ladder unit to every call would occasionally reduce the loss of life and property in a big city, but at what cost? Cities cannot eliminate loss of life due to fire; good management can only minimize it, given their allotted budget. Thus life and death are affected each time a public safety unit's operating budget is set, and the strategic importance of operating budgets and policies can scarcely be overstated.

In banks, grocery stores, mail-order houses, and fast-food chains, profit margins are low. The operations function employs a large fraction of the work force and spends a large fraction of the money. If operating costs are not held tightly in check, there will be no profit. On the other hand, if the service is not reliable and fast, sales will be lost. Even the nature of the advertising depends on how reliable and fast the service is. Top management must establish the image they wish to portray to customers and pass this decision to operations through policy guidelines. Thus the operations area is central to the strategy of these organizations.

Operations management is even more clearly of strategic importance in manufacturing. Manufacturing firms typically use most of their yearly expenditures in support of operations. In addition, they have most of their assets tied up in plant, equipment, and inventory. Of course, these assets must earn a return if the firm is going to be able to attract capital in the future. The importance of these assets in corporate decision making is illustrated in Table 17-1, in which the relative size of cost of sales, inventory, and plant and equipment are shown for five very large manufacturing companies. Cost of sales refers to the cost to produce and transport the goods that resulted in the yearly sales figure. All figures for assets are book value, meaning historical cost for inventory and cost less depreciation for plant and equipment. The four firms represent both high and low values for inventories and plant and equipment, as a percent of total assets.

Inventories can amount to nearly half of the total assets if the product line is broad and must be supported by a full line of spare parts (McDonnell-Douglas).

TABLE 17-1   COST OF SALES AND ASSET FIGURES FOR SOME MANUFACTURING COMPANIES

	International Harvester	McDonnell-Douglas	Firestone	Alcoa	IBM
Total sales	$3601[a]	$8111	$3866	$5263	$40180
Cost of sales	3325	6754	2852	4176	16395
(as % of sales)	92.3	83.3	73.7	79.3	40.8
Inventory	619	1905	455	551	4381
(as % of assets)	18.4	39.8	16.7	8.9	11.8
Plant and equipment	837	1014	1053	3267	9330
(as % of assets)	24.9	21.2	38.6	52.1	25.1
Total assets	3362	4792	2729	6267	37243

[a] Figures are in millions of dollars. The source is the annual report, 1983, for each company.

Plant and equipment can be half of the assets in a process industry that requires very expensive facilities (Firestone and Alcoa). IBM's inventory plus plant and equipment seems low as a percent because rental machines, also supported by operations, is a large fraction of total assets. International Harvester's asset percentages are lower than in the past because they have been in financial difficulty and have reduced assets.

Another indication of the strategic importance of operations management is its effect on the economy. For example, at the end of 1983, the book value of inventories in the United States was $514.3 billion.[1] As a reference point, GNP for 1983 was $3310.5 billion. Using an inventory carrying cost rate of (say) 25%, we can see that inventory carrying costs are roughly equal to 4% of GNP. New plant and equipment expenditures totaled $303.2 billion in 1983 or about 9% of GNP. The overall investment in inventories and plant and equipment indicates that properly managing these assets is crucial to the economy as well as the firm.

The strategic impact of operations management can also be seen in the relation of the organization to the outside world. In the next several paragraphs, we will examine strategic operations decisions concerning employment policies, government regulation, and interaction with foreign governments. As with nearly all important decisions, both tangible and intangible trade-offs will be involved. For example, the firm's employment policies generate an image for the organization in the local community. A firm that maintains stable employment at good wages can usually count on having a good image in the community. That is one of the (largely intangible) benefits from using inventory rather than hiring and layoffs to smooth out demand fluctuations. Because the operations area employs most of the people in many organizations, the operations manager is in the public relations business, like it or not.

Even a firm with a stable employment policy may reach a time in an economic downturn when layoffs are necessary to protect the organization and the jobs of those that remain. Deciding when to use layoffs is not easy, but it is important. One of the inputs into the decision is a quantitative cost analysis, as discussed in Chapter 9. Sound judgment, considering the long-run good of the organization, employees, and the community, is another input.

Another way in which operations interact with the outside world is by causing or ceasing to cause pollution. Both legal and ethical considerations are involved in allocating money to pollution-abatement investments. The decisions are not always clear-cut. A firm should stop dumping poisonous chemicals into a stream at a level that endangers human life, but how clean should they make the stream? The stream can be made as pure as it was above the plant, but the customer will have to pay much more for the product. Cars can be made to

---

[1] The source for all the numbers in this paragraph is the *Survey of Current Business*, U.S. Department of Commerce, January, February, and May 1984.

produce fewer air pollutants, but if they burn more gasoline as a result, the overall effect on the environment is unclear.

Regulations on pollution are promulgated by state and federal government agencies. The Environmental Protection Agency (EPA) acts to recommend allowable pollutant levels to Congress and the President, and to ensure that companies act in accordance with such regulations. Since the operations area is responsible for meeting the requirements of government regulations, it is important for operations managers to understand the regulatory process. In addition to the EPA, the Occupational Safety and Health Agency (OSHA) defines working conditions for many large and small organizations. There are many other state and federal regulatory agencies that are important to operations managers in certain industries.

Following the rules is not the only task for the manager; investments must be planned to minimize the cost of meeting regulations. Some managers argue (and lobby) against regulations in an attempt to try to change them or postpone their implementation. Dealing with the government is the task of top management, but planning within the regulations is the task of all operations managers, thoughout the organization.

In multinational organizations, interacting with several national governments is necessary. The tax structure, tariffs, attitudes, and regulations of those governments must be a part of any major facility location decision. For example, some countries give favorable tax and tariff rates to companies that establish production facilities in their countries. In addition, sales in the country are easier to generate if there is a significant local operation. The firm is more visible, and customers may prefer dealing with a company that is willing to create jobs in the country. A plant in country A may not have as low a unit cost as one in country B, but the plant may be justified based on its positive effect on sales and negative effect on tariffs in country A.

Some facilities are located in other countries to obtain a low labor cost. The attitude of the government (what is the risk of nationalization?), the quality level that can be obtained, and the difficulty of managing from afar must be considered, in addition to the extra transportation cost implied by shipping units thousands of miles. Such decisions change the basic way in which the company does business, so they are, indeed, strategic decisions. The decision to become a complex multinational firm is often justified, but it cannot be made lightly. The role of the operations manager in such decisions is to understand the total effect on the production and delivery of the goods or services, at the same time that the marketing manager plans the sales, worldwide, of the product line.

Long-range strategic plans must simultaneously consider: What and to whom will we sell? How will we make it and deliver it? How will the business be financed? Marketing, operations, and finance are inextricably tied together. In this chapter, we will see that strategic planning must involve all three areas, even for very small, one-location concerns. We will discuss methods of making such strategic plans, from the point of view of both top management and operations management.

TABLE 17-2 PARTIAL LIST OF POLICY-LEVEL OPERATIONS DECISIONS

1. Method of organizing for production and delivery of goods and services. (Chapters 2, 3, 5, 6, 14, and 15)

2. Rate of return required by investments of different riskiness and type, including inventories. (Chapters 10, 13, and Section 17-2)

3. Location of inventory and customer service facilities, such as warehouses or retail stores. (Chapters 7 and 13)

4. Capacity and location of productive facilities such as plants, including international locations, and the plan for their long-term use. (Chapters 4 and 7)

5. Facility design, including type of layout to be used, and the plan for using those facilities to satisfy customers' demands. (Chapters 4, 5, and Section 17-2)

6. Basic method of satisfying customer demands: from inventory, by special order, by appointment, or some other method. (Chapters 10, 11, 12, 13, and 14)

7. Personnel policies regarding stability of employment, work situation, pay, and so on. (Chapters 6 and 9)

8. The level of quality to be maintained. (Chapter 16)

To conclude this section, we will give a partial list of operations area decisions that should reach the policy level and be used to influence daily operations. The interaction of operations with marketing and finance will be easily identified. The list, including the connection to chapters in the text, is given in Table 17-2.

Review Problems

Each of the following statements is not always true. Briefly state why this is so.

1. Better management of assets means that inventories should be reduced, especially for firms with as much as half of their assets tied up in inventory.

2. Dealing with and planning for government regulation is a task for top management alone.

3. In a consumer service organization such as a supermarket, attracting the customer is the most important thing; thus marketing, not operations, is the key strategic functional area.

Solutions

1. Inventories should be set at a level commensurate with the value they provide in customer service. Some companies should have more than half of their assets in inventories while others should have much less. A reduction in inventory may be counterproductive. (It is still often true that, with careful management, inventory can be reduced without ill effects.)

2. Since investment decisions about pollution abatement and work-safety rules are usually implemented at lower levels, all operations managers must be aware of and plan for government regulations.

3. All marketing efforts are worthless if the service is unacceptable. Further, the profit of the firm is strongly influenced by the cost performance of the operations of the firm. Both marketing and operations are of strategic importance in this setting.

17-2 INVESTING IN OPERATIONS TO MEET STRATEGIC GOALS

Strategic planning usually involves investing money in operations to meet the long-term goals of the organization. In this section, we will discuss some ways of selecting the operations to invest in, considering the organization's financial position and marketing and operational strengths. This process must use a long planning horizon. The financing of the operations and the marketability of the products must be considered simultaneously with the operations investment. That is, what products (or services) do we want to be making and selling in (say) 5 to 10 years, and how can we finance the necessary investments? Current decisions regarding operations must be made in such a way that the organization stays on the track specified by the strategic plan.

This section contains two main parts. First, we discuss a method for categorizing the organization's operations and products into several groups (called *strategic business units* or SBUs) for strategic planning. A method for assessing the future value of each SBU will be discussed. The second part of this section discusses ways of selecting among investments in different strategic business units. This selection process will need to balance current profits against future profits, consider the amount of risk the organization can take, and analyze the value of an operations investment in an uncertain future.

Strategic Business Units

In developing a strategic plan, an organization typically begins by dividing their total business into *strategic business units* (SBUs). An SBU is a set of products that use similar means and methods of production and are sold to similar types of customers. The number of SBUs must be large enough that significant differences in production or marketing opportunities are not lost by aggregation, and small enough that attention can be given to each SBU regarding market growth predictions, technological forecasting, and competitive position analysis.

For example, a company that makes athletic shoes might define one SBU as "high-priced training shoes for runners." There would be several styles in that category, and they would be sold both to teams and to individuals. Another SBU would be hiking boots, which would be sold almost entirely to individuals, so the marketing plans would be very different. Again, there would be several individual styles in the category. Yet another SBU might be the casual shoe market, and an athletic shoe company might have low-priced training shoes in this category. The production process and materials would be different from high-priced training shoes, and the marketing plan would be different. Each of these three SBUs would have different growth patterns, marketing plans, and production requirements, and a strategic plan should consider each one separately.

A key part of the organization's strategy is the allocation of investments among these SBUs, both for maintenance of current business and development of new thrusts. It is therefore necessary to determine what opportunities exist for *strategic investments* in each SBU over the next few years. (The exact length of time to be used depends on the particular industry.) The manager responsible for an SBU must identify these opportunities and flesh them out, estimating the required resources, probability of success or failure, and so on.

Questions of particular interest in evaluating a strategic investment include:

1. How large will the market be for the product or service and how fast will it grow?
2. Does the product or service fit with our production and marketing strengths? That is, do we have a comparative advantage, and what does the competition look like? Further, does it help us to utilize more fully some of our existing facilities?
3. Based on the answer to question 2, and our current position, what share of the market can we expect to attain?
4. What is the nature and extent of the risks involved?

Based on the answers to questions such as these, a firm can allocate its two scarce resources (capital and managerial/technical talent) among strategic thrusts. A balance must also be maintained between investments for improvement of current operations and strategic investments for the future.

In profit-making organizations and in most not-for-profit organizations, current operations generate the funds necessary to keep the organization going, making strategic investments possible. To guarantee the organization's viability, some investments must be made in current operations, perhaps thereby excluding some longer-term strategic investments. However, just as some potential strategic investments are rejected, some current operations will be phased out through time as they lose their potential to generate funds.

Management must be certain that strategic investments are made so that new, attractive operations are in place when old operations are phased out. It may be desirable to require a different rate of return for current operations than for strategic thrusts into new areas, in order to obtain this continued viability (and perhaps growth) through time. These required rates of return may change through time, as the situation changes.

Selecting SBU Investments in a Competitive Setting

Many methods have been suggested to select which SBUs to favor with continued investment. See Hax and Majluf (1982, 1983a, and 1983b) for discussion and further references. One argument is that, due to economies of scale, the firm with the highest market share will have a competitive advantage due to their lower cost. Thus firms should try to dominate their industry. Porter (1980) refers to this as *cost leadership,* one of three generic strategies he presents.

The notion of a cost advantage because of market domination is rooted in the *learning curve.* Learning curves were discussed by psychologists in the nineteenth century, applied to animals and individuals. Industrial engineers observed *organizational learning* in the 1950s, whereby cost declines as an organization makes more of an item. Cost-saving ideas stay with an organization even after the individual whose idea it is leaves. (An organizational learning curve is often referred to as an *experience curve.*)

Learning curves (or experience curves) can be used to predict cost performance. The most common mathematical relationship is a negative exponential form (Hax and Majluf, 1982):

$$C_t = C_0 \left(\frac{P_t}{P_0} \right)^{-a} \tag{1}$$

where C_0, C_t = cost per unit, corrected for inflation, at times 0 and t

P_0, P_t = accumulated production volume at time 0 and time t

a = constant, which reflects the elasticity of unit costs to accumulated volume

If an organization cuts its cost to 80% (20% reduction) each time its accumulated volume doubles, then $a = 0.322$. To see this, set $C_t/C_0 = 0.8$, $P_t/P_0 = 2$, and solve for a:

$$0.8 = \frac{C_t}{C_0} = \left(\frac{P_t}{P_0} \right)^{-a} = 2^{-a}$$

Taking logarithms (base 2) of both sides, we obtain

$$\log_2 0.8 = -a = -0.322$$

There is an a value for any percent cost reduction. If costs are reduced to (90%, 85%, 80%, 75%, 70%) each time production doubles, then a is equal to (0.152, 0.234, 0.322, 0.415, 0.515), respectively.

Learning curves are used in cost accounting to predict future costs. They are used by strategists to predict the advantage of having a larger market share than one's competitors. Notice that when a total market increases, everyone's costs decline, so there is no competitive advantage. However, it still is advantageous to be in industries that are growing, since the organization wishes to have a growth in profits. Thus organizations would like to invest in SBUs for which the worldwide market is growing and in which their market share is relatively large. (The rationale is that a big slice of a big pie is the way to get the most pie.) This implies a four-way breakdown of SBUs, shown in Table 17-3.

An SBU identified as type 1 would receive favored treatment in investment dollars, since the firm would be solidifying a position that should reap future

TABLE 17-3 CATEGORIZATION OF SBUs

Market Share (Our Slice)	GROWTH OF MARKET (FUTURE SIZE OF PIE)	
	High	Low
High	Type 1	Type 2
Low	Type 3	Type 4

benefits. An SBU identified as type 4 would not receive investment funds unless they could promise a very fast return. Type 2 has been called a *cash cow,* meaning that the firm can make money for a long time without investing further. Since the market is not growing, it may not be worthwhile to push that SBU for the future. The firm may choose to let market share decline ("harvest" market share) while generating cash for strategic investments. Type 3 is chosen for major investment only if there is some way to obtain an increased market share.

Concentrating on market share and growth is the essence of the cost leadership strategy. However, this may be too simplistic. A firm may have a strategic advantage because of experience in a related area. For example, computer control is such a large and growing fraction of the cost of military aircraft that a computer manufacturer might be the principal contractor for a fighter plane, in spite of having no air frame production experience.

Porter (1980) describes two generic strategies in addition to cost leadership: *differentiation* and *targeting*. In these situations a niche is selected considering the competitors' products and actions, and the firm hopes to maintain high margins. There are many companies that continue to make the best product in the market, maintain a low market share, but operate at a large profit, because of their ability to charge a high price. The firm may in fact enjoy and utilitize its smallness.

To deal a little better with the complexities of strategic investment, a firm can use something like Table 17-4 to evaluate investment proposals. Table 17-

TABLE 17-4 EXAMPLES OF REQUIRED RATES OF RETURN FOR OPERATIONS INVESTMENT PROPOSALS

Fit with Organizational Strengths	BUSINESS ATTRACTIVENESS		
	High	Medium	Low
High	15%	20%	25%
Medium	20%	25%	30%
Low	30%	35%	40%

4 attempts to answer the question: Should this proposed use of capital be approved? The numbers, which are only examples, are the expected rates of return that are required to gain approval.

Business attractiveness is meant to include several factors. The total industry sales for the product line and the growth rate of that total market would be two of the factors. If the organization is already in the business under study, the current profitability of the line would be a factor in deciding whether to invest more money in that line. Who the competitors are, and how likely they are to make a big push in the area, are also factors. For some firms with large sales and profit swings due to seasonal or economic cycles, a product (or service) line that is up when the other products are down would be valuable. Some businesses choose to give each factor a numerical weight, so that business attractiveness can be measured quantitatively.

Fit with organizational strengths is also meant to include many factors, and a numerical scale could be developed for it as well. The questions to be considered would include:

1. What is the current market share (if the organization is currently making the product)?
2. Can the current sales force or distribution channel market the product (if it is new)?
3. Does the organization have a technological advantage based on technical expertise, previous experience, and/or special facilities?
4. Are there any special reasons why the organization can produce and distribute the product cheaper or faster than the competition?

In different situations, different factors might be included, and management would have the option of adjusting the numerical value if there was a reason to do so. In any case, many factors can be included, and having them written down ahead of time reduces the chance of overlooking a key aspect of the investment.

The numbers given in Table 17-4 are only examples, and they would vary based on a firm's cost of capital and ability to withstand losses. The form of the table and the numbers would be set by top management as a guiding policy for lower-level managers. Individual investment decisions are routinely made on lower operating levels, although the overall strategic plan must be viewed by top management to guarantee a balanced portfolio of projects.

Both present and future operations can be evaluated using a chart similar to Table 17-4, including cost-cutting proposals, basic research programs, and projects to improve a current product. The two inputs to be rationed, managerial/technical personnel and capital, can be reduced to dollar terms, although the scarcity of each input may have to be considered separately.

The attractiveness/fit approach of Table 17-4 emphasizes the fact that market potential and operations expertise should interact to help form a financial policy for allocation of scarce resources. The approach should be viewed as a guideline, rather than the final word for investment decisions. Many other factors are likely to be of importance, including the degree and type of risk present in an investment.

The most common way to think about risk is *financial risk*: Will the project earn 2% or 20% or some other return? Financial risk often occurs because of other risks. For example, in an operations investment, what will it cost to build the facility? Will the raw materials needed to operate the facility be available, and at what cost? (This is called *supply risk*.) How many units will we be able to sell per year? What will it cost to produce the product, per unit, once the facility is in operation? Will our favored position (taxes, sales, etc.) in a foreign investment continue?

An operations manager cannot avoid risk. In fact, risky investments are often very attractive. An organization should consider risky strategic investments where, because of its sales force, technical staff, or management expertise, the risk is lower to them than to other organizations. The marketplace usually pays a premium to risk takers, and a firm can obtain that premium by seizing well-chosen risks. For example, a firm that successfully operates four overseas assembly plants and sells its products in country A is better prepared than most to take the risk of building a plant in country A.

An important example of risk in an operations investment occurs when we are considering what type of facilities are to be built and the method of managing them. A long-range forecast of what products will be sold in the future by an organization is necessary for this process, as well as a forecast of what new technologies will be available. A plant that is designed for minimum-cost production using current technology may be inflexible to change, and it may become a burden. This is referred to as the "millstone" effect by Skinner (1969). The company may soon have an obsolete plant on its hands. On the other hand, a flexible facility, easily adapted to change, may have too high an average unit cost to be competitive in a static market.

A related strategic consideration in investing in operations involves the degree of *vertical integration* (see Porter, 1980). Vertical integration involves owning more links of the chain stretching from raw materials to production and distribution of a product. For example, GTE, a producer of light bulbs, recently purchased two glass plants from Corning. The argument against vertical integration is that the firm is inflexible and unable to change with the market.

Similar arguments apply to the method of managing operations. A management style of allowing decentralized decisions in production and distribution may allow a firm to respond quickly to changes in the market, but the costs may be higher than if all potential savings of centralized purchasing and distribution are realized. The appropriate organization depends on what the market demands currently and will demand in the future. There is no correct way to design facilities and organizations for the long term, but the considerations raised in this section must be part of the decision.

We have introduced the concept of SBUs (strategic business units) as a method of organization for strategic planning. The evaluation of market size, market share, business attractiveness, organizational fit, risk, and flexibility have been proposed as primary considerations in identifying SBUs to be favored, and selecting opportunities within SBUs. This foray into business policy is very limited, and many other considerations come into play. The examples in the next section illustrate these principles and the interplay of operations, marketing, and finance in strategic decision making.

Review Problems

A manufacturing firm is considering increasing its investment in inventory, placing more inventory in stocking points that are close to the customer.

1. What is the nature of the risk in such an investment?
2. The term *balance* is used to refer to planning both investments for short-term return and strategic investments to guarantee the organization's viability in the distant future. On which side of that dichotomy does an inventory investment lie? Why?
3. Can inventory be a burden to the company in the future, in the same way that an obsolete plant can be a burden?

Solutions

1. There is financial risk because the date of the sale is uncertain, so the rate of return is uncertain. Obsolescence is much more likely to occur if inventory is increased and moved closer to the customer. On the other hand, if more inventory is held, service will improve, and if demand suddenly increases, the firm will be in a good position to gain market share.
2. An inventory investment is almost always a short-term investment (for 2 years or less). An exception is a move to buy raw-material inventory (and sources of raw materials) to protect long-term supply.
3. Yes, in exactly the same way as an obsolete plant. The company faces the future with a large amount of assets that have less value than their cost. Unless these assets are able to produce sufficient revenue, the firm may have difficulty raising needed capital.

17-3 EXAMPLES

Worldwide Metal Products Producer

A producer of a wide variety of metal products had been slipping in market share and profitability. European Metals was the third largest firm in the European market and was considering divesting that business. Their customer service was poor. The largest competitor delivered products within 4 weeks. European Metals promised 6-week delivery but kept the promise only half of the time.

Their production cycle took 10 weeks, so they had to keep large amounts of finished goods inventory.

The firm produced 500 semifinished items, but accessories that were used in finishing the products meant that they had a total of 20,000 finished items. They always could produce a finished product from a semifinished product in less than 2 weeks. Finally, the firm was only earning 7% on the accounting book value of its assets. They had an offer to buy the operation for 40% of the book value.

European Metals recognized that the return on book value is not an appropriate way to determine whether or not to sell a facility. The book value is a fiction; an actual offer is real. Since European Metals was earning a good return on the realizable value, the parent firm decided not to sell, even though they had a small market share. However, they were concerned about the source of the small (and declining) market share–poor service.

The firm invested in new, automated equipment that cut the manufacturing cycle to 2 weeks, by dramatically reducing both setup time and processing time. This allows a make-to-order business, so that finished goods inventory can be cut dramatically. In fact, the total inventory reduction exceeded the cost of the new machinery. The facility changes were appropriate even though they represented "excess" capacity. The facility was maintained because, even though they did not dominate the industry, the changes allowed improved marketing as well as improved production. Finally, the experience gained in automated equipment should imply future benefits for the firm.

Personal Computers

A large, vertically integrated computer manufacturer changed its strategy in the early 1980s and decided to go after the personal computer (PC) market. Even though vertical integration is its overall strategy, they used a different approach for the PC market.

The PC group buys components from many suppliers and assembles and tests personal computers. They can produce PCs quickly, and they were able to begin producing soon after the decision to proceed was made. The firm felt that (1) they had to enter the market quickly, and (2) they had to be able to change products quickly. That implied a production approach with mostly purchased materials. They rejected the idea of vertical integration for this SBU.

The firm had less experience with PCs than their competitors. Thus one might predict a high-cost position. But they had more experience in engineering design for computers in general, and their technical expertise carried over to this product, as did their quality image, product testing knowledge, and part of their marketing skill. A simplistic view of learning curves or market share could not be used to analyze the decision.

The ideas of vertical integration, learning or experience curves, market share, market growth, business attractiveness, and fit with our organization can all be used to help think about the decision. But the ideas must be tempered with managerial judgment.

Health Planning Agency

A state health planning agency has reviewed the usage of acute cancer-care wards (and some other facilities) in the state. They found that many such facilities were utilized to less than 50% of capacity, while others were over capacity. They felt they had two options: (1) impose a rule requiring that any proposed acute cancer-care ward must be approved by the state agency, which will approve only wards with expected usage above a minimum level, or (2) allow each hospital to act independently.

The considerations are almost endless, and the future of the health care system will be affected in a major way. Some of the arguments against central controls are as follows. Fully utilized facilities will tend to be in the cities, so access will not be as easy for many rural patients. Some rural patients may even refuse to go to the city, so the quality of care will not be equalized. Further, doctors may prefer to practice in hospitals with many advanced facilities, so hospitals that are not allowed advanced facilities may have trouble attracting medical staff.

On the other side of the argument, the American Medical Association and the specialty groups within it publish utilization figures (number of cases) that are necessary, in their opinion, to provide enough experience to maintain the skill levels of the staff. If the state agency allows hospitals to proceed on their own, low quality may occur as a result of underutilization. Also, it is expensive from society's view to duplicate high-priced medical facilities, especially when they will not be fully utilized.

The question is: To what extent should operations area investments be centralized to force economies of scale? The financial implications are clear, but there are also implications for the consumer. If there are fewer facilities, advertising may be used to reduce the anxiety of going to a distant medical center for care. The health agency in the foregoing example must make a far-reaching decision about the long-term future of health operations. This is a case where not to act is simply choosing one of the alternatives.

The state agency is placed in the position of deciding what SBUs are attractive for the medical units in their state. They must consider the degree to which a new unit fits into an existing medical unit in terms of professional staff, laboratory facilities, and so on. They must consider the risk of obsolescence; that risk is reduced if fewer dollars are invested statewide in one type of facility. The state agency must consider the well-being of all the people they serve. They must hold total costs down or everyone's medical insurance skyrockets. They must provide access to good care for all people, but they cannot provide equally good access for all. Finally, they must use a long-range view to plan the health care system, including its operations and financing, for several years into the future.

Cosmetic Manufacturer

The designer of the product line for a cosmetic manufacturer had final authority on all product-line decisions, and frequently made quick judgments, with little or no lead time, about product-line changes. After deciding that now was the time to change from pastels to bold colors (or the reverse), production would cease, materials would be changed, and some inventory would be scrapped. The complete changeover to the new product line would be accomplished in a week or so. Recent profit pressures had called this practice into question. The company was interested in reducing production cost as part of a strategic plan to sustain profits.

Quick changes in the product line with little regard for the cost might be termed a *bold stroke,* used to get the edge on the competition. This approach made sense when the product cost was a very small percent of the price, as was true in the cosmetic industry. A key question is: Is this approach still appropriate? The cost must be assessed and compared to the benefit. (An estimate of the benefit will be hard to obtain.) A person with a feel for the market is invaluable. However, many people have tried their own bold stroke, only to have it backfire.

The cosmetic company should try to establish communication between product design and production. As much advance planning as possible should be done. If none is possible, production should plan its production methods and inventories knowing the environment it is in. That is, someone must adapt if the profit potential is to be realized. Until now, it appears that strategic planning has been done, with a short time horizon, by the product design group, and production has always been the group that had to adapt. As the industry becomes more competitive, a more formal strategic planning process, including production's inputs, may be necessary.

Review Problem

Briefly describe an organization with which you are familiar. Describe its basic options regarding the products (or services) and customers it will have in the future. Also describe its options regarding the manner in which it will organize and invest to produce and deliver those goods or services. Try to choose an example that has an important decision point at hand, as in the four examples above.

17-4 THE FUTURE

Even though no prediction of the future can be completely accurate, much can be gained by thinking about the future. Operations management strategies may be selected partially based on their efficacy in each of several likely future scenarios. This section will examine a few trends in operations management that appear likely to continue. Further, we will see that the methods of analysis discussed in this text will hold in those scenarios. Operations management will be perhaps more important in the future, and the skills needed will include many of the same skills used today and discussed in this book.

Perhaps the most significant change in the next few years will relate to the attitudes of both managers and workers toward their work, their organizations, and their lives. One aspect of this is that organizations will attempt to more fully utilize the abilities of the work force, including them in more decision making and giving them part of the benefits through gainsharing and similar approaches (see Chapter 6). A second aspect is the composition of the work force, both demographically and psychologically. In the 1990s, 47% of the work force will be female and 45% will be parents of children under 18 (see Bohen, 1983). Issues such as child care, flextime, and job sharing will be important, so that people can contribute both to organizations and their families. This will also affect managers and technical staff, since many two-career families will find it hard to maintain the pace required to get to the top. Organizations will have to adjust to managers and professionals who need to stay in one location for family reasons. The individuals may have to accept a slower path up the ladder than that available to the worker who can put the organization first in his or her life.

Societal issues will continue to be important. Mintzberg (1982) argues that although *efficiency* is a value-free word in theory (one can efficiently achieve social goals), in fact the measurability of cost and the lack of measurability of quality of life means that a drive for efficiency really becomes a drive for low cost. We would add that managers' short stays in their jobs often lead to short time horizons as well as cost-oriented goals (see Hayes and Abernathy, 1980). Longer planning horizons will be used in the next few years, since they help organizations make competitive and strategic plans. As managers increase their use of judgment based on years of operational experience, items that are qualitative in nature will be more readily included in analyses. Quantitative techniques will not (and should not) become less common; they are highly valuable decision aids. They will be *decision support systems* rather than decision systems.

Another significant change in the future in operations will be the use of information processing. As information processing becomes available cheaply, functions such as inventory control and production scheduling may become more sophisticated in small organizations. Soon, computers will have interface compatibility with each other on a large scale, and automatic orders can go from a customer to its major suppliers, with promised delivery dates being sent back immediately. The increased visibility into orders and inventory will help reduce, but not eliminate, variability of forecasting and of scheduling.

Automation, and capital-intensive operations in general, will continue to grow. Plants with few (not zero) workers exist today, and they will become more common in the future. Even though personnel problems are reduced in these plants, other problems remain: capacity planning, inventory and distribution planning, production scheduling, and plant layout, for example. Operations managers will face a similar set of problems, but with new opportunities for innovation.

The trend toward automation does not imply a permanently high rate of unemployment in the future. Another trend—the increasing importance of the service sector—will help to counteract the loss of jobs due to automation. The service sector has grown to the point where it constitutes three-fourths of the jobs in the United States. The service sector is much more labor-intensive than manufacturing, so the slack in jobs created by automation should be taken up by the service sector. As we have seen throughout this text, operations management skills are and will be needed in the service sector. Personnel management is, of course, important, but so is layout, aggregate and capacity planning, scheduling, inventory, and quality control. In fact, quality control is often more complex in a service setting than in a manufacturing plant.

The set of goods and services to be produced in the future will change for several reasons. Because of energy conservation, material shortages, increasing costs, and other factors, some items will face decreasing demand. Products will have to be redesigned, and some companies must plan for shrinkage, not growth. Also, due to increasing pressure for return on assets, stockholders may push companies into reducing assets to get a higher return on the ones that remain. Pruning a product line or facilities slowly, over time, is an important process that should not be viewed negatively.

Increasing the quality of life and maintaining profitability (and viability) of organizations does not depend on sustained growth. Some organizations will grow creatively, and others will shrink, hopefully also creatively. Modifying operations through time to fit with a shrinking or growing organization will be an important part of intermediate and long-range planning.

Inflation rates have been more highly variable during the last 10 years than they were during the preceding 50 or so years. High inflation rates make investments in physical assets, including inventory, relatively more attractive. However, such investments may face an increased risk of obsolescence, requiring the manager to trade off that risk against the future saving of capital. In other words, the issues and methods of the trade-off analysis look the same in inflationary times—only the numbers change.

Finally, as a systems view of problems and organizations is taken, managers will be forced to include more factors in their decision making. The interaction of marketing and production will be analyzed; the flow of materials may be designed using an overall view from raw materials to consumer goods, and sociopolitical effects of doing business in an international setting will be within the realm of many operations managers. In complex situations such as these, an optimal solution will have little meaning, but managers can use analytical methods to help them find a satisfactory one.

Operations managers will be necessary in each of these views of the future, and they will be doing things similar to what they do now. They may be in the service industry rather than manufacturing; they may use a higher cost of capital; they will have access to more sophisticated information processing; but the heart of most manufacturing and service industries will still be the production and delivery of goods and services. As a red-bearded professor once said: "There's making it and selling it; and everything else is just keeping score."

PROBLEMS

*1. Why is the operations area of strategic importance in:
   (a) Hospitals?
   (b) A construction company?
   (c) An automobile manufacturer?

2. Select a large manufacturing company and examine their annual reports for the past 5 years. For each year, compute the information given in Table 17-1. Write a brief report commenting on the relative size of cost of sales, inventories, and plant and equipment, as well as any trends in those variables over the 5-year period. What possible explanations are there for unusually high values?

3. Following the pattern described in Problem 2, perform a comparative analysis for three or four large firms in the same manufacturing industry. (For example, examine Chrysler, Ford, and General Motors, or Goodyear, Firestone, and Goodrich.) Which company seems to have the best operations management? What makes you think so?

4. Examine a recent issue of *Survey of Current Business*. Comment on the size of total inventory, expenditures for plant and equipment, and the inventory/sales ratio. Also comment on the pattern of these variables over the past 12 months.

*5. How, and in relation to what decisions (give examples), must operations managers interact with
   (a) Government agencies?
   (b) Foreign governments?

6. Consider Table 17-2, which lists some policy-level operations decisions.
   (a) Which of the eight decisions involve the finance area? How so?
   (b) Which of the eight decisions involve the marketing area? How so?
   (c) What important decisions do you think should be added to the list?

*7. (a) What is an SBU and what is the purpose of using SBUs?
   (b) Give some possible SBUs in (i) an automobile manufacturer, (ii) a business school, and (iii) a furniture manufacturer.

8. What considerations are included in Table 17-4 that are not included in Table 17-3? What considerations are not adequately included in either one, in your opinion?

*9. In considering an operations area investment:
   (a) What is balance and why is it important?
   (b) Why is risk not necessarily bad?

10. Consider the Personal Computers example from Section 17-3.
   (a) List the pros and cons of entering the personal computer market at the time discussed.
   (b) Comment on the *business attractives* and *fit with the organization* of the decision.

*11. Consider the Health Planning Agency example of Section 17-3.
   (a) List the pros and cons of limiting the number of cancer-care facilities (alternative 1).
   (b) How would quality of care be affected by selecting alternative 2?

12. In the future of operations management:
   (a) Why will changes in information processing be important? In what industries do you think the effect will be present?
   (b) Why does the trend to automation not necessarily imply a high rate of unemployment?
   (c) Less growth, energy conservation, and higher inflation rates (than during most of this century) will affect operations management decisions but not the importance of operations management. How and why?

*13. **(a)** If the ABC Company made its first unit with $10 cost and its second with $8, what a value is implied for equation (1)? (The cost declined to 80% as the accumulated output doubled.)
   (b) What prediction would be made, using the learning rate from part (a), for the cost of the eighth unit?
   (c) Do you feel comfortable using a learning rate estimated using only 2 units?

14. It has been suggested that learning may level off as a product becomes mature. Suppose that the learning model of this chapter applies only for the first 1000 units. Thereafter, the unit cost stays constant. Briefly describe some implications that this would have for strategy formulation.

REFERENCES

Annual Reports (1983) for Alcoa, Firestone, IBM, International Harvester, and McDonnell-Douglas.

BOHEN, H., *Corporate Employment Policies Affecting Families and Children: The United States and Europe.* New York: Aspen Institute for Humanistic Studies, 1983.

HAX, A., AND N. MAJLUF, "Competitive Cost Dynamics: The Experience Curve." *Interfaces,* Vol. 12, No. 5 (October 1982).

HAX, A., AND N. MAJLUF, "The Use of the Growth-Share Matrix in Strategic Planning." *Interfaces,* Vol. 13, No. 1 (February 1983a).

HAX, A., AND N. MAJLUF, "The Use of the Industry Attractiveness-Business Strength Matrix in Strategic Planning." *Interfaces,* Vol. 13, No. 2 (April 1983b).

HAYES, R., AND W. ABERNATHY, "Managing Our Way to Economic Decline." *Harvard Business Review,* July–August 1980.

MINTZBERG, H., "A Note on That Dirty Word 'Efficiency'." *Interfaces,* Vol. 12, No. 5 (October 1982).

NAISBITT, J., *Megatrends: Ten New Directions Transforming Our Lives.* New York: Warner Books, 1982.

PORTER, M., *Competitive Strategy: Techniques for Analyzing Industries and Competitors.* New York: Free Press, 1980.

SKINNER, W., "Manufacturing—Missing Link in Corporate Strategy." *Harvard Business Review,* May–June 1969.

SKINNER, W., "The Focused Factory." *Harvard Business Review,* May–June 1974.

Survey of Current Business, U.S. Department of Commerce, February 1984.

PART V

Technical Appendices

Appendix A. Probabilistic models of service and waiting facilities
Appendix B. Simulation
Appendix C. Linear programming
Appendix D. Tables

Part V is devoted to tools that are applicable in many different areas of operations management. The concepts of the queuing models discussed in Appendix A are fundamental to some of the design and capacity decisions discussed in Chapters 5 and 7, as well as the scheduling decisions of Chapters 11, 12, and 14. Simulation (Appendix B) is also used for these problems, and in understanding large-scale systems of the type discussed in Chapter 13.

The order of presentation of A and B is significant, since queuing theory models (A) are often supplemented or replaced by simulation (B).

Linear programming (Appendix C) is an allocation method used in plant and warehouse location and capacity decisions (Chapter 7), production planning at an aggregate level (Chapter 9), work scheduling (Chapter 14), and a number of other planning and decision situations.

Each of these appendices is designed to teach or review a single tool or problem-solving approach. This makes them different from the chapter text, which is oriented toward a variety of decisions faced by operations managers at various levels in an organization. Appendix D is a compilation of a few useful statistical tables and a table of present values.

APPENDIX A

Probabilistic Models of Service and Waiting Facilities

When customers arrive, the potential for delivery of a good or service is finally complete. The capability to satisfy that demand has been carefully planned (one hopes), so that the appropriate personnel and supplies are available. However, customers seldom arrive at a uniform rate. Consequently, there are always periods of idle capacity, interspersed with periods when customers outnumber servers, and a waiting line builds.

This feast-or-famine effect is observed even if arrivals are more or less steady, as in a dentist's office where patients arrive according to a schedule. The usual cause of delay is the difference in service times among the customers. A single longer-than-average service time overlaps with the time allotted for the next service, and thereby causes a waiting line that persists until shorter service times reduce it. This discussion points out a general principle of waiting lines:

Waiting lines are caused by variability in either the rate of arrivals or the rate of service, or both. Therefore, over the long run, a service system will have both idle capacity and waiting lines.

A *stochastic model* is a set of mathematical equations that use probability distributions to (1) describe the variability in arrival and service rates and (2) predict the resulting effects on both servers and customers. Thus the input to a stochastic model includes probability distributions of arrival and service rates, and the output includes probability distributions of busy servers and waiting customers. These outputs are the mathematical version of the feast-or-famine effect in real systems.

There are many examples of *stochastic processes* in management, and many of them may be characterized as "customer meets server." In the most obvious examples, customers and servers are people (retail stores, doctors' offices, hamburger stands). However, machines or other inanimate objects are sometimes the server (automatic toll booth, computer systems, telephones) or the customer (cars waiting for repair, jobs waiting to be done).

As a consequence of this generality, stochastic models are used in several chapters of this book. In this appendix, we shall only use examples with people. The first part explains and illustrates some important planning concepts which may be understood on an intuitive basis. These concepts deal with averages (such as average utilization of servers) and do not require any notions of probability distributions. The second part presents formulas for predicting the size of the waiting line, based on use of the Poisson probability law.

A-1 PLANNING PRINCIPLES: SYSTEMS IN STEADY STATE

There are a number of principles that are particularly useful for planning service system capacity, but they require the very important assumption that the system is in steady state.

> **Definition:** *A system is said to be in steady state if (1) the number of servers, the average arrival rate, and the average service rate are not changing, (2) the average arrival rate is less than the average service rate times the number of servers, and (3) these conditions have existed for a substantial period of time. (See the following discussion.) The opposite of steady state is transience, which refers to the behavior of the system during the period following some change.*

The *pipeline principle* states that the steady-state average rate of flow through a system must be equal to the intake rate in the long run. Thus the rate of admissions to a hospital equals the rate of discharges plus deaths, and the number of college admissions equals the graduates plus dropouts, in the long run. This may seem too simple to be important, but it is sometimes overlooked. During the transient period following an increase in the size of the entering class, the admission rate exceeds the graduation plus dropout rate, but steady state is restored by the time the first of the larger classes has reached graduation.

Figure A-1 shows a typical service system with a single waiting line. The pipeline principle is incorporated in that diagram by making sure that the average inflow equals the average outflow at each point in the system. For example, the rate at which customers demand service (λ) equals the rate at which they join the queue (AR) plus the turnaway rate (unmet demand).

The Greek letter ρ is used to denote the *utilization factor,* which refers to the fraction of the servers' time that is used productively, on the average. Therefore, $1 - \rho$ is the fraction of idle time. We assume that all servers are identical. The average service rate capacity of each server is called μ. Because μ is the average output rate of a server when 100% utilized, then $\mu\rho$ must be the effective average output rate per server, when idle time is factored in. The

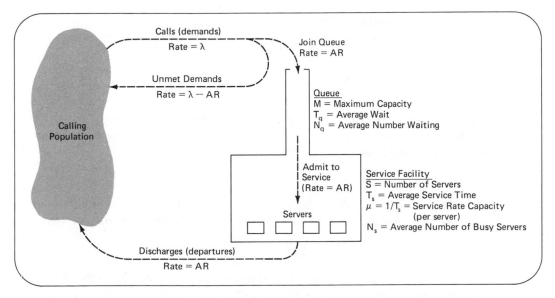

Figure A-1   Schematic of a service system with a single waiting line.

effective output rate of a facility with S servers is, therefore, $S\mu\rho$. However, according to the pipeline principle, the average output rate must equal the average input rate (or admission rate), denoted AR. Therefore,

$$\text{average input rate} = \text{average output rate}$$
$$\text{AR} = \rho S\mu$$

which may be rearranged to give the following formula for the utilization factor:

$$\frac{\text{average utilization}}{\text{factor}} = \frac{\text{average input rate}}{\text{maximum average output rate}}$$

$$\rho = \frac{\text{AR}}{S\mu}$$

The following principles are all variations on the utilization factor formula:

Minimum Capacity. Since utilization cannot exceed 100% ($\rho < 1.0$), then $\text{AR}/S\mu < 1.0$, which may be rearranged as

$$\frac{\text{number of}}{\text{servers}} > \frac{\text{input rate}}{\text{output rate capacity per server}}$$

$$S > \frac{\text{AR}}{\mu}$$

Occupied Servers. There are S servers. Since ρ is the fraction of servers who are busy, $S\rho$ must be the average number who are busy, denoted N_s, so $N_s = S\rho$. Using the previous formula for ρ, the S cancels out. The result is

$$\begin{aligned} \text{average number} \\ \text{of servers who} \\ \text{are busy} \end{aligned} = \frac{\text{input rate}}{\text{output rate capacity per server}}$$

$$N_s = \frac{\text{AR}}{\mu}$$

Customers Being Served. Since there is one customer for each busy server, then, on the average, the number of customers in the process of being served is equal to N_s, the number of busy servers.

The *average service time per customer,* denoted T_s, is often easier to measure than the service rate, μ. Therefore, it is worthwhile to note that

$$T_s \equiv \frac{1}{\mu}$$

Consequently, each of the preceding formulas can be stated in terms of T_s. For example, the occupancy of the service facility is $N_s = \text{AR}/\mu = \text{AR} \cdot T_s$ customers.

Customers in the Queue. Just as $N_s = \text{AR} \cdot T_s$, the average waiting time per customer (T_q) is related to average queue length (N_q) by

$$\begin{aligned} \text{average} \\ \text{queue} \\ \text{length} \end{aligned} = \left(\begin{aligned} \text{average rate} \\ \text{of joining} \\ \text{queue} \end{aligned} \right) \left(\begin{aligned} \text{average} \\ \text{waiting} \\ \text{time} \end{aligned} \right)$$

$$N_q = \text{AR} \cdot T_q$$

Of course, if there is a maximum queue length (M), the average cannot exceed the maximum. This would apply in the case of a drive-in bank if cars are turned away when the line backs up into the street.

In summary, we have assumed that there are S identical servers that are always available. Both arrivals and service may be random. However, the *average* service capacity of each server does not change with time, nor does the average rate of arrivals. The resulting steady-state analysis has given us the following formulas:

$$\begin{aligned} \text{average} \\ \text{utilization} \\ \text{factor} \end{aligned} = \frac{\text{admission rate}}{\text{service capacity}} = \frac{\text{busy servers}}{\text{total servers}} \quad (1)$$

$$\rho = \frac{\text{AR}}{S\mu} = \frac{N_s}{S}$$

$$\begin{aligned} \text{demand} \\ \text{arrival} \\ \text{rate} \end{aligned} \geqslant \begin{aligned} \text{rate of} \\ \text{joining} \\ \text{queue} \end{aligned} < \begin{aligned} \text{service} \\ \text{rate} \\ \text{capability} \end{aligned} \quad (2)$$

$$\lambda \quad \geqslant \quad \text{AR} \quad < S\mu \text{ (or } S/T_s)$$

$$\begin{array}{ccc} \begin{matrix} \text{number of} \\ \text{servers} \end{matrix} & \geqslant & \begin{matrix} \text{average} \\ \text{number of} \\ \text{occupied} \\ \text{servers} \end{matrix} & = & \left(\begin{matrix} \text{average} \\ \text{admission} \\ \text{rate} \end{matrix} \right) \left(\begin{matrix} \text{average} \\ \text{service} \\ \text{time} \end{matrix} \right) \end{array} \quad (3)$$

$$S \quad \geqslant \quad N_s \quad = \quad \text{AR} \cdot T_s \ (\text{or AR}/\mu)$$

$$\begin{array}{ccc} \begin{matrix} \text{maximum} \\ \text{queue size} \end{matrix} & \geqslant & \begin{matrix} \text{average} \\ \text{queue} \\ \text{size} \end{matrix} & = & \left(\begin{matrix} \text{rate of} \\ \text{joining} \\ \text{queue} \end{matrix} \right) \left(\begin{matrix} \text{average} \\ \text{time in} \\ \text{queue} \end{matrix} \right) \end{array} \quad (4)$$

$$M \quad \geqslant \quad N_q \quad = \quad \text{AR} \cdot T_q$$

These formulas hold for any service system in steady state, no matter what probability laws govern the variability of arrivals and service time. However, there is a missing link between equations (3) and (4): The average waiting time (T_q) must be related to the average occupancy level of the service facility (N_s), since waiting lines become a serious problem in facilities that are nearly full, on the average. *One of the most important decisions in designing a service system is how much excess capacity to provide as a safety margin to keep waiting lines at a reasonable level.* Unfortunately, the trade-off between capacity and waiting lines is very complex and requires substantial analysis. Before pursuing those relationships, we will consider a few applications of the principles discussed so far.

Review Problems

1. The average car spends 10 seconds in the toll station on Murkey Turnpike. There are three toll booths. How much traffic can the station handle?

2. A 450-bed hospital expects to admit 18,250 patients next year, each averaging 8 days of hospital stay. Are there sufficient beds? How many beds will be empty? What would happen to hospital utilization if 10 more beds were added?

3. An airline telephone reservation service has been designed to hold calls whenever a clerk is not available. The design goal is an average waiting time of less than 3 minutes. Approximately 200 calls per hour are to be handled. How many calls must the system be able to place on hold?

4. On Murkey Turnpike (Review Problem 1) the maximum rate of traffic flow is 20 cars per minute, occurring between 5:15 and 5:30 P.M. on Friday. The rate is 17 per minute during the 15-minute periods before 5:15 and after 5:30 P.M. Describe the transient behavior of the toll-booth waiting line during the peak.

Solutions

1. All traffic must pass through the station, so the arrival rate is equal to the admission rate. Equation (2) therefore says that $\lambda < S\mu = (3)(\frac{1}{10}) = 0.3$ car per second, or 18 per minute.

2. Each bed may be viewed as a server, so $S = 450$. AR $= 18{,}250/365 =$

50 per day, and $T_s = 8$ days. Therefore, from equation (3), $N_s = (50)(8) = 400$ beds occupied, on the average, so 50 will be empty. This 50 beds is a safety margin since *actual* hospital census will vary daily. Using equation (1), occupancy will average $\rho = 400/450$, or 89%. If there are 10 more beds, unless either admissions or length of stay changes, there will still be $N_s = 400$ occupied, so $\rho = 400/460 = 87\%$ utilization.

3. If all customers are willing to wait, $\lambda_q = 200$ per hour, or 3.333 calls per minute. Using equation (4), $N_q = \lambda_q T_q = (3.33)(3) = 10$ calls waiting, *on the average*. The actual number waiting will vary from this average, so the queue capacity must be larger than 10. (The next section gives information on the extra margin of safety.)

4. During the peak period, the arrival rate exceeds the service capability by 2 cars per minute, so the waiting line grows at this average rate. The number of cars waiting increases by about $(2)(15) = 30$ over the 15-minute peak interval, on the average.

A-2 WAITING TIME: QUEUING THEORY APPROACH

Our previous discussion pointed out that waiting time is influenced by variability in arrivals and service. Accordingly, we must explicitly model these two random variables in order to predict waiting time. The derivation of the relationships is too involved for this appendix. Instead, we shall state a few of these results without proof, and work through some examples to show how they can be used. They are based on the assumptions that (1) arrivals per unit time follow the Poisson probability distribution[1] (as before, the mean arrival rate $= \lambda$), and (2) service times are governed by the exponential probability distribution[1] (with mean $T_s = 1/\mu$). Together, we shall refer to these assumptions as the *Markov property*. (3) The third assumption is that all servers are identical, which was also assumed in the previous section. These assumptions are made for convenience; without them, the analysis becomes very cumbersome, if not downright impossible. Because they are fairly restrictive assumptions, the models to be described are often not accurate in the strictest sense. Nevertheless, the models do have substantial value for several reasons: (1) together with the steady-state formulas of the previous section, the queuing theory models often provide a reasonable approximation, thus assuring that the capacity decision is in the right ballpark; (2) the results usually provide an upper bound estimate of average waiting time, when the assumptions of the model are not realistic; and (3) the general nature of the trade-off between service capacity and queue length can be studied with these limited models, demonstrating several very general principles.

Figure A-2 summarizes the kind of system that we shall study. (The results of the preceding sections are also included in the diagram.) The three elements

---

[1] See Appendix D, Tables 4 and 5, for brief descriptions of these probability laws.

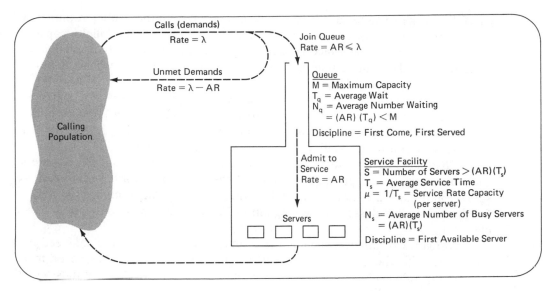

Figure A-2 Schematic with summary of steady-state relationships.

are (1) the calling population (often referred to as the service population), (2) the queue, and (3) the service facility. We shall discuss each of these in turn.

When the *calling population* is large compared to the number of customers in the queue and service facility ($N \gg N_q + N_s$), the demand rate varies randomly about the mean value λ, regardless of the actual number in the queue. This is referred to as an *infinite-population* ($N = \infty$) *model.* In contrast, suppose that N is only twice as large as $N_q + N_s$; then on the average the calling population is reduced by half (the other half are waiting for service or being served), so the arrival rate is also down by 50%. *Only the infinite population model is considered here.* However, it is reasonable to use such a model as long as $N_s + N_q < (0.01)(N)$ (which implies that less than 1% of the population is in the service system, on the average).

Since the population is infinite, there is no theoretical limit to the length of the waiting line unless a maximum queue capacity (M) is specified. In that case, we have a *finite queue* model. When the queue reaches the maximum capacity of the waiting area, it is assumed that arrivals are turned away. These customers are lost to the system (served by a competitor, for example). When the waiting area once again has space available, arrivals resume at the same average rate as before (no loss of goodwill). The average rate of joining the queue (AR) is therefore lower than the demand rate λ by a percentage equal to the probability that the queue is full.

In many situations there is no practical limit on the size of the queue. This is true, for example, when the queue is really a list of names of people waiting to be called for service. It is also true for many service facilities, which are carefully designed to have substantial excess capacity in the waiting room. This is referred to as an *infinite capacity queue*. Of course, for the infinite capacity queue model, $\lambda = AR$, since no demands are turned away. Incidentally, we shall see that the waiting-time formulas are somewhat simpler when no limit is assumed for the queue length.

In the *service facility* are S identical servers. (Of course, $S = 1$ if there is a single server.) Each serves one customer at a time, on a first come, first served basis, averaging T_s time units per customer (not including idle time). The average service rate capacity per server, denoted μ, is simply $1/T_s$.

Customers may be served on a priority basis, with K classes of customers, each class having a separate queue. Class 1 has top priority for the next available server, and class 2 is not served unless the class 1 queue is empty, and so on for the remaining classes. (The diagram in Figure A-2 depicts only one priority class.)

Networks of queues, such as the example in Figure A-3, are analyzed one at a time with the output of one subsystem supplying input to one or more succeeding subsystems. Of course, the total output of each facility must equal its input (the pipeline principle).

The formulas for various queuing systems are contained in Table A-1. Although they may look difficult, most of the work is eliminated by reference to Table A-2. The rest of the computations are easy to perform with a hand calculator.

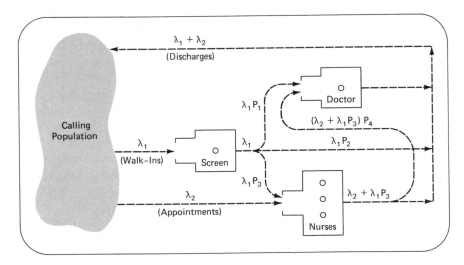

Figure A-3 Service network: a clinic with a screener who decides whether walk-in patients should see the doctor (Probability P_1), a nurse (Probability P_3), or nobody, $(P_2)^a$.

    [a] All patients who have an appointment see a nurse. Nurses' patients either see the doctor (probability P_4) or go home.

TABLE A-1 SUMMARY OF SOME QUEUING FORMULAS BASED ON THE MARKOV PROPERTY[a]

Model	Number of Servers, S	Calling Population, N	Maximum Queue, M	Number of Priority Classes, K	% Turned Away, P_{full}	Admission Rate, AR	Number of Occupied Servers, N_s	Average Number in Queue, N_q	Waiting Time, T_q
I	1	∞	∞	1	0	$AR = \lambda$	$\dfrac{\lambda}{\mu}$	$\dfrac{\rho^2}{1-\rho}$	$\dfrac{N_q}{\lambda}$
II	S	∞	∞	1	0	$AR = \lambda$	$\dfrac{\lambda}{\mu}$	(See Table A-2)	$\dfrac{N_q}{\lambda}$
III	S	∞	M	1	$\dfrac{\rho^M(1-\rho)}{A-\rho^{M+1}}$	$AR = \lambda(1 - P_{full})$	$\dfrac{AR}{\mu}$	$\dfrac{\rho}{1-\rho}\left\{\dfrac{1-[\rho^M(M-M\rho+1)]}{A-\rho^{M+1}}\right\}$	$\dfrac{N_q}{AR}$
IV	S	∞	∞	K	0	$AR = \lambda$	$\dfrac{\lambda}{\mu}$	$\dfrac{\rho_k}{(A)(B_{k-1})(B_k)}$ $k = 1, \ldots, K$	$\dfrac{N_{qk}}{\lambda_k}$ $k = 1, \ldots, K$

[a] Definitions:

λ = average arrival rate   (λ_k = arrival rate of priority k customers)

μ = average service rate capacity per server

$\rho = \dfrac{\lambda}{S\mu}$ ($\rho_k = \lambda_k/S\mu$ for priority k customers, and $\rho = \Sigma \rho_k$)

$A = \dfrac{\rho/(1-\rho)}{N_q \text{ from Table A-2}}$ (this number, A, has no physical meaning; it is just an intermediate calculation)

$B_k = B_{k-1} - \rho_k$ ($B_0 = 1$; the numbers B_k are also intermediate calculations, without meaning)

TABLE A-2 AVERAGE NUMBER IN WAITING LINE (N_q), WITH 95TH AND 99TH PERCENTILES[a] FOR MODEL II, TABLE A-1

UTILIZATION FACTOR

Servers	0.10	0.20	0.30	0.40	0.50	0.60	0.70	0.75	0.80	0.85	0.90	0.95	0.98
1	0.011	0.050	0.129	0.267	0.500	0.900	1.633	2.250	3.200	4.817	8.100	18.050	48.020
	0 0	0 1	1 2	2 4	3 5	4 8	7 11	9 15	12 19	17 27	27 42	57 88	147 226
2	0.002	0.017	0.059	0.152	0.333	0.675	1.345	1.929	2.844	4.426	7.674	17.587	47.535
	0 0	0 1	0 2	1 3	2 5	4 7	6 11	8 14	11 19	16 26	26 42	56 88	146 226
3	0.000	0.006	0.030	0.094	0.237	0.532	1.149	1.703	2.589	4.139	7.354	17.233	47.160
	0 0	0 0	0 1	1 2	2 4	3 6	6 10	8 14	11 18	16 26	26 41	56 87	146 226
4	0.000	0.002	0.016	0.060	0.174	0.431	1.000	1.528	2.386	3.906	7.090	16.937	46.844
	0 0	0 0	0 1	0 2	1 4	3 6	6 10	8 13	11 18	16 26	26 41	56 87	146 225
5	0.000	0.001	0.009	0.040	0.130	0.354	0.882	1.385	2.216	3.709	6.862	16.678	46.566
	0 0	0 0	0 0	0 1	1 3	3 6	5 10	7 13	10 17	15 25	25 41	55 87	145 225
6	0.000	0.000	0.005	0.027	0.099	0.295	0.784	1.265	2.071	3.536	6.661	16.446	46.314
	0 0	0 0	0 0	0 1	0 3	2 5	5 9	7 13	10 17	15 25	25 40	55 86	145 225
7	0.000	0.000	0.003	0.018	0.076	0.248	0.702	1.161	1.944	3.383	6.480	16.235	46.084
	0 0	0 0	0 0	0 1	0 2	2 5	5 9	7 12	10 17	15 25	25 40	55 86	145 224
8	0.000	0.000	0.002	0.012	0.059	0.209	0.631	1.071	1.831	3.245	6.314	16.039	45.870
	0 0	0 0	0 0	0 0	0 2	2 5	4 9	6 12	9 17	15 24	25 40	55 86	145 224
9	0.000	0.000	0.001	0.008	0.046	0.178	0.571	0.991	1.729	3.118	6.161	15.857	45.669
	0 0	0 0	0 0	0 0	0 2	1 4	4 8	6 12	9 16	14 24	24 40	54 86	144 224
10	0.000	0.000	0.000	0.006	0.036	0.152	0.517	0.920	1.637	3.003	6.019	15.686	45.480
	0 0	0 0	0 0	0 0	0 1	1 4	4 8	6 11	9 16	14 24	24 39	54 86	144 224
11	0.000	0.000	0.000	0.004	0.028	0.130	0.471	0.856	1.553	2.895	5.886	15.525	45.300
	0 0	0 0	0 0	0 0	0 1	1 4	3 8	6 11	9 16	14 24	24 39	54 85	144 224
12	0.000	0.000	0.000	0.003	0.022	0.112	0.429	0.798	1.475	2.796	5.760	15.371	45.129
	0 0	0 0	0 0	0 0	0 1	0 3	3 8	5 11	8 16	14 23	24 39	54 85	144 223
13	0.000	0.000	0.000	0.002	0.018	0.097	0.392	0.746	1.404	2.702	5.642	15.226	44.965
	0 0	0 0	0 0	0 0	0 1	0 3	3 7	5 11	8 15	13 23	24 39	54 85	144 223
14	0.000	0.000	0.000	0.001	0.014	0.084	0.359	0.698	1.338	2.615	5.530	15.086	44.808
	0 0	0 0	0 0	0 0	0 0	0 3	3 7	5 10	8 15	13 23	23 39	53 85	143 223
15	0.000	0.000	0.000	0.001	0.011	0.072	0.329	0.654	1.277	2.533	5.424	14.952	44.656
	0 0	0 0	0 0	0 0	0 0	0 3	2 7	5 10	8 15	13 23	23 38	53 85	143 223

16	44.510 / 143 223	14.824 / 53 84	5.322 / 23 38	2.455 / 13 23	1.220 / 8 15	0.614 / 4 10	0.303 / 2 7	0.063 / 0 2	0.009 / 0 0	0.001 / 0 0	0.000 / 0 0	0.000 / 0 0	0.000 / 0 0
17	44.369 / 143 223	14.700 / 53 84	5.225 / 23 38	2.381 / 13 23	1.166 / 7 15	0.577 / 4 10	0.278 / 2 6	0.055 / 0 2	0.007 / 0 0	0.000 / 0 0	0.000 / 0 0	0.000 / 0 0	0.000 / 0 0
18	44.232 / 143 222	14.580 / 53 84	5.132 / 23 38	2.312 / 12 22	1.116 / 7 14	0.542 / 4 10	0.256 / 2 6	0.048 / 0 2	0.006 / 0 0	0.000 / 0 0	0.000 / 0 0	0.000 / 0 0	0.000 / 0 0
19	44.099 / 143 222	14.465 / 53 84	5.043 / 23 38	2.245 / 12 22	1.069 / 7 14	0.511 / 4 9	0.236 / 1 6	0.041 / 0 1	0.005 / 0 0	0.000 / 0 0	0.000 / 0 0	0.000 / 0 0	0.000 / 0 0
20	43.970 / 142 222	14.353 / 53 84	4.957 / 22 38	2.182 / 12 22	1.024 / 7 14	0.481 / 4 9	0.218 / 1 6	0.036 / 0 1	0.004 / 0 0	0.000 / 0 0	0.000 / 0 0	0.000 / 0 0	0.000 / 0 0
25	43.371 / 142 221	13.839 / 52 83	4.571 / 22 37	1.905 / 11 21	0.836 / 6 13	0.362 / 3 8	0.148 / 0 5	0.019 / 0 0	0.001 / 0 0	0.000 / 0 0	0.000 / 0 0	0.000 / 0 0	0.000 / 0 0
30	42.834 / 141 221	13.386 / 51 82	4.243 / 21 36	1.680 / 10 20	0.691 / 5 12	0.276 / 2 7	0.102 / 0 4	0.010 / 0 0	0.000 / 0 0	0.000 / 0 0	0.000 / 0 0	0.000 / 0 0	0.000 / 0 0
35	42.344 / 141 220	12.979 / 50 82	3.957 / 20 35	1.491 / 10 20	0.577 / 4 11	0.213 / 1 6	0.072 / 0 3	0.005 / 0 0	0.000 / 0 0	0.000 / 0 0	0.000 / 0 0	0.000 / 0 0	0.000 / 0 0
40	41.892 / 140 220	12.609 / 50 81	3.704 / 20 35	1.331 / 9 19	0.485 / 3 11	0.166 / 0 5	0.051 / 0 2	0.003 / 0 0	0.000 / 0 0	0.000 / 0 0	0.000 / 0 0	0.000 / 0 0	0.000 / 0 0
50	41.075 / 139 219	11.953 / 49 80	3.275 / 18 34	1.075 / 8 18	0.348 / 2 9	0.102 / 0 4	0.026 / 0 0	0.001 / 0 0	0.000 / 0 0	0.000 / 0 0	0.000 / 0 0	0.000 / 0 0	0.000 / 0 0

$$N_q = \frac{\rho(\lambda/\mu)^s/[S!(1-\rho)^2]}{\frac{(\lambda/\mu)^s}{S!(1-\rho)} + \sum_{n=0}^{s-1}\frac{(\lambda/\mu)^n}{n!}}$$

$$P(\text{queue} > q) = (1-\rho)N_q\rho^q$$

$$P(\text{wait} > t) = \left(\frac{1-\rho}{\rho}\right)N_q e^{-S\mu(1-\rho)t}$$

[a] Key: The decimal numbers are N_q values, and the integers are $q(95)$ and $q(99)$. I.e. the probability is >95% that the queue is $\le q(95)$, and similarly for $q(99)$.

The City Walk-In Clinic

Three categories of patients are treated at City Clinic, arriving at a rate of 10, 15, and 20 per 8-hour day, respectively. All patients are walk-ins, since this clinic does not accept appointments. Average service rate capacity is 25 per day for each of the two nurse practitioners who staff the clinic. The first category of patients is the primary target population for the facility. However, all patients are currently served on a first come, first served basis, regardless of category. Some thought has been given to limiting access by reducing the waiting room to a capacity of 10 patients and sending overflow patients to a neighboring clinic.

Analysis 1 (no priorities, infinite queue). Under current policy, there are no priorities ($K = 1$), and no stated limit on queue size ($M = \infty$) or population ($N = \infty$). Therefore, our first analysis will use Model II in Table A-1, with $\lambda = AR = 10 + 15 + 20 = 45$ admissions per day. The average number of occupied servers is, therefore, $N_s = \lambda/\mu = 45/25 = 1.8$, which means that the two nurse practitioners ($S = 2$) are busy 90% of the time ($\rho = 1.8/2 = 90\%$).

To find the average queue size (N_q), we look in Table A-2, in the row for $S = 2$ servers. Reading across the top, we find the column for which $\rho = 0.90$. Where the $S = 2$ row and the $\rho = 0.9$ column intersect, we find $N_q = 7.674$ patients waiting, on the average. Returning to Table A-1, the final instruction for Model II is to calculate the average patient waiting time as $T_q = N_q/\lambda = 7.674/45 = 0.1705$ day $= 1.36$ hours at 8 hours per day. This very high waiting time indicates why they are considering limiting the arrivals.

When we found $N_q = 7.674$ in Table A-2, there were two other numbers, 26 and 42, immediately below. These are the 95th and 99th percentile points from the probability distribution of the waiting line. Consequently, we know that there is about a 5% chance that the waiting line will exceed 26 people, so their suggested policy of limiting the line to 10 people will have a large effect.

Analysis 2 (finite queue). With a queue limit of $M = 10$, Model III of Table A-1 gives a formula for the percent of patients who are turned away.

$$P_{\text{full}} = \frac{\rho^M(1 - \rho)}{A - \rho^{M+1}}$$

In this formula, the factor A is required, and its definition is given in the notes at the bottom of Table A-1:

$$A = \frac{\rho/(1 - \rho)}{N_q \text{ from Table A-2}}$$

Now, from analysis 1, we know that $\rho = 0.9$, and the N_q value from Table A-2 is 7.674. Plugging these into the two equations above, the result is

$$A = \frac{0.9/0.1}{7.674} = 1.173$$

$$\rho^M = 0.9^{10} = 0.3487$$

$$P_{\text{full}} = \frac{\rho^M(1-\rho)}{A - \rho^{M+1}} = \frac{0.3487(0.1)}{1.173 - (0.9)(0.3487)} = \frac{0.03487}{0.8591} = 0.0406$$

Therefore, about 4% of arrivals will be turned away. According to Model III, the admission rate will be $\text{AR} = \lambda(1 - P_{\text{full}}) = 43.2$ per day (4% below the demand rate of 45), and the average queue will be

$$
\begin{aligned}
N_q &= \frac{\rho}{1-\rho}\left\{\frac{1 - [\rho^M(M - M\rho + 1)]}{A - \rho^{M+1}}\right\} \\
&= \frac{0.9}{0.1}\left\{\frac{1 - [0.3487(10 - 9 + 1)]}{0.8591}\right\} = 3.17
\end{aligned}
$$

The average wait is $T_q = N_q/\text{AR} = 3.17/43.2 = 0.073$ day $= 0.59$ hour. Thus the model predicts that this small reduction in arrivals will decrease the average waiting time by almost 60% (from 1.4 to 0.6 hour). *This surprisingly large decrease is because the patients turned away would have had long waits, since their arrival occurred when the line would have been 10 or more.*

Analysis 3 (priorities). The three categories of City Clinic's patients might be given different priorities. Category 1 is the primary target population. In choosing the next patient from the queue, if the clinic wished to give top priority to these patients, second priority to category 2, and third to category 3, model IV of Table A-1 applies. Using $K = 3$ priorities, we follow the instructions in the table: $N_s = \lambda/\mu = 1.8$, and $A - 1.173$ (from analysis 2), and we calculate the factors ρ_k, B_k, and N_{qk} as follows:

k	$\rho_k = \dfrac{\lambda_k}{S\mu}$	$B_k = B_{k-1} - \rho_k$	$N_{qk} = \dfrac{\rho_k}{AB_{k-1}B_k}$
0		$B_0 = 1.0$	
1	$10/50 = 0.2$	$B_1 = B_0 - \rho_1 = 0.8$	$\dfrac{0.2}{(A)(1)(0.8)} = 0.213$
2	$15/50 = 0.3$	$B_2 = B_1 - \rho_2 = 0.5$	$\dfrac{0.3}{A(0.8)(0.5)} = 0.640$
3	$20/50 = 0.4$	$B_3 = B_2 - \rho_3 = 0.1$	$\dfrac{0.4}{A(0.5)(0.1)} = 6.821$
			Total $= 7.674$

We note from these computations that the average number waiting is still 7.674, unchanged by the priority system: but *the waiting line is disproportionately category 3 patients* (6.82/7.67 = 89% in the queue are category 3, versus $\lambda_3/\lambda = 20/45 = 44\%$ of the arrivals). The waiting times are $N_{qk}/\lambda_k = 0.213/10 = 0.0213$ day or 0.17 hour for category 1, 0.34 hour for category 2, and 2.73 hours for category 3.

Conclusions for City Clinic. We have no evidence that the Markov property accurately describes the arrivals and service times, so these analyses must be viewed as only approximate. The two proposals to deal with the unacceptably long waits may be contrasted as egalitarian (analysis 2 turns away 4% of *all* patient categories) versus selective (analysis 3 makes life miserable for category 3 patients). Note, however, that the egalitarian approach results in a loss of 4% of patient revenues, with a corresponding increase in idle time.

The result of the clinic analysis provides an example of a very important *principle of waiting time versus idle time*: Waiting times can be reduced by increasing the relative service capacity. This may be accomplished by reducing the arrival rate, or increasing the number of servers or their work pace (service rate). All these actions will increase the average idle time of the servers.

Optimization

The cost trade-off between idle time and waiting time may be illustrated by considering two options for decreasing patient congestion at the City Clinic: (1) increase the number of nurse practitioners, or (2) decrease the number of patients served. To keep the analysis simple, the infinite-queue model without priority classes will be used. Because option (2) varies the size of the population served, the analysis is done on a cost-per-arrival basis.

The *cost of the clinic* is assumed to have three components: fixed cost (F), cost per additional server (C_s), and marginal cost per patient served (C_p). The cost per server includes the salaries of the nurse practitioners, and the variable overhead for supporting them. The marginal cost per patient served is very small, mostly attributable to supplies and record keeping. Fixed cost refers to the fixed overhead of the clinic, also small in comparison to the cost per additional server. The total daily cost is

$$F + SC_s + \lambda C_p$$

and the average cost per arrival is

$$AC = \frac{F + SC_s}{\lambda} + C_p$$

The *opportunity cost to the consumer* is assumed to be proportional to time spent in the clinic (since type and quality of service are assumed fixed, as are location, hours of operation, etc.). Therefore, if C_w is the cost to the consumer per hour of waiting, $C_w T_q$ is the average consumer's opportunity cost per arrival.

For City Clinic, we shall use $F = \$200$ per day, $C_s = \$150$ per server per day, and $C_p = \$6$ per arrival. The two values $C_w = \$2$ per hour and $C_w = \$10$ per hour are used to provide a range for this hard-to-measure parameter.

Table A-3 shows the total average cost per arrival. Assuming that all the costs are passed on to the consumer, if the consumer's waiting time is valued at $2 per hour, the current policy of $\lambda = 45$, $S = 2$ is better than the others, since it achieves the lowest total cost of $19.84 per visit. However, the conclusion is different when $C_w = \$10$ per hour, for which the direct cost of increasing the number of servers to three is more than offset by the reduction in waiting-time costs.

TABLE A-3 COSTS OF OPERATION AND WAITING AT CITY CLINIC

	COST OF CLINIC				COST OF WAITING				TOTAL COST PER ARRIVAL	
Servers, S	Patients Per Day, λ	Cost Per Arrival, AC	ρ	Queue, N_q	Wait, T_q (Hours)	Cost: $C_w = 2$	$C_w = 10$	$C_w = 2$	$C_w = 10$
2	45	17.11	0.9	7.674	1.364	2.73	13.64	19.84	30.75
3	45	20.44	0.6	0.53	0.094	0.19	0.94	20.63	21.38
4	45	23.78	0.45	0.11	0.020	0.04	0.20	23.82	23.98
2	40	19.25	0.8	2.84	0.568	1.14	5.68	20.39	24.93
2	35	22	0.7	1.34	0.306	0.61	3.06	22.61	25.06
2	30	25.67	0.6	0.67	0.179	0.36	1.79	26.03	27.46
2	25	30.8	0.5	0.33	0.106	0.21	1.06	31.01	31.86

Sensitivity Analysis

A disproportionate reduction in waiting time occurs when changes are made to a system that is near saturation. For example, in Table A-3 an increase from two to three servers (50%) cut waiting time from 1.364 to 0.094 hour (93%), and a reduction in the demand rate from 45 to 40 (11%) cut the delay by 0.8 hour, or 58%. This is a very important phenomenon to remember, because it points out that *waiting lines can be very sensitive to small changes in the system parameters, especially if there is very little slack capacity.*

Many services are provided on an appointment basis, which reduces the randomness in the arrival process. Moreover, some services can be delivered in a fixed amount of time, or with only a small variation. How does this affect the waiting line? The answer is: Shorter average waits result whenever randomness is reduced in either arrivals or service time. Therefore, use of the formulas presented here represents a conservative analysis, in that waiting times should be smaller than calculated when appointment systems are present.

There are many queuing situations in which mathematical models are difficult or impossible to derive. When a more precise model is needed, simulation is often used (see Appendix B).

Review Problems

1. What is the difference between a finite-queue model and a finite-population model?
2. Which gives larger N_q values, finite or infinite population models? Why?
3. The average car spends 10 seconds in a toll station on Murkey Turnpike. There are three toll booths in the station.
   (a) What is the average number of cars in the waiting line when the traffic flow averages 14 cars per minute? 16? 18? 20?

   (b) If the average flow peaks at 16.2 cars per minute, suggest how large
        the toll-plaza capacity should be for waiting cars.
4. A typist works for five executives, each of whom generates an average of
   five dictated (tape-recorded) jobs per hour.
   (a) Explain why this is not a finite-population model with $N = 5$.
   (b) What must the typist's service rate be?

Solutions

1. Finite-queue models place a limit on the length of the waiting line, regardless
   of the number of potential customers. Finite-population models assume
   that the number of customers is small enough that the waiting line represents
   a significant portion of the total population.

2. Infinite. In a finite-population model, the arrival rate slows down as the
   queue builds up, simply because there are fewer potential customers in the
   calling population (they are in the queue instead).

3. (a) There are $S = 3$ toll booths. $T_s = 10$ seconds, so $\mu = 6$ per minute
        per toll booth. For $\lambda = 14$ per minute, $\rho = \lambda/S\mu = 14/(3)(6) = 0.78$.
        From Table A-2, with $S = 3$ and a utilization factor of 0.78, we find
        that N_q is between 1.7 and 2.6 cars. Interpolation yields 2.4 cars waiting,
        on the average. For $\lambda = 16$, $\rho = 0.89$, and $N_q = 7.1$ cars. There is
        no steady-state solution for 18 and 20 cars per hour, since ρ is no longer
        less than 1.00.
   (b) At 16.2 cars per minute, $\rho = 0.9$ and the average line is 7.4 cars. The
        length of the line will reach 26 cars about 5% of the time, and 41 cars
        about 1% of the time. Therefore, the waiting area should hold about
        40 cars if the peak rate is one that persists for any length of time.

4. (a) The population is not the executives. It is the jobs they generate. The
        rate of arrival of those jobs is not affected by the typist's queue of
        tapes. However, it might be a finite-queue model if there is a limit on
        the number of available tapes.
   (b) At least $(5)(5) = 25$ per hour.

A-3 Summary

The formulas in this appendix represent only a small part of the body of available queuing theory models. We have concentrated on steady-state models, which describe systems that are unchanging in their service capabilities and are subjected to randomly varying streams of inputs (customers) whose service time needs are also randomly varying. Because of the restrictive assumptions entailed in the Markov property, these models are very seldom accurate enough for more than a ballpark analysis.

In an article about attempts to apply queuing theory, Byrd (1978) described a series of frustrations in matching up the assumptions against reality. The examples he chose were diverse—a bookstore, a pinball parlor, a drugstore, a stop light, and so on. In each case, the textbook models seemed inadequate. In a rejoinder to that piece, Bhat (1978) pointed to a huge body of literature on applications of queuing theory. But he also made a significant point: "If a better solution is unnecessary for the problem at hand, one should not hesitate to stop with a 'quick and dirty' one." The applications of queuing theory in this text follow that philosophy. The models help us to learn certain things about a number of situations in operations management, but we must avoid accepting their advice too literally.

PROBLEMS

*1. Identify which of the following statements are accurate descriptions of a system in steady state. For each false statement, explain why it is false.
  (a) Arrivals are not varying in frequency.
  (b) The number of servers is constant.
  (c) The service time is the same for all customers.
  (d) The waiting line has achieved its ultimate level and is no longer changing.
  (e) The average input rate equals the average output rate.

2. This problem is intended to point out the nonlinear nature of the queuing theory models.
  (a) For $S = 5$ servers, look up the average number waiting for the ρ values 0.1, 0.3, 0.5, 0.7, 0.8, and 0.9, and plot N_q against ρ.
  (b) Interpret what you see in your plot, remembering that ρ represents the utilization of the servers.
  (c) For a given number of servers, there are only two ways that the utilization factor can be altered. What are they?
  (d) A five-server system currently has a workload that keeps the servers occupied 70% of the time. Suppose that the workload increased so that the utilization became 90%. From your answer to part (a), what is the percentage increase in the average waiting line? Compare that to the percentage increase in the workload, and comment.
  (e) What might a fast-food restaurant do to increase the service rate, μ?

*3. The U.R. Trukin Company manufactures shirts, and employs one person to inspect and perform any necessary rework. The inspector can operate at the rate of 10,000 shirts per month.
  (a) Using Model I in Table A-1, compute the average number of shirts waiting for inspection if the production rate is 8000 per month.
  (b) What is the percentage of idle time for the inspector?
  (c) Answer parts (a) and (b) if the production rate is 9000.
  (d) Compare the increase in the workload (λ) to the increase in the waiting line, between parts (a) and (c).

(e) Do you think the Markov property holds for this example? What is its most questionable assumption here?

(f) Given your answer to part (d), in which direction are your estimates of the average queue biased? Why?

4. A public health agency in Venezuela is providing free polio vaccine. Arrivals of people seem to be random throughout the day, with an average of 288 per day. The public health nurse can provide up to 360 doses per day. The clinic is open 6 hours a day, but they give doses to all persons waiting at closing time.

(a) How large should their waiting area be? Explain your answer.

(b) The service time is not actually random. In fact, the service always takes *exactly* 1 minute. In what direction does this change your answer?

(c) Criticize your answer to part (a) from the point of view of the steady-state assumption.

*5. A service system has $\lambda = 40$ arrivals per hour and $\mu = 15$ customers can be served per hour by each server. Each server costs $12 per hour in wages and fringe benefits.

(a) What is the theoretical minimum number of servers?

(b) How many servers are required to keep waiting time to less than 5 minutes on the average?

(c) Express your answer to part (b) as a payroll cost per customer served.

(d) If customers value their own time at $8 per hour, would they prefer that the system have three servers or four? (Assume that the saving of having fewer servers is passed on to the customer.)

6. One of the work stations in the Duke Manufacturing Company shop is manned by Pete Salt. He is a specialist in machine parts finishing and receives jobs from many departments of the company, on an irregular basis. He receives an average of 10 jobs per day, and the pileup of unfinished jobs awaiting his attention amounts to eight jobs, on the average.

(a) Estimate his idle time (percent). (Use either the Model I formulas or Table A-2, and solve for ρ.) [*Note:* If you cannot answer part (a), assume that the answer is 10% and continue.]

(b) Estimate Pete's service rate capability, μ.

(c) If I have a job for Pete (with no special priority), how long will it be before he begins to work on the job?

(d) What would be the average number of jobs in the waiting line if another equivalent worker were permanently assigned to help Pete?

7. Two professors each have private secretaries (don't we wish) who can type four pages per hour. The professors each generate three pages of work per hour. What benefit would there be if they pooled their typing between the two secretaries? Explain why this difference occurs.

*8. A barbershop has two barbers, each of whom can serve five customers per hour. A total of eight customers per hour arrive at the shop on the average.

(a) If 60% of the customers want barber 1, 40% want barber 2, and no customer will accept a barber other than their preferred barber, how long does the average customer wait?

(b) If all customers would take the next available barber, how long would the average customer wait?

(c) In words, why is the answer to part (b) less than the answer to part (a)? Would it still be true if the customers were divided equally?

*9. A hospital admits an average of 10 new patients per day, with an average stay of 8 days. A first come, first served waiting list is used for patients categorized as urgent admissions, as opposed to emergency patients and elective admissions. About 20% of patients are admitted through the waiting list, whereas the other 80% are either scheduled or admitted immediately. The average urgent patient waits 2 days for admission. The following questions may be answered by using equations (1) to (4), without reference to any of the models in Table A-1.

(a) How many beds do you think this hospital probably has?

(b) How many beds are full, on the average?

(c) How many names are on the waiting list, on the average?

10. A bank has one drive-in window. The average drive-in customer spends 4 minutes at the window. There are 13.5 customers per hour who wish to use the drive-in window. What is the average size of the waiting line if

(a) There is no limit on the number of cars allowed in line?

(b) There is a limit of four cars?

11. Tasty Bakers has 10 mixing machines that are in almost constant use. They are operated by one person, who adds the appropriate ingredients, sets the timer, and then departs to load other mixers. When the timer stops the mixer, the operator empties the contents and cleans the machine, if necessary. This service requires an average of 1 minute in total. The amount of mixing time averages 19 minutes.

(a) What is the rate of demand for service, per machine?

(b) What is the total hourly demand rate?

(c) Using Model I, Table A-1, what is the average number of mixers waiting for service?

(d) Is the infinite population assumption of Model I adequate in this case? Discuss.

*12. In a job shop, there are two priority classes—normal orders and hot orders. Usually, 10% of orders are classified as hot, and when such an order arrives at a machine center, it is processed on the first available machine, regardless of how many normal orders are waiting. If two or more hot orders are in the queue, the hot orders are processed in the order in which they arrived.

(a) Estimate the average waiting time at a machine center with $S = 10$ identical machines, when $\lambda = 18$ jobs per day, $\mu = 2$ jobs per day per machine, and the hot-order system is not in use.

(b) Suppose that 10% of the jobs are hot orders and the hot order system is in use. Estimate the average wait for hot and normal orders.

13. The Skunk Hollow Service Station is the only supplier of gasoline for the friendly community of Skunk Hollow. The station has been open 12 hours per day, serving an average of 14 customers per hour with one gas pump. During a recent gas shortage, customers began to "top off the tank" for fear of being caught short of gasoline if and when SHSS ran out. The net effect was to *double the frequency of visits* to the service station, but each visit required only *half of the usual amount of gasoline*.

    (a) Using the following data, calculate the length of the waiting line before and during the crisis.

    Before the gas crisis:

    Time to take the customer's order = 10 seconds
    Time to pump gas = 2 minutes (average)
    Time to receive payment and write up credit card slip = 50 seconds (average)
    Arrival rate = 14 per hour (average)

    Changes during the gas crisis:

    Time to pump gas = 1 minute (average)
    Arrival rate = 28 per hour (average)

    (b) What would be the effect on the waiting line of adding another gas pump during the crisis? Be sure to state your assumptions about the arrangements for waiting customers. (Assume that there are enough attendants to avoid delay between customers.)

14. The Quik Job Shop currently has four employees and 20 machines. All employees are expert on each of the 20 machines. Each job usually involves several steps to complete. Once they are begun, jobs are carried straight through to completion by one employee. The wide variety of jobs leads to a wide variety of "processing times" (total time required to finish a job) once the job is actually begun. The average is about 2.7 hours per job. Quik employees work 8 hour days. There are approximately eight new jobs each day.

    (a) Estimate the average "flow time" (time from receipt of order until finish of job).

    (b) List the assumptions that you must make to get an answer to part (a).

    (c) One employee will retire in 2 weeks. What will happen to the average flow time in the weeks following her departure, assuming that she is not replaced?

*15. A family practice medical clinic employs a receptionist, a nurse clinician (NC), and a physician (MD). The receptionist has been trained to screen patients as to whether they should see the NC or the MD. There are, of course, some errors, so the NC sees some patients who must then go to the physician. A diagram of patient flow is shown below.

λ = arrival rate of patients = 30 per hour

P_1 = fraction who go to nurse clinician = 2/3

P_2 = fraction of NC patients who must also see the physician = 0.15

μ_S = service rate of the receptionist/screener = 40 per hour

μ_D = service rate of the MD = 15 per hour

μ_N = service rate of the NC = 30 per hour

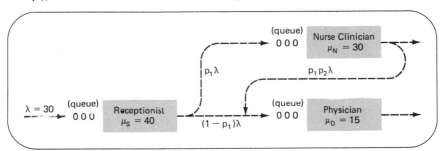

We wish to eliminate, using queuing theory:
(a) The average waiting time in each queue.
(b) The average time in the entire system for each of the three patient paths.
(c) The overall average time in the system.
(d) The idle time of each server, per hour.
(e) The impact of having two physicians instead of one, sharing the same queue on a "first MD available" basis.

16. A community has 10 ambulances. It is now considering reorganizing (decentralizing) its ambulance service into three districts each with three ambulances, rather than its present arrangement of a central dispatching location. This would reduce the number to nine ambulances. Under the present arrangement, when an ambulance is available, it can answer and complete a call in 30 minutes (average), from time of dispatch until final arrival at the emergency room. Under the proposed system, carefully dividing the districts into units with equal populations, ambulances will be able to answer and complete calls in 20 minutes, on the average. Both estimates include an average of 6 minutes on the scene (loading the patient) and 8 minutes travel time to the nearest emergency center. There are presently 10 calls (demands) per hour. This is not expected to change in the near future. However, under the new district arrangement, district A has 3.0 calls per hour, and B and C each have 3.5. The city officials realize that they cannot split an ambulance, and the traffic arrangements make it impossible to have

three districts with equal call rates. Medical experts are pressing for decentralization because they believe the 10-minute reduction in travel time will significantly reduce deaths and injuries. Would you recommend decentralizing and eliminating one ambulance? A criterion for measuring the effectiveness of a system should emphasize the response time. The accompanying diagram was constructed to show the major events in an average call for an ambulance.

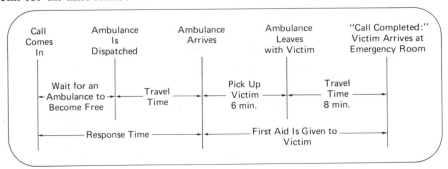

REFERENCES

BHAT, U. N., "The Value of Queuing Theory, a Rejoinder." *Interfaces,* Vol. 8, No. 3 (1978).

BYRD, J., "The Value of Queuing Theory." *Interfaces,* Vol. 8, No. 3 (1978).

COOPER, R. B., *Introduction to Queuing Theory,* 2nd ed. New York: Elsevier North-Holland, 1981.

HILLIER, F. S., AND G. J. LIEBERMAN, *Operations Research,* 3rd ed. San Francisco: Holden-Day, 1980, Chaps. 9 and 10.

APPENDIX B

Simulation

New ideas often go untried because of the expense and difficulty of implementing changes in an operation, especially when the ultimate benefits are in doubt. Experimentation is also risky in an operating system, since frequent changes can bring confusion and disharmony among the employees and customers alike.

An alternative is to experiment on a model of the system. This book includes a variety of models useful in operations management. Each chapter has presented one or more verbal, mathematical, or diagrammatic models. Each of these models simulates a portion of an operation by representing one or more important aspects of reality. The manager can then experiment on the model, rather than the real system.

The models studied in other parts of this book have two elements in common: they are often simplistic in their representation of reality and they are fairly easy to manipulate, often yielding optimal solutions. However, there is a class of models which do not fit that pattern, and they are generally referred to as *simulation models*. The typical simulation model is neither overly simplistic nor easily optimized. In fact, as the complexity of the model is increased to mirror reality, the concept of optimality may vanish entirely because there are so many aspects of the problem that one may find it impossible to define *best*. Unfortunately, this trade-off between simplicity and solvability seems unavoidable. Nevertheless, realistic, complex simulation models are used by operations managers as a laboratory for experimentation, trying out different ideas and observing the impact on system performance. The guiding principles of such experiments may be summarized as follows.

1. We may not be able to define what we mean by *optimal,* but we will surely recognize which ideas have worked out, when we see the results.

2. We can generate alternative solutions by the dozen, but it is impossible for us to work through all the ramifications of our proposed changes. What we need is a good model so that we can evaluate and compare those solutions systematically.

Simulation has been used in a wide variety of situations: in manufacturing, service, military, and environmental analysis; investigating inanimate systems such as computers, biological systems such as rivers, and human systems such as hospital maternity wards; addressing problems ranging from the mundane (who gets Saturday off next week?) to the grandiose (when will the world's population level off?). The advent of the large-scale electronic digital computer has been accompanied by growth in the use of simulation, a trend that will probably continue.

There are many special-purpose computer languages for simulation, available (at a cost) from computer companies and other vendors. We shall not discuss any of them in detail here. They are very powerful in that a simple command can set up all the details required to simulate a complicated process, such as keeping track of the people in a waiting line. Law and Kelton (1982) describe the advantages and disadvantages of many of the commonly available languages and Henriksen (1983) discusses their future development.

This appendix introduces the concepts of descriptive simulation modeling. The general approach makes very little use of mathematics: the major operations are addition, subtraction, and certain logic elements such as "if." The models attain their complexity by stringing together as many of these simple elements as are necessary to give an adequate represention of reality. The basic concepts will be introduced in Section B-1 through elementary examples that may be carried out by the reader. The Monte Carlo method, used to include the element of randomness in a simulation model, is described in Section B-2. Simulation experiments often generate large amounts of data, which must be analyzed in much the same way as data collected in real experiments. Section B-3 summarizes a few important aspects of analysis of simulated data, and the final sections bring us back to reality by discussing how to assess a simulation model's validity, or lack thereof, and the interplay between a simulation model and management.

B-1 SIMULATION USING HISTORICAL DATA

In analyzing a problem, a manager must determine what variables are of interest, considering the decisions that must be made. With simulation, this determination is crucial both in designing the model and in determining how it will be used. We shall base our discussion on a simple example of management in a medical clinic. The focus is on the punctuality of the doctors at the beginning of the day and how it affects patient delays. The model that results is very narrowly focused on this issue, and will therefore require modification in order to address other interesting questions of clinic management.

Simulation Exercise

The data in Table B-1 were collected during three different days of the week of January 7, 1985, at the Carthage Medical Clinic. We are going to make use of these data to explore the impact of various changes in the way service is provided to patients. Of particular interest is the appropriate number of doctors and the time of day at which service should begin (doctor arrival time).

Problem 1 What would be the number of patients present upon the doctor's arrival if he or she were to arrive at 1:30 P.M.? At 1:15 P.M.?

Analysis The simulation model is a set of two assumptions:

    1. The arrival of patients will not be influenced by the doctor's absence, as long as he or she arrives before 1:30 P.M.

    2. The historical data are representative of future clinic sessions.

Under these assumptions, Table B-1 shows that there would be four patients present at 1:30 P.M. on day 1, five on day 2, and three on the third day. That concludes the "1:30" simulation. The average is $\bar{x} = (4 + 5 + 3)/3 = 4.00$ patients, and the standard deviation is $s = \sqrt{[(4 - 4)^2 + (5 - 4)^2 + (3 - 4)^2]/(3 - 1)} = 1.00$ patient. These two statistics

TABLE B-1 FIRST 10 PATIENTS ON THREE TYPICAL DAYS
(OPENING TIME = 1:00 P.M.)

Patient	DAY 1 Arrival Time, T (P.M.)	DAY 1 Service Duration, T_s (Minutes)	DAY 2 T	DAY 2 T_s	DAY 3 T	DAY 3 T_s
P1	1:05	15	1:00	20	1:15	5
P2	1:15	15	1:05	15	1:20	20
P3	1:20	10	1:15	10	1:30	15
P4	1:30	10	1:15	15	1:35	15
P5	1:45	15	1:25	10	1:50	20
P6	1:45	5	1:40	15	1:50	10
P7	1:50	10	1:45	5	2:05	10
P8	1:55	5	2:00	5	2:20	15
P9	2:05	15	2:15	20	2:25	5
P10	2:10	20	2:15	15	2:30	20

provide a rough summary of the three simulated days. (Of course, if more data were available, it would be simple to "run" the simulation for more days.)

The same simulation, stopping at 1:15 P.M., results in 2, 4, and 1 patients, for an average of 2.33 patients and a standard deviation of 1.53.

This example points out that, when a random element is present, a simulation (like a real experiment) must be repeated a sufficient number of times to represent adequately the range of possible outcomes. The results can then be summarized just like real data.

Let us define a few terms that are commonly used to describe a simulation. All simulations may be viewed as a series of *activities* (in the example, patients receiving service from the doctor) representing interactions between *entities* (patients and doctors) and separated by *events* (clinic opens, patient 1 arrives, patient 2 arrives, etc., and doctor arrives).

The events of the simulation occur at instants of time at which there is a change in the *status* of the system (e.g., another patient is added to the queue, or the doctor arrives). In general, when an event occurs, it is because of a change in an *attribute* of some entity. Each entity has a set of attributes. The attributes of a patient include an arrival time, a status in the clinic (waiting, seeing a doctor, etc.), and any other description necessary for the simulation to progress. Thus, depending on the complexity of the simulation, one may or may not wish to include the patient's disease, age, sex, and so on, as attributes.

The simulator (you) has access to information that would not be available in the real situation. The arrival times of patients is a case in point; it would not be fair to have the doctor arrive simultaneously with (say) the third patient each day, because in reality the arrival time of the third patient is not known until it occurs. Therefore, it is important to distinguish between a *real schedule* (e.g., agreed-upon time or appointment for the patient to arrive, which may be violated by the patient arriving early or late) and the *simulation's calendar of future events* (in this case, the actual arrival times of patients and the doctor). The real schedule was not explained in the example. There might have been no schedule (patients just walk in) or perhaps two patients were given a 1:00 appointment with two more at 1:15 and so on, but their arrivals were not punctual.

Problem 2   Suppose that there are two doctors, and each doctor can serve any patient. There are no appointments. In this example, to keep the simulation short, assume that the clinic doors close at 2:00 P.M. but each doctor stays until there are no more patients to be seen. What events will there be in a simulated day? What attributes should we assign to each entity to keep track of the events?

Analysis   Arrivals of patients and doctors are events, as are the beginning and ending of service for each patient, opening and closing the clinic doors, departure of each doctor, and final closure of the clinic when the last patient and doctor depart. These fall into two categories, depending on whether the simulator can know, before the simulation begins, when they will occur:

Externally Determined (Exogenous) Events	Internally Determined (Endogenous) Events
Clinic opens	Patient's service begins
Patient arrives	Patient's service ends
Doctor arrives	Doctor departs
Clinic doors close	Clinic closes

To process the simulation, the following attributes would be useful:

Patient's attributes:
   Status (waiting, being served)
   Arrival time (time of day)
   Service time (duration of service)
Doctor's attributes:
   Status (absent, idle, serving "patient N")
   Arrival time
   Time when current service will end

With these attributes we can tell, at any instant of the day, whether any event is to occur. For example, at a given time in the simulation, to determine whether a patient's service is to begin, we can ask: "Are there any idle doctors?" The entire simulation is a series of questions like this, along with instructions on what to do next, depending on whether the answer is yes or no.

Problem 3 Using the description from Problem 2, simulate day 1 (from Table B-1) assuming that one doctor arrives at 1:15 and the second at 1:30.

Analysis Since we have eight categories of events to keep track of, it is important to be systematic. Table B-2 shows the status of the simulated clinic every 5 minutes for all of day 1. It very carefully lists each event, one at a time. For example, at 1:30, five events occur: a patient arrival, a doctor arrival, a patient departure, and two patients begin to receive service. This causes some apparently unnecessary writing (both doctors become idle, briefly, even though patients are waiting), but this systematic approach pays off in reduction of errors.

There are many ways to summarize the results of a simulation. In the analysis of the first question, we accentuated one property (number of patients in queue at 1:30 P.M.) by presenting an average and a standard deviation. Problem 3 has left us with substantial detail for one day (rather than three); in summarizing the results, a picture of how the day progressed might be more useful than an average calculated over different times within the one day. Figure B-1 is a Gantt chart (see Chapter 11) of the day's operation, focusing on the three permanent aspects of the system (two doctors, one queue). Note that the summary does not include the instantaneous idle times or queue buildups that occurred in Table B-2 because of our one-event-at-a-time process. Instead, the last status recorded at each time is used as representative for the entire subsequent interval.

TABLE B-2 WORKSHEET FOR SIMULATING ONE DAY

Time	Event	DOCTOR STATUS		Queue
		Doc 1	Doc 2	
1:00	Opening	Absent	Absent	Empty
1:05	P1 arrives	Absent	Absent	P1
1:10		Absent	Absent	P1
1:15	P2 arrives	Absent	Absent	P1 and 2
	Doc 1 arrives	Idle	Absent	P1 and 2
	P1 begins	P1 until 1:30	Absent	P2
1:20	P3 arrives	P1 until 1:30	Absent	P2 and 3
1:25		P1 until 1:30	Absent	P2 and 3
1:30	P4 arrives	P1 until 1:30	Absent	P2–4
	Doc 2 arrives	P1 until 1:30	Idle	P2–4
	P1 departs	Idle	Idle	P2–4
	P2 begins	Idle	P2 until 1:45	P3 and 4
	P3 begins	P3 until 1:40	P2 until 1:45	P4
1:35		P3 until 1:40	P2 until 1:45	P4
1:40	P3 departs	Idle	P2 until 1:45	P4
	P4 begins	P4 until 1:50	P2 until 1:45	Empty
1:45	P5 arrives	P4 until 1:50	P2 until 1:45	P5
	P6 arrives	P4 until 1:50	P2 until 1:45	P5 and 6
	P2 departs	P4 until 1:50	Idle	P5 and 6
	P5 begins	P4 until 1:50	P5 until 2:00	P6
1:50	P7 arrives	P4 until 1:50	P5 until 2:00	P6 and 7
	P4 departs	Idle	P5 until 2:00	P6 and 7
	P6 begins	P6 until 1:55	P5 until 2:00	P7
1:55	P8 arrives	P6 until 1:55	P5 until 2:00	P7 and 8
	P6 departs	Idle	P5 until 2:00	P7 and 8
	P7 begins	P7 until 2:05	P5 until 2:00	P8
2:00	Doors close	P7 until 2:05	P5 until 2:00	P8
	P5 departs	P7 until 2:05	Idle	P8
	P8 begins	P7 until 2:05	P8 until 2:05	Empty
2:05	P7 departs	Idle	P8 until 2:05	Empty
	P8 departs	Idle	Idle	Empty
	Doc 1 departs	Absent	Idle	Empty
	Doc 2 departs	Absent	Absent	Empty

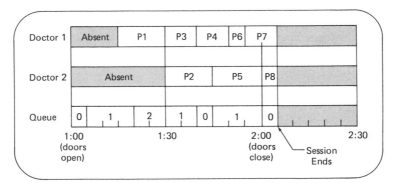

Figure B-1 Gantt chart for displaying one day's results.

The experiences of each patient could also be represented on Gantt charts. This would be particularly effective if there were several stages through which each patient must pass (check in, check up, write check, check out). However, for this example we want to focus attention on waiting times, so they have been summarized in Table B-3. The pattern is intuitively appealing: early patients have longer waiting times because of late doctors, but the arrival of the second doctor quickly reduces waiting times. However, one should not place too much confidence in this pattern, since it is based only on one day's experience.

How could this simulation be used by the clinic manager? Presuming that the clinic has been adequately represented (a heroic assumption for such a simple example) and that a few more days have been simulated, questions such as the following could be addressed:

TABLE B-3 WORKSHEET FOR SUMMARIZING ONE DAY'S SIMULATION

| Patient | FROM TABLE B-1 | | FROM TABLE B-2 | | Waiting Time (Minutes) |
	Arrival Time	Service Duration	Service Begins	Service Ends	
P1	1:05	15	1:15	1:30	10
P2	1:15	15	1:30	1:45	15
P3	1:20	10	1:30	1:40	10
P4	1:30	10	1:40	1:50	10
P5	1:45	15	1:45	2:00	0
P6	1:45	5	1:50	1:55	5
P7	1:50	10	1:55	2:05	5
P8	1:55	5	2:00	2:05	5
P9	2:05	15	Too late		
P10	2:10	20	Too late		

Total waiting time = 60 minutes

Average = 60/8 = 7.5 minutes per patient

Standard deviation = 4.63 minutes per patient

1. What are the "best" times for the doctors to arrive?
2. Can one doctor handle the load *within* reasonable bounds on patient waiting times?
3. If the patient load varies predictably by day of the week, how can we staff to take advantage of the pattern?

Additional experimental questions might include:

4. At what patient load would an additional doctor be required?
5. What would be the effect of replacing one doctor by a physician's assistant, who would work at a different pace and require periodic supervision and consultation?

Questions 4 and 5 would require changes in the simulation. How could we generate patient arrivals at a faster rate? How could we simulate service time of a physician's assistant without historical data (such as Table B-1)? We would need data on the productivity of a physician's assistant, and patients would have to be categorized by service needed. Furthermore, some new events must be added to the simulation to account for consultations between doctor and assistant. The consultations can be incorporated as events, using the concepts we have discussed previously. However, where historical data are insufficient, unavailable, or too old to be relevant, we must generate artificial data to use in a simulation. This is the topic of the next section, where the Monte Carlo technique is described.

Consider what we have done to create the simulated day depicted in Tables B-2 and B-3 and Figure B-1. Implicitly, we have followed a set of instructions that moved us through the day in 5-minute steps. It is important to be able to write down those steps, if we wish to turn the calculations over to someone else, either for computer coding or manual processing. Table B-4 contains a set of instructions for the clinic simulation.

Step 7 in Table B-4 shows how this simulation keeps time. The variable *t* is the *clock*, and it moves forward in increments of 5 simulated minutes. This is called a *time-step* simulation. Of course, if 5-minute intervals are too long, so that some events of interest are likely to occur more than once in an interval, we could decrease the length of the step to 1 minute or any other duration that is suitable. The shorter the interval, the more computations that are required to cover a simulated day, so one should specify the longest reasonable interval.

Another alternative is to use an *event-step simulation*, in which timekeeping is based on a calendar of future simulated events. Step 7 would read "set *t* equal to the time of the next scheduled event." This approach is particularly useful when there are long intervals of no activity followed by periods when events occur rapidly. Although our examples are based on the time-step approach, the discussion applies equally to event-step simulation.

TABLE B-4 INSTRUCTIONS FOR THE CLINIC SIMULATION, USING A WORKSHEET SUCH AS TABLE B-2

1. Begin day. t = 1:00 P.M., all doctors are absent, queue empty.
2. If any patients have just arrived, enter their ID numbers in the queue list.
3. If any doctors have just arrived, change them from absent to idle.
4. If any patients are to depart now, change their doctors from busy to idle.
5. If there are both idle doctors and waiting patients, remove the next patient from the queue and place with an idle doctor. Note the patient's (future) departure time by adding service time to t. Change doctor from idle to busy.
6. Repeat step 5 until queue is empty or all doctors are busy.
7. $t = t + 5$ (move clock forward 5 minutes).
8. Repeat steps 2 to 7 until closing time.
9. After closing time, repeat steps 4, 5, 6, and 7 until all patients have departed, sending idle doctors home when the queue is empty.

Review Problems

1. What limitations are there in using historical data in a simulation?
2. Follow the instructions in Table B-4 and the steps in Table B-2 to see if they match up.
3. What new activities, entities, attributes, and events would be introduced if a physician's assistant were used instead of one of the doctors? (A physician's assistant can serve most of the functions of a doctor, but must consult the doctor periodically and might turn a patient over to the doctor if the case is too complicated.)

Solutions

1. Historical data may be irrelevant for the questions being studied. For example, one would not expect that patients will continue to arrive in the same pattern if an appointment system were instituted or modified.

2.

Time	Step Number (Table B-4)	Action (Table B-2)
1:00	1	Opening
	2	Nothing
	3	Nothing
	4	Nothing
	5	Nothing
	6	Nothing
	7	t = 1:05
1:05	2	P1 arrives, joins queue
	3–6	Nothing
	7	t = 1:10
1:10	2–6	Nothing
	7	t = 1:15

1:15	2	P2 arrives, joins queue
	3	Doctor 1 arrives, idle
	4	Nothing
	5	Doctor 1 begins with P1
	6	P2 remains in queue
	7	$t = 1:20$

And so on. Thus Table B-2 does match with the steps in Table B-4.

3. New entity: Physician's assistant

   New activities: Consultation

   Interrupted service (a new type of patient delay)

   New events: Service halts temporarily

   Service resumes

   Patient transferred from assistant to doctor

   New attributes: Patient status now includes "interrupted" and "transferred," as well as "waiting" and "being served." A new attribute is whether the patient's needs can be met by the assistant.

   Doctor and assistant status both now include "in consultation."

B-2 SIMULATING WITH ARTIFICIAL DATA—MONTE CARLO

One purpose of simulation is to experiment with ideas and situations that have never occurred before. Obtaining historical data is impossible in such circumstances, but it is often possible to describe an unknown situation by using a probability distribution. For example, one might study the pattern of occurrences of traffic accidents and conclude that the number of accidents per hour has the Poisson probability distribution,[1] with a mean value that varies with the time of day, day of week, and weather conditions. Simulating the occurrence of accidents 10 years in the future would then involve forecasting the average rate and using a method known as *Monte Carlo* to generate simulated data with all the patterns of today's accidents, but using a rate corresponding to the 10-year forecast and randomness that is governed by the Poisson probability distribution. The same method could generate a series of simulated equipment failures to test a proposed maintenance system or a series of demands to test a new inventory control system.

The idea of Monte Carlo is quite simple. The first step is to find or create a device, like a roulette wheel, which takes on different states randomly (where it stops, nobody knows). A coin is the simplest device, and is quite an effective simulator of the boy/girl outcome in childbirth. This device is not perfect, of

[1] Four probability distributions are described in Appendix D, Tables 2 through 5.

TABLE B-5 PROBABILITY DISTRIBUTION OF DAILY HOT DOG
DEMANDS

Hot dogs	0	1	2	3	4
Probability	0.30	0.40	0.20	0.07	0.03
Peg numbers (Figure B-2)	01–30	31–70	71–90	91–97	98–00

course, since the heads/tails outcomes are equally likely, whereas more boys are born than girls.

The second step in Monte Carlo is to match the outcomes of the random device with outcomes of the process being simulated. This must be done in a way such that the simulated events will have the correct probability of occurring.

Suppose that we randomize with a wheel of fortune, with 100 pegs arrayed with perfect symmetry about the periphery and a single pointer fixed in position. This device has 100 equally likely outcomes, which may be divided up any way we wish, in order to mimic a real process. Consider the probability distribution of daily demand for hot dogs at Joe's Convenient Corner Stand in South Porcupine, Ontario (Table B-5), which was derived from a study of historical sales. We could simulate daily demands by painting the wheel of fortune as shown in Figure B-2 (making certain to use weightless paint). There should be 30 pegs in the sector labeled ''0 hot dogs,'' 40 pegs in the ''1 hot dog'' sector; and so on.

If each peg is labeled with a two-digit number (from 00 to 99), one convenient

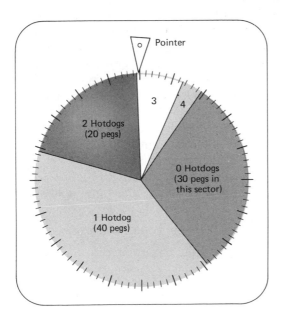

Figure B-2 Wheel of fortune, with 100 pegs, for generating simulated hot-dog demands.

assignment of pegs to "hot dogs demanded" is shown in Table B-5. There are two important relationships between the peg numbers and the probabilities in Table B-5. First, one peg = 1% of probability (since there are 100 equally likely pegs), so 30 pegs were assigned to achieve a 30% probability of zero demand, and so on. Second, the peg numbers correspond to the cumulative probability of hot dog demand. That is, the probability of one or fewer hot dogs is $0.30 + 0.40 = 0.70$, the same as the last peg number assigned to one hot dog. This comes about because of the way we arranged the peg assignment, and it can always be done that way. We shall use this *cumulative probability assignment* again, as soon as we have divested ourselves of the rather awkward wheel of fortune.

Physical devices have many drawbacks as random-number generators. One of the main drawbacks is that they do not fit into a computer very well. Fortunately, mathematical formulas are commonly available to generate *pseudo-random numbers,* which can be made to appear completely random for long periods of time. These numbers are decimal fractions equally distributed between zero and 1, exactly fitting the requirements of our "cumulative probability assignment" method. Thus, in using a computer simulation language, one supplies the computer with the probability distribution, and it performs Monte Carlo by spinning its pseudo-random-number generator and matching the resulting number (the counterpart of a peg in the wheel of fortune) against the cumulative probability. Table B-6 shows the same random-number assignment as Table B-5, except using a decimal notation for the pegs. Suppose that the pseudo-random-number generator spewed forth the following 5 numbers: 0.53076, 0.67675, 0.11682, 0.80779, and 0.18002. The first number, 0.53076, falls in the "1 hot dog" interval in Table B-6, so Joe sells one simulated hot dog on the first simulated day. The second day also has 1 sale, and the remaining days have sales of 0, 2, and 0 hot dogs, respectively.

There are many variations on the Monte Carlo theme, but they all have cumulative probability assignment as a basis. For example, we have only used discrete variables (number of hot dogs) in our example, but continuous variables (time, distance, etc.) may be simulated as well. Figure B-3 shows the cumulative probability distribution of the distance each hot dog is thrown after the first bite, and the dashed line indicates how the random number 0.74217 is matched to the distance of 60 meters (a very bad hot dog).

Manual simulations can also take advantage of Monte Carlo (as you will see in the Review Problem below), by using tables of random digits such as

TABLE B-6 RANDOM-NUMBER ASSIGNMENT BY THE
CUMULATIVE PROBABILITY RULE

Hot dogs	0	1	2	3	4
Probability	0.30	0.40	0.20	0.07	0.03
Random numbers	0–0.3	0.3–0.7	0.7–0.9	0.9–0.97	0.97–1.0

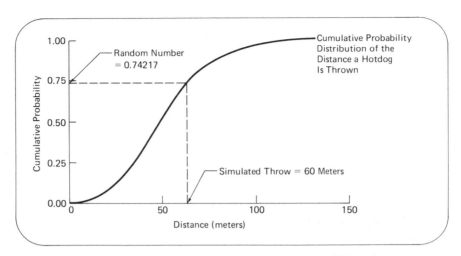

Figure B-3 Monte Carlo simulation of a continuous variable (the distance a hotdog is thrown).

Table 1, Appendix D. One merely reads successive numbers from the table, rather than spinning the wheel of fortune.

Looking back, we see that Monte Carlo simulation requires two things—a random-number generator and a probability distribution describing the entity to be simulated. The random-number generator is easily obtained, as described above, for both manual and computer simulation. The probability distribution must be obtained by the simulator (you) in one way or another. At the beginning of this section, one method was mentioned—try to identify a known probability distribution (such as Poisson, normal, etc.) from historical data and modify it as necessary to fit the situation being simulated. Sometimes only an opinion is available. For example, a foreman may be able to give an estimate of how long a job will take, and may also be able to give optimistic and pessimistic time estimates. There are several methods for incorporating such rough data into a simulation, which we shall not pursue.

The data generated by the Monte Carlo method can be used in exactly the same way as the real data in the examples of Section B-1. Monte Carlo can therefore be viewed as a method for generating enough realistic data so that adequate experimentation can be done with a simulation model.

Review Problems

1. The accompanying table gives a list of random digits and probabilities for times between arrivals and service times for patients at the Carthage Clinic. Generate the first five patients arrivals, recording an arrival time and a service time for each. (Remember, the doors open at 1:00 P.M.) To use the random digits, first insert a decimal point (so that 3513 becomes 0.3513). Use the first column of numbers to generate the five Δt values.

		TIME BETWEEN ARRIVALS		SERVICE DURATION	
Random Digits		Δt (Minutes)	Probability	Time (Minutes)	Probability
3513	2883	0	0.17	0	0
6976	0882	5	0.40	5	0.20
9847	4311	10	0.20	10	0.23
1622	2741	15	0.23	15	0.37
3874	2020	20	0	20	0.20

2. Use the simulated times you generated in Review Problem 1 to simulate the first five arrivals, using a table like Table B-2 to keep track of the simulated activities.

Solutions

1. First, construct cumulative probability tables:

TIME BETWEEN ARRIVALS		SERVICE DURATION	
Δt	Cumulative Probability	Service Time	Cumulative Probability
0	0.0001–0.1700	5	0.0001–0.2000
5	0.1701–0.5700	10	0.2001–0.4300
10	0.5701–0.7700	15	0.4301–0.8000
15	0.7701–0.0000	20	0.8001–0.0000

Next, use the random numbers to generate arrivals and service times.

Patient	Random Number	Δt	Arrival Time	Random Number	Service Time
P1	0.3513	5	1:05	0.2883	10
P2	0.6976	10	1:15	0.0882	5
P3	0.9847	15	1:30	0.4311	15
P4	0.1622	0	1:30	0.2741	10
P5	0.3874	5	1:35	0.2020	10

2. Follow the same method as in Table B-2.

B-3 ANALYSIS OF THE RESULTS OF A SIMULATION

Randomness is put into a simulation to reflect reality. Just as two days in a clinic are never alike, the same simulation will lead to different results if a new set of random numbers is used. (In fact, you may already have noticed in the examples that you get answers different from ours by applying the same set of random numbers in a different order.) However, one of the reasons for simulation is to try out different ideas; that entails changing the simulation itself. Experimenting with different arrival schedules for physicians is an example. Because of these two causes of different simulated outcomes, one must use care in interpreting the results, separating the effects of randomness from the changes due to the new ideas being tried. This requires the use of statistics. In the medical clinic simulation, for example, after many simulated days, one could summarize the waiting times of patients in several ways, including an average, a range, or a histogram. Any or all of these might be used, but their degree of precision depends on how many days have been simulated. For example, suppose that 50 days were simulated, the average total waiting time of patients was $\bar{x} = 70$ patient-minutes per day, and the standard deviation was $s = 14$ patient-minutes per day. Then, if $n \geqslant 30$, a 95% confidence interval[2] is

$$95\% \text{ confidence interval} = \bar{x} \pm \frac{1.96s}{\sqrt{n}} = 70 \pm \frac{1.96(14)}{\sqrt{50}}$$

$$= 70 \pm 3.9$$

(1)

That is, we have 95% confidence that the true mean value of patient delay per day lies in the interval between 66.1 and 73.9. This precision of ± 3.9 is probably good enough for this particular situation. However, if greater precision is needed, the simulation can be extended to a larger sample of days, and an estimate of the total number of simulated days required (including the 50 already simulated) is[3]

$$\text{required sample size} = n = \left(\frac{1.96s}{\text{desired precision}}\right)^2$$

(2)

Thus, to achieve a precision of ± 2.0 patient minutes per day,

$$n = \left[\frac{(1.96)(14)}{2.0}\right]^2 = 188$$

or 138, in addition to the 50 days we have already simulated.

Unfortunately, confidence intervals are not always as straightforward as this. Suppose that we wanted the average waiting time per patient (rather than per day). This is easily calculated from the simulated data, but the confidence

---

[2] For $n < 30$, one must use the t distribution with $n - 1$ degrees of freedom to replace the value 1.96 in equation (1). See Appendix D for the normal and t distributions. A reader unfamiliar with confidence intervals and hypothesis testing should consult any standard statistics text, such as Dyckman and Thomas (1977).

[3] This is derived by solving the equation

$$\pm \text{ desired precision} = \frac{\pm 1.96s}{\sqrt{n}}$$

A z value other than 1.96 (from the normal probability distribution) could be used if one wished to use some confidence level other than 95%. Also, the t distribution should be used if s was estimated from a pilot study with fewer than 30 observations.

interval is not given by equation (1). The reason is that equation (1) assumes that there are n statistically independent observations, which is incorrect in this case because the waiting times of any two successive patients are likely to be correlated, since they encounter almost the same waiting line. This difficulty is called *autocorrelation*, since the variable (patient wait) is correlated with its own previous and subsequent values. Methods for handling autocorrelated data can be quite simple or very complicated, and the reader is advised to pursue a reference such as Law and Kelton (1982, Chap. 10) or Schruben (1983).

Comparing Different Experiments

So far, we have talked about describing the results of one repeated simulation. Contrasting two or more alternatives is usually the goal of a simulation, so that the manager can select the best option to implement in the real system. This is one place where simulation has a unique advantage over actual experiments: *several ideas may be tested under absolutely identical circumstances* by careful design. In the clinic simulation, exactly the same patients can be sent to the clinic, whether there is one doctor or two, regardless of when the doctors arrive, and so on. This is a very valuable feature, and it can be used in many ways. (How else, for example, could a general have the opportunity to fight the same battle several times to evaluate different tactics?)

When two experiments are carried out under identical circumstances, except for differences that are introduced by the experimenter, they are said to be *paired comparisons*. This gives us a statistical advantage, since the observed differences are not likely to be due to the randomness of the inputs, which were the same for both experiments.

There are several special formulas for comparing the two experiments. For example, if x_i is the outcome of repetition i of experiment X, and y_i is its twin for experiment Y, the difference between $\bar{x}$ and $\bar{y}$ may be tested for statistical significance by calculating $d_i = x_i - y_i$ for each repetition i, and then calculating the mean $\bar{d}$ and standard deviation s_d of the d_i values. Then, if $n \geq 30$, we may conclude that[4]

$$\begin{matrix} x \text{ and } y \text{ are} \\ \text{significantly} \\ \text{different} \end{matrix} \quad \text{if} \quad \frac{|\bar{d}|}{s_d/\sqrt{n}} > 1.96 \quad\quad (3)$$

For example, if we wished to compare the clinic as we simulated it (two doctors, one arriving at 1:15, one at 1:30) to the same clinic with one doctor arriving at 1:00 P.M., then x_i might be patient waiting minutes on day i in the two-doctor configuration, and y_i the corresponding number for the same day with one doctor. Then $d_1 = x_1 - y_1 =$ the difference in patient waiting time on day 1, and

---

[4] For $n < 30$, one must use the t distribution to replace the value of 1.96 in this equation. The value of 1.96 was chosen from the normal probability law, assuming that one accepts a 5% probability of Type I error, and that a two-sided test is appropriate.

similarly for day 2, day 3, and so on. We would then calculate an average and standard deviation of the d values and plug into (3) to see if one on-time doctor is significantly better (or worse) than two late ones, as regards average patient delays.

Review Problems

Elmer's Job Shop was the site of a simulation demonstration by a computer software company. In simulating Elmer's job shop, a new priority system was used to decide on the order of job processing. The results were expressed as an average and a standard deviation of the daily number of jobs completed. (Several other measures were also reported, such as work-in-process inventory, average lateness, etc.) Based on a simulation of 30 days, the results were $\bar{x} = 42.2$ jobs completed per day, and $s = 18.4$

1. Construct a 95% confidence interval.
2. What sample size would be required to cut the width of the confidence interval by half?
3. A second simulation run was made, using a different priority scheme but using exactly the same set of jobs, processing times, etc. (Only the order of processing was altered.) Based on the data in the accompanying table, are the two priority schemes significantly different?

SIMULATION RESULTS: JOBS COMPLETED
PER DAY

| | PRIORITY SCHEME | | Difference: |
Day	A	B	$d = A - B$
5	84	89	−5
2	28	31	−3
3	37	35	+2
⋮	⋮	⋮	⋮
30	55	60	−5
Average	42.2	46.6	−4.4
Standard deviation	18.4	14.2	9.3

Solutions

1. Using equation (1),

$$\bar{x} \pm \frac{1.96s}{\sqrt{n}} = 42.2 \pm \frac{(1.96)(18.4)}{\sqrt{30}} = 42.2 \pm 6.58$$

Thus, if the simulation were run an infinite number of times, the average job completion rate would most probably fall within 6.58 of the current estimate of 42.2 jobs per day.

2. To cut the width by half, the precision must be $6.58/2 = 3.29$, and, using equation (2),

$$n = \left(\frac{1.96s}{\text{desired precision}}\right)^2$$

$$= \left[\frac{(1.96)(18.4)}{3.29}\right]^2$$

$$= 120$$

3. Using equation (3), $\bar{d} = -4.4$, $s_d = 9.3$, and $n = 30$, so

$$\frac{|\bar{d}|}{s_d/\sqrt{n}} = \frac{4.4}{9.3/\sqrt{30}} = 2.59$$

which is greater than 1.96, so the two priority schemes do give significantly different results.

Note that the average under priority scheme B *lies within the confidence interval* of scheme A, computed in problem 1. One might conclude from this that the two schemes are *not* significantly different, at least as far as a 30-day sample can indicate. However, using the identical set of jobs in the second simulation increased the contrast, which is why we were able to conclude that the difference is statistically significant. That is the whole idea of paired comparisons.

B-4 VALIDITY

Validity is the first priority in model building. If the model cannot be trusted, it will be of no use. However, validity comes in degrees, and it is not practical to strive for a perfect model (if there is such a thing), since development time and effort would be unjustifiably expensive. Validity must be defined and evaluated in relationship to the intended use of the model.

Evaluation of model validity, often called validation, may be visualized as consisting of three stages (Law and Kelton 1982, Chap. 10):

1. Comparing the assumptions of the model to existing theory, known research findings, and intuition. (Choose the best possible building blocks for the model.)
2. Subject these assumptions, one at a time, to empirical (statistical) tests, whenever possible.
3. Test the overall model's performance and its predictive power when compared to management intuition and a variety of real data.

The first two stages refer to the details of model construction, whereas the third involves a look at the performance of the package. These three stages are applied repeatedly during model development and testing, prior to any decision making based on the model.

Theoretically, model-improvement effort should cease at the point where the marginal cost of further improvement exceeds the marginal gain achieved through better decision making made possible by a better model. Practically speaking, it is usually impossible to be precise as to when this balance occurs, so the trade-off is based on judgment. This means that the decision maker should be involved throughout development of a model, passing judgment on the adequacy of assumptions as they are incorporated in the model.

As an example of the three stages of validation, consider the clinic example from Section B-1. One of the assumptions was that patients, once in the waiting room, do not get angry and leave if waiting time becomes lengthy. One could appeal to research findings on this question, if they exist, or one could ask someone who works in the clinic how often they believe people leave. (That would be a stage 1 validity test.) If it seems to be a significant issue, one could conduct an on-site experiment (a stage 2 validity test) to observe the circumstances under which and likelihood that people leave.

A third approach would be to incorporate, in the model, a probability of leaving the queue. Because it is difficult or impossible to accurately estimate such a probability value from real data, one should carry out a sensitivity analysis; that is, vary the probability of departure and see how influential it is on the results and on the decisions we might make based on the model. This is a stage 3 analysis, because it focuses on overall model performance.

Stage 3 for the clinic example would also include a test to see whether the model behaves like a real system. One method would be to configure the model to mimic an existing clinic, and test whether the simulated waiting times were similar to the actual waiting times. A variety of statistical tests are available for this kind of comparison, including the paired-comparison test of the averages described in the previous section.

It is also desirable to put the model through its paces by trying out many different ideas, and seeing whether the model's predictions make sense. For example, does an increase in the doctor's lateness result in an increase in patient delays? Does a reduction in the variability of patient arrivals reduce idle time? Or, in general, does the model behave like a real system, in the judgment of the manager? A formal version of this approach is called a *Turing test*, in which a knowledgeable manager is presented with two sets of data and required to decide which one came from a model and which from a real system. The manager is allowed to ask for more data. If the manager cannot tell the difference, the model passes the test.

If a model fails a validity test, one must consider the possible sources of error:

1. Model design.

2. Model programming or execution.

3. Data input (including the random-number generator, if one is used).

4. Interpretation of the results.

5. Use of the model.

It is easy to lose sight of 4 and 5. It may happen, for example, that the model is rejected because its results contradict the intuition of the manager. Two possibilities should be investigated: were the results improperly presented; and are there one or more alternative explanations of the unexpected findings that were not fully explored? One should also ask whether the model is being used improperly, in a way not intended by its designers. It is always worthwhile to consider these possibilities before beginning a detailed investigation of the sort suggested by error sources 1, 2, and 3.

We have see that validity has many facets: from minute details to overall model performance, from correct interpretation of output to correct use of the model, and from accurate inputs to accurate predictions. Unfortunately, this problem is compounded by the multiplicity of information generated by the model. A clinic model might be valid with regard to average waiting time but not be accurate in predicting physician idle time. And there might be several other kinds of data generated by the model. Thus we have come full circle. One of the reasons for using a simulation approach is the complexity of the situation to be modeled. Now, we find that the resulting model complexity also makes it difficult to interpret the results. Such is life.

Review Problems

1. In the three stages of validity testing, what is the major characteristic that sets stage 3 apart from 1 and 2?

2. If the output of a simulation model does not make intuitive sense to a manager, what next?

Solutions

1. The first two stages consist of tests of parts of the model, whereas the final stage looks at the performance of the model as a whole.

2. The model should not (and will not) be used in making decisions until the manager trusts it. Thus either the model must be improved, or the manager's intuition will change because of insights provided by the model, or else the whole thing will be junked.

B-5 FINDING SOLUTIONS

Solutions to problems are created or discovered by people—the role of a simulation model is to aid in evaluating alternative ideas. But the ideas must come from the manager. Naylor and Shauland (1976) report on many different uses of corporate simulation models, in a variety of industries. The process of interaction between manager and model has been studied formally. Little (1970) proposed what he calls a *decision calculus* governing the managerial use of models. He uses an advertising-media planning model as an example to show how a manager will use a model, providing that it is easily available and gives useful answers. The model may be consulted in many different ways on the same issue, so that its role is to supply information to the decision maker rather than to make decisions.

If management is to obtain the needed information, the simulation runs[5] must be carefully planned in advance, because of the complex, multifaceted nature of most simulations. The tools of *experimental design* may be applied to experiments on a simulation model in the same way as in real systems. Shannon (1975, pp. 144–169) summarizes some of the methods of experimental design that may be applied to simulation. This includes issues of sample size, choosing alternatives to test, and methods of statistical analysis.

Because there is typically an enormous number of possible combinations of ideas that management may wish to try, a systematic *search* method is often useful. For example, if a naval task force is simulated to try to determine the most effective antisubmarine protection using a combination of antisubmarine warfare (ASW) surface ships and aircraft, one could limit the number of alternatives by using a *grid search*. Figure B-4 indicates how the search for the best combination might proceed. The admirals have suggested the range of up to 100 aircraft and up to 20 ASW ships. As a first phase, a coarse grid is developed, varying the number of ships in increments of 5 and aircraft in increments of 25, in order to determine an overall picture of effectiveness of protection. A second phase follows, selecting points on a finer grid, near the best solution from the first phase. For example, if phase 1 found that 75 aircraft and 10 ships was best, phase 2 could try combinations of 6, 8, 10, 12, and 14 ships, and 60, 70, 80, and 90 aircraft. If desired, additional phases could follow, using progressively finer grids.

The dark loop in the diagram was drawn to exclude solutions that were felt to be unacceptable (either too few or too many total ASW crews). Therefore, phase 1 consists of 10 simulation runs, corresponding to the 10 points inside the loop, and phase 2 (as described above) consists of 20 runs. As a review problem will show, this tactic of varying the grid density substantially reduces the number of simulation runs by avoiding detailed search of nonoptimal regions.

Other methods have been devised for guiding the selection of alternative solutions to simulate. Efficiency becomes increasingly important as the dimensions of the problem are increased. For example, if the ASW grid had a four-dimensional space of helicopters, fixed-wing aircraft, surface ASW ships, and ASW submarines,

---

[5] A simulation run is the use of a simulation model with one particular set of parameters. For example, a clinic simulation run would have a specified number of doctors, a given average rate of arrivals, and so on, and could consist of any prespecified number of simulated days.

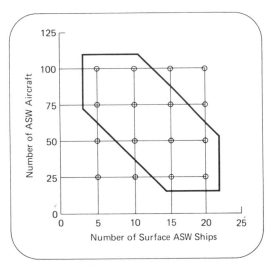

Figure B-4 Grid of alternative solutions to the convoy protection problem.

the coarse grid might have $4^4 = 256$ points instead of $4^2 = 16$ as in Figure B-4. Shannon (1975, pp. 169–176) describes several heuristic approaches to searching for optimal solutions, including *steepest-ascent* methods, and *second-order* designs, both of which use the limited information of a few simulations to determine the next alternative to try. Heuristic methods are useful in problems such as warehouse location (see Chapter 7), where the number of possible alternatives is, for practical purposes, infinite. Shanthikumar and Sargent (1983) present an overview of approaches that mix analytical and simulation models.

Review Problems

1. In the antisubmarine warfare example of this section, how many alternatives are there in all possible combinations of from 5 to 20 ships and 25 to 100 aircraft?

2. Referring to Figure B-4, roughly what percent of these alternatives are eliminated by staying within the loop?

3. Suppose that the two-phase grid search described in the text found that 70 aircraft and 12 ships was the best system. Design a third phase which varies both ships and aircraft with a grid spacing of 1. How many simulations would be run in phase 3? Altogether in the three phases?

4. Comparing Review Problems 1 and 3, roughly what percentage reduction has the three-phase search achieved?

Solutions

1. In the range 5 to 20, there are 16 possible numbers of ships (5, 6, . . . , 20). For each of these, there are from 25 to 100 aircraft, or 76 choices, so the total is (16)(76) = 1216 alternatives.

2. In Figure B-4, with the grid shown, 6 out of 16 choices are outside the line. Therefore, about 37.5% of the alternatives have been excluded.

3. As described, phase 1 simulated the 10 alternatives inside the loop, and phase 2 consisted of the 20 alternatives achieved by trying 60, 70, 80, and 90 aircraft, and 6, 8, 10, 12, and 14 ships. Phase 3 would vary aircraft from 61 to 79 and ships from 11 to 13, for a total of $(19)(3) = 57$ runs. The three phases therefore consist of $10 + 20 + 57 = 87$ runs.

4. $87/1216 = 0.0715$, so the three-phase search eliminated all but 7.15% of the alternatives, a 92.85% reduction.

B-6 Summary

Simulation is in daily use by manufacturers, the military, health planners, engineers, utility companies, and many others. The models range from simple and hand-computed to very complex computer programs. Even the most complex simulation is composed of fairly simple elements. However, the difficulty of interpreting the results can be substantial, because of the many possible sources of randomness and the complexity of interactions when many variables are put together.

In order to make effective use of a simulation model, a manager must be willing to invest time in its design and development. Trade-offs must be made between degree of detail and cost (size) of the model. Since these decisions require an understanding both of the model and of its intended use, they must be made by an intended user, who must develop a good understanding of the model during its development.

Access to simulation becomes increasingly convenient as interactive computer systems improve. Quick response to a manager's request is an important attribute of any management tool, and simulation is no exception. This requires careful attention to programming, so that the input is easy for the manager to provide, and the output is readily understood. Because randomness is an integral part of Monte Carlo simulation, analysis of simulated data may require statistical methods. The techniques may be either simple or sophisticated, depending on the complexity of the model and the number of different inputs and outputs. In using a simulation to search for an optimal solution, careful attention to the rules for selecting which alternatives are to be simulated (and which should be ignored) can have a dramatic effect on the cost of the search.

Simulation has been used in many of the areas covered in this book. Most notable are warehouse location, job-shop management, and design of service facilities.

PROBLEMS

1. The following table describes the probability distribution of service times at a hamburger stand. Using the given random numbers, simulate service times for three customers.

Minutes	5	10	15	20	25
Probability	0.15	0.3	0.25	0.2	0.1

Random numbers
    0.06248   0.92317   0.45473   0.51124

2. At Joe's Barbershop, 40% of the customers will accept only barber 1, 30% want barber 2, and 30% will accept either barber. Generate five customers, using Monte Carlo to determine which category each belongs to, using the following random numbers: 0.567, 0.246, 0.979, 0.895, and 0.098.

*3. Haircuts take a varying amount of time. The following data describe the experience at Joe's Barbershop:

Haircut time (minutes):	15–20	20–25	25–30	30–35
Number of customers:	121	134	130	115

(a) Convert these data to relative frequencies (probabilities) and set up a random-number assignment table similar to Table B-6.
(b) Generate five simulated haircut times, using the random numbers 0.784, 0.611, 0.874, 0.200, and 0.798.
(c) Plot the cumulative probability from your table, following the format of Figure B-3. Draw a smooth curve through the points you have plotted.
(d) Use the five random numbers from part (b) to generate five simulated haircut times from your graph, using the method shown in Figure B-3.

4. An orange-juice stand has demand for oranges and orange juice with the following probability mass function:

Orange Demand (Oranges per Customer)	Probability	Juice Demand (Cups per Customer)	Probability
1	0.3	1	0.1
2	0.3	2	0.5
3	0.2	3	0.1
4	0.2	4	0.3

(a) Set up random-number assignment tables for simulating demand for whole oranges and for juice.
(b) 20% of the customers buy only oranges, 70% buy only juice, and 10% buy both. Simulate three customers. First simulate whether the purchase is oranges, juice, or both. Then generate the simulated quantity or quantities. Use the following random numbers: 0.351, 0.697, 0.984, 0.162, 0.387, 0.288, 0.088, and 0.431.
(c) Of what use could this type of simulation be to the owners of the stand? What additional data would be needed?

*5. (This problem refers to the PERT/CPM method from Chapter 3.) The accompanying PERT diagram describes a very simple project consisting of three activities. The activities have been done many times before. The probabilities in the accompanying table are a summary of historical activity times.

(a) Using the random numbers given (read down the columns), simulate the entire project once. (i) What was the completion time of the project? (ii) What was the critical path?

(b) Repeat part (a) two more times and use the results to estimate the *expected* completion time of the project.

(c) You have been asked to find a completion time deadline that you can be 80% certain of meeting. How would you use the simulation to find such a deadline?

(d) What are the most important assumptions you are making in using this simulation?

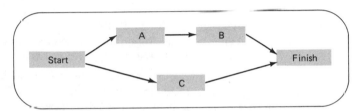

PROBABILITIES

Activity Time (Weeks)	Activity A	Activity B	Activity C
1	0	0.2	0
2	0.4	0.6	0
3	0.4	0.1	0.2
4	0.1	0.1	0.4
5	0.1	0	0.4
Expected value (weeks)	2.9	2.1	4.2

Random numbers:

0.96589	0.88727	0.72655
0.03477	0.29528	0.63956
0.72898	0.32411	0.88861
0.39420	0.94211	0.58042
0.47743	0.60156	0.38037

*6. The normal probability distribution may be simulated by using the cumulative probability method. The random-number assignment may be done by using the normal probability table, Table 2, Appendix D.

(a) Look up the z values corresponding to each of the following random numbers, treating the random numbers as cumulative probabilities: 0.885, 0.274, 0.998, 0.036, and 0.655.

(b) The diameter of machined parts from a certain process is normally distributed with mean 10 centimeters and standard deviation 0.0010 centimeter. Convert the z values from part (a) into simulated diameters.

7. If a variable has the exponential probability distribution, and its mean value is $\bar{x}$, the cumulative probability function is

$$\text{probability of } x \text{ or less} = 1 - e^{-x/\bar{x}}$$

In using the Monte Carlo method, the variable x is simulated by using the cumulative probability function as in Figure B-3. This is the same as solving for x in the following equation, in which RN stands for random number:

$$\text{RN} = \text{probability of } x \text{ or less}$$

(a) Solve this equation for x using the exponential probability distribution. (*Hint:* Use logarithms.)

(b) Generate five service times from the exponential distribution if the average service time is 10 minutes per customer, using the random numbers 0.567, 0.246, 0.979, 0.895, and 0.098.

*8. (a) The average life of an incandescent bulb is 1200 hours, with standard deviation 50 hours. Using the random number 0.9342, generate a simulated bulb lifetime, assuming that bulb life is normally distributed.

(b) The process of part (a) was repeated 40 times; the average simulated bulb life was 1160 hours and the standard deviation was 52 hours. Is there any reason to believe that the random numbers are not random? Explain.

9. The history of machine breakdowns was simulated under two different repair policies. Policy 1 had scheduled maintenance twice a month, whereas policy 2 had weekly maintenance. The simulated numbers of breakdowns per week are listed below. They were generated using the same sequence of random numbers for each policy. Are the results significantly different at the 95% level?

| | BREAKDOWNS | |
Week	Policy 1	Policy 2
1	20	19
2	23	21
3	18	14
4	14	15
5	20	17

*10. A simulation was set up of a simple waiting-line situation with four servers, in order to compare several different working schedules. Before using the simulation, a simple test of validity was devised, in which all servers were given identical characteristics and the simulated customers arrived according to a Poisson process, with exponential service times. The simulation could then be compared to a queuing theory model. (See Appendix A.) Suppose that the simulation gave a queue length 10% lower than the queuing theory model. What two questions must you ask before you may make a judgment about the accuracy of the simulation?

11. An extensive study of the patient arrivals at Friendly Clinic showed that the Poisson probability distribution described the arrivals per day quite accurately. The average rate of arrivals has been 48 per day. In a simulation of the clinic, the average rate of arrivals was 46 per day, and the standard deviation was 6. These statistics were gathered over 220 simulated days. Is the simulated average significantly different from the actual?

*12. A simulation of a job shop showed that 42.3 jobs could be finished per day, on the average. The standard deviation was 8.7 jobs per day, and the number of days simulated was 4.
   (a) Calculate a confidence interval for these results.
   (b) How many days should be simulated to achieve a precision of ±2.0 on the average?

*13. At Silver Shirt Corporation, an inspector is stationed at the end of the production line. Shirts arrive at the inspector at 2-minute intervals. There are three categories of shirts, in the eyes of the inspector—good (no further work needed), rework (minor touch-up required), and reject (major repair needed). The inspector spends the least amount of time on rejects, since they are usually easy to discover and are then set aside. The greatest amount of time is spent on the rework shirts, since the inspector does the touch-up. The accompanying table shows the relative frequency of each category, and the time per shirt.

Category	Frequency (%)	Time per Shirt (Minutes)
Good	85	1.8
Rework	10	2.3
Reject	5	1.0

   (a) Use Monte Carlo to generate 10 simulated shirts. Use the following random numbers: 0.567, 0.246, 0.979, 0.895, 0.098, 0.784, 0.611, 0.874, 0.900, and 0.798.
   (b) Simulate the arrival and processing of these 10 shirts, and show the results on a Gantt chart, similar to Figure B-1.
   (c) Write a set of instructions describing this simulation as was done in Table B-4.
   (d) How would the simulation be altered if the times given in the table

were averages per shirt and we had a probability distribution of times for each category of shirt?

14. High Rise Ski Association is planning a new ski area. As part of the planning process, they have contracted with you to build a simulation model to determine the congestion to be anticipated at the bottom of the ski lifts. As the first step in this job, you were asked to concentrate on a single lift. The congestion is known to vary with the time of day, and to increase when the lift has to be stopped. The lift almost never breaks down, but it stops whenever a customer makes a serious error in entering or leaving a chair.

   (a) What data do you need?

   (b) List in English phrases the major blocks in the simulation.

15. Following a recent college convocation there was a reception. At the reception a queuing problem arose that will have to be solved prior to next year's convocation. In particular, the punch and cookie line moved much too slowly throughout the reception, particularly in the first half-hour. The data are as follows.

   1. There are three service facilities (two alcoholic punches, one nonalcoholic; cookies are available at all three stations).

   2. During the first half-hour, service at any station takes either $\frac{1}{2}$ minute (no cookies) with probability 0.1, or 1 minute (with cookies) with probability 0.9. During the remaining 1 hour, service at any station takes $\frac{1}{2}$ minute with probability 0.6, and 1 minute with probability 0.4.

   3. During the first half-hour, persons arrive every minute in numbers as follows:

      6 with probability 0.2   9 with probability 0.1
      7 with probability 0.3   10 with probability 0.1
      8 with probability 0.2   11 with probability 0.1

   During the remaining 1 hour the probabilities are:

      0 with probability 0.2
      1 with probability 0.4
      2 with probability 0.2
      3 with probability 0.2

   Each customer, at any time, either chooses the nonalcoholic punch (with probability 0.023) and goes directly to that line, or chooses the alcoholic punch (with probability 0.977) and goes to the shorter of the two lines. The customers are served on a first come, first served basis.

   (a) What are the entities and their attributes?

   (b) Set up all random-number assignment tables.

   (c) Indicate how the simulation would proceed (i.e., in what order would various steps of the simulation be taken?). Briefly, what differences are there between the first half-hour and the last hour? What time unit should be used, and why?

16. A typing pool consists of four typists and one supervisor/typist. They receive a variety of work, which is sorted into two priorities by the supervisor. The top-priority work is done on a first come, first served basis, but the second-priority jobs are performed by selecting the shortest job first. At the beginning of each day, the waiting pile of priority 2 work is searched. Any job that has waited longer than 7 days is moved to priority 1, where it joins the first come, first served queue according to the date it was received by the pool. Work arrives according to the following probability law every hour:

Jobs per hour	0	1	2	3	4
Probability	0.2	0.3	0.2	0.2	0.1

One-fourth of the jobs are top priority, on the average. Estimated job length is normally distributed with mean 1.5 hours and standard deviation 0.5 hour.

(a) Set up the random-number assignment tables, and demonstrate how each one works using the following random numbers: 0.82338, 0.29840, 0.55626, 0.60977, and 0.35137.

(b) List the important events for a simulation of the pool, with a brief English description of what occurs in the simulation at each event.

*17. OJ is an orange juice stand at Girdle Beach. Each evening, the owners place an order for the number of oranges to be delivered on the following morning. Each morning, they squeeze part of the oranges into juice, two oranges per cup. During the day, they sell both oranges and juice. If their supply of juice runs out, they squeeze additional oranges on demand. This slows down their service rate by 50%, and sometimes causes long waiting lines as a result. At the end of the day, leftover juice is disposed of, and leftover oranges are stored until the following day. If OJ runs out of both oranges and juice, they close for the day, and their competitors gladly take the thirsty customers.

A computer simulation program was written, with the objective of helping to decide on the following two issues: how many unsqueezed oranges to stock at the beginning of the day, and how much juice to squeeze before opening.

(a) What information should the computer report to aid in this decision?

(b) What information must be given to the computer in order for it to perform the simulation?

(c) Given that demand for oranges varies between 200 and 400 per day, and demand for juice varies between 800 and 1000 cups per day, design a two- or three-stage grid search that will find a good solution in 20 computer runs or less, assuming that a single objective function can be defined (such as expected profit per day).

(d) Use your strategy from part (c) to search for the optimal solution to the following equation, in which F = oranges (fruit) and J = juice.

$$\text{profit} = 13F + 36J - \frac{FJ}{200} - \frac{F^2}{100} - \frac{J^2}{50} - 17{,}800$$

(*Note:* This equation was made up to simulate a computer simulation. As you plug in the values, pretend that you are giving them to a computer and obtaining output from a simulation.)

(**e**) Observing your results in part (d), what would you do next—stop or continue the search? Explain.

18. The chief administrative officer of Midvale General Hospital has read about simulation, and believes the maternity ward can be simulated. The present layout is as shown in the accompanying diagram.

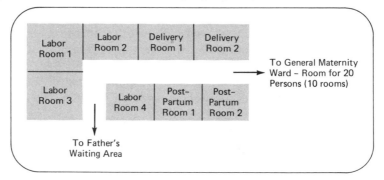

Given:

1. Delivery room 2 can handle Caesarean and regular deliveries. Delivery room 1 can handle only regular delivery.
2. Labor rooms and postpartum rooms can be used interchangeably, but the administration prefers not to do so.
3. Postpartum recovery can use general ward rooms, but they prefer not to do so.

The objectives are:

1. Minimize the number of times that a delivery must be performed in a room not designed for that purpose.
2. Minimize the number of times postpartum recovery must be done in a room not designed for that purpose.
3. Minimize the number of times a patient in labor has to wait in the general maternity ward.
4. Minimize cost.

The hospital administrator thinks that the first three objectives may be inconsistent with the fourth, and is considering the following plans, most of which will require money.

A. Prepare delivery room 2 for Caesarean deliveries—cost, $4000.
B. Prepare labor room 4 so that it can serve as either a labor room or a postpartum room—cost, $2000.

C. Prepare one room in the general maternity ward for use as a postpartum room—cost, $4000.
D. Eliminate the waiting area (visitors would wait in the main lobby and be paged), creating two new rooms, one labor room and one postpartum room—cost, $6000.
E. Leave the system as is—no cost.

The investigation was initiated when, for the first time in recent years, there were two Caesarean patients at the same time. As a consultant to the administrator, you are to:

(a) Describe (using a flowchart or numbered steps) the simulation. Be sure to show what output would be required. Fine detail is not necessary.
(b) Show how random numbers would be used to generate values of each random variable.
(c) Starting with no rooms filled, simulate 2 hours of operation. Begin by listing entities and attributes. You have the following data:
    (i)   Regular delivery time is normally distributed with an average of 1 hour and standard deviation of 0.2 hour.
   (ii) Caesarean delivery time is normally distributed with an average of 2 hours and a standard deviation of 0.3 hour.
  (iii) The number of arrivals is Poisson-distributed with a mean of 0.5 per quarter-hour, or 2 per hour. Assume that arrivals occur at the beginning of the quarter-hour, and use 15 minutes as the time unit (i.e., round other occurrences to the nearest 15-minute interval). Always assign patients to rooms on a first come, first served basis.
  (iv) One of every 10 arrivals is for a Caesarean.
   (v) Time in the labor room (for regular delivery) is normally distributed with mean $= 5$, $\sigma = 1$. (Assume that there is no false labor.) Caesareans spend exactly 1 hour in a labor room.
  (vi) Time in the postpartum room is 1 hour for 80% of the patients, and 2 hours for the remaining 20%.
 (vii) Length of stay for a regular delivery patient in the general ward is 3 days 50% of the time, 4 days 20%, 5 days 20%, and 7 days 10%. Caesarean patients always stay 10 days.
(d) Comment on the validity of assumptions, approximations, and the data. Also, how useful would the first day's simulated data be?
(e) Suppose that the output of the simulation is as follows:

OBJECTIVE NUMBER

Plan	(1)	(2)	(3)	(4)
A	0.04	5.0	12	4000
B	0.10	4.0	16	2000
C	0.10	3.0	11	4000
D	0.10	3.0	8	6000
E	0.10	5.0	12	0

where (1) is the average number of times per year a delivery is performed in an inappropriate room, (2) and (3) are the same for objectives 2 and 3, and (4) is the additional cost of the plan. Which plan do you choose? Why?

(f) Are the data useful if we want to consider doing two of the plans? Comment briefly.

(g) In addition to building plans, could we use the simulation to test anything else?

REFERENCES

DYCKMAN, T. R., AND L. J. THOMAS, *Fundamental Statistics for Business and Economics*. Englewood Cliffs, N.J.: Prentice-Hall, 1977.

HENRIKSEN, J. O., "The Integrated Simulation Environment (Simulation Software of the 1990s)." *Operations Research*, Vol. 31, No. 6 (1983).

LAW, A. M., AND W. D. KELTON, *Simulation Modeling and Analysis*. New York: McGraw-Hill, 1982.

LITTLE, J. D. C., "Models and Managers: The Concept of a Decision Calculus." *Management Science*, Vol. 16, No. 8 (1970).

MORGENTHALER, G. W., "The Theory and Application of Simulation in Operations Research," in *Progress in Operations Research*, Vol. I, R. L. Ackoff, ed. New York: Wiley, 1961, pp. 366–372.

NAYLOR, T. H., AND H. SHAULAND, "A Survey of Users of Corporate Planning Models." *Management Science*, Vol. 22, No. 9 (1976), p. 927.

SCHRUBEN, L., "Confidence Interval Estimation Using Standardized Time Series." *Operations Research*, Vol. 31, No. 6 (1983).

SHANNON, R. E., *Systems Simulation, the Art and Science*. Englewood Cliffs, N.J.: Prentice-Hall, 1975.

SHANTHIKUMAR, J. G., AND R. G. SARGENT, "A Unifying View of Hybrid Simulation/Analytic Models and Modeling." *Operations Research*, Vol. 31, No. 6 (1983).

APPENDIX C

Linear Programming

Linear programming (LP) is one of a very few mathematical tools that can be used in the solution of a wide variety of large, complex managerial problems. For example:

> An oil refinery can vary its product mix by its choice among the different grades of crude oil available from various parts of the world. Also important is the process selected, since parameters such as temperature will affect the yield. As prices and demands vary, an LP recommends which inputs and processes to use in order to maximize profits.

> Livestock gain in value as they grow, but the rate of gain depends in part on their feed. Choice of the proper combination of ingredients to maximize the net gain in value can be expressed as an LP.

> A firm that distributes products over a large territory faces an unimaginably large number of choices in deciding how best to meet demand from its network of warehouses. Each warehouse has a limited stock of items, and demands often cannot be met from the nearest warehouse. If there are 25 warehouses and 1000 customers, there are 25,000 possible matchups between customer and warehouse. LP can quickly recommend shipping quantities and destinations so as to minimize the cost of distribution.

These are just a sample of the managerial problems that have been addressed successfully by linear programming. A few others are described throughout this text. Project scheduling can be improved by allocating funds appropriately among the most critical tasks so as to most effectively reduce the overall project duration

(Chapter 3). Production planning over a year or more can reduce costs by careful timing of the use of overtime and inventory to control changes in the size of the work force (Chapter 9). In the short run, personnel work schedules must take into account not only the production schedule, but also assigned vacations, absenteeism, worker preferences for days off, and other considerations (Chapter 14).

Besides recommending solutions to problems like these, LP can supply useful information for managerial decisions that cannot be solved by LP. In Chapter 7, for example, production capacity and facility location decisions are discussed. Because of the variety of nonquantifiable factors involved in these decisions, models such as LP are not used to make the decisions. Nevertheless, one aspect of the decision is the future operating cost as demands change and new capacity or new location decisions are put into effect. Using LP to simulate how the firm would operate under various scenarios is one way to supply this part of the information.

Chapter 15 describes another situation where LP is only part of the decision. However, in this case it is one of several models that are tied together into an integrated decision system for production and distribution.

The simplex algorithm and its successors are used to solve LP problems. It is extremely efficient, and commercially available computer programs can solve problems with thousands of variables. Some applications, such as the distribution problem described earlier, have special solution methods that are faster and easier than simplex. However, the emphasis of this appendix is not on solution methods, but rather on formulation and managerial use of the solutions. Therefore, the description of simplex is very brief and no mention is made of other solution techniques.

The goal of this appendix is to explain the two most important aspects of LP for a manager: formulation (converting managerial problems into LPs) and use of the solution. This requires at least an intuitive grasp of the method of solution, for the following reason. Solutions are not decisions. Models can seldom capture enough of reality to be trusted without careful scrutiny. Changes are often required to bring the model's recommendations into line with reality. Without a feeling for the way an LP will respond to changes, a manager would be ineffective in such interactions.

To develop this intuition, Section C-1 introduces LP with a simple example that can be solved on a graph. This shows how LP finds a solution that satisfies all the restrictions specified by the user and still manages to maximize profits or minimize costs. More important, it demonstrates how the answer changes when the restrictions are modified. This is called *sensitivity analysis* and forms the basis for managerial use of LP.

Section C-2 explains the simplex algorithm on which computer LP programs are based. The first two subsections, "Standard LP Format" and "Slack and Surplus Variables" should be read carefully, but the rest of the section may be skipped without loss of continuity. Section C-2 also introduces sensitivity analysis from the point of view of simplex.

Formulating managerial problems as LP problems is the topic of Section C-3, using a manufacturing problem as an example. Given the large number of restrictions to be embodied in the LP, a classification scheme is presented to help assure that no important restrictions are forgotten.

The final section is extremely important to a manager, since it describes the output typically available from a computer LP package, and shows how a number of important managerial questions can be approached using this information. Computer outputs are also included in some of the problems. As Geoffrion (1976) has pointed out, the so-called optimal solution produced by an LP is only part of its value; LP can also be used by a manager to develop insight into the problem, and to modify the solution in light of information that could not be included in the LP model.

C-1 GRAPHICAL INTRODUCTION TO LINEAR PROGRAMMING

Managerial problems can be characterized by the goals and restrictions one must face in making a decision. Linear programming models represent these elements in two ways: each LP has an objective function and a set of constraints. Maximizing profits or minimizing costs are common objectives, but others are often used. There can be an enormous number of constraints in an LP, and each one represents either a restriction or a goal specified by the manager. The resulting mathematical problem may require several pages of formulas just to represent the decision situation.

There are two criteria that a problem must satisfy in order to qualify as an LP. First, the objective and the constraints must be expressed as linear equations. Second, the variables must be continuous (fractional values must have some meaning). Most applications violate the second criterion, but rounding off often suffices. For example, if an LP recommends production of 4123.7 units of an item, it probably makes little difference whether we make 4123 or 4124. The following example illustrates formulation and solution of an LP.

Tasty Toothpaste Company

The Tasty Toothpaste Company manufactures two kinds of toothpaste in quantities measured in units equivalent to 1000 five-ounce tubes. Formula X is sold to discount stores under several house brands at a net profit of $50 per unit, whereas formula Y is Tasty's own brand, which nets $60 profit per unit. Sales of X have been forecasted for the upcoming month to be no more than 50,000 units, whereas Y is expected to have sales of up to 10,000 units. Both of these figures would normally be accepted as feasible sales goals. Management needs to make production quantity decisions for each product. Therefore, the *variables* are x = quantity (thousands) of product X and y = quantity of product Y.

However, there is a temporary but critical shortage of the secret ingredient that gives Tasty its taste. There are only 100,000 ounces available for use in producing next month's toothpaste. Steps have been taken to assure an adequate supply thereafter. Product X requires 2 ounces of flavoring per unit, whereas Y uses 4 ounces per unit. Therefore, 50,000 units of X and 10,000 of Y would require $2x + 4y = (2)(50) + (4)(10) = 100 + 40 = 140$ thousand ounces of flavoring. Since only 100,000 are available, we must decide on the best compromise between the two products, and the solution must satisfy a constraint:

$$2x + 4y \leqslant 100 \quad \text{(flavor limit)} \tag{1}$$

The words "flavor limit" have been added as a label to describe the constraint for future discussion.

There are standing contracts for 40,000 units of house brands per month. This represents a lower limit on production. The market strategy of the company is to emphasize the house brands, a market segment in which they wish to strengthen their position. It was decided, therefore, that no more than one-fourth of the production beyond the 40,000-unit minimum should be formula Y, Tasty's own brand. The mathematical expression of this is

$$\tfrac{1}{4}(x + y - 40) \geqslant y$$

in which $x + y$ represents the total production, so $x + y - 40$ is the amount of production beyond 40,000 units.

The standard format of a linear programming constraint has all the variables on the left side. The policy constraint on product mix can be rearranged into the required format as follows:

$$x + y - 40 \geqslant 4y$$
$$x + y - 4y \geqslant 40$$
$$x - 3y \geqslant 40 \quad \text{(policy limit)} \tag{2}$$

The standing contracts can be represented by another constraint, $x \geqslant 40$. However, constraint (2) already forces x to equal or exceed 40. To see this, rewrite (2) as $x \geqslant 40 + 3y$, which exceeds 40 whenever y is positive. Because of this, the constraint $x \geqslant 40$ is not needed and is referred to as a *redundant* constraint.

We now face six restrictions or constraints in finding the best compromise solution for the upcoming month. They consist of the inequalities (1) and (2), and the following upper and lower limits:

$$x \leqslant 50 \quad \text{(market limit)} \tag{3}$$

$$y \leqslant 10 \quad \text{(market limit)} \tag{4}$$

$$x \geqslant 0 \quad \text{(nonnegativity limit)} \tag{5}$$

$$y \geqslant 0 \quad \text{(nonnegativity limit)} \tag{6}$$

Constraint (5) is redundant for the same reason that $x \geqslant 40$ is redundant. Nevertheless, it is customary to include a nonnegativity constraint for each variable. In fact, it is done automatically in LP computer packages.

Constraints (1) to (6) can be conveniently summarized on a graph, since there are only two variables. Figure C-1 shows all the constraints discussed so

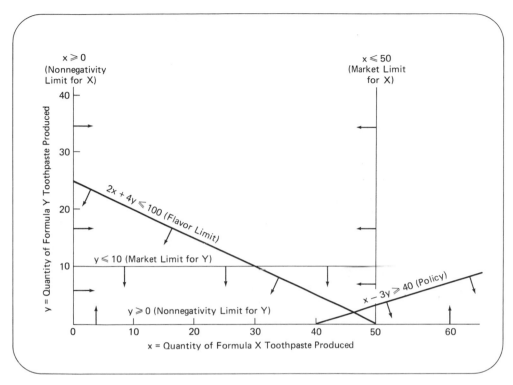

Figure C-1 Graph of Tasty Toothpaste's problem.

far. For example, constraint (1) is plotted by finding two points and drawing a straight line, as follows: (a) if we set $x = 0$, then $2x + 4y = 0 + 4y = 100$, so $y = 100/4 = 25$; (b) setting $y = 0$, $2x + 4y = 2x + 0 = 100$, so $x = 100/2 = 50$. Thus the flavor limit passes through the Y axis at $x = 0$, $y = 25$, and through the X axis at $x = 50$, $y = 0$. The arrows pointing downward from the flavor limit indicate that the area below that line satisfies the less-than part of the constraint. For example, the origin $x = 0$, $y = 0$ has $2x + 4y = 0 + 0 = 0$, which is certainly $\leqslant 100$. However, the point at which $x = 50$ and $y = 30$ is above the flavor line on the graph, and $2x + 4y = (2)(50) + (4)(30) = 100 + 120 = 220$, well above the available quantity of flavoring.

A solution must satisfy all the constraints. In Figure C-2 we have shaded all the areas excluded by the constraints, paying careful attention to the direction of the arrows in Figure C-1. The remaining area is a small triangle, indicating that x will be between 40 and 50, and y will be 2 units or less. This area is called the *feasible region*. (It is not always a triangle, as will be seen in the Review Problems.)

The *objective function* in this example is the profit, which is $50 for each unit of X and $60 for Y, or

$$50x + 60y = \text{profit} \quad \text{(to maximize)} \tag{7}$$

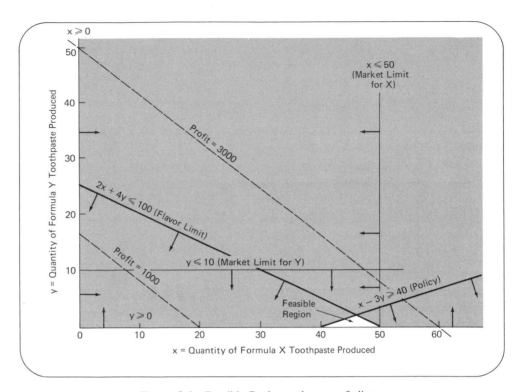

Figure C-2   Feasible Region and two profit lines.

The *optimal solution* in this case will be a point in the feasible region that maximizes profit. (In other examples the objective may be to minimize cost.) Equation (7) represents another straight line, but unlike the constraints, the objective function can move. For example, two profit lines have been plotted as dashed lines in Figure C-2. The one labeled profit = 1000 was obtained by arbitrarily selecting a profit of 1000, inserting 1000 on the right side of equation (7), and plotting the resulting equation $50x + 60y = 1000$. This initial guess proved fruitless since the profit line missed the feasible region altogether. Similarly, the line labeled profit = 3000 overshoots the feasible region.

Before seeking the optimal solution, let us examine these two profit lines. First, they are parallel. Thus, when we try another profit line, it will be parallel to these two. Second, the higher profit is the line that is to the upper right. Therefore, we want to find a profit line that passes through the feasible region, remains parallel to the two already plotted, and is as far to the upper right as possible. By visual inspection, we can see that the optimal solution will be at the rightmost corner of the feasible region, where $x = 50$, $y = 0$, for a profit of $(50)(50) + (60)(0) = 2500$ thousand dollars.

Discussion

Every two-variable LP can be graphed. The feasible region always has straight sides, although it is sometimes open in one direction. Improvements in the objective function correspond to moving a straight line across the graph in a parallel manner. Moving in one direction will minimize the objective function, wheras the opposite direction maximizes.

Because we want to move the objective function line as far as we can, but still have at least part of it in the feasible region, *one of the corners will always be an optimal solution* except in unusual circumstances. This indicates a great shortcut—we can ignore all of the feasible region except the corners.

Sometimes an entire side of the feasible region can be optimal, as illustrated in Problem 3. In that case, there are at least two optimal corners and many other equally optimal solutions. It is also possible that there may be no optimal solution, or no solution at all. The first case occurs when the feasible region has an opening in a direction such that the objective function can improve indefinitely. The second case happens if inconsistent constraints are given so that there is no feasible region. Both of these situations indicate that the formulation is incorrect.

Which corner is optimal depends on the slope of the objective function and the shape of the feasible region. This interaction between objective function and constraints can lead to unexpected results. For example, the Tasty Toothpaste LP appears very simple:

$$\text{maximize } 50x + 60y$$

subject to the constraints

$$2x + 4y \leq 100$$
$$x - 3y \geq 40$$
$$x \leq 50$$
$$y \leq 10$$

and the nonnegativity constraints $x \geq 0$ and $y \geq 0$. At first glance it would seem appropriate to produce as much Y as possible because it has the higher contribution. Nevertheless, the optimal solution is $x = 50$, $y = 0$. This is optimal because Y requires twice as much of the scarce flavor ingredient.

In general, the solution to an LP depends as much on the constraints as on the objective function. Because the solution depends so heavily on the constraints, it is prudent to study how changes in the constraints will affect the answer. This is called sensitivity analysis, and the review problems are examples of questions that can be addressed. We will return to this topic in Sections C-2 and C-4. It is the most important element for proper managerial use of LP.

Realistic problems often involve hundreds or thousands of variables, so the graphical approach cannot be used. There may be thousands of constraints, making it difficult to find any solution, let alone an optimal one. Fortunately, the graphical method is only a teaching device, and computer programs are widely available to do the job. Just like the graphical method, they consider only corner points, but they operate in a "hyperspace" with dimension equal to the number of variables in the problem. The constraints are "hyperplanes" rather than lines. Interpreting computer output is discussed in Section C-4.

As we have observed, optimal LP solutions will be corner points. However, the corners of the feasible region will often have fractional values for the variables. Therefore, LP answers must often be rounded off to obtain whole-number (integer) answers. Usually, these changes are minor. However, there are many problems where rounding off can give bad or even meaningless answers. Suppose that production has a setup cost of $250. Then the variable that represents the setup cost must either be zero (if there is no production) or 250 (if production takes place). Other values are meaningless. Integer programming methods have been developed for this type of problem but are not covered in this text.

Review Problems

1. The optimal solution to Tasty Toothpaste was $x = 50$, $y = 0$. Locate this point in Figure C-1, and mark it with a small circle.
   (a) The market limit for Y was 10,000 units. What would happen to the optimal solution if this were changed to 5000? 15,000?
   (b) The market limit for X was 50,000. What would happen if this were changed to 48,000?
   (c) What effect does the "policy limit" constraint have on the optimal solution?

2. Suppose that management changed the "policy limit" constraint by dropping the limitation on y, but retaining 40 as a lower limit for x. Draw the new feasible region.

3. Suppose that the objective function were $50x + 200y$. Find the optimal solution to the problem as modified in Review Problem 2.

4. Answer Review Problem 1 for the solution to Review Problem 3.

Solutions

1. (a) The $y = 10$ line does not touch the feasible region. Moving it up or down by 5 units will not affect the feasible region (and hence the optimal solution) at all. Had this constraint been absent, the solution would have been the same. This is a redundant constraint.
   (b) Moving the market limit of X to 48 would clip off the right-hand corner of the feasible region. The new solution would occur where the line $x = 48$ intersects the flavor limit. Since we know that x is 48 at the intersection, to find y we can solve equation (1): $2(48) + 4y = 100$, so $y = (100 - 96)/4 = 1$. The new solution would be $x = 48$, $y = 1$. The profit would be $50(48) + 60(1) = 2460$, a drop of 40 attributable to the 1-unit decrease in the market limit for X.

(c) None. The optimal solution occurred at the intersection of the flavor limit, the market limit for X and the nonnegativity limit for Y. As long as we use this objective function and the other constraints, the same solution would be optimal even if the policy limit constraint were omitted.

2. In miniature,

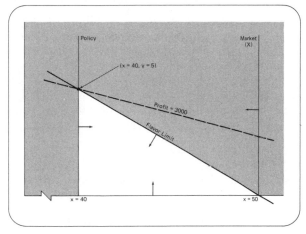

3. The profit $= 3000$ line is now much nearer the horizontal, running from $x = 0$, $y = 15$ to $x = 60$, $y = 0$. This line is plotted in the solution to Review Problem 2. This profit line brings us to the peak of the triangle, which is $x = 40$, $y = 5$, for a profit of $(50)(40) + (200)(5) = 3000$ thousand dollars.

4. (a) Same as Review Problem 1(a).
   (b) $x \le 50$ now has no effect, since the optimal solution has changed corners in the feasible region.
   (c) The policy constraint is now crucial. If we change it at all, the peak of the triangular feasible region would move.

C-2 THE SIMPLEX METHOD FOR SOLVING A LINEAR PROGRAM

LP can be viewed as a computer program that solves a particular kind of mathematical problem. The solution can be found by the *simplex method*, which is based on the same concepts as the simultaneous solution of two or more linear equations. LP problems typically have more unknowns (variables) than equations (constraints). Because of this, the problem usually has an infinite number of possible solutions. The goal of the simplex method is to find the best (optimal) solution. It accomplishes that goal quickly and efficiently by limiting the search to corner points that improve the solution. How this is done is the subject of this section. The reader uninterested in the details of the simplex method should read the first two subsections and then skip to Section C-3.

Standard LP Format

In the preceding section it was stated that the standard LP format requires that all the variables appear on the left side of each equation or inequality. In this section the reason for that requirement will become clear as we introduce the idea of a tableau for LP computation. As a definition:

An LP in standard format *has linear constraints (equations and/or inequalities) arranged so that all variables are on the left side and a nonnegative constant on the right. It also has a linear objective function. All variables are constrained to be nonnegative.*

The policy constraint on product mix provided an example of rearranging so that variables are on the left. Achieving nonnegative right-hand sides (abbreviated RHS) is a little trickier. Consider, for example, a constraint

$$x + y \geq -20$$

To get rid of the negative right-hand-side constant, we multiply both sides of the constraint by -1. In the example above this changes the constraint to

$$-x - y \leq 20$$

Multiplying by -1 changes the *sense* of the inequality. In this case, $\geq$ becomes $\leq$.

Now consider an objective function with a constant. Suppose the objective were to minimize a cost function that has a fixed element. For example, $9x - 2y + 150$ (to minimize) has a fixed element of 150. The standard LP format requires that we delete the 150. This is of little concern to us because a solution that minimizes the variable costs $9x - 2y$ also minimizes the cost function with fixed cost added. Therefore, when we get the solution, we can simply add 150.

Slack and Surplus Variables

The simplex method works only with equations, so our first task is to convert all $\leq$ and $\geq$ constraints to equalities. Continuing with the Tasty Toothpaste example, constraints (1) and (2) were stated earlier as

$$2x + 4y \leq 100 \tag{1}$$

$$x - 3y \geq 40 \tag{2}$$

In equation (1), if the left side is less than the right side (which is allowed by $\leq$), the difference is termed *slack*. That is, if we define w to be the slack variable for constraint (1), then

$$w = 100 - (2x + 4y)$$

Rearranging this to get the variables on the left side, the result is

$$2x + 4y + w = 100 \tag{8}$$

We have made constraint (1) an equality by explicitly including the slack.

The slack variable w must not be allowed to be negative. To see why, substitute $w = -5$ into equation (8):

$$2x + 4y - 5 = 100$$

$$2x + 4y = 105$$

Thus, if $w = -5$, $2x + 4y$ equals 105, which is not allowed in the original problem. To prevent this, constraint (1) is replaced by equality (8) and the nonnegativity requirement $w \geq 0$.

Constraint (2) may also be replaced by an equality, but this time we must subtract a slack variable, since the left side is allowed to be greater than the right side. For $\geq$ constraints, the difference between the two sides is called *surplus* (or negative slack). Let v be the surplus variable for (2). Then (2) is replaced by two requirements:

$$x - 3y - v = 40 \tag{9}$$

$$v \geq 0$$

The general rule is to convert each $\leq$ constraint to $=$ by adding a slack variable, and to convert each $\geq$ to $=$ by subtracting a surplus variable. Slack and surplus variables must be constrained to be nonnegative.

Slack and surplus variables have real meanings. For example, the slack variable in equation (8) represents the quantity of the secret flavor ingredient left unused by our choice of production quantities x and y. The surplus variable in (9) represents the amount by which the policy limit on product mix is exceeded (oversatisfied). It is important to keep these interpretations in mind.

At corner points, the constraints that intersect have zero slack or surplus. For example, in Figure C-2 the point $x = 50$, $y = 0$ has zero slack for the two constraints $x \leq 50$ and $2x + 4y \leq 100$, whereas the policy constraint and the market limit for y pass some distance from this point—their slack and surplus variables are not zero. In the Review Problems, we found that changes in some of the constraints had no effect on the solutiuon. *The solution is sensitive to changes in any constraint that has zero slack, and not sensitive if the slack or surplus exceeds zero.*

The Tableau

In the preceding section, the Tasty Toothpaste LP was solved graphically. We saw that two of the constraints did not affect the optimal solution. In this section, for simplicity, those two constraints, $x \leq 50$ and $y \leq 10$, are ignored. The resulting LP, including slack and surplus variables, may be summarized in standard LP format as:

$$\text{Max} \quad 50x + 60y \tag{7}$$

s.t.

$$2x + 4y + w = 100 \tag{8}$$

$$x - 3y - v = 40 \tag{9}$$

$$x, y, w, v \geq 0 \tag{10}$$

in which *Max* means to maximize (we use *Min* if the objective is to minimize) and *s.t.* means "subject to the following constraints being satisfied". Constraint (10) indicates that each of the variables is to be prevented from being negative.

For computation, the problem data are displayed in a *tableau*. An LP tableau is a table with numbers arranged in horizontal rows and vertical columns. Table C-1 is a tableau corresponding to the LP equations (7) to (9). Each row corresponds to a constraint except row 1, the objective function. Each column (except the last) represents a variable. The RHS column contains the constants from the right-hand sides of the equations.

TABLE C-1 TABLEAU FOR TASTY TOOTHPASTE

Eq. No.	Row No.	x	y	w	v	RHS
(7)	1	Max 50	60	0	0	
(8)	2	2	4	1	0	100
(9)	3	1	−3	0	−1	40

As computations proceed the tableau is changed. The columns always represent information about the variables, but the rows and the RHS column are altered in their interpretation, as we shall see later.

Notice that the nonnegativity constraints (10) are not in the tableau. LP computer programs assume that all variables must be nonnegative. (Some programs do have special instructions for handling variables that can be negative.)

The property that makes LP difficult to solve is that all the constraints must be satisfied simultaneously rather than one at a time. The tableau makes it easy to find these solutions.

For example, consider the following solution to equation (8): $w = 100$, $x = 0$, and $y = 0$. To see why this solution is of particular interest, examine the column labeled w in the tableau. Notice that all but one of the entries in this column are 0. This means that choosing a quantity for w will have no effect on any equation other than row 2. If each equation could be solved in this manner, simultaneous solution would be a breeze.

However, if we try to solve equation (9) this way, we run into trouble. The variable v has 0 in all but one row; it has an effect only on equation (9). Unfortunately, the -1 in row 3 results in the solution $x = 0$, $y = 0$, and $v = -40$. This is not an allowable solution to equation (9) because of the negative value of v. One way to avoid this difficulty is to augment the tableau with artificial variables.

Augmenting the Initial Tableau: Artificial Variables

Artificial variables differ from slack and surplus variables in one important way; they have no meaning in the originial problem and therefore must be required to be zero in the final solution. The artificial variable we are about to introduce represents the amount by which constraint (9) is violated. That is why it must be zero when we are finished.

Equation (9) is changed by adding the artificial variable A:

$$x - 3y - v + A = 40 \qquad (11)$$

This equation can be solved as easily as (8) was, $x = 0$, $y = 0$, $v = 0$, and $A = 40$. This solution does not satisfy equation (9). We are counting on A being zero in future solutions because when A is zero, equations (9) and (11) are identical.

Table C-2 shows the augmented tableau. Notice that the artificial variable A looks like a slack variable for row 3 except for the large negative coefficient in the objective function. Since the objective is to maximize row 1, the artificial variable has been given a profit contribution that is so negative that an optimal solution method will drive it to zero.

TABLE C-2   AUGMENTED TABLEAU FOR TASTY TOOTHPASTE

Eq. No.	Row No.	x	y	w	v	A	RHS
(7)	1	Max 50	60	0	0	−10,000	
(8)	2	2	4	1	0	0	100
(11)	3	1	−3	0	−1	1	40

The initial solution to an augmented tableau is to set each slack and artificial variable equal to its corresponding RHS quantity. For Table C-2 the solution is $w = 100$, $A = 40$. All the other variables are zero in this solution.

Each equation that has no slack variable must be given its own artificial variable. They are needed only for equality and greater-than-or-equal-to constraints. In a maximization problem, the objective function coefficients for artificial variables are large and negative. For minimization, they are large and positive.

The "Net Change" Objective Function

Is this solution optimal? The augmented tableau of Table C-2 is not yet ready for this question. For example, row 1 seems to indicate that x is worth 50 per unit, y is worth 60, and so on. Remember, however, that the initial solution has $A = 40$; any change in x or y may change A as well. Which of the variables will have the greatest impact on the objective function when the change in A is taken into account?

A was created for row 3. In that row, the coefficients for x and A have the same sign. They are substitutes in the "consumption of RHS 3." Increasing x will decrease A. On the other hand, both y and v have negative row 3 coefficients, so they do not substitute for A. In fact, increasing either of these variables would increase A.

To adjust the objective function to reflect these effects, we multiply row 3 by 10,000 and add the result to row 1. The justification for this step is that row 3 represents the abilities of all variables to reduce A, which increases profit by 10,000 per unit. The result is shown in Table C-3.

TABLE C-3   FIRST SIMPLEX TABLEAU FOR TASTY TOOTHPASTE

Row No.	x	y	w	v	A	RHS
1	Max 10,050	−29,940	0	−10,000	0	400,000
2	2	4	1	0	0	100
3	1	−3	0	−1	1	40

The first-row entry for x is now 10,050, reflecting the fact that x yields 50 in direct profits and 10,000 indirectly by reducing A. Variable y now looks like a terrible investment, since the gain of 60 has been offset by a loss of 30,000 because to increase y by 1 unit requires increasing A by 3.

The RHS column now has an entry of 400,000. Its interpretation will be given below. The tableau is now in a form suitable for optimization by the simplex method. Hence it is called the *first simplex tableau*.

Interpreting a Simplex Tableau

The simplex tableau should be thought of in a new way: it represents a solution. The tableau in Table C-3 represents the solution $w = 100$, $A = 40$, profit = −400,000. Notice that the RHS column contains these numbers, with the exception of row 1, which is the negative of the profit. That is, 100 units of v at zero return and 40 of A at a return of −10,000 is $0 + (−10,000)(40) = −400,000$, compared to $+400,000$ in row 1. Henceforth, as we move through simplex iterations:

> *The RHS column contains the current solution.*

Now you can see why the RHS values must be nonnegative in the standard LP format. The RHS is the initial solution, and we want it to satisfy the nonnegativity requirements for the variables.

In this tableau we already know which variables correspond to the RHS values ($w = 100$ and $A = 40$). How could we pick out these variables if someone gave us another tableau? Observe the w and A columns; they are different from the others. There is a single entry of 1 in each of these columns, and the rest of the entries are zero. That is called a *unit column*. In the w column, the 1 is in the row with a RHS of 100. In this solution, w and A are referred to as the *basic* variables because they alone define the solution. The rest of the variables are zero. In general;

> *The basic variables have unit columns. Each basic variable has a 1 in "its" row and zeros in the rest of the rows. Each RHS is the current solution for "its" basic variable.*

In this new interpretation, the basic variables have taken possession of the rows. As we shall see, all the numbers in the tableau tell us something about the basic variables.

The rest of the variables are called *nonbasic*. They are all zero in the solution represented by the tableau. However, the tableau contains information about the nonbasic variables. For example, as we saw previously:

The first row contains the net rates of increase in the objective function that would result from increases in the nonbasic variables.

This information is vital if we want to know how to improve the solution. But changing a variable affects more than the objective function. It also affects the basic variables. (That is why we need *net* changes in row 1.) As we shall illustrate:

If a nonbasic variable is increased, its column contains the net rates of substitution (decrease) of the basic variables.

Now that a tableau has been identified with a current solution, it remains to show how to find the best solution. If the solution is to be improved, it is by changing the nonbasic[1] variables. One way of carrying this out is called the simplex method.

The Simplex Method

Row 1 of Table C-3 shows clearly that x is the most profitable variable in the tableau. However, it is currently nonbasic and therefore equal to zero. We designate x as the *entering variable* because we want to bring it into the solution. We have just used

The Simplex Criterion for Optimality: As long as there are any positive coefficients in the first row of a maximization problem, the solution can be improved. If all row 1 coefficients are zero or negative, the solution is optimal. (The opposite signs apply for minimization.)

The next task is to find a new solution with x in it. The method uses two columns: the x column and the RHS. Consider the possibility of increasing x from its current value of 0. Reading down the x column, it is apparent that each unit increase in x would require 2 units of RHS from row 2 and 1 unit from row 3.

How far can we increase x? The RHS values represent basic variables, so we must stop increasing x before any RHS becomes negative.

Consider row 2. The RHS is 100 and each unit of x substitutes for 2 of these. Therefore, if x increases by $100/2 = 50$, the RHS will decrease to zero. Any further increase in x would drive the RHS negative, which is not allowed. Similarly, in row 3 the allowable range of increase for x is $40/1 = 40$. Therefore, to avoid negative RHS values in both rows, x cannot exceed either 40 or 50, so it is limited to the smaller of the two numbers, or 40.

---

[1] There is one basic variable per row. Therefore, there is only one solution for a given set of basic variables. New solutions are found by bringing in a nonbasic variable.

When $x = 40$ is reached, the RHS of row 3 is reduced to zero and the variable that it represents becomes nonbasic. Since A is basic in row 3, it is the *departing variable*. In short, 40 units of x have displaced A as a basic variable. The objective function should improve by 10,050 for each unit of x, or $(40)(10,050) = 402,000$.

This example has shown how to improve the solution. A formal statement of this procedure follows:

> *Simplex step 1:* To find the entering variable, choose any variable with a $+$ sign in row 1, for maximization, or a $-$ sign for minimization.
>
> *Simplex step 2:* To find the departing variable:
> (a) divide each RHS value (except row 1) by the corresponding entry in the column of the entering variable. Ignore ratios with zero or negative denominators.
> (b) Find the row with the smallest ratio. Call that the departing row. The basic variable for that row is the departing variable.
> (c) If all rows have negative or zero denominators, abandon the problem. There is no limit on the entering variable, so the solution is unbounded.

Once the entering and departing variables have been identified, a new tableau is needed to represent the new solution. This requires a bit of algebra. First, we define

> The pivot element: *the number at the intersection of the column of the entering variable and the row of the departing variable.*

In our example, we wish to make x a basic variable in row 3. The pivot element is therefore the number 1 in the x column.

To make x basic, we must give it a unit column with a 1 in row 3. There is already a 1 in row 3 of the x column. (If not, we would divide each number in row 3 by the pivot element.) Now to get the zeros for the rest of the unit column. How can we get a zero in row 1 of the x column? This is done as follows:

$$\text{new row 1} = \text{old row 1} - (10{,}050)(\text{new row 3})$$

That is:

	x	y	w	v	A	RHS
Old row 1 =	10,050	−29,940	0	−10,000	0	400,000
10,050 (new row 3) =	10,050	−30,150	0	−10,050	10,050	402,000
Subtract to get	0	210	0	50	−10,500	−2,000

The same procedure is used to process row 2, so that

$$\text{new row 2} = \text{old row 2} - (2)(\text{new row 3})$$

The results are shown in Table C-4.

TABLE C-4   SECOND SIMPLEX TABLEAU FOR TASTY TOOTHPASTE

Row No.	x	y	w	v	A	RHS
1	0	210	0	50	−10,050	−2,000
2	0	10	1	2	−2	20
3	1	−3	0	−1	1	40

In deriving the new tableau we have performed

Simplex step 3: the *pivot step.*
   (a) Divide each number in the departing row by the pivot element. Call the result the new departing row.
   (b) Process all the remaining rows starting with row 1. That is, for each row i except the departing row:
       (1) In the column of the entering variable, locate the number in row i. Call it B.
       (2) Multiply the new departing row by B and subtract the result from row i. That is, new row i = old row i − (B)(new departing row)

The three simplex steps constitute the simplex method. When step 3 is completed, there is a new tableau, so steps 1, 2, and 3 can be repeated. This continues until step 1 fails because no variable can improve the objective function. Then the simplex criterion is satisfied and the algorithm terminates.

Possible Outcomes for the Simplex Method

Outcome 1. No feasible solution. (Artificial variables remain in the solution.) *Problem:* The constraints are inconsistent. *Example:* $x + y = 10$ and $x + y = 20$ are inconsistent, because $x + y$ cannot be both 10 and 20 at the same time. *Remedy:* Either give up in despair, or reformulate the problem.

Outcome 2. Solution is unbounded. (All ratios in step 2a are negative or have zero denominators.) *Problem:* The constraints are not sufficient to prevent the optimum from being positive or negative infinity. *Example:* Maximize $z = x + y$ with the constraint $x - y = 10$. Note that $x = 100,010$, $y = 100,000$ is feasible, as are any numbers such that x exceeds y by 10 units. *Remedy:* You have probably left out a real-world constraint on available resources. Reformulate the problem.

Outcome 3. Optimal solution found. This is the desired outcome. Although the final basic solution is optimal, there may be more than one optimal solution. This may be ascertained by looking at the final objective function row:

(a) If any (one or more) nonbasic variable has a coefficient of zero in the final objective function, the solution reported by the LP is only one of an infinite number of optimal solutions.

(b) All these optimal solutions achieve the same value of the objective function, so we can choose among them based on facts not included in the LP formulation.

(c) The alternative optimal solutions are found by "bringing in" any of the nonbasic variables that have a zero in the final objective function equation.

Sensitivity Analysis of the Optimal Solution

If an LP formulation is changed, it stands to reason that the optimal solution will also change. Sensitivity analysis explores the link between the problem and its optimal solution. This is very important to a manager because values used in the formulation may be estimates or may be changed by management action. Section C-4 describes sensitivity analysis based on the output from a typical LP computer program. The following briefly illustrates how sensitivity information is obtained from the simplex tableau.

For illustration, we will consider forcing a nonoptimal (nonbasic) variable into the solution. That is, on reflection a manager may require production of an unprofitable item to round out a product line. The analysis follows from simplex step 2. Increasing an entering variable has *linear* effects on the objective function value and on the basic variables. Simplex step 2 will also yield a departing variable, so the effect is linear over a limited range; it ends when one of the basic variables is driven to zero.

The rates of change are given in the column of the nonbasic variable in the optimal simplex tableau. Row 1 is the rate at which the objective function value changes. This is called the *reduced cost*. The other rows are the net rates of substitution for the basic variables.

There are many other questions that a manager might wish to address using sensitivity analysis. Some of them use the idea just explained for nonbasic variables. For example, changing a RHS value can be shown to be equivalent to forcing a nonbasic slack into the solution. Section C-4 describes the most common sensitivity outputs from computer LP packages and their application.

Discussion

Computer programs are widely available to do all the work discussed in this section (and more). These programs are based on the simplex method (or other similar approach), which derives its efficiency by (1) moving from one basic solution to another, and (2) using the simplex criterion to assure that each move improves the objective function. The program stops when no more improvements are possible and reports an optimal, feasible, basic solution (if one exists). The tableau that accompanies the solution contains all the information needed to study modifications of that solution.

The Tasty Toothpaste LP was graphed in Figure C-2 in the previous section. We have now generated two tableaus, and each is a solution. The first, Table C-3, has both x and y equal to zero (they are nonbasic). That is the origin in Figure C-2. The second, Table C-4, has $x = 40$ and $y = 0$ which is the lower left corner of the feasible region in the graph. *The basic solutions generated by simplex tableaus correspond to corner points of the graph. If all artificial variables are zero, a tableau solution is a corner point of the feasible region.*

Review Problems

1. What is the solution given by Table C-4? (How much of each variable and at what profit?)
2. According to simplex step 1, Table C-4 indicates that either y or v could be the next entering variable. Which one would you choose? Why?
3. Let v be the entering variable. Using simplex step 2, determine the departing variable.
4. Using simplex step 3, find a new tableau.
5. Is this solution optimal? How can you tell?
6. Locate the solution to Review Problem 4 in Figure C-2 in the preceding section. Does this confirm your answer to Review Problem 5?
7. How much would profits drop if we forced the LP to produce 1 unit of Y?

Solutions

1. The basic variables are $x = 40$ and $w = 20$. The net profit is 2000.
2. We may as well choose the one with the highest net profit, which is y at 210 per unit.
3. Despite the answer to Review Problem 2, we have chosen v as the entering variable. First, check row 2: $20/2 = 10$. Row 3: $40/(-1) = $ negative. Ignore the negative number. The departing row is row 2 and the departing variable is w.
4. The pivot element is 2. The new tableau is shown in Table C-5. Note the

TABLE C-5 THIRD SIMPLEX TABLEAU FOR TASTY TOOTHPASTE AND THE FORMULATION WITH SLACK, SURPLUS, AND ARTIFICIAL VARIABLES

Row No.	x	y	w	v	A	RHS
1	0	-40	-25	0	$-10,000$	$-2,500$
2	0	5	0.5	1	-1	10
3	1	2	0.5	0	0	50

$$\text{Max} \quad 50x + 60y \qquad\qquad - 10,000A$$
$$\text{s.t.} \qquad 2x + 4y + w \qquad\qquad = 100$$
$$x - 3y \qquad\quad -v + A = 40$$
$$x, y, w, v \geq 0$$

role played by the column of the entering variable v: in Table C-4, the number 2 is the pivot element, and the numbers 50 and -1 play the role of B when rows 1 and 3 are processed in simplex step 3(b), respectively.

5. This solution is optimal because all row 1 coefficients are negative or zero. (If we had introduced y first, v would still have a positive coefficient; it would enter in the next iteration and y would depart.)

6. Table C-5 corresponds to $x = 50$, $y = 0$, the lower right point in the feasible region of the graph. This does confirm the solution to Review Problem 5 because we proved graphically that this is the optimal solution.

7. If y were the entering variable, the objective function would drop by $40 per unit (the reduced cost in row 1).

C-3 LINEAR PROGRAMMING FORMULATIONS

In this section we will address the questions asked most frequently by people who have some understanding of LP and are faced with making use of it for the first time. The case of the Rockwell Stone Corporation is used to bring most of these questions to a practical level. Although it is a simplified version of allocation of resources to production, it has complications of the kind often encountered in full-scale problems. It is also large enough that one is pleased to use a computer for its solution. Rockwell Stone is an example of a multistage production planning problem, of the type discussed in Chapter 12.

There are a number of standard LP formulations, and many of them are used in this text. For the convenience of the student interested in practicing the important art of formulation, and for the instructor who wishes to include more examples, here is a directory of LP formulations in this text.

Project scheduling: Section 3-2. Data from Problems 11 and 15 in Chapter 3 can be used as examples.

Transportation/distribution problem: Section 7-5 (which includes a mixed-integer formulation), Problems 15 to 18 in Chapter 7. Also, see Problems 15 and 21 in this appendix.

Multiple-period production–inventory–workforce scheduling: Section 9-4, Problem 16 in Chapter 9, and the Handicraft Jewelers caselet.

Personnel scheduling: Section 14-1, Problem 10 in Chapter 14.

Assignment problem: Section 14-3, Problems 18 and 19 in Chapter 14.

LP embedded in a decision system: Section 15-2.

Product mix: this section and Problems 12, 13, 16, 18, and 19.

Blending with quality constraints: in this appendix, Problem 17 and the Red Brand Canners caselet.

Nonlinear objectives functions with diseconomies of scale: in this appendix, Problems 14 and 15.

Rockwell Stone, Inc.

The Rockwell Stone Corporation makes two models of rock crushers. Sales of these two products and spare crusher blades (they do not sell any parts other than crusher blades) are handled through an internal sales department. Forecasts of the demand for the upcoming quarter are as follows:

Item	Description	Selling Price	Demand Forecast (Next Quarter)
BS1	Rock crusher, light	$14,000	250
BS2	Rock crusher, heavy	46,000	150
P2	Crusher blade, replacement	3,400	5,000

In the fabrication part of the plant, raw materials are processed into parts that then go to the assembly area, where they are stored until needed. In addition to the fabricated parts, assembly of a rock crusher requires two subassemblies, which are purchased from an outside supplier. Another supplier offers part P4 for sale, but Rockwell currently makes all the P4 it needs. The decision as to whether to make or buy this part is currently being considered. The fabrication and assembly requirements, listing the materials required for assembly of each of the two products and manufacture of each part, are:

Part	RAW MATERIALS REQUIRED PER PART		Labor Hours per Part
	RM1	RM2	
P1	25	0	0.1
P2	37	700	2.0
P3	0	12	2.0
P4	0	170	25.0

Crusher Model	PARTS REQUIRED PER ROCK CRUSHER				SUBASSEMBLIES		Labor
	P1	P2	P3	P4	SA1	SA2	
BS1	3	2	4	2	1	0	0.3
BS2	6	5	4	1	2	1	1.0

For items that may be purchased, the prices and availabilities are:

Item	Price	Purchase Limit
P4	$ 1,035	No limit
SA1	3,150	450
SA2	18,000	No limit
RM1	5	750,000
RM2	5	No limit
LABOR	$8.50/hr	No limit

Although the data seem to indicate maximum sales of 250 + 150 = 400 rock crushers, there is some degree of substitutibility between the two models. Maximum total sales have been estimated to be 360. The firm has set a minimum production goal of 300 rock crushers. The purchasing manager has been given a budget of $7.2 million, from which the required subassemblies and raw materials must be purchased. The budget restriction would not apply to purchase of part type P4, even if Rockwell decides to buy it as mentioned above.

Formulating the Multistage Production LP

The remainder of this section is devoted to understanding the complete formulation of this problem, which is shown (later) in Table C-6.

How Does One Decide What the Variables Should Be? Variables are created for every decision or recommendation that is to come from the LP. Rockwell Stone wants to know what quantity of each part to fabricate, how many subassemblies and raw materials to purchase, and how many rock crushers to assemble. They further desire a recommended quantity of part P2 to fabricate for sale, and of P4 to purchase from the outside supplier. We will use Rockwell's notation wherever possible, so that BS1 will stand for the quantity of model 1 rock crushers to be produced, P1 the quantity of type 1 parts to be fabricated, and so on. In addition, the number of part type 2 to be sold as spares will be designated SPARE, and BUY will be the quantity of type 4 parts purchased from the outside.

How Are Objectives and Constraints Formulated? The first step is to list, in English, all the restrictions that the solution must satisfy. Each of these restrictions will be represented by one (or sometimes more than one) equation or inequality. Management must also specify its objectives, first verbally, then quantitatively. It will then be up to the computer to find a solution that satisfies all the restrictions, and also optimizes the objective function.

    There is a convenient categorization scheme which helps the user determine whether the LP formulation contains all the necessary constraints. The categories are: accounting constraints, facts-of-life constraints, policy constraints, and objective function.

    1. *Accounting constraints.* These are equations that tie the variables together. Without these constraints, the LP might recommend producing rock crushers but no type 1 parts. To prevent such a ridiculous recommendation, we must account for the parts that will be required in production of rock crushers. In English, and then in mathematical terms, the constraint for type 1 parts (P1) is:

$$\text{type 1 parts required} = 3 \text{ for each BS1} + 6 \text{ for each BS2}$$

$$\text{P1} = 3 \text{ BS1} + 6 \text{ BS2} \tag{12}$$

To see if this would prevent the error described above, set $BS1 = 10$ and $BS2 = 20$, and note that this gives us $P1 = (3)(10) + (6)(20) = 150$, which is just enough type 1 parts to produce 10 model 1 rock crushers and 20 of model 2.

For part type 2 (P2) there are three uses: assembly of two types of rock crushers and sales for spare parts. Equation (13) will account for the type 2 parts used in assembly of BS1 and BS2 crushers, and will also require production of the quantity required for spares. Equations (14) and (15) give the accounting constraints for P3 and P4.

$$P2 = 2\ BS1 + 5\ BS2 + 1\ SPARE \qquad (13)$$

$$P3 = 4\ BS1 + 4\ BS2 \qquad (14)$$

$$P4 = 2\ BS1 + 1\ BS2 - 1\ BUY \qquad (15)$$

2. *Facts-of-life constraints.* Because of a limited market for rock crushers, we can sell no more than 250 of type 1 and 150 of type 2. Therefore, explicit upper limits must be placed on BS1 and BS2, which may be accomplished as follows:

$$BS1 \leq 250 \qquad (16)$$

$$BS2 \leq 150 \qquad (17)$$

Another fact-of-life constraint is that no more than 360 rock crushers can be sold in total because they are partial substitutes for one another. This is formulated as

$$BS1 + BS2 \leq 360 \qquad (18)$$

Although the examples of facts-of-life constraints have been inequalities, this is not always so. For example, a permanent contract to produce an exact quantity of an item would be an equality constraint. Also, the numbers used in these constraints may sometimes be more appropriately termed *guesses,* as the actual fact may not be known. (The market constraint is an example of an educated guess.)

3. *Policy constraints.* A budget is an example of a policy constraint imposed on the solution by a management decision. The following expresses the budget for the purchase of raw materials and subassemblies:

$$3150\ SA1 + 18,000\ SA2 + 5\ RM1 + 5\ RM2 \leq 7,200,000 \qquad (19)$$

Notice that an inequality has been used to express the budget as an upper limit. A slack variable for this inequality would represent budgeted funds not used in the LP solution.

Company policy also requires a minimum output of at least 300 rock crushers. Therefore, another policy constraint is

$$BS1 + BS2 \geq 300 \qquad (20)$$

4. *The objective function.* If the objective is to maximize net contribution to fixed cost and profit, the objective function is

$$14{,}000 \text{ BS1} + 46{,}000 \text{ BS2} + 3400 \text{ SPARE}$$
$$- 1035 \text{ BUY} - 3150 \text{ SA1} - 18{,}000 \text{ SA2} - 5 \text{ RM1} \qquad (21)$$
$$- 5 \text{ RM2} - 8.50 \text{ LABOR}$$

Table C-6 summarizes the Rockwell Stone LP formulation, including all the constraints discussed above and several others that were formulated from the verbal description in the same manner.

TABLE C-6 FORMULATION FOR ROCKWELL STONE, INC.

Equation Number	Row Number		
(21)	1	Max	14,000 BS1 + 46,000 BS2 + 3400 SPARE − 1035 BUY − 3150 SA1 − 18,000 SA2 − 5 RM1 − 5 RM2 − 8.50 LABOR
(12)	2		P1 − 3 BS1 − 6 BS2 = 0
(13)	3		P2 − 2 BS1 − 5 BS2 − SPARE = 0
(14)	4		P3 − 4 BS1 − 4 BS2 = 0
(15)	5		P4 − 2 BS1 − BS2 + BUY = 0
	6		SA1 − BS1 − 2 BS2 = 0
	7		SA2 − BS2 = 0
	8		RM1 − 25 P1 − 37 P2 = 0
	9		RM2 − 700 P2 − 12 P3 − 170 P4 = 0
	10		LABOR − 0.3 BS1 − 1.0 BS2 − 0.1 P1 − 2 P2 − 2 P3 − 25 P4 = 0
(18)	11		BS1 + BS2 ≤ 360
(20)	12		BS1 + BS2 ≥ 300
(19)	13		3150 SA1 + 18,000 SA2 + 5 RM1 + 5 RM2 ≤ 7,200,000
(16)	14		BS1 ≤ 250
(17)	15		BS2 ≤ 150
	16		SPARE ≤ 5000
	17		SA1 ≤ 450
	18		RM1 ≤ 750,000

How Are Constraints Tested? Equation (12) was tested earlier in this section by plugging numbers in for each variable, and seeing whether the results matched the verbal description. This is an important step, because it is very easy to write constraints incorrectly or backward. For example, the statement, "Each BS1 takes three P1, two P2, four P3, and two P4" might be written, erroneously,

Erroneous formula: BS1 = 3 P1 + 2 P2 + 4 P3 + 2 P4

To see why this is wrong, plug in P1 = 3, P2 = 2, P3 = 4, and P4 = 2 and see if you get BS1 = 1. (You don't!) The correct formulation requires four equations, one for each part. They are equations (12)–(15). When the same numbers are plugged in, each of the four equations balances.

How Can the Entire Formulation Be Checked? This is a very important question, because it is the interaction of the many variables and constraints that make a large-scale problem difficult to solve. Checking the constraints one at a time does not guarantee that the final formulation is complete and accurate. Final testing of the model is done by running the computer program and examining the results. It is at this stage that errors of omission are often discovered. For example, if one or more accounting constraints have been omitted, the LP will recommend an impossible solution such as, "Produce 200 rock crushers and sell them all, but minimize costs by not buying any subassemblies." Such a solution would result if the rows labeled SUB1 and SUB2 in Table C-6 were omitted.

How Can We Tell Whether the Output Makes Sense? Making sense from the LP answer is the subject of the next section. This question requires us to go beyond learning how to read the answer; we must learn how to determine the implications of answers that appear unreasonable, because LP solutions may radically alter one's view of the problem.

Summary

An LP user must go through a rather involved process to translate a problem into mathematical terms that a computer can understand. The variables for the LP correspond to every detailed decision that is part of the problem being analyzed. The constraints correspond to restrictions put on the situation by *facts of life* and *policies,* but must also include equations to tie the variables together in a way that forces the LP *to account for all the interactions* among the decisions. One should check each constraint individually by plugging in reasonable values of the decisions variables. The entire formulation is tested by examining the output to determine whether it makes sense, and changing the formulation if necessary.

To complete a formulation, the numbers used in the equations must be obtained. These include the technological coefficients which express the formula or recipe for the products, and the constants which appear on the right-hand side of the equations. Some of these numbers may require substantial effort to collect. Estimation will often have to suffice, especially if the linear equations are only approximations to the real situation. The next section deals with methods of determining how crucial these estimates are, and how influential the resulting errors may be on the solution.

Review Problems

1. Test equation (15) by plugging in BS1 = 10, BS2 = 20, and BUY = 15. How many type 4 parts would be fabricated, according to (15)? Would this be sufficient to produce 10 BS1 and 20 BS2?

2. What are the accounting constraints [other than equations (12), (13), (14), and (15)] in the Rockwell Stone problem? Say them in English, and verify

that they are contained in the summary of the formulation shown in Table C-6.

3. Each Champburger takes three slices of bread, two beef patties, and one pickle. Show that the following formula is not correct, and write a correct set of expressions.

$$\text{BURGS} = 3\,\text{BREAD} + 2\,\text{BEEFS} + 1\,\text{PICKLE}$$

Solutions

1. P4 = 2 BS1 + 1 BS2 − 1 BUY
   P4 = (2)(10) + (1)(20) − (1)(15)
   P4 = 20 + 20 − 15
   P4 = 25
   Yes. Each BS1 takes 2 P4, so 20 are needed there, and 20 are also needed for producing 20 BS2, for a total of 40. However, 15 are procured through purchasing (BUY = 15), so 25 is a sufficient number to fabricate.

2. In Table C-6, rows 6 to 10 are accounting constraints. For row 6 an English expression is "The number of SA1 needed is 1 for each BS1 and 2 for each BS2." Mathematically, this is

$$\text{SA1} = 1\,\text{BS1} + 2\,\text{BS2}$$

   which is transformed to row 6 in Table C-6 by subtracting 1 BS1 and 2 BS2 from both sides.

3. If the formula were correct, then BREAD = 3, BEEFS = 2, and PICKLE = 1 should lead to BURG = 1.

$$1 = (3)(3) + (2)(2) + (1)(1)$$
$$1 = 9 + 4 + 1 = 14$$

   Since this does not check, the formula is wrong. The correct formulas are

$$\text{BREAD} = 3\,\text{BURGS}$$
$$\text{BEEFS} = 2\,\text{BURGS}$$
$$\text{PICKLE} = 1\,\text{BURGS}$$

   which reads, "the number of bread slices equals 3 for each burger, the number of beef patties equals 2 for each burger," and so on. Checking these formulas, we have

$$3 = (3)(1)$$
$$2 = (2)(1)$$
$$1 = (1)(1)$$

C-4 MANAGERIAL USE OF LP SOLUTIONS

The Rockwell Stone LP was formulated by a manager named Tom Dirk. The optimal solution for Rockwell Stone is shown in Table C-7. The objective function value (net contribution) is $280,315. The recommended production quantities

TABLE C-7 OPTIMAL SOLUTION AND SENSITIVITY ANALYSIS FOR ROCKWELL STONE

OBJECTIVE FUNCTION VALUE = 280,315.00

| | | | OBJECTIVE COEFFICIENT RANGES | | |
VARIABLE	SOLUTION	REDUCED COST	CURRENT COEF.	ALLOWED INCREASE	ALLOWED DECREASE
BS1	250	0.00	14,000	INFINITY	146.20
BS2	100	0.00	46,000	292.40	1,083.40
SPARE	0	302.00	3,400	302.00	INFINITY
BUY	600	0.00	−1,035	INFINITY	27.50
SA1	450	0.00	−3,150	INFINITY	541.70
SA2	100	0.00	−18,000	292.40	1,083.40
RM1	70,750	0.00	−5	7.90	3.23
RM2	716,800	0.00	−5	0.16	0.31
LABOR	5,110	0.00	−8.5	1.10	52.21
P1	1,350	0.00	0.0	INFINITY	180.57
P2	1,000	0.00	0.0	292.40	216.68
P3	1,400	0.00	0.0	INFINITY	73.10
P4	0	27.50	0.0	27.50	INFINITY

| | | | RIGHT-HAND-SIDE RANGES | | |
ROW	SLACK/ SURPLUS	DUAL PRICES	CURRENT RHS	ALLOWED INCREASE	ALLOWED DECREASE
2	0	−125.85	0	358.00	1,350.00
3	0	−3,702.00	0	12.14	1,000.00
4	0	−77.00	0	745.83	1,400.00
5	0	−1,035.00	0	INFINITY	600.00
6	0	−3,691.70	0	100.00	2.39
7	0	−18,000.00	0	2.49	100.00
8	0	−5.00	0	8,950.00	70,750.00
9	0	−5.00	0	8,950.00	716,800.00
10	0	−8.50	0	INFINITY	5,110.00
11	10	0.00	360	INFINITY	10.00
12	50	0.00	300	50.00	INFINITY
13	44,750	0.00	7,200,000	INFINITY	44,750.00
14	0	146.20	250	20.00	4.17
15	50	0.00	150	INFINITY	50.00
16	5,000	0.00	5,000	INFINITY	5,000.00
17	0	541.70	450	2.05	100.00
18	679,250	0.00	750,000	INFINITY	679,250.00

are (see the column labeled SOLUTION) BS1 = 250 type 1 rock crushers, BS2 = 100 of type 2, SPARE = 0 crusher blades to be produced as spares, and so on.

There are two controversial recommendations. First, P4 = 0 and BUY = 600 indicate that all parts of type P4 should be purchased from the outside supplier. Second, SPARE = 0 suggests going out of the business of supplying spare crusher blades. Tom realized that management would object to these solutions because they violate a long-standing policy, "We service what we sell."

This puts Tom in a difficult position. Having proposed that the LP can solve Rockwell Stone's production planning problem, he must either justify these recommendations or change them. He decided to talk the situation over with Dean Smalley, a friend who had been with the company 5 years longer than he.

Dean: The boss sure isn't going to like this solution. We have always produced spare crusher blades. It is part of our image. You had better change your model if you want to get anywhere.

Tom: Well, I could add a constraint such as SPARE ≥ 50 and run the LP again. Maybe I'll do several runs with different values of SPARE and make a graph of net profits as a function of the level of production of SPARE.

Dean: That would be a good idea, but the news of your LP has already leaked out and started a controversy over going out of the business of spare blades.

Tom: So now I'm the center of a controversy. Maybe I ought to look for some ideas that could improve my image with top management. According to the LP output (Table C-7) the market limit of 250 for the Rock Crusher model BS1 has been reached in the solution. I wonder if we could make more money if this market were larger? Should I recommend that Rockwell Stone undertake a marketing promotion for model BS1?

Sensitivity Analysis

As the conversation continued, Tom realized that there were many things that he would like to know about the LP recommendations. Sensitivity analysis is a method of analyzing a solution, and LP is one of a very few management science techniques where sensitivity analysis is directly available in the output. For example, the marketing promotion is an option that did not occur to Tom when formulating the LP. Sensitivity analysis is one way to decide whether the effort and expense of such a campaign would be justified.

In this section, sensitivity analysis is defined as changing one element of the problem and watching what happens to the optimal solution. Even with this one-at-a-time restriction, a rich variety of questions can be addressed. The following symbols are used to simplify the description:

$$X = \text{variables}$$
$$C = \text{objective function coefficients (one for each } X)$$
$$\text{RHS} = \text{constants on the right-hand side of the constraints}$$
$$Z = \text{value of the objective function}$$
$$Z^*, X^* = \text{optimal values of } Z \text{ and } X$$

The Sensitivity Game

Sensitivity analysis can be viewed as a game between a manager and an LP. First, the manager specifies a problem formulation and the LP solves it. Then the manager changes the problem. The LP's response is to find a new optimal solution. Sensitivity analysis is trying to anticipate the LP's next move. Becoming adept at this game allows one to answer many interesting questions with very little work.

As in chess, each player has a set of pieces to move. The manager's pieces are the coefficients of the model, such as the RHS and C values. The LP's pieces are the X values. *The manager is allowed to change only one parameter of the problem at each move, but the LP is allowed to change any or all of the variables in its response.*

The manager has two additional moves that can be very powerful—add a new constraint or a new variable to the formulation. However, LP's ability to modify all the variables at once allows it to make very complex responses that are difficult to anticipate.

The object of the game for the LP is to maintain the best solution possible (either the highest or lowest Z^*). The manager has many goals, and plays the game to get a solution that satisfies them as well as possible. Among the manager's goals are testing different opportunities, such as changes in selling prices or marketing campaigns to increase demand. Playing the sensitivity game allows the manager to evaluate the marginal benefits or costs of future plans. Of particular interest is the opportunity cost associated with an action (or lack of action).

Shadow Prices and Opportunity Costs

Profits and losses are usually given by the optimal objective function value Z^*. An opportunity cost is a potential improvement in Z^* if management were able to ease one of the restrictions. Linear programs give a great deal of information about opportunity costs, but it is usually disguised under jargon adopted years ago. DUAL PRICE and REDUCED COST are examples. A generic term for this concept is shadow price.

> The shadow price *is the* net *rate of change of* Z^* *in response to a change in the formulation. Shadow prices are opportunity costs.*

The word *net* is emphasized as a reminder that the LP is allowed to change all X values in order to achieve a new Z^*. This section is devoted to finding shadow prices in the LP output and learning how to apply them to managerial problems.

Modifying Constraints

Tom spent the first part of the meeting explaining the LP formulation (Table C-6) to Dean. Then they began to work on questions concerning the solution (Table C-7).

Dean: The LP said to produce 250 BS1 rock crushers. More production is impossible because of the market constraint of 250 (row 14 of Table C-6). The way I look at it, your idea of expanding the market for BS1 should be of interest since the LP recommends making as much as the market will bear. But your model has other restrictions. For example, the supply of raw material RM1 is restricted to 750,000 units (row 18). Which would be more profitable, promoting BS1 sales or buying additional RM1?

Tom: I think we can solve this one quickly. The LP output (Table C-7) shows no slack in row 14 and a slack of 697,250 in row 18. Since there are tons of RM1 left over, we surely don't want to recommend buying more right now. My textbook calls this the principle of *complementary slackness:*

Principle 1. *Constraints that have slack in the optimal solution must have zero shadow prices. And constraints with nonzero shadow prices must have zero slack.* A constraint with zero slack is called a *binding constraint.*

Dean: Yes, I agree with that. But how do we decide whether to go for more BS1 sales? How much more profit can be generated?

Tom: There are several ways to find opportunity costs in LP. Here's the way for constraints:

Principle 2. *DUAL PRICES are shadow prices for the constraints.*

The DUAL PRICE for row 14 is 146.20 in the output, so that is the opportunity cost of this market limit. Additional sales of BS1 would increase profits at a rate of up to $146.20 per unit sold. The cost of the promotion would have to be paid for from this increase.

Dean: Some of the DUAL PRICES are negative. Does this indicate that profits decrease?

Tom: Yes. But there is a way to tell whether a given change is going to be bad or good without getting confused by the signs of the shadow prices.

Principle 3. *Changes that reduce the size of the feasible region cannot be favorable. Changes that increase the feasible region cannot be harmful.* The feasible region becomes smaller if you reduce the RHS of a $\leq$ constraint or increase the RHS of a $\geq$ constraint.

It helps to reflect on the graphs in Section C-1. If part of the feasible region is chopped off by moving a constraint, there are two possibilities. If the optimal solution was in the portion chopped off, the LP is forced to find a new solution in the smaller feasible region. And it must choose one that it had previously rejected! Thus, whether minimizing or maximizing, the solution will be worse than before. The other possibility is that the chopped-off segment does not contain the optimal solution. Having escaped the hatchet, the previous solution remains optimal. The only way that an improved solution can be found is if new area is added to the feasible region.

Dean: It think I get it. Adding BS1 demand would give the LP more choices. The LP could still choose 250 if that were optimal, so adding demand can't hurt. So the shadow price of increasing demand must represent higher profit or lower cost. But how far can we increase sales at a unit gain of $146.20?

Principle 4. *Z^* changes linearly as a RHS value is changed within a limited range.* The RIGHT-HAND-SIDE RANGES section of the output shows these limits. The shadow price indicates the rate of change.

Tom: For the BS1 market (row 14) the ALLOWED INCREASE is 20. Therefore, the first 20 units (or less) of additional demand will increase profits by $146.20 per unit.

Dean: I see that the ALLOWED DECREASE is 4.17. Does this mean that the first 4.17 BS1 sales lost to competitors would reduce profit at a rate of $146.20?

Tom: Yes. The opportunity cost of a constraint is the same in both directions. The only difference is that profits go up if sales increase, and down if sales decrease.

Dean: But what if the change exceeds the range?

Tom: It turns out that we can always hedge our bets. Even though the shadow price is not valid beyond the range, a limit can be given:

Principle 5. *If the shadow price indicates that a RHS change is favorable within the specified range, it is less favorable beyond. Or, if it is unfavorable, going beyond the range makes it worse.*

So if the promotion would increase demand by 30 units, profits would increase by *no more than* $(146.2)(30) = 4386$. If that is not high enough to justify the effort, no more analysis is needed. But if 4286 is more than the cost of the promotion, we would want to run the LP again with a higher BS1 market limit to see how much profits actually increase.

Dean: So the shadow price is an optimistic estimate. Is that always true? It seems pretty risky to assume that one rule applies in every situation.

Tom: It always applies in LP problems. The reasoning behind principle 5 is as follows. In the sensitivity game, LP attains the best possible response to management's move. Available resources and production quantities of all the products are juggled until the best way to produce more BS1 within the given constraints is found. Therefore, 146.2 is the highest return that can be attained on additional sales of BS1. At the end of the range, LP has exhausted the optimal strategy it was using. To meet additional BS1 demand LP must use an inferior strategy, so returns will be lower.

Dean: Let me try to summarize what we have gone over. BS1's upper limit of 250 is binding; it is restricting the optimal solution and has no slack. Its shadow price (DUAL PRICE) of 146.2 is the opportunity cost of this limit as long as demand is between $250 - 4.17 = 245.83$ and $250 + 20 = 270$. Above 270, the shadow price is an upper limit on profits from additional demand. Below 245.83 the shadow price is a lower limit on lost profits.

Tom: That's right. You can also examine the limit on RM1 given in row 18 in the same way. Its DUAL PRICE is zero and its slack is 679,250. If you look at the range, you will see that this zero shadow price holds as long as there is slack.

Dean: Yes. That was your complementary slackness notion. When the slack is gone, there can be a shadow price. Right?

Tom: Right.

Modifying the Nonnegativity Constraints

Dean: Let's quit beating around the bush. What about spare crusher blades? The LP says to make none. How do I find the shadow price for changing that one? RM1 and BS1 were easy because they had upper limits in the constraints, so we just looked at the DUAL PRICES. But SPARE doesn't have a limit.

Tom: Actually, it does. It has a lower limit of zero, and that is binding.

Principle 6. *REDUCED COSTS are the shadow prices for the nonnegativity constraints.* Because the nonnegativity constraints are $\geqslant$, increasing them makes Z^* worse.

So, for every spare produced, profits will decrease by at least \$302. That's the REDUCED COST of SPARE in the output.

Dean: That doesn't seem correct. We sell them for \$3400 and that is supposed to cover the costs of materials and labor and still allow for a profit margin.

Tom: The \$3400 does not take into account the fact that some of the materials used to make spares might be needed for making something else that is more profitable. But the shadow price does take other products into account. The LP prices things according to their most profitable use. We can force production by adding a constraint such as SPARE $\geq$ 10, and the LP will recommend a different solution. It might even change all the production quantities. Whatever it does will squeeze out the highest possible profits, but they will still be lower by at least 302 per spare produced.

Dean: What about the range? How do we know how many spares could be produced at an opportunity cost of $302?

Tom: The output in Table C-7 does not give the range over which the REDUCED COST is valid. There is no good reason for this omission; it's a tradition. However, there is a range, and if SPARE is increased too far, the REDUCED COST changes in a way that is less favorable (principle 5). Since the LP is maximizing profits in this case, the loss per unit would increase if SPARE goes beyond the range.

The Two Meanings of a Shadow Price

Dean: OK, let's say that you are right; we would lose $302 per unit by producing spares. I have two reasons why we should produce them anyway. First, a loss of $302 is small compared to the price of $3400, and it's probably worth it to be able to offer the service. Second, if that's all it takes, I'll bet that we could get approval for a price increase so that sales cover costs. What would your LP say to that?

Tom: If the selling price of spares is increased more than $302, that would offset the opportunity cost and LP would recommend production. I can't tell you how many spares it would recommend, but the LP would no longer see it as a losing proposition. You can see in the output that the ALLOWED INCREASE in the OBJECTIVE COEFFICIENT is 302.

Dean: Yes, I see that in the table. So a new price of 3400 + 302 = $3702 would make SPARE break even.

Tom: That's right. The $302 has two meanings. It is the opportunity cost of forcing the LP to produce spares by adding a constraint, and it is also the price increase that would make it optimal to produce spares.

Dean: I understand that. It even makes sense. I would do the same. If someone offered to compensate me for my loss, I would be willing to go along with production of a financial loser. But what about the ALLOWED DECREASE column? Why does it say INFINITY?

Tom: It means that we can decrease the price as much as we want without changing the optimal solution. Cutting the selling price would only make spare blades less profitable, so the LP would still recommend against production.

Dean: That makes sense too. Now I want to follow up on the two meanings of REDUCED COSTS. You said that it is an opportunity cost of producing more spares than optimal, and it is also the price change that would make it optimal to produce more. Right?

Tom: Right.

Dean: Do all the shadow prices have two meanings? Take the DUAL PRICE of the BS1 market limit (row 14). Wait, let me try. Let's see. If the opportunity cost of increasing the RHS is $146.20, then that is the price I would pay to increase the market.

Tom: That is a good way to put it. Every shadow price has two meanings, one as an opportunity cost and the other as a price change. In the BS1 example, the price change applies to a variable that is not in the LP at the moment, namely a variable to represent demand generated by a promotion. If it were included, and its cost were less than $146.20, the LP would take advantage of it. If the cost exceeded $146.20, its optimal quantity would be zero. No promotion.

Modifying the Variables

Having learned how to evaluate changes in SPARE and BS1, it occurred to Dean that there may be a great opportunity for additional profit with the other major product, BS2. In the formulation, its net unit contribution of $46,000 is by far the highest of any product. Even so, its optimal production quantity is 100 units, which is 50 units less than its market limit in row 15. Unlike BS1, the market for BS2 has a zero opportunity cost (DUAL PRICE, row 15) because there are 50 units of slack in the constraint.

> *Dean:* Leaving 50 units of unmet demand in the BS2 market could be bad for the corporate image. Why is BS2 production below the market? What would happen if we increase it? In the table its REDUCED COST is zero. Does that mean that we can increase it at no cost?
>
> *Tom:* No. Remember principle 6. The REDUCED COST tells us what happens if the nonnegativity constraint BS2 $\geq$ 0 is increased. Since BS2 is already 100, nothing happens. That is why the REDUCED COST is zero.
>
> *Dean:* Then how can we evaluate an increase in BS2?
>
> *Tom:* Let's see what we can learn from the OBJECTIVE COEFFICIENT RANGES.

Principle 7. In maximization problems, increasing an objective coefficient C more than the ALLOWED INCREASE causes the corresponding X^* to increase; decreasing C more than ALLOWED DECREASE will reduce X^*. (In minimization problems, the opposite is true.) *Changes within*

> *the allowed range have no effect on the optimal quantities X^*. With-in the range, if dC is the change in C, then the change in Z^* is $(X^*)(dC)$, and the change in X^* is zero.*

The coefficient for BS2 is its selling price of \$46,000. If that goes up by more than the ALLOWED INCREASE of \$292.40, the LP will choose a new solution that has greater production of type 2 rock crushers.

Dean: I see what you are saying, but I can't for the life of me understand where that number came from.

Tom: It's not easy. That's one of the beauties of LP. It is always looking for the most profitable way to use the resources. It has evaluated other alternatives as well as the optimal solution. The \$292.40 comes from knowing the next-best alternative.

Graphically, changing one objective coefficient tilts the objective function. A small tilt has no effect on the choice of the optimal corner. The increase of 292.4 is just enough to make LP indifferent between the current solution and producing more BS2.

Dean: I guess I'll have to take your word for it. But I still want to know the same information about BS2 as we learned about SPARE. We lose \$302 per unit to produce SPARE, and the same \$302 could be added to the selling price to motivate the LP into producing spares. Does the same trick work for BS2?

Tom: Yes. The price changes in the OBJECTIVE COEFFICIENT RANGE section are also shadow prices. The optimal production of BS2 is 100. If we added a constraint such as BS2 $\geq$ 110, the extra 10 units would cost us at least \$292.40 each in lost profits. The LP would come back with a different optimal solution, and its objective function would be lower by 10 times \$292.40 or more.

Dean: So the \$292.40 does double duty. It is the opportunity cost of producing more BS2 than is optimal, and it is also the price change required to make it optimal to produce more BS2. Right?

Tom: Right. And all the other OBJECTIVE COEFFICIENT ALLOWED INCREASES and DECREASES have double meanings, too.

Dean: This opportunity cost must hold for a range of BS2 values, but I don't see the range in the output.

Tom: Some computer programs give you the range for this kind of sensitivity analysis. The one I used does not. So we have to hedge our bets using principle 5. That's why I said it would cost *at least* \$292.40 per unit.

Dean: You are telling me that all shadow prices are optimistic estimates of the opportunity cost if the range is exceeded.

Tom: That's right. It holds for DUAL PRICES, REDUCED COSTS, and the shadow prices we have just found in the OBJECTIVE COEFFICIENT RANGES.

Dean: What about decreasing BS2? If more BS2 costs $292.40 per unit, then if we produced less we would *gain* $292.40 per unit. Right?

Tom: No. The LP chose BS2 = 100 to maximize profits, so profits will drop whenever we impose a different solution.

Principle 8. *Forcing a variable away from its optimal quantity X* cannot improve Z*.*

Think of it this way. If the selling price drops by more than the ALLOWED DECREASE of $1083.40, the optimal BS2 production will decrease. Why does the price have to decrease so far to get a reduction in output? Because the last unit of BS2 generated a net profit of $1083.40. So that is the opportunity cost of decreasing production.

Dean: OK. The opportunity cost of increasing BS2 is $292.40 and the opportunity cost of decreasing it is $1083.40. And these same figures are the price changes that would make it optimal to increase or decrease BS2 production.

Tom: That's right.

Dean: Those numbers seem to be pulled out of a hat. How does the LP know that we would lose $1083.40 if we produce less BS2?

Tom: It figures out the best way to use the resources that would become available if BS2 production were reduced. The LP uses that information to find the optimal solution in the first place, so pricing out a change is very easy. My textbook summarizes it this way:

Principle 9. *The shadow price for a new constraint to change X* is numerically equal to the OBJECTIVE COEFFICIENT ALLOWED INCREASE or DECREASE that would encourage a change in the same direction. (Or the opportunity cost of a forced change is the same as the price adjustment needed to motivate the change.)*

This is complicated enough to make it worthwhile to list the four cases to which it applies.

For maximization,

        shadow price for   OBJECTIVE COEFFICIENT
        new constraint   = ALLOWED
        increasing X*   INCREASE

shadow price for   OBJECTIVE COEFFICIENT
new constraint   = ALLOWED
decreasing X*   DECREASE

For minimization,

shadow price for   OBJECTIVE COEFFICIENT
new constraint   = ALLOWED
increasing X*   DECREASE

shadow price for   OBJECTIVE COEFFICIENT
new constraint   = ALLOWED
decreasing X*   INCREASE

And, in keeping with principle 8, each of these shadow prices represents a rate at which Z^* is *worsened*.

Dean: I'm trying to apply the same reasoning to the other product, BS1, but the table seems confusing. To find the price change that would cause an increase in BS1, I look at the OBJECTIVE COEFFICIENT ALLOWED INCREASE, but the table says that it is INFINITY. Is that really true?

Tom: When you see an INFINITY, it means that you are up against some problem constraint. Remember that for SPARE, there was no price decrease large enough to motivate less production because production was already zero. The nonnegativity constraint stops SPARE from going lower, regardless of price.

Dean: I get it. The market constraint for BS1 was 250 units (row 14 in Table C-6) and even an infinite price increase is not large enough to make LP violate that constraint.

Tom: That's right.

Dean: Now I've got you trapped. At the beginning of this meeting we decided that a promotion could increase the market for BS1, and the opportunity cost of not doing the promotion was the DUAL PRICE of $146.20. But now principle 9 tells me that the OBJECTIVE COEFFICIENT ALLOWED INCREASE is supposed to equal the opportunity cost, and that is INFINITY, not $146.20. How do you explain that?

Tom: That's a tough one. But there is an explanation. Sensitivity analysis assumes that we change only one part of the formulation at a time, and let LP do the rest. Principles 2, 3, and 4 assumed that we changed one RHS value. Row 14 was the one that affected BS1. Principle 7 assumes that we change one objective coefficient. The price of BS1 is an example.
    Principle 9 assumes that we add one new constraint such as BS2 ≥ 110, and leave all the original constraints as they are. But we cannot add a constraint to force BS1 above 250 without violating row 14.

Dean: I don't see what's so different. Can't we just add a constraint like BS1 ≥ 255 to get more BS1 production?

Tom: No. Not without changing the existing constraint, because BS1 cannot be both greater than 255 and less than 250 at the same time. That is why the opportunity cost of increasing BS1 is infinity. If you go above 250, *there is no solution.*

Dean: Your LP seems pretty simpleminded if it doesn't know that it must change the upper limit if a new constraint is added.

Tom: You are right; it is simpleminded in that respect. Some LP packages are more sophisticated in the way that upper limits are handled. But it really doesn't matter. The information we wanted about BS1 was there. We just had to remember to look in row 14 where the market limit was.

Thanks for your help. You have given me some ideas for my report. I am going to prepare cost trade-offs for spare blades, different levels of BS2 output, and for the idea of promoting BS1 sales.

Dean: Glad to help. While you are at it, why don't you look at the possibility of producing extra units of the part P1? I understand that there is a market for it, too.

Interpreting Equality Constraints

We have used a number from every section of Table C-7, and most of them have been used twice! However, the principles have not dealt with equality constraints. Principle 3 has warned us to expect shadow prices of opposite direction for ≥ constraints compared to ≤. It turns out that = constraints can have DUAL PRICES of either sign. How can we tell whether an increase in the RHS of an equality is good or bad?

In the formulation of Table C-6, rows 2 to 10 are the accounting constraints that tie together the products, components, parts, subassemblies, raw materials, and labor. In the solution of Table C-7, the SLACK is 0 for each of these rows; equalities have no slack!

Row 2 has a DUAL PRICE of −125.85. DUAL PRICE relates to changes in the RHS, so consider what it would mean if the RHS of row 2 were increased from 0 to 1. Then it would read

$$\text{Row 2:}\quad \text{P1} - 3\,\text{BS1} - 6\,\text{BS2} = 1$$

In English, production of part type 1 is now required to exceed the assembly requirements by 1 unit. Therefore, the DUAL PRICE of −125.85 is the opportunity cost of producing extra units of P1. If management wishes to have a supply of P1 for repairs, each unit produced would lower profits by 125.85. If they are sold as spare parts, the selling price should exceed $125.85 to cover costs.

In this example it was obvious that additional P1 must represent a cost rather than a profit since there is no provision in the formulation for selling it.

In other cases, it may not be so obvious whether a change will be advantageous or detrimental to the objective function.

Principle 10. *By convention, a positive DUAL PRICE represents an improvement to the objective function when the RHS is increased.* (This does not apply to REDUCED COSTS.)

Therefore, to be consistent with principle 3 the DUAL PRICE should be positive for $\leq$ and negative for $\geq$. If you ever encounter an output with the signs reversed for $\leq$ and $\geq$ DUAL PRICES, you can simply reverse the signs of all DUAL PRICES and use principle 10. Before applying a shadow price, it is always wise to examine what the change means, as in the preceding example.

Summary

The Rockwell Stone example has illustrated that a large number of relevant management issues can be addressed through LP. With a good understanding of the output a great deal of work can be saved. The shadow prices may be used as opportunity costs to evaluate changes in the formulation such as increased demand or decreased supply of material. Even beyond their valid ranges, the shadow prices can be used to obtain limits on the change in Z^*.

Opportunity costs associated with the restrictions of the problem are called shadow prices. Shadow prices represent the rate of change of the optimal objective function value Z^*. Ignoring the signs, DUAL PRICES are shadow prices for changing the RHS values, and REDUCED COSTS are shadow prices for the nonnegativity constraints.

A RHS value usually represents some resource that is in limited supply or a goal that management has set. The shadow price evaluates the opportunity cost of staying within the constraint and at the same time is an upper limit on how much management should be willing to pay to relax the constraint.

The nonnegativity constraints affect only the variables that have an optimal value of zero. Their shadow prices tell us how much the objective function value will be damaged by introducing a nonoptimal variable into the solution. At the same time, the shadow price equals the change in the objective coefficient that would make it optimal to bring that variable into the solution.

Changing a RHS value affects Z^* and X^* linearly over a range. Changes in one direction improve Z^* and the other direction makes Z^* worse. The same shadow price applies to both directions. This is also true for the nonnegativity constraints, although the ranges are not given in the output.

A constraint can be added to the formulation to force a variable X to move away from its optimal value X^*. Either increasing or decreasing X leads to *worse* values for Z^* (lower if maximizing, higher if minimizing). The shadow price for increasing X is different than for decreasing it. The ranges are not given in the LP output shown in this text.

In every case, if a change goes beyond the range where the shadow price is valid, the shadow price provides an overoptimistic estimate of the effect on Z^*.

The objective coefficients C can vary over a range given in the output without affecting X^* at all. Beyond the range, X^* will change in the direction that is motivated by the change in C. For example, to increase a particular X^*, we could increase its profit (or decrease its cost) by more than the allowable change.

Commercially available LP packages allow one to design the output to suit the application. This is particularly important because many applications are so large that output such as Table C-7 would be voluminous. As with any aid to decision making, the report should be designed to present the most relevant material only and in a format that is easy to understand. As you may have gathered from this discussion, that may not be an easy task.

Review Problems

1. Interpret the output in Table C-7 for row 12.

2. What would happen to the solution if the cost of labor were to decrease by 0.5? 2.0?

3. The LP recommended that Rockwell Stone purchase 450 units of subassembly SA1, which is all of the available supply. If additional units of SA1 are available from another source, how much would we be willing to pay, and how many units would we buy at that price? What would we do with them?

4. Rockwell is considering putting some of the 450 SA1 units aside for sale as spare parts. Use the shadow price of row 6 to determine how much this will cost.

5. Use principle 9 to find the cost per unit of decreasing SA1 from its optimal purchase quantity. Why is this answer different from that for Review Problem 4?

Solutions

1. Row 12 is a lower limit of 300 on production of rock crushers. It is the only $\geq$ constraint in the formulation (other than the nonnegativity constraints). The entry 50 in the SLACK/SURPLUS column means that the limit of 300 in row 12 is exceeded by 50 units. The DUAL PRICE is zero over a range determined by the SURPLUS.

2. If the objective coefficient of LABOR is between $-8.5 - 52.21 = -60.71$ and $-8.5 + 1.1 = -7.4$, there will be no change in the production quantities. Lowering costs by 0.5 changes the coefficient to -8.0, which is within this range, so X^* does not change. However, LABOR = 5110, so lowering its unit cost by 0.5 would increase net contribution by $(0.5)(5110) = 2555$.
   If the labor cost decreases by 2.0, its objective coefficient falls outside the range, so a new solution will result, using more LABOR.

3. The limit of 450 units for SA1 is given in row 17. The Dual Price is $541.70,

which is valid if the available quantity increases by 2.05 units or less. However, the objective function includes the current purchase price of $3150, so we would be willing to pay up to $3150 + $541.70 or $3691.70 per unit for 2 additional units of SA1. These units would be used to increase production of BS2 rock crushers, since BS1 is already at its upper limit of 250.

4. Increasing the RHS of row 6 would mean that more units of SA1 are to be purchased than are used for assembly. The difference can be set aside for sale as spares (or for any other use). Row 6 of Table C-7 indicates that the objective function will decrease by $3691.70 per unit for the first 100 units that are set aside in this way. The reason for the decrease is that there will be less production of rock crushers if some of the SA1s are set aside. (Note that this is the same answer as problem 3.)

5. The shadow price of decreasing SA1 is the OBJECTIVE FUNCTION ALLOWED DECREASE = 541.70. In this case, we save (avoid) the purchase cost of $3150, which is not true in problem 3.

   In contrast (as we saw in Review Problems 3 and 4) the row 6 shadow price allows SA1 production to differ from requirements for rock crusher assembly. The decreased RHS represents SA1 that we use but do not produce. The Review Problem 4 shadow price is the saving in production cost by obtaining SA1 elsewhere.

CASELET: RED BRAND CANNERS[2]

One Monday morning, Mr. Mitchell Gordon, vice-president of operations, asked the controller, the sales manager, and the production manager to meet with him to discuss the amount of tomato products to pack that season. The tomato crop, which had been purchased at planting, was beginning to arrive at the cannery, and packing operations would have to be started by the following Monday. Red Brand Canners was a medium-sized company which canned and distributed a variety of fruit and vegetable products under private brands in the western states.

Mr. William Cooper, the controller, and Mr. Charles Myers, the sales manager, were the first to arrive in Mr. Gordon's office. Dan Tucker, the production manager, came in a few minutes later and said that he had picked up Produce Inspection's latest estimate of the quality of the incoming tomatoes. According to their report, about 20% of the crop was grade A quality and the remaining portion of the 3,000,000-pound crop was grade B.

---

[2] Reprinted from *Stanford Business Cases 1977* with permission of the publishers, Stanford University Graduate School of Business, © 1977 and by the Board of Trustees of the Leland Stanford Junior University.

Gordon asked Myers about the demand for tomato products for the coming year. Myers replied that they could sell all of the whole canned tomatoes they could produce. The expected demand for tomato juice and tomato paste, on the other hand, was limited. The sales manager then passed around the latest demand forecast, which is shown in Exhibit 1. He reminded the group that the selling prices had been set in light of the long-term marketing strategy of the company, and potential sales had been forecasted at these prices.

Bill Cooper, after looking at Myers' estimates of demand, said that it looked like the company "should do quite well (on the tomato crop) this year." With the new accounting system that had been set up, he had been able to compute the contribution for each product, and according to his analysis the incremental profit on the whole tomatoes was greater than for any other tomato product. In May, after Red Brand had signed contracts agreeing to purchase the grower's production at an average delivered price of 6 cents per pound, Cooper had computed the tomato products' contributions (see Exhibit 2).

Dan Tucker brought to Cooper's attention that although there was ample production capacity, it was impossible to produce all whole tomatoes, as too small a portion of the tomato crop was grade A quality. Red Brand used a numerical scale to record the quality of both raw produce and prepared products. This scale ran from zero to ten, the higher number representing better quality. Rating tomatoes according to this scale, grade A tomatoes averaged nine points per pound and grade B tomatoes averaged five points per pound. Tucker noted that the minimum average input quality for canned whole tomatoes was eight and for juice it was six points per pound. Paste could be made entirely from grade B tomatoes. This quality-point requirement meant that whole tomato production was limited to 800,000 pounds.

Gordon stated that this was not a real limitation. He had been recently solicited to purchase 80,000 pounds of grade A tomatoes at $8\frac{1}{2}$ cents per pound and at that time had turned down the offer. He felt, however, that the tomatoes were still available.

Myers, who had been doing some calculations, said that although he agreed that the company "should do quite well this year," it would not be canning whole tomatoes. It seemed to him that the tomato cost should be allocated on the basis of quality and quantity rather than by quantity only as Cooper had done. Therefore, he had recomputed the marginal profit on this basis (see Exhibit 3), and from his results, Red Brand should use 2,000,000 pounds of grade B tomatoes for paste, and the remaining 400,000 pounds of grade B tomatoes and all the grade A tomatoes for juice. If the demand expectations were realized, a contribution of $48,000 would be made on this year's tomato crop.

Required

1. Check Myers' production plan to see if his $48,000 figure is correct.
2. Formulate an LP that allocates the 3 million pound crop to the three products.
3. The objective is to maximize profits. Decide on objective function coefficients based on cost accounting principles, keeping in mind Cooper's and Meyers' cost-allocation schemes.
4. Solve the LP if you have a computer package available.
5. Whether or not you solve the LP, discuss how LP can help them to decide on the option for 80,000 more grade A tomatoes.

EXHIBIT 1 SALES DATA

Product	Selling Price per Case	Demand Forecast (Cases)
Whole tomatoes	$4.00	800,000
Tomato juice	4.50	50,000
Tomato paste	3.80	80,000

EXHIBIT 2 PRODUCT ITEM PROFITABILITY (PER CASE)

Product	Whole Tomatoes	Tomato Juice	Tomato Paste
Selling price	$4.00	$4.50	$3.80
Variable costs			
Direct labor	1.18	1.32	0.54
Variable OHD	0.24	0.36	0.26
Variable selling	0.40	0.85	0.38
Packaging material	0.70	0.65	0.77
Fruit	1.08	1.20	1.50
Total variable costs	3.60	4.38	3.45
Contribution	0.40	0.12	0.35
Less allocated OHD	0.28	0.21	0.23
Net profit	0.12	(0.09)	0.12

Product usage is as given below:

Product	Pounds per Case
Whole tomatoes	18
Tomato juice	20
Tomato paste	25

EXHIBIT 3 MARGINAL ANALYSIS OF TOMATO PRODUCTS

Z = cost per pound of grade A tomatoes in cents

Y = cost per pound of grade B tomatoes in cents

(1) $(600{,}000 \text{ lb} \times Z) + (2{,}400{,}000 \text{ lb} \times Y)$
     $= (3{,}000{,}000 \text{ lb} \times 6 \text{ cents/lb})$

(2) $\dfrac{Z}{9} = \dfrac{Y}{5}$

Z = 9.32 cents per pound

Y = 5.18 cents per pound

Product	Canned Whole Tomatoes	Tomato Juice	Tomato Paste
Selling price	$4.00	$4.50	$3.80
Variable cost (excluding tomato costs)	2.52	3.18	1.95
	$1.48	$1.32	$1.85
Tomato cost	1.49	1.24	1.30
Marginal profit	($0.01)	$0.08	$0.55

PROBLEMS

*1. Consider the following LP:

$$\text{minimize} \quad X_1 + X_2$$
$$\text{subject to (2):} \quad X_1 + 2X_2 \leq 12$$
$$(3): \quad 2X_1 + X_2 \leq 10$$
$$(4): \quad X_1 + 3X_2 \geq 4$$
$$(5): \quad 3X_1 + X_2 \geq 5$$

(a) Check each of the following solutions for feasibility. (Are the constraints satisfied?)

Solution 1: $X_1 = 0$ $X_2 = 0$ Solution 5: $X_1 = 5$ $X_2 = 0$

Solution 2: $X_1 = 0$ $X_2 = 5$ Solution 6: $X_1 = 1$ $X_2 = 1$

Solution 3: $X_1 = 0$ $X_2 = 6$ Solution 7: $X_1 = 2$ $X_2 = 2$

Solution 4: $X_1 = 4$ $X_2 = 0$ Solution 8: $X_1 = 4$ $X_2 = 4$

(b) Find the objective function value for each of the feasible solutions shown above.

(c) Plot constraints (2) to (5) on a graph similar to Figure C-1. Be sure to include the arrows to indicate which side of each line satisfies the inequality.

(d) Plot the points from part (a), and verify your answer to (a).

(e) Plot the objective function for the two values $X_1 + X_2 = 1$ and $X_1 + X_2 = 10$. Then find the optimal solution, remembering that this is a minimization problem.

2. Consider the LP in Problem 1.
   (a) Insert slack and/or surplus variables to convert all constraints to equalities.
   (b) Calculate the quantities of each slack and/or surplus variable for each solution given in part (a) of Problem 1.
   (c) Is it true that a negative value of a slack or surplus variable occurs if and only if an inequality constraint is violated? Show how you know.

*3. Consider the following LP:

$$\text{maximize} \quad 2X_1 + 2X_2$$

$$\text{subject to (2):} \quad 2X_1 + X_2 \leqslant 20$$

$$\text{(3):} \quad X_1 + X_2 \leqslant 12$$

$$\text{(4):} \quad X_1 + 2X_2 \leqslant 20$$

   (a) Check the following solutions for feasibility and give their objective function values: $X_1 = 8$, $X_2 = 4$; $X_1 = 6$, $X_2 = 6$; and $X_1 = 4$, $X_2 = 8$.
   (b) What two properties do all these solutions have in common?
   (c) Graph the constraints, plot the three points from part (a), and plot the objective function at $2X_1 + 2X_2 = 30$.
   (d) Verify that all three solutions from part (a) are optimal.
   (e) If you had the final tableau from a simplex solution to this problem, how would you know that more than one optimal solution exists?

4. (a) Solve the following LP graphically:

$$\text{maximize} \ N + M$$

$$\text{subject to (2):} \quad 2N + 0.5M \leqslant 200$$

$$\text{(3):} \quad N + M \leqslant 200$$

$$\text{(4):} \quad 0.05N + 0.25M \leqslant 20$$

   (b) Identify which of the constraints can be changed with no effect on the optimal solution.
   (c) Change the right-hand-side for (2) to 220 and estimate the amount of change in the objective function.

5. Consider the following LP:

$$\text{maximize} \quad 10X_1 + 9X_2$$

$$\text{subject to (2):} \quad 0.7X_1 + X_2 \leqslant 630$$

$$\text{(3):} \quad 3X_1 + 5X_2 \leqslant 3600$$

$$\text{(4):} \quad 3X_1 + 2X_2 \leqslant 2124$$

$$\text{(5):} \quad X_1 + 2.5X_2 \leqslant 1350$$

   (a) Solve this LP graphically.

   (b) Include, as constraint (6), $X_1 + X_2 \geq 1000$ on your graph and comment
       on the impossible situation in which you find yourself.
6. Below is the computer output and a graph of a two-variable LP that minimizes
   a cost function. The purpose of this problem is to see how the sensitivity
   analysis looks on a graph.
   (a) The optimal objective function value (cost) is 2.5. Plot the objective
       function equation $X + 4Y = 2.5$. What X and Y are optimal?
   (b) The ALLOWED INCREASE of the objective coefficient of X is 2.2,
       which would increase the unit cost of X from 1.0 (now) to 3.2. The
       objective function value would be $3.2(2.5) + 4(0) = 8.0$ for the current
       X and Y solution. Plot the new objective function $3.2X + 4Y = 8$.
       What X and Y are optimal? What would happen if the coefficient of X
       were 3.21? (No need to plot.) Explain what the ALLOWED INCREASE
       $= 2.2$ means based on this exercise.
   (c) Instead of changing the objective coefficients, how else could we force
       the solution $X = \frac{5}{6}$ to be optimal by adding a $\leq$ constraint? What would
       the objective function value be? Based on this, compute the opportunity
       cost per unit change in X. Compare your answer to part (b) and comment
       on principle 9 of Section C-4.

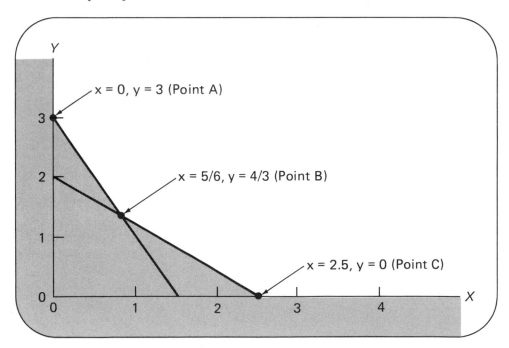

(d) Ignoring parts (b) and (c), consider decreasing the RHS of row 3. Use principle 3 of Section C-4 to predict whether this will be good or bad. According to the output, what effect will this have? Over what range?

(e) Add the constraint $4X + 5Y \geqslant 9$ to the graph and compute the new optimal solution. How much has it changed per unit change in RHS? Compare to part (d).

(f) Repeat part (e) for a RHS of 4 and use your results to comment on principle 5 in Section C-4.

(g) Without computation (and ignoring the foregoing) explain what would happen if we forced Y to increase by imposing a constraint such as $Y \geqslant 1$. What would happen to cost (quantitative)? What would happen to X (qualitative, referring to the graph)?

(h) Using the same approach as part (g), explain what happens if the RHS of row 2 is increased.

$$\text{MIN} \qquad X + 4Y$$
$$\text{SUBJECT TO}$$
$$(2) \quad 2X + Y \geqslant 3$$
$$(3) \quad 4X + 5Y \geqslant 10$$

OBJECTIVE FUNCTION VALUE = 2.5

OBJECTIVE COEFFICIENT RANGES

VARIABLE	SOLUTION	REDUCED COST	CURRENT COEF.	ALLOWED INCREASE	ALLOWED DECREASE
X	2.50	0.00	1.00	2.20	1.00
Y	0.00	2.75	4.00	INFINITY	2.75

RIGHT-HAND-SIDE RANGES

ROW	SLACK/ SURPLUS	DUAL PRICES	CURRENT RHS	ALLOWED INCREASE	ALLOWED DECREASE
2.	2.00	0.00	3.00	2.00	INFINITY
3.	0.00	−0.25	10.00	INFINITY	4.00

---

*7. Consider the following LP:

$$\text{maximize} \quad 10X_1 + 9X_2$$
$$\text{subject to (2):} \quad 0.7X_1 + X_2 \leqslant 630$$
$$(3): \quad X_1 + 5X_2 \leqslant 3600$$
$$(4): \quad 3X_1 + 2X_2 \leqslant 2124$$
$$(5): \quad X_1 + 2.5X_2 \leqslant 1350$$

We are going to evaluate a particular basic solution to see whether it is feasible, and whether it is optimal.

(a) Change all constraints to equalities by inserting slack and/or surplus variables. Call them S_1, S_2, S_3, and S_4.

(b) Write a tableau for this problem.

(c) Interpret the solution implied by the tableau.

(d) What are the quantities of the nonbasic variables?

(e) Is the solution feasible?

(f) Is it optimal?

(g) Would it be optimal if the objective were minimization?

8. Problem 7 should be done before this one. All equation numbers refer to the LP developed in that problem, with slack variables having been added to each constraint. We are going to bring X_1 into the basis and eliminate S_1. This is not the choice that the simplex method would make, and we shall see why.

(a) Using X_1 as the entering variable and S_1 as the departing variable, carry out simplex step 3 on the objective function and row 2.

(b) Is the simplex criterion for optimality satisfied?

(c) What are the quantities of X_1 and X_2 in this solution?

(d) Substitute your answer from part (c) into the original LP equations and explain why this is not the optimal solution to the LP.

(e) What should the departing variable have been instead of S_1?

*9. Use the simplex method to show that the optimal solution to the LP in Problem 7 is $X_1 = 540$, $X_2 = 252$. (Note that this exercise is solved graphically in Problem 5.)

10. Solve the following LP using the simplex method. (This is identical to the problem solved graphically in Problem 4.)

$$\text{Objective function:} \quad N + M \text{ (to maximize)}$$
$$\text{Constraints:} \quad 2N + 0.5M + SP = 200$$
$$N + M + SC = 200$$
$$0.05N + 0.25M + ST = 20$$

11. Use the simplex method to solve the minimization LP in Problem 6.

*12. Blizzard's Clam Chowder comes in two varieties. New England and Manhattan. The ingredients are as follows for 1 liter of soup.
New England: 2 potatoes, one clam, 0.85 liter water, 0.05 liter tomato sauce.
Manhattan: 0.5 potato, one clam, 0.65 liter water, 0.25 liter tomato sauce. Clams cost $0.10 each, tomato costs $0.60 per liter, potatoes cost $0.03 each, and water is so cheap that we can ignore it in this problem. At Blizzard, the current stocks of ingredients are 200,000 potatoes, 200,000 clams, 20,000 liters of tomato sauce, and unlimited water. The two varieties

of soup sell for the same price and their current stock will not saturate the markets.

(a) Make up a one-letter symbol for each ingredient and each product. Define them carefully in words.

(b) Write the constraints that account for the ingredients used.

(c) Test your constraints in part (b) using the quantities of ingredients for 1 liter of New England and 1 liter of Manhattan.

(d) If Blizzard was planning a production run of New England Chowder only, how many liters could they make using only the current stock of ingredients? Which ingredients will be left over?

(e) Answer part (d) for a run of Manhattan Chowder, assuming that no New England Chowder is made.

(f) Assuming that all leftover ingredients must be discarded, how could Blizzard get the most profit out of their current stock without purchasing additional ingredients? (Formulate an LP to help them with this decision, but do not solve it.)

*13. (This problem requires data from, but not a solution to, Problem 12.) The management of Blizzard's Clam Chowder Company found the linear program approach interesting, but it did not solve their real problem. They plan production on a quarterly basis. At the end of each quarter, any leftover soup is deducted from the demand forecast for the next quarter. Then production plans and purchasing decisions are made based on not allowing production to exceed the modified demand forecast. Current prices and current inventories of ingredients left from the previous period also enter the decision. However, these plans are never precisely carried out because Blizzard procures the ingredients by contracting to purchase the entire harvest (of potatoes, clams or tomatoes) from farmers and clammers in the region, and the delivered quantities usually vary from expectations. Furthermore, production plans are modified whenever the demand deviates significantly from the forecast. As a consequence, it is not uncommon to have leftover ingredients and/or leftover soup as the new planning period approaches. Leftover ingredients are treated as free (no cost) resources in their quarterly plan.

   The clam chowder demand forecast for the upcoming quarter is 500,000 liters of New England and 450,000 liters of Manhattan, to sell at $1.05 and $1.00 per liter, respectively. Data on ingredient prices and stocks are given in Problem 12. There are 50,000 liters of leftover Manhattan and no leftover New England Clam Chowder.

(a) In an LP formulation for clam chowder production planning, why is it important to use a different variable for potatoes to be purchased than for potatoes to be used from current stocks?

(b) Carefully define the variables for this problem, making up a one- or two-letter symbol for each one.

(c) Write the constraints and state them in words.

(d) What objective function should be used? Why? Formulate and explain it.

(e) Categorize each constraint as either accounting, fact of life, or policy (see Section C-3) and discuss briefly.

(f) There is an obvious optimal solution to this problem. Can you find it? Explain.

14. (This problem requires a solution to Problem 13.) At a meeting of all the management personnel of Blizzard's Clam Chowder Company, the purchasing manager pointed out that the company cannot obtain unlimited supplies of potatoes at $0.03 each. Often they will have to go as high as $0.04 or $0.05 to obtain the required quantities. In the upcoming quarter, it is estimated (a very rough guess) that up to 150,000 potatoes can be obtain at $0.03, and an additional 300,000 potatoes will be available at $0.05.

(a) As the inventor of the LP in Problem 13, explain how you could incorporate this consideration in your formulation. [*Hint:* Consider your answer to part (a) of Problem 13, treating the $0.03 potatoes as a limited resource.]

(b) If all ingredients had nonlinear prices and limited quantities, why may the solution "produce enough to satisfy all demand" not be optimal?

*15. The Acme Company has three plants and four warehouses. The following data have been obtained for aggregate planning for the coming quarter; all figures are in units of one thousand.

Plant	Unit Production Cost	Plant Capacity	Warehouse	Demand
A	$1.00	1200	1	700
B	$1.20	1200	2	400
C	$0.90	500	3	600
			4	500

UNIT TRANSPORTATION COST

To: From:	1	2	3	4
A	0.10	0.15	0.40	0.30
B	0.50	0.20	0.25	0.20
C	0.25	0.45	0.30	0.25

Average selling price = $1.50 thousand at all warehouses.

(a) Suppose that the objective is to minimize cost, with upper limits on production due to the plant capacities, and upper limits on amounts shipped so that each warehouse receives no more than the expected demand. Explain why the optimal solution to that problem is zero— produce nothing. How should the demand constraints be stated to prevent this from happening?

(b) Suppose that the objective is to maximize contribution to fixed cost and profit. What kind of constraint should be used to relate demand to production: equality, upper limit, or lower limit? Explain.

(c) Formulate this problem as an LP to maximize contribution, using the variables A1, A2, and so on, to represent the quantities produced at plant A and shipped to warehouse 1 and warehouse 2, and so on for all 12 combinations of plant-to-warehouse shipments.

(d) The company does not wish to spend more than $400,000 on transportation. Incorporate this budget in your LP.

(e) Up to 50,000 units of additional capacity are available at plant location C at an additional cost of $0.05 per unit actually used. Modify your LP to allow it to choose whether or not to use the additional capacity.

16. The SFWP corporation produces 500 different products. One area of their operation consists of four departments: stamping, forming, welding, and painting. These four departments are referred to in the company as Group 42. Three different products are produced in Group 42, and the company is interested in reevaluating the production mix. Their aggregate production plan has set upper limits on the production rate in these departments by specifying the number of employees and not allowing any extra shifts or overtime during the current month. However, the demands for these items, as estimated from sales trends, are increasing.

(a) Formulate an LP to recommend the daily production of each item, using the data in the accompanying tables.

(b) Management is considering shifting some workers between departments in Group 42. How could the LP output be used to help decide on where exchanges would be desirable? [Not a new LP, just the solution of the LP in part (a).]

(c) Would your answer for part (b) also hold for personnel exchanges between groups within the company? Explain.

TIME REQUIRED PER ITEM PRODUCED (SECONDS)

Item	Stamping	Forming	Welding	Painting	Marginal Contributions to Profit
A	6	15	10	10	$0.020
B	3	5	20	8	0.030
C	10	6	8	25	0.025

AVAILABLE MANPOWER (50 MINUTES PER HOUR, 8 HOURS PER SHIFT)

Department	Employees	Time Available (Seconds)
Stamping	1.5	36,000
Forming	2	48,000
Welding	2	48,000
Painting	2.5	60,000

17. Four kinds of grain are mixed for cattle feed, with the goal of maximizing net dollar gain per month, defined as value of the beef minus the cost of the feed. Certain nutrients must be held within prespecified allowances, some by law, and others for the health of the animals. Formulate an LP to recommend the proportions to be used in the feed mix, using the following data. A, B, and C are three nutrients.

Grain Types	Cost per Pound	NUTRIENT CONTENT (UNITS PER POUND)			Dollar Value of Weight Gain Contribution (per Pound of Feed)
		A	B	C	
1	$0.10	0.1	0.05	0.3	$2.00
2	0.20	0.6	0.01	0.2	3.00
3	0.25	0.4	0.2	0.1	5.00
4	0.30	0.5	0.03	0.1	7.00

Nutrients	Minimum Units per Pound of Feed Mix	Maximum Units per Pound of Feed Mix
A	0.3	None
B	None	0.1
C	0.2	0.25

*18. The Seemore Cement Company makes two grades of cement. Each grade has a minimum production quantity to satisfy a contract they have with Smidt Builders. The minimums are 5000 tons of grade A and 4000 of grade B. Each ton of grade A is composed of 0.5 ton of ingredient 1, 0.3 ton of ingredient 2, and 0.2 ton of ingredient 3. The composition of grade B is 0.4, 0.2, and 0.4 of ingredients 1, 2, and 3. Each ton of grade A sells for $200 and costs $20 to manufacture, exclusive of raw materials. Grade B also costs $20 to manufacture, but sells for $170 per ton. Cement ingredients 1 and 3 are available in unlimited quantity, but 2 is available only up to 15,000 tons.
  (a) Formulate an LP with the information given above. Be sure to define your variables.
  (b) This LP formulation is incomplete. What information would be needed to complete it?
  (c) Using either numbers (you make them up) or letters (math symbols) complete the formulation.

19. A farm family owns 100 acres of land and has $15,000 in funds available for investment. Its members can produce a total of 3500 worker-hours worth of labor during the winter months and 4000 worker-hours during the summer. If any of these worker-hours are not needed, younger members of the family will use them to work on a neighboring farm for $3.80 per hour during the winter months and $4.10 per hour during the summer.

Cash income may be obtained from three crops and two types of livestock: dairy cows and laying hens. No investment funds are needed for the crops. However, each cow will require an investment outlay of $400 and each hen will require $3. Each cow will require 1.5 acres of land, 100 worker-hours of work during the winter months, and another 50 worker-hours during the summer (i.e., 150 for the year total). Each cow will produce a net annual cash income of $400 for the family. The corresponding figures for each hen are: no acreage, 0.6 worker-hour during the winter, 0.3 more worker-hour during the summer (0.9 total for the year), and an annual net cash income of $2. The chicken house can accommodate a maximum of 3000 hens, and the size of the barn limits the herd to a maximum of 32 cows.

Estimated worker-hours and income per acre planted in each of the three crops are as follows:

	Soybeans	Corn	Oats
Winter worker-hours	20	35	10
Summer worker-hours	50	75	40
Net annual cash income ($)	175	300	120

The family wishes to determine how much acreage should be planted in each of the crops and how many cows and hens should be kept to maximize its net cash income.

(a) Formulate an LP to help them with this problem.

(b) Based on the results of your LP (if the output were available), how could they decide whether to consider expansion of the cow barn?

(c) What advice could you give them based on the shadow price of the constraint on available land?

*20. The table on the next page shows the solution to the Blizzard's Clam Chowder problem. (It is useful, but not necessary, to have done Problem 12 before this one. Data for this problem are described there.)

NENG = thousands of liters of New England Clam Chowder produced

MNHTN = thousands of liters of Manhattan Clam Chowder produced

(a) What is the optimal solution? How much of each ingredient is left over? (Notice that all variables are in thousands.)

(b) Suppose that 20,000 more potatoes were available at no cost. How much more soup could be produced?

(c) Repeat part (b) for 20,000 additional clams, and again for 20,000 liters of tomato sauce, each time assuming that only one ingredient is increased.

(d) Disregarding parts (b) and (c), suppose that a recount of the potato inventory yielded only 180,000. What should the change in total output be?

(e) Repeat part (d), assuming 200,000 potatoes and 180,000 clams, then 140,000 clams, then 70,000 clams.

(f) Ignoring parts (b) to (e), suppose that the market for New England Chowder will only allow sales of 50,000 liters. What will the optimal total production be, and how many liters of Manhattan does this imply?

(g) Ignoring parts (b) to (f), suppose that the selling price of New England is $1.05 per liter, compared to $1.00 for Manhattan. Is the solution in part (a) optimal? Explain.

MAX   NENG +   MNHTN
SUBJECT TO
(2)   2 NENG + 0.5 MNHTN ≤ 200   (potatoes)
(3)   NENG +   MNHTN ≤ 200   (clams)
(4)   0.05 NENG + 0.25 MNHTN ≤ 20   (tomato sauce)

OBJECTIVE FUNCTION VALUE = 147.37

OBJECTIVE COEFFICIENT RANGES

VARIABLE	SOLUTION	REDUCED COST	CURRENT COEF.	ALLOWED INCREASE	ALLOWED DECREASE
NENG	84.21	0	1.00	3.00	0.80
MNHTN	63.16	0	1.00	4.00	0.75

RIGHT-HAND-SIDE RANGES

ROW	SLACK/ SURPLUS	DUAL PRICES	CURRENT RHS	ALLOWED INCREASE	ALLOWED DECREASE
2.	0	0.421	200	125.00	160.00
3.	52.63	0	200	INFINITY	52.63
4.	0	3.158	20	16.67	15.00

21. (Problem 15 should be done prior to this one, although it is not absolutely necessary.) The table on the next page shows the solution to the Acme Company's production and distribution problem without considering the possibility of additional capacity at plant *C*.

(a) What is the optimal plant-to-warehouse distribution pattern?

(b) Are there any other optimal solutions? Explain.

(c) What is the net contribution for the quarter?

(d) Would a larger transportation budget allow higher net quarterly profits? Would that be a good investment? How much would you recommend adding to or deleting from the transportation budget?

(e) How much more profit would Acme obtain if capacity of plant *C* were expanded by 50 thousand units? Would this be a good opportunity if each unit of increased capacity cost $0.05 each quarter?

(f) The shipment of 700 units from plant *A* to warehouse 1 was criticized as being excessive. If A1 is forced to be smaller, will profits increase or decline? At what rate?

$$\text{MAX } .4\,A1 + .35\,A2 + .1\,A3 + .2\,A4 - .2\,B1 + .1\,B2$$
$$+ .05\,B3 + .1\,B4 + .35\,C1 + .15\,C2 + .3\,C3 + .35\,C4$$

SUBJECT TO		
$A1 + A2 + A3 + A4 \leq 1200$	(2)
$B1 + B2 + B3 + B4 \leq 1200$	(3)
$C1 + C2 + C3 + C4 \leq 500$	(4)
$A1 + B1 + C1 \leq 700$	(5)
$A2 + B2 + C2 \leq 400$	(6)
$A3 + B3 + C3 \leq 600$	(7)
$A4 + B4 + C4 \leq 500$	(8)

$$.1\,A1 + .15\,A2 + .4\,A3 + .3\,A4 + .5\,B1 + .2\,B2 \qquad (9)$$
$$+ .25\,B3 + .2\,B4 + .25\,C1 + .45\,C2 + .3\,C3 + .25\,C4 \leq 400$$

OBJECTIVE FUNCTION VALUE = 632

			OBJECTIVE COEFFICIENT RANGES		
VARIABLE	SOLUTION	REDUCED COST	CURRENT COEF.	ALLOWED INCREASE	ALLOWED DECREASE
A1	700	0	0.40	INFINITY	0.24
A2	400	0	0.35	INFINITY	0.18
A3	0	0.06	0.10	0.06	INFINITY
A4	100	0	0.20	0.18	0.06
B1	0	0.06	−0.20	0.60	INFINITY
B2	0	0.18	0.10	0.18	INFINITY
B3	40	0	0.05	0	0.05
B4	400	0	0.10	0.06	0
C1	0	0.24	0.35	0.24	INFINITY
C2	0	0.42	0.15	0.42	INFINITY
C3	500	0	0.30	INFINITY	0
C4	0	0	0.35	0	INFINITY

			RIGHT-HAND-SIDE RANGES		
ROW	SLACK/ SURPLUS	DUAL PRICES	CURRENT RHS	ALLOWED INCREASE	ALLOWED DECREASE
2.	0	0.080	1200	100.00	100
3.	760	0	1200	INFINITY	760
4.	0	0.240	500	33.33	300
5.	0	0.300	700	100.00	400
6.	0	0.240	400	100.00	300
7.	60	0	600	INFINITY	60
8.	0	0.060	500	50.00	75
9.	0	0.200	400	15.00	10

REFERENCES

DYCKMAN, T. R., AND L. J. THOMAS, *Algebra and Calculus for Business*. Englewood Cliffs, N.J.: Prentice-Hall, 1974.

EPPEN, G. D., AND F. J. GOULD, *Introductory Management Science*. Englewood Cliffs, N.J.: Prentice-Hall, 1984.

GEOFFRION, A. M., "The Purpose of Mathematical Programming Is Insight, Not Numbers." *Interfaces,* Vol. 7, No. 1 (1976), pp. 81–92.

HILLIER, F. S., AND G. J. LIEBERMAN, *Operations Research,* 3rd ed. San Francisco: Holden-Day, 1980.

SCHRAGE, L., *Linear Programming Models with LINDO*. Palo Alto, Calif.: Scientific Press, 1981.

WAGNER, H., *Principles of Operations Research,* 2nd ed. Englewood Cliffs, N.J.: Prentice-Hall, 1975.

APPENDIX D

Tables

TABLE 1   RANDOM NUMBERS

09 18 82 00 97	32 82 53 95 27	04 22 08 63 04	83 38 98 73 74	64 27 85 80 44
90 04 58 54 97	51 98 15 06 54	94 93 88 19 97	91 87 07 61 50	68 47 66 46 59
73 18 95 02 07	47 67 72 62 69	62 29 06 44 64	27 12 46 70 18	41 36 18 27 60
75 76 87 64 90	20 97 18 17 49	90 42 91 22 72	95 37 50 58 71	93 82 34 31 78
54 01 64 40 56	66 28 13 10 03	00 68 22 73 98	20 71 45 32 95	07 70 61 78 13
08 35 86 99 10	78 54 24 27 85	13 66 15 88 73	04 61 89 75 53	31 22 30 84 20
28 30 60 32 64	81 33 31 05 91	40 51 00 78 93	32 60 46 04 75	94 11 90 18 40
53 84 08 62 33	81 59 41 36 28	51 21 59 02 90	28 46 66 87 95	77 76 22 07 91
91 75 75 37 41	61 61 36 22 69	50 26 39 02 12	55 78 17 65 14	83 48 34 70 55
89 41 59 26 94	00 39 75 83 91	12 60 71 76 46	48 94 97 23 06	83 48 34 70 55
				94 54 13 74 08
77 51 30 38 20	86 83 42 99 01	68 41 48 27 74	51 90 81 39 80	72 89 35 55 07
19 50 23 71 74	69 97 92 02 88	55 21 02 97 73	74 28 77 52 51	65 34 46 74 15
21 81 85 93 13	93 27 88 17 57	05 68 67 31 56	07 08 28 50 46	31 85 33 84 52
51 47 46 64 99	68 10 72 36 21	94 04 99 13 45	42 83 60 91 91	08 00 74 54 49
99 55 96 83 31	62 53 52 41 70	69 77 71 28 30	74 81 97 81 42	43 86 07 28 34
33 71 34 80 07	93 58 47 28 69	51 92 66 47 21	58 30 32 98 22	93 17 49 39 72
85 27 48 68 93	11 30 32 92 70	28 83 43 41 37	73 51 59 04 00	71 14 84 36 43
84 13 38 96 40	44 03 55 21 66	73 85 27 00 91	61 22 26 05 61	62 32 71 84 23
56 73 21 62 34	17 39 59 61 31	10 12 39 16 22	85 49 65 75 60	81 60 41 88 80
65 13 85 68 06	87 64 88 52 61	34 31 36 58 61	45 87 52 10 69	85 64 44 72 77
38 00 10 21 76	81 71 91 17 11	71 60 29 29 37	74 21 96 40 49	65 58 44 96 98
37 40 29 63 97	01 30 47 75 86	56 27 11 00 86	47 32 46 26 05	40 03 03 74 38
97 12 54 03 48	87 08 33 14 17	21 81 53 92 50	75 23 76 20 47	15 50 12 95 78
21 82 64 11 34	47 14 33 40 72	64 63 88 59 02	49 13 90 64 41	03 85 65 45 52
73 13 54 27 42	95 71 90 90 35	85 79 47 42 96	08 78 98 81 56	64 69 11 92 02
07 63 87 79 29	03 06 11 80 72	96 20 74 41 56	23 82 19 95 38	04 71 36 69 94
60 52 88 34 41	07 95 41 98 14	59 17 52 06 95	05 53 35 21 39	61 21 20 64 55
83 59 63 56 55	06 95 89 29 83	05 12 80 97 19	77 43 35 37 83	92 30 15 04 98
10 85 06 27 46	99 59 91 05 07	13 49 90 63 19	53 07 57 18 39	06 41 01 93 62
39 82 09 89 52	43 62 26 31 47	64 42 18 08 14	43 80 00 93 51	31 02 47 31 67
59 58 00 64 78	75 58 97 88 00	88 83 55 44 86	23 76 80 61 56	04 11 10 84 08
38 50 80 73 41	23 79 34 87 63	90 82 29 70 22	17 71 90 42 07	95 95 44 99 53
30 69 27 06 68	94 68 81 61 27	56 19 68 00 91	82 06 76 34 00	05 46 26 92 00
65 44 39 56 59	18 28 82 74 37	49 63 22 40 41	08 33 76 56 76	96 29 99 08 36
27 26 75 02 64	13 19 27 22 94	07 47 74 46 06	17 98 54 89 11	97 34 13 03 58
91 30 70 69 91	19 07 22 42 10	36 69 95 37 28	28 82 53 57 93	28 97 66 62 52
68 43 49 46 88	84 47 31 36 22	62 12 69 84 08	12 84 38 25 90	09 81 59 31 46
48 90 81 58 77	54 74 52 45 91	35 70 00 47 54	83 82 45 26 92	54 13 05 51 60
06 91 34 51 97	42 67 27 86 01	11 88 30 95 28	63 01 19 89 01	14 97 44 03 44
10 45 51 60 19	14 21 03 37 12	91 34 23 78 21	88 32 58 08 51	43 66 77 08 83
12 88 39 73 43	65 02 76 11 84	04 28 50 13 92	17 97 41 50 77	90 71 22 67 69
21 77 83 09 76	38 80 73 69 61	31 64 94 20 96	63 28 10 20 23	08 81 64 74 49
19 52 35 95 15	65 12 25 96 59	86 28 36 82 58	69 57 21 37 98	16 43 59 15 29
67 24 55 26 70	35 58 31 65 63	79 24 68 66 86	76 46 33 42 22	26 65 59 08 02
60 58 44 73 77	07 50 03 79 92	45 13 42 65 29	28 78 08 36 37	41 32 64 43 44
53 85 34 13 77	36 06 69 48 50	58 83 87 38 59	49 36 47 33 31	96 24 04 36 42
24 63 73 87 36	74 38 48 93 42	52 62 30 79 92	12 36 91 86 01	03 74 28 38 73
83 08 01 24 51	38 99 22 28 15	07 75 95 17 77	97 37 72 75 85	51 97 23 78 67
16 44 42 43 34	36 15 19 90 73	27 49 37 09 39	85 13 03 25 52	54 84 65 47 59
60 79 01 81 57	57 17 86 57 62	11 16 17 85 76	45 81 95 29 79	65 13 00 48 60

SOURCE: Reproduced by permission from tables of the RAND Corporation in A Million Random Digits with 100,000 Normal Deviates (New York: Free Press, 1955).

TABLE 2   NORMAL DISTRIBUTION (UPPER TAIL)

Areas under the Normal Curve from Z to ∞

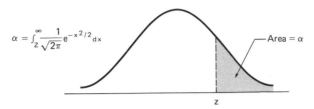

$$\alpha = \int_z^\infty \frac{1}{\sqrt{2\pi}} e^{-x^2/2} dx$$

Area = α

z	0.00	0.01	0.02	0.03	0.04	0.05	0.06	0.07	0.08	0.09
0.0	0.5000	0.4960	0.4920	0.4880	0.4840	0.4801	0.4761	0.4721	0.4681	0.4641
0.1	0.4602	0.4562	0.4522	0.4483	0.4443	0.4404	0.4364	0.4325	0.4286	0.4247
0.2	0.4207	0.4168	0.4129	0.4090	0.4052	0.4013	0.3974	0.3936	0.3897	0.3859
0.3	0.3821	0.3783	0.3745	0.3707	0.3669	0.3632	0.3594	0.3557	0.3520	0.3483
0.4	0.3446	0.3409	0.3372	0.3336	0.3300	0.3264	0.3228	0.3192	0.3156	0.3121
0.5	0.3085	0.3050	0.3015	0.2981	0.2946	0.2912	0.2877	0.2843	0.2810	0.2776
0.6	0.2743	0.2709	0.2676	0.2643	0.2611	0.2578	0.2546	0.2514	0.2483	0.2451
0.7	0.2420	0.2389	0.2358	0.2327	0.2296	0.2266	0.2236	0.2206	0.2177	0.2148
0.8	0.2119	0.2090	0.2061	0.2033	0.2005	0.1977	0.1949	0.1922	0.1894	0.1867
0.9	0.1841	0.1814	0.1788	0.1762	0.1736	0.1711	0.1685	0.1660	0.1635	0.1611
1.0	0.1587	0.1562	0.1539	0.1515	0.1492	0.1469	0.1446	0.1423	0.1401	0.1379
1.1	0.1357	0.1335	0.1314	0.1292	0.1271	0.1251	0.1230	0.1210	0.1190	0.1170
1.2	0.1151	0.1131	0.1112	0.1093	0.1075	0.1056	0.1038	0.1020	0.1003	0.0985
1.3	0.0968	0.0951	0.0934	0.0918	0.0901	0.0885	0.0869	0.0853	0.0838	0.0823
1.4	0.0808	0.0793	0.0778	0.0764	0.0749	0.0735	0.0721	0.0708	0.0694	0.0681
1.5	0.0668	0.0655	0.0643	0.0630	0.0618	0.0606	0.0594	0.0582	0.0571	0.0559
1.6	0.0548	0.0537	0.0526	0.0516	0.0505	0.0495	0.0485	0.0475	0.0465	0.0455
1.7	0.0446	0.0436	0.0427	0.0418	0.0409	0.0401	0.0392	0.0384	0.0375	0.0367
1.8	0.0359	0.0351	0.0344	0.0336	0.0329	0.0322	0.0314	0.0307	0.0301	0.0294
1.9	0.0287	0.0281	0.0274	0.0268	0.0262	0.0256	0.0250	0.0244	0.0239	0.0233
2.0	0.0228	0.0222	0.0217	0.0212	0.0207	0.0202	0.0197	0.0192	0.0188	0.0183
2.1	0.0179	0.0174	0.0170	0.0166	0.0162	0.0158	0.0154	0.0150	0.0146	0.0143
2.2	0.0139	0.0136	0.0132	0.0129	0.0125	0.0122	0.0119	0.0116	0.0113	0.0110
2.3	0.0107	0.0104	0.0102	0.00990	0.00964	0.00939	0.00914	0.00889	0.00866	0.00842
2.4	0.00820	0.00798	0.00776	0.00755	0.00734	0.00714	0.00695	0.00676	0.00657	0.00639
2.5	0.00621	0.00604	0.00587	0.00570	0.00554	0.00539	0.00523	0.00508	0.00494	0.00480
2.6	0.00466	0.00453	0.00440	0.00427	0.00415	0.00402	0.00391	0.00379	0.00368	0.00357
2.7	0.00347	0.00336	0.00326	0.00317	0.00307	0.00298	0.00289	0.00280	0.00272	0.00264
2.8	0.00256	0.00248	0.00240	0.00233	0.00226	0.00219	0.00212	0.00205	0.00199	0.00193
2.9	0.00187	0.00181	0.00175	0.00169	0.00164	0.00159	0.00154	0.00149	0.00144	0.00139

z	0.0	0.1	0.2	0.3	0.4	0.5	0.6	0.7	0.8	0.9
3	0.00135	0.0^3968^a	0.0^3687	0.0^3483	0.0^3337	0.0^3233	0.0^3159	0.0^3108	0.0^4723	0.0^4481
4	0.0^4317	0.0^4207	0.0^4133	0.0^5854	0.0^5541	0.0^5340	0.0^5211	0.0^5130	0.0^6793	0.0^6479
5	0.0^6287	0.0^6170	0.0^7996	0.0^7579	0.0^7333	0.0^7190	0.0^7107	0.0^8599	0.0^8332	0.0^8182
6	0.0^9987	0.0^9530	0.0^9282	0.0^9149	$0.0^{10}777$	$0.0^{10}402$	$0.0^{10}206$	$0.0^{10}104$	$0.0^{11}523$	$0.0^{11}260$

z	PROBABILITY	
1.282	0.100	
1.645	0.050	Most frequently
1.960	0.025	encountered probabilities
2.326	0.010	
2.576	0.005	

[a] Note: 0.0^3968 means three zeros before the 968, or 0.000968.

TABLE 3 STUDENT t DISTRIBUTION (UPPER TAIL)

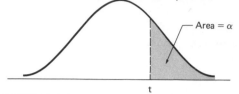

Area = α

Areas under the Student Curve from to to ∞,
for a Specified Number of Degrees of Freedom

The following table provides the values of t that correspond to a given probability (area) between t and $+\infty$ (or $-t$ and $-\infty$) for a specified number of degrees of freedom.

Degrees of Freedom	ONE-TAIL PROBABILITY (AREA)							
	0.40	0.25	0.10	0.05	0.025	0.01	0.005	0.001
1	0.325	1.000	3.078	6.314	12.706	31.821	63.657	318.31
2	0.289	0.816	1.886	2.920	4.303	6.965	9.925	22.326
3	0.277	0.765	1.638	2.353	3.182	4.541	5.841	10.213
4	0.271	0.741	1.533	2.132	2.776	3.747	4.604	7.173
5	0.267	0.727	1.476	2.015	2.571	3.365	4.032	5.893
6	0.265	0.718	1.440	1.943	2.447	3.143	3.707	5.208
7	0.263	0.711	1.415	1.895	2.365	2.998	3.499	4.785
8	0.262	0.706	1.397	1.860	2.306	2.896	3.355	4.501
9	0.261	0.703	1.383	1.833	2.262	2.821	3.250	4.297
10	0.260	0.700	1.372	1.812	2.228	2.764	3.169	4.144
11	0.260	0.697	1.363	1.796	2.201	2.718	3.106	4.025
12	0.259	0.695	1.356	1.782	2.179	2.681	3.055	3.930
13	0.259	0.694	1.350	1.771	2.160	2.650	3.012	3.852
14	0.258	0.692	1.345	1.761	2.145	2.624	2.977	3.787
15	0.258	0.691	1.341	1.753	2.131	2.602	2.947	3.733
16	0.258	0.690	1.337	1.746	2.120	2.583	2.921	3.686
17	0.257	0.689	1.333	1.740	2.110	2.567	2.898	3.646
18	0.257	0.688	1.330	1.734	2.101	2.552	2.878	3.610
19	0.257	0.688	1.328	1.729	2.093	2.539	2.861	3.579
20	0.257	0.687	1.325	1.725	2.086	2.528	2.845	3.552
21	0.257	0.686	1.323	1.721	2.080	2.518	2.831	3.527
22	0.256	0.686	1.321	1.717	2.074	2.508	2.819	3.505
23	0.256	0.685	1.319	1.714	2.069	2.500	2.807	3.485
24	0.256	0.685	1.318	1.711	2.064	2.492	2.797	3.467
25	0.256	0.684	1.316	1.708	2.060	2.485	2.787	3.450
26	0.256	0.684	1.315	1.706	2.056	2.479	2.779	3.435
27	0.256	0.684	1.314	1.703	2.052	2.473	2.771	3.421
28	0.256	0.683	1.313	1.701	2.048	2.467	2.763	3.408
29	0.256	0.683	1.311	1.699	2.045	2.462	2.756	3.396
30	0.256	0.683	1.310	1.697	2.042	2.457	2.750	3.385
40	0.255	0.681	1.303	1.684	2.021	2.423	2.704	3.307
60	0.254	0.679	1.296	1.671	2.000	2.390	2.660	3.232
120	0.254	0.677	1.289	1.658	1.980	2.358	2.617	3.160
∞	0.253	0.674	1.282	1.645	1.960	2.326	2.576	3.090

SOURCE: E. S. Pearson and H. O. Hartley, Biometrika Tables for Statisticians, Vol. 1, 1966, London, by permission.

TABLE 4 EXPONENTIAL DISTRIBUTION (LOWER TAIL)

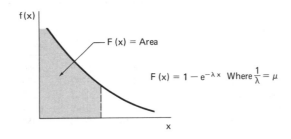

$$F(x) = 1 - e^{-\lambda x} \quad \text{Where } \frac{1}{\lambda} = \mu$$

Area under the Exponential Curve between 0 and X

λx	$F(x)$	λx	$F(x)$	λx	$F(x)$	λx	$F(x)$
0.0	0.00	1.0	0.63	2.0	0.86	4.0	0.982
0.1	0.10	1.1	0.67	2.2	0.89	4.5	0.989
0.2	0.18	1.2	0.70	2.4	0.91	5.0	0.993
0.3	0.26	1.3	0.73	2.6	0.92	5.5	0.996
0.4	0.33	1.4	0.75	2.8	0.94	6.0	0.998
0.5	0.39	1.5	0.78	3.0	0.95	6.5	0.9985
0.6	0.45	1.6	0.80	3.2	0.96	7.0	0.9991
0.7	0.50	1.7	0.82	3.4	0.97	8.0	0.9997
0.8	0.55	1.8	0.83	3.6	0.97	9.0	0.9999
0.9	0.59	1.9	0.85	3.8	0.98	10.0	0.99995

TABLE 5 POISSON DISTRIBUTION

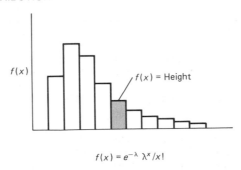

$$f(x) = e^{-\lambda} \lambda^x / x!$$

The table gives the probability of exactly x occurrences for given expected value λ.

x	0.005	0.01	0.02	0.03	0.04	0.05	0.06	0.07	0.08	0.09
0	.9950	.9900	.9802	.9704	.9608	.9512	.9418	.9324	.9231	.9139
1	.0050	.0099	.0192	.0291	.0384	.0476	.0565	.0653	.0738	.0823
2	.0000	.0000	.0002	.0004	.0008	.0012	.0017	.0023	.0030	.0037
3	.0000	.0000	.0000	.0000	.0000	.0000	.0000	.0001	.0001	.0001

TABLE 5   (continued)

					λ					
x	0.1	0.2	0.3	0.4	0.5	0.6	0.7	0.8	0.9	1.0
0	.9048	.8187	.7408	.6703	.6065	.5488	.4966	.4493	.4066	.3679
1	.0905	.1637	.2222	.2681	.3033	.3293	.3476	.3595	.3659	.3679
2	.0045	.0164	.0333	.0536	.0758	.0988	.1217	.1438	.1647	.1839
3	.0002	.0011	.0033	.0072	.0126	.0198	.0284	.0383	.0494	.0613
4	.0000	.0001	.0002	.0007	.0016	.0030	.0050	.0077	.0111	.0153
5	.0000	.0000	.0000	.0001	.0002	.0004	.0007	.0012	.0020	.0031
6	.0000	.0000	.0000	.0000	.0000	.0000	.0001	.0002	.0003	.0005
7	.0000	.0000	.0000	.0000	.0000	.0000	.0000	.0000	.0000	.0001

					λ					
x	1.1	1.2	1.3	1.4	1.5	1.6	1.7	1.8	1.9	2.0
0	.3329	.3012	.2725	.2466	.2231	.2019	.1827	.1653	.1496	.1353
1	.3662	.3614	.3543	.3452	.3347	.3230	.3106	.2975	.2842	.2707
2	.2014	.2169	.2303	.2417	.2510	.2584	.2640	.2678	.2700	.2707
3	.0738	.0867	.0998	.1128	.1255	.1378	.1496	.1607	.1710	.1804
4	.0203	.0260	.0324	.0395	.0471	.0551	.0636	.0723	.0812	.0902
5	.0045	.0062	.0084	.0111	.0141	.0176	.0216	.0260	.0309	.0361
6	.0008	.0012	.0018	.0026	.0035	.0047	.0061	.0078	.0098	.0120
7	.0001	.0002	.0003	.0005	.0008	.0011	.0015	.0020	.0027	.0034
8	.0000	.0000	.0001	.0001	.0001	.0002	.0003	.0005	.0006	.0009
9	.0000	.0000	.0000	.0000	.0000	.0000	.0001	.0001	.0001	.0002

					λ					
x	2.1	2.2	2.3	2.4	2.5	2.6	2.7	2.8	2.9	3.0
0	.1225	.1108	.1003	.0907	.0821	.0743	.0672	.0608	.0550	.0498
1	.2572	.2438	.2306	.2177	.2052	.1931	.1815	.1703	.1596	.1494
2	.2700	.2681	.2652	.2613	.2565	.2510	.2450	.2384	.2314	.2240
3	.1890	.1966	.2033	.2090	.2138	.2176	.2205	.2225	.2237	.2240
4	.0992	.1082	.1169	.1254	.1336	.1414	.1488	.1557	.1622	.1680
5	.0417	.0476	.0538	.0602	.0668	.0735	.0804	.0872	.0940	.1008
6	.0146	.0174	.0206	.0241	.0278	.0319	.0362	.0407	.0455	.0504
7	.0044	.0055	.0068	.0083	.0099	.0118	.0139	.0163	.0188	.0216
8	.0011	.0015	.0019	.0025	.0031	.0038	.0047	.0057	.0068	.0081
9	.0003	.0004	.0005	.0007	.0009	.0011	.0014	.0018	.0022	.0027
10	.0001	.0001	.0001	.0002	.0002	.0003	.0004	.0005	.0006	.0008
11	.0000	.0000	.0000	.0000	.0000	.0001	.0001	.0001	.0002	.0002
12	.0000	.0000	.0000	.0000	.0000	.0000	.0000	.0000	.0000	.0001

TABLE 5   (continued)

					λ					
x	3.1	3.2	3.3	3.4	3.5	3.6	3.7	3.8	3.9	4.0
0	.0450	.0408	.0369	.0334	.0302	.0273	.0247	.0224	.0202	.0183
1	.1397	.1304	.1217	.1135	.1057	.0984	.0915	.0850	.0789	.0733
2	.2165	.2087	.2008	.1929	.1850	.1771	.1692	.1615	.1539	.1465
3	.2237	.2226	.2209	.2186	.2158	.2125	.2087	.2046	.2001	.1954
4	.1734	.1781	.1823	.1858	.1888	.1912	.1931	.1944	.1951	.1954
5	.1075	.1140	.1203	.1264	.1322	.1377	.1429	.1477	.1522	.1563
6	.0555	.0608	.0662	.0716	.0771	.0826	.0881	.0936	.0989	.1042
7	.0246	.0278	.0312	.0348	.0385	.0425	.0466	.0508	.0551	.0595
8	.0095	.0111	.0129	.0148	.0169	.0191	.0215	.0241	.0269	.0298
9	.0033	.0040	.0047	.0056	.0066	.0076	.0089	.0102	.0116	.0132
10	.0010	.0013	.0016	.0019	.0023	.0028	.0033	.0039	.0045	.0053
11	.0003	.0004	.0005	.0006	.0007	.0009	.0011	.0013	.0016	.0019
12	.0001	.0001	.0001	.0002	.0002	.0003	.0003	.0004	.0005	.0006
13	.0000	.0000	.0000	.0000	.0001	.0001	.0001	.0001	.0002	.0002
14	.0000	.0000	.0000	.0000	.0000	.0000	.0000	.0000	.0000	.0001

					λ					
x	4.1	4.2	4.3	4.4	4.5	4.6	4.7	4.8	4.9	5.0
0	.0166	.0150	.0136	.0123	.0111	.0101	.0091	.0082	.0074	.0067
1	.0679	.0630	.0583	.0540	.0500	.0462	.0427	.0395	.0365	.0337
2	.1393	.1323	.1254	.1188	.1125	.1063	.1005	.0948	.0894	.0842
3	.1904	.1852	.1798	.1743	.1687	.1631	.1574	.1517	.1460	.1404
4	.1951	.1944	.1933	.1917	.1898	.1875	.1849	.1820	.1789	.1755
5	.1600	.1633	.1662	.1687	.1708	.1725	.1738	.1747	.1753	.1755
6	.1093	.1143	.1191	.1237	.1281	.1323	.1362	.1398	.1432	.1462
7	.0640	.0686	.0732	.0778	.0824	.0869	.0914	.0959	.1002	.1044
8	.0328	.0360	.0393	.0428	.0463	.0500	.0537	.0575	.0614	.0653
9	.0150	.0168	.0188	.0209	.0232	.0255	.0280	.0307	.0334	.0363
10	.0061	.0071	.0081	.0092	.0104	.0118	.0132	.0147	.0164	.0181
11	.0023	.0027	.0032	.0037	.0043	.0049	.0056	.0064	.0073	.0082
12	.0008	.0009	.0011	.0014	.0016	.0019	.0022	.0026	.0030	.0034
13	.0002	.0003	.0004	.0005	.0006	.0007	.0008	.0009	.0011	.0013
14	.0001	.0001	.0001	.0001	.0002	.0002	.0003	.0003	.0004	.0005
15	.0000	.0000	.0000	.0000	.0001	.0001	.0001	.0001	.0001	.0002

TABLE 5 (continued)

λ

x	5.1	5.2	5.3	5.4	5.5	5.6	5.7	5.8	5.9	6.0
0	.0061	.0055	.0050	.0045	.0041	.0037	.0033	.0030	.0027	.0025
1	.0311	.0287	.0265	.0244	.0225	.0207	.0191	.0176	.0162	.0149
2	.0793	.0746	.0701	.0659	.0618	.0580	.0544	.0509	.0477	.0446
3	.1348	.1293	.1239	.1185	.1133	.1082	.1033	.0985	.0938	.0892
4	.1719	.1681	.1641	.1600	.1558	.1515	.1472	.1428	.1383	.1339
5	.1753	.1748	.1740	.1728	.1714	.1697	.1678	.1656	.1632	.1606
6	.1490	.1515	.1537	.1555	.1571	.1584	.1594	.1601	.1605	.1606
7	.1086	.1125	.1163	.1200	.1234	.1267	.1298	.1326	.1353	.1377
8	.0692	.0731	.0771	.0810	.0849	.0887	.0925	.0962	.0998	.1033
9	.0392	.0423	.0454	.0486	.0519	.0552	.0586	.0620	.0654	.0688
10	.0200	.0220	.0241	.0262	.0285	.0309	.0334	.0359	.0386	.0413
11	.0093	.0104	.0116	.0129	.0143	.0157	.0173	.0190	.0207	.0225
12	.0039	.0045	.0051	.0058	.0065	.0073	.0082	.0092	.0102	.0113
13	.0015	.0018	.0021	.0024	.0028	.0032	.0036	.0041	.0046	.0052
14	.0006	.0007	.0008	.0009	.0011	.0013	.0015	.0017	.0019	.0022
15	.0002	.0002	.0003	.0003	.0004	.0005	.0006	.0007	.0008	.0009
16	.0001	.0001	.0001	.0001	.0001	.0002	.0002	.0002	.0003	.0003
17	.0000	.0000	.0000	.0000	.0000	.0001	.0001	.0001	.0001	.0001

λ

x	6.1	6.2	6.3	6.4	6.5	6.6	6.7	6.8	6.9	7.0
0	.0022	.0020	.0018	.0017	.0015	.0014	.0012	.0011	.0010	.0009
1	.0137	.0126	.0116	.0106	.0098	.0090	.0082	.0076	.0070	.0064
2	.0417	.0390	.0364	.0340	.0318	.0296	.0276	.0258	.0240	.0223
3	.0848	.0806	.0765	.0726	.0688	.0652	.0617	.0584	.0552	.0521
4	.1294	.1249	.1205	.1162	.1118	.1076	.1034	.0992	.0952	.0912
5	.1579	.1549	.1519	.1487	.1454	.1420	.1385	.1349	.1314	.1277
6	.1605	.1601	.1595	.1586	.1575	.1562	.1546	.1529	.1511	.1490
7	.1399	.1418	.1435	.1450	.1462	.1472	.1480	.1486	.1489	.1490
8	.1066	.1099	.1130	.1160	.1188	.1215	.1240	.1263	.1284	.1304
9	.0723	.0757	.0791	.0825	.0858	.0891	.0923	.0954	.0985	.1014
10	.0441	.0469	.0498	.0528	.0558	.0588	.0618	.0649	.0679	.0710
11	.0245	.0265	.0285	.0307	.0330	.0353	.0377	.0401	.0426	.0452
12	.0124	.0137	.0150	.0164	.0179	.0194	.0210	.0227	.0245	.0264
13	.0058	.0065	.0073	.0081	.0089	.0098	.0108	.0119	.0130	.0142
14	.0025	.0029	.0033	.0037	.0041	.0046	.0052	.0058	.0064	.0071
15	.0010	.0012	.0014	.0016	.0018	.0020	.0023	.0026	.0029	.0033
16	.0004	.0005	.0005	.0006	.0007	.0008	.0010	.0011	.0013	.0014
17	.0001	.0002	.0002	.0002	.0003	.0003	.0004	.0004	.0005	.0006
18	.0000	.0001	.0001	.0001	.0001	.0001	.0001	.0002	.0002	.0002
19	.0000	.0000	.0000	.0000	.0000	.0000	.0000	.0001	.0001	.0001

TABLE 5   (continued)

						λ				
x	7.1	7.2	7.3	7.4	7.5	7.6	7.7	7.8	7.9	8.0
0	.0008	.0007	.0007	.0006	.0006	.0005	.0005	.0004	.0004	.0003
1	.0059	.0054	.0049	.0045	.0041	.0038	.0035	.0032	.0029	.0027
2	.0208	.0194	.0180	.0167	.0156	.0145	.0134	.0125	.0116	.0107
3	.0492	.0464	.0438	.0413	.0389	.0366	.0345	.0324	.0305	.0286
4	.0874	.0836	.0799	.0764	.0729	.0696	.0663	.0632	.0602	.0573
5	.1241	.1204	.1167	.1130	.1094	.1057	.1021	.0986	.0951	.0916
6	.1468	.1445	.1420	.1394	.1367	.1339	.1311	.1282	.1252	.1221
7	.1489	.1486	.1481	.1474	.1465	.1454	.1442	.1428	.1413	.1396
8	.1321	.1337	.1351	.1363	.1373	.1382	.1388	.1392	.1395	.1396
9	.1042	.1070	.1096	.1121	.1144	.1167	.1187	.1207	.1224	.1241
10	.0740	.0770	.0800	.0829	.0858	.0887	.0914	.0941	.0967	.0993
11	.0478	.0504	.0531	.0558	.0585	.0613	.0640	.0667	.0695	.0722
12	.0283	.0303	.0323	.0344	.0366	.0388	.0411	.0434	.0457	.0481
13	.0154	.0168	.0181	.0196	.0211	.0227	.0243	.0260	.0278	.0296
14	.0078	.0086	.0095	.0104	.0113	.0123	.0134	.0145	.0157	.0169
15	.0037	.0041	.0046	.0051	.0057	.0062	.0069	.0075	.0083	.0090
16	.0016	.0019	.0021	.0024	.0026	.0030	.0033	.0037	.0041	.0045
17	.0007	.0008	.0009	.0010	.0012	.0013	.0015	.0017	.0019	.0021
18	.0003	.0003	.0004	.0004	.0005	.0006	.0006	.0007	.0008	.0009
19	.0001	.0001	.0001	.0002	.0002	.0002	.0003	.0003	.0003	.0004
20	.0000	.0000	.0001	.0001	.0001	.0001	.0001	.0001	.0001	.0002
21	.0000	.0000	.0000	.0000	.0000	.0000	.0000	.0000	.0001	.0001

						λ				
x	8.1	8.2	8.3	8.4	8.5	8.6	8.7	8.8	8.9	9.0
0	.0003	.0003	.0002	.0002	.0002	.0002	.0002	.0002	.0001	.0001
1	.0025	.0023	.0021	.0019	.0017	.0016	.0014	.0013	.0012	.0011
2	.0100	.0092	.0086	.0079	.0074	.0068	.0063	.0058	.0054	.0050
3	.0269	.0252	.0237	.0222	.0208	.0195	.0183	.0171	.0160	.0150
4	.0544	.0517	.0491	.0466	.0443	.0420	.0398	.0377	.0357	.0337
5	.0882	.0849	.0816	.0784	.0752	.0722	.0692	.0663	.0635	.0607
6	.1191	.1160	.1128	.1097	.1066	.1034	.1003	.0972	.0941	.0911
7	.1378	.1358	.1338	.1317	.1294	.1271	.1247	.1222	.1197	.1171
8	.1395	.1392	.1388	.1382	.1375	.1366	.1356	.1344	.1332	.1318
9	.1256	.1269	.1280	.1290	.1299	.1306	.1311	.1315	.1317	.1318
10	.1017	.1040	.1063	.1084	.1104	.1123	.1140	.1157	.1172	.1186
11	.0749	.0776	.0802	.0828	.0853	.0878	.0902	.0925	.0948	.0970
12	.0505	.0530	.0555	.0579	.0604	.0629	.0654	.0679	.0703	.0728
13	.0315	.0334	.0354	.0374	.0395	.0416	.0438	.0459	.0481	.0504
14	.0182	.0196	.0210	.0225	.0240	.0256	.0272	.0289	.0306	.0324

TABLE 5   (continued)

15	.0098	.0107	.0116	.0126	.0136	.0147	.0158	.0169	.0182	.0194
16	.0050	.0055	.0060	.0066	.0072	.0079	.0086	.0093	.0101	.0109
17	.0024	.0026	.0029	.0033	.0036	.0040	.0044	.0048	.0053	.0058
18	.0011	.0012	.0014	.0015	.0017	.0019	.0021	.0024	.0026	.0029
19	.0005	.0005	.0006	.0007	.0008	.0009	.0010	.0011	.0012	.0014
20	.0002	.0002	.0002	.0003	.0003	.0004	.0004	.0005	.0005	.0006
21	.0001	.0001	.0001	.0001	.0001	.0002	.0002	.0002	.0002	.0003
22	.0000	.0000	.0000	.0000	.0001	.0001	.0001	.0001	.0001	.0001

λ

x	9.1	9.2	9.3	9.4	9.5	9.6	9.7	9.8	9.9	10.0
0	.0001	.0001	.0001	.0001	.0001	.0001	.0001	.0001	.0001	.0000
1	.0010	.0009	.0009	.0008	.0007	.0007	.0006	.0005	.0005	.0005
2	.0046	.0043	.0040	.0037	.0034	.0031	.0029	.0027	.0025	.0023
3	.0140	.0131	.0123	.0115	.00107	.0100	.0093	.0087	.0081	.0076
4	.0319	.0302	.0285	.0269	.00254	.0240	.0226	.0213	.0201	.0189
5	.0581	.0555	.0530	.0506	.0483	.0460	.0439	.0418	.0398	.0378
6	.0881	.0851	.0822	.0793	.0764	.0736	.0709	.0682	.0656	.0631
7	.1145	.1118	.1091	.1064	.1037	.1010	.0982	.0955	.0928	.0901
8	.1302	.1286	.1269	.1251	.1232	.1212	.1191	.1170	.1148	.1126
9	.1317	.1315	.1311	.1306	.1300	.1293	.1284	.1274	.1263	.1251
10	.1198	.1210	.1219	.1228	.1235	.1241	.1245	.1249	.1250	.1251
11	.0991	.1012	.1031	.1049	.1067	.1083	.1098	.1112	.1125	.1137
12	.0752	.0776	.0799	.0822	.0844	.0866	.0888	.0908	.0928	.0948
13	.0526	.0549	.0472	.0594	.0617	.0640	.0662	.0685	.0707	.0729
14	.0342	.0361	.0380	.0399	.0419	.0439	.0459	.0479	.0500	.0521
15	.0208	.0221	.0235	.0250	.0265	.0281	.0297	.0313	.0330	.0347
16	.0118	.0127	.0137	.0147	.0157	.0168	.0180	.0192	.0204	.0217
17	.0063	.0069	.0075	.0081	.0088	.0095	.0103	.0111	.0119	.0128
18	.0032	.0035	.0039	.0042	.0046	.0051	.0055	.0060	.0065	.0071
19	.0015	.0017	.0019	.0021	.0023	.0026	.0028	.0031	.0034	.0037
20	.0007	.0008	.0009	.0010	.0011	.0012	.0014	.0015	.0017	.0019
21	.0003	.0003	.0004	.0004	.0005	.0006	.0006	.0007	.0008	.0009
22	.0001	.0001	.0002	.0002	.0002	.0002	.0003	.0003	.0004	.0004
23	.0000	.0001	.0001	.0001	.0001	.0001	.0001	.0001	.0002	.0002
24	.0000	.0000	.0000	.0000	.0000	.0000	.0000	.0001	.0001	.0001

TABLE 6A   PRESENT VALUE OF A SINGLE PAYMENT OF $1 AT THE END OF PERIOD T

						DISCOUNT RATE									
T	1%	2%	4%	6%	8%	10%	12%	14%	15%	16%	18%	20%	22%	24%	25%
1	0.990	0.980	0.962	0.943	0.926	0.909	0.893	0.877	0.870	0.862	0.847	0.833	0.820	0.806	0.800
2	0.980	0.961	0.925	0.890	0.857	0.826	0.797	0.769	0.756	0.743	0.718	0.694	0.672	0.650	0.640
3	0.971	0.942	0.889	0.840	0.794	0.751	0.712	0.675	0.658	0.641	0.609	0.579	0.551	0.524	0.512
4	0.961	0.924	0.855	0.792	0.735	0.683	0.636	0.592	0.572	0.552	0.516	0.482	0.451	0.423	0.410
5	0.951	0.906	0.822	0.747	0.681	0.621	0.567	0.519	0.497	0.476	0.437	0.402	0.370	0.341	0.328
6	0.942	0.888	0.790	0.705	0.630	0.564	0.507	0.456	0.432	0.410	0.370	0.335	0.303	0.275	0.262
7	0.933	0.871	0.760	0.665	0.583	0.513	0.452	0.400	0.376	0.354	0.314	0.279	0.249	0.222	0.210
8	0.923	0.853	0.731	0.627	0.540	0.467	0.404	0.351	0.327	0.305	0.266	0.233	0.204	0.179	0.168
9	0.914	0.837	0.703	0.592	0.500	0.424	0.361	0.308	0.284	0.263	0.225	0.194	0.167	0.144	0.134
10	0.905	0.820	0.676	0.558	0.463	0.386	0.322	0.270	0.247	0.227	0.191	0.162	0.137	0.116	0.107
11	0.896	0.804	0.650	0.527	0.429	0.350	0.287	0.237	0.215	0.195	0.162	0.135	0.112	0.094	0.086
12	0.887	0.788	0.625	0.497	0.397	0.319	0.257	0.208	0.187	0.168	0.137	0.112	0.092	0.076	0.069
13	0.879	0.773	0.601	0.469	0.368	0.290	0.229	0.182	0.163	0.145	0.116	0.093	0.075	0.061	0.055
14	0.870	0.758	0.577	0.442	0.340	0.263	0.205	0.160	0.141	0.125	0.099	0.078	0.062	0.049	0.044
15	0.861	0.743	0.555	0.417	0.315	0.239	0.183	0.140	0.123	0.108	0.084	0.065	0.051	0.040	0.035
16	0.853	0.728	0.534	0.394	0.292	0.218	0.163	0.123	0.107	0.093	0.071	0.054	0.042	0.032	0.028
17	0.844	0.714	0.513	0.371	0.270	0.198	0.146	0.108	0.093	0.080	0.060	0.045	0.034	0.026	0.023
18	0.836	0.700	0.494	0.350	0.250	0.180	0.130	0.095	0.081	0.069	0.051	0.038	0.028	0.021	0.018
19	0.828	0.686	0.475	0.331	0.232	0.164	0.116	0.083	0.070	0.060	0.043	0.031	0.023	0.017	0.014
20	0.820	0.673	0.456	0.312	0.215	0.149	0.104	0.073	0.061	0.051	0.037	0.026	0.019	0.014	0.012
21	0.811	0.660	0.439	0.294	0.199	0.135	0.093	0.064	0.053	0.044	0.031	0.022	0.015	0.011	0.009
22	0.803	0.647	0.422	0.278	0.184	0.123	0.083	0.056	0.046	0.038	0.026	0.018	0.013	0.009	0.007
23	0.795	0.634	0.406	0.262	0.170	0.112	0.074	0.049	0.040	0.033	0.022	0.015	0.010	0.007	0.006
24	0.788	0.622	0.390	0.247	0.158	0.102	0.066	0.043	0.035	0.028	0.019	0.013	0.008	0.006	0.005
25	0.780	0.610	0.375	0.233	0.146	0.092	0.059	0.038	0.030	0.024	0.016	0.010	0.007	0.005	0.004

TABLE 6B PRESENT VALUE OF AN ANNUITY CONSISTING OF $1 PAYMENTS AT THE END OF EACH OF THE NEXT *T* PERIODS

							DISCOUNT RATE								
T	1%	2%	4%	6%	8%	10%	12%	14%	15%	16%	18%	20%	22%	24%	25%
1	0.990	0.980	0.962	0.943	0.926	0.909	0.893	0.877	0.870	0.862	0.847	0.833	0.820	0.806	0.800
2	1.970	1.942	1.886	1.833	1.783	1.736	1.690	1.647	1.626	1.605	1.566	1.528	1.492	1.457	1.440
3	2.941	2.884	2.775	2.673	2.577	2.487	2.402	2.322	2.283	2.246	2.174	2.106	2.042	1.981	1.952
4	3.902	3.808	3.630	3.465	3.312	3.170	3.037	2.914	2.855	2.798	2.690	2.589	2.494	2.404	2.362
5	4.853	4.713	4.452	4.212	3.993	3.791	3.605	3.433	3.352	3.274	3.127	2.991	2.864	2.745	2.689
6	5.795	5.601	5.242	4.917	4.623	4.355	4.111	3.889	3.784	3.685	3.498	3.326	3.167	3.020	2.951
7	6.728	6.472	6.002	5.582	5.206	4.868	4.564	4.288	4.160	4.039	3.812	3.605	3.416	3.242	3.161
8	7.652	7.325	6.733	6.210	5.747	5.335	4.968	4.639	4.487	4.344	4.078	3.837	3.619	3.421	3.329
9	8.566	8.162	7.435	6.802	6.247	5.759	5.328	4.946	4.772	4.607	4.303	4.031	3.786	3.566	3.463
10	9.471	8.983	8.111	7.360	6.710	6.145	5.650	5.216	5.019	4.833	4.494	4.192	3.923	3.682	3.571
11	10.368	9.787	8.760	7.887	7.139	6.495	5.937	5.453	5.234	5.029	4.656	4.327	4.035	3.776	3.656
12	11.255	10.575	9.385	8.384	7.536	6.814	6.194	5.660	5.421	5.197	4.793	4.439	4.127	3.851	3.725
13	12.135	11.343	9.986	8.853	7.904	7.103	6.424	5.842	5.583	5.342	4.910	4.533	4.203	3.912	3.780
14	13.004	12.106	10.563	9.295	8.244	7.367	6.628	6.002	5.724	5.468	5.008	4.611	4.265	3.962	3.824
15	13.865	12.849	11.118	9.712	8.559	7.606	6.811	6.142	5.847	5.575	5.092	4.675	4.315	4.001	3.859
16	14.718	13.578	11.652	10.106	8.851	7.824	6.974	6.265	5.954	5.669	5.162	4.730	4.357	4.033	3.887
17	15.562	14.292	12.166	10.477	9.122	8.022	7.120	6.373	6.047	5.749	5.222	4.775	4.391	4.059	3.910
18	16.398	14.992	12.659	10.828	9.372	8.201	7.250	6.467	6.128	5.818	5.273	4.812	4.419	4.080	3.928
19	17.226	15.678	13.134	11.158	9.604	8.365	7.366	6.550	6.198	5.877	5.316	4.844	4.442	4.097	3.942
20	18.046	16.351	13.590	11.470	9.818	8.514	7.469	6.623	6.259	5.929	5.353	4.870	4.460	4.110	3.954
21	18.857	17.011	14.029	11.764	10.017	8.649	7.562	6.687	6.312	5.973	5.384	4.891	4.476	4.121	3.963
22	19.660	17.658	14.451	12.042	10.201	8.772	7.645	6.743	6.359	6.011	5.410	4.909	4.488	4.130	3.970
23	20.456	18.292	14.857	12.303	10.371	8.883	7.718	6.792	6.399	6.044	5.432	4.925	4.499	4.137	3.976
24	21.243	18.914	15.247	12.550	10.529	8.985	7.784	6.835	6.434	6.073	5.451	4.937	4.507	4.143	3.981
25	22.023	19.523	15.622	12.783	10.675	9.077	7.843	6.873	6.464	6.097	5.467	4.948	4.514	4.147	3.985

Solutions
to Starred Problems

1. Check clearing; credit operations; facility design to allow customer interface as well as smooth operations; worker scheduling; cost control.

3. The agency can perform more or improved services if it is efficient.

6. Services cannot be inventoried in the usual sense of the word. Thus supply-demand coordination is achieved in different ways.

8. Frequent pick-ups and deliveries improve service but increase costs. More collection points provide easier access (better service) but at an increased cost.

10. Air-conditioning manufacturing; Christmas card production.

11. Minimize cost; provide a wide range of services; maintain good community relations; maintain high quality. The first goal conflicts with the others.

15. **(a)** To provide cost, feasibility, and quality information.
    (b) Projected sales volume and its seasonality, sales price, and distribution information.
    (c) In addition to (a), lead times to first shipment, production quantities possible, source and quality of material supply, packaging information.

---

[1] There are many questions for which more than one answer is possible. Rather than making that statement every time it is appropriate, we have made it once, here. Further, the answers given here will be very brief and, therefore, on occasion will be incomplete.

CHAPTER 2

1. One store, since one layout has little effect on the rest of the system.
4. (a) Tactical, since major expenses for an intermediate time horizon are committed.
   (b) Strategic, since a large amount of resources is committed for a long time.
   (c) Detailed, since the economic impact is low and the time horizon is short.
   (d) Probably tactical, since the system would be reviewed every year or so.
6. Trucking expense will increase, but inventories and emergency orders will decline.
10. They should choose 200; TC (200) = 125.0
12. The computer could minimize cost by satisfying none of the demand. (Set all $X_{ij} = 0$.)
14. Simulation can include relationships too complex for mathematical models. Simulation models help managers rather than make decisions.
17. $12.78 \approx 13$ is the breakeven point; the firm should find out who their customers might be and try to estimate the average return more carefully.
19. 120,408.
20. Buy the trucks; present value of rental payments = $6,549,000.
22. (a) More attractive, since there is one additional value component. (The salvage value will exceed the loss of tax savings due to reduced depreciation.)
    (b) More attractive, since the tax saving is received earlier and thus has a larger present value.

CHAPTER 3

3. (a) Activity C is shown as starting later than its ES.
   (b) B and D are most worrisome (no slack). A has 2 units of slack and is probably least worrisome.
4. (a)

Activity	ES	EF	LS	LF	Slack
E	0	5	5	10	5
F	0	4	7	11	7
G	0	9	3	12	3
A	5	10	10	15	5
B	4	8	11	15	7
C	9	17	12	20	3
D	10	15	15	20	5

   (b) Critical path = G, C for $9 + 8 = 17$ days.

(c) Path EA has less slack than FB, and is therefore probably more likely to delay D.

(d) 17 days. Probably too low because it doesn't recognize that the critical path might shift. Time estimates may be wrong.

6. (a) Critical path = 3, 4, 6, completed at time 9 (i.e., week 45).

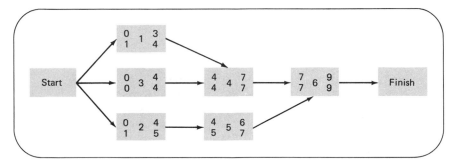

(b) 9 is too low. Variability in student progress will slow down the average.

8. (a) Activities B, F, H and I have 3 days of slack, the smallest for noncritical activities.

(b) More than 2 days, 5 days and 5 days, respectively.

(c) (i) F (up by 2) and H (up by 2)
(ii) none

10. (a) No. The LS for D is 14.

(b) Activity F has 7 days of slack.

(c) 5 days

11. (a) 32 hours

(b) 24 hours at $310

13. (a) Critical path is C, E, F for 35 days. D and B have slack of 4 days.

(b) If Cobalt unit is shut down when accelerator is delivered, speed electricians up by 2 days, saving $200.

16. (a) $\bar{x} = 27$, $s = 2.867$

(b) 85%

(c) Actual probability is probably lower than 85%.

CHAPTER 4

2. All three are design problems.

4. Mainly, how the firm will respond to high demand (using overtime, inventory, extra shifts or subcontracting). Others might include how easy it will be to add products to the product line and how quickly the firm can respond to rush orders.

7. The plant must be designed to be cost effective for the current and possible future product lines.

10. The investment earns 21.4% (before tax). The manager might turn it down if he had no way to obtain the money or if the money could be used in a more attractive investment.

12. Many extra channels are possible on cable TV. Some local advertising might be sent by cable TV (food ads, for example). If some advertising is lost, the price of both the newspaper and remaining advertising may have to increase.

14. Disposable Income—positive coefficient.
    Advertising Budget—positive coefficient.
    Relative price compared to industry—negative coefficient.

CHAPTER 5

3.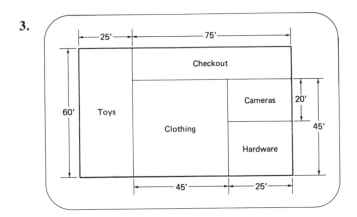

6.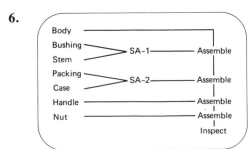

8. (a) 30 seconds
   (b) 7 hours/760 items or 35 seconds per item, for a balance delay of 35.7%.
   (c) Yes. Combine stations 3 and 4.
   (d) 3

(e) 2 per minute. To improve, try to transfer a task from station 2 to station 3.

(f) 0.25; because the stations cannot be made to have identical cycle times.

9. (a) Station 1 = A, C, D, J; Station 2 = E, K; Station 3 = L, B; Station 4 = G, I, H; Station 5 = F, M; Station 6 = N

   (b) Balance delay = 16.7%

12. Flexible manufacturing is the automated version of cellular manufacturing. A cellular layout might form four cells with doctors, physicians' assistants, nurses, and practical nurses. A central reception area would funnel patients to one of the cells, where, for most patients, their entire needs would be fulfilled. The advantage is less travel time for patients and perhaps better privacy. A disadvantage is that specialization may not be easy to incorporate.

14. (a) − $9,568,000

    (b) − $6,438,000

    (c) + $11,818,000

15. + $9,005,000

17. The jobs created may not be designed for the people who lost jobs. Some industrial cities may have a permanently lower number of jobs. Training and relocation programs may be insufficient.

CHAPTER 6

1. Both. Autonomy is the unique element.

4. "Stopwatch" measures activity times. "Work sampling" estimates "proportion of time spent in each category of activity."

6. (a) 0.20

   (b) 0.1012

   (c) 1537 in total, or 1477 more than the pilot study.

9. Two examples are to guarantee that no one will lose jobs or pay and to give cash awards for good ideas.

11. (a) 1.04

    (b) The product may have changed; the labor force may be different; they may have new capital equipment.

12. (a) 20 P1's and 6⅔ P2's. (The fraction would be a partially completed unit.)

    (b) P2 may be more profitable; they may want to maintain a significant presence in both market segments.

13. (a) 20 P2's and zero P1's.

    (b) The small machine might be more profitable, or they may want to maintain a presence in both markets.

16. Group incentives can be directed more easily toward the goals of the organization, and people have a need to belong to and contribute to a group. Individual goals may be preferred because the individual can see the immediate reward and because it is easier to see how to improve vis-à-vis that incentive.

CHAPTER 7

2. Property and construction cost; system-wide transportation costs; socio-economic composition of the three schools; usefulness of the new site for community activities.

4. (a) Build 2000, expand if demand is high. Expected net present value = $3,968,000

(b) Break-even probability = 0.405

7. (a) $1200; T_q = 0.8 months

(b) 4.8 jobs per month.

(c) T_q = 11.67, 20.0, 28.3 and 45.0 for the four λ values. Average monthly profit = 1050, 1200, 1275, and 1350.

(d) If an increase to 4.8 or more (but less than or equal to the 4.95 they can handle) can be assured, profits will increase slightly.

(e) They might increase price and keep the same size crew.

10. (a) N_q = 2.250 so 5 chairs are needed.

(b) 9 is the 95th percentile, so 18 chairs are needed.

(c) T_q = 0.75 hour.

12. 0.64 hour or about 38 minutes, using two pairs.

14. (a) Number of truck bays, number of trucks, or throughput capability.

(b) Cost of the facility and of operating the facility; number of spare trucks needed to maintain readiness; overtime cost if regular throughput capacity is insufficient.

(c) The trucks' regular repair and breakdown rates; time to perform maintenance of various types; costs mentioned in (b).

16. Minimize $1500X_{A1} + 1400X_{A2} + \cdots + 1650X_{C3} + 1800X_{C4}$

subject to
$$X_{A1} + X_{B1} + X_{C1} = 2500$$
$$X_{A2} + X_{B2} + X_{C2} = 3000$$
$$X_{A3} + X_{B3} + X_{C3} = 5000$$
$$X_{A4} + X_{B4} + X_{C4} = 2000$$
$$X_{A1} + X_{A2} + X_{A3} + X_{A4} \leq 5000$$
$$X_{B1} + X_{B2} + X_{B3} + X_{B4} \leq 5000$$
$$X_{C1} + X_{C2} + X_{C3} + X_{C4} \leq 5000$$

To consider D, replace all X_{Ci} variables with X_{Di}, using 1400, 1500, 1650, and 1700 as objective function coefficients.

18. (a) Prediction of future demand patterns, construction and operating costs; the "presence" effect of either plant.

    (b) Consider net contribution attributable to the new plant. Without it, the firm will lose some sales. Do an investment analysis.

20. Simulation represents a real situation and allows us to test alternatives generated by a manager. A heuristic program generates good alternatives to be tested by some (perhaps a simulation) model.

23. (a) There are several possible reasons. One is that by word of mouth you hear that "I'm traveling on Instant Airlines." Another is that the larger-capacity airline is less likely to be full and turn customers away.

    (b) The firm that changes first will add seats and gain market share, in the short run, more than proportionally to the share of seats. The other firm will retaliate by adding capacity. In the long run they may settle into their old shares, with lower occupancy rates, and lose money.

CHAPTER 8

3. Analysis of the data using a mathematical model.

7. Mary wins. Her forecast has almost completely discounted the (now irrelevant) data from before the drop in demand.

9. (a) $S_1 = 18.4$; $MAD_1 = 3.87$

   (b) They should use a high α value for a while. Sales personnel may have "grass roots" information that could improve the forecast.

10. (a) 183 ± 25

    (b) 189.6 ± 28.5

13. (a) Sales dropped rapidly during periods 1 to 6; the regression estimates are $a_6 = 129.5$ and $b_6 = -16.9$.

    (b) Ignoring periods 1 to 5, $a_6 = 110.7$ and $b_6 = 5.0$.

    (c) To weight six months of data, $R_A = \frac{2}{7} = 0.286$ should be about right. $R_B = 0.05$ is between the two values suggested in equations (11) and (12).

    (d)

Period	6	7	8	9	10	11
a_t	110	116.5	118.3	125	133	136
b_t	5.0	5.25	4.66	5.02	5.52	5.10

15. (a) $\bar{x} = 6.5$, $\Sigma x^2 = 650$, $\Sigma xy = 5137$, $\bar{y} = 62.0$, $n = 12$, $b = 2.105$, $a = 48.318$

    (b) The sum of the absolute errors is 33.6, so $MAD = 2.8$.

17. (a) 1.097

(b) Use an exponentially weighted average of the Wednesday centered averages.

18. (a)

Month	Sept.	Oct.	Nov.	Dec.	Jan.
Cake	99,000	108,000	126,000	117,000	72,000
Frosting	57,200	63,600	75,600	71,500	44,800

(b) The final quarter is Oct.–Dec., so the forecast is (108,000 + 126,000 + 117,000) = 351,000 for cake mix and 210,700 for frosting.

(c)

	Cake	Frosting
Deseasonalize:	94,000/1.1 = 85,455	52,727
$e_t =$	85,455 − 90,000 = −4,545	727
$a_t =$	90,000 + (0.1)(−4,545) = 89,546	52,073
$b_t =$	0	1,000 + 0.01(727) = 1,007
$a_t + b_t =$	89,546	53,080
Multiply times Oct. seasonal:	107,455	63,696

(d) Average the two seasonal factors. One might want to weight the individual factors by sales volume.

20. Using equation (17), forecast = 6.52. But this is the forecast of the natural logarithm of registrations, in thousand. Thus

$$\text{forecast} = e^{6.52} = 679 \text{ thousand}$$

CHAPTER 9

2. Backlogging demand, scheduling consumers, price promotions to level demand, diversify product line.

5. (a) Inventory cost of bottles (not wine)
Additional production equipment
Additional warehouse space

(b) Second shift startup and premium wage.
Frequent changeovers due to low inventory

(c) Oversupply

(d) Shortages

7. (a) 40 units

(b) Average requirements change for June–December only. The new values are 4.76, 4.71, 4.38, 4.48, 4.46, 4.50, and 5.04 for June through December, respectively, and 5.04 is the highest.

(c) 40 units causes horizon to jump to December.

(d) No change.

9. (a) Cumulative Requirements = 130, 240, 380, 480.

(b) Yes

(c) Peak output would be reduced (may save some overtime). Inventory is less in month 2 and the same elsewhere. Yes, this is an improvement.

10. (a) Steepest production curve in months 5 and 6.
   (b) 18.75 units per month.
   (c) Month 10
   (d) Follow given plan in months 1–4. Then follow a constant production rate through month 10, meeting the same ending inventory. This reduces inventory cost, reduces peak production rate, and saves a layoff at end of month 6.

13. (a) Produce 5875 per month. Total cost = $1,428,000 composed of $1,260,000 for holding inventory and $168,000 for overtime.
   (b) $1,270,000 composed of $1,000,000 for holding inventory, $50,000 for hiring/firing and $220,000 second shift.
   (c) Part (b) leaves 3000 more units of inventory than part (a). If this difference is carried one month, the cost advantage of part (b) virtually disappears.

15. (a) $m^* = 5$ months (largest integer in 5.84). Therefore, $2(m^* + 1) = 12$, and seasonal layoffs can be used (rule 1 in Table 9-3).
   (b) Beginning of month 11 at the earliest (rule 4).
   (c) At least 6 months (rule 6).
   (d) Layoffs at end of month 4 (rule 3) and hiring at end of month 10 (see part b).
   (e) Current work force can produce $(5000)(4) = 20,000$ through month 4, whereas demand = 21,000.
   (f) Hiring/firing is a cheaper way to increase production for periods above $l^* = 1.0$ month.
   (g) Hire fewer workers, earlier, because there will be a layoff in period 5 (rule 6).
   (h) Plan 1 = $660, plan 2 = $580, plan 3 = $810.
   (i) Plan 2 violates this principle, but is $80 cheaper than plan 1.

17. (a) $(61 - 5)/6 = 9.33$ per month.
   (b) Backlog exceeds 15 in period 5.
   (c) MCP = produce 9.4 per month for first 5 months, which stays within specified bounds.
   (d) The violation of the minimum backlog by 1 truck in month 3 seems a small price to pay for keeping the work force steady.

CHAPTER 10

5. (a) Larger orders last longer, yielding less frequent transactions.
   (b) Larger orders increase cycle stock, $Q/2$.
   (c) Do a Q^+ type of approach, as in Section 10-3.

7. (a) $Q^* = 1000$ lb.
   (b) $Q^* = 223.6$ lb, $D^\$ = \$200,000$ per year, TVC $= \$894.4$ per year, and $n = 22.4$ orders per year.
   (c) Higher inventory cost for titanium implies smaller Q.

9. At the cheaper price, $C_1 = \$3.90$ and $Q^* = 277$, which exceeds 200 and is therefore optimal.

11. (a) Both items have the same costs, but different demands D, so they cannot have the same Q^*.
    (b) Perhaps, although some other considerations, such as quantity discounts, might be present.

13. Using equation (19), $Q = 250$ items which should be placed on the last order before the price increase.

15. (a) $Q^* = 400$
    (b) $n = 4000/400 = 10$ per year
    (c) Safety stock $= z\sigma_u = (2.33)(48) = 112$
    (d) (C_1)(safety stock) $= \$280$
    (e) Cutting $\overline{LT}$ by 50% saves nothing *in this case,* since σ_u is not affected. Cutting $\sigma(LT)$ by 50% saves half of \$280, or \$140.

18. (a) $\sigma_u = 80$, $z = (600 - 400)/80 = 2.5$, Probability $= 0.0062$. $n = 10$ orders per year, so there are $(10)(0.0062) = 0.062$ stockout per year.
    (b) Using $C_B \approx \$350$ in equations (12), (13), and (14), $R = 664$.

20. (a) Let $c =$ cost. Then "optimal stockout probability" $= (c - 0.9c)/(0.3c + 0 + c - 0.9c) = 0.25$. Therefore, the rule is to stock enough to meet all demand 75% of the time.
    (b) Using Table 5, Appendix D, the order should be for 13 loaves to keep the cumulative stockout probability below 0.25. (The cumulative probability is $(0.0729 + \cdots + 0.0001) = 0.2085$ for demand of 13 or more.)
    (c) This is not a one-shot opportunity. Future demand may depend on keeping a high service level.

22. (a) $1649/6 = 274.83$ per week, so $D = 14,291$ per year
    (b) Orders placed on Tuesday of week 1, Wednesday of week 3, and Tuesday of week 5. Orders arrive on Tuesday of week 2, Wednesday of week 5. Shortage of 22 on Tuesday of week 5.
    (c) No shortages. Orders for 533 on Monday of week 1, 542 on Monday of week 3, 528 on Monday of week 5. Orders received on Monday of weeks 2 and 5.
    (d) $R - \overline{u} = 550 - (2)(274.83) = 0.33$ or zero, so the Q, R system has no safety stock in part (b). $TI - (T)(\overline{d}) - \overline{u} = 1100 - 2(274.83) - 2(274.83) = 0.66$, so there is also none in part (c).

CHAPTER 11

1. (a) 29,623
   (b) 37.0 days
   (c) 74.1 days
   (d) 21,491; 2.686; 53.7; EOQ formula gives 20,947.

3. (a) Since supervisors have other productive tasks, an opportunity cost should be assigned to their time spent on changeovers.
   (b) Increase, since C_T will increase.

5. (a) 0.674 week
   (b) 202 of A; 135 of B; 67 of C.
   (c) 0.2 week.

8. (a) TMAX/FT* is 2.33 for family A and 1 for family B; these values are rounded to 2 and 1; 8.4 weeks is the total family production time for A and 4.7 is the value for B. The 8.4 for A is broken into two runs of 4.2 weeks each with product one getting 3.25 weeks of each 4.2.
   (b) The chart produces A1, A2, B3, B4, A1, A2, then it is idle, then it starts again with A1. The times of changeovers are 3.25, 4.2, 7.0, 8.9, 12.15, 13.10, and 14.0

10. (a) TMAX/FT* values (1.0, 3.0, 2.5, 2.7, and 2.0) are very close to the multiples used in both plans.

   (b)
A	BD	CE	BD	CE	BD	Plan 2
A	BCD	E	BCD	E	BCD	Plan 1

   (c)
2	$4\frac{2}{3}$	7	$4\frac{2}{3}$	7	$4\frac{2}{3}$	Plan 2 (numbers are working days)
2	8	2	8	2	8	Plan 1 (numbers are working days)

12. (a) 2.6 weeks
    (b) Production is -60, 1140, 980, 440 for fruity, wintergreen, spearmint, and bubblegum. The -60 indicates production should be zero for that item; the runout times for other items should be shortened by 60/2250 weeks, but the difference is small here.

15. (a) No
    (b) J1 starts on M1 and J2 starts on M2, at time zero. At time 4 both remaining tasks are started and makespan is reduced to 8.
    (c) 8

17. (a) Type M2, since one of each of J1, J2, and J3 would require 13 days on M2, but 6 and 7 on M1 and M3, respectively.
    (b) All jobs can be done by day 20. In our chart, the new machine will work on J2, 2 (second job of type J2), then J1, 2 and J3, 2, finishing its work at day 19. The old M2 is done on day 14.

19. (a) (i) ABCDE; A is 1 hour late and E is 5 hours late.
        (ii) CBDAE; A is 4.5 hours late and E is 5 hours late.

       (iii) AEBCD; A is 1 hour late, E is 1.5 hours late, and C is 0.5 hour
           late.
  (b) FCFS or SOT
  (c) FCFS
  (d) DS/RO
  (e) Results apply to this set of jobs.

21. (a) 2 per day per machine
  (b) $N_q = 16.678$
  (c) The Markov assumption, steady state, FCFS discipline, single waiting
     line, infinite population, and arrival and service rates independent of
     queue size.
  (d) Lower, since SOT moves jobs through more quickly.

CHAPTER 12

2. MRP provides a planned completion time and an order release time. Then
if a capacity utilization plan is obtained it can foresee potential bottlenecks.
The effects of a trial schedule can be observed.

4. (a) Safety time.
  (b) External independent demand for a component or reject allowance.
  (c) Yes, so that frequent shortages will not cause constant replanning of the
     master schedule.

7. (i) One plant's product may be a subassembly.
  (ii) The product demand may be predictable only to semifinished stage, with
     color, fabric, or options being added for a specific customer.

9. (i) A master production schedule known well in advance.
  (ii) A multistage manufacturing process.
  (iii) Lead times that are not highly variable.
  (iv) Small reject allowances and small independent demand for components.

12. By the end of day zero, we must have on hand or on order 400 units of
TM75, 600 units of TM 112, and only 3200 units of RM 1 (because 4000
units will be in-process in the TM products).

14. (a) Level 1 contains A, level 2 contains C and D, level 3 contains B and
     F, and level 4 contains E.
  (b) 600 of B, 400 of C, 100 of D, 1900 of E, and 1100 of F.
  (c) 1200 units in week 4 and 700 units in week 6.

17. (a) The figure has six levels with (SYS 1 and SYS 2) on level 1, (SUB 1,
     SUB 2 and SUB 4) on level 2, (RM 2, SUB 3 and COMP 4) on level 3,
     (COMP 1 and COMP 3) on level 4, (COMP 2) on level 5, and (RM 1
     and RM 3) on level 6. There are 25 entries on level 6, 13 for SYS 1
     and 12 for SYS 2.

(b) 86

(c) Much simpler.

18. (a) On-hand inventory first becomes negative in periods 16, 6, 4, 4, 14, and 4 for SYS 1, SYS 2, SUB 1, SUB 2, SUB 4, and SUB 3, respectively. The first order releases for those products (in the same order as above) are two periods before, for quantities of 1000, 2000, 2090, 2064, 1029 and 3068.

(b) Order releases could allow for rejects and the computer would be programmed to receive only 90% or 80%.

19. All answers are in order for: SYS 1, SYS 2, SUB 1, SUB 2, SUB 3, and SUB 4.

(a) 100, 200, 310, 508, 309, 103

(b) 245, 400, 431, 552, 352, 185

(c) 2, 2, 1, 1, 1, 2 (to the nearest week). Runs should be made more often for finished items (every 2 weeks) and components should be scheduled in a lot-for-lot manner.

20. (a) The labor hours needed per week during the first 15 weeks are: 0; 5055.4; 5055.4; 1800; 1800; 0; 0; 0; 0; 0; 0; 8609.3; 8609.3; 2700; 2700.

(b) Reduce lot sizes.

(c) Not using the current lot sizes; on average, however, they need 2262.

29. (a) $800 with 2 products; $40,000 with 100 products.

(b) Lot size of 10 units and four boxes of inventory per product. These might be reduced toward the goals of 1 unit and zero inventory.

31. One unit, zero, and 100% good items.

CHAPTER 13

1. All three cycles are time lags between needing an item and having it available. Procurement—material supplier and plant. Replenishment—plant and DC. Order—DC and retail outlet. See Section 13-1 for discussion.

3. Only proposal 1 is justified. Net annual saving = $100,208.

5. (a) True, because the risk of obsolescence and several costs depend on the nature of the item.

(b) False, since the value added in transportation may be significant.

(c) False, since dead stock may be claimed as a tax loss.

7. (a) False, since the carrying cost may be very low or instant service may be required.

(b) False, because revenue may be lost due to lack of product availability.

9. (a) 0.0137

(b) 2.21

(c) 3,885 at retail; 1,765 at the DC.

11. C_B = \$20. Inventory is 629 and 58 units for items 1 and 2 respectively. Stockouts per year is 0.05 for both items. Total values are \$3,022,500 in inventory and 275 stockouts per year. C_B = \$200. The corresponding values are 665; 63; 0.005; \$3,237,500; and 27.5.

14. (a) High-cost, low-demand items where a slight delay is not too costly.
    (b) Inventory is reduced. Speed of response is increased, and transportation cost may rise.

16. (a) 3,600,000 − 2,100,000 = \$1,500,000
    (b) No, since \$400,000 > (0.2)(1,500,000).
    (c) No. The inventory saving would be even lower.

CHAPTER 14

3. They increase congestion.

6. (a) Total demand = 74 workdays per week, compared to (14)(5) = 70 available. Thus we need 4 days of part-time help.
   (b) At least 2.
   (c) Pick up the half days on Monday and Friday.
   (d) Advantage is that the entire full-time crew would *not* be present on any day. Disadvantage is that 3 different part-timers need to be trained.
   (e) Days off Monday through Sunday = 5, 3, 0, 4, 4, 6, 6 = 28 total.
   (f) Only Wednesday requires part time help.

7. (a) 3500/250 = 14 crews.
   (b) 300 Monday, 100 Tuesday.
   (c) Days off are: Weeks 1 and 2 have Wed. and Sun., weeks 3–6 have Thurs. and Sun., weeks 7–10 have Fri. & Sun., and weeks 11–14 have Sat. & Sun.
   (d) Same as (c) except week 1 is Mon. & Sun. instead of Wed. & Sun.
   (e) Solution (d) leaves an extra 50 tons uncollected at the end of Monday and Tuesday.

12. (a) Groups 1–7 take weeks 1–7 day shift, groups 8–14 do the same but evenings, and 15–21 the same but nights. Rotate after finishing week 7 of the schedule.
    (b) 5

13. (a) 10 minutes, with 2 and 5 intervals allocated to established and new customer office visits, respectively.
    (b) If you allow 30 minutes per broker for breaks, etc., there should be (2400 − 150 − 75)/10 = 217 intervals, or more if we allow for no-shows.
    (c) Total demand = 1650 minutes, so idle time = 750 minutes per day or 150 per broker per day.

(d) Allowing 150 minutes personal time, $(750 - 150)/50 = 12$ (or fewer) in addition to the 15 already allocated in part (c).

(e) Away from heavy demand times. Toward the junior members, as they have fewer established customers.

14. (a) Fri. through Thurs. = 155, 128, 115, 131, 152, 163, 164.

(b) 157, 140, 137, 146, 156, 156, 155.

(c) The current pattern is above certified capacity on Thursday, and leaves only 1 bed safety margin.

(d) Yes. Up to 4 more patients can be in the hospital without exceeding 160.

17. (a) *Day shift:* 3 on duty every day except 4 on duty during week 1 (Thurs.–Sat.), week 2 (Sun., and Fri.–Sat.), week 3 (Sun., Mon. and Sat.), week 4 (Sun.–Tues.).
Evenings: 2 every day except 3 during week 5 (Mon.–Wed.) and week 6 (Tues.–Thurs.).
Nights: 1 every day except 2 during week 7 (Wed.–Fri.).

(b) Groups 1 and 6 have 5 nights, and the other groups have 6. There are also differences in evenings and days.

(c) Advantage—regularity. Disadvantage—vacation planning and uneven work loads by day of week do not fit in. May need part time help because of this.

CHAPTER 15

1. Job descriptions can be used to ensure that all tasks are assigned to someone. Cost accounting can be used to give division managers objectives that are consistent with company-wide goals. Information systems can be used to provide timely information, to allow a manager to correct problems before it is too late.

3. A manager with responsibilities in two or more areas would have more than one boss. Diverse goals are kept in mind, but managers may spend more time dealing with two bosses, to the detriment of problem-solving efforts.

6. An average of 7 furnaces ($2\frac{1}{3}$ per plant) is needed. The $40 per ton penalty would be paid only if one plant does not have enough warehouses it can ship to at a cost within $40 of other plants. Examining Figure 15-2 (and recalling the $320 and $310 production costs) we see that each plant has at least two furnaces' worth of production within $40 of the other two plants on production plus transportation costs.

9. Nine furnaces will be kept warm all year. Inventory will exist in small amounts in month 10. LPs will be used to select warm furnace locations (by trial and error) and to determine the monthly production and shipping schedule. The lower portions of Figure 15-2 would still apply.

12. **(a)** Goal: Keep average time between an ambulance call and the patient's treatment low. The purpose is to save lives, and the organization can follow up by keeping data to see if the goal is met.
    (b) Goal: Keep average actual cost below standard cost. The variance can be used to follow up on cost performance.
    (c) Goal: Reduce distribution costs (which are thought to be excessive). The data are used to see what performance level is being attained and isolate areas for improvement.

14. "Bugs" show up before the organization must depend on the system. The disadvantages are the cost of two systems and the temporary loss of efficiency if the new system turns out to be superior.

CHAPTER 16

7. The process will be out of control part of the time, and during these intervals much more than 1% of the points will fall outside the limits.

9. **(a)** $n = 175$, $c = 3$ comes satisfactorily close to achieving α and β.
    (b) Slightly over 50% probability of acceptance. The OC curve can be drawn through the points ($f = 0$, $P_a = 1.0$), ($f = 0.01$, $P_a = 0.9$), ($f = 0.021$, $P_a = 0.5$), ($f = 0.05$, $P_a = 0.025$).
    (c) AOQL $= (1.9424)(1/175 - 1/5000) = 0.0107$.

11. **(a)** The sample size n is reduced by 55 for $\beta = 5\%$ and by 83 for $\beta = 10\%$.
    (b) For $\beta = 1\%$, AOQL $= 0.025$; for $\beta = 5\%$, AOQL $= 0.0265$; for $\beta = 10\%$, AOQL $= 0.0288$, so AOQL increases very little.

14. **(a)** No. C_{ins} lies between $f_{min} C_{def}$ and $f_{max} C_{def}$.
    (b) Consider "almost zero" inspection; i.e., infrequent checks to make sure quality has not slipped.

17. **(a)** 0.0123 or 1.23% $=$ AOQL
    (b) $(0.008)(0.15) + (0.012)(0.40) + (0.006)(0.40) + (0.002)(0.05) = 0.0085$
    (c) AOQL is an upper limit on the long-run fraction defective in outgoing batches. Therefore (a) should be higher than (b), and it was.

19. Only (e) can be said to be true. Parts (a) and (b) are false, and the others cannot be judged from an AOQ curve.

22. **(a)** Batch five.
    (b) Batch 1 is rejected on the fourth defective.
    (c) Single $=$ 150 inspected per batch. Sequential averages 90.6.

23. **(a)** 30 ± 10.74, assuming the data describe the process when it is in control.
    (b) Yes. 30 ± 24 would be the limits.
    (c) *Weekly:* Yes. Same as part (a), because of the central limit theorem.
    Daily: Yes, but not using the normal distribution. Choose the upper 5th percentile from a histogram.

25. No. A 2-sigma shift brings the tolerance limits to within 1.33σ of the mean, which would put more than 9% of the parts out-of-tolerance.

26. (a) $(5.078)(0.003) = 0.0152$

(b) To detect variability in the process that might not change the average size.

28. (a) Using $z = 2.33$ and 1.645, $n = 135$

(b) 0.0398

(c) $p = 0.0398$ corresponds to $(.0398)(135) = 5.37$ defective items, so $n = 135$, $c = 5$ is the plan from (a) and (b). Using $c = 5$ in Table 16-1, $n_\alpha = 131.7$ and $n_\beta = 131.1$ which is very close to $n = 135$ from part (a). In the text, we didn't stop at $c = 5$ because μ_β/μ_α was slightly higher than LTPD/AQL.

CHAPTER 17

1. (a) Facilities are very expensive, so utilization must be high if costs are to be controlled.

(b) Idle time must be kept low (by proper scheduling) to meet completion time and cost contract values.

(c) The operations area spends the money; cost and quality determine both short-run and long-run profitability.

5. (a) Regulatory agencies cause constraints on product and process design. Other agencies have rules regarding work situations.

(b) Tax incentives and tariff rates are stated or negotiated. Locations are chosen in conjunction with industrial development agencies. Local arrangements are made for fire and police protection and other services.

7. (a) A set of products that uses similar technology and is sold to a specific type of customer; SBU's are used to help plan strategic operations and marketing efforts.

(b) (i) Subcompact inexpensive cars; compact inexpensive cars; compact luxury cars.

(ii) Associate degrees with bookkeeping skills; bachelor's degrees with technical training in (say) accounting; Ph.D.'s with research skills.

(iii) Expensive traditional dining room furniture; expensive modern dining room furniture; inexpensive traditional dining room furniture.

9. (a) Investments should provide for short-term income and for strategic, long-term planning goals; balance could also mean that risky projects are mixed with those having a fairly certain return (or with projects that are "negatively correlated" to the risky project).

(b) Risky investments often have a higher expected return.

11. (a) PROS: Better care because of higher volume; lower cost.
   CONS: Poor access for some people and for some physicians.
   (b) The physicians will have less practice, but the patients might be more comfortable closer to home. The total effect is hard to predict.
13. (a) 0.322
   (b) $5.12
   (c) No.

APPENDIX A

1. (a) False. Arrival frequency *varies* according to the Poisson probability law. Only the *mean* arrival rate is assumed constant.
   (b) True.
   (c) False. Same argument as (a).
   (d) False. Same argument as (a).
   (e) True, over the *long run*.
3. (a) N_q = 3.2 shirts.
   (b) 20%.
   (c) 8.1 shirts and 10%.
   (d) 12.5% increase in shirts leads to 153% increase in queue.
   (e) No. Shirts probably arrive at a fairly uniform rate.
   (f) The answers are too high, since there is less variability than assumed.
5. (a) 3.
   (b) For S = 4, T_q = 1.2 minutes.
   (c) (4)(12)/40 = $1.20 per customer.
   (d) Four is preferred. Three servers increases T_q by 8.9 minutes per visit, which is more expensive at $8 per hour than the additional $0.30 per visit needed to pay the extra server.
8. (a) T_q = 4.8 hours for barber 1 and 0.36 hours for barber 2, for an average of (0.6)(4.8) + (0.4)(0.36) = 3.02 hours.
   (b) T_q = 0.36 hours.
   (c) In (a), barber 2 is frequently idle when customers are waiting for barber 1. This would also be true if they were equally popular.
9. (a) More than 80. S > (AR)(T_s) = 80.
   (b) N_s = 80.
   (c) AR = (.2)(10) = 2 per day, N_q = AR T_q = 4 patients.
12. (a) S = 10, N_q = 6.019, T_q = 0.334 days.
   (b) Use model IV with K = 2. N_{q1} = 0.066, N_{q2} = 5.954, T_{q1} = 0.037 day, and T_{q2} = 0.37 day, so hot orders wait one-tenth as long as regular orders.
15. (a) T_q values at the receptionist = 4.5 minutes, nurse clinician = 4.0 minutes, and physician = 26 minutes.

(b) Count T_q and T_s.

  Path 1:   (NC only) = 12 minutes

  Path 2:   (NC, MD) = 42 minutes

  Path 3:   (MD only) = 36 minutes

(c) 23 minutes.

(d) Receptionist is idle 0.25 hour per hour, NC = 0.33 and MD = 0.13.

(e) Reduces T_q to 0.9 minute for MD, but increases MD idle time to 1.13 doc-hours per hour (0.567 each).

APPENDIX B

---

3. **(a)**

Time (minutes)	15–20	20–25	25–30	30–35
Random numbers	.001–.242	.243–.510	.511–.770	.771–.000

(b) Customer 1 = 30–35; 2 = 25–30; 3 = 30–35; 4 = 15–20; 5 = 30–35

(c) The plot is zero out to t = 15 minutes, then a straight line from (P = 0 at t = 15) to (P = 1.0 at t = 35), then a horizontal line at P = 1.0 beyond t = 35.

(d) 31 minutes, 27 minutes, 32, 19 and 31.

5. **(a)** 5 weeks for A, 1 week for B, 5 weeks for C. Critical path = AB = 6 weeks.

(b) A = 2, B = 2, C = 5 for completion in 5 weeks.

  A = 2, B = 2, C = 5, same result.

  Average = (6 + 5 + 5)/3 = 5.33 weeks.

(c) Repeat 100 times and find the 80th percentile.

(d) Activity times statistically independent; historical distributions are accurate for the future.

6. **(a)** P = .885 corresponds to z = +1.2; .274 implies z = −0.6, and the other 3 are +2.9, −1.8 and +0.4.

(b) Part 1 = 10 + z(0.0010) = 10.0012, and the rest are 9.9994, 10.0029, 9.9982 and 10.0004.

8. **(a)** z = 1.5, so life = 1200 + 1.5(50) = 1275.

(b) Using equation (1), 1160 ± 1.96(52)/$\sqrt{40}$ does not include 1200, so the simulated value is suspiciously low.

10. Queuing model assumes steady state; did the simulation? Is 10% statistically significant?

12. **(a)** Since n = 4 is much less than 30, we must use the t distribution in equations (1) and (2).

$$42.3 \pm 3.182(8.7)/\sqrt{4} = 42.3 \pm 13.84$$

(b) n = $[3.182(8.7)/2.0]^2$ = 192

13. **(a)** Good = .001 − .850; rework = .851 − .950; reject = .951 − .000.

  Shirt 1 = good, 2 = G, 3 = reject, 4 = rework, 5 = G, 6 = G, 7 = G, 8 = rework, 9 = rework, 10 = G.

(b)

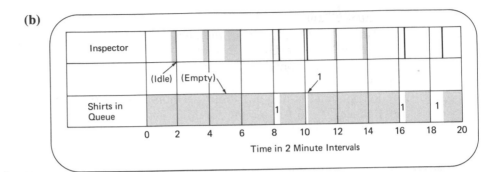

(c) 1. Set clock at zero ($t = 0$), inspector = idle, queue = empty.
2. Add 1 shirt to queue.
3. If Inspector is free and queue is empty, inspector = idle.
4. If Inspector is free and queue is not empty, take shirt from queue and compute next time when inspector will be free (that is, $t +$ inspection time). Write this down as an attribute of the inspector.
5. If Inspector is busy but will be free before next arrival, then move clock forward to time when inspector is free and repeat steps 3, 4, 5.
6. Move clock to next shirt arrival and repeat steps 2–6.

(d) After each shirt's category was generated, as in part (a), a second random number would be used to generate its processing time from the probability distribution corresponding to the category.

17. **(a)** Mean and variance of sales, wastage, procurements, lost sales, waiting line.
(b) Probability distributions of demands by time of day, and service times.
(c) Stage 1 (nine runs):
Oranges = 250, 300, 350 and juice = 850, 900, 950.
Stage 2 (eight runs):
Oranges = best from stage 1 $\pm$ 25, juice = best $\pm$ 25
Stage 3 (three runs):
Explore three points near the best from stage 2.
(d) Best stage 1 is oranges = 350, juice = 850, profit = 187.5
Best stage 2 is oranges = 375, juice = 850, profit = 225
Best stage 3 is oranges = 400, juice = 850, profit = 250
(e) Continue searching, increasing oranges by 25 until profit declines.

APPENDIX C

1. **(a)** Solutions 1, 6, and 8 are infeasible.
(b) Solution 2, $Z = 5$. Solution 3, $Z = 6$. Solution 4, $Z = 4$. Solution 5, $Z = 5$. Solution 7, $Z = 4$.

(c), (d) and (e)

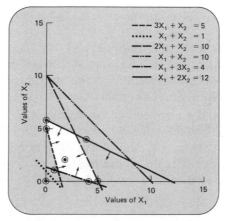

The optimum (minimum) occurs at the lower left corner, at the intersection of the two lines $3X_1 + X_2 = 5$ and $X_1 + 3X_2 = 4$. Solving them simultaneously (or carefully reading the graph) yields the solution $X_1 = 1.375$ and $X_2 = 0.875$, for an objective function value of 2.25.

3. **(a)** All feasible. Z value is 24 for each solution.
   (b) Same Z and same value (of 12) for constraint (3).
   (c)

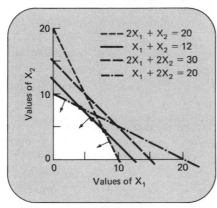

   (d) The objective function is parallel to the constraint $X_1 + X_2 = 12$, and so all points on that line have the same objective function value. The objective function is increasing as we move up to the right, so all three points are optimal.
   (e) There would be a zero among the objective function coefficients of the nonbasic variables.

7. **(a)** and **(b):** Only slacks are needed.

Row No.	X_1		X_2	S_1	S_2	S_3	S_4	RHS
1	Max	10	9	0	0	0	0	0
2		0.7	1	1	0	0	0	630
3		3	5	0	1	0	0	3600
4		3	2	0	0	1	0	2124
5		1	2.5	0	0	0	1	1350

(c) Objective function value $= 0$, $S_1 = 630$, $S_2 = 3600$, $S_3 = 2124$, $S_4 = 1350$.

(d) $X_1 = 0$, $X_2 = 0$ are nonbasic.

(e) Yes. All variables including slacks are nonnegative.

(f) No. Two positive numbers in row 1.

(g) Yes. No negative numbers in row 1.

9. Working from the tableau in Problem 7, let X_1 be the entering variable. The ratios of RHS/"X_1 column" are as follows. Row 2: $630/0.7 = 900$, row 3: $3600/3 = 1200$, row 4: $2124/3 = 708$, row 5: $1350/1 = 1350$. The minimum is 708, so row 4 is the departing row and S_3, being basic in row 4, is the departing variable. The pivot element is in the X_1 column, row 4, or 3.0.

Row No.	X_1	X_2	S_1	S_2	S_3	S_4	RHS
1	0	2.333	0	0	-3.333	0	-7080
2	0	0.533	1	0	-0.233	0	134.4
3	0	3	0	1	-1	0	1476
4	1	0.667	0	0	0.333	0	708
5	0	1.833	0	0	-0.333	1	642

X_2 is the entering variable now. The ratios are as follows. Row 2: $134.4/0.533 = 252$, row 3: 492, row 4: 1062, row 5: 350.2, so row 2 and S_1 are departing, and 0.533 is the pivot element.

Row No.	X_1	X_2	S_1	S_2	S_3	S_4	RHS
1	0	0	-4.3750	0	-2.31250	0	-7668
2	0	1	1.8750	0	-0.43750	0	252
3	0	0	-5.6250	1	0.31250	0	720
4	1	0	-1.2500	0	0.62500	0	540
5	0	0	-3.4375	0	0.46875	1	180

12. (a) $P =$ number of potatoes used in production. $C =$ same, for clams, and $T =$ same, for liters of tomato sauce. $N =$ liters of New England Chowder produced, $M =$ same for Manhattan.

(b) $P = 2N + 0.5M$, $C = N + M$, $T = 0.05N + 0.25M$.

(c) Using $N = 1$ and $M = 1$, we get $P = 2.5$ potatoes, $C = 2$ clams and $T = 0.3$ liter, which is just what's needed.

(d) 100,000 liters of N, with 100,000 clams and 15,000 liters of sauce left over.

(e) 80,000 liters of M with 160,000 potatoes and 120,000 clams left over.

(f) All costs are sunk and revenue is equal for both products, so maximize total production $= N + M$, subject to constraints in part (b) and $P \leqslant 200,000$, $C \leqslant 200,000$ and $T \leqslant 20,000$.

13. (a) They have different prices.

(b) LP, LC, LT $=$ leftover potatoes, clams, and tomato sauce used in production. PP, PC, PT $=$ purchased potatoes (etc.) used. $N =$ liters of New England produced, $M =$ same, Manhattan.

(c) LP $+$ PP $= 2N + 0.5M$, LC $+$ PC $= N + M$, LT $+$ PT $= 0.05N +$

0.25M, LP $\leq$ 200,000, LC $\leq$ 200,000, LT $\leq$ 20,000, $N \leq$ 500,000, $M \leq$ 400,000.

(d) Maximize 1.05N + 1.00M − 0.03PP − 0.10PC − 0.60PT

(e) The first 3 are accounting, the next 3 are facts of life, and the last 2 are both policy and facts of life.

(f) With the prices given, both products have a positive net return. Buy as much as is needed for production to meet demand.

15. **(a)** This solution achieves zero cost. Change the demand constraints to "equalities".

(b) Upper limit, allowing the LP to select product mix.

(c) Maximize .40 A1 + .35 A2 + .10 A3 + .20 A4 − .20 B1 + .10 B2 + .05 B3 + .10 B4 + .35 C1 + .15 C2 + .30 C3 + .35 C4, Subject to A1 + A2 + A3 + A4 $\leq$ 1200; B1 + B2 + B3 + B4 $\leq$ 1200; C1 + C2 + C3 + C4 $\leq$ 500; A1 + B1 + C1 $\leq$ 700; A2 + B2 + C2 $\leq$ 400; A3 + B3 + C3 $\leq$ 600; A4 + B4 + C4 $\leq$ 500

(d) .10 A1 + .15 A2 + ⋯ + .25 C4 $\leq$ 400

(e) Y = additional capacity; $Y \leq$ 50 and change the plant C constraint to C1 + C2 + C3 $\leq$ 500 + Y, and add − 0.05Y to the objective function.

18. **(a)** X_A = tons of cement A (similarly X_B); Y_1 = tons of ingredient 1 (similarly Y_2, Y_3). Maximize 180X_A + 150X_B subject to Y_1 = 0.5X_A + 0.4X_B; Y_2 = 0.3X_A + 0.2X_B; Y_3 = 0.2X_A + 0.4X_B; $Y_2 \leq$ 15,000; $X_A \geq$ 5000; $X_B \geq$ 4000.

(b) Upper limits on sales, and costs of ingredients.

(c) Maximize 180X_A + 150X_B − $C_1 X_1$ − $C_2 X_2$ − $C_3 X_3$ subject to $X_A \leq U_A$; $X_B \leq U_B$; and the constraints in (a).

20. **(a)** 84,210 liters of New England and 63,160 of Manhattan. Leftovers = 52.63 thousand clams.

(b) (0.421)(20) = 8.42 thousand liters of chowder.

(c) Additional clams are of no use. An additional 20 thousand liters of tomato sauce exceeds the range of the shadow price, so *no more than* (3.158)(20) = 63.16 thousand liters.

(d) Decrease by (0.421)(20) = 8.42 thousand liters.

(e) (i) No change. (ii) and (iii) Can't tell because the change exceeds the ALLOWED DECREASE.

(f) The shadow price for decreasing NENG is 0.80, so the objective function (chowder output) decreases by at least (0.8)(84.21 − 50) = 27.37, so the new output would be 147.37 − 27.37 = 120 or less. Since NENG = 50, MNHTN = 120 − 50 = 70 or less.

(g) Yes, it is still optimal. The ALLOWED INCREASE of NENG's objective coefficient is 3.0.

Index